India

(Bhāratīya Gaṇarājya)

Under Siege;
The Enemy Within

A Concise History

Dr Mohan Ragbeer

सत्यमेव जयते

Satyameva Jayaté (only truth prevails)

ISBN:1506123619

ISBN-13: 9781506123615

DEDICATION

To my late Parents, my sister Mahadai and her husband Tulla--my mentors and role models who inspired *"The Indelible Red Stain"*, which includes part of this history--and to my extended and scattered family who nurtured their ancestral culture in many lands: UK, USA, Canada, India, the Caribbean, and maintained the heritage, reflected here, despite enormous obstacles placed before them by heartless conquerors.

To young people everywhere, Indians above all, who ought to know something of this history, recent and remote, so that they can understand why India is close to losing the chance to become truly independent.

To my wife, Mary, for her meticulous editing, patience and support.

To my children, for constant inspiration.

To my friends for critical appraisal of this work; and

To the numerous heroes I have not named, of all backgrounds and religions, who have given their best, often their lives, in the cause of India's freedom, and those who strive for tolerance, peace and prosperity for all.

Mohan Ragbeer

Table of Contents

Acknowledgments

My parents ensured that their eight children had a solid background in Indian tradition, in all its variety. My father died when I was only seven, but his instructions stayed with me, reinforced by my mother and my elder siblings, and by Dr Brahmam, my mentor, and the late Sri Latchmanji—the scholarly farmer, with whom I boarded for a time, and who taught Hindi, Sanskrit and the *Vaidas*. They fed my curiosity and steered the search for truth, which has sustained me throughout my life. They virtually wrote this book.

Mary, my wife, confidante and critic, and David, our son have been supportive throughout; so also the five children of my first marriage, and my many nieces and nephews, in Canada, USA, UK and Guyana.

Special thanks to Fatlind Melani of *Indo Caribbean World*, Thornhill, Ontario, Canada, for the Cover design. Harry Ramkhelawan, publisher and editor of *ICWorld*, gave sterling help.

I thank the members of the 1961 expedition to Wappai, British Guiana (now Guyana) whose interest in, and lack of knowledge of the heritage of Indians—then over 50% of their compatriots—stimulated further historical review of pre-independence India; they gave me the chance of presenting them a version of that history free of the pervasive distortions by British and secular Indian historians, who tend to deny India's Hindu heritage, and whom I had learned to avoid quite early.

I thank my late friend, Joseph Young, a prominent Canadian, a teacher, author and senior Olympic starter and official, who after reading the first draft confessed that he had been taught, at home and at school, that the British had civilised Indians, having found them, in their 17th century voyages of exploration, at the same "primitive" stage of growth as the aborigines of Africa, America and Australia! His revelation answered many questions I had had for decades about North American stereotypes about India and Indians. He apologised and urged its publication so that others can learn this truth, as it dispelled so many contradictions in his dealings with Indians—especially Hindus—that traditional sources had failed to clarify and nearly always patronised. His enthusiasm is reward enough for the labour spent.

Several Indian and British contacts gave data on Indian history and the *British Rāja*, endorsing accounts by Dr Brahmam and others and guiding my research. I thank them: teachers, colleagues, friends, and must separate the decent and diligent British majority from the aristocrats and their acolytes who, with rare exceptions, are the villains and the objects of my criticisms of the British. *Mohan Ragbeer, 2014*

Introduction

"Scant justice is done to India's position in the world by those European histories which recount the exploits of her invaders and leave the impression that her own people were a feeble dreamy folk, surrendered from the rest of mankind by their seas and mountain frontiers. Such a picture takes no account of the intellectual conquests of the Hindus." *Sir C N E Eliot, British diplomat*

The recording or interpretation of history is a noble challenge; those who would analyse events and personalities and add their contribution to the growth of thought, humanity and virtue, deserve our appreciation. I think of Ferdowsi. He was a Persian poet who authored the historical epic, the *Shahnameh,* which he began in 977 CE, exactly a thousand years before I started this. He finished his, thirty years later, compiled from the collective wisdom of earlier and contemporary generations of scholars, to present the past, analyse its lessons, so as to guide the present wisely and reduce future error. For it is in today's actions that we either improve or degrade tomorrow.

To Ferdowsi and his contemporaries in Persian and Indian culture—as by then India had rescued the Parsi victims of Islamic *jihad*—the cruelty, cupidity, cheating, prevarication and lust shown by the conquerors, wasted human talent, which would have been better directed to achieve truth, honesty, justice and wisdom that with other virtues might be fostered to fulfil the promise inherent in man's gift of humanity. This was the core position of ancient Vaidic authors and the heroes of the great Indian epics, the *Ramayana* and *Mahabharata,* which together with other writings, then and later, tell the history of India.

Al Beruni, early 11th century astronomer, wrote *Tariq al Hind* (*A history of India*) which became known all over Europe, then awakening. He credited Indians with key discoveries in Mathematics and Science. Thanks to him, modern efforts to ignore or deny these are easily countered, but have to overcome the lingering anti-India and anti-Hindu falsehoods by British writers: James Mill (1815), Thomas Macaulay (1835) and, in the following decades, Max Müller, their acolytes and numerous others fed on their distortions, whether Americans or Germans, or Anglophile and "secular" Indian academics of the last century, now scattered worldwide. Arabs were thus credited for the knowledge and discoveries: in algebra, other mathematics, medicine, anatomy, navigation etc. that they had brought to enlighten Europe. This misleading attribution has stubbornly persisted in western records and continues to serve the cause of anti-Hindu activists, inside and outside India. Diligent corrections continue to be made by many scholars, as listed in the *Bibliography*, including analysts like Seidenberg, Srivasta,

Klostermeier, Frawley, Rajaram, Talageri, Kak, Arya and others, including the findings of the Archaeological Survey of India.

Early in the 19th century when "Germany" was a web of small weak surrogates of Austria and France and seeking a national identity, its scholars "adopted" the Hindu *Vaidas* as an ancient source of organised wisdom. Wilhelm von Humboldt, for example, the Prussian educator and founder of the University of Berlin, described the *Bhagavad Gita* as *"the loftiest and deepest thing the world has to show."* Other German scholars shared his view. When Max Müller wrongly concluded that "arya" in the *Vaidas* referred to a noble race, and launched the aryan invasion theory of Indian origin, Germany finally "found" its long sought roots and named itself an aryan race. The British used Müller's findings to distort Indian history, while recent archaeological finds support the Vaidas.

This publication covers salient features of Indian history and should assist those readers and teachers who wish to know and to introduce to their students a brief portrayal of that history, free of the distortions and inventions devised by the British *Rāja* to divide and subjugate Indians, after the failed 1857 War of Indian Independence. Those distortions still pervade Indian history textbooks, written by prominent UK-trained historians, including Indians schooled in the British tradition, who consciously or not, maintain the perfidy. In Pakistan, historians are even now repeating the British model of denial and substitution (Wynbrandt).

My interest is historical, genetic, ancestral and transcendental. It began with a childhood fascination with scriptural and other heroes imbued in me by great raconteurs, such as my mother, her Tamil-speaking friend—whose rapid-fire stories my mother translated into Hindi—and later my guru and Vaidic teacher, Sri Latchmanji.

My teachers told intriguing tales of early kingdoms, of courage and honour, and of fearsome strange machines, aerial chariots and exploding weapons used in Rāma's struggle against Rāvana and in the war described in the *Ramāyana,* one of the world's great epics, which describes anti-gravity vehicles and atomic weapons. Later we heard of the Indian mathematical and scientific achievers who, as Einstein observed, invented the basis of our civilisation. Yet, no one in the wider society, of which I was a part, all those decades, knew or cared or would even believe they had existed.

From these early exposures I came to understand something of ancient societal organisation, religion, linguistics, computational methods and the integration of these into a coherent whole; I was consumed by the enduring mysteries and metaphors. The lessons came at a time when I was a sponge for things new and illuminating, stirring my curiosity, indiscriminately. So I learned almost indiscriminately.

The lessons from these humble yet profound sources were a stimulating and solid base, and sharpened understanding of the universe and our place in it. Its infinite perspective facilitated reaching for the soul hidden deep to the superficialities that seemed to beguile the majorities of today. Most helpfully, I learned about India from north to south and of the significance of the *Vaidic* concept of the stages of our lives on earth, of the ages and cycles of the Universe, and of *Kaliyuga*, the age we had entered just over five millennia ago. Our elders had learned to cope, despite anti-Hindu propaganda, and the rulers' perversions of religion and history. They had accepted the pressures of colonial society and the karmic realities of their own immediate history of indenture and contact with the materialistic, militaristic forces of Christianity and Islam—two young cultures, 19 and 13 centuries old, jostling for supremacy and religious monopoly. Europeans, they found, thrived on fighting, like pugilists. Christianity had become dominant, owning or controlling the world's resources, which WWII would consume. Victory was tempered with alarm when Wahhabi Islam emerged as owners of one of the world's richest deposits of oil, which soon dominated the global economy and provided sources of friction, and a war chest for Wahhabis.

Later, my friend and physician colleague, Dr Brahmam, gave me a tour of Indian history, a saga without end, spiritual and secular, with many absorbing sights, from the zenith to the nadir of human achievement and behaviour, from grand to shameful, from tolerance to bigotry. They are tales of freedom and conquest, wealth and poverty, valour and cowardice, trust and deceit, and the whole panoply of human experience in vibrant colour, from "pre-history" to the present. India, he confirmed, was an ancient crucible of creativity in mathematics, sciences, agriculture, religion, grammar, medicine, engineering, transportation, philosophy and government. It attracted raiders, the last of them British, with the collusion of influential or opportunistic Indians. They not only continued Christian and Islamic aims to destroy Indian religions— and, in trying, massacred tens of millions of Indians—but continued to distort and denigrate India's true history, substitute it with Müller's mythical "aryan invasion" and create the secular religion of *Hinduphobia* that rules and threatens to fragment India further, if unchecked.

The partition of India could have been avoided, but for Islamist ambitions, militancy, secular confusion, Hindu pusillanimity and British aristocratic biases, falsification, self-interest, greed and a brutish policy of control, still expressed, although more subtly. By the time I met him, the Cold War was well under way. He re-ignited the flame of curiosity, especially his fascination for the unsolved mysteries of flight, space and the universe, described as *fact*, not fable, in the epics. But the language used in translations reflected the technology and vocabulary of the later millennia in which they were done, not the more remote period of invention or development. Thus, many terms had no modern equivalent; for example, of the sixteen or so alloys mentioned in the construction of ancient flying machines, only three have a modern equivalent. Similarly the word "car" or "chariot" was used for all vehicles and "arrow" for missiles of various types, from ordinary arrows to bullets, flame throwers and rockets, and other personal and mass explosive projectiles.

I was born in the Indian Diaspora, in the last days of the British *Rāja*. My parents were pragmatic Hindus in the *Vaidic* tradition. They had a degree of nationalism that I had thought common to all Indians. Apart from Sri Latchmanji and Dr Brahmam, I had met several learned men, two of whom were historians, who confirmed the British resolve to fragment India and effect Lord Macaulay's plan to destroy Hinduism by educating middle class Indians in English only and luring them to Christianity and British ways. South Indian and Vaidic history would be treated as myth, and its antiquity denied while the recency (less than 1000 years) of British civilisation and imperialist designs would be suppressed. They achieved this by destroying the structure of Indian education, then restrictively channelling middle-class Indians to higher study of anglocentric curricula, where subterfuge and bogus theorising passed off as knowledge created by officially sponsored "scholars", most with aristocratic roots or links.

These deceivers were employees of the British East India Company. One of the earliest was James Mill (father of John Stuart Mill, the philosopher,) who wrote an influential condemnatory history of India 200 years ago, without ever going there. Macaulay went to India, two decades later, and served the BEICo. The distortions of these two framed British policy towards India. Later, the *Rāja* taught the deceptions to the trusting Indian masses, already cowed by centuries of Islamic rule, and so eager for learning as a means to escape oppression that they would have done anything to access whatever was presented as required knowledge. They knew nothing of the falsification and bias that would make them toadies: an educated, privileged, mostly urban, anglophilic middle class, learning of ancestral history and culture only as taught pejoratively and derisively in British schools, even today.

Some of these schools were started by Indian teachers beguiled by British dominance in India into believing that all British citizens had the same attributes of high social stature and education, free of the prejudices and divisions so pervasive and transparent among Indians. They believed that British education was "ancient" and would improve them and society, little realising that British authorities had been systematically expropriating, not just valuables, but knowledge in science, mathematics, philosophy, engineering, language, healing arts and others, passing them off as their own, even though the Arab sources had presented them as Indian work. In the absence of contrary views, naive Indian students, from the 19th century onwards, would believe that the only valid things were those that the British had just taught them.

The invention of the printing press revolutionised communication and contributed enormously to rapid intellectual advances in Europe, especially the Reformation. Later, naval and industrial revolutions placed Britain at the van of manufacturing and military nations.

Anglo-educated Indians often spurned their own people and incongruously aped British attitudes and culture, even food, except for one crucial particular: skin colour. The father of Sri Aurobindo illustrates this perfectly. In his disdain for Indian culture, he zealously adopted all things British, raising his children to be perfect little *"coconuts"* (brown outside, white inside). Yet Aurobindo rejected this anglomania and became a freedom fighter, writer, Hindu philosopher, yogi and teacher.

In a sense, a rather cruel sense, the British surpassed their aim and left behind, as an independent nation, a people that is fractured, scheming and untrustworthy, ignorant of their history, more Islamic than Hindu in outlook, with a westernised middle and upper class, often more British than the British had been in the 200 years they ruled India. The offspring of these brown Englishmen today ape Americans even more sedulously, down to their worst vices. We see them in the works of Indian writers like Vikram Seth, Nobel laureate Vidia Naipaul, formerly of Trinidad, Salman Rushdie, Rohinton Mistry and, increasingly, in the flesh, among the staff of Indian and Western universities, colleges, clinics, governments and corporations, including popular media.

Today Indian scholars gravitate to the West, where they meet, and often fail to greet their look-alike contemporaries from the Diaspora. They have joined a highly visible part of the over 20 million diasporal Indians—a significant segment of the "model minority". Those from India tend to populate tribal islands isolated by *jāt* (subtribe), region or language, or occupation, especially academics. They insulate themselves by acronyms such as PIO (*people of Indian origin*) and NRI (*non-resident Indian*), waking up to their identity and the reality of having become part of the Diaspora, when they rise in their jobs to collide with the glass ceiling that Blacks had so poignantly described in the last century, which few outside of politics have been able to penetrate consistently.

Attempts to unite Indians to common action continue to be quite frustrating. Recently, BK Agnihotri, a former Indian Ambassador-at-large, admitted, in relation to a visit to the USA, *"I turned down an invitation to California because three different Indian organisations invited me for the same program; now they are joining together and sending me another invitation. All the organisations have their use and value but for common causes they must join together and work together."* Earlier in the same interview he had noted *"There are 20 million plus Indians living abroad but there is a lack of communication between them in America... For example, the Indians in the Caribbean don't know their counterparts here and the Indian Americans here don't want to know about their Caribbean counterparts. I invited the President of Guyana and the people in Surinam to come here and meet the Indian American community here. In fact it's amazing how much more in touch with their cultural heritage people from Guyana and the Caribbean are"!*

The summary history that follows includes the views and analyses of an eclectic mix of scholars, who have studied and rejected anglocentric manipulations of ancient Indian history and the origins of its religions and peoples, now bolstered by new evidence from modern science, space exploration and archaeology.

It is fairly certain that Indian social and political development, in this iteration, had progressed over many millennia, from the primal hunter-gatherer or Stone Age man to cultivators of fertile riverain fields, after mastery of basic agricultural techniques. Settlements allowed groups to develop—from small oligarchies to large kingdoms—expanding from tribal enclaves to large entities sustaining many millions, along the major river systems and their fertile basins. In the north and west, these were the Saraswati, Sindhu (Indus), Ganga, Yamuna, Mahanadi and others, until the Saraswati "disappeared" about 4000 years ago. In the east the Brahmaputra, centrally, the great rivers, Narmada and Tapti, and south the Godavari, Krishna, Kaveri and others, were centres of growth in commerce and religion, recovering after loss by post-ice age flooding of the ancient Kumari (*Lemuria*) continent (*Kumari Kandam*). See map, p 9.

Social amelioration progressed steadily, as enterprise and trade with neighbours brought wealth, so that, by the last millennium BCE, kingdoms had begun the first steps to unification, with initiatives from Magadha (modern Bengal, Bihar and eastern UP), and its southern neighbours Videha and Vidarbha. On Chandragupta Maurya's accession to the throne of Magadha, his son Ashoka and the Prime Minister, Chanukya (Kautilya), a professor at the University of Taxashila (and likely Nālandā), expanded the kingdom to include most of India, and reclaim Afghanistan into the Mauryan Empire (Gandhāra was an Indian kingdom at the time of the *Mahābhārata* War). This ushered in two centuries of progress, religious tolerance and growth in knowledge in astronomy, mathematics, agriculture, engineering, medicine and so on.

Long before this, Indians, South and North, had begun to explore astronomy and natural phenomena, developing intricate and complex mathematics *(ganita),* religious philosophy and grammar which had led to the multiple and sequential discoveries that laid the foundations of modern science. By the third millennium BCE scholars had propounded the main elements of computational and line mathematics, and celestial data sought to the extent possible without instruments, revealing physical principles and notions of time (see p. 39). In the 14th century, Sayāna, a Vijayanagara official using such *Purānic* data calculated the speed of light as 186,000 miles/sec., a result that physicist S. Kak called "the most astonishing 'blind hit' in the history of science" *(Bibliography).*

In time, Indian knowledge and religious philosophies, her wealth and fame spread throughout its areas of influence and attracted many foreigners—from those seeking enlightenment and knowledge to those craving wealth and power. But millennia of uncontrolled growth; deforestation; natural disasters from tectonic shifts; rain and wind; human greed and conflict; and finally, two to three centuries of drought ended the Saraswati/Sindhu civilisation. Early refugees settled east along the great central rivers far from the areas of disaster: Ganga, Yamuna, Brahmaputra, and south along the ones listed, and their tributaries. The lower Indus settlements survived in Sindh. PT Srinivas Iyengar (*Bibliography*) described this changing geography and showed that populations traditionally mixed on both sides of the Vindhya Mountains. A British writer, VA Smith (1917), wrongly concluded that Vindhya had divided north and south India into dissimilar races and cultures, matching 19th century Bishop Caldwell's guess of a *"dravidian race"* dominant in South India, the foil to North India's equally mythical *"aryans"*. The British exploited this hypothesis in its vigorous efforts to divide the peoples of north and south India. Jesus (Christ) arrived as a youth and studied religion at Nālandā and Taxashila (Faber-Kaiser).

Waves of invasions after the Gupta period changed the Indian landscape and culture until the British conquest, by arms and subterfuges, brought the subcontinent to its knees and left it broken, benighted, confused and dominated by corrupt, callous and aristocratic adventurers. Their successors continue brazenly to oppress their fellows and are well on the way to serve India, thoroughly and suitably seasoned, on a platter, to the new imperialists, the USA. This subversive attitude had earlier given the Tamil DMK party—*Dravida Munnetra Kazhagam (Dravidian Progress Federation),* founded in 1949 by CN Annadurai—a rationale for promoting a separate country, *Dravidasthan,* even though, linguistically, Tamil, Malayalam, Kannada, Telugu—all classical southern languages—share features with Sanskrit. They are rich too in literature and religious lore, Tamil being noted for its *Sangam* literature. The DMK, up to 1962, did promote *Dravidasthan,* despite lack of persuasive evidence, relying on the sagas of the fabled *Lemuria,* said to stretch from India southwest to Madagascar, thence east to Australia. Much of this was lowland and included Sundaland, which sank over many millennia from flooding and marine disasters expected in an active seismic zone. The 1962 war between India and China led the DMK to choose India, and in 1963 it dropped its claim for separation. Recent revival of the continental construct has followed submarine findings suggesting 10,000 years old structures; this coincided with soured relationships with the INC (Tamil Tigers murder of Rajiv Gandhi) and escalation of a militant and divisive Christian proselytism among Tamils.

Ancient geography presented on modern maps is not as the ancients saw it. Today's maps are refined from numerous technological advances: geo-political, computational, land, air, space, photography, etc. The coverage of the ancient east, even by prestigious western magazines, like *National Geographic*, remains sketchy and ignores the triumphs of ancient oriental civilisations, non-white, pre-Greek and pre-Christian. They prefer the standard biases—people, writers, rulers, religions—towards British, American and Judaeo-Christian beliefs, which many, including Canadian media, use to publicise Indian atheists, leftists and other non-Hindus, who persist in blaming Hinduism for *all* of India's social "ills".

Even "great" Western Universities distort this region, perhaps because funding agencies may react negatively to accounts that favour *dharmic* religions, or criticise Europeans, or contradict old British dogma, or reveal their perfidy. (Corporate sponsors react similarly and often withdraw support when the results of a study contradict theirs.) Ideally, knowledge and its diffusion should be above such pettiness, but perhaps the wrong bodies have reached the pinnacles of power. Was it ever any better? My excursions into history suggest that little has changed where human motivation is concerned, that lust and greed seem to express the paramount drives of ambitious men and women, just as it had been at the dawn of history. Was the Jewish metaphor of Eve and the apple not an example of bribery, greed and exploitation of lust? Krishna' theme in the *Bhagavad Gita* includes specific condemnation of these qualities.

Note: The timelines given are those of British in India, and generally rejected by *dharmic* scholars, who rely on scriptures and epics, references to astronomical or historical events, and the continuum of the *Vaidic* calendar which gives the age of the *Universe* as 155.5 trillion years! Most written records of this recent civilisation, estimated to be about 12,000 years old, were lost in the Islamic destruction of libraries at Nālanda and Taxashila, and temples elsewhere. The Bibliography includes detailed treatises on this subject.

"Make peace with your past so it won't screw up the present" is an old injunction whose origin is lost in time. The *Mundok Upanishad 3-1-6* advises, *Satyameva Jayate Nanritam* i.e. Only the truth triumphs!

Partition of India, 1947 (bold lines); India light grey; Others dark grey) Modified from http://www.columbia.edu/itc/mealac/pritchett/00maplinks/modern/maps1947/

Post-Partition: Area of India: 1,269,338 sq,m (3,283,590 sq,km.);
West Pakistan 310,401 sq.m.; East Pakistan (Bangladesh) 55,598 sq.m.
For population data see p. 485

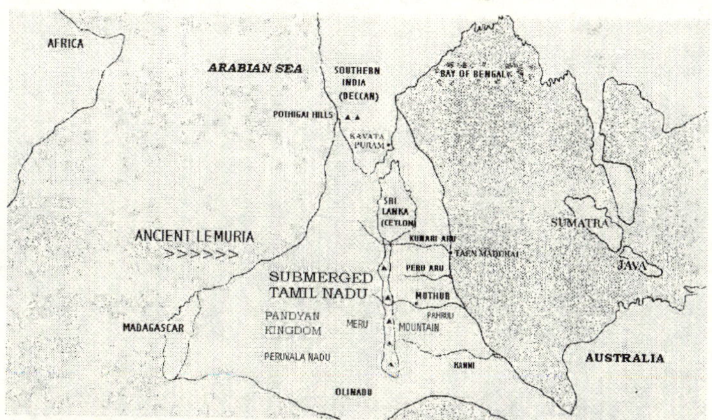

Antediluvian Kumari continent (Lemuria), South India (Nirojansakthivel; see also Parameswaran). The 19th century German biologist, Ernst Haeckel, believed that Lemuria was the origin of the human species and agreed with Darwinian theory; from studies in embryology, he proposed that "ontogeny recapitulates phylogeny"

Satellite view reveals valley of ancient Saraswati, now lying buried. The Indus River is at top left; Himalayas top right. (NASA)

Mesolithic Rock Shelters, Bhimbetka, Central India (VS Wakankar 1957)
(Photo by Raveesh Vyas)

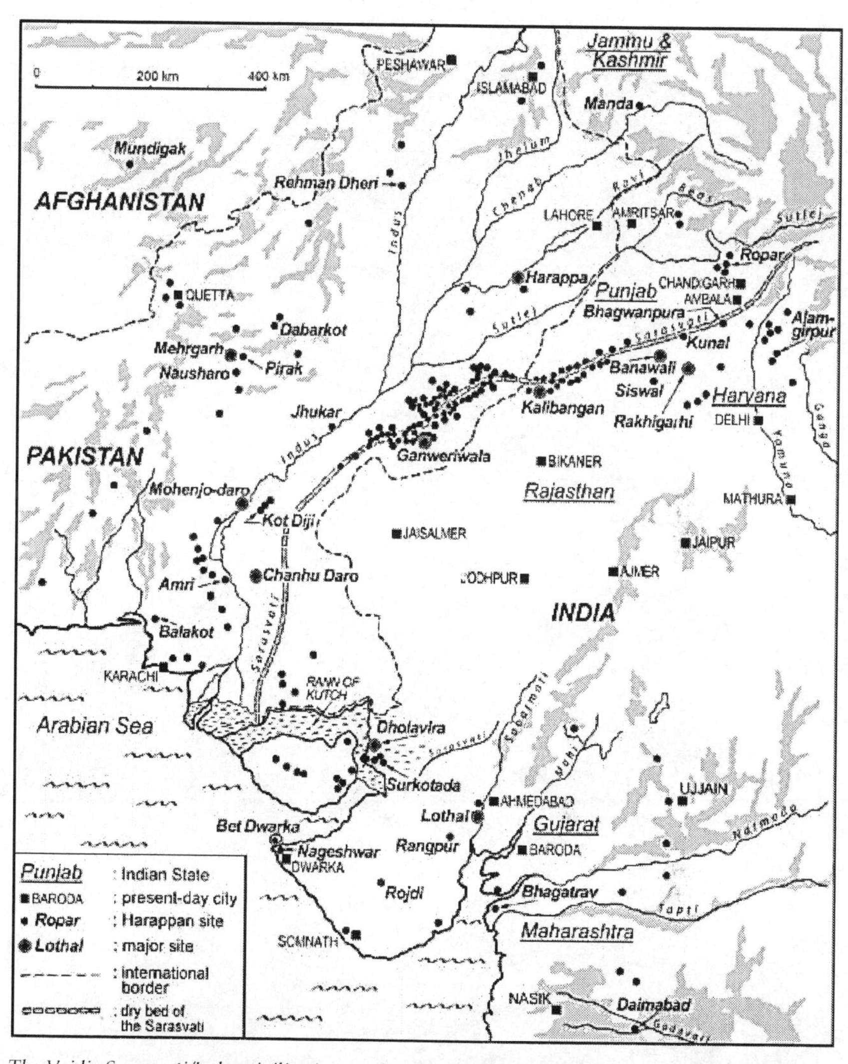

The Vaidic Saraswati/Indus civilisation, settlements so far identified, shown in relation to modern states and cities. Note the heavy concentration along the Saraswati River (shown schematically) as it coursed through Rājasthān. (See satellite photo, p. 10, above)

Source: htp://www.gsbkerala.com/swriverbed.jpg)

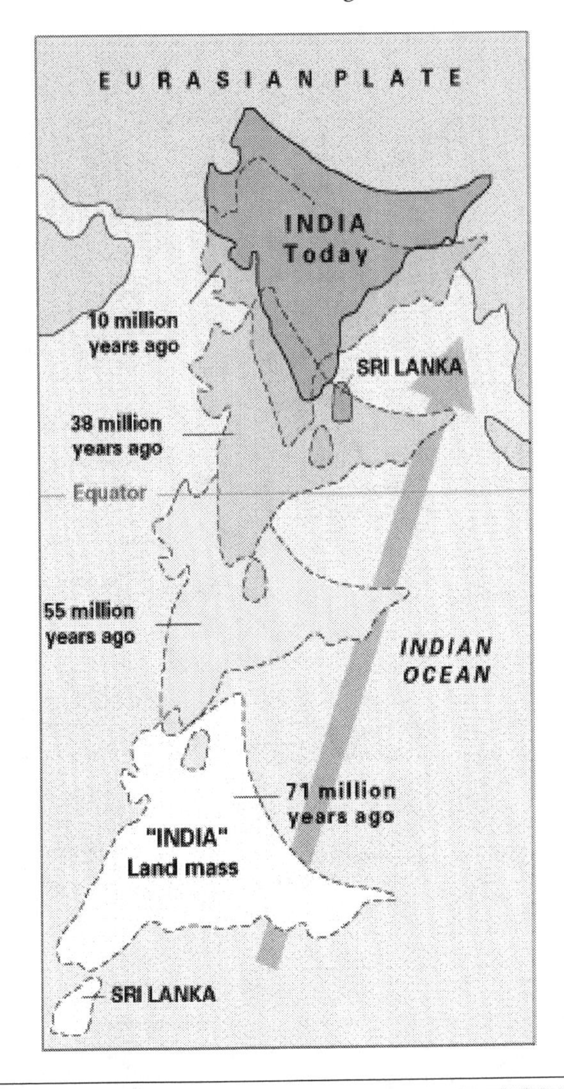

India, after separation from Pangaea, showing the continental drift that set its course, as shown, to collide eventually with the Eurasian plate and raise the Himalayas range, a journey of ca. 71M years. (Himalaya Formation, source www.usgs.org). *The Indian tectonic plate continues to drift north at 40-50mm/year, spawning numerous minor earthquakes (below M_w 4, on Moment Magnitude scale) periodic damaging ones (over 5 M_w), and catastrophes occasionally, at strengths over 7M_w. The India plate is pushing against the Eurasian in a wide arc from the Sulaiman Range in Pakistan, along the Himalayas to the Arakan Range that forms the boundary between Myanmar and India and Bangladesh. In the past, severe quakes have occurred along this line. Quetta was levelled in 1935 by a magnitude M_w 7.6 earthquake which left 30,000 people dead (USGS). In 1934, an M_w8 earthquake caused extensive damage in Nepal and Bihar. The number of deaths was 10,700 to 12,000, with 7,253 recorded in Bihar. Other have occurred elsewhere along the contact line.*

Prologue

"India was China's and the world's teacher in philosophy, religion, imaginative literature, trigonometry, quadratic equations, grammar, phonetics and chess. India inspired Boccaccio, Schopenhauer and Emerson". Lin Yutang (1895-1976)

"The science of yoga was born at a time when mankind was more enlightened and could easily grasp truths and ideas for which our best, our more advanced western thinkers are still groping" Anon

A brief discourse on Indian History

Dr Brahmam, a scholarly and urbane south Indian physician, had contracted with the British Colonial Office to work in British Guiana (BG) for three years, and had thus followed in the same path as hundreds of thousands of his countrymen who had gone before him, in the past century, to build the Indian Diaspora. The only difference was that he was an "*officer*", not a "slave", of the same Crown that had become synonymous with one of the worst forms of human abuse in modern civilisation. Having realised this, he had concluded, like other observers, that the behaviour of the British aristocracy in Guiana was a simple replicate of their hegemony in India and the Empire, and that what he would find in the streets and farmlands of BG—albeit on a much smaller scale—was no different from what existed in rural India among cotton growers or urban workers, struggling to eke out a living from the scraps of Empire.

And what was worse was that the British had systematically lied that things were much better under them and had taught these lies as fact to millions of eager aspiring Indian learners, rearing them to be loyal anglophiles, pleased to have been selected and elevated a rung or two above their countrymen, "respected by their fellows and bosses as good *brown Englishmen,* loyal to a young and thievish race of aristocratic strangers! It's been a terrible deception!" Dr Brahmam pounded his clenched right fist into the left palm, as he spoke.

"What British taught us as history of India is *criminal* omission and distortion; what's worse, eminent *Indian* professors *today* (1960) still teach this same nonsense from the same old English textbooks and repeat it in their own modern work! No change! Most don't know Sanskrit, and will berate anyone studying it, rather than praise them for maintaining the cultural connection. Most are socialists and embraced secularism since this freed them from what they called the bondage of religion and Sanskrit, yet they worship Marxism, like slaves. They're worse than the Brits who brain-washed them. They dismiss *Vaidas* as myth, but the real myths are their history books. *Vaidas* deal with the universe, spirituality and man's hopes and yearning for enlightenment," he stressed. "They are internationally renowned for the depth and breadth of coverage, beauty of language and imagery, and originality. The style is inspirational and universal; appeal of spiritual and scientific message has influenced subsequent religious philosophies[1]. *Sāma Vaida* is written as a song and represents earliest form of music known to man. *Vaidas* detail actions and methods of behaviour to protect civil life, communities, environment, and to ensure health, prevent and treat disease; they are a model for this age. Invaders and religious fanatics suppressed them for a millennium, so they are unknown in West, and more so among secular Indians, however educated; secularists and atheists continue to assault and reject this ancient wisdom."

"That's more or less what Mr Yesu Das told us at Berbice High seventeen years ago; he refused to teach Indian history."

We were at his flat at Taylor Hall, University College of the West Indies, Jamaica, sipping "white ladies" made to his personal recipé. He had just begun a fellowship in cardiology at the University Hospital where I was a resident. We had drifted to the discussion on a casual comment I had made about the aloofness of expatriate Indian businessmen—mostly Sindhis—who dominated Kingston's *Club India*. He had visited once only, and stayed away since, as he had found the members shallow and clannish, except re business, and, despite trying, could not find common ground for discourse, outside their *jāt*.

Being South Indian did not help. That had spurred him to review our historical evolution, and, warming to a subject that fascinated him, he continued, "We don't know for sure how old our civilisation is, but it seems reasonable that when the last ice age ended we lost a lot of developed areas along the coasts from flooding, and maybe people too, especially when the great rivers were formed from melting Himalayan snows and ice. Those who survived must have picked up the pieces by memory and simply started 'new' in India or they took what they knew to foreign places where they'd fled. But the way things developed up to the time the Muslims invaded, and from the literature that survives, Bhārata did make great strides in recouping the lost knowledge. But who knows what we lost when Islam destroyed those old Universities at Nālandā and Taxila? Or when Roman armies destroyed library at Alexandria, or when Catholics burned books and Popes held Inquisitions, and Hitler burned books, and Brits burned Hindi writings?"

"I've always marvelled at the descriptions of flying machines in the *Rāmāyana* and *Mahābhārata*; they sounded just like helicopters, VTOL's

---

[1]The *Vaidas*—my preferred English rendering as it matches the Sanskrit pronunciation and spelling—meaning *wisdom* or *knowledge*, consist of the *Rg, Atharva, Yajur and Sāma Vaidas and* are this civilisation's earliest literary and philosophical works. They stimulated the two Sanskrit epics, the *Ramāyana* and *Mahābhārata*, the latter including the *Bhagavad Gita*. They are complemented by the *Vaishnava, Shiva* and *Shakta Agamas*.

and conventional aeroplanes, or even flying 'saucers.' I remember specially the one about Bhīma in his shining aerial car, perhaps because I have a cousin named Bhīma, and I was an impressionable six when I heard this, and had not yet seen an aeroplane. So I imagined him in a boxy old Austin with wings, but now I see it as the clearest description of a space rocket."[2]

He chuckled and chanted verses in Sanskrit, the ringing consonants precisely mimicking the thundering sound of a soaring machine. He added, "*Vaidas* also refer many times to flying machines. Bhavabhuti, in millennium before Christ, quoted older references to *Pushpaka*, an aerial chariot, which carried people to Ayodhya, where, he said, sky was full of awesome flying-machines flashing yellow lights. Your teacher was right; you won't read these things in English textbooks. They worked very hard to twist peoples' minds to believe that Indians were illiterate until they brought schooling, and today their disciples still pass on that lie! James Mill perfected that tradition with his 1815 book of half-truths. And the American Miss Mayo didn't even get half the truth in her 1927 book of pure filth misnamed *Mother India*."

I did not know that one then, but I was excited and delighted to hear finally an affirmation of a view that had haunted me from the time when I first heard it, which had steered me away from pejorative accounts of India presented in my schoolbook, Williamson's history of the British Empire, whose chapter on India Mr Yesu Das, a historian, had condemned as British 'mythology'! What I had learned instead were the stories my parents had told us and the accounts given by my guru, *chacha* (uncle) Latchmanji from his study of the *Vaidas* and from writings by Vyāsa, Vālmiki, Manu, Baudhāyana, Sushruta, Tulsidās, Chanukya, Charaka, Aryābhatta, Brahmagupta and others, whose stories were the real history that he had collected over many years, with great difficulty.

More recently I had read accounts given by or about Sir William Jones, Asiatic Society founder, and by Indian critics of British occupation like Swāmi Dayānanda Saraswati, Sri Aurobindo, Swāmi Vivekānanda, Bāl Gangādhar Tilak, Rabindranāth Tāgore, Sarojini Naidu, Subhās Chandra Bose, the Mahātma, Radhakrishnan, Nehru and verbal opinions of others, including my brother-in law Tulla Hardeen and Dr JB Singh.

"The best name is Bhārata; remember that!" *Chacha* Latchman had advised, "India is a corruption of Indus or Sindhu by foreigners and Hindu is a corruption of Sindhu, because those Persians and Arabs and

---

[2] "Bhima flew along in his car, resplendent as the sun and loud as thunder...The flying chariot shone like a flame in the night sky of summer...it swept by like a comet... It was as if two suns were shining. Then the chariot rose up and all the heaven brightened." *Mahabharata*, quoted by DH Childress, *The Anti- Gravity Handbook*."

Turks apparently couldn't pronounce letter 's'. Vaidic culture was everywhere in that region, even parts of what you call Afghanistan and Iran, even to the Baluchis and ancient Arabs before Mohamed. You good at Geography; check your map."

Chacha had said much that was new to me, but mention of the atlas recalled my drawing maps of many countries, including India, for our 4th standard class at DeHoop primary school. I smiled; he continued, "You must be careful with what British say. After they conquered Mughals and realised that Hindus had no reason to become Christian, they set out to ruin us by destroying rural industry, and so they did; they gave all land to zamindars and turned thriving family food farms to opium and cane plantations and forced Chinese to use opium; they destroyed village economies, health centres and, worst of all, Hindu schools; and called *Vaidic* learning slavery and teachers tyrants! They ordered schooling in English only, but built no schools. So millions of children got no schooling, and without food farms, not even charity at time of famine. I teach today, like my father and grandfather did, in the old gurukuls; I break their law; they can jail me! If you must learn what they teach about India, learn it to pass tests, but remember, most are lies. Yesu Das is right; don't forget: *Vaidic* religion stresses *learning, true learning*; all *varnas* had to learn, even Sudras."

"Who were the *mlechchas,* chacha? They are not listed with the varnas; are they the ones the Mahābhārata called barbarians? "

"*Vaidic* peoples used that word for anyone who was foreign or who was crude and rough-behaved. Barbarians, some yes, not all."

Now years later I was hearing more of this doubt.

"But where do you get something reliable, in English, which I could read more quickly?" I asked Dr Brahmam.

"In English, I don't know," he sighed. "English books tend to be anti-Hindu, even by Hindus like Radhakrishnan; there are many books in Hindi, Marathi, Tamil, Bengali and other Indian languages. Tamil and Telugu are classical languages and still spoken; Malayalam is 90% Sanskrit and Kannada 40%. Some books have been translated into English. Read Swami Dayānanda—you have his name, I see— and PT Iyengar's excellent history, which Venkata Rao completed, and I'll lend you Sastri's book on South India. Then there's Munshi Premchand; his real name is Dhanpat Rai Srivastava; he wrote about the common people and their troubles; British banned his 1910 book, *Soz-e-Watan* (Nation's Lament), calling it seditious and burnt all copies, just like Popes and Hitler! He is great writer, in Urdu and Hindi; collected stories in Hindi called *Mānsarovar*. And Vinayak Savarkar, PB Desai and of course Gandhi, Nehru, Tilak, or better yet, go to *Vaidas* or *Agamas* directly; only you need guidance to spot the many insertions made to suit Brits."

He rocked his head from side to side as he spoke. "*Vaidas* are oldest known roots of knowledge in this world, as old as Creation itself; without philosophical change, scholars say; some feel that insertions have been made in *smritis* also, especially *Manusmriti, Upanishads* and *Purānas,* to make Hinduism look bad; also reference about Muhammad is insertion, I think. Original Sanskrit versions remain intact, they say, but who knows how much Brahmins bribed by British messed up in last two centuries? So you can't trust what's in English, or even Hindi sometimes. But with so many Indian languages, British could only tamper with texts they want to teach; these they sent everywhere. Then Gandhi translated *Gita* into Gujarati. Germans loved *Gita* and *Upanishads.* Humboldt and von Schlegel and Schopenhauer called these '*the production of the highest human wisdom*' with superhuman ideas. He called Sanskrit literature '*greatest gift of our century*' and '*Aum its supreme symbol,*' but not Müller; he distorted and mistranslated *Vaidas*. British stooge!" He hissed.[3].

"Today everybody reads Nehru's book but he repeats British propaganda. He's pro-British, I think, more Muslim than Hindu, probably anti-Hindu; he calls himself and associates new breed of 'secularist'; they want to reform or even ignore Hinduism; but they leave Islam intact, at least for now, I think because Marx wrote 100 years ago—1853, I think—that villages based on Hinduism and caste must be destroyed to 'cleanse' India, and secularists and atheists will do that. British destroyed villages but promoted caste to divide more easily. Today many Indian intellectuals demean Hindus because British educated and brain-washed them to hate India and treat Hinduism as petty myths and us Indians as primitive tribes; British tried to convert Hindus and bribed them with jobs. You know, the Brits promoted only some Hindus, mostly those who observe caste rigidly, and made each *jāt* feel special, to prevent unity; just look at how they strut in BG!"

"I know about British caste, only they call it *hierarchy,* blessed by God; at school we used to joke about Elizabethan hierarchy in our Shakespeare classes. They firmly believed in the *Chain of Being* and included everything from God and angels at the top to the lowliest plant at the bottom. There was this picture of a tree, bearing each rank on a branch, from serf to lord. Caste at its best, we said. I told that to some

[3] Muhammad Umar, Muslim scholar, in *The Review of Religions*, May/June 1993. Vol. LXXXVIII No. 5/6 names the source of the Muhammad prophesy as Bhavishyat Purana Vol. 3, verse 3. *Purānas* are collections of old tales of gods and heroes from different ages. We had learnt that the *Bhagavad Gita* crystallised Vaidic and Hindu wisdom and that we would 'never regret' living our lives by its precepts. The non-Indian population had never heard of it in the way we had heard so much of the teachings of Christ and generally scoffed at its mention, as they did at all things Indian. So I was astonished to hear the Rev. JB Cropper of the Canadian Presbyterian Church recommending it heartily.

students here when I was in Arts; they mocked me. I reminded them that most of Britain's wealthy were the lordly, and that most white colonials were middle or low class folk, who, like Vaidic Indians, paid taxes to the upper class. A few got titles by military deeds, piracy or rarely, if they got very rich, by marrying needy higher caste partners." (Ragbeer)

"Yes; widespread practice; all cultures; that was how detested moneylenders like Rothschilds aggrandised themselves to become world's most powerful family! Indian caste system did *allow* Vaishya and Shudra to do business, trade, commerce and get as rich as they wanted; rulers then preyed on them for loans and taxes! *Varna* by itself is no bar to learning or enterprise. India is full of rich Shudras; only untouchables yet to be uplifted. *Varna* is mostly horizontal, not vertical like British *Chain*. Some say that one of India's greatest dynasties, the Mauryan, was founded by Shudras. But power comes from Money; soon Money will be strongest caste, but rich men will hoard it only for themselves!"

"But what does Nehru hope that secularists will do that can't be done by Hindus? India's past greatness came from Hindus and Buddhists, not communists!"

"He and his people think Hindus will oppose socialism, reject reform on caste and women's rights, without discourse, and reject education aimed to address those issues," he observed.

"But I thought it was the orthodox Muslim who rejected education of women! Caste as practised now in India *is* a burden; it's not Hindu, not the way *we* learned about Hinduism. We learned about *"varna"* from the *Vaidas* and *Bhāgavad Gita;* I can still hear *guru* Latchmanji and later Pandit Dowlat Ram Chaubé reading and explaining *varna* as four divisions of labour based on qualities and abilities of persons, and *not* on birthright or any rigid scheme; one can move from one *varna* to another depending on circumstances, abilities, and so on, just as Jagan moved from a *shudra* (labourer) to a *Kshatriya* (administrator) or my friend Sharma from *brahmin* (teacher, which he's not) to a trader (*vaishya*)."

"When Buddhism fell, the Mughals and British, and before them Brahmins distorted concept and used caste to make divisions that would profit them and pass on and keep permanent. British favoured Brahmins and Kshatriyas, gave them new powers over others and employed them as *sipahis* (sepoys); this made caste rigid. Brits passed off *Smritis* as scripture and authority, because they could easily tamper with them, but *Smritis* are works of man, called *purusheya,* which deal with human aspects of society and rules for living at specific periods; they are not *Shruti* – which is *apurusheya,* not made by man, and presumed scriptural! Some claim that British suppressed revisions of *Manusmriti* to hide regular changes and updates that kept up with new laws and changing customs."

"Many colonies, like BG and Trinidad, got rid of the worst aspects of the British brand of caste, although some survive. What's often denounced as caste are social and economic imbalances found in all societies. It's sheer ignorance; British suppression of Hindi language and *Vaidic* education led to this. There's no society more casteist than Brits."

"Right," Dr Brahmam affirmed. "Indian government should tackle caste head-on and not ignore it or continue to punish *all* Hindus, like British and Muslims did. British were confused by India; they found a society with huge economy, advanced philosophy beyond their own, math outside their grasp that only a few like Newton could understand, ideas they'd never had, but stole them, and an enterprising people, even under Mughals. They were too immature—just a teenager culture, after all; they didn't know how to manage the shock, whose advice they should follow, whether to act as trustee as per Burke, or to play role of guardian, utilitarian or even despot; none would have worked.

"Then they seized idea of religious conversion, to destroy power of Hindus; that is today's secularism. Socialist Government and Marxists made secularism upper and middle class city religion, dressed it up with big words and fancy concepts and imaginary fears of Hindutva; they forgot that we Hindus, Buddhists and Jains rescued the tormented and persecuted from everywhere—Jews, Christians, Parsis, and others, including Muslims. They forget that Ashoka Maurya created world's first socialist government, with full control of all means of production, over *2000 years before Marx*; but he also limited the emperor's powers and fully supported peoples' rights; in this he was democratic.

"Islam and British stole our land and lived the high life. Secularism is fashionable, because it allows freedom to flout social and religious discipline and morals that the *Gita* teaches; that will degrade India and make it easier for western conquerors, USA or USSR. So blind they are; they're raising people, especially privileged women, who do PhDs in psychology or sociology, history or politics, usually abroad, and litter our literature with condemnations, neologisms and obscure phrases that require further papers to explain! This way they get academic jobs and keep tenure, while trashing their people and heritage; even the best is guilty, like Radhakrishnan. They take themselves so seriously, they don't realise how ridiculous they are. They're the new quislings, like Qasim, Jafar, Jaichandra, Mir Sadiq, Nawab Abdul Gafoor Khan, Ratipal, Ranamal, Kunwar Mansingh and their kind, before and since, who betrayed our country to Mughals and British for bribes; US and UK love and honour that kind and will use them to conquer India once more."

"I've met some who fit that description." I said. "They don't hear the ridicule or see the derogatory smirks. Even from the little I know those Indians are ignorant when they attack Hindus who quote the *Vaidas,* and wrong to dismiss *Vaidic* history simply because it's Hindu, while they slavishly accept other views just because they're non-Hindu or trendy, especially the new powers.[4] Like our fearless premier, Dr Jagan, who doesn't want to hear anything about Hindus or Hinduism."

"Yes, indeed! Secularists ridicule study of Sanskrit, don't study *Vaidas*, *Rāmāyana* or *Gita* yet dismiss their content, accept European versions of everything, and give Hindu scholars dirty looks and names, in true colonial style, attack being the best form of defence. Because they're anti-religion, they accept Darwin's evolution hypothesis, quite ignorant of the fact that this is in keeping with *Vaidas*, which speak of ten major *evolutionary* avatars[5] in Hinduism. So they look stupid when they deny or downplay anything that glorifies India's past, as if progress to the point of great wealth that attracted invaders happened by chance or in vacuum. Also they miss how closely avatars match morphology of species from dawn of life, from seabed to land, and from fins to feet! We know too little to discard even our myths. West formulated Atomic theory just last century. Kanadā deduced this over 2000 years ago, and that is using British compressed timing; truth may put in another one or two thousand years back. Other ancients talked of atoms and void."

"My old Bio Prof. Millott would love this! He's the Brit who condemned all doctors, and medical students, as dumb and greedy."

"I've met some like that and of course he's partly right. But doesn't he know that British propaganda educated us mainly for government jobs, that Indian students faithfully crammed false British version of 'facts' to pass examinations? Indian scholars rank British teaching above Indian,

---

[4]"Romila Thapar, a leftist Indian historian paradoxically favoured by and prospering in the capitalist West, seems to fit this description perfectly," he agreed. "She built a career on an anti-Hindu, pro-US, pro-Islam and pro-Aryan-invasion portrayal of Indian history, knowing little of Sanskrit or the *Vaidas*." Despite her bias, or because of it, and far left orientation, she has been recognised by the US Library of Congress as a referee on the history of India, over the objections of Indo-Americans.

[5] The *major* Prophets are, in order of their coming: *Matsya*, fish; *Kumura* tortoise; *Vahara* boar; *Nārasimha* man-lion; *Vamana* dwarf; *Parshuram* an imperfect man; *Rāma*, physically a perfect man; *Krishna*, the son of a Virgin; *Buddha* (first millennium BCE); and *Kalki*, who is yet to appear, though some claim that he is today's Satya Sai Baba of South India. Some Baha'i claim Baha'u'llah for this role and Ahmadiyyas propose Ghulam Ahmed. Hinduism recognises several others as prophets, including Mahavir, Jesus Christ, Mohamed and Nanak." Madame H. P. Blavatsky in "*The Secret Doctrine*" (Theosophical Press, 1888) wrote, *"In this list of avatars we can trace the gradual evolution and transformation of all species out of the ante-Silurian mud of Darwin to the zodiacal "beasts "of the Babylonian god Oannes. Beginning with the Azoic time in which Brahma implants the creative germ, we pass through the Palaeozoic and Mesozoic period, covered by His first and second incarnations as the Fish and Tortoise; and the Cenozoic which is embraced by the incarnations in animal and semi-human forms of the Boar and Man-Lion; and we come to the fifth and crowning geological period, designated as the "era of mind," or "age of man," whose symbol in Hindu mythology is the Dwarf—the first attempt of nature to create man."*

even what's wrong, and continue to teach them, with great force and passion, condemning anyone who disagrees. Some even call themselves scientists, yet fail in the first task of a scientist, which is to be objective and consider *all* evidence. They fear Hindus educated in Sanskrit and versed in *Vaidas,* belittle those who demand change in these old curricula, when they should be fearing Islam which is much more sinister and militant; they forget that Islamists have let them down again and again; it's very fragile religion, easily driven to senseless violence by anarchists; I'm afraid that Wahhabi doctrines from Arabia will spread."

"Wahhabi? I know about wallabies; not Wahhabis. What are these?"

"Muslims who follow severe doctrine of Mohammed ibn Abdul Wahhab, mid-18th century mullah who restricted Sunni Islam to teachings of first three generations of Islamic leaders, called *salafi,* means old, who had contact with prophet; *Wahhabism* is fundamentalist sect of *salafis.* Wahhab was expelled from one Arabian tribe or another for extremism but went to Nejd in Arabia and made pact of mutual support with tribe leader ibn Saud, ancestor of family that rules Arabia today.

"Chief danger is that oil will make Saudis rich and give them lots of money to take over *madrassahs* in Arabia, Middle East, Pakistan and beyond. Soviets will keep them in check, but I fear for India under Nehru's blind pro-Islam leadership, since Wahhabis believe that Islam must reject and even destroy all non-Muslim ideas and beliefs; they even condemn Muslim groups like Ahmadiyyas, Shi'a and Sufi. Wahhabism is big threat to India and to whole world, if it begins to spread."

"Wow! That's frightening. Extremism is a danger in any religion but worst in Islam, which seems free with *jihad* and *fatwa,* and promises of great rewards in heaven for murder or suicide done for 'religion'. There are some radical Muslims in this country, but the vast majority are peaceful and friendly; I've never heard of any Wahhabis."

"They won't spread easily until they get big money to train children to be fanatics by teenage, when hormones turn boys hungry for sex. So far they're only in Arabia, the older people, clerics and Bedouins, even though you'll find *salafis* in Egypt and other Muslim countries that have *Muslim Brotherhood.* India has *Jamaat-e-islami,* started by a zealot named Abu Ala Maudoodi who wanted an independent sharia state. *Vaidic* strengths can protect India, especially with *ahimsa* in Hinduism, Buddhism, Jainism and tolerance of religions, beliefs and peoples. You know, India spread culture over most of Asia without making any big enemies. They did this because after migrating somewhere they adapted to local customs and let people choose, whether in China, Bali or Indonesia. Gupta Rāja Vikramaditya brought Indian culture and learning to Arabia; it's said he made *Ka'aba* a Hindu temple, which explains Mohammed's reference to smashing *murtis.* Vikram created prosperity and was liked, according to pre-Islam poets. So when nations invaded India it was not to punish her, but to rob her!"

"I have to thank my parents and *nana* for their knowledge and insight and my teachers Ben Yesu Das and *chacha* Latchmanji, who opened doors for me, and others who cared. Mr. Das gave us a choice of what to study, where the facts were not so badly distorted or contested, and steered us in the direction of tolerance and neighbourliness. I think he was unique and rather brave among teachers of that time; he would have been replaced for sure by a white teacher, if the war was not on."

"In India we had only one syllabus and most of teachers were already two, three generations brain-washed! French and others were more open to India and gave fairer accounts. La Fontaine copied *Panchatantra* fables for his book; read Louis Jacolliot, a French envoy to India, or Madame Blavatsky, Annie Besant, or *The Story of Civilisation* by the American, Will Durant; better, get Hindi poetry of Subhadra Kumari Chauhan, and others not available in West. You *must* go outside British and righteous seculars and Marxist Indian historians, if you want truth and inspiration. Most of them today merely echo old British propaganda, gang up on anyone who is Hindu; they generally know too little about religion, much less Hinduism, to be fair. If they have any religion it's sanitised view of Islam. Marx wanted to destroy India. You must go there and see for yourself. India cannot be taught; it must be experienced! And yet your people have a much better grasp of Indian history and heritage than people in India! Especially our secularists and middle class!"

"I wondered about that; I know about the British: Jones, Hastings, Clive, Mill, Wellesley, Macaulay, Müller, Monier Williams, Kipling and that lot. And I've read Americans Sheridan, William Bryan, Mark Twain[6] and others. I suspect that some of the doctors here, Grewal, Stracey, Shenolikar, Bhattacharya and others know only the British version of things and are proper *coconuts*. That would explain why they're shy of talking with us, and why they con their patients; I heard they were shocked to find that the two senior hospital administrators, Balkaran Singh and Indar Persaud, were staunch Hindus, like Balwant Singh, the lab director, and Nehaul, the Deputy CMO."

---

[6]*"This is indeed India! The land of dreams and romance, of fabulous wealth and fabulous poverty, of splendour and rags, of palaces and hovels, of famine and pestilence, of genii and giants and Aladdin lamps, of tigers and elephants, the cobra and the jungle, the country of a hundred nations and a hundred tongues, of a thousand religions and two million gods, cradle of the human race, birthplace of human speech, mother of history, grandmother of legend, great-grandmother of tradition, whose yesterdays bear date with the mouldering antiquities of the rest of the nations – the one sole country under the sun that is endowed with an imperishable interest for alien prince and alien peasant, for lettered and ignorant, wise and fool, rich and poor, bond and free, the one land that all men desire to see, and having seen once, by even a glimpse, would not give that glimpse for the shows of all the rest of the globe combined.* Mark Twain, *Following the Equator*, 1896

"Balkaran took them to a *Maha Sabha* function." Brahmam recalled, chuckling. "That was awkward; I'm afraid my colleagues had no clue what was happening. They didn't go back! But ordinary Indians still treat these fellows like gods."

"I noticed that. But tell me; is Nehru Communist, like Jagan?"

"Not really; he's Attlee-walla, *vāmpanthi* (leftist). His policies make many best-qualified Indians leave India. British rejected socialism ten years ago, but it *survives* in India. *Everything British survives in India*," he said regretfully. "We celebrate British and Islam's heroes and writers, instead of Indian ones, in place names. You'll see Victoria, Shakespeare, Nelson, Newton, Clive, Dalhousie,[7] Akbar, etc. rather than Aryābhatta, Pānini, Bhāskara, Bhikaji Cāma, Lakshmi Bai, Tantia Tope, Madan Mohan, Tilak, Banerjea, Rai, and a million others. Libraries in India still promote British, Greek and Roman literature and science, even Arabic; and the schools, especially private schools for rich, have mainly British curricula and slavish copycat methods, even their clothes. Where do you find genuine Sanskrit epics and classics, which came before all these and gave rise to them? Where is *ganita, Vaidic* science, or *agnihotra*? These are sciences, which we invented. Shri Aurobindo felt that *Sanatan Dharma* must return to India if India is to survive. I agree with him."

"British historian Toynbee said something similar; but are the secularists so brain-washed that they don't know the best of India's *Vaidic* heritage? Even Nehru admitted India's greatness and how much that derived from Hindutva."

"Yes, Nehru does[8], but more Marxist secularists do not. It will be long struggle to restore primacy of *Vaidas*, but we have to do it. What I fear most is that secularists will enrich themselves, condemn Hindus in books and publications, which West will gladly print, and fail to educate villagers; India's strength is in villages, not cities; villages are 70% or more of India; they are real Bharat; *cities suck its blood*. We have to give country back to villages. Coming here I expected to find lost people, in spite of what the recruiter said. But I found instead that he understated the incredible preservation of *Vaidic* wisdom, which most Indian cities have lost. I even see things from *Atharva Vaida* which we learned to ridicule in medical school, but they work: for fevers, injuries, mental

---

[7]After independence, the Dalhousie Square was named B.B.D. Bagh - after martyrs: Benoy, Badal and Dinesh.

[8]Despite his secular politics J. Nehru recognized India's Hindu heritage without allowing himself to use "*Hindu*" or "*Vaidic*" when he lamented: "*How few of us know of these great achievements of our past, how few realize that if India was great in thought and philosophy, she was equally great in action. Most westerners still imagine ancient history is largely concerned with the Mediterranean countries, and medieval and modern history is dominated by the quarrelsome little continent of Europe.*"

health, arthritis and so on. The loyalty of Indian migrants to their heritage in these European colonies is truly amazing, and shames us in India. This is partly why my colleagues cannot relate to Indians here. Also, your good relations with Muslims prove *Vaidic* life style is not anti-Islam, as some say; in fact its tolerance is its strength, as Swami Vivekānanda so pithily proclaimed decades ago and Swami Prakashānanda has documented in greater detail more recently."[9]

"You'll find the same in Trinidad, Mauritius, Fiji, and Suriname where Indians did better and preserved language; the Dutch apparently did not ban studies in Hindi. As for Muslims, a few have begun to distort history and claim origin from Pakistan, giving it an ancient identity! So soon, they're only 12 years old![10] This is sheer ignorance. Some even pretend to be Arabic, especially the radical ones. All ordinary Muslims I know are embarrassed by this."

"There is so much ignorance even among the educated. You must tell them that there is no need to pretend; an interchange of peoples took place for millennia along the trading cities of the Arabian coast. Arabs and Yemenis and Persians resemble Indians."

We talked at great length of how India had founded a great civilisation many millennia before Christ, and had become a leading power in the ancient world, with an "almost perfect language and most tolerant and peaceful religions, which Congress leaders today are afraid to explore or accept. Some of this is because they're not certain as to what is not corrupted or changed. For instance, the British say the Mauryans reigned from 322 BCE, a date given by a judge named Pargiter around 1900; he was chair of Asiatic Society and came to this date by making assumptions of how long the rule of Nandas and others lasted; he took great pains to make it fit in Christian calendar; his error is still widely taught. Hindu sources give 1541 BCE as the date! (See Fn 9).

"They call Vaidic scholars who dissent fanatics, and claim that all Brahmins support caste and militancy. Utter nonsense! Secularists hold power, but they weaken Indian culture. The scriptures are our strength. We must preserve that! We must be fearless in telling our story, despite Christian evangelists from America. I don't think that Nehru has the skill or the will to set rules, but sooner or later India must or its culture and religions will suffer. The one that will be assaulted first is Hinduism. It's already begun in South India and in the east and will spread."

---

[9]"Swami Vivekānanda (1863-1902) ; see Bibliography for Prakashānada Saraswati.

[10] This conversation took place in April 1960; if anything , modern Pakistani historians have become more insistent, and in many ways irrational, in pushing the falsehood of an "ancient" Pakistan, distorting Indian history, just as the British had done! (Wynbrandt).

Chapter 1

"Prajāpatir vai idam sit/tasya vag dvitiyā asit;/Vag vai parāmam Brahmā." (In the beginning was Brahma; /with whom was Vag or the Word; /And the Word was Brahma) *Rg Vaida*

"I am proud to belong to a religion that has taught the world both tolerance and universal acceptance." *Swami Vivekananda*

"The world is led by intelligence, is established in intelligence...The support is intelligence. Brahman is intelligence." *Aiteriya Upanishad 3: iii, translated by* V.Jayaram

Origins

The culture of India[11] is very old and at various times had spread to most of South Asia, Afghanistan, Indo-China, Indonesia and parts of Iran, and influenced China, Tibet and the Philippines. Since 1924, excavations and reconstructions of ruins along the Sindhu and recently rediscovered Saraswati Rivers—see maps pp 9-11—confirm that Indian civilisation is much older than is currently taught in the west, and in many Indian schools, and more closely matches accounts and dates given in the *Vaidas* than those in the revisionist propaganda of the British and their Indian acolytes.

The first hominids are said to have originated in East Africa 2-3 million years ago and spread to Asia leaving traces which can be used to characterise and age them.[12] It would take most of the subsequent 2 million years for various evolutionary human forms to develop, including *Homo erectus, Homo habilis* and others to *Homo sapiens,* until about 200,000 BCE, when *Homo sapiens sapiens* emerged in East Africa.

Stone artefacts two million years old have been found in northern India, and evidence of elephants and other animals; hand axes and other tools 0.5 million years old have been found in Punjab and Tamil Nadu, and a culture known as Soan was defined 400,000 years ago similar to other cultures in African and Asian sites. In time, hominids in Northern India learned to use hand tools and by 470,000 BCE could be found over much of India, from north to south. *Homo erectus* appeared around 360,000 BCE and learned to use fire, like those in China. Their successors *Homo sapiens* became dominant in Africa and Asia until *Homo sapiens sapiens* spread and, like their fore-runners, mingled with earlier species.

---

[11]It is hoped that readers will be encouraged to consult sources closer to the *Vaidas* and other authentic Indian sources, mindful that records in most western and even Indian universities, many Indian textbooks and many educated Indians, especially secular ones, still believe, write and teach erroneous 19th century British propaganda. The *Bibliography* hopefully includes enough authorities to correct this, but resistance remains rigid.

[12] The science of dating artefacts is still imprecise but estimates will bear a fairly stable relationship if measuring errors are skewed all in the same direction. DNA traces add verification to historical research on population movements.

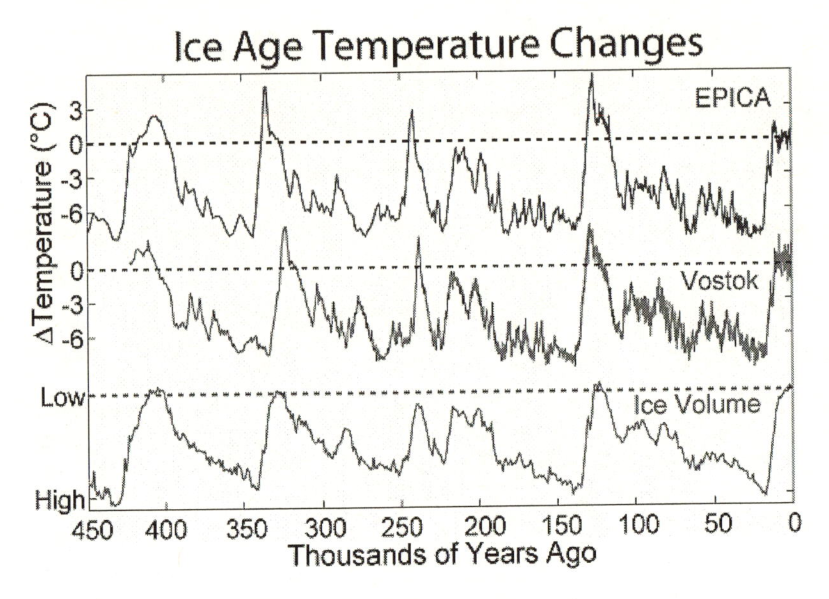

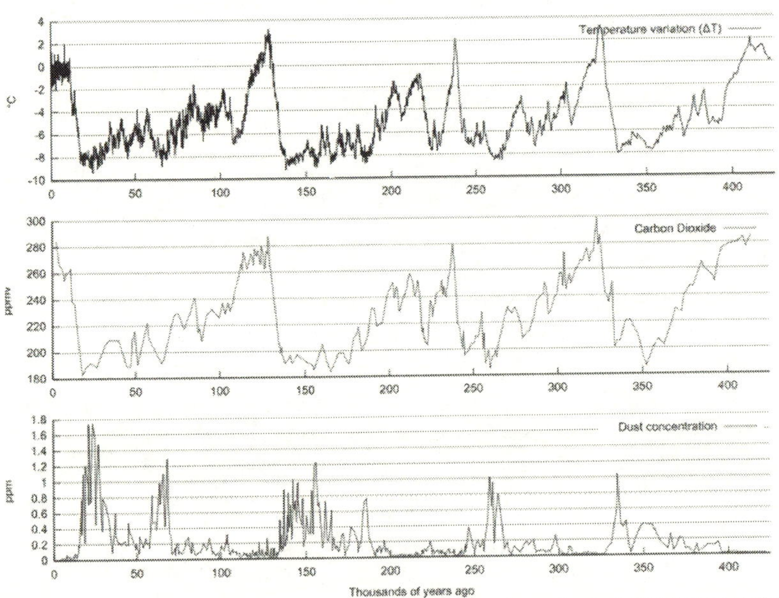

The Earth's orbital eccentricity, tilt, and precession vary in a pattern over thousands of years. The IPCC notes that Milankovitch cycles drove the ice age cycles; CO_2 followed temperature change "with a lag of some hundreds of years" (visible on a graph more zoomed in than this); and that as a feedback amplified temperature change. Among other factors, CO_2 is more soluble in colder than in warmer waters. (2010-06-20 13:2 [UTC]. Author Vostok-ice-core-petit.png: NOAA derivative work: Autopilot [Robert A. Rhode])

They were hunter-gatherers similar to the Barama Caribs of the Guyana forests and various groups deep in the Amazon and Congolese hinterlands. Their growth could have been affected by the ice age, which began *circa* 75,000 BCE, changed the world, and perhaps cleansed it. The charts give a perspective of climate trends for many thousand years and aid understanding of the events. The deep freeze and lowering of sea level exposed continental shelves and land masses in various shallow seas worldwide. East and south of India a vast area is said to have appeared known as *Sundaland* incorporating all of Indonesia, the Philippines and Southeast Asia which with India formed a contiguous land mass—a Greater India—stretching from the Himalayas to the western edge of the Pacific Ocean, and separated from Australia by a strait, across which people could have readily migrated. The relative warmth of this vast subcontinent had kept the land habitable and productive throughout the period of glaciation. The massive Himalayan glaciers so locked in the huge volume of moisture that early Vaidic observers likened the phenomenon to a giant serpent that had ringed the Himalayas and barricaded its waters, creating the aridity of early northern and north-western India.

Indians generally survived the ice-age, during which people were organised as tribes, mainly hunter-gatherers, and, as they adapted to the environment, gradually developed skills in various occupations which would later identify them. The south exploited the plentiful deposits of iron ore for tools and cookware, while copper was similarly used in the north. This specialisation would in time facilitate the classification of available skills into the system of four *varnas (see p.42).* Painted-rock shelters of ca. 40,000 BCE and earlier—perhaps as long ago as the Palaeolithic age—have been found in central India and the Deccan, and primitive cave art in many locations, some quite elaborate, included pictures of a hunter on a horse and warriors on horses and elephants. Coastal tribes learned navigation, which led to marine exploration and migration to Australia and the Pacific islands, presumably from the shores of Sundaland, and the Kumari sub-continent (p.6), to find less arid lands during the long ice age, which lasted so many generations that it appeared permanent. Many tribes appeared to have roamed north of the Himalayas and settled in the Middle East and southern Europe, about 35,000 BCE and later; this roughly coincided with the migration of various Asian tribes to the Americas across the frozen Bering Sea.

Some believe that migrations had also followed natural sea routes, established in the past from study of winds and ocean currents. The 1947 *Kon-tiki* expedition under Thor Heyerdahl, in a balsa raft, and his other voyages established the fact that the Pacific could be crossed in pre-Columbian sea-craft. However, the *Rāmāyana* (p.15, footnote 2) suggests that man had invented and used flying machines much earlier for long journeys. When and why they disappeared is another mystery raised by study of the *Vaidas* and Indian epics.[14]

Kon-tiki raft

According to the *Vaidas,* Indian civilisations had developed along various rivers and coastlines, with growth of cities and ports, as civilisation advanced to the Neolithic period. Settlements became feasible and more plentiful as agriculture developed, tools were refined, animals tamed and exploited for food, for example milk, and for work. Cities carried on a brisk trade with neighbours, and later, with countries farther away, in agricultural produce—grains and cotton—salt and artisanry. The main Indian port on the Arabian Sea was Dwaraka, a city of Lord Krishna, on the Gulf of Kacch, where submerged ruins of a complex city have been identified validating the *Vaidic* account. (The much later Mathura is also a city of Krishna.)

It is known that the glacial period ended about 12,000 years ago. Melting Himalayan snows enlarged the many rivers that resulted, converting arid northern India into fertile and productive lands. The major streams were the massive *Saraswati, Sindhu, Ganga and Brahmaputra* in the north and east; the *Narmada, Tapti* and *Mahanadi* centrally and the *Godavari, Krishna* and *Kaveri* in the south The major kingdoms developed along them in the next centuries.

When the globe thawed around 10,000 BCE, the melting ice and increased rainfall from convection and wind movements that sprang from the warming waters, and tectonic shifts, raised sea levels over 300 feet, drowning lowland, converting rivers to seas, and seas to oceans, resulting in the topography we know today. The extensive consequential flooding of low coastal lands by high seas, and of the hinterland by river courses, destroyed much, including readily accessible evidence of antediluvian civilisations; some were indeed identified and explored in the last 90 years, at first desultorily and presented as curiosities in British

---

[14] The migration dates are approximate and roughly coincide with modern estimates of the disappearance of large animals in several continents. Did man, the ultimate predator, bring about some species extinction such as he is causing today and do these migrations represent his search for new sources of food? We will await the verdict of palaeontologists. The suggestion of early flight is also noted later in the book.

versions of Indian history, but rather more objectively and extensively in the past six decades, by Indians in the Archaeological Survey of India. At the same time, linguists, especially Sanskritists, probed the *Vaidas* and scientists applied new knowledge to study humans and their records. These suggest that the Dwaraka ruins are at least 9,000-11,000 years old.

The Himalayan torrents—the metaphor of the serpents slain by Indra—swelled the Indus and Saraswati river courses, both mentioned in the *Rg Vaida 1, 32,* and promoted developments for the next several millennia. Many city states grew and thrived along their banks; these are now collectively called the Saraswati/Indus civilisation (see map p.11).

Many settlements were undoubtedly lost in the floods, especially along low-lying river valleys and in coastal regions less than 300-400 feet above sea level. Presumably escape was possible and could account for the tribal settlements in the highlands of Indonesia and Australia. The *Manusmriti* records the help given by Matsya, an avatar of Vishnu, who guided Manu and others to escape the flood and resettle the land, rather like the later story of Noah, the Jew. (*The Bible, Genesis Ch. 6-9*; see also *Shatpatha Brāhmana 1, 8:1-6*)

Gradually civilisation resumed as various skills re-developed and recovery continued in all phases of activity with development of new settlements, villages, cities and kingdoms. In time, the floods abated and a more stable form of the waterways developed, permitting long-term planning and the development of a new civilisation.

The British had dismissed as myth Vaidic accounts of these cities, until the ruins of the first two, Harappa and Mohenjo-Daro, were identified in 1924, and subsequently many more (p.11). Similarly, those settlements thrived that had sprung up on the banks of the Yamuna and Ganga Rivers, on the Brahmaputra further east, and along the Vindhyan and Deccan rivers in central and south India. Streams also flowed from the Himalayas north, west and east, to nourish lands between them and the Persian Gulf and south central Asia. Thus was provided the ample fresh water needed to sustain large Asian populations, which in India became increasingly complex, as growing knowledge and technology influenced societal development.

At the end of the ice age, India's population was about one million and the world's estimated at 4 million. Indians gradually began to cultivate grains—barley and wheat among the earliest, as agricultural knowledge had survived the glaciation—domesticate animals, build cities, study the heavens and to develop a guiding philosophy. In the following millennia, their beliefs became the foundation of the four *Vaidas,* which represent not only original and unique spiritual and intellectual insights, but some of the most sublime and riveting poetry in the world, composed in Sanskrit, the ancient Indian *lingua franca.*

A depiction of Matsya, an avatar of Vishnu, leading Manu to escape the flood

From these works and the great epics of the age, the *Rāmāyana* and *Mahābhārata*, it seems clear that the civilisations of the Saraswati, Indus and the Ganga valleys—and contemporaneous coastal settlements, which had submerged in the great flood—had perfected the philosophy presented in the Vaidas, nurturing it, through the vicissitudes of life, time and place, spreading it from its base in western India to the cities and kingdoms of the lower Ganga and Brahmaputra and their tributaries, and south throughout India.

The course of the Saraswati River crossed lush grasslands and forests in northern India, as it flowed from the Himalayas to the Arabian Sea; it lay east of the Sindhu (Indus) River and almost parallel to it, with the Yamuna among its tributaries. West of the Sindhu were the dry highlands where Baluchi, Pashtu, Afghan and other tribes roamed to the borders of Persia. These peoples have remained in tight clans, rarely sharing in the social and economic growth of the settled kingdoms to the east, south and west.

Prosperity spawned larger and more complex communities along the banks of the Saraswati and Indus Rivers, and likely others not yet discovered. The *Rg Vaida* tells of them and of the region drained by these large rivers and their five main tributaries: *Shatadru (Sutlej), Vipasa (Beas), Asikni (Chenab), Parosni (Ravi), Vitasta (Jhelum).*[15] The Ganga and Yamuna Rivers and their tributaries also developed great religious significance as

[15] *Saptasindhu (seven rivers)*; the five main tributaries, *paanch ab*, (five rivers, in Hindi), gave the region its English rendition, Punjab, now shared by India and Pakistan.

suggested in one of many references in the *Mahābhārata* (1:172, 8761) *"They who drink the waters of these seven streams: Ganga, Yamuna, Saraswati, Vitasta, Sarayu, Gomati, and Gandaki, are, cleansed of all their sins."*[16] Similar, if not greater powers were ascribed to the Narmada River.

Indians: traditional regional attires

The sub-continent was heavily forested, rich in animal life, with numerous rivers and fertile valleys. Each tribe in the earliest days held territory collectively, exploited its resources to benefit all and defended it. The tribes were each led by a *rāja* (king), guided by administrators (Brahmins or learned men), and frequently raided one another's livestock. For nomadic tribes the size of the herd expressed their owner's wealth, and it seems certain that early conflicts might have erupted not only in response to raids but over grazing rights. As settlement consolidated along the great rivers, rules and conventions were framed to control land use and minimise conflicts, but the opposing positions of grain and stock farmers would remain an enduring challenge, as in other parts of the world.

Geographic features of mountain, river or forest created natural boundaries and provided security; yet weaker tribes often fell to expansionist or greedy neighbours. Marriage among ruling families was a more civilised way of acquiring and strengthening territory. As morality, virtue and ideas of justice matured with the intercession of divine guidance, violence would be scrutinised and its use to solve problems censured, (via *avatars*)[17] At times, however, it would erupt with regrettable results. The settlements, though often far apart, showed common features united by commerce, religion, language, and other beliefs and practices. The first of these old settlements was discovered in 1924 at Harappa in Punjab, and Mohenjodaro and Mehrgarh in Sindh. The discovery of skeletons led Mortimer Wheeler, briefly head of

[16] Translated by Kisari Mohan Ganguli. 1883-96

[17] *"Bee chakram prithoi aishai ta khestraaeh Vishnu mansai das sayaan throvaah so asaya keeryo janaas oeroo khashatra so janama chakaar (8)"* meaning "Whenever sinful ways rise up in the world and noble behaviour vanishes, just as the moon disappears on the darkest night, there will appear Vishnu as a prominent Prophet from the Kshatriya Clan and will manifest in consecutive form through 10 Prophets to restore the ways of virtue to the ailing world." *Rg Vaida (i): Mandala 7, Ush 5, Mantra 5.*

archaeological survey of India, then under the British, to conclude that they were victims of invaders into India, in line with a popular though discredited 19th century British belief that Indian culture had been shaped by outsiders: Max Müller's "aryan invasion" hypothesis. This was widely publicised—despite rejection by Indian scholars— especially after Wheeler returned to a professorship in London.

Hardly had it been published than this view was shown to be erroneous by others, using Wheeler's own technique of stratigraphy, which clearly showed that the skeletons were of different eras and bore no marks of violence. Nevertheless, the belief survived as gospel, as it supported the cause of the British imperialists and continues to permeate major writings about the ancient Saraswati-Sindhu (Indus) civilisation, including accounts in encyclopaedias.

Water reservoir at Dholavira, Saraswati civilisation. (Photo Rama's Arrow)

In the last six decades numerous other sites have been found, including Lothal, Rakhigari, Dholavira, Dwaraka (the great port near the mouth of the Saraswati River at the Rann of Kacch on the Arabian Sea) and others mentioned in Hindu texts[18]. The use of satellite imagery has been invaluable in confirming the location of cities that sank after the ice age ended. Computer models of ancient Arabian Sea coastlines confirm subsidence of wide areas of land in Gujarat near the Rann of Kacch which were once above sea level. This includes Dwaraka, now reckoned to be about 12,000 years old—which tallies with Plato's estimate of the period of the flooding of Atlantis—and other sites of the Saraswati civilisation, dated between 7000 and 12,000 years old, conforming to Vaidic accounts and consistent with the current dating of Vaidic Sanskrit

[18]See p.9 and *http://www.youtube.com/watch?v=d733X4nYHW*

as at least 8000 years old. The discovery of Dwaraka lends support to the Tamil *Kaliththokai,* which tells of *Kumari Kandam,* the legendary "continent" ruled by Pandyas and Cheras for 10,000 years before it became swallowed by the rising Indian Ocean.

The Saraswati-Sindhu cities had paved streets, laid out in a grid pattern—like Manhattan, New York, or Santo Domingo, Hispaniola, which was the first western city so laid out, in 1498—large brick buildings, granaries and other warehouses, piped water, indoor plumbing, sewage disposal and other features, like most modern cities, but ironically lacking in many parts of India today. In addition, many homes had brick altars used in *Vaidic* ceremonial worship of Lord Shiva, and clay figurines of females probably representing *Shakti.* Of note is the exactness of the dimensions of the vessels used for the ritual fire *(agnihotra)* and the composition of the herbs *(sāmagri)* used to create its fragrant and health-giving vapours (Narang).

The numerous scientific and structural innovations found in these ancient cities confirmed the advanced knowledge of mathematics and science possessed by the builders, thus predating the earliest Greek science by several millennia. Indeed the close similarities between what is claimed as Greek achievements of the millennium before Christ and the earlier work of Indians in the sciences, medicine and mathematics, and the antiquity of the latter suggest that there was a wide and deep transfer of knowledge between Indians and Greeks; many Greeks, like Euclid, may have, in the normal course of scholarship, contributed to the solution of problems in geometry, or shared their expertise. It is pertinent to note the relationship between mathematics and Vaidic and other religious thought; the similarity between Hindu and Greek gods including their mountain abodes, Mount Meru and Mount Olympus, respectively; the names of heroes and heroines; how closely the plot line of the *Iliad* follows that of the *Ramayana,* and the same for many stories.

The needs and tenets of Indian religions could have driven the search for mathematical solutions, or perhaps the reverse. Whichever it was, Indian religions are partly based on several practices supported by biosciences and mathematics. Their development was extensively studied and documented in Indian classical literature, particularly the *Shastras* and *Sutras,* of which the *Sulbasutras,* by various authors at different times, most likely as early as the fourth millennium BCE, record specifics in great detail, long before others in Mesopotamia, Egypt or Greece. There is scholarly evidence that Indian mathematics was the source of the knowledge used in ancient Egypt and Babylonia (Seidenberg) and later adopted by Arabs, who combined Indian algebra (*beez ganita*) with their own and some from other sources—including the geometric algebra of the Greek Diophantus—and published as *Al gebr* by Al Khorazmi (780-850 CE).

To illustrate, the arithmetical concepts of zero, uniform digits 1-9 and place value were taken from India to Arabia along with other scientific ideas. The Arabs called the numerals "*hindsa*" (Indian). This practice continues in Saudi Arabia, where in 1982 Arabic scholars freely acknowledged that they had learned mathematics from India, yet Europe and America continued to call it *Arabic*, though recently *"Hindu-Arabic"* has begun to appear. Also mystifying are the claims of Muslims in Pakistan, Central Asia and elsewhere that Arabs followed the Quran and "invented" modern science, mathematics, computers and so on! These themes, however, were already covered in ancient India, in the context of *Triskandh Jyotisha,* before the end of the 1st millennium BCE, before Greek contributions to Mathematics and more than fifteen hundred years before Islam.

In the first millennium CE in Europe, the clergy were islands of learning within seas of illiteracy, ignorance and the pagan beliefs of the Dark Ages. As Greek declined in the Roman Empire, the main source of new knowledge was the Arab conquerors, who had by the eighth century militarily advanced to the south of France and occupied the Iberian Peninsula (*map, p.110*). By the 9th century, they had introduced and disseminated learning on a variety of themes via Latin: mathematics, sciences, medicine, architecture, astronomy and grammar. Church scholars slowly came to learn the value of the new way of reckoning and adopted them, as the Middle Ages gave way to the Renaissance, and education slowly spread, bringing the flood of knowledge, with periodic updates, to the lay population, as travel and conquest increased.

Arabs were given credit for new knowledge and discoveries in agriculture, algebra, anatomy, astronomy, mathematics, medicine, navigation etc. This misleading attribution has stubbornly persisted in western records, unopposed by Indian secularists and anti-Hindu activists from within and outside India, perhaps due to their erroneous anglocentric learning. Diligent corrections were made by many scholars, as listed in the *Bibliography,* including analysts like Arya, Gautier, Seidenberg, Srivasta, Klostermeier, Frawley, Rajaram, Elst, Talageri and many others, including the Archaeological Survey of India. The *Vaidas* and *Agamas* provide original knowledge, but the pall of darkness clouding this knowledge remains, so powerfully entrenched have the foundations of distraction and deception laid by the British become, despite repeated corrections from contrary scientific, linguistic and archaeological evidence.

Lord Siva weds Goddess Meenakshi, Lord Vishnu Hands over his Sister. (These names are not original to the Vaidas but a later adoption.)

Gateway at Harappa (http://www.crystalinks.com/induscivilization.html)

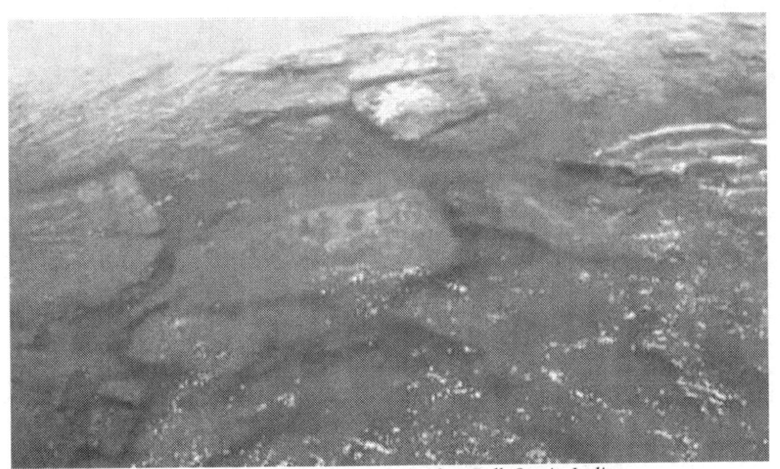

Stone slabs at site of Rama's Bridge, Palk Strait, India

Coin of the Bactrian King Agathocles, showing Hindu deities Vasudeva-Krishna and Balarama-Samkarshana, Brahmi script.

A depiction of Krishna with herdsmen, gopis and cows, Pahari Painting, (Smithsonian)

Chapter 2

"I think that the Aryan Invasion theory in its classic form is dead."
Richard Villems, geneticist, Estonian Biocentre

"In the RgVeda we shall have before us more real antiquity than in all the inscriptions of Egypt or Ninevah....the Veda is the oldest book in existence..." Max Muller, 1859

"What is found herein may also be found in other sources. What is not found herein does not matter."
The Mahabharata

Discovery; Growth; Organisation: kingdoms rise and fall

From the beginnings of Indian civilisation, inquiring and observant minds—the first of an unending line of scholars—had marvelled at the richness of earthly life, the myriad forms of living things, animal and plant, that covered the land, how they inter-related, propagated and survived. They pondered the meaning of life, and probed its origin, purpose, rhythms and cycles. The sun, moon and other heavenly bodies, with their unique periodicities, had stimulated wonderment and speculation. In due course, reaction moved from awe to scientific examination and determination of the properties of physical and metaphysical phenomena, which led to the concept of an inclusive and extensive, eventually limitless universe. Above all, they puzzled over the creation of all the wondrous complexity and diversity that they saw each day.

By study and contemplation the sages[19] of that remote era—among whom were the peripatetic "wise men" (scientists) who communed among the many tribes they visited—developed theories of the nature of the universe and of its creation as a coherent whole, one that saw the universe in each person and each one as part of the ultimate *Creator.* They integrated the wisdom and observations of their forebears who, in previous iterations of civilisation, had noted the succession of *avatars* who had appeared, at critical stages of evolution, to guide living creatures. Eventually they had revealed to mankind this lineage and thereby some of the mystery of Creation, including concepts of the *Universal Presence* or *Supreme Force – Brahmān*—that had made it possible, of which they were a part, and with which they could reunite through

---

[19]*Saksat krtdharmanah rsayo babhuvuh* (Nirukta, 1:20), that is, *"Rsis (Rishis) were born who visualized universal laws of nature in the form of the Vaidas."* (Trans. by Prof. Ravi Prakash Arya, Indian Foundation for Vaidic Science, New Delhi). One of the foremost was Nārada Muni, a peripatetic sage, known for his unique musical instrument, the *veena,* songs in praise of Vishnu and authorship of the *Pāncharātra* (dealing with deity worship in temples), *Nāradsmriti* dealing with jurisprudence, and*Nārada Bhakti Sutra* dealing with *Bhakti yoga.* He is noted for the ability to move between material and spiritual spheres and is discussed widely in the *Bhāgavad Purana* and *Ramāyana.*

good works. They recorded this knowledge—from the end of the Ice Age, when Manu, guided by Matsya, the avatar, had led their ancestors towards high ground and away from floods; they kept the knowledge sacrosanct and passed it on down the generations, with names for each function and functionary, attribute and place, and each discovery. Yet too many records have been lost to allow conclusion of how much is allegory, how much fact, or the conflation of events of different epochs.

The *Taitteriya Brahmana* (a segment of the *Ayurvaida*) appeared ca. 10,000 BCE—one of the first "religious" treatises, if not the first by a human in this civilisation; it contained observations of celestial bodies that allowed fairly accurate dating. It confirmed the inquisitive nature of the people and marked the emergence of a philosophy of life and of norms for a happy and productive society that would surmount obstacles, mental and physical, and endure.

Seers *(rishis)*, enlightened by deep meditation and revelation received the sacred scriptures, the four *Vaidas* (from *vid*, to know): *Rg, Sāma, Yajur and Atharva,* the quintessential wisdom of Creation and the foundation of the philosophy called *Sanatan Dharma,* later called Hinduism, a Persian neologism. These they organised as four major religious works or *srutis,* meaning *what is heard,* since early transmission was entirely oral: *Samhitas,* hymns to praise and glorify God and sounds to invoke His presence; *Brahmanas* to describe ways of giving thanks and rituals for worship; records of the philosophy, styled *Aranyaka,* literally *in the forest*—perhaps a reflection of the environment of their growth; and interpretations, *Upanishads,* literally *"at the feet of..."* of which the most profound and famous is the *Bhagavad-Gita,* narrated and explained by Krishna himself.

The Sanskrit language was perfected in the process and enriched with words and phrases to describe living things and their attributes; physical and social entities; objects; actions or abstractions—thoughts, concepts, moods, emotions, behaviours, and so on. They were used in song to express views on the weighty matters that troubled people. Centres of learning developed and temples for assembly, knowledge-sharing discourse and worship. Heads of governments and administrators thus acquired tools to codify human behaviour, to avoid personal or group conflict, and to order and manage the activities of rulers and citizens so as to promote growth of peaceful and secure communities, while preserving their autonomy, as tribes or kingdoms or republics.

By this time, Indians probing astronomical and mathematical themes, had begun to elaborate on such abstractions as the nature of time and of civilisations and the influence of natural forces on their many iterations. The current cycle of development had accelerated with the end of the ice age.

Research into mathematical puzzles and abstract ideas, such as relationships, and social amelioration, were a prelude to physical development. Mastery of the abstract led to concrete results such as the unique understanding of natural phenomena that Hinduism asserts. For example, Hindus came to understand the movement of galaxies and their component stars and planets; phases of the moon (which they correctly related to movement of the earth around the sun); expression of abstract concepts like infinity and zero (the keys to *all* science, as Einstein declared); and solution of mathematical problems necessary to explain natural phenomena, concepts and features of religion, and to perform *Vaidic* rites.

Thus Hinduism's roots in mathematics and science spurred research into astronomy, enabling scientists to document and name solar systems, constellations, galaxies etc. and to suggest the size and age of the universe, despite lacking the sophisticated instruments and methods of today. According to the Vaidas the universe is over 155 trillion years old, the length of one Brahma era (RP Arya). This period is divided into eras each with a special name. But life as we know it did not appear until 1,973 billion years ago; that period is called one *Kalpa* or *Sristi* Era. Life is said to have started as elements in a primitive soup and slowly evolved over this time to what we have today; science accepts this. In that time numerous species have come and gone[20].

Each *Kalpa* is divided into 16 periods of about 120 million years (120,533,107), called *Manvantaras.* (Notice how the Hindu numbering system could handle huge figures before any other culture. Rome, and most developed nations of that time and for centuries to come, had trouble computing past a thousand, which is as nothing in astronomy.) *Manvantaras* are divided into four *ages* (or *yugas* in Sanskrit): *Krita, Tretha, Dwapar and Kali.* The year 3102 BCE began *Kali Yuga,* the Iron Age, the last of four in this cycle, starting the period of decline when hypocrisy and conflict will be paramount and human existence threatened.

The *Satpatha Brahmana* describes the journey up to the Himalayas led by Manu to escape the great flood (cf Noah), and the subsequent emergence of the *pāncha jaña* (five tribes): *Anu, Druhyu, Pūru, Turvaśa and Yadu*—as described in the *Vaidas.* Vaidic philosophy matured among

[20]Each religion has a unique starting date; Abrahamic religions suggest a start between 3613 and 5500 BCE (Judaism). By contrast the *Vaidas* date the Universe at 155.5 *trillion* years and the Mayans 24 *trillion* years. Some Christians today attempt a rational approach to the Biblical "days" accepting the obvious error of equating divine "days" with earth days of 24 hours. Hindus believe that the creator's "day" (Brahma day) is 50M years. Current science ages the universe as 13.798 ± 0.03B years. *(See Arya, Vaidic Calendar).*

these peoples, who were described by specific attributes; those of exemplary character—with mastery of the complexities of spiritual and religious thought—were called "noble" (*arya* in Sanskrit), a personal descriptor, not the name of a tribe, as a later European, Max Müller, would mistranslate, launching a grave historical error *(Ch.15)*[21].

Each of the five major tribes was linked with a major geographic area: Anūs with Punjab; Druhyus with Afghanistan, northwest India and Gandhāra; Purus with the valleys of the Yamuna and Gangā rivers; Turvaśas with Bengal, Bihar and Orissa; and Yadus with Gujarat and Rajasthan (the area between Mathura on the Yamuna, and Dwaraka and Somnāth in Kathiawar on the Arabian Sea). The *Purānas* record many wars among these, mainly in the name of *dharma*, the commanding morality and virtue in Hinduism. The Purus are said to have been the least culpable of the five, while the Yadus were the ones most often "at fault". As a result of some of these wars large numbers of Druhyus and Anūs migrated to the Middle East, Central Asia and Europe, founding civilisations in various localities, as far as Britain, taking with them the features of Vaidic Hinduism, a migration theory supported by modern genetics.

The Rg Vaida records many conflicts that have influenced the direction of Indian and world history, for example, the *War of Ten Kings* (*Dasharajnya War*), ca. 7200 BCE, resulting in the exile or migration of

---

[21] Thus they are no different from contemporaneous or later noble groups that subscribed to Vaidic values. Nor is there any evidence for supposing them to be of non-Indian origin, as Roman Catholic Bishop Caldwell hypothesised in the 19th century, suggesting that southern Indians were the original inhabitants and belonged to a separate race, which he called *Dravidian*, corrupting a common adjective, *dravida* (dark), in the same way that Müller had done for *arya*. These spurious inventions divided Indians into two non-existing races of northern "Aryans" and southern "Dravidians" to suit a usurper's agenda; this continues to plague the land to this day; it is sad to read in several blogs the profound ignorance of many Indians commenting on Hindu topics. So it is with Christianity, which developed among the Jews of Palestine, and under duress in Rome, but became the dominant religion of the Roman Empire, the rest of Europe and Asian Russia, after Constantine adopted it. Islam developed in Arabia and soon spread by trade and war to the Middle East, Mediterranean states, India, East Indies and Africa.

many of the defeated rulers and their retinue.[23] Most went west and founded kingdoms from Persia to Europe.[24] For India this marked an important step in the growth of monarchy—in this case the *Puru-Bhārata* dynasty of north India—and its influence on the development of the regional valleys to the west, east and south: Helmand, Saraswati-Indus, Yamuna-Ganga, Narmada and others. It affected religious thought, and its scope qualifies it as a major event of Indian history, worthy of the same epic treatment as the *Rāmāyana* or *Mahābhārata*. The philosophical basis of Hinduism is thus buried in antiquity.

Development was not always smooth. From time immemorial , tribes and kingdoms have clashed over "rights" of one kind or another, and it seemed that humans—especially their leaders—could not remain for long in tranquillity or contentment, but became restless, suffused with feelings of rancour, anger, greed, envy and other base qualities. These were the exact opposite of those deemed laudable human traits and of the *Vaidic* principles of *sat, chit* and *ānanda*—existence, conscious intelligence and bliss—inherent qualities of *Brahmān,* the Universal Presence (not the same as *brahmin,* the varna). Differences were settled by negotiation but those that resulted in war got wider publicity and provided material for all kinds of religious, artistic and other expression.

The kingdoms advanced over the following millennia through religious, technological and agricultural discoveries in many fields. Commercial developments included product preservation and warehousing, which stimulated trade with neighbours, in surplus and in specialties derived from various arts, including healing arts[25] and crafts, and from agricultural, engineering and other practices and products. An unknown part of the vast knowledge accumulated in these times has been lost, due to the destruction of universities, temples and libraries by

---

[23] See S.D. Kulkarni: *Shri Bhagavan Vaidavyasa Itihasa Samshodhana Mandira*, Bombay, (now Mumbai), India, 1994.

[24] The losers in this and later wars became slaves, or found refuge in hills and forests—shunned by victors as outcasts (? today's low castes), or exiled to Asia and Europe, retaining their customs and practices in the same way as recent Indians in the Diaspora, despite changes of language. These and other massive movements took place over several millennia and spawned cultures with linguistic and religious similarities to their parents in India complete with the pantheon of 'god' and 'goddess' figures. These émigrés are said to include inhabitants of the Mediterranean and Middle East, the Druids of northern Europe, and German, Finnish, Scandinavian, and other tribes. Studies of M-DNA and R genes in various populations tend to support this. Pre-Christian migrations are paralleled by the massive shifts of European tribes that occurred in the fifth century CE (see p.56 & Ch. 5).

[25] "The science of yoga was born at a time when mankind was more enlightened and could easily grasp truths and ideas for which our best, our more advanced western thinkers are still groping." (Anon.).

Islamic invaders, and the undermining of Indian education by Mughals and the British in the last millennium[26].

To facilitate dissemination of Vaidic knowledge—which had been kept intact by successive generations of rote learners, as was customary before writing became standard, and the printing press was invented—the sage Vyāsa put the four *Vaidas* in writing and wrote a simpler version, sometimes called the *Fifth Vaida,* to which other writings were added, together forming the *Smriti Vaidas.* These were quite extensive, recording knowledge and updating advances. They covered the histories and attributes of stable communities and orderly societies, including considerations of human character and behaviour, good and evil. Sanskrit, the language of these books, spread from north to south, among all peoples, facilitating communication and study, and may have given rise to the Indo-European group of languages, as people moved, for various reasons, to the Middle East and Europe. (S.P. Arya)

In due course, *Vaidic* societies found it necessary to classify citizens according to their abilities and occupations, creating a useful inventory of skills in the land. People were grouped into four large categories or *varnas: Brahmin, Kshatriya, Vaishya and Shudra* , perhaps the world's first attempt to enumerate and classify a nation's labour pool and provide a basis for planning, organising labour, skills appraisal and managing production by government, academia, industry and business.

At the time, the controlling *varna* was that of the rulers and soldiers *(Kshatriya),* claiming attachment to the Sun *(Surya),* Moon *(Chandra)* or Fire *(Agni),* giving rise to sub-groups *Suryavanshi, Chandravanshi* (Somavanshi, or Ailas) and *Agnivanshi.* The best known of the Suryavanshi were people of the Raghu clan, associated with the Sun and originating in lands east of the zero meridian, which astronomers had placed at Ujjain. Rāma, titled the 7th avatar of Vishnu, was born into this clan. The Chandravansha were various ruling families of the Bh*ārata, Kuru, Pāndava, Yadu, Puru,* and other lineages, all originating from lands west of Ujjain and associated with Chandra, the Moon. It is important to stress that the varnas represented occupations for which anyone could qualify by appropriate education and training and not simply through heredity. All persons were born equal though being born of a father involved in a certain occupation would give one an insider's chance of

---

[26] Sir William Jones, one of the first late 18th century students of Indian culture, founder of the Asiatic Society, noted "*... a stronger affinity* (between Sanskrit, Latin and Greek) *than could possibly have been produced by accident; so strong, indeed, that no philologer could examine them all three, without first believing them to have sprung from some common source...The Sanskrit language is of wonderful structure, more perfect than the Greek, more copious than the Latin and more exquisitely refined than either.*"

following in his line of work, as parental training would be guaranteed, or if no scope or interest existed in pursuing other interests offered by society. As noted earlier, the system was a horizontal arrangement with freedom to move from one *varna* to another based on qualifications. Until society provided the full range of training and mobility, apprenticeships with family or friends would govern choices, limit separation, and lead to closely-knit communities, and encourage closed-shop occupations.

The expansion of families *(jātis)* fuelled the growth of tribes and with the slow progress of universal education the concept and practices of *varna* became distorted and later merged with the European idea of "caste" (Portuguese *"casta"*). It degenerated from a useful catalogue of national human resources and job descriptions to a justification of demeaning and troubling vertical hierarchical practices like the *Chain of Being (p.172)*. These served, at first, the special interests of Brahmins, who in the process played a seminal role in advancing education, science and learning generally. But they did not spread this knowledge to the masses capable of absorbing and benefitting from it, and were content to see the traits of labour merge with social class and wrongly ascribed to heredity, a feature seized by the British to divide the teachers and pandits from the general population, and so keep the majority subjugated.

In the process, women—who held a pride of place in Vaidic society, from Creator to mother and leader of the household—were devalued, like the poor, particularly so during the periods of Muslim and European domination, which brought them to their lowest station in history. Vaidic philosophy and practices showed reverence to *Viraj*, the Female Creative force derived from *Purusha*, the incarnation of the Supreme. Deified females include Parvati, Saraswati and Lakshmi, figures known by many other names and by the numerous forms in which they are represented and venerated throughout Indian society. Vaidic women studied scriptures and performed religious rites, but became subservient in later history. Women of the Middle East and Europe are still oppressed by men, apart from those born in aristocracy and luxury; the attitude of Muslim men to women of all lands is haughty and dismissive (see later chapters), survives today, and is often lethally expressed.

Among Hindus today, Brahmins are the likeliest *varna* to claim that heredity is the source of wisdom and social class, trumping education and the doctrine of equality at birth. The *Vajrasuchika Upanishad* stresses, however, that a true Brahmin is not born but achieves this status because he has knowledge and has realised Brahmān, the *Supreme Truth*, directly.

By the 5th millennium BCE, north Indian kings and rulers, in craving power, had begun to show intolerance, envy, hate, lust, ambition, despotism, and so on, in breach of *Vaidic* principles and conduct, deviating so much from the path of *dharma* or righteousness that an avatar had arrived to guide them back to a moral and righteous way of life. Rāma, a model of nobility and virtue—later regarded as the seventh avatar of God in His role as preserver (Vishnu)—was born in Ayodhya into the Raghu clan with a mission to show mankind, by precept and example, how to regain *dharmic* focus and live full and just lives.

His story is beautifully told in two classic epics, one by Vālmiki, in Sanskrit, called *The Rāmāyana,* the other much later in Hindi by Tulsidās, generally known as *The Rāmacharitmānas.* They describe India of that time, its status and principles, and highlight the decline in human morality. They relate the life and work of Rāma and his mission to eliminate evil and establish a code of interpersonal behaviour that reflected the best and noblest of virtues. These included altruism; respect for others and security of their welfare; goodness; fair and just dealing; and rightness, within a social, economic and religious framework throughout the land, that respected and had a place and a role for *everyone*[27]. Rama is shown as *arya sarva samascaiva sadaiva priyadarsanah.*[28] ("a noble person who worked for the equality of all and was dear to everyone") This, after all, was the prime virtue of a model citizen as told in the Vaidas.

The *Rāmāyana* is universally known and widely available, and provides a good start for anyone learning the story of Hinduism. The events it describes in grand poetic style are said to have taken place eons before the date given for the "Creation" (p. 47) according to the Jews, Christians and Muslims![29] What remains unclear is whether there was one visit by this avatar in Tretha Yuga or more recently, five or six millennia ago, or two appearances. How much of this old knowledge was lost cannot be readily ascertained. To illustrate, South Indian stories tell of sunken cities off the coast of Andhra Pradesh and of the *"Rāma Empire"* that had developed air and possibly space travel. The sage Nārada is portrayed as a travelling monk with the ability to visit distant worlds or planets (*lokas* in Sanskrit), as we had earlier noted. The *Ramāyana* tells too of the land bridge across the Palk Strait between the south eastern tip of India and Lanka—now crossed by railroad and

---

[27] *"Peaceful lived the righteous people, rich in wealth in merit high, /Envy dwelt not in their bosoms and their accents shaped no lie, /Fathers with their happy households owned their cattle, corn, and gold, /Galling penury and famine in Ayodhya had no hold, /Neighbours lived in mutual kindness helpful with their ample wealth, /None who begged the wasted refuse, none who lived by fraud and stealth!"* The *Rāmāyana*, translated and condensed by Romesh C. Dutt, 19th Century CE.

[28] Ramāyana, quoted by Francois Gautier

[29] *"It does not behoove us, who were only savages and barbarians when these Indian and Chinese peoples were civilized and learned, to dispute their antiquity."* Voltaire, French philosopher, (1694-1778)

ferry—and the more familiar tales of Hanumān's flight from south India to Mount Nanga Parbat at the western end of the Himalayas to fetch the herbs that would heal the fallen Lachman, Rama's brother, in their epic struggle against Ravana of Lanka. The tales of speed and flight suggested that this ancient civilisation had discovered aeronautics and an anti-gravity, solar or other source of power, e.g. mercury ions for space propulsion. They seemed to have had commercial relations globally and contact with Atlantis. What calamity ended it is still subject of speculation.

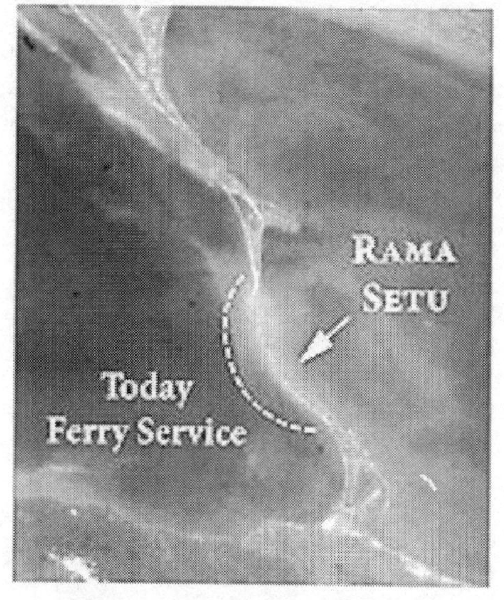

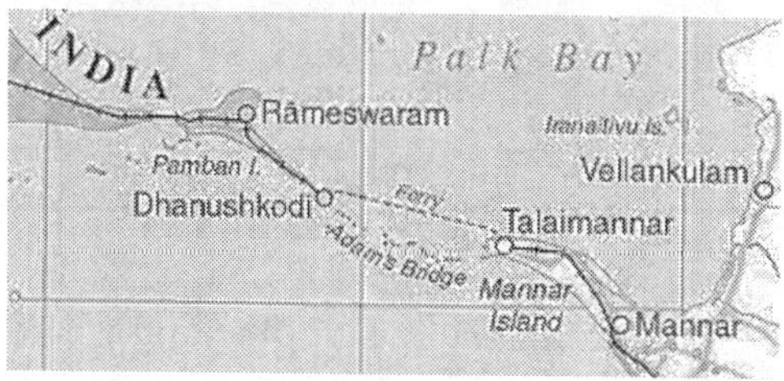

British dogma classified all stories in Indian epics and scriptures as myth while accepting imaginative Biblical tales such as Noah's exploits with an ark-ful of animals; Moses leading an impossible and irascible 600,000 Jews through a *desert* for 40 years after parting the Red Sea; Samson's strength residing in his hair; Joshua and the walls of Jericho; human pregnancy at age 100; men living to age 700 years or more, and like "miracles", all ultimately ascribed to "acts of God". If indeed these are believable, how much more so are the technical feats by Rāma and his retinue?[31] The accuracy of any assertion today, as always, rests on the balance of probabilities, so far as they are known. Many do accept that there was a protohistoric character called Rāma; whether he did all he is said to have done in the Ramāyana is a matter of sifting fact from fiction, with full knowledge. (See Satish Prakash, and (http://defenceforumindia.com *forum/religion-culture/25895-greatest-kings-indian-history).*

[31] The efforts of Swami Dayānanda and others in the late 19th century to restore the study of the *Vaidas* marked the beginning of a rough road to restore that knowledge base, ironically resisted today by secular and converted Indians, heavily shielded from this past, who grew up to deny their Hindu roots, like Indian Muslims, and simplistically denigrate as "fundamentalists" all those who quote or seek to restore it. Hanuman, for example could have been an intelligent early human, with some ape-like features, not a literal monkey!

Just as evidence of Rama's existence is incomplete, so too is the full story of Jesus' "missing" eighteen or so years, and much of the detail of all great lives and events of ancient Judaeo-Christian history. Writing made it easier to keep abreast of events and modern technology affords multiple media for recording them. Historians prefer primary sources of information, but often have to rely on secondary or tertiary ones that may blur the boundaries between truth and "a good story". However, the same credence should apply to the stories of all protohistoric personalities, in all cultures, instead of the Western practice of crediting Judaeo-Christian and Islamic accounts and doubting others, especially from the older, more mature cultures of the east, and elsewhere, with a strong oral history. The truth is that the evidence for or against anything is often incomplete and is always affected—accepted, denied, hidden or suppressed—by religious or political priorities. In the case of Indian and other protohistory, which was severely compromised by British agendas, one can adopt a "wait and see" policy in the hope that science will continue to discover new data to further clarify historical "myths".

At that time, Indians ranged from the Persian border to the Bay of Bengal and from the Himalayas to Ceylon, organised as tribes, principalities and kingdoms, which flourished in well-built cities and related farming districts along the great rivers: the Saraswati, Sindhu (the name Indus was used later by invaders) in the northwest; Ganga and Yamuna in the north; Brahmaputra in the east; Narmada,[32] Tapti and Mahanadi in the centre; and Godavari, Krishna, Kaveri and others in the south.

Barley, rice, cotton, other grains, sesame and grasses had become major agricultural industries, along with the rearing of cattle, sheep, goats, horses and camels. This was well before the Egyptians had built their first pyramid, circa 2600 BCE. Indians traded among themselves and externally, some to distant areas, east and west, as noted, having developed expertise in crafts, agriculture, astronomy, mathematics—pure and applied—science, religion and architecture. They promoted scholarship, the arts, especially music, dance, song, poetry and writing. Agricultural production fuelled prosperity. Rice cultivation began in eastern India and spread to China by 5000 BCE.

Trade with the Middle and Far East and with Indonesia was evident by 4000 BCE. India's population had reached nearly two million then—20% of the world's peoples—many of whom had become wealthy and influential. Dwaraka on the Arabian Sea in Gujarat, (see map, p. 11), was most likely at this time the major seaport for trade south and west with

[32]To many Hindus absolution requires *immersion* in Ganga, but just *looking* at the Narmada suffices.

neighbouring kingdoms, and further afield with Persian Gulf states, the Middle East, the Mediterranean and Europe, and Africa via the Red Sea. Many of the links seemed to have been with Indian traders or migrants who had established settlements and kingdoms in foreign regions. *Vaidic* philosophy spread with the migrants, a logical inference from the similar names of deities and forms of worship in Mediterranean countries such as Anatolia (Turkey), Crete, Greece, Rome, Egypt and others, which also displayed a matriarchal order and multiple deities.

By the time of Krishna's advent late in the fourth millennium BCE, the large number of tribes within the five major groups had consolidated into sixteen or so larger or major powers, along with satellite or smaller allied principalities and chiefdoms (satrapies).

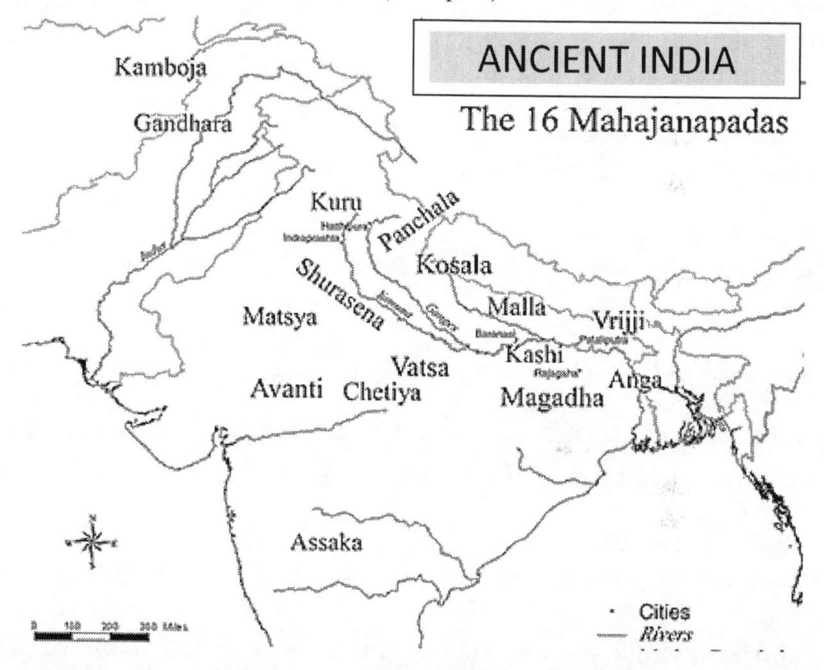

These powers were later styled *mahājanapadas* (महाजनपद -*mahā*, great; *janapada*, "tribe's foothold"), and extended from Afghanistan to the Burmese border. From west to east, these were: Kamboja, Gandhāra, Kuru, Panchala, Kosala, Malla, Kashi, Magadha, Vrijji (Vajji), Anga and Vatsa (Vamsa); and south from Kuru: Shurasena, Machcha (Matsya), Avanti, Chetiya and Assaka. South of Assaka and not included among these sixteen, but just as important for Indian history, were the lands south of the Manjira River, where the Pandyas, and later the Cholas and Cheras, had established prosperous kingdoms with extensions in the Malay peninsula, southeast Asia and Indonesia. Tamil literature shows the strong south Indian influence on Hindu culture as far back as the Saraswati/Indus period.

The Vaidas mention these *mahājanapadas*. The date on British maps—e.g., the one shown on p.47 was given as 600 BCE—is almost certainly much too late, as it was assigned by bias to conform to the age of the earth given by Archbishop Ussher of Armagh, Ireland, who claimed that creation had occurred in 4004 BC! (Rajaram & Frawley, Prakashānanda and others.) During the centuries of Muslim and British rule, the old Hindu kingdoms are sketchily mentioned, dismissed as myths, if cited, and perverted to serve the British agenda. Buddhist and Jain literature describe them, but Muslims and the British ignored or trashed Indian records, while the latter imposed a distorted version of Indian history, and ensured its entrenchment in Indian scholarship. Corrections have been slow, despite the findings of the last fifty years from archaeology and satellite imaging. The following brief notes on each of these entities are culled from various sources and one hopes that the main truths are preserved, and that amplifying and/or corroborative information would emerge from new archaeological and other investigative work.

Kamboja was said to have been located on either sides of the Hindu Kush in the Western Himalayas. In early scriptures and literature, Kamboja is often mentioned along with *Gandhara, Darada* and the *Bahlikas*. The people of Kamboja had both north Indian and Iranian traits, and were warlike. They eventually migrated to South East Asia, perhaps as a result of invasion or internal conflict, and founded what is modern Cambodia, a multi-ethnic society.

Gandhāra was known in Vaidic literature, its people having settled first in the area between the Kubha and Indus Rivers, later crossing the latter to occupy the Punjab. They were an aggressive and warlike people, like those of Kamboja. The kingdom is said to have been founded by the son of Aruddha, who was known as Gandhāra. The wife of the Kaurava king Dritharastra, of Mahābhārata fame, was a Gandhāra princess.

The *Kurus* have a long and in many ways distinguished history; they are an offshoot of the Puru-Bhārata tribe, which developed on both sides of the western Himalayas in the region of modern Haryana and Punjab, stretching north towards Jammu and Kashmir. Kuru, son of Samvarsana, founded Kururashtra in Kurukshetra, in the area between the Saraswati and Ganges Rivers; it had two *parts, Kuru-Jangala and Kuru Proper*. (It is believed that some Kuru chieftains "fled" India with their following, fearing reprisals from the Pāndavas after their loss in the Mahābhārata war, and were ancestors of the Kureshi [Qureshi] tribe that ruled Mecca in Mohamed's time, and to which Mohamed belonged.) The Kurus were the archetypal "healthy, wealthy and wise" rulers. In the millennium before Christ, about the 5th century BCE, they changed the traditional monarchic form of government to a republic, one of many monarchies to do so, like their eastern neighbour the Pānchalas, perhaps influenced by the reforms stirred by the rise of Buddhism and Jainism and the changes these advocated. The most significant drawback was that they did not introduce universal suffrage, believing, like Athenians, that a person must qualify for the right and privilege of voting. A century later, the Mauryan Prime Minister, Chanukya, would remark in *Arthashastra* that "the Kurus, like their neighbour, the Pānchalas, governed according to a *Rāja shabdopajivin* (king consul) type of constitution."

The region east of the Kurus, between the Himalayas and Ganga River, was the domain of the *Pānchalas*, today corresponding roughly to Uttaranchal and Himachal Pradesh. Originally a monarchy, Pānchala became a republic in the 5th Century BCE.

Kosala was about 70 miles to the northwest of present day Gorakhpur in Uttar Pradesh, bounded south by the Ganga River, north by the Himalayas and in the east by the River Gandak. Raja Prasenjit was an early ruler; his son, Vidudabha, succeeded him and concluded a union with Magadha. Kosala is famous in ancient Hindu literature for the prominent cities of Ayodhya, Saketa and Sravasta, the first as Rāma's birthplace.

The *Kashis* settled in territory on the River Ganga between the Varuna and Asi rivers, hence the name Varanasi. Before the rise of Buddhism Kashi held a dominant position among the sixteen *janapadas* but became known as Kosala as Buddhism gained ground. The *Matsya Purāna* mentions it as Kausika or Kausaka.

The *Mallas* had established a republic in what is today eastern Uttar Pradesh and north Bihar, before the advent of Mahavira (Jainism) and Siddhartha (Buddhism), and had become quite powerful. The republic consisted of nine provinces, two of which, Pava and Kusinārā, became renowned as the places where the Buddha had his last meal before passing away at Kusinārā.

Magadha occupied the region corresponding to modern West Bengal, Jharkhand, parts of southern Bihar and eastern Madhya Pradesh, and is referred to in the *Atharva Vaida*. King Pramaganda is its only ruler mentioned in the *Vaidas*. According to the *Mahābhārata* (see also below) Magadha became well-known in the war at Kurukshetra under Rāja Bimbisāra and later his son Ajātasatru. It became a major empire, conquering the Licchavis, an independent clan which had their capital at Vaishali, the birthplace of Mahavira and later well-known to Buddhists as the place where Buddha gave his last sermon. It was the headquarters of the powerful republic of *Vajjis*. The Licchavi kingdom was an important centre of cultural and political activities. The Licchavis moved to Nepal after their defeat.

Vrijji was a composite of eight or nine allied north Indian tribes, which settled the area corresponding to northern Bengal, east of the Mallas. The most prominent of the nine were the Licchavis, Vedehans, Jnatrikas and Vajjis.

The *Atharva Vaida* mentions the kingdom of *Anga*, located roughly at the site of the present day Bihar and some parts of West Bengal, between the Ganga and Champa rivers, the latter separating it from Magadha to the south. Anga was an important centre of trade and commerce and one of the chief cities of ancient India.

Considered to be an offshoot of the Kurus, the kingdom of *Vatsa* (or Vamsa in *Prakrit*) occupied the region of the confluence of the Yamuna and Ganga Rivers in Uttar Pradesh, its centre Prayag, corresponding to modern Allahabad. The capital was known as Kaushāmbi, a prosperous commercial city, and a transportation hub between north and south. Like others in that millennium, its king, Udayana, adopted Buddhism, which became the kingdom's religion.

Shurasena occupied the west side of river Yamuna. Its capital was Mathura, Lord Krishna's birthplace and a major centre of Hinduism. It occupied an area corresponding to the modern Braj region of Uttar Pradesh and was prominent in the *Mahābhārata*. In the time of Buddha, Raja Avantiputra, its ruler, became a disciple and promoted Buddhism throughout his kingdom. With time, Shurasena was annexed by the Magadha Empire.

The kingdom of *Matsya* or Machcha in Rajasthan was founded by Raja Virata in the region of modern Jaipur, Alwar and Bharatpur, with Viratanagara the capital. Matsya was once a part of the Chedi kingdom. It lay west of the Yamuna and south of the Kurus. Rama's eldest son, Lau, ruled the kingdom in his time. There were several areas called Matsya, not unlikely as the word means fish; it is associated with Satyavati, daughter of a fisherman who married Santanu, the ancestor of the *Mahābhārata's* warring families, the Kauravas and Pāndavas.

Avanti was a major kingdom in Vaidic times and occupied both banks of the Vetravati River (modern Betwa) corresponding to a part of modern Madhya Pradesh. Its capital Ujjain is an ancient centre of education and the location of the zero meridian. It took the side of the Kauravas in the Mahābhārata war and lost both its kings, Vinda and Anuvinda in fighting against Arjuna. It became a prominent Buddhist centre and was incorporated in the Empire of Magadha.

The Chedi/Cheti kingdom is mentioned in the Rg Vaida, thus establishing its antiquity. Its ancient location corresponds to modern Bundelkhand and part of Madhya Pradesh, along the Vetravati River and south of the Yamuna River. It was allied to the Kurus in the Mahābhārata war in which many Chedi princes lost their lives. The king, Sisupal, was a cousin of Krishna and lost his life during a ritual *Rajasuya* sacrifice held by Yudisthir, the chief of the Pāndavas. The Chedis are said to have settled later in the mountains of Nepal.

The kingdom of *Ashmaka* (Assaka in Pāli) corresponds to modern Maharashtra, central and south India, between the Godavari River and its tributary Manjira. The capital, Potana, was on the Godavari. Ashmaka was the only *mahājanapada* south of the rugged Vindhya Range. The region became famous later as the birthplace of the precocious 5th century mathematician and astronomer Aryābhatta.

Following Rāma's mission, the kingdoms along the great rivers prospered and expanded. But with success and power they drifted inexorably into the state of *adharma,*[33] foregoing the principles laid out by Rāma, and ignoring the social and community precepts detailed by *Manu. D*riven by self-aggrandisement and the lust for wealth and power, that grew with corruption; families fractured and societies deteriorated morally and spiritually. With internecine war threatening the Ganga-Yamuna *doab* and Saraswati regions, Lord Krishna, the 8th avatar of Vishnu, came among them and proceeded to restore moral and spiritual order, reaffirming the tenets of Vaidic *dharma (Bhagavad Gita)* as war between the dominant Kauravas and Pāndavas became inevitable.

Krishna was the religious protagonist and strategist depicted in the *Mahābhārata,* and author of the *Bhāgavad Gita,* which forms part of that major work, and was guru to Arjuna, its hero. The *Mahābhārata* describes and discusses the causes and outcomes of the Great War between the Pāndavas and Kauravas—descendants of Satyavati and Santanu—and their numerous allies. In the *Gita* Krishna explains man's role in the universe and his duty to ensure that right prevails over wrong. In addressing the concerns of the righteous Arjuna, commander of the Pāndava forces facing a family war that he abhors, Krishna explains that righteous duty or *dharma* sometimes includes fighting friends and relatives who behave unjustly, or bring great harm to their people, especially since rulers should ensure the welfare and protection of all their people. They had a duty to take every available measure to avoid war; but if war becomes inevitable, only warriors must fight, be equally

---

[33] The prefix "a" before a Sanskrit or Hindi noun gives it an opposite meaning.

prepared, use fair means, avoid attacking the wounded or harming innocents, and above all, use no underhand methods.

Illustration of the battle of Kurukshetra: Arjuna, the Pāndava commander, is seen at left behind Krishna, his charioteer. Karna, commander of the Kauravas, is at right. (www.philamuseum.org/collections/permanent/70158.htm)

The *Mahābhārata* outlines Krishna's mission among people to restore their focus on *dharma*. After a great cleansing of the forces of evil, honour and morality prevailed for a time under the victors, the Pāndavas. But the cost in lives was enormous. In addition, many losing kings, fearing reprisals from the victors, are said to have migrated with their followers to found kingdoms in distant lands.

Krishna's older brother, Balarāma, was associated with his work and regarded also as an avatar. He was of fair complexion in contrast to Krishna's, (illustrating the lack of a colour bias, a strong lesson for today's Indians). They had begun their mission in Mathura by restoring King Ugrasena to the throne of Mathura. Krishna "died" in 3102 BCE, the beginning of *Kaliyuga*. The ancient Indian calendar starts at this date, thus making 2010 the 5082nd year of *Kaliyuga*.

Vaidic civilisation regained its prosperity following the Mahābhārata wars, but kingdoms in the next millennium inevitably became more and more mercenary. Newer generations forgot the ideals for which the war was fought, became more selfish and abused their natural resources. Prosperity is a beguiling condition and no doubt led to misleading ideologies and distortion of values, as it does today, reproving those in power. In such a state, selfishness and greed trump good sense, and leaders lose sight of their responsibility to safeguard the weak, using them instead as pawns in a power game. The poor became poorer, and the rich fattened on their labour, a sad human condition that persists and is prominent today, despite all the pratings of an advanced civilisation.

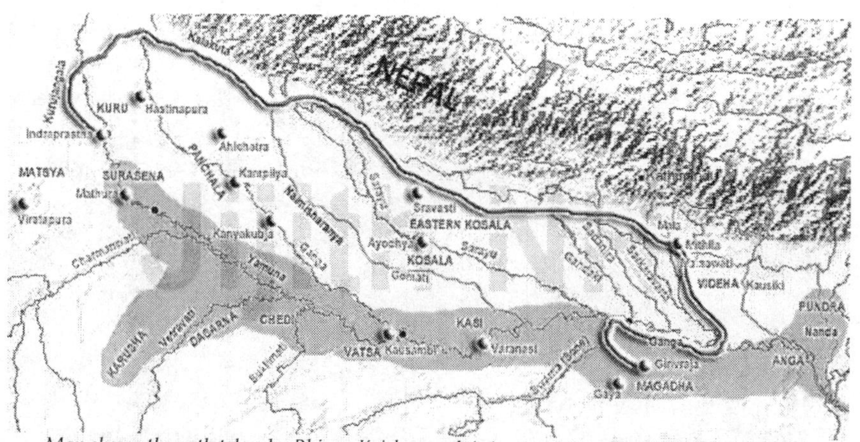

Map shows the path taken by Bhima, Krishna and Arjuna to Magadha, the kingdom of Raja Jarasandha, a dark band stretching from Shurasena east to Pundra and lying south of the kingdoms of Kuru-Panchala and Kosala-Videha (Mahābhārata).

The Saraswati-Sindhu (S-S, or Indus Valley) city states were highly developed at the time the civilisation suddenly ended ca. 2000 BCE.[34] Site excavations began in 1924 with Sir John Marshall's discovery of relics at Harappa and started the slow process of identification, aided by Mortimer Wheeler's findings in 1946, and later by India's S. R. Rao, the foremost authority on this archaeology. These have tended to confirm Vaidic accounts and their extensive commentaries, which the British had purposely dismissed in the 19th century as mythology[35] . Harappa was 5-6,000 years old, and its excavations show features of *modern* industrial cities, with complex irrigation and fire and flood control. A textile industry, based on cotton, so far as can be interpreted, traded among sister cities and externally with the Middle East and Egypt. The cities were united, and conflict rare.

The civilisation prospered for millennia and expanded, while public morals declined as expected during Kali Yuga. Population pressures, clearing of forests and weak leadership led to uncontrolled use of

---

[34] Urban development ante-dates those of west Asia and the Mediterranean and thus supports the authenticity of India's claim to have led the world to modernity, perhaps a bit too spiritedly, exhausting its resources by overzealous materialism and selfish pursuit of influence and power, much as we have been seeing in the USA since the advent of Ronald Reagan, the rather shallow pawn of adventurers and materialists, recapitulating the grossest errors of the past, heralding the two Bushes, who compounded his errors!

[35] See Ch. 15. Today's Indian secularists—most of whom are either atheists or communists, or both, who became submerged by the waves of Marxist fervour between the world Wars and especially after WWII, as decolonisation became a reality—come from the 15% of urban or privileged persons educated in the British tradition, and continue a campaign to denounce Hinduism or any notion of *Vaidic* rebirth or attempt to recognise the reality that over 80% of Indians are Hindus, and that *all* indigenous Indians share a Hindu ancestry, that welcomed others, regardless of religion.

resources and climate change—with prolonged droughts over 2-3 centuries prior to 2000 BCE, perhaps due to monsoon shifts eastward. Societal standards declined and the civilisation collapsed, as natural forces convulsed, most likely a massive earthquake along the fault line in Gujarat, bringing a catastrophic end to the beleaguered Saraswati-Sindhu civilisation. People fled east and south and shared this fate with contemporaries in a vast area of some 600,000 square miles (>1.5M sq. Km) stretching from eastern UP to Iran and south to the Godavari valley, thus larger than the total area of Mesopotamia and Egypt[36]. The Akkadian civilisation of south Mesopotamia also ended abruptly about the same time. Here too it is likely that societal decline and the ignoring of warnings of natural disasters ended the civilisation, as we have begun to see globally in this age of climate change and man's increasing infractions against the earth, and aversion to reform.

Wheeler suggested that the collapse was due to invasion by "*Aryans*"—the 19th century invention by Max Müller (see later), who, as noted, mistranslated the epithet, *arya,* meaning noble, a quality of persons, and used the word for the name of a mythical *race* of "*Aryans*", who must have invaded the country and acculturated it, *without trace*—see Ch. 15. This error was exactly what the British invader wanted; it justified their conquest as that of just another civilising invader, this time Christian, and was widely publicised. It is still held today by anti-Hindu westerners *and Indians,* and defended by academics at eminent British, Indian, US and Canadian universities—including Oxford, London, Harvard, Yale, California and Toronto—and almost every university in Europe. It pervades museums and encyclopaedias and is taught and rewarded with MAs and PhDs, despite the powerful and mounting evidence against it, from religious, linguistic and textual, to physical, especially archaeological, now that the physical evidence unearthed is less likely to be tainted by pre-judgment or vested interest, and genetics.

There is still much to be clarified in the narratives and philosophic treatises given in the Vaidas and epics. Many modern secular historians, Indian and non-Indian, especially in the West, continue to deny their authenticity or antiquity, preferring to continue a vested position to treat them as myths, or, at best, attach timelines that conform to Biblical accounts, ancient Jewish history being considered authentic! (But see Vidal). Incredibly no shame is attached to today's claimants, especially in the media, who admit to ignorance of mathematics or science and to mystification by the cosmos, an admission that is getting more common yearly in the popular western media of television and radio talk shows, where ignorance and naiveté replace wisdom, and the wise are ignored.

---

[36] See writings of archaeologist, S.R. Rao.

Academics like Arthur Basham and his following also regard the *Vaidas* and epics as myth, thus devaluing arguments based on them – or on the *Agamas*. This following includes Thapar—footnote, p. 20—the Indian *communist* historian who has conquered the West and who has allegedly opposed any revision of Indian school readers; her book on ancient Indian history is a required text.

Romain Rolland (1866-1944), French Nobel laureate, author of *"Life of Ramakrishna"*, thinker, and professor of the history of music at the Sorbonne, observed however, *"Religious faith in the case of the Hindus has never been allowed to run counter to scientific laws, moreover the former is never made a condition for the knowledge they teach, but they are always scrupulously careful to take into consideration the possibility that by reason both the agnostic and atheist may attain truth in their own way."* Such tolerance may surprise religious dogmatists in the West, and anti-Hindu Indians, but it is an integral part of Vedantic belief.

Nurtured by British propaganda, descendants of the major *Vaidic* tribes were brainwashed to regard themselves as the descendants of the central Asian conqueror, distinct from other Indians. Thus privileged, they distanced themselves from other Indians and from their own heritage. They continue to use the adjective "arya" incorrectly as a proper noun for a "race" rather than correctly for a quality of character possessed and fostered by *any* worthy individual, of any time. Today the invasion theory is rejected by conscientious scholars, and convincing evidence exists for the opposite: that ancient Indians migrated *to* lands west and north as a result of various domestic cataclysms.

The discovery of the Saraswati river bed and the ruins of its many cities beneath the Rajasthan desert in the very places described in the *Rg Vaida* should now permanently dispel the British myth and establish the truths in the great epics, *Ramayana* (of uncertain antiquity: see Satish Prakash), and *Mahabharata* (4th millennium BCE, 3102,) and the lessons of the heroes whose lives are reviewed there. These texts have always included true *itihaas* (history) and not only *kavya*, myth and metaphor, the way they have been promulgated for 200 years; (the *kavya* is a poetic work similar to English ballads and French *chansons* of the 12th and 13th centuries. (See Carpentier de Gourdon; Rajaram; Michel, and others.)

Indians are only now realising that their real ancestors were indigenous Indians, and not mythical invaders from central Asia. Regrettably, the doubters are among the most influential political and historical figures in India and the West. They have been joined by Pakistan, which for the last three decades or more, has applied oil wealth donations from Arabia to support those opposed to attempts to correct Indian history, beginning with reform of school textbooks. (It should be clear that Islam is a viable religion and its followers do not need to convince anyone, nor indeed does any religion have to justify itself; each should be respected. No religion can justify its claim to exclusivity or a sacred mission to infiltrate, undermine and destroy others by violence. In this respect Hinduism is the least aggressive, though detractors invariably quote lines from the *Mahābhārata* war against this claim. Violent verses can be found aplenty in the writings of all religions).

An "invasion" cast doubts on the Indian origin of the *Vaidas,* allowing division of Indians from a historical mixed race to one of light-skinned invaders and dark-skinned natives, and making British claims more convincing and Britons more reputable (but see above note re Krishna and Balarāma). Promulgating race created an anglocentric India, permitting a population of two hundred thousand or so British aristocrats and their servants to enslave nearly 300 million people, roughly the same ratio as planters to slaves in European plantations in British colonies, including the USA! Until recently, controversy raged between these two views of the antecedents of India's peoples and the originators of its languages—Sanskrit, Hindi and others—the Vaidas, other literature and religious doctrines, pitting Indian learned men, with words as their weapons, against the British—beefed up by Islamists, atheists and secularists—with cannonballs and "coconuts" as theirs! So far few Indians converted by British brainwashing have given the time or resources to analyse Britain's anti-Hindu claims.

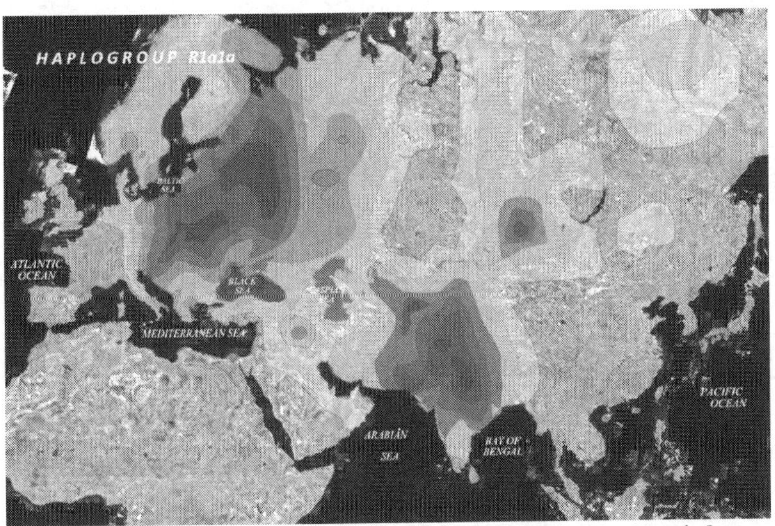

Dispersal of R1a1a gene, adapted from Underhill et al (2009).Credit :User:Hxseek; Same as R-M 17

Chapter 3

"The acceptance of such views would create a revolution in our view of history as shattering as that in science caused by Einstein's theory of relativity. It would make ancient India perhaps the oldest, largest and most central of ancient cultures." David Frawley

"We can now assert, with the power of hindsight, that Indian linguists in the 5th century BC knew and understood more than Western linguists in the 19th century AD. Can one not extend this conclusion and claim that it is probable that Indian linguists are still ahead of their Western colleagues, and may continue to be so in the next century?" Frits Staal

Post-Saraswati India; the religions

The great epics and raconteurs tell many heroic tales of the wise and not-so-wise who came to the thrones of India. By 2000 BCE, Europeans of presumed Indian or central Asian origin: Celts, Lithuanians, Slavs, Ukrainians; the Akkads of Mesopotamia (founded by Sargon); the Kassites and the Babylonians under Indatu (a contemporary of Varanasi's Divodas), were following patterns and practices similar to those in *Vaidic* India in areas of cosmology, astronomy and theology; and in marriage and other sacraments and social practices. The world population had reached 27 million, of which 5 million (22%) were Indians; (note that throughout history Indians would comprise roughly a fifth of humanity, until Islamic and British rule reduced it to a sixth.)

Long before the final disappearance of the huge Saraswati River in ca. 2000 BCE and the flooding of the Sindhu, the population had responded to the droughts by migrating, as mentioned above, before the final catastrophe forced the evacuation of the remaining millions from their doomed cities. Migrants are believed to have found refuge among the Chaldeans, the Mitanni of Syria and others in central Asia, the Middle and Far East and possibly Eastern Europe, whose deities and practices were the same as those described in the *Vaidas*. For example at Boghaz Koi in Turkey, stone inscriptions include such names as Mitra, Varuna, Indra and the Nasatyas (Ashvins)—all *Vaidic* deities.

In India, the centres of civilisation moved to the Ganges/Yamuna valley, even as other Hindu kingdoms in the south: Chola, Pallava, Pandya etc., were developing and establishing trade and other relations with countries of the Middle and Far East, where Indian migrants or exiles had settled and established colonies—in much the same way as modern migrants keep contact and carry on trade with their country of origin. In Egypt, the Valley of the Kings was becoming a major cemetery, and in the Pacific, Polynesians were spreading throughout the archipelagos, and Mayan and other tribes were advancing culturally in

Mexico and adjacent lands.[37] As time passed, the knowledge lost by Indians was replaced; it re-accumulated and crystallised in diverse fields, driven by the continuing desire to understand and explain natural phenomena, to guide spiritual, religious and scientific exploration, to organise various sectors of society and to improve government. The Vaidic religion spread throughout the land and was rendered in many languages, with formalised worship that applied physical and chemical sciences, for example, as in *Agnihotra,* to preserve health, air quality and Nature (Narang).

Sages and teachers found innovative ways to store the knowledge gained, conduct studies to obtain reproducible results, compile analyses and reports, and exchange information. By the end of the second millennium BCE, intellectual ferment had led to the establishment of many centres of learning throughout India, prime among them the world's first residential universities at Nālandā, Bihar and at Taxashila (Taxila), Punjab.

The great Sanskrit grammarian, Pānini, composed the famed *Ashtadhyāyi,* the world's first treatise on grammar and language. As material and structural developments expanded, the relationships and interactions among people became more complex. With the increase in knowledge, important social, political and legal principles evolved to address the uses and abuses of power, ensure fairness and equality of treatment in interpersonal matters, and establish the supremacy of law. These would expand and find more eloquent expression and application under Ashoka Maurya.

In the centuries between the end of the Saraswati civilisation and the Mauryans, the major kingdoms had seen steady progress in the various fields of endeavour and learning that contribute to development of an organised and progressive society. Populations grew along the great northern rivers: Ganga, Indus and their many large tributaries, and on the major central and Deccan streams, the Arabian Sea coast and Bay of Bengal. In politics and government the world's first democratic federal republic was formed in the last millennium BCE—Videha, Magadha and Bihar—and lacked in one particular: the enfranchised did not include the lower or poorer classes, and prosperity did not spread to all who may have contributed to individual and national wealth. The lowest classes remained in need, with social pressure rising as their numbers grew.

Education advanced with the establishment of universities, where students from all over India and many foreign lands including Greece and Rome studied the subjects then developed, both secular and

---

[37] The Classic Mayan civilisation ended in the 9th C. CE, presumably from drought or other natural disaster.

religious: mathematics, science, astrology, astronomy, grammar, logic, language, medicine, metaphysics, religion (Hinduism and its later variants, Buddhism and Jainism), philosophy, history etc. Indian regions and kingdoms differed in language but shared *Vaidic* traditions and traded extensively. Regional customs and practices including dress and cuisine developed according to geography, climate, social and economic factors; some of these have naturally persisted and are identifiable among diasporal Indians worldwide. The most distinctive feature was the variety of languages, which surprisingly puzzled many anglophone non-Indians raised in British colonies, unaware of the size of India and the diversity of its dialects and regional languages. For example, the small continent of Europe has at least twenty significant languages and many dialects. Why then would one marvel at the variety in India?

Varanasi, the holy city of the Hindus on the sacred Ganga River, rose to great prominence. Scholarship flourished even among the ruling class. For example, Shuchi, the King of Magadha, wrote about his studies in astronomy in a book titled the *Jyotisha Vaidanga,* published in 1255 BCE. Elsewhere, about this time, Zarathustra founded the Parsi religion in Persia. Its scripture, the *Zend Avesta,* contained passages identical to those in the *Rg* and *Atharva Vaidas.* The stress on good versus evil established the dualism of this and other religions that emerged in western Asia.

Further west Egyptian pharaohs of the 18th dynasty took their armies south to quell the rising power of Nubians, and successfully indoctrinated them to Egyptian ways. More than a century later, Moses led a horde[38] of cantankerous Jews out of Egypt—circa 1250 BCE—and Greeks battled Trojans, in 1200 BCE, over a kidnapped woman, who, however, seemed rather fond of her kidnapper. In 1124 BCE, Nebuchadnezzar I, the Elamite emperor, moved his capital to Babylon, then the largest city in the world. By 1000 BCE, the world's population had reached 50 million and Europe was a collection of numerous primitive, unlettered and warring tribes.

At this time, trade had grown between India and the Middle East. From the port at Supāra (Ophir) on the Arabian Sea near today's Mumbai, Indians traded with King Hiram of Phoenicia and with Jewish King Solomon. A little later, in 950 BCE, India accepted Jewish settlers

---

[38]The Bible quotes 600,000 (Exodus 12:37) excluding women and children, J Gebhart however revised this to a more realistic 7000, citing translation and other problems in the English version. He stressed particularly the logistic nightmare of keeping 600,000 frustrated Jews for 40 years in an inhospitable desert. The basis of Gebhart's figure is clearly reasonable. *See http://www.ancient-hebrew.org/39_exodus.html.* A similar analysis of Genesis Ch. 6-9, which describes the legend, shows its many implausibilities and inconsistences, supporting the conclusion that the tale is a parable of God's wrath.

who would achieve fame and fortune in the spice industry in Cochin. Many intermarried with Indians to create the "black Jews", who endured the discrimination of later arrivals, the "white" Jews, who were escaping various Eurasian calamities, especially the Muslim-Christian wars. By this time too, transportation technology, e.g., the spoked-wheel chariot and horse-drawn freighter—widely used in India for over two thousand years—had become established in central Asia, the Ukraine and other regions in the west where Indians had settled. Later, these vehicles would reach, and be adapted by societies north and south of the Mediterranean Sea, from Turkey to the Maghreb, and east to Egypt.

About the same time as David had established his reign over the region that is today's Palestine, Lebanon and Israel, the Greeks had begun to use iron to replace bronze, which had gotten scarce due to a shortage of tin, thus consolidating the western Iron Age, which in India had begun in 3102 BCE. In this era, the Chinese adopted the Hindu *jyotisha* (zodiac) system, calling it *Shiu* (ca. 850 BCE). In the Middle East, Phoenicians had long dominated Mediterranean Sea lanes and thereby the sea trade. The Greeks held their first Olympic games in Athens (776 BCE), even as Pharoanic Egypt had devolved into a series of fractious entities, under Libyan and other warlords.

The armies of Nubia (Kush) under Piye (he later adopted the ancient name of Thutmose III), invaded Egypt and held Memphis; his brother Shabako extended control over all Egypt and soon restored Egyptian values and culture, just in time to face the Assyrians, under Sennacherib, pouring bloodthirsty armies into Palestine, in the early 7th century BCE. Sennacherib, poised to sack Jerusalem, then under Hezekiah, retreated on learning of a Nubian advance to assist the Jewish king. Although Hezekiah saved Jerusalem and the Jews, he would succumb to the westward expansion of Nebuchadnezzar II of Babylon, in 597 BCE, and be destroyed, along with Judah, ten years later, when citizens rebelled. Survivors were exiled to Babylon. The subjugation of Phoenicia followed.

At this time the major kingdoms of India were prospering and had advanced in learning. But as in all human endeavours this progress did not bring benefits to all. Exploitation of the underprivileged had become systemic. Once again, the disparities in living standards and the plight of the poor became a principal social concern, and as the number of the oppressed increased and rulers continued waging inter-tribal wars, two avatars, Jainism's Mahavira Vardhamana and Siddhartha Gautama rose to prominence—perhaps a century or more apart—in the millennium (or more) BCE. (Later British accounts give dates as 5-6 centuries BCE, based mainly on Müller's linguistic guesses and Pargiter's estimates (p. 24).

As *Vaidic* themes developed and would become the cornerstone of Hinduism, other lines of thinking had developed which had become distinct religions and have contributed to Hinduism today. Some of the narratives refer to events, beliefs and personalities in the story of Creation and of man's understanding of the Universe, and of the role played by the Creator in maintaining the integrity of His creation. They vary from the superhuman to the mythical; although lost in the history of previous civilisations they provide puzzling glimpses of that heritage. Some stories survived the passage of time, embellished or minimised as raconteurs devised, but usually maintaining a certain theme and concept of Creator and Creation.

Deities were personified as beings who could change shape at will, some depicted with multiple limbs and other parts, human or other, each performing a particular function and possessing magical abilities to illustrate their powers, which they could display at will. They granted boons when moved to do so, including waking the dead, conferring special attributes to protect or prolong life, sometimes spanning *yugas* and *manvantaras,* akin to Gods and their avatars. Whatever the manifestation, the accretion or the subtraction, one central theme remained. The Creator or Godhead is Brahmān, the *Universal Presence,* the Divine Ground and the centre of the perennial philosophy, which gives rise to the view that all major religions share a common universal truth and aims for their adherents, chief among which is union with the Godhead. They include the dharmic Indian religions—Hinduism, Jainism, Buddhism—and elsewhere Judaism. Shaktism, the variant of Hinduism in which the female occupies the prime position in the Godhead, i.e. Brahmān, stretches to pre-history and appears in the Saraswati/Indus civilisation. Although eclipsed for a time by the *Vaidas,* it has regained its stature and shares with Vaishnavism and Shaivism prominence in Hindu devotions.[39]

Shramanism developed at the same time as the Vaidas as the belief system of religious renunciants and gave rise to Jainism, Buddhism and Yoga, with dominant ideas of *samsāra,* the cycle of birth and death, and *moksha,* freedom from that cycle. Its followers were known for diligence, asceticism, and discipline in work and life styles, in some ways analogous to the *sanyasi* stage of Brahmānism, that aspect of Hinduism that emphasised doctrine and rituals. The *Taittiriya Aranyaka* (2,7:1) used the word quite early in Hinduism to mean "performance of austerities," while Buddhists linked it with curbing evil: *"samitattā pāpānaŋ 'samaṇo' ti pavuccati;"* i.e. *"a samaṇa is one who has silenced evil."* (*Dhammapada*, v. 265)

[39]Later, *Taoism Confucianism, Christianity, Islam, Sikhism, Baha'i* will show similar features; Shaktism became popular through Mme H Blavatsky, Annie Besant and A. Huxley.

Mahāvir

The origin of Jainism is shrouded in prehistoric mists; it became prominent with the rise of Mahavira, the 24th *tirthankara* (ford maker) and his immediate predecessor. The extension of spiritual doctrines and the struggle for righteousness, unity and equality in a multi-faceted society had given rise to novel philosophies: atheism, Jainism Buddhism etc., which stemmed from the *Vaidas* and incorporated parallel beliefs, or borrowed from, and enhanced one another. The missions of the previous 23 Jain *tirthankaras* had taken perhaps a millennium and held to the central theme of *ahimsa* (no harm). The lessons of Jainism's 24th *tirthankara,* Mahavira (also spelled Mahabir), were contemporaneous with the teachings and attainment of enlightenment by Siddhartha Gautama, who perfected Buddhism. His teachings spread through East and South Asia. Centuries later, it stimulated Jesus Christ, the Jewish student at Nālanda University, to adopt pacifism and to enunciate his *Beatitudes*.

The ancient belief system of Jainism rests on a concrete understanding of the workings of *karma,* its effects on the living soul (*jiva*), and the conditions for extinguishing action and the soul's release. Jains view the soul as a living substance that combines with various kinds of non-living matter and through action accumulates particles that adhere to it and determine its fate. Thus, most of perceptible matter is attached in some way to living souls and is thereby alive; the greatest accretions come from hostile acts against other living beings. The ultimate Jain discipline, therefore, rests on absolute nonviolence (*ahimsa*) against any *living* being. Jains have gone so far as to classify beings based on how many of the five senses they possess—touch, taste, smell, sight, and hearing, as follows:

(i) five senses: humans, animals, heavenly and hellish beings
(ii) four senses: flies, bees, etc.
(iii) three senses: ants, lice, etc.
(iv) two senses: worms, leaches, etc.
(v) one sense: vegetables, water, air, earth, fire etc.

Apart from *ahimsa,* Jains advocate vegetarianism and asceticism in the search for righteousness and final union with the Universal Presence, i.e. *nirvana* (salvation), the state of bliss one attains when finally freed from the cycles of birth and death. Mahavira attained *nirvana* and also *kevala*, a state of absolute knowledge or awareness. There is some debate concerning the Jain view of *karma* and that of Hinduism and Buddhism, the former seeing *karma* as *the* cause of the soul's travail. (See Radhakrishnan, and other religious treatises).

Buddha, unlike Mahavira, had no known fore-runner, although he is said to have had nearly thirty. He was born Siddhartha, a Hindu, the son of King Śuddhodana[40] of Kapilavastu, capital of Shakya—later annexed by the kingdom of Kosala during Buddha's lifetime. Purānic history identifies him as the grandson of Sañjaya, the narrator of the *Mahābhārata* conflict. He was descended from Ikshvaku, the fabled early king, of the Surya clan, a grandson of Vivasvan (Surya) and son of Vaivasvata Manu. This dynasty is in the *Sūryavaṁśa* line (Solar dynasty), and includes former kings Harishchandra, Dilīpa, Sagara, Raghu, Rāma and Prasenjit, before the Buddha. Raghu was so famed that his line was given its own name, *Raghuvaṁśa*. Gautama was Buddha's family name. His mother, Queen Mahā Maya (*Māyādevī*), was a Shakya princess.

Legend has it that on the night Siddhartha was conceived, Queen Maya dreamt that a white elephant with six white tusks had entered her right side. Siddhartha was born ten months later. As was the Shakya tradition, his mother left Kapilavastu for her father's home kingdom to give birth. However, she is said to have given birth on the way, at

The birth of the Buddha, symbolised

[40]The dating of these avatars as ca. 600 BCE is guesswork by 19th century British evangelists (see later Macaulay and Müller). Even if this is near true, Jainism's prior 23 tirthankaras and other authorities must have followed one another over many centuries, perhaps a millennium or more, placing the start of the movement to close to the time of the collapse of the Saraswati civilisation. As time passes, a clearer picture will emerge as archaeology provides new data for these and other historical events in Europe and Asia. Until then dates of early events will remain tentative.

Lumbini, in a garden beneath a *sal* tree.

The foundation of Buddhism lies in the *Four Noble Truths*, at whose core is *dukkha*, a concept that cannot be reduced to a single word in English, involving three ideas: *pain*, physical or mental and its cause or relief from it; *changeability*; and *dependence*, along with the many variations and conditions to which each is susceptible. To the Buddhist, this is an insight that comes from immersion and action, from living the doctrines and walking the path.

These two major reformers, Mahāvira and Buddha, and disciples like Buddhist scholar, Nāgārjuna, preached against the evils that permeated human society and expounded philosophies that emphasised respect for life in all its forms, proposing that each individual could achieve an enlightened state by eliminating greed, corruption, enmity and delusions—the plague of nations. They supported other religious figures who were warning against specific evils such as gambling, as people seemed taken with *ashtapada*, a board game played with dice.

In deference to the Laws of Manu – *Manusmriti* – the socio-cultural and general guide, dice were discarded and the game evolved into the two-sided strategy game *shaturanga*, the forerunner of chess. Their teachings updated and amended the *Manusmriti*, adding values and new frames of reference for human interaction, thus enriching the social and spiritual spheres. A gradual breakdown of Sanskrit as a spoken language began as both movements took to writing in Prakrit, especially Pāli, the vernacular; Sanskrit retained its status as a refined priestly language and has remained so to this day. Other philosophies of the time had developed before or alongside the *Vaidas*—the *Ajivika* and *Cārvāka*, particularly—which rejected the *Vaidas* and stressed asceticism.

This was in line with some of the views of Mahavir and Buddha and can be grouped with them as non-Vaidic or *Nāstika*, in contrast to those six creeds of Hinduism which are pro-Vaidic or *Āstika*: Nyāyá, Vaiśeṣika, Sāṃkhya, Yoga, Mimāṃsā and Vedānta. The Ajivika and Cārvāka were largely atheists, and their asceticism ran to austere lengths, including the belief that asceticism alone can sever the continuation of births and deaths. Vocal sects of ascetic atheists were known in the south; one Ajita went about naked for the most part, cursed a lot, denounced religion, preached materialism and believed in the inevitable end of everything! The influence of the *Ajivika* lasted for a millennium in a section of Mysore; not much is known about them as little remains in writing of their doctrine.[41] Makkhali Gosālā was either the founder or a major

[41]For detailed treatment of the religious ferment of this time and analyses of various systems, see Prakashānanda, Radhakrishnan, Talageri etc. and major religious texts of Hinduism: the *Vaidas, Upanishads, Purānas, Ramayana and Mahābhārata (Bhagavad Gita)*.

figure in the growth of *Ajivika*. The legend his birth is uncannily similar to that of Christ. His parents, Bhaddā and Mankhali, were poor and had come to the village of Saravaṇa, where she gave birth in the only place they could find, a cowshed *(gosālā)*, belonging to Gobahula, a rich man.

At about the same time, Lao-tze *Tao-te Ching* established Taoism in China; his emphasis on simplicity and selflessness shaped Chinese life and spirituality from then on and spread to adjacent countries. Later, Kung Fu (Confucius) would emerge and enunciate new principles that attracted the powerful and the ruling class and became a blueprint for upper class Chinese education and conduct. In India, many of the fables in the *Panchatantra* were known, written or collected by Vishnu Sharma.

Other great works of that time included some of the *Upanishads,* and an amazing textbook of Ayurvaidic medical practice by the physician Sushruta, of Varanasi, acclaimed as the "father" of surgery[42]. His work encompassed the broadest range of subjects such as the diagnostic process, medical ethics, toxicology, psychiatry, surgical anaesthesia, midwifery, embryology, cosmetic surgery, antiseptics, use of styptics, surgical implements, and specific topics such as hernias, fistulae, cataract extractions, lithiasis, the pulse, classification of burns, therapeutic uses of garlic, and others.

The spread of this and other health systems—including *Siddha* and *Unani,* now in the *Department of Ayurveda, Yoga and Naturopathy, Unani, Siddha and Homoeopathy (AYUSH),* of the Ministry of Health and Family Welfare, Government of India—and the spread of education, and their consolidation in centres of learning and excellence, attracted students and visitors from all over the world. Scientific successes in agriculture, engineering (e.g. irrigation and drainage projects) and in meteorology became widely known; they inevitably enticed foreign invaders who coveted India's wealth and resources, both human and material. The Parsi king, Darius I, invaded the Indus Valley in 518 BCE. This was perhaps a kind of homecoming, as their ancestors might have originated there over a millennium earlier. His stay soon ended, and he withdrew.

India's population was then 25% of the world's 100 million, probably the highest percentage of Indians ever achieved.

Sometime after, about 478 BCE, or likely much earlier, the Gujarati King, Sinhabahu, exiled his son Vijaya, who sailed to Sri Lanka with 700 followers and settled Sri Lanka. In Greece, Socrates became famous; his disciple Plato would start the Athens Academy, and Hippocrates

---

[42]Arabs, on order by Caliph Haroun al Rashid (788–809), copied many Indian texts including *Samhitas* of Sushruta and Charaka, two famous Indian physicians and teachers of different periods; they called Al-Zahrawi, 936–1013CE, the *"father of surgery"*.

develop the code of medical conduct still in use; it is said that he was familiar with the Sushruta School of Ayurvaidic Medicine.

Like Darius, Alexander of Macedonia tried to conquer India, reached the Punjab in 326 BCE, defeated the Puru king, after several attempts, but could advance no further. He withdrew; many of his troops deserted to remain behind, but not before he had massacred thousands of children and women—in addition to over a hundred thousand killed in the war—in retaliation for each of the two wounds he had suffered, one a thrust to his chest that was stopped by his sternum, saving his life. Some say that his homosexuality had made him hostile to women and children, who were thus easily victimised. Failing to cross the Beas River into Punjab, he took his army down the Indus and captured several cities including Multan.

At the delta, he split his army into three and led one group across the Gedrosian desert to Babylon. A year and a half later, on the eve of his invasion of Arabia in 323 BCE, he developed a febrile illness, almost certainly the cerebral form of falciparum malaria, and died within two weeks. His companion and deputy, Hephaistion, had curiously died earlier of a similar fever contracted in the mountains north of Babylon.

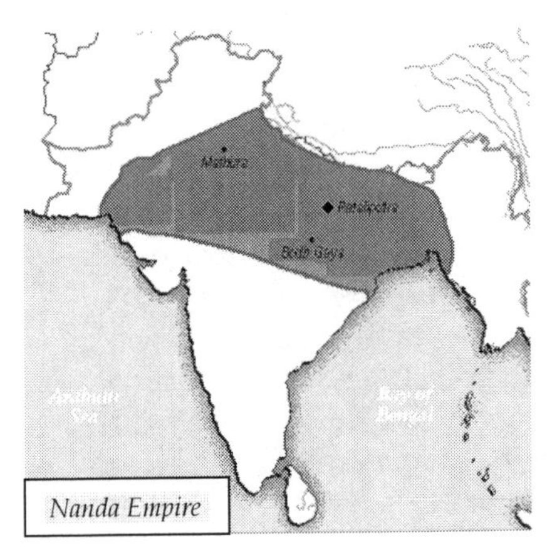
Nanda Empire

The Mauryan dynasty started when Chandragupta deposed King Dhana Nanda of Magadha, in 321 BCE (as dated by the British, but disputed by Prakashānanda, Frawley, Rajaram and others). Chandragupta was an astute general and ruler who came under the influence of two imposing personages, first Prime Minister Chanakya (Kautilya) of Magadha whose book, *Arthashastra,* written two decades earlier, described the art and practice of government, gave details on administering an empire, and is said to have inspired Machiavelli's *The Prince*. The second was Jainacharya Bhadrabahu, who preached the Jain doctrine of respect for, and preservation of all life, vegetarianism, and asceticism to attain *moksha*. The king was so impressed that he abdicated and became a Jain monk! By then the Empire included most of India, Gandhara and parts of Persia and Central Asia, taking advantage of the destabilisation of north Indian kingdoms by Greek invaders. His son, Bhindusara, pursued Indian unification, by conquest of the remaining kingdoms and smaller tribal chieftainships. His Empire extended from the Indus east to Burma, and from Gandhāra south to Mysore; it excluded Kālinga, and the Chola kingdom at the extreme south (map, p. 69).

The Macedonian empire fractured on Alexander's death; the eastern part came under one of his generals, Seleucus Nicator, who failed in attempts to retain or expand his Indian holdings, and made peace with the Indian emperor. The *Purānas* identified him as Samudragupta of the later Gupta period (Saraswati, P.), but he was called Chandragupta by the British, who not only had great difficulty with Indian names, but also misunderstood the numbers, and contracted the time period of this dynasty, deliberately it seems, to make it coincide with Alexander's visit. Seleucus ceded all Indian and Afghan territories, and a daughter in marriage to Maurya. He received 500 elephants, which would later prove a vital asset in his defeat of Demetrius of Macedon, at Ipsus in Phrygia.

Formal relations developed between these two Empires, previously established at an academic level, and ambassadors were exchanged, as with other Mediterranean states, including Egypt, spreading new awareness of India. Pliny the Elder wrote, *"But [India] has been treated of by several other Greek writers who resided at the courts of Indian kings, such, for instance, as Megasthenes, and by Dionysius, who was sent thither by Philadelphus*[43]*, expressly for the purpose: all of whom have enlarged upon the power and vast resources of these nations."* (Pliny, *Natural History*, Ch. 21.) Megasthenes served Seleucus as envoy to India.

Strabo, a Greek of Anatolia (*Strabo XV, I: 53-56),* wrote: *"Megasthenes, the ambassador to the Mauryans representing the Greek ruler Seleucus, a successor to Alexander of Macedonia, describes a large disciplined population under Chandragupta, who live simply, honestly, and do not know writing(!). The Indians all live frugally, especially when in camp. They dislike a great undisciplined multitude, and consequently they observe good order. Theft is of very rare occurrence. Megasthenes says that...* (in a camp of) *400,000 men, thefts reported on any one day did not exceed the value of two hundred drachmae*[44] *and this among a people who have no written laws, but are ignorant of writing, and must therefore in all the business of life trust to memory..."*

Strabo was sceptical and trashed these accounts, commenting, *"Generally speaking the men who have written on the affairs of India were a set of liars. Deimachos is first, Megasthenes comes the next."* Diodorus also held similar opinions about Megasthenes. (See Saraswati, P., Art. 33).

The Mauryans reached the apex of their power and influence under Ashoka, Chandragupta's grandson, who ruled for 41 years (273-232 BCE,

---

[43] Ptolemy II was dubbed Philadelphus on marrying his natural sister Arsinoe II, who in fact was the proper *philadelpha,* having previously married her brother. Ptolemy II is mentioned in Ashoka's *Edicts* and may have been introduced to Buddhism.

[44] 1 drachma of that time was equivalent to about $5.50 US in 1960.

by British timeline, Indian 1200 years earlier). Overcome by the horror of his victory over his neighbour, Kalinga, in the seventh year of his reign, he renounced invasive war, sparing the Cholas and holding them as tributary. He converted to Buddhism, consolidated his empire, initiating administrative reforms, establishing the world's first socialist democracy in which the state controlled all means of production, long before Marx proposed this. He placed curbs on royal powers, assured citizens' rights, reformed taxation, expanded infrastructure, law and order, discouraged casteism and improved diplomatic relations with neighbours. He sent peace missions as far as the Mediterranean countries and religious missions to China, Sri Lanka and Southeast Asia; his son Mahendra led the mission to Sri Lanka.

The result of this attention to the spiritual was that Buddhism became the most renowned religion, spreading to China and SE Asia. But, despite adopting Buddhist and Jain ideas, Ashoka kept Hindu priests and ministers as courtiers; the religions thus existed side by side without discrimination. The philosophy of *ahimsa* spread throughout the land. Prosperity increased. Ashoka's name and work became the most celebrated in the civilised world.

His injunctions and messages to his subjects were carved on stone pillars and erected in major centres of population (see map p 70); perhaps the best known is the pillar at Sārnath, whose lion capital was chosen as modern India's national emblem *(see picture back of title page).* Many today feel that a study of Ashoka's edicts might guide our generation towards a more caring political philosophy, to elevate man above and away from the twin dangers of communism and corporate capitalism. The Mauryans changed to building in stone after fire destroyed the wooden buildings of Pataliputra,[45] the capital city (today's Patna). The Chinese at this time were building the Great Wall, one of the world's marvels of engineering.

In his book Kautilya recorded various advances: air conditioning *(variyantra)*; and advanced metallurgical methods to extract metals, prepare alloys and assay metals for purity; these skills were based on data and practices that no doubt had survived the fall of the Saraswati/Indus civilisation nearly 2000 years earlier. Under the Mauryans new skills and industries developed in metallurgy, tool- and die-making, cement manufacture, construction design, engineering technology, masonry, transportation and haulage, to create the buildings, dams, canals, bridges, sculptures and monuments that changed the landscape and marked the hand of man. Many of these

[45] Half of Tokyo was destroyed in one major WWII raid by incendiary bombs because the city was built of wood.

structures survive to this day. These had relied heavily on advances in Mathematics and Sciences.

The life of dynasties is invariably limited. But the fall of the Mauryans came rather suddenly, having lasted 137 years, felled by weakness that comes with intrigue and internal conflict as the dynasty decayed under successors with limited vision and ability, more egotistical and power-seeking than keen on unity and growth. This disunity would defeat numerous future dynasties and power-brokers.

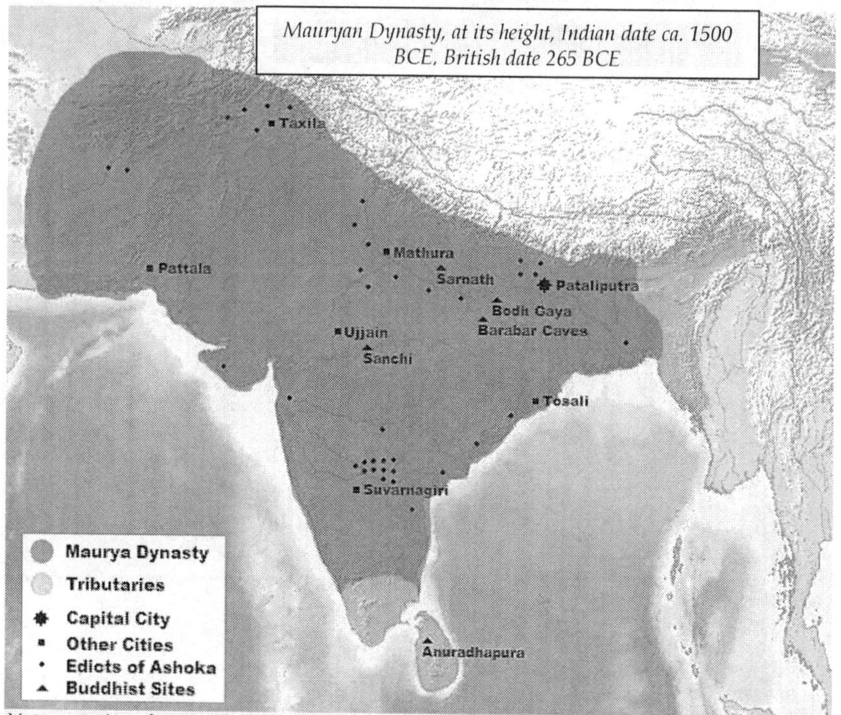

Note exception of extreme south, the area of modern Tamil Nadu and Sri Lanka, whose invasion was stayed by Asoka's horror at Kalinga bloodshed. However they seem to have submitted to Mauryan authority and became tributary states. (See Prakashānanda Saraswati re dates).

At the fall of the Mauryans, the Empire reverted to the original kingdoms or something close. The last conquest, Kalinga, (Orissa), was the first to return to her former greatness. Under Khāravēla (193-170 BCE, British timeline) , its army regained its former strength. He was the third and best known emperor of the Mahameghavahana dynasty; his story is partly preserved in the *Hātigumphā* (Elephant Cave)—seventeen lines carved in Brahmi script on the wall of a cave in the Udayagiri hills outside Bhubaneswar, Orissa (Odisha).

During Khāravēla's reign, the Chedi dynasty regained power and restored the glory that Kalinga had lost in the cruel war with Ashoka, and expanded its maritime reach by trade with Sinhala (Sri Lanka), Burma (Myanmar), Siam (Thailand), Kamboja (Cambodia), Bali, Vietnam, Borneo, Samudra (Sumatra) and Jabadwipa (Java). He waged successful campaigns against Anga, Satavahanas, Magadha and Pandya (Andhra Pradesh), and expanded Kalinga to the Ganges and Kaveri (see *map p.74*)

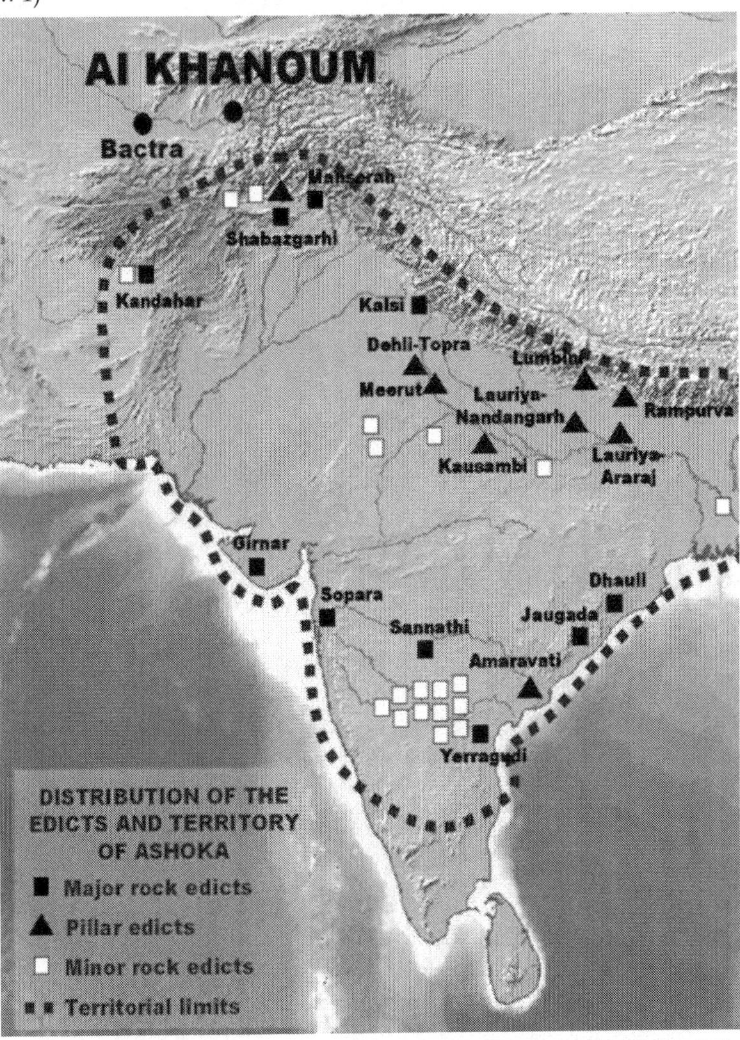

The distribution of the Edicts of Ashoka is a concrete indication of the extent of his rule. Those at Kandahar were written in Greek and Aramaic, and bordered the existing Hellenistic city of AI Khanoum.
(http://commons.wikimedia.org/wiki/User:PHGCO)

Chapter 4

"Just as branches of a peacock and jewel-stone of a snake are placed at the highest place of the body (forehead), similarly the position of Ganit is highest in all the branches of Vaidas and Shastras."

Vaidanga Jyotisha, ca. 1000 BC, quoted Srivasta

In addition to the Babylonian antecedents of Greek science, there existed Indian antecedents.

Subash Kak, Louisiana State University, USA

It is more important to prevent the occurrence of disease than to seek a cure.

Charaka, Indian physician to Kushan court

Cholas, Christ, Kushans; the heliocentric earth

The Chola Empire was founded in southern India (modern Tamil Nadu), sometime during or before the Mauryan reign, grew and became noted for its sound government, artistic achievements and agricultural enterprises with some of the most impressive irrigation and other water management works of that time. One outstanding hydro-engineering feat was the great stone dam (the grand anicut, or *kallanai*) built in the first century CE by Raja Karikala, on the Kaveri River about 12 miles from Tiruchirapalli. It is one of the oldest functioning water management structures in the world. It was expanded by the British in the 19th century and stands as a symbol of Indian engineering. Copies of

this design were made centuries later by others, including the British occupiers. This achievement is perhaps not unexpected, since modern exploration of ancient Dholavira, one of the cities of the Saraswati civilisation, showed water management systems dating back about 3300 BCE.

Besides art, the Chola Empire produced numerous religious dissertations on various themes in Hinduism and Buddhism; it thrived for over 1445 years, one of the longest in history, until broken up by invading Muslims from the north, in 1300 CE.

The *Vikrama Samvat*[46] Hindu era and calendar started in 57 BCE. The Kushans, a Mongolian Buddhist group, began their assault on India in 50 BCE, and later succeeded in annexing northwest India, Afghanistan and parts of their northern neighbours, which they held for 270 years. The victory of the Kushans was an important lesson, later ignored by regional Indian kings, who put clan and local power over their own security and "national" integrity. United India was able to repel invaders who had nibbled at her borders for millennia, and few Indian kings realised, like the ruler of Magadha, hearing of Alexander, that a threat to Gandhara and Punjab was a threat to his people 2000 miles away. The zeal and overwhelming desire of the Kushan raiders were more than enough for a region to overcome alone, and so Kushans were able to seize a treasure.

At the beginning of the first century CE, a bright young Jewish student of religion, Yesu (Jesus) Christ (ca. 4 BCE-30CE), from Bethlehem and Nazareth, in Judea, Palestine, arrived in India to study with Buddhist, Jain and Hindu preceptors at Nālandā and Taxāshila Universities (Faber-Kaiser). He stayed for over a decade and a half—the "missing years" of the New Testament—and travelled widely on religious missions after completing over a decade of study. He was of humble birth, but traced his ancestry to Jewish king David.

Returning to Palestine, his mature peace-oriented teachings were understandably closer to those of Indian philosophies than to Judaism. It incorporated Buddhist and Jain principles, especially *ahimsa,* which he preached, much to the discomfiture of Jewish high priests who had waited for a person with his charisma to lead them in war against Roman hegemony. He completed three years spreading his contrarian doctrine of *peace and love*, captivating audiences in all Palestine. But the Jewish hierarchy rejected him as *the* Messiah, the promised one, and, given the choice to save one man from crucifixion at a certain Passover, chose the convict and rebel, Barabbas.

Jesus was crucified, but taken down from the cross after just a few hours—too few to cause death by this method, unless he had massive injuries, for which there was no evidence—and was released to Joseph of Arimathea, a man of wealth and influence; Jesus survived to return to India. The *Ahmadiyyas* of Kashmir show proof that Jesus of Nazareth had

---

[46]This marks the triumph of Vikramaditya over the *Sakas*, who had ousted his father, Gardabhilla, king of Ujjain.

come to India in search of the ten lost tribes of Israel, had studied religious philosophies with Buddhists, Jains, Hindus and Ajivikas, and undertaken at least four overland journeys and pilgrimages throughout India before returning to Palestine. His *Beatitudes, ahimsa* and other teachings bear striking concordance with those of Indian religions. He returned to India after his "death" to preach and live in Kashmir, married and had children, according to the Ahmadiyyas, who claim him as an ancestor and protect a tomb in Srinagar said to be his.[47]

Meanwhile, his twelve disciples in Palestine had accepted him as the Messiah and preached his doctrine throughout the Roman Empire. After many vicissitudes, it became the official religion with Constantine's Edict of Milan, in 313 AD. Rome declared tolerance of all religions, including paganism, and lived amicably with them. Constantine's nephew, Julian, became Augustus briefly and tried to revive the traditional Roman religions and rebuild the temple. He wanted all religions to co-exist, but died two years later. After this, Christianity eventually displaced all other religions in the Empire, increasingly with violence. Emperor Theodosius adopted Trinitarianism and destroyed the Greek temples in 391 AD. In time, Christianity grew to command the largest, richest and most powerful following in the western world, perhaps not quite the way Christ would have wanted, and certainly not with the numerous schisms and wars fought in his name. Romans used his birth to define a new calendar era (*Anno Domini*, AD, now *Christian era*, CE).

India then had about 35 million people, a fifth of the world's population. She had established Shaivite colonies in Funan, on the Mekong Delta—where Kaundinya, an Indian Brahmin, became the first king—and others, a century later in Cambodia[48] and Malaysia. Funan thrived for centuries as a business and trading centre, attracting shipping, from China in the north to Persia in the west, especially under the Sassanids. Further south, Prince Ajishaka of Gujarat had invaded Java and founded colonies.

A few years later China's Emperor Ming Di (ruled 58-76CE) converted to Buddhism and brought the religion to China where Indian monks directed the building of a temple in Hunan (Henan Sheng).The Chinese leader Zhang Qian led the development of the "Silk Roads" to

---

[47]Andreas Faber-Kaiser names people among the Ahmadiyyas claiming kinship with Jesus and illustrates a sepulchre with his remains. They also claim to be custodian of Mary's tomb. It is interesting that the most powerful attempt to convert Indians to Christianity is happening today, headed by Rome after decades of priming by Mother Teresa! The ten lost tribes, the unconverted, most likely settled in Kashmir and the Eurasian Diaspora.

[48] A variant of Kamboja, an ancient region of Northwest India, Afghanistan and Iran, whose people are said to have migrated to surrounding lands and settled in Funan, which included the area of modern Cambodia. King Norodom Sihanouk acknowledged his ancient bond with Indian Kambojis on a visit to India in 1955.

the Middle East and Roman Empire, then nearing its zenith, just a few years before Zhang's contemporaries invented paper in 105 CE. Across the Pacific, in the western hemisphere, the population of Teotihuacan, Mexico had reached 100,000 and the city covered 11 square miles.

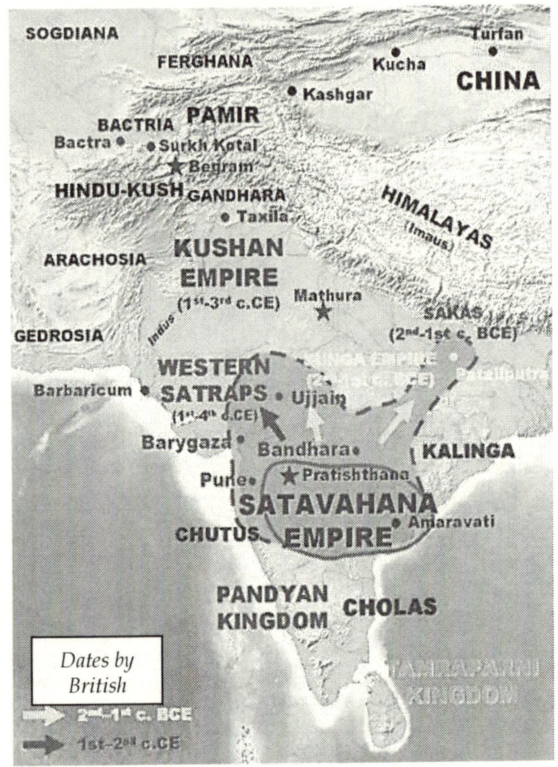

Meanwhile, the Buddhist Kushans had been raiding India's north since the Mauryans fell. But they had little success until the reign of Kanishka I (100-144 CE), son of Vima Kadphises. Kanishka expanded his empire along the Indus into northern India (Kashmir to Gujarat), and into Central Asia to the Tarim Basin and parts of western China. He promoted *Mahayana* Buddhism and its architecture, and built a huge *stupa* in Peshawar, measuring 286 feet in diameter, and 591-689 feet tall. (The building of shrines had been a common practice among warriors of that time, usually to commemorate an important victory, and explains the large number of stupas, temples, mosques and so on). He supported Greco-Buddhist (Gandhāra School) and Hindu art (Mathura School) and followed the Persian cult of *Mithra*.

At the start of his rule, Kanishka convened the Fourth Buddhist Council with 500 monks under Vasumitra, who wrote a commentary on Buddhist philosophy known as the *Mahā Vibhāṣā* or The Great Exegesis. This helped to spread Buddhism in Kashmir and led to the rendering of the Pāli text into Sanskrit—the language of Hinduism—as Sanskrit allowed wider dissemination of these writings. Missionaries thus spread Buddhism throughout the Empire, and beyond, to China, in whose capital, Louyang (Henan province), Kanishka founded a translation agency. A monk, Lokasema, translated several texts into Chinese.

The Kushans were a tolerant people; their coins showed Hindu, Buddhist, and Persian deities. They adopted Indian customs, including Ayurvaidic medical and health practices, which Charaka (ca 80-180 CE), physician to the Kushan king—and contemporary of Roman physician Galen—promoted vigorously with his textbook of medicine, the *Charaka Sāmhita.* The work carried on the practices of Sushruta and the principles of Ayurvaidic medicine that had become widely known; it included a code of conduct for doctors.[49]

Many treatises on various religious subjects emerged and led to formation of many sects. Religious discourses flourished in many parts of the country and new commentaries—*Samhitas, Agamas, etc.* on ancient treatises—revived interest in them and created new movements and personalities e.g., Shandilya[50] and followers who wrote on the *Pancharatra* and stirred a rebirth in the worship of Vishnu. Commerce grew internationally, expanding as new routes to China, the Middle East and the Mediterranean were established, including the "silk roads" developed by Zhang Qian, by 100 AD. The invention of paper affected every nation, as did Rome's expansion, which reached its zenith in 117 AD. In time, paper replaced palm leaves that Sinhalese Buddhists had used and tree bark of the Hindus. Towards the end of their rule, the Kushans came under growing influence of the new Sassanid regime that would dominate Persia for over four hundred years. In India, Prince Shatakarni of Andhra ended the Shaka reign in Gujarat.

The Greek astronomer Ptolemy visited India—where he was called *Asura Maya*—near the end of the second century and lectured on solar astronomy *(Surya Siddhanta)* to University students. He had studied the heavens and, contrary to Aristotle, had proposed a flat earth theory of the Universe (geocentricity), with the earth at its centre and all heavenly bodies rotating around it, beginning with the oceans, from inside out. However, his hypothesis could not explain the heavenly data; he thus invented explanations, including reverse motion of some bodies. Various imaginative and often poignant depictions of the inhabited earth were given, to the credit of the cartographers, considering that exploration was not yet fashionable, and quite dangerous—not just from fear of

[49] It includes this timeless advice: *"A physician who fails to enter the body of a patient with the lamp of knowledge and understanding can never treat diseases. He should first study all the factors, including environment, which influence a patient's disease, and then prescribe treatment. It is more important to prevent the occurrence of disease than to seek a cure."*

[50] Promoter of *Pancharatra* doctrines, *Bhakti sutras,* on worship of *Vishnu.* The central teaching is that the deity manifests in five forms: *Para, Vyūha, Vibhava, Antaryamin,* and *Archa,* which show how *Parabrahma,* the formless God can be brought into interaction with humanity.

falling over the edge of Ocean—but the tools for safe ocean voyages were yet to come.

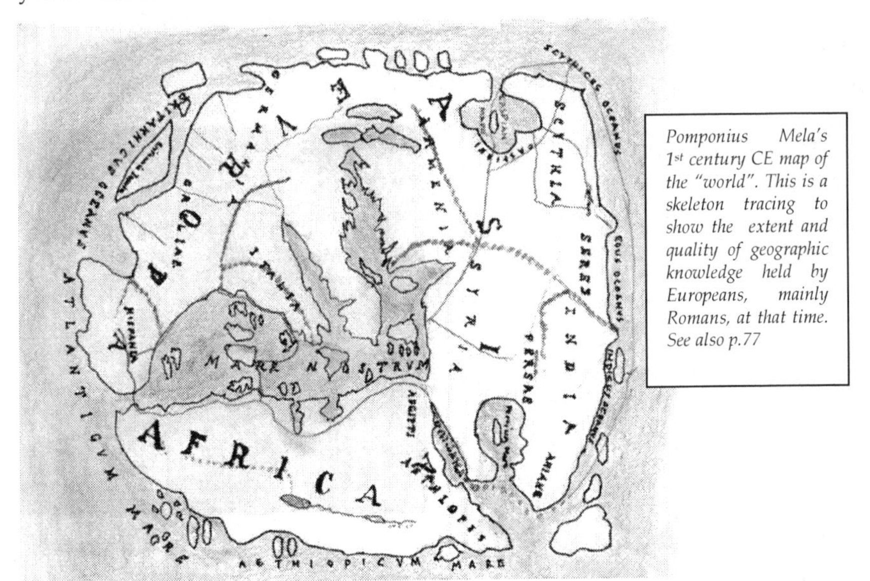

Pomponius Mela's 1st century CE map of the "world". This is a skeleton tracing to show the extent and quality of geographic knowledge held by Europeans, mainly Romans, at that time. *See also p.77*

Like his predecessors—from Anaximander in the 7th century BCE, Eratosthenes and Posidonius (two polymaths), and Ptolemy, to those of the 15th Century CE—Pomponius Mela, in the 1st century CE, saw the world as a flat plate around the Mediterranean, which he pompously, but accurately perhaps, called *Mare Nostrum* (our sea), giving national names to the indentations from it e.g., Libyan, Aegean, Adriatic Seas, but Britannic Ocean for the water west of Britain, continuous with the Atlantic, to conform to the notion of an envelopping ocean. He was the first to divide the world into habitable zones: a central torrid zone, two temperate and two frigid zones. Of these, only the temperate ones were considered habitable! (An 1898 reconstruction of his map shows the geographic limitations and errors that would survive until the late 15th century, despite contradictions from India and China.)

Eratosthenes of Cyrene, (276-194 BCE), librarian of Alexandria, mathematician and geographer, had earlier shown the world as a rectangle with Europe larger than Asia, the Mediterranean fairly represented, China unnamed and India forming the eastern Asian boundary with Ocean as a straight north-south line inclining slightly to the West as it moved up to join the Northern Ocean (Arctic, not so conceived then). While allowing for the primitive state of geographic knowledge at that time, it is disappointing that many geographers, Eratosthenes excepted, ignored oriental knowledge that was already available by that date, from Aristotle, Alexander, Megasthenes, Seleucus etc. and, notably, Indian teachers and astronomers in Greece. Modern renditions of ancient history have done little to remedy this oversight and outdated western guesswork has far more influence than Asian evidence in versions of Asian history, achievements and scholarship.

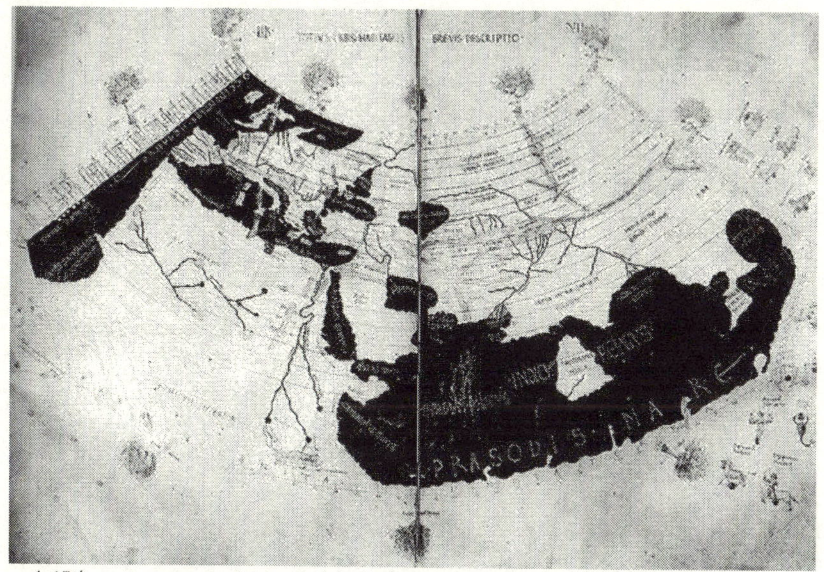

A 15th century manuscript copy of the Ptolemy world map, reconstituted from Ptolemy's Geographia (circa 150CE) Ocean and Seas are shown in black.

Ptolemy in his *Geographia* was probably the first to show features of central Asia and India, with the Indus and Ganges fairly well depicted and good positioning of the Amu Darya and Syr Darya. He had travelled to Taxila, India, having heard of, or been "invited" to the university there, but shows none of the other great rivers of the region, neither west (Helmand) nor East (Brahmaputra) nor of China. For the rest, Ptolemy's map was no better and hardly an advance on the one drawn by Posidonius some 50 years earlier. A 6th century "world" map by Cosmas Indicopleustes (*India voyager*) shows the world as a rectangle shaped like a tabernacle in the middle of Ocean, with the Mediterranean Sea and Gibraltar in the west, the Aegean, Adriatic and Euxine (Black) Seas in the east, the Nile to the south and the Euphrates and Tigris Rivers flowing into the Persian Gulf. Intuitively, he had placed Paradise in the far east!

The narrow ideas of the world and universe then current were definitively debunked by Aryābhatta in 499 CE, but incredibly retained until the 17th century, within the Roman church, which had declared as heresy all things eastern. Surprisingly, astronomers from Kerala writing in the 14th century overlooked the work of Aryābhatta, but recognised the contributions of Bhāskara, who had written a book titled *Aryābhattiya*

Bhashya. Were it not for European commercial craving for Indian and oriental spices, and the huge profits they brought, it may have remained so. Not to be outdone, American Lutherans in Missouri maintained a belief in the geocentric universe well into the 20th century; surveys have shown that up to 20% of people in the West still believe in a flat earth! The Flat Earth Society epitomises this and stoutly rejects the facts.

In the 3rd century CE, Plotinus, an Egyptian-Greek philosopher and religious scholar, was teaching *"ahimsa, karma, vegetarianism, reincarnation and belief in a Supreme Force, both immanent and transcendent,"* all basic Hindu tenets. His work influenced later Islamic and European thought.

The Pallava dynasty (ca. 250-885 CE) developed in Tamil Nadu, and built monuments and temples, including the *Kailasa Kamakshi* temple complex at Kanchi, the capital.

The fourth century CE dawned with the rise of the Imperial Gupta dynasty in the north of India which would flourish from 320-540 CE. Its origin coincided with the acceptance of Christianity as the religion of the Roman Empire (see Ch. 6). The Guptas replaced the Kushans, and India began a period of renewed strength, unity and prosperity recapturing much of the glory of the Mauryans. This period is regarded by some as the *Classical Age* since it established norms for architecture, literature, art and philosophy. All religious Hindu and Buddhist groups were accepted and the regime exerted control over most of India. Srigupta I, the founder, was the ruler of Magadha (modern Bihar) from 270 to 290 CE, and established the dynasty, with Pataliputra (Patna) as its capital. He and his son, Ghatotkacha (290-305 CE), have left very few artefacts to show for their respective rules, unlike their successors, each of whom minted individual coins.

Ghatotkacha's son, Chandragupta I (305-325 CE), strengthened the kingdom by marrying princess Kumaradevi of the powerful and prestigious Lichchavi family, the rulers of Mithila, the capital of Videha, ancient home of Sitā, wife of Rāma. The Lichchavi dynasty later established a Hindu kingdom in Nepal, which ruled for 550 years to 900 CE, and became the major intellectual and commercial link between South and Central Asia. Chandragupta's marriage increased his power and resources, enabling him to gain control of the entire Ganges valley and to be crowned Emperor *(Maharajadhiraja)*.

He quickly extended his sway over most of India. Religion prospered and Vaishnavism, Saivism and Buddhism grew. However, it was his son Vikramaditya, Chandragupta II (375-414 CE), who became the best-known of the Guptas. more tales are told of him than of any other ruler of India, some regarding him the greatest of the Hindu monarchs. He consolidated his father's gains, and during his reign—and that of his son Kumaragupta—India reached a peak of opulence and prestige that spread internationally: in the Middle East, Mediterranean, Africa and the rest of Asia. Europe was then a congeries of rough nomadic tribes, nibbling at the borders of the Roman Empire.

Thus began a long period of political stability, internal security, economic expansion and prosperity. Trade and religion expanded west by land into the Sassanid Empire and Central Asia, the Levant, and the Eastern and Western Roman Empires, and by sea to Aden, the west coast of Arabia (Hejaz), Egypt and the other North African provinces of Rome. At the same time Christianity was spreading throughout the Roman Empire. Once it became the sole state religion, it inevitably clashed with *Vaidic* doctrines outside India—in Greece, Anatolia, the Middle East, Egypt and Arabia—e.g., reincarnation and what some believe were other Vaidic expressions of spirituality. So it was not surprising that the new converts would carry out acts of vandalism and iconoclasm against non-Christians in the name of Christ, such as the destruction of Hellenic temples in Greece and elsewhere, beginning with Roman Emperor Theodosius in 391 CE, as already noted.

It is a tenacious failing that humans tend to express their new-found beliefs far more virulently than born adherents, as if to exorcise the spirits of their former religion, from shame or hate or the need to convince themselves and others of their commitment. And although the Greeks adopted Christianity, mostly by force, they still celebrated their pre-Christian heritage, complete with gods and goddesses, and its rich literature—unlike Indian converts to Islam living in Pakistan and India today—earning the wrath of iconoclasts long thereafter.[51]

---

[51]On this subject Dr Brahmam, who had studied convert behaviour, observed, "Muslims pretend that the world began with Islam and that Hinduism and all its complexities did not exist before Mohamed, yet they reach into *Purānas* to find a prediction—by insertion, I think—to justify Mohamed's place in the line of prophets! In the same way, secular Indians do not want Vaidic scholars, Indian or foreign, to correct our history as British taught it. These critics," he sneered, "forget that it was British educators who planned curricula and wrote textbooks, which they used to turn us into *coconuts*! You know, *Qutb Minar* was built by Guptas, not Muslims, to celebrate Arab links. Evidence from coins, wall inscriptions, ceramics etc., which they suppress, shows that *Ka'aba* was pre-Islamic *Vaidic* shrine set up by Guptas. You know, Romans did not really lose their Empire; they gave up a crumbling militarist one, decimated by disease, for one based on *faith*, not might, and for this Constantine must be seen as a seer, to recognise the power of faith as a greater and cheaper tool of conquest and wealth than arms and armies! Convert the rulers and sit back while they wage wars against the pagans and bring you converts!"

"That's a highly original thought!" I said, impressed. "Popes did become militaristic and support wars to conquer territory and to destroy other beliefs, bad or good, up to today. The loss of Britain to Henry VIII was just another of numerous schisms in Christianity. Today's RC Church is larger and more powerful than the Roman Empire ever was. Muslims would improve on this with *Dawah* and *Jihad*!" *(Conversations at UCWI, 1960)*

Leisure activities developed in all India as industrial and agricultural prosperity increased. Centuries earlier, the popular *ashtapada*—the four-handed war game played with dice—evolved to *shaturanga*, the two-person forerunner of chess (p.64). At a more intimate level another two-person game benefited enormously from the publication of Vatsyāyana's *Kāmasutra*, a treatise presenting human sexuality and physical love as essential for married bliss and success. *Kāmasutra* described details of sexual intercourse and the numerous positions in which the act could be consummated, many possible only by exponents of Yoga in its many forms, thus justifying the practices of this branch of Medicine!

The Guptas supported learning, from research to dissemination: in mathematics, language, art, culture, and the sciences, pure and applied. They promoted agriculture, commerce and trade, local and foreign. The best known paintings of this period can be found among the murals in the Ajanta caves, noted for rich and detailed depiction of nature, people, dress, atmosphere and mood, including the rich and sensuous life of Gupta India. The frescoes also show Siddhartha (Buddha) dressed in the style that Nehru has made popular today, called the *chudidara pyjama*. Gupta styles influenced Buddhist art all over Asia.

Indian epics—including lasting literature such as Vishnu Sharma's amazing collection of fables, the *Panchatantra*[52]—have inspired centuries of European and West Asian writers like Aesop, Boccaccio, Chaucer, Dante, La Fontaine, Shakespeare, Ibn Sena, Omar Khayyam and myriad others, to this day. Books by Kalidāsa *e.g. Meghaduta, Kumarsamhita, and Shakuntala,* the Sanskrit dramas, *Mrichchhakatika* and *Mudra Rakshasa,* were written down in this period. Many new works were added to the religious library, and the law books of Brihaspati were composed at this period. Architecture flourished and several major temples were constructed, lavishly outfitted and embellished, and in later years provided rich targets for looting and destruction by Muslim invaders.

After the third century, Indian trade shifted from emphasis on west Asia and Europe to South-East Asia and China. Developments were taking place elsewhere in various ways that would affect India and Asia generally. In the northwest, Hunas (Hephtalites) and Sakas (Scythians) continued to harass border areas. The Guptas held their territories, old and new, repelling the invaders, and established good relations with

---

[52]Burzoe, physician and vizier to Khosrau I, the revered and highly cultured 6th century Sassanid king (501-579, rule 48 years), translated *Panchatantra* into Persian; this version was translated into Arabic by Ibn al-Mafuqqa under the title *Kalila and Dimna* or *The Fables of Bidpai* and became paramount among Arab writings. Original Persian works prior to the Islamic period are few, ?destroyed by conquerors along with Zoroastrianism. Omar Khayyam is well-known in the West for his Rubaiyat. Persian literature would flourish during the Mughal Akbar's time when many Sanskrit works were translated into Persian.

their neighbour, the Sassanids[53] of Persia, who claimed Baluchistan as an eastern boundary and had considerable trade and other relations with Indian territories, including Sindh.

The Buddhist patriarch, Bodhidharma (450-535 CE), of South India founded *Ch'an* Buddhism in China (*Zen* in Japan). Christianity spread in Europe throughout the Roman Empire, dominated by the authority of the Emperors, albeit rife with patrician intrigues, until the Protestant Reformation split the Church, over 1000 years later.

Popes, however, from the dawn of Christianity and the creation of the bishopric of Rome, assumed the succession of Peter and Christ's role on earth; *sacerdotalism* became rooted. Popes issued periodic edicts, some after due reflection, others unsupported by Christ's teachings, but perhaps based on statements by disciples or their successors, or mostly, it seems, on temporal/political expediency. Thus Catholicism acquired accretions over time. One was the rejection of the notion of reincarnation by the Council of Ferrara-Florence (438-445), and affirmed by the Council of Constantinople, a century later, stating categorically that the "soul" did not exist prior to conception, a claim no more valid than its opposite. The Council of Lyons II repeated this in 1274 CE.

Far away, and not directly related, Polynesians explored the Pacific in open outrigger canoes, reaching Hawaii and Easter Island, while Peru completed the 150 feet high Sun temple of Moche. Meanwhile, Europe, composed largely of illiterate and hungry Germanic and Scandinavian tribes, seethed with unrest and bloody border intrusions, aiming to share in the life style of the civilised Roman Empires.

While Gupta armies were repelling Hephtalite forces at the borders, universities were being established in the heartland to advance and spread knowledge, especially in Mathematics and Astronomy. In 499 CE, Aryābhatta I, (476-ca 550 CE), a youthful mathematician and astronomer, wrote his astonishing work, the *Aryābhattiya*, the world's first treatise on arithmetic, algebra, and plane and spherical trigonometry. Aryābhatta was probably born in Ashmaka (Maharashtra) and studied astronomy at Nālandā University. His achievements included description of *sine*;

[53] The Sassanid Empire (226—651) was a Parsi kingdom established by Ardashir I on the defeat of Artabanus IV, king of Parthia. It ended when Yazdegerd III lost his 14-year struggle against Islamic invaders. At its height, the empire, named the *Eranshahr* (dominion of the Iranians) covered lands from modern eastern Turkey to western Pakistan. It practised a rigid, hereditary caste system, strictly enforced, under the supreme ruler or *Shahanshah*. The layers consisted of *Priests, Warriors, Secretaries and Commoners*, with little mobility between them; in this it differed from the practice in India, which was not conceived as hereditary and inter-caste mobility was recognised, but later discouraged by Brahmins when they gained ascendancy, and society regressed under their exploitation.

rendering *pi* as 3.1416, the value in common use today; explanation of eclipses; and revelation that the earth was continuously spinning on a north-south axis, each rotation taking 24 hours, and that it orbited the sun in 365.3586805 days, the duration of a solar year. He showed that Earth was one of several spherical planets in parallel elliptical solar orbits, which explained gravity and the "dance" of celestial bodies.

Aryābhatta was barely 20, when he made some of these stunning discoveries, without a telescope, and over a thousand years before Newton described gravity, and the Vatican denounced Galileo for supporting Copernicus's independent postulate of a heliocentric universe. Western cultures credit this pair with these astronomical findings, unaware of Aryābhatta's earlier work; they credit Arabs and others with his mathematical achievements, despite the clear attribution of that body of knowledge to Indians by Muslim scholar Ibn Sena.

In 499 CE, Aryābhatta toured Mesopotamia, Arabia, the Levant and probably the Byzantine Empire to teach Indian numerals, script and mathematics, and their application to accounting practices, doubtless to facilitate commerce and trade by establishing a uniform system and language of accounting. India then had 50 million people, 26% of the world's population and was a dominant force in higher education, culture and commerce. His book, *Aryābhattiya,* comprised 121 rhyming stanzas, was translated from Sanskrit into Latin and thus became available to Roman and Arabic scholars, and eventually to Europeans, enabling them finally to accomplish complex calculations such as fractions; decimals; square and cube roots; areas of triangles and other geometric shapes; volume of spheres; relationships; trigonometric functions, and so on. Other Indian mathematicians of that period included Varāhamihira, whose treatise, *Bhrihata Sāmhita*, dealt with the decimal system.[54]

Europeans outside the Mediterranean uncritically credited the Arabs as originators of the wealth of knowledge in mathematics, science and language that they had brought and spread. European lack of language skills and innate regard for martial peoples kept them for a millennium from discovering the fountains of knowledge and culture that lay east of Arabia; they have yet to acknowledge their debt to the writings of Aryābhatta, his predecessors of previous millennia—Āpastamba, Baudhāyana et al, and his successors like Brahmagupta, Bhāskara, Rāmanuj and the other Indian luminaries in mathematics, astronomy and grammar, who had enlightened the ancient and modern world.

---

[54] Their work would be extended by many brilliant successors down to the present day and be consolidated in the Indian Institutes of Technology (IIT's) that the Indian Government has established as superior places of learning and research.

The influence of Chandragupta II had reached Mesopotamia, the Roman Empire and Arabia. His emissaries were a dominant presence in Mecca, where the ruling Qureshis used Indian mathematics, after Aryābhatta's lectures, to achieve consistency in the division of spoils after raids (*ghazw* or *razzias*). Some Indian scholars had speculated that Qureshi descended from Kurus of India and that the Ka'aba was a pagan or Hindu shrine and place of pilgrimage, with many jewelled *murtis* (statues) and *mandalas*. The annual pilgrimage boosted city revenues, even as it does today. It became Islam's primary shrine on Mohamed's conquest of Mecca, a model of conquest, conversion and desecration of holy buildings that had been practised by the Roman Christians throughout the Empire, and also characterised the Islamist approach to Hindu temples ever since. The great Sanskrit poet and dramatist, Kalidāsa, lived at this time.

By the end of the fifth century, the Gupta Empire was in decline, in spite of heroic efforts of the later Guptas: Skanda, Kumar, Buddha, Vainya and Bhanu, to repel the relentless Hunas (Hephtalites). In Europe, the Western Roman Empire had just ended, falling to Germanic pagans seizing lands in Gaul, Hispania and Britain. It would be a century or more before these would rise above their innate brutality to begin to form organised realms and attain a status similar to the same vulnerable small nation states to which the collapse of the cultured Gupta Empire would bring India. Local Indian leaders, it seemed, had tired of prosperity and unity as part of the great and admired nation forged by the Guptas, more sophisticated and complex than the Roman Empire, more learned and advanced in science, mathematics, language, philosophy, religion and engineering than Greece or Egypt. Regional leaders put tribal and other local and emotional interests above the prestige, power and security that the Empire had brought.

So often in human history does decadence that comes with power and prosperity undermine the progress already made, and the newly privileged seek to control and direct their territory even at risk of losing it. India was weakened by internal dissension and scheming among subject rulers, whose forebears had wisely united with the Guptas to achieve a strong Empire. Greater individual control might bring greater immediate profit, but only until aliens, seeking India's wealth, amassed the force needed to intensify border raids, the tactic that the Germanic tribes had used against the Roman Empire so successfully.

By the middle of the sixth century CE, the Gupta Empire had disintegrated and India came once again under individual regional kings, great and small. These ambitious leaders underestimated how vulnerable fragmentation would make them, and realised this only too late, when the border regions of the Empire fell to the Hunas, Toramana and his son Mihirakula, who left a legacy of anti-Buddhist atrocities. The Huns held north India until expelled, ca. 533 CE, by the armies of the Aulikar Rajas Yashovarman of Malwa and Ishanavarman of Kanauj. Persians and Turks later crushed the Hunas in Iran.

The 6th-century Alexandrian traveller Cosmas Indicopleustes agreed that the Hephtalites in India had reached the zenith of their power under Mihirakula, whom 7th-century Chinese traveller Hiuen-tsang described in his *The Record of the Western Regions* as a "quick talent and naturally brave. He subdued all the neighbouring provinces without exception." If so, he was one of a long line of land-grabbing adventurers in the tradition of Nebuchadnezzar, Darius, Alexander, Maurya, Caesar, Gupta, Charlemagne, Genghis Khan and latterly, the Mughals, British, Napoleon and Hitler. But few had the sustained triumphs of that war-mongering mercantilist collective, the British aristocracy.

The following centuries saw the emergence and flowering of the Chalukya dynasty in Gujarat and adjacent regions of western India (two eras: ca 543-757CE and 975-1189 CE), begun under Pulakeshin I. In Japan, Emperor Kimmei officially recognised Buddhism, and in Arabia, Mohammed (570-632CE) was developing the religion of Islam. At this time, Brahmagupta, the great astronomer (598-665), wrote the 25-chapter *Brahma Sphuta Siddhanta* on Hindu astronomy, gravity and complex mathematics, extending the work of Aryābhatta.

Soon after, the Buddhist king Harshavardhana (ruled 606-44) regained control of North and central India from Baluchistan to the Narmada River, south of which the Chalukya Empire prospered under Pulakeshin II. Learning flourished throughout the land, centred at Nālandā, Taxashila, Pataliputra, Ujjain, Madras (Chennai) and a dozen other cities. Nālandā University was estimated to have over 1,500 teachers, some 10,000 residents, and thousands of manuscripts. Many prolific writers emerged, prominent among them Banabhatta, author of *Harshacharita* (story of King Harsha) and *Kadambari*. Vagbhata, a physician, wrote the *Ashtanga Sangraha* on Ayurvaida; a succession of religious writers, centred in Tamil Nadu, composed thousands of songs and poems in praise of Nārayana, Rāma and Krishna which were collected as *Nalayira Divya Prabandham*.

The Gupta period had seen enormous strides in applied sciences. One example was the unique metallurgical innovation, rust-proofing, shown in the 23-foot high iron pillar at Delhi, which has survived rust-free for some 2000 years. This technology matured in the following centuries and was used to construct rust-proof iron beams, posts and girders for large buildings, such as the temples at Puri and Konarak.

India had become widely known for the high quality of its steel—from Kushan and Harshavardhana periods—and had developed a method to extract zinc from its ore and make an alloy of copper, lead and tin *(bidari)*.[56] In his book, *Science in Medieval India,* A. Rahman noted that Indian science allowed them to make the best cannon in the world; the leading factory was located at Jaigarh, Jaipur, Rajasthan.

The Chinese pilgrim Hiuen-Tsang (Huan Zang) toured India and wrote extensively about his travels. By the middle of the seventh century more than 60 Chinese monks had travelled to India (taking full advantage of the hospitality of the Buddhist temple that the Pallava King, Narasinha Varman, had built at Nagapatam for Chinese merchants and visiting monks); 400 Sanskrit works had been translated into Chinese, continuing the work of earlier Kushans, of which three hundred and eighty survive today.

Meanwhile Hinduism had spread to Indonesia and Buddhism to Indochina, Afghanistan, Central Asia, China, Korea and Japan. At this time the Arabs had begun to spread their new religion, Islam, by *dawah* (request) and *jihad,* that is, the *lesser jihad,* or aggression against others, not the personal or *greater jihad,* which consists of introspection. They began in Mesopotamia, then the Levant and the Byzantine Empire and moved west through North Africa. They took with them—wherever their raiding armies went, west, south, north and east from their bases, first in Medina, later in Damascus and Baghdad—Indian knowledge of sciences, mathematics and medicine, gleaned from the *Aryābhattiya* (499 CE), the *Brahma Sphuta Siddhanta* of Brahmagupta, and from others. This knowledge would ironically help Islamic marauders many centuries later in their conquest of the Indian sub-continent.

To understand the profound changes that were to consume India, and indeed the world, one has to recall developments in Europe, the explosion of militancy, the spread of Christianity, the fall of the Western Roman Empire, the rise of a belligerent Islam and the many schisms in each that led to Roman usurpation and distortion of Christianity, the cultivation of Papal hegemony, the capture and control of Islam by a friction-ridden Caliphate, and the contests for power and trade in India and commercial domination of the Orient.

[56] The exact age of the Delhi Iron Pillar is uncertain; some assign it to the Gupta period of Chandragupta II Vikramaditya, but others, including Professor Kak of Louisiana State University, place it in the century before Christ, ca 50 BCE.

The main stupa (reliquary) of Śāriputra, a disciple of Buddha, in Nālandā University, Bihar, India. This and Taxashila, north Punjab were the first University centres for religious and academic learning in India and the world; they attracted students from many countries, especially China, Middle East, Greece and other Mediterranean states

Chanakya, administrator of Mauryans and author of Arthashastra, a book on governance, which Machiavelli is said to have used as a source for his book, "The Prince".

The Pillar at Sārnath

The pillar (right) at Sārnath (Sannathi. see map p. 70), one of India's symbols of Independence, contains one of Ashoka's instructions. It reads: *"Esahi vidhi ya iyam: dhammena palana, dhammena vidhane, dhammena sukhiyana, dhammena gotiti"*. This translates to:
"For this is my rule: government by the law, of the law; prosperity by the law, protection by the law."

Chapter 5

Thou art Peter and upon this rock I will build my church. Matthew's Gospel: 16:18

"From Persia to the Chinese Sea, from the icy regions of Siberia to the islands of Java and Borneo, from Oceania to Socotra, India has propagated her beliefs, her tales and her civilization. She has left indelible imprints on one-fourth of the human race in the course of a long succession of centuries. She has the right to reclaim in universal history the rank that ignorance has refused her for a long time and to hold her place amongst the great nations summarising and symbolising the spirit of Humanity."

Sylvain Levi

Roman decline; the Great Migration and Indian history.

After the Romans had conquered Europe, Latin, and later Greek became the major languages of learning. But it would be more than a millennium before education came within reach of the non-priestly classes, who knew *"no Latin and less Greek"*. The lettered people of Europe were Christian clergy and Greco-Roman and Jewish philosophers and scribes. Learning gave Christians prestige and protection when Emperor Constantine accepted Christianity in 313 CE, and Theodosius I on 27 February, 380 decreed it to be *the* official religion of the Empire, turning the lawbreakers of yesterday into today's saints!

The literature of Greeks and Romans gradually spread to monasteries and libraries throughout the Empire, where they joined the prior writings of scholars whose prose and poetry were well known. Some books included the stories of little known cultures such as the Hindus, Buddhists and Chinese, and those of Egypt and middle Africa (North Africa being part of the Roman Empire). Prior to that time knowledge was transmitted mainly orally, verbatim, notwithstanding the use of papyrus, silk, bamboo, banana and other leaves and tree bark for writing. Stone carvings, used by Ashoka, had limits. Scholars, regardless of origin, wanting to study histories, had to be physically present at the foot of the teacher to learn, by rote, and to maintain the integrity of the record, and only then to try to understand it.[57]

Roman conquest had stopped short of "Germania": the realms of the "barbaric" Saxons, Angles, Jutes, Goths, Vandals and others. Many of these who later came under Roman rule would convert to Christianity between the 4th and 7th centuries, but tribes of the eastern Baltic region would resist until the 13th-14th centuries. Their religious rituals were similar to those of the Vaidas; and words and names in their languages,

---

[57]The Sanskrit and Hindi word *Upanishad* means literally "at the feet of..." I saw this process first hand in Saudi Arabia in the 1980s where children crammed the Quran and were expected to progress at a certain rate; they were tested daily on recall and the best "memories" were channelled into religious service.

described as Indo-European, bore striking concordance in meaning and pronunciation to Sanskrit.

At the end of the first century CE, the Roman Empire, with Trajan at its head, had reached a high level of prosperity, with relative peace, sustained by a large regular army, under command of aristocrats supported by well-paid, literate centurions. The Empire occupied the Mediterranean countries, the Balkans and parts of northwest Europe. Waves of invasion of Britain spanning a century—under Caesar, Claudius, Flavius and Hadrian—had conquered Britain north to the River Tyne where Hadrian had built a wall due west to Solway Firth.

The Roman Empire thus extended from the Iberian Peninsula in the west to Mesopotamia in the east, and exerted influence over Africa south to the Niger. It was variably tolerant to all religions, which helped to avoid social clashes. The main one was the centuries-old religious conflict with the Jews which ended in 136 CE, with the devastation of Judea and the crushing of the revolt led by Rabbi Kokhba, a militant anti-Roman, who had been hailed by the Jews as the long-awaited messiah and had succeeded, by a mixture of discipline, fortitude and religious zeal, in expelling the Romans for two years!

Germanic tribesmen cf Anglo-Saxon ancestors, from Philip Clüver's Germania Antiqua (1616) Plate 17

Christians were becoming a growing headache to the Romans, starting with the ministries of Christ's disciple, Peter, their first leader and "Pope"; thereafter it grew among the masses, perhaps as the natural reaction of simple people to the misery and violence that they saw each day, as ambitious men vied for power. In turn, citizens of the Empire viewed Christian behaviour and practices as hostile, largely because of presumed secrecy and the strange practices, both what Christians did and what they omitted, such as failing to celebrate Roman feast days, omitting to make the customary sacrifices or honouring the Emperor as a god. Thus they were generally suspected of being everything, from deviants to traitors. Citizens complained against them, often anonymously.

Authorities initially underplayed this reaction. Trajan (98-117), in particular, advised his governors to show some tolerance, to ignore anonymous complaints but punish wrong-doing. In the first century of Christianity, many of the leaders, including several disciples, were so punished. At least sixteen were martyred, beginning with Stephen in Jerusalem, and Peter and Paul in Rome. The attitude of rulers generally continued to be more reactive than persecutory; but that began to change when a band of citizens in Lyon rallied to murder Christians in their homes, and would no doubt have succeeded, if authorities had not intervened to prevent it.

Christians continued to face hostility in the second and third centuries, increasing as public pressure mounted and ambitious generals, craving ultimate power, sought to placate their citizens to gain popularity, even as the fortunes of the Empire were becoming shaky and invaders more insistent. Considering the belief systems of the Romans, it was not unexpected that their citizens would blame the reclusive Christians and their unpatriotic religious beliefs and practices, for angering Roman gods, and causing, not only economic decline and foreign incursions that were costly to reverse, but the violent outbreaks of "plagues." These were the classic scourges: the plague proper, small pox, measles and similar infections—which raged between 165-180 CE, killing over five million people and decimating the army.

Marcus Aurelius, Emperor then, summoned to Rome the renowned physician, Galen, to help with the sick and control the epidemic. Galen had advanced his knowledge of anatomy and physiology, comparable to that of Charaka, the contemporaneous Ayurvaidic physician to the court of the Kushan Emperor in northern India. But neither knew of the existence of pathogenic bacteria and viruses and the epidemiology of the diseases they caused; people would have to wait for over 1700 years for that knowledge. So Galen was powerless to help stem the waves of death or the outbreaks that came to bear his name as *Galen's epidemic.*

The scope of knowledge was extremely limited in the first century, travel and research constricted, and Europeans would have to wait many lifetimes for Bacon and Descartes to provide direction to learning by defining inductive and deductive reasoning respectively. But by then, certain practices had become standard and attitudes hardened, notably among the successors to Peter's religion, Christianity, which regrettably evolved away from Christ—who became a figurehead—and changed to a political hegemony, the Papacy. It soon developed into a colonising state, later a global Empire, with its exclusive centre in Rome, its own diplomatic service, its own bank etc.—until Mussolini restricted it in 1929 to religion and to the Vatican. By then it had accumulated huge estates and enormous wealth, from taxing adherents (tithes) and soliciting donations, which people were coerced into giving, by being either shamed or threatened with hell, or fear of something worse. In time the organism became more important than the message, and Christ increasingly irrelevant. This became so obvious that many preachers have declaimed that were Christ to reappear today, he would almost certainly be crucified by the Roman Catholic Church, if some other Christian group didn't get him first!

Invaders from Germanic and other northern tribes seeking new lands for their growing populations, and wanting to share the higher standard of living in the Empire, had been breaching the Empire's borders since the time of Trajan. But they were checked by superior Roman forces and by the Danube and Rhine Rivers, which aided the defenders. The epidemics had a lasting impact on Romans as their armies suffered huge losses, which weakened defences and allowed major intrusions, even though border tribes had also been sapped by disease. Military use of mercenaries, aliens and Christians increased.

By the third century CE, the problems were proving unwieldy and divisive. Decius was Emperor at Rome's millennium celebration in 248 CE. Three years later, his death and his son's, while defending against the Goths, plus unrest in the provinces and civil squabbling among generals, led in 260 CE to a division of the Empire into three parts: Gallic Empire in the northwest, Roman centrally and Palmyrene in Asia Minor, the Levant and Egypt. Indeed, when the Palmyrene emperor Odeanthus died in 267 CE, his wife Zenobia assumed leadership, expelled the Roman prefect and ruled until 274. She fell to the Emperor Aurelian, who had already ousted Tetricus, successor to Gallic Emperor Postumus (261-68), and reunited the Empire. But the unrest grew. The history of the period is uncertain in detail, but it is clear that the next century saw frequent civil wars among the ambitious, and loss of defensive capacity against invaders.

Christians had, by then, become inured to local discrimination in the Empire, even when emperors had left them unmolested. In the 250s decade, amid rising animosities, Emperors Decius and Valerian passed laws compelling Christians to make the required sacrifices to Roman gods or face imprisonment and execution. Emperor Gallienus changed these in 260 CE, issuing an edict of tolerance toward Christians that relieved them, until Diocletian became Emperor in 284 CE and ruled to 305 CE. He began drastic changes, first retiring Christians from the army, replacing any in service close to him, and dealing harshly with the Gnostics. Of these, the Manichaeans were the most prominent and widespread, perhaps more than Christians, since their doctrine had spread to the borders of India. Soon, with support of Emperor Galerius and a favourable "sign" received from the god Apollo, Diocletian began to prosecute Christians and other minorities. It is probable that this was one of the times that feeding Christians to the lions in the Coliseum had become a popular sport and distraction, as perhaps it had been in 250 CE.

Christians had managed to weather decades of turbulence and the ups and downs of their relationship with rulers. But they were neither unified nor free of controversy. The disciples, apostles and their converts had taken the message of Christ, unfortunately with much amendment and changed emphases, throughout Roman Africa, Egypt, parts of Europe and the Middle East, from bases in the Mediterranean, facilitated by the international use of Greek, the language used by Paul in his *Epistles*.

Variations in theme and practice stemmed in various degrees from the seed (the message), the soil (the listeners) and the sowers (the 70 evangelists that Jesus had appointed to spread the word—St *Luke's Gospel, 10, 1-24*). By the middle of the third century, the focus of these missions had gone through enough generations, personalities, trials and soul-searching to modify Christ's original message in ways ennobling and confusing, liberal and strict. So it was not surprising that the hottest dispute was between the two fundamental doctrines of *Unitarianism* and *Trinitarianism* which stood at the very heart of the beliefs. (The modern Pentecostals tend to be *Non-Trinitarians* or *Unitarians*, as are Mormons, Christian Scientists, Jehovah's Witnesses, Church of God, Jews, Iglesia ni Cristo members, and other Protestant sects.)

In 284 CE, Diocletian had become Emperor and promptly addressed the festering problem of maladministration and political instability that had troubled the Empire for most of that century. Civil wars still raged in many locations, as regional generals sought power; but, in fighting among themselves, they had placed the Empire at greater risk from invaders, forcing it to accept them as settlers. Conspiracies and infighting had been features of Roman high society for centuries, and various emperors had tried in vain to end them, from Vespasian, in the first century CE, to Gallienus in the third.

Diocletian divided the administration into Western and Eastern Empires, with Rome and Byzantium the respective capitals. Each had an Augustus and a Caesar who divided responsibility between them: Diocletian and Galerius shared the East and Maximian and Constantius Chlorus the West. This arrangement came to be known as the Tetrarchy and stabilised the Empire for two decades. It did not prevent skirmishes with intruders along the borders, but it created definitive jurisdictions for each ruler, permitting him to defend exclusively against aliens, yet in a position to give help where needed. Romans had lost the ability to secure their western borders.

Diocletian allowed persecution of Christians in 303 CE, but two years later he and Maximian abdicated, ending the Tetrarchy and giving way to Constantius and Galerius. With Constantius' death in 306 CE, his son Constantine took his position; but this was not easy sailing, and for the next six years various civil struggles took place for power, at the end of which Constantine and Licinius emerged Emperors. This is an important event in Christianity, as in 313, they issued the Edict of Milan, which proclaimed tolerance of all religions throughout the Empire and stopped the persecution of Christians.

Icon re First Council of Nicaea, 325CE

Constantine accepted Christianity and became the first Christian Emperor of Rome. Almost at once he stepped into a Christological schism: *Unitarianism* versus *Trinitarianism*. Unitarianism (*Arianism*) was championed by Arius, an ascetic priest, born in Cyrene, Libya, and head of the Coptic church of Baucalis in Alexandria, Egypt. He held that God was Supreme and that Jesus Christ, though "perfect", was the son who ranked below the Father and carried out His behests. Trinitarians believed that Jesus had equal status with the Father and that the Holy Spirit was also a man. The dispute occupied prelates and became a primary concern at the First Ecumenical Council convened by Emperor Constantine I and held on May 20, 325 CE, at Nicaea, Eastern Roman Empire (modern Iznik, Turkey).

The Council decided, whimsically, it seemed, in favour of Trinitarianism, which entrenched dogma, guaranteed continuing schism and seemed to negate Christ's own words. For centuries, Unitarians would be persecuted, scandalising the noble teachings of Jesus Christ.

The Council and Emperors announced many changes over the next decades and supervised their adherence. Pagans were forbidden their customary practices, especially sacrifices, temple worship, consultations with fortune-tellers and other occult practices. At the same time, prelates gained many exemptions, for example, taxes and public service for them and family, trial by lay courts, and the right to use Church property as their own. One peculiar right of Christians was that a prostitute could only have Christian clients! The Council of Laodicea in 364 CE made Sunday the Christian Sabbath instead of Saturday, and relaxing at home on a Saturday was deemed a sin!

Constantine in 326 CE had made Byzantium the main capital of the Empire and changed its name to Constantinople. Rome remained the religious centre. In 380 CE *Trinitarian Catholicism* was emphasised as the sole state religion of the Roman Empire. By then, most of the Goths who had become Christians had chosen to be *Arians,* the name by which *Unitarians* became better known.

In the following year, the Council of Constantinople announced that the "*Holy Spirit*" was divine, justifying the Trinity. Theodosius I banned paganism or reconversion to paganism, or even visiting temples, and ordered the looting and arson of temples. Many of the raids were led by priests, e.g. Ambrosius of Milan and the famous John Chrysostom in Palestine, while Augustine—later sanctified for his dedication to duty—immolated pagans in Algeria, and Hypatius copied him in Bithynia.

Needless to say, other non-Christians, including Jews, were also targeted and persecuted in a way early Christians never were. It didn't help the Jews that they were reviled for other reasons, among which was their success in private business, in competition with the Roman state. This actually led to an early edict by Constantius II in the mid-fourth century restricting Jewish activity and freedom in social and employment practices. Male Jews could not marry Christians nor try to convert them; the converted stood to lose his/her property; non-Jewish slaves owned by Jews would be seized and a Jew could be executed for circumcising a slave. Women could not leave government jobs to work with Jews, a curious decree, considering the reputation of Jewish bosses for thrift!

Egregious acts were numerous and the extent of persecution, atrocities and the wanton destruction over the next centuries—including denial of rights, dismissal from jobs at all ranks, book-burning, trashing libraries—would have made Christ weep. Theodosius went so far as to label all non-Christians as "insane"—perhaps in its original sense of "unhealthy". The inhumanity of these acts—approved by Emperors and Popes, in the name of God—defies rational thinking and denies Christ's teachings; nevertheless, they are quoted by believers as divine doctrine.

Not all temples were burned. Some were converted to churches; some to stables or other non-religious use. The Temple of Aphrodite, in Constantinople, received special treatment and became a brothel! Christian priests were so zealous they tried to lynch Nestor, the Patriarch of that city—appointed by Theodosius I—who disagreed with the interpretation of Jesus as God, as it would tend to contradict his humanity, a major pillar of Christianity. His views on Christ were opposed by many Nicenes, and quite vehemently by the Coptic Archbishop Cyril, Patriarch of Alexandria, who, acting for Pope Celestine, had dishonourably gotten the Council of Ephesus, in 431 CE, to declare Nestor a heretic, before Nestor's supporters from the Eastern Church had arrived and could vote!

The Papacy quickly became a tool of the Emperor, as Constantine might originally have conceived it, and was used to great effect. Thus, starting with the rule of Theodosius I, the most inhuman acts of persecution against non-Christians took place in the next two centuries, with persistent assaults, confiscation of property, family disruption, pillage, exile, imprisonment, executions and book burning in almost every city in the Roman Empire, east and west. In 364, Emperor Jovian burned books in the library of Antioch, Valens attacked Greeks and their knowledge base throughout the Empire, and book-burning was celebrated in town squares.

Most European tribes knocking at Rome's door at the time were pagan—deemed by Theodosius as "loathsome, heretic, stupid and blind"—seeking to enter an Empire gripped by a new-found creed, and therefore ultra-righteous, as only converts could be. The tribes had also remained nomadic, but craved the amenities and higher living standard of the Romans enough to accept the terms of migration and settlement, viz., to become Christian and join the Roman armies.

The incursions into the Roman Empire—part of the *great migration* that forever changed the character of Europe—involved various German, Scandinavian, East European and West Asian tribes which had been gnawing at the northern borders of the Roman Empire for centuries. As noted, the Empire suffered several calamities in the second century: epidemics, economic recessions and natural physical disasters. Border defences further weakened, allowing "barbarians" to become bolder and more intrusive. Eventually, some of those encroaching on the Balkans were permitted to settle depleted areas south of the Danube—in Pannonia, Moesia, Dacia and later Thrace—first the Vandals, then Goths and others, including the Huns. Their numbers grew as Roman power got weaker, and by the fifth century, they had gained control over much of the Western Roman Empire.

In northern Europe, Jutes, Angles, Saxons, Burgundians, Franks and some Suevis had, by the same time migrated from the Danish peninsula and the Low Countries to Gaul, and across the North Sea and English Channel to Britannia, two provinces of the Western Roman Empire. They had, no doubt, left to escape climate changes and constant and increasing flooding of their estuarine and low coastal homelands, from the Elbe to the Meuse Rivers, and the Danish peninsula, home of the Angles and Jutes. Bede, a Northumbrian Benedictine monk and one of the earliest historians of Britain, claims in his *Historia ecclesiastica gentis Anglorum* that the entire mainland population of Angles (modern SE Denmark) had migrated to Britannia by the early 5th century. Angles, Saxons and Jutes plus a smattering of other Germanic peoples settled the eastern half of the island.

Sapped by internal divisions and by the inadequacy of Roman defence against foreigners, the youthful and timid Emperor Honorius was unable to defend Britannia. Rome withdrew between 383 and 410 CE, allowing SE Britain to fall to Danes (Angles) and Germans (Saxons). Although Roman Britons might have tried to unite for defence and to preserve their life-style and culture, the province, and thereafter the whole region, began a period of decline—the "dark ages"—fragmented, illiterate, with loss of values, no sense of direction or moral purpose, quarrelling among themselves, and unable to resist the waves of barbarians. The Roman system of law and order collapsed; appeals to Gaul resulted in only temporary and partial relief.

With the collapse of Roman rule, the Picts, Scots and Celts also seized the opportunity to invade from north of Hadrian's Wall; they occupied all lands west of the Pennines, Wales and the southwest. The Angles held on to the eastern half, from Firth of Forth (Northumbria) in the north to the midlands, Norfolk and Suffolk. The Saxons occupied England from south of Suffolk to Bristol, while the Jutes populated the southeast, mainly today's Sussex and Kent.

The survivors, Romano-Britons and Romans, lamented the losses, as local leaders seized portions of the province, just as later Anglo-Indians would long for the return of the British to India. The schism, caused by the rejection of the Christian doctrine of *Pelagianism*[58]—which Gauls and Britons had adopted—divided the population along sectarian lines and was a major barrier to unification. Angles, Saxon and Jute invaders uprooted the existing population and rejected their religion. They remained illiterate pagans, largely rural, organised under local chiefs,

---

[58]Pelagius taught that mankind was basically good, had free will and could find God and earn salvation without another's intervention. He rejected the doctrine of original sin, which underpins Roman Christianity, as championed by Augustine, whose arguments persuaded the Council of Carthage in 418 CE to deem Pelagianism as heresy.

and continued their traditions; they converted to Christianity reluctantly and slowly, by pressure and expediency, carried by the wave of change.

King Arthur *(Arthur Pendragon,* pictured left, stylised*)* is said to have appeared during this period of the dark ages, perhaps the 5th-6th century, in Wales (Wessex), as ruler of an idyllic and noble kingdom, and fought against the Saxon invaders. He is a dominant figure in the mythology of Britain, with Boadicea (1st century, who fought the Romans), and previously Lear (8th C BCE) and others. His legend remains credible and influential, although it is doubtful that the expanded stories of either him or his retinue of knights, pretty damsels and wizards are any more than engaging and wistful after-dinner fairy tales, popular before producers of shows for modern television adopted mythology as fact and distorted knowledge for good.

The first Anglo-Saxon kingdoms arose in Northumbria in the 6th century—Bernicia, from the Forth to the Tees rivers, and in Deira, its southern neighbour. In 634 CE, King Oswald, son of Æthelfrit, united the two as the kingdom of Northumbria, an Anglo-Saxon first, two years after the death of Mohamed, and decades after the fall of India's Guptas.

The following centuries were rife with myth and inter-tribal struggles; the farm-based economy grew until the Vikings invaded in the 11th century and took control of most Anglo-Saxon and central Celtic lands, or accepted tributes from them (*danegeld*). Denmark's Canute became king in 1016, led England well, but his successors were less popular, until the third, Edward the Confessor, his stepson, became king in 1042. He had no child; it is said that he had offered the succession to William of Normandy, where he had spent many years, but the *Witenagemot* (Wise Council) appointed Harold Godwinson, Earl of Wessex, instead. Hardly pausing, William invaded that same year, and Harold was killed at Hastings. That ended the line of Anglo-Saxon kings but the intrigue, the killings and seizures of lands, often with the help of the Church, continued!

Europe outside the Roman Empire was illiterate in the dark ages, apart from the learning of Christian clerics and Jewish scribes. Books were few, mainly laboriously hand-written religious texts used to spread the gospel. Those wealthy enough to afford an education in Latin often learned to read and write. In time, following the reforms of Charlemagne, writing in Latin spread among lay Christians, adapted to some local dialects, e.g. the Icelandic sagas: the stories of the Vikings. Writing did exist as rune stones and cave art (popular in India, the Far East, China, native America etc., ages earlier), and came to Scandinavia with Christianity in the 11th century.

The Romans had earlier allowed the Franks, Burgundians and Visigoths to migrate into Gaul, but they had proved an internal problem as they moved about to avoid Roman ridicule for their crude ways, and settled in a relatively uncontrolled manner. The Franks, however, seemed least sensitive and related more amicably with their hosts; many became allied with the ruling class, especially through service in the army, which allowed some to achieve high rank, including generalships.

Emperors demanded loyalty at all times, and conversion to Christianity, when the Empire became Christian. The Romans controlled movements, though uneasily, but received a major blow when relays of German tribes: Vandals, Burgundians, Alans, Suevis and others, invaded in 406 CE, irretrievably damaging Roman defences, already threatened by squabbling among ambitious and aristocratic Romans, commanding armies of uncertain loyalty and an eclectic mix of Romans, mercenaries and migrants. Julius Caesar in his time had noted the violence of the Germanic tribes and the frequency of wars, features noted too by earlier historians, including Tacitus who had said that the *"Germans have no taste for peace..."* (A little reflexion would have shown the same for Romans!)

The Balkans had seen a steady growth of migrants: Vandals, Goths, Gepidae, Suevi and other German and Baltic tribes, Sarmatians from East Europe, followed by the Slavs, Huns, Alans and Khwarazmians of West Asia. The Vandals originated in East Europe, south of the Baltic Sea in regions corresponding to modern Poland and nearby territories; they had been migrating since the first century CE, had reached the Roman Empire in the third and were allowed to settle in Dacia (modern Bulgaria). In time, conflicts with newly arriving Goths forced them to leave. They went west across Europe, into Gaul and were allowed to settle in Aquitaine, until displaced by Goths and Franks. By the 5th century, they had reached Spain, probably about the same time as the Alans and Suevi, who had invaded Gaul in 406, the latter settling in the region that is modern Portugal.

Driven from Spain by the Goths, Vandals crossed the Straits of Gibraltar, succeeded in conquering Roman Africa, and established their capital in Carthage. From this stronghold, they launched sallies into the Mediterranean islands west of Italy, gaining control of several, attacked Rome and Greece, and sacked Rome in 455 CE. This further weakened the Western Empire that the Huns under Attila had threatened a few years earlier, but had spared because of risks from famine and disease—most likely malaria and plague—which had sapped the Roman army. The Western Empire fell by 500 CE, while the East (Byzantine Empire) survived for a thousand more years. The Vandals prevailed in Africa until the 6th century CE, when Justinian regained the territories, but the two halves of the Empire remained separate.

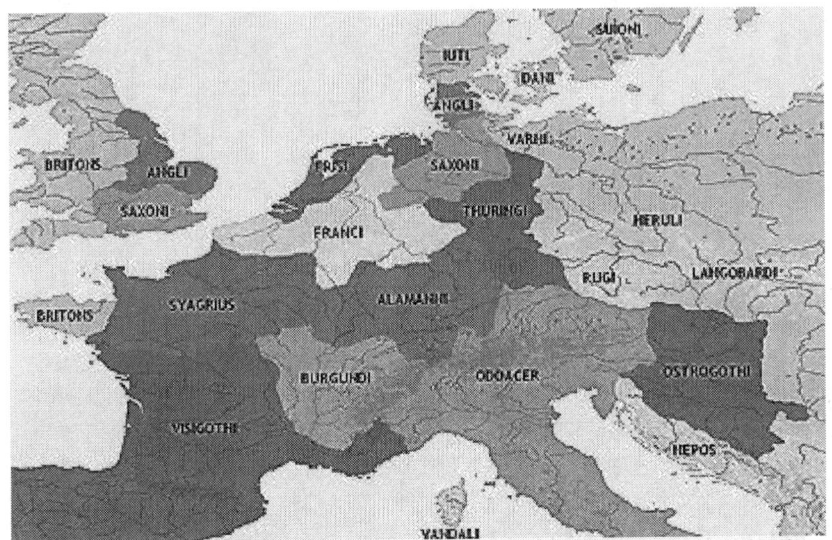

Western Europe, 480 CE showing the spread and dominance of German tribes. Note that the outlines and boundaries given are modern while the knowledge at that time permitted maps no better than shown on pages 76 and 77.

Back in 376 CE, large numbers of Goths had crossed the Danube and, after many skirmishes with the Romans under Emperor Valens, had been allowed to settle in the Balkans as *foederati* (allies). They had become a new source of soldiers for Roman armies, displacing the Vandals, who had left after clashing with the Goths, hoping to find greener, healthier and friendlier pastures, and to escape local discrimination. Goths, facing a similar bias, had revolted in 378, killing their benefactor, Valens, at Hadrianopolis (Adrianople), and gradually had become more numerous and prominent in the Balkans.

A century earlier, they had tried to do just this. Having amassed a large fleet to raid the Eastern Empire, they had sailed from the Black Sea through the Bosphorus to the capital, Byzantium, but failed to take it or the city of Cyzicus across the Propontis (Sea of Marmara). They went south through the Hellespont (Dardanelles) to Greece, where they sacked Athens, Corinth, Argos and Sparta. Emperor Gallienus marched east to stop them but was too late to prevent the plunder of the Grecian cities. He found the Goths at Nessos and defeated them in probably the bloodiest battle of that time.[59] This restrained the Goths for many decades. But by the end of the fourth century their fortunes had improved and they returned.

They had by then split into two groups: Visigoths (western), to whom most of the above applied, and the Ostrogoths (eastern), most of whom went east to Asia Minor (modern Turkey). But some remained or later migrated west, allied with other German tribes, and would, by the end of the 5th century, gain control of the Balkans and of Italy. The Huns, a large confederation of many sovereign tribes, organised like the Indians, had by this time occupied a vast area from East Europe to West Asia, and had subdued tribes as they went west, including the Alans, a large Iranian tribe settled in the Steppes, between the Aral and Caspian Seas. They had found the western migration and the loosely-defended or empty Balkans so much easier than tackling the southern and eastern lands of the Sassanids of Persia, who had repelled them, and earlier in the mid-third century, had seized Antioch in the Byzantine Empire, as a show of strength and a warning of Sassanid intentions in the region.

In India, the Gupta Empire was at its height and controlled territory to the centre of Afghanistan; it had strong commercial bonds with the Sassanids, Arabians and the Romans, and trading relationships afar, with and through the Radhanite Jews (*? from the 'lost' ten tribes*), who controlled much of the trade in silks, spices and other oriental goods, by sea and land, in Eurasia and between Europe, the Orient and East Indies.

By the 5th century, Huns commanded an Empire that extended from the Danube River to the Baltic Sea, and east to the Don River, towards Georgia and Armenia, the extent corresponding to the western part of old Scythia. They had their greatest triumphs under Attila and his brother, Bleda. Having subdued the Eastern Empire of Theodosius by 443, Attila led the Huns against the Western Empire, then under Emperor Aetius, who, ironically, had earlier befriended the brothers.

But experience, including the habitual intrigues among ruling Roman families, had changed Attila into an enemy of Rome and success had made him arrogant. In 451 CE, Frankish forces joined with Aetius to defeat Attila at the Battle of the Catalaunian Plains near Orléans, NW Gaul, ending his attempt to conquer Gaul. Three years later, a coalition of German tribes defeated the Huns at the Battle of Nedao, in the Balkan

---

[59]Some confusion exists between Nessos, on the Aegean in Macedonia, and Naissus, the Serbian city Nish, and whether there was a battle at each place against the Goths, the former won by Gallienus, the latter by Claudius, who claimed the victory and adopted the cognomen Gothicus. Gallienus was murdered in 268. There was likely only one war: that at Nessos, but Gallienus "died" before he could claim the honour!

province of Pannonia, ending their prominence as a European conqueror. As the Western Empire buckled in Gaul, Clovis, the ruler of the Merovingians (Salian Franks), moved against Syagrius (430–487 CE), the last Roman official in Gaul, and defeated him, thus ending Roman rule in that province. Clovis I united the Frankish tribes, became king (509-11), and was the first Frankish king to convert to Christianity.

In 475 CE, a year after he had become the Western Emperor, Julius Nepos was deposed by his military commander Orestes—a German migrant with a Roman wife—who appointed his young son Romulus as Emperor. A year later, Romulus was ousted by a rival German officer, Flavius Odoacer (433-493), who thus became the first migrant German king of Italy (476-493 CE), and ruled, paying lip service to Nepos. His ascent to power marked the effective end of the Western Roman Empire.

There had been a brief recovery for Rome between 457 and 461, when Emperor Majorian had re-captured Aquitaine from the Visigoths, the Rhone valley from the Burgundians and the Iberian Peninsula (Hispania) from the Vandals and the Suevi, but he could not sustain the victories. The territories reverted to the Germanic tribal settlers, who would grow in strength and numbers and come to dominate all of Gaul, and eventually replace the Romans.

Odoacer ruled until the Ostrogoths defeated him in 493 CE, in a war endorsed by the Byzantine Emperor Zeno. Their rule continued, although precariously, until the Byzantine Emperor Justinian I, born into a peasant family in Macedonia, successfully campaigned between 553 and 563 to regain most of the Western Empire. But the wars so drained manpower and resources that northern Italy fell fairly easily to the Lombards, who held them until defeated by Charlemagne, over two centuries later, in 774 CE. The Romans in the Byzantine Empire fared much better. By the sixth century, they had crushed the Huns, who fled west to northern Italy and joined the Lombards. Justinian I was Emperor from 527 to 565 CE, and in a well-planned and spirited campaign re-captured the lost western provinces, except Gaul and Hispania, and brought them under Byzantine rule for the next two centuries.

The Lombards, like the Scandinavian Suevis, had migrated south from northern Europe to the fringes of the Roman Empire, and were allowed to settle in Pannonia (Balkans). Their trek had taken six centuries during which they had battled other migrant Germans, finally defeating the Gepids in or near Pannonia. In 568, they moved to northern Italy, settling in the Po valley. The Huns joined them later and in time disappeared into the north Italian melting pot and became absorbed into papal Christianity and Roman ways. Likewise the foreign conquerors, nearly all German nomads, became settled, adopting the Roman life style they had craved, the language, mores and social norms, achieving some literacy, and almost to a man, Christianity.

During its existence, the Roman Empire was the most powerful economic, cultural, and military force in Europe. Heraclius ruled from 610 to 641 CE and replaced Latin with Greek as the Empire's primary language. Militarily, he campaigned against the Sassanids, regaining lands in Asia Minor up to the Dardanelles that the Sassanids had conquered, just in time to face Islamic hordes thundering out of Arabia, under General Khalid ibn al Walīd, the envoy of political Islam.

Huns in battle with the Alans, by Peter Johann Nepomuk Geiger. 1873; The Alans, an Iranian people who lived east of the Black Sea, were Europe's first line of defence against the Huns. They were dislocated and settled throughout the Roman Empire.

L: Iron Pillar, Delhi, rust-free for ~2000 years; see footnote 56, p.85

Below: Buddha, Bamiyan cave, Afghanistan, destroyed in 2001 CE by Taliban

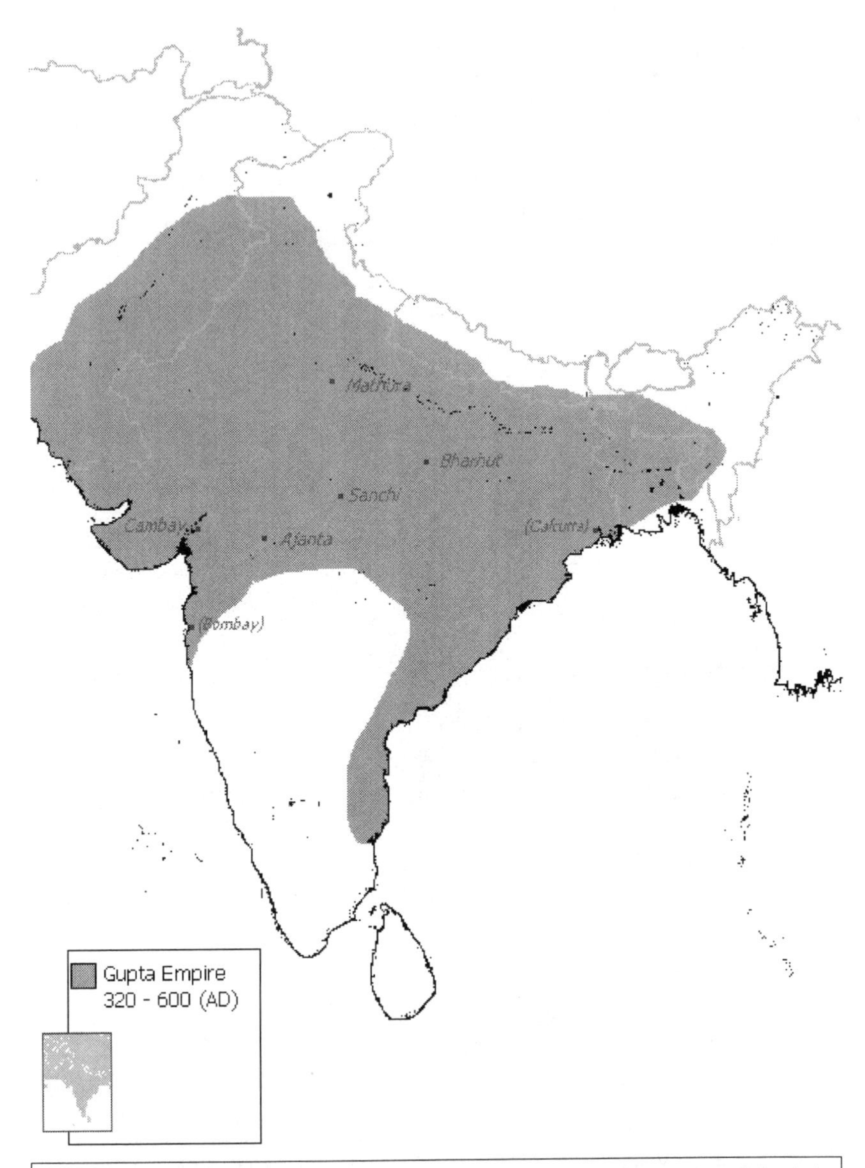

Gupta Empire (Arab Hafez, en.Wikipedia) The capital was at Pataliputra (modern Patna), on the Ganga River in modern Bihar; the empire covered over 3.5million sq.km (1.351M sq.m.); Gupta rule brought peace, stability and prosperity for 250 years; it conducted commerce with a large area, from the Mediterranean to the Far East and China; many immediate neighbours were beneficial tributary states. Its decline began by 550CE and was complete a few decades later.

Chapter 6

"...When we are passed away and gone, Allah remains the One and Eternal. Whoever sits down to the feast of life must, before it is over, drink of the cup of death....How much better then is it to die with honour than to live with infamy." *Babur, 1527*

"...the quarrelsome little continent of Europe" Jawaharlal Nehru

It is a tenacious failing that humans tend to express their new-found beliefs far more virulently than born adherents, as if to exorcise the spirits of their former religion, from shame or hate or the need to convince themselves and others of their commitment. Author p.79

Islamic expansion; rise of Papacy; Europe's dark ages

The eighth century brought the first waves of Muslim raiders from across the Arabian Sea to the Maharashtra coast of India resulting in skirmishes that would continue for three hundred years. Muslims had begun expanding, with Mohammed's campaigns across Arabia which aimed to convert or else destroy the Christians and Jewish tribes that had settled the oasis of Khaybar, and further south in or near Medina (formerly Yathrib). The Jewish tribes of Medina were the Banu Nadir (date farmers), Banu Qaynuqa (metal workers, including goldsmiths and weapons makers) and Banu Qurayza (vintners). They had fled to Arabia, escaping the destruction of Judea by Romans in the second century, joining the descendants of those who had fled the conquest of Palestine in 597 BCE by Nebuchadnezzar of Babylon, and ten years later, when Jerusalem was destroyed. Large numbers had escaped to Egypt, and others were taken to Babylon and dispersed elsewhere, as their northern brethren has been, over a century earlier by the Assyrians.

In Arabia, most had kept their way of life and occupations, and prospered, providing additional services as teachers and scribes. They however suffered from a peculiar hatred of one another, what Jews called *sinat chinam,* or groundless hatred, a phenomenon that is as old as Jewry! This ancient hate allowed Mohamed to divide and conquer them in a systematic series of wars against each tribe in turn, and in three years destroyed them, even the weapons makers!

He eliminated the men who did not convert, and enslaved the women and children, who were made to serve the Muslims as *dhimmis,* especially in agriculture. Some Medina Jews, especially Banu Qurayza, and those of Khaybar, joined with the Qureshi in Mecca, opposing Mohamed's message and claim of prophethood. They joined in two battles against him, but lost, giving him control of Mecca, the domain of his natal tribe, where he made many converts. Mohamed continued his mission to unite the Bedouins, Arabia's scattered tribes, of every religion, under the banner of Islam. He secured the Ka'aba, purging it of its long-standing "idols" and other non-Islamic icons, and instilled in his converts a zeal for belief and booty that would turn them into vicious raiding forces and forge an expansive empire that would extend from the Iberian Peninsula to the East Indies.

In 628 the Byzantines under Heraclius had counterattacked and driven the Sassanids back to the eastern border from which they had invaded in 602 and conquered Asia Minor, the Levant and Egypt. Heraclius' armies freed these provinces. Khosrau II, the Sassanid king, surrendered after his final defeat at Nineveh, and was assassinated soon after, an act which destabilised the defeated Empire even further. Mohamed found this to his advantage, but he died in 632 before he could personally exploit it. Modern Saudi clerics claim that before he died, the prophet had revealed himself to the emperors and kings around, inviting them to accept Islam. They even produced the *dawah* (invitation): "*In the name of Allah, the Beneficent, the Merciful. From Muhammad, the Messenger of Allah, to the great Kisra of Iran. Peace be upon him, who seeks truth and expresses belief in Allah and in His Prophet and testifies that there is no god but Allah and that He has no partner, and who believes that Muhammad is His servant and Prophet. Under the Command of Allah, I invite you to Him. He has sent me for the guidance of all people so that I may warn them all of His wrath and may present the unbelievers with an ultimatum. Embrace Islam so that you may remain safe. And if you refuse to accept Islam, you will be responsible for the sins of the Magi.*" Refusal of a dawah would be followed by a *jihad.*

Abu Bakr, Mohamed's father-in-law, was the first of the four caliphs (632-4)—known as the *Rashidun* ("rightly-guided") Caliphate (632-661), the first four Commanders of the faithful *(Amir al-Mu'minin*). The others were Umar ibn Al-Khattāb (634–644), Uthman bin Affan (644-56) and Ali ibn Abu Ṭālib (656–661). Abu Bakr was opposed by several tribes, which General Khālid ibn al-Walīd, the new Commander of Muslim forces, overcame in a series of bloody confrontations, the *Ridda Wars*. By 633, he had brought nearly all Arabian dissenters, headless, into the Muslim union, enabling Abu Bakr to begin the *jihad* against his neighbours.

The aggressors were heartened to learn that raids from Eastern Arabia into Mesopotamia, in the early 630s, had already netted much booty. Thus, the new campaigns would not only spread Islam, but enrich the leadership. Medina rewarded the leader of these raids, Muthana ibn Harith, with the position of Commander of the eastern section of the country. Abu Bakr then launched Khalid on one of the most relentless and prolonged campaigns of military conquest known to that time. But the failure of the Caliphate to set up a governance structure would haunt Islam thereafter, with power struggles and killings often determining the successor. Umar, Uthman, Ali, and many after, were assassinated.

The first foreign prey were the northern and eastern Arab tribes, the Ghassanids and Lakhmids, two opposing Christian groups that were client states of the Byzantines and Sassanids respectively. Once they were over-run, Syria was taken from the Byzantines, and Mesopotamia occupied. The assault on the Sassanids coincided with a period of instability, following the murder of Khosrau II in 628 by his son, and the frequent changes of ruler during the next four years. Finally, in 632, the year of Mohamed's death, the Sassanid crown went to the minor, Yazdegerd III, a grandson of Khosrau II, a choice that left power in the hands of a regent. The Sassanid Empire, already weakened by two decades of war against the Byzantines, became increasingly vulnerable.

On Abu Bakr's death in 634, Umar ibn al-Khattāb succeeded to the Caliphate, and from his seat in Medina directed a master plan of attacks against the two neighbouring Empires. Khalid, a skilled tactician, fully exploited their ravaged state of imperial defences and depleted resources caused by nearly three decades of war. The assault on Persia followed, and, by 644, the Sassanid Empire had collapsed. The dynasty ended in 651, its fall hastened by the loss of powerful former Parthian allies, who had found it expedient to conclude treaties with the Arabs. (It is worth recalling that by the end of the second century CE the Parthians had cooperated with the Eastern Roman Emperor to end the Seleucid dynasty—precursor to the Sassanids). Egypt was conquered next and the campaign carried west across North Africa to the Roman city of Carthage (modern Tunis). By the middle of the seventh century Muslims had conquered the Mediterranean, Africa and the Iberian Peninsula. They turned their attention east and attacked the Hephthalites, Afghans and the peoples of the Aral region by land, while naval forces took the war to India's west coast, where repeated losses kept them at bay.

The Umayyad dynasty, 661-750 CE, was initiated by the sixth caliph, Muawiyah ibn Abu Sufyan, a Qureshi, and a late convert to Islam. Emir of Syria for many years, he expanded the Caliphate, spreading Islam to Asia Minor, North Africa, Spain, Central and West Asia, and India, by warfare, and Southeast Asia and the East Indies, by trade (Fatah).

In 721 CE, the Umayyad Caliphate embarked on the conquest of Europe, planning pincer-like movements from Hispania into Aquitaine in the west and thence across Gaul and barbarian lands—then divided largely among the Franks (Neustrians and Austrasians), Burgundians, Alamannis (Swabians), Thuringians, Bavarians, Slavs and others. They would connect eventually with the armies invading from the east that had started from the Levant, Mesopotamia and Persia, advancing north through the Caucasus to Khazaria, thence westwards, along the north shore of the Euxine (Black) Sea to the Carpathians, and into Slavic territories and Byzantine provinces. Salients from the western armies would overrun Italy, and those from the Levant would enter Asia Minor to crush the Byzantine Empire. Supremely confident of success, they would thus gain control of the Eurasian world; see Ptolemy's map p.77. Meanwhile attacks would continue by land and by sea against India, the last stronghold before China, the two great repositories of untold wealth.

Aquitaine, in southwest Gaul, had been settled in the fifth century by Visigoths. Invading Islamists, chiefly the arrogant Arabs, who had followed the Berbers, thought little of the German nomads and were surprised when their leader, Odo, the Duke of Aquitaine, defeated the army of Al-Samh ibn Malik al-Khawlani at Toulouse, in 721, with loss of many crack Islamic warriors; it was the first major defeat in their expansion from Arabia. The victory earned Odo the Pope's appreciation.

Regarding this loss as an aberration, Muslims regrouped and rode into Aquitaine eleven years later, this time with greater success, firstly in the Pyrenees against Uthman ibn Naissa, a Berber chief and Odo's son-in-law, whom Odo had pledged to help but could not, having to defend against his erstwhile Frankish ally, Charles Martel of Neustria, who had chosen that very time to attack Aquitaine.

The previous two centuries had seen major consolidation of rule by Germanic tribes that had replaced the Romans in Gaul. Tribal leaders smartly realised that embracing Christianity would bring them the support of the Pope, a position that had changed radically since Constantine's adoption of Christianity, and the diktats of the Council of Nicaea. The Christianising of the two Roman Empires transferred power to the Church and gave them the right to own property while sparing church officials and their families the burden of paying taxes. Their first acquisition was the gift of a palace from Constantine, which would be the Pope's residence for nearly a thousand years, until the Papacy moved to Avignon. While most of the earlier popes had faced the definite prospect of martyrdom, and often courted it to prove their steadfastness, the fortunes of the papacy reversed dramatically; it acquired influence and glamour, especially after the Emperor Theodosius had deemed Christianity the sole religion, reaffirmed the Nicene Creed and ordered the persecution of non-converts.

In the fourth century, the Roman Emperor Julian had permitted German tribes, especially Salian Franks, to settle in northeastern Gaul as *foederati* (allies). Initially they had followed traditional nomadic practices but a century later, under Merovius, decided to expand from their base rather than move out to "fresh pastures"; they had noted the growing weakness of Roman defences, the increases in the Frankish population and in the number of their military leaders in high Roman positions.

Merovingian Franks began campaigns and fought many battles, gaining control over neighbouring tribes, including other Franks, until

Clovis I, Merovius' grandson, ousted the Romans in 486 CE by defeating Syagrius, the Roman head of the rump state of Soissons, the last of the Roman-held regions of northern Gaul, between the Marne and the Seine Rivers. Clovis united the Salian Franks in 511 and later converted to Roman Christianity (*Trinitarianism*)—in contrast to other Germanic leaders who had accepted *Unitarianism* (Arianism)—a factor that might have gained him favour with the Roman papacy and aristocracy, as he later expanded his control over all Gaul. He had not converted easily, and did so only when he saw the intimacy of the relationship between Church leaders and the imperial hierarchy of emerging European states.

By the early eighth century, the Franks had become quite strong and dominated Western Europe, both economically and militarily. They controlled the territory from Austrasia (*eastern land,* roughly the northern Rhineland and Low Countries) and Swabia (south-west Germany, land of the *Suevi*[60]), to Neustria (*new land) in* northern Gaul, and had an ambivalent, generally rival relationship with the Visigoths of Aquitaine. (All these had been part of the Roman province of Gaul following Julius Caesar's many conquests five hundred years earlier). Charles Martel—needing a strong permanent army to prepare for the inevitable attack from Islamic strongholds in Iberia, whence they had already raided Aquitaine—seized idle Church lands to secure finance. This angered the Pope but Charles was in no danger of excommunication, as the Papacy was quite fearful of the Muslims and in growing need of a strong friend.

In 732, Islamic armies under Emir Abdul Rahman al Ghafiqi entered Bordeaux, and defeated Odo, then nearing 80. He escaped north, warned Martel, who marched with him against the invaders, Odo having accepted his overlordship. In 732, they defeated the Emir's forces at Tours (Poitiers) and watched them retreat to the Iberian Peninsula. This victory united the Franks and Visigoths under Charles, initiating the Carolingian lineage and supplanting the Merovingians, whose last king Childeric, Charles' grandfather, had been deposed on orders of Pope Stephen II, and replaced by Charles' father Pepin, the first Frankish king to be anointed by a Pope. By then, the epithet Salian had been dropped as a descriptor. By 737 CE, the Frankish kingdom incorporated most of Gaul, including parts of the Rhineland, Alamannia and Bavaria, and Burgundy, which would be consolidated in the next decades.

The Islamic army had been inexplicably humbled. Invading Aquitaine at Toulouse was seen as a routine raid against infidels for spoils, and territory for taxation. They were surprised at the discipline and quality of the resistance, being unaware of the true strength of the

---

[60]A section of the Suevis, an Elbe-Baltic Germanic tribe, had migrated to the Iberian Peninsula and settled the area, now northern Portugal and the Spanish panhandle.

Frankish kingdoms and of the many changes Charles Martel had made that could derail Islamic ambitions. With help from King Liutprand of Lombardy, Italy, Charles expelled the Umayyads from Provence, sending a Duke from Marseilles, an Islamic ally, into an Alpine exile. In this way, Charles gained Provence for the Franks. In 737, he engaged the Umayyads at Narbonne, where they had landed a fleet, and defeated them soundly, leaving the task of seizure of the town and future consolidation of his conquests to his sons, Carloman and Pepin. This would fall to the latter, when Carloman, after six years in joint rule with Pepin, elected religion and retired to Italy; Pepin became king.

The Islamists had made many errors, not the least of which was their arrogance, magnified by religious zeal and their sense of superiority as Arabs. They had underestimated Charles' ability to fight on their terms, so were again surprised, when, despite their change in tactics, they were hammered in their second venture against him. The *Arab Chronicles*, a history of that age, confirmed Arabs' ignorance of the growth of Frankish military might, until the Battle of Tours enlightened them. The Caliph could not believe that his veteran army, led by a most distinguished commander, could be defeated so soundly. The English bigot, historian Edward Creasy, in the late 19th century—a prime age for exhibitions of Anglo-Saxon biases—listed Tours as one of the *"fifteen decisive battles of the world"*, and explained the defeat as an inevitable triumph of Christian Europeans over barbarians, since the Arabs had lost despite every advantage: strength, time, place and circumstance, and had prepared well to avoid the errors of Toulouse. Creasy no doubt exaggerated, but after Narbonne, and the subsequent expansion of Frankish power and territory under Charlemagne, Islamists left northern Europe alone, prepared to wait, reluctantly, for a more propitious time. It did not help their cause that the Berbers resented the emir's preference for Arabs, revolted and seized Africa, from Morocco to Egypt.

The Popes had meanwhile slowly become king-makers in Europe. In the previous century the pace of Islamic conquests in the Levant, Middle East, Africa and Iberia had been so alarming that they had feared an imminent invasion. Odo's victory at Toulouse halted that advance, relieved the tension and pleased the papacy.

Popes had relished the growth of Christianity among the Germanic tribes that had settled in Gaul, and were especially satisfied that several of them had changed from *Arianism* to *Trinitarianism*. They had closely followed the rise of the Merovingians and their westward expansion, and when Charles conquered the Saxons, his eastern neighbours, and forced them to exchange paganism for Christianity, Popes were more than delighted to have an ally who could bring Gaul into the Roman fold once more, and perhaps restore the fallen Western Empire.

With Islamists at bay, Pepin turned to assisting the Pope, who had complained about the Lombards' seizure of Papal lands. The Lombards (*Longobardi*), with Huns and other small tribes, had become firmly settled in the fertile Po valley in northern Italy and had expanded by the end of the sixth century to include dukedoms in the centre of Italy and to the south, beyond the cities controlled by Rome. The Lombards had grown in strength, and as the Romans got weaker, had, in 751, seized Ravenna and the associated Byzantine exarchate, which had been for centuries the political capital of the Western Roman Empire, thus effectively cutting Roman communications with Constantinople.

The Church had recognised the rising power of the Franks and had granted preferences and titles to Martel and Pepin, especially the latter. Pope Stephen II had travelled to Paris to bless his coronation, after he had displaced the nominal king, Childeric III, the last of the Merovingians. Pepin subdued Lombardy and restored to the Papacy the Byzantine exarchate—the lands between Ravenna and Rome—but left the kingdom itself intact. The Papacy gained control of Lazio, Romagna, Umbria, and Marche, known as the "Papal States" of Italy, which it would hold until 1870. This *"Donation of Pepin"* legitimised the secular rule of the Pope over these states. Pepin then moved west and conquered Septimania, to complete his father's defeat of the Umayyads at Narbonne and brought Aquitaine under Frankish rule.

The relationship with the Papacy became closer and stronger when the Franks came under Charlemagne—reign 768 to 814—and their territories increased.

Meanwhile the Byzantine Empire had come under the rule of a Syrian line of Emperors, the Isaurians, which held sway from 711 to 802. They fought the Muslims in the Levant and Asia Minor and the Bulgars in the Balkans, repelling the former but losing territory to the latter. For sixty years Isaurian emperors effected the most punishing iconoclasm of the time, in the belief that purging would glorify them, purify the realms, boost faith, and preserve them against paganism and Islam.

Charlemagne's ardent and unquestioning faith—unusual today in one so talented, but understandable then, with "enlightenment" yet to come—led him to support these severe acts of iconoclasm, which were terminated in 787 CE by the second Council of Nicaea. Charlemagne expanded the Western Empire, became King of Italy after defeating the Lombards and reaffirming the Papal States. He expanded all Frankish borders in a constant campaign that eventually brought into the Empire Catalan, Saxony, Frisia and lands east, to the lower Elbe and the western borders of Bohemia, Moravia and Pannonia, and the Dalmatian strip on the Adriatic Sea.

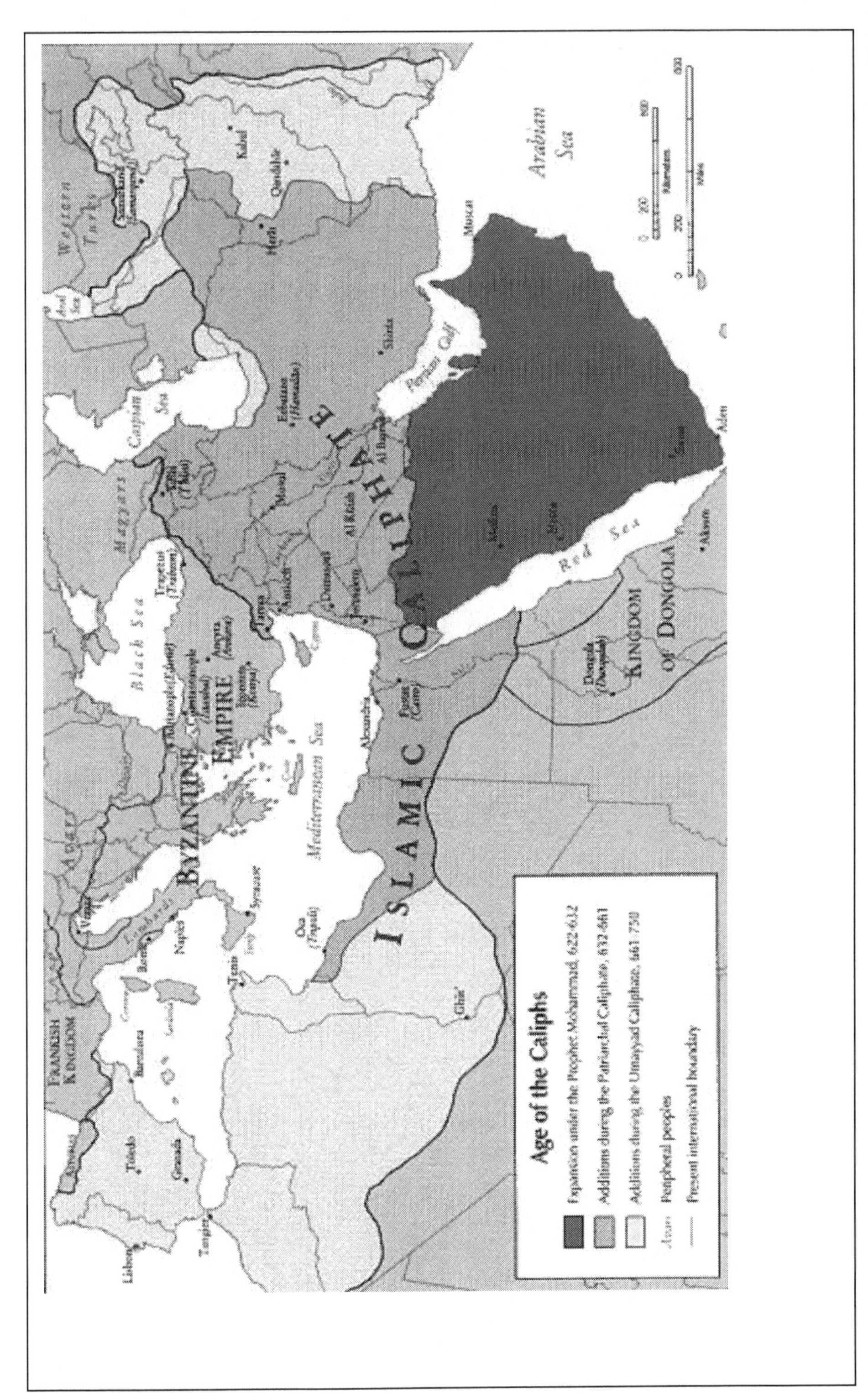
Age of the Caliphs
Expansion under the Prophet Mohammad, 622-632
Additions during the Patriarchal Caliphate, 632-661
Additions during the Umayyad Caliphate, 661-750
Peripheral peoples
Present international boundary
ISLAMIC CALIPHATE
BYZANTINE EMPIRE
KINGDOM OF DONGOLA
FRANKISH KINGDOM
Western Turks
Magyars
Black Sea
Caspian Sea
Mediterranean Sea
Red Sea
Persian Gulf
Arabian Sea

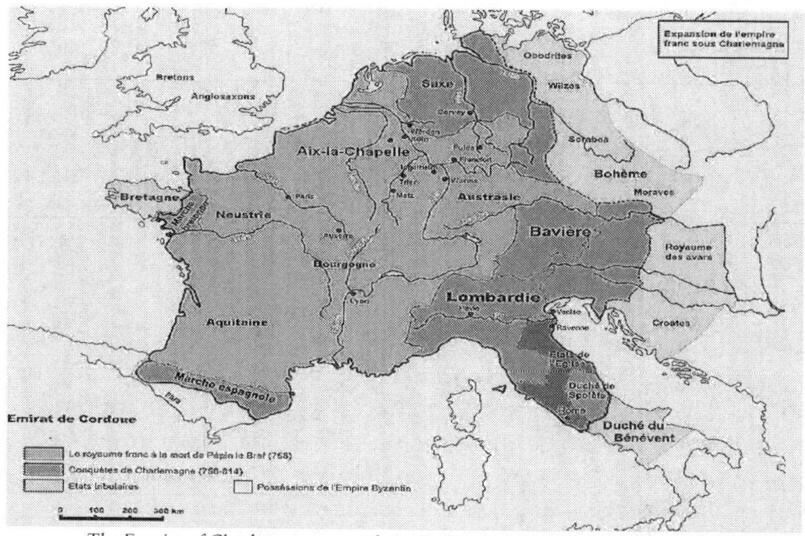

The Empire of Charlemagne, a modern display (credit: vincde 15, Wikipedia)

This extent of Empire corresponds to modern France, northern Spain and Portugal, the Low Countries, parts of Denmark, Switzerland, West Germany, Slovenia, northern Italy, Sardinia and the Balearic Islands. In 800 CE, Pope Leo III anointed Charlemagne the *Holy Roman Emperor*, the first Imperial title-holder in the west for over 300 years.

Charlemagne zealously promoted Roman Catholicism and condemned many to death for failure to convert, a more severe verdict than Mohammed would have imposed, and one that Christ would have rejected. This fanaticism was a major weakness; but then it fitted nicely with the ambitions of the Papacy, which profited handsomely from land grants in every major city, each coming with a congregation to support bishoprics and finance the exalted life-styles of the prelates. Thus Charlemagne earned the praise and blessings of Popes, not their criticism. He made important changes in economics. Facing a shortage of gold following the loss of Venice to the Byzantines—and thus control of trade routes to Africa—he switched coinage from the gold *sou* to a silver standard, introducing the *libra, solidus and denarius* (£.s.d.) The denominations had a ratio of 1:20:240 thus one pound of silver was 20 solidi or 240 denarii. In this he was supported by Offa, king of Mercia, an Anglo-Saxon kingdom in central Britain, where the coinage became known as the *pound, shilling and pence* system (*sterling*), and survived to the mid-20th century with the abbreviation £.s.d. unchanged.

Charlemagne also prohibited the charging of interest on loans as being anti-Christian, a measure aimed to curb Jewish exploitation of citizens, ostensibly to avoid clashes with religious beliefs, but undoubtedly pleasing to those who relied on borrowing to finance daily activities, especially in trade and commerce. By these and other work—including construction and architectural design—hardly any aspect of daily life escaped his reformist attention, throughout the Frankish Empire, thus casting light on the deep darkness of Europe.

Charlemagne's success flowed not just from his superb military skills, but from the talent that he had assembled to achieve his aims and manage his empire, his patronage of the arts, his love of learning and his pursuit of quality, in all aspects of life. His *Admonitio generalis* is an example of his dedication to religious instruction of his subjects and illustrates his desire to foster education, including his children's, and spread knowledge through wide reading, which required an improved and uniform writing style. In his military and political skills, his religious commitment, and his desire to communicate, he approached Ashoka Maurya of India who, over a millennium earlier, had united India and used etchings on stone monuments to spread timely advice to his people.

From the start of his reign, Charlemagne had collected to his service the best officials and scholars of Europe, particularly those with flawless writing skills, a thing he lacked and cherished, and which he promoted as a critical tool of communication and instruction. Script at that time was uneven and dissimilar. He initiated reforms that enhanced the legibility and uniformity of writing, thus improving the value of books, whose production depended entirely on hand-copies. The innovations resulted in the Carolingian *minuscule* script, accomplished under supervision of one of Charlemagne's most trusted advisors and scholars, Alcuin, called *the Albino,* who achieved many advances at that time. (The script was forerunner of the Times script so popular today). This signalled the beginning of European enlightenment, roughly *1500 years after* a mature script had been in scholarly use in India and up to 3000 years since Pānini's seminal work on Grammar.

Alcuin (Latin: Alcuinus Flaccus, 735- 804) was an unusual cleric, writer and teacher, from York, Northumbria. He was an Anglian by ultimate tribal origin, of humble birth, and was considered the foremost scholar in Europe. His recruitment showed Charlemagne's reach, even into a former enemy's camps, to find men of talent. He was known as much for hiring talented Saxons as for executing those who rejected Christianity! In 796 Alcuin was appointed abbot of Tours, where he remained until his death, as the "most learned man anywhere to be found", a principal leader of the Carolingian renaissance, according to Einhard's *Life of Charlemagne. (*Alcuin had recruited Einhard, a multi-talented German scholar, also of humble birth, who achieved fame as Charlemagne's biographer.)

Composite picture showing stages of La Chanson de Roland ("The Song of Roland"), an early 12th CE French Poem, the oldest known, on the death of the hero, Roland, at the Battle of Roncevaux in 778 CE between Charlemagne and the Muslims of Spain.

Alcuin documented the first Viking raid on Northumbria in 793 CE, at the island of Lindisfarne in the North Sea just off the coast of the kingdom, where an abbey had been established. The destruction of the holy place tainted the reputation of the Vikings for over a millennium, but they shared the barbarism, crudeness and illiteracy of other European tribes of that period, for whom raiding was a major economic activity, as it was for Arabs. Indeed more killing was done in the name of the Church and Islam than for pagan gods, a fact that is often forgotten.

It may be, perhaps, that those who believed in Papal polemics and the dogma preached in Christ's name, would forgive the killings, and excuse the use of coercion as a tool of conversion, however much it distorted his principles and teachings. Observers would repeat the

Church bias against Vikings and tend to forget the bravery and daring they displayed to journey in small vulnerable ships, no bigger than large canoes, across the northern ocean to Greenland and North America, venturing close to the edge of the world, at a time when the earth was seen as flat and the known land mass surrounded by a wild ocean. Nor would they recall that their ancestors had travelled some of the same routes, raided others' property, despoiled their land and abused their women and children. No migrant or invading tribe was free of this taint.

On Charlemagne's death, the Empire passed to his heirs and before long various changes, claims and intrigues among greedy and less intellectually gifted successors fractured the Carolingian Empire into a western Frankish and an eastern Germanic-Slavic kingdom, each under an heir (cf earlier Mauryans and Guptas of India).

By 888 CE, the disintegration was almost complete. The title of Holy Roman Emperor fell into disuse in the following decades, until Otto I of Germany claimed the throne of Italy and was crowned Emperor in 962 CE. The title survived among his descendants for 844 years, until the Empire dissolved in 1806, having disintegrated much earlier into a collection of small, autonomous and competing states, similar to the fragments of the Mauryan and Gupta Empires in India, the Sassanids in Persia and Abbasid Caliphate in Mesopotamia.

European rulers, flush with power, were perhaps excused for believing that becoming Christian had given them the right to make *all* appointments, not just those of tax collectors, civil servants and merchants, but senior clergy also, as they were major beneficiaries of the state. This created a conflict with the Pope who felt that only he was qualified to make senior Church appointments, to spare them the prospect and difficulty of split allegiances (conflicts of interest). A schism inevitably resulted—called the *Investiture Controversy,* or realistically *Contest,* for that's what it was—as Popes and Kings fought for primacy, in the Holy Roman Empire and in Britain.

The early 12th century brought Pope Calixtus II and Emperor Henry V to a meeting at the upper Rhine city of Worms. (This was perhaps the oldest city in Germany, having been founded by the ancient Celts, and related to the 5th century BCE *La Tène* culture north of Lake Neuchâtel, Helvetia—modern Switzerland. Germanic tribes overran it during their *great migration* into the Roman Empire in the fourth and fifth centuries CE). An agreement was reached at Worms, the *Concordat of Worms* (Latin, *Pactum Calixtinum*), which accepted the separate authority and jurisdiction of kings and popes. But despite this, European states, especially small ones, would have to endure five further centuries of wars of invasion and consolidation in Europe, until the 1648 *Peace of Westphalia.* By its terms, Europeans agreed to recognise the sovereignty

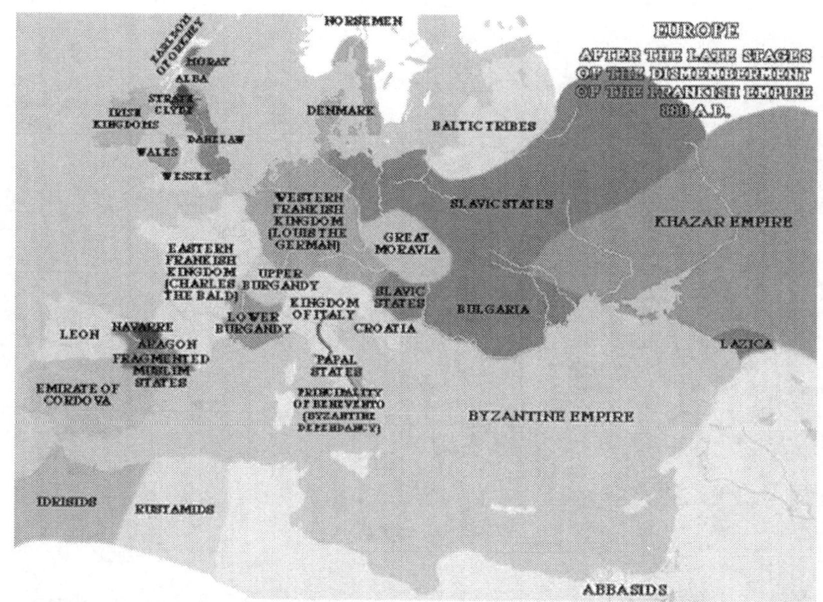

Rendition of 9th CE European states on modern map. Note interchanged labelling of "eastern" and "western" Frankish kingdoms

of nations and grant one another freedom from outside interference in their domestic affairs, thus discouraging casual raids, expansionism and Empire building. Not that it worked, but it did lay the foundations for international law and release of captive states held solely by might, such as Holland's final release from Spain.

The account given above describes some significant changes that led to Europe's emergence, and its ascendancy a millennium later. Its rise is very recent, analogous to a brash teenager, now at age 19 (19 centuries), while Islam is just 13, compared with the centenarians of Asia Minor, East and South Asia, or the Middle East and Egypt. Reviews of Europe's timeline show its youth and flawed assumptions, e.g. the folly of assigning a date for creation, compared with India's maturity, its more scientific approach from the beginning, and the advanced civilisation that had developed there, dating back to antiquity, well before the literal date of the Abrahamic creation. The British timeline for Hindu culture is thus uniformly disputed and by all ancient Indian records, wrong (see later chapters). This "developmental age" comparison is rarely made in modern histories, especially those with a western, racial or anti-Hindu bias, regardless of their origin or authorship.

Left: Rabanus Maurus, Alcuin and Archbishop Otgar of Mainz as Rabanus dedicates his work to the prelate. (Carolingian MSS, c. 831)

Below: Martin Luther defending his views before the Reichstag in Worms, April 1521. He was excommunicated by Pope Leo X in January, 1521. This effectively heralded the Reformation. Luther was contemporary of John Calvin, the French Protestant reformer and of Erasmus of Holland.

Sushruta, Indian father of Surgery, at work. Note students, 6th century, BCE

Chapter 7

"But where religion is goaded on by rapine and rapine serves as a handmaid to religion, the propelling force that is generated by these together is only equalled by the profundity of human misery and devastation they leave behind them in their march." VD Savarkar

"How often have I not heard on the evening air, her moans of wailing complaint that seemed to rise from desert marshes, sombre pathways, river banks, or woody shades etc. Was it the voice of the past, returning to weep o'er a lost civilization and an extinguished grandeur?" Louis Jacolliot, India

"United we stand, divided we fall." Winston Churchill

India, after the Guptas; the foreign raiders

In the 7th century, as the Umayyads were rampaging through the Middle East and advancing towards India, Harshavardhan, the King of Malwa, united the small principalities and republics of Northern India that had emerged, a century earlier, from the fall of the Gupta Empire. Harsha had won support of most of northern India by agreements and coercion, but was held in check at the Narmada River where Pulakeshin II had consolidated the Chalukya Empire, extending from south of the River towards the southern tip of India barring a triangle ruled by the Cholas. A lasting truce was struck which allowed Pulakeshin to defend successfully against Muslim raiders.

Caliph Umar, having conquered the Sassanid Empire, which then included western Baluchistan, halted to provide time to consolidate the seizures, careful not to expand faster than the administrative capability of the Caliphate. Then he sent a series of sorties against the Hephthalites[61], who had gained control over significant parts of Northwest India following the collapse of the Gupta Empire. Umar attacked the tribes east of Persia and Afghanistan, and along India's borders, whose defence had now fallen to individual frontier states. (The analogy with the forays of Germanic tribes, Slavs and Huns across the Danube into the Byzantine Empire is close indeed).

The first recorded overland raids into India by the Umayyads came from bases in Iran, then a Parsi state, and from Baluchistan, whose peoples practised Hinduism and Buddhism. Islamic forces met strong resistance from King Rai (Rasil) of Sindh, but aid from Iraq helped them to prevail at the battle of Rasil, somewhere west of the Indus, near Alor (modern Sukkur, Sindh). Rai fled east across the river to reorganise his defences, but for various reasons, Umar stopped his own advance at the west bank of the Indus. The Achaemenids of the 6th century BCE had

---

[61]Also called White Huns (*Huna* in Sanskrit), their origins are not clear and several postulates are current, the most likely being the Hindu Kush and the region of the Amu Darya. They are distinct ethnically from Attila's tribe and may be kin to the Kushans. Another group, the Red Huns, may be so-called from their favoured colour.

similarly advanced from Persia and conquered territory to the west bank of the Indus but had ventured no further.

The Rai Dynasty (c. 489–690 CE) never recovered its former strength or glory. It had once occupied the entire northwest and west of India—Kashmir, Kandahar, Makran, Daybul and cities along the Indus and Saraswati rivers (Saraswati/Indus civilisation), including Mohenjodaro, Mehrgarh, the lower Indus sites—and south to Surat and the delta of the Indus. It had occupied over 600,000 square miles (1,553,993 km^2), an area nearly twice that of modern Pakistan, and was a traditional and loyal protector of Hinduism and its culture.

Proximity of ancient Persia and Sindh (Hindustan)

The governor of Iraq at that time, the cruel al-Hajjaj (*bone-crusher*) ibn Yousef had failed to capture Gandhāra in the late 7th to early 8th century and faced hostility from non-Arab Muslims in Persia, whom he had antagonised by his brutality. But the desire of the Caliph to gain control of the Indus River and its peoples spawned new campaigns. A sea venture had become more difficult due to the ruthless and ubiquitous Mid corsairs who roamed the Arabian Sea in their *bawarij* boats, harassing all ships. According to Tha'alībī in *Laṭ'āif*, al Hajjaj was one of four men known to have killed over 100,000 people; the others were Abu Harb, Abu Muslim and Babak!

Al Biruni in *"From The Remaining Signs of Past Centuries"* gave this example of how al Hajjaj treated the defeated: *"When Qutaibah bin Muslim under the command of al-Hajjaj ibn Yousef was sent to Khwarazmia* (greater Iran, modern Uzbekistan) *with a military expedition and conquered it for the second time, he swiftly killed anyone who wrote the Khwarazmian native language or knew of the Khwarazmian heritage, history, and culture. He then killed all their Zoroastrian priests and burned and wasted their books, until gradually the illiterate only remained, who knew nothing of writing, and hence their history was mostly forgotten." (See also* Ragbeer*: The Indelible Red Stain, Bk* 2, Ch.3: "Language as coloniser").

In 712 CE, al-Hajjaj sent a strong force from Persia under his 17-year-old nephew (or cousin) Muhammad Bin Qasim along the coastal route into Sindh. Qasim seized the city of Daybul (Karachi), slew all defenders, collected the women and children as hostages and slaves, and sent a fifth of the booty to al-Hajjaj, according to *razzia* rules. He garrisoned the city, *destroyed the temple and built a mosque on the ruins*.[62] This act was often repeated. Similarly, Christians had built churches on pagan shrines in Europe and converted temples to basilicas. Islamists built on churches in the Levant, Africa and the Mediterranean, and centuries later in Asia Minor and the Balkans, with the establishment of the Ottoman Empire.

Qasim moved north along the Indus subduing towns all the way to Multan, meeting little resistance from the predominantly unarmed and pacifist Sindhi Buddhists and Hindu civilians. When he was opposed later at Brahmanābad and Multan, he dealt harshly with the population, killed all fighters, enslaved civilians, desecrated or destroyed temples and replaced them with mosques. Multan was known as the *House of Gold*, home of the great *Sun Mandir,* with capacity of some 6000 persons; it was looted and destroyed. Thus was consolidated the pattern of looting, razing temples and replacing them with mosques; raiding would reach new excesses of cruelty and barbarity under the Ghaznids, Ghorids, the sultans of India, and later Mughals and the British.

From Sindhi strongholds, Islamists carried out regular and frequent *razzias* into the rich provinces of Rājputāna and Punjab. Strong forces raided Gujarat and Maharashtra, but were beaten back by the Chalukya armies at Navasari, Gujarat, in 739, seven years after the Franks had stopped the European advance of Islamic forces at Tours (Poitiers). But while Franks had driven them out of Gaul and Italy, Indian victors incredibly allowed them to stay and keep their Indus "trading" posts—perhaps for profit, a passion with Sindhis, equal to that of the Jews—only to regret later their failure to abolish the threat, when they had the chance. Understandably captivated by the richness of the prize, the raiders returned in greater strength, hoping that each raid would help them expand and strengthen their base to fatten themselves, like parasites, off the sweat and labour of others, as the Romans had done in the west, until their demise as the dominant world power of their time.

India's traditional bonds have been its strong dharmic traditions—Hinduism, Buddhism and Jainism—regardless of political systems, whether kingdom, republic, dictatorship, democracy, theocracy or other. In fact, it was possible for many different systems to co-exist in unions that were founded on a shared set of values. This was common in India and the neighbouring lands it controlled at various times, such as Gandhāra, Nepal, Kamboja, or those that its culture had inspired, such as Burma (Myanmar), SE Asia (Indochina) and Indonesia. At times some of these elements were brought together under a unified rule persuaded by

[62] Similarly Roman Emperor Hadrian rekindled the wrath of the Jews by planning to build a temple of Jupiter on the ruins of the temple of Jerusalem.

the argument that shared beliefs and religions provided a sound basis for social and political organisation, with security and prosperity for all.

Such instances tended to begin as kratocracies converting to the more benign geniocracies, but rarely into true democracies, perhaps because the sophistication needed to grasp the complexities of governance was missing at large. It was possible that popular government might naturally develop in certain areas, while a more dictatorial style might be better in another. Generally though, a good government saw that justice and equality were available to all, as illustrated by Ashoka's reign. Yet the poor continue to be overlooked.

Over time, different groups had seen the strong and numerous take advantage of the weak and few. At critical times when greed had misdirected human endeavour, strong and able rulers had emerged to show that social unity could provide security and allow better prospects than one could expect in a vassal or tributary state. As border kingdoms, which had lost the relative cohesiveness of the Guptas, discovered too late, they could not alone defend against the rising numbers of raiders that became so plentiful that they seemed to represent virtually all Asia.

To the southwest Islamic corsairs had continually raided states bordering the Arabian Sea, harrying Indian cities, from Sindh to Maharashtra. Their retreat after defeat at Navasari had been brief. The magnet of Indian wealth, its lush vegetation, comfortable lifestyle and the spur of Islamic *jihad* brought them back, in greater numbers and with heightened resolve, to continue the *razzia* tradition. For three centuries they persisted, with fanatical zeal, becoming more intense as their numbers and generations increased. Religious fervour took on new dimensions as leadership changed, pet beliefs solidified, and religious factions developed, led by charismatic men with personal aims and horizons, for which Islamic dogma was well-crafted and would be a potent spur. Roman emperors had, in like manner, usurped Christian leadership, first by serving the Papacy, then by installing favourites locally and in Rome, in a ruthless symbiosis. India yielded when governments weakened through schisms among constituent rulers, a condition that had crippled the Western Roman Empire.

On the overthrow of the Umayyad Caliphate in 750 CE, the Abbasids—descendants of Mohammed's uncle, Abbas ibn Abd al-Muttalib—gained control of all Muslim conquests except for al Andalus, which Umayyads would control until 1031 CE. Abbasids moved the capital of the Caliphate from Kufa to the new city of Baghdad and ruled relatively unopposed for two centuries, until forced to yield more and more power to non-Arab warlords of central Asia, retaining only nominal authority, mainly in education and cultural affairs. This was similar to the recognition given by Rome to converted European tribal leaders. The later disintegration of the Holy Roman Empire that Otto had ruled would show similar features.

Haroun al Rashid became the 5th Abbasid caliph of Baghdad from 786 to 809 CE, and was known for relative tolerance, promotion of culture, religion, science, music and the arts. The caliphate extended from Persia across North Africa to southern Spain; the Byzantine Empire became his tributary. His rule coincided with that of Charlemagne, who had become king of the Franks and of Italy. Charlemagne respected Haroun, a regard that was reciprocated; they exchanged many gifts, Charlemagne notably receiving novelty clocks and albino elephants. Haroun had diplomatic and cultural exchanges with his neighbours and with eastern powers, including India and China. When he became ill, an Indian physician, named Mankah, arrived in Baghdad to treat him.

Meanwhile changes had taken place in the Ganges Valley as the Bengali Pāla dynasty came to power and would rule for 424 years. The dynasty was founded in Gauda by a Buddhist Gopāla, a general, who was elected in 750 by Bengali chiefs to bring an end to the decades of chaos that had followed the death of Raja Shashanka, the general who had seized the eastern Gupta lands in the late sixth century from the weakening empire. This was notably the first election of a king in India since the period of the Mahājanapadas.

Gopāla restored orderly rule and was followed in 770 by his son, Dharmapāla, who ruled for 40 years and expanded the kingdom to include the lower Brahmaputra, the entire Ganga, Yamuna, Indus and Kabul valleys, and south to the Narmada River. With these victories Dharmapāla called himself *Uttarapathasvamin* (lord of the North). He displaced the Gurjara-Pratiharas and clashed with the Rashtrakutas of Karnataka (753-982), a Hindu-Jain lineage, which had developed simultaneously, after overthrowing their overlords, the Chalukyas.

An Arab traveller, Suleiman, adjudged the Rashtrakutas Empire in 850CE, then under Amoghavarsha I (ruled 814-878CE), among the top four in the (Eurasian) world, the others being the Byzantine Empire, the Caliphate and the Chinese Empire. Amoghavarsha is known as one of the great kings of India. His fame is based on the quality of his long and mostly peaceful reign, religious tolerance, the sponsorship of literature—including his contribution to the first major work in Kannada, *Kavirajamarga,* and others in Sanskrit (contrast the illiteracy of European kings). He supported architecture—Kailasanath Temple at Ellora, sculptures in Elephanta caves and other Jain temples in Karnataka—and the work of several celebrated intellectuals including mathematicians Mahaviracharya (*Ganita-sara-samgraha,*) and Virasena; Shakatayan and scholar Srivijaya; a language expert; and several Jain teachers, collectively called Jinasena. Mahavir is known for his pithy remark on the central role of Mathematics *(ganit)* in all learning: *"What is the use of much speaking. Whatever object exists in this moving and non-moving world, cannot be understood without the base of Ganit."*

The Rashtrakutas expanded their empire north to Kanauj, at that time controlled by the Gurjara-Pritiharas, and also targeted by Dharmapāla, creating a three-way contest for the annexation of that land. Control of the contact areas of central India changed hands at times. Thus the Empire that was once united—first under the Mauryans, some two millennia earlier, and then the Guptas, until two centuries ago—was now reconstituted as three units, each trying to be the sole controller.

And while they squabbled, these followers of the three pacifist religions, one of the most tenacious military doctrines, Islam, now under the Abbasid Caliphate, was breaching the western and northern borders of India, having gained control of all Persia and rapidly eliminated the religion of Zarathustra *(Parsi)*. This base enabled it to occupy parts of the western Indian province of Sindh, and push into Multan and Punjab in a coordinated campaign maintained by the Caliphate. In much the same way, Christianity, in its militant Roman form, was conquering all European tribes and had begun to fight successful wars against Islam on several western fronts. Europe was thus poised to cross a threshold from darkness into knowledge that would equip it to challenge the world.

It seems remarkable that at almost the exact time when Indians were facing deadly Islamic invasions that the combined might of the Gurjaras, Pritiharas, Pālas and Rashtrakutas—which could have easily destroyed the Islamic invaders—was focussed on internal wars of expansion, a misuse of energy and manpower that India would regret to this day. Nor did they learn a lesson in prevention, as subsequent history will poignantly show how Indians were authors of their own misery, even as they are today, slipping into a vulnerable, disjointed and confused state, which foreigners would find easy to overcome, by combining bribery and force of arms and exploiting the cupidity of the privileged classes.

Marching from Bengal and Bihar, Dharmapāla's son Devapāla, showed great military skill and expanded the empire, ruling for 40 years. He secured sovereignty over Gandhara, the Ganga valley, northeast India and expanded his sway over parts of Burma, Nepal and strips of China; he marched south into eastern Deccan, where the Chalukyas held him at bay. But in time, Devapala completed the rout of the Gurjara and Pritiharas, and Rashtrakutas in central India, expanding control to the eastern limits of Rajasthan.

Devapala's successors lost some ground initially but soon regained it. The dynasty lasted until 1174, through twenty rulers, crumbling in the last years, as if unable to sustain such a long and worthy run. Finally, they gave way to Sena rule, restricted to Bengal mainly, to be succeeded by the Deva dynasty, which would be the last Hindu rulers of Bengal before the coming of the Muslim Khiljis. The Pāla Empire improved education, restored Nālandā University and built a second university at Vikramshila, Bihar. They perfected the Bengali-Bihar language, expanded Buddhism to surrounding countries and patronised the arts. Their non-military contributions were similar to those of the Rashtrakutas in literature, the arts and architecture. The unrestrained movement of peoples from south to north and vice versa followed millennia-old travel routes crossing rivers and mountains that later Europeans would find daunting.

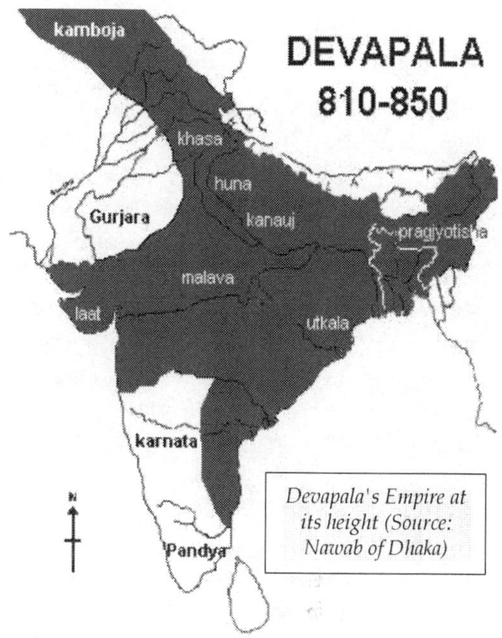

Devapala's Empire at its height (Source: Nawab of Dhaka)

The sustained military actions by the Turks which would erupt in India had disrupted life in Eurasia, destroyed trade along the silk routes and scattered many huge groups, like the Radhanite Jews, who had traded for centuries in spices, silks and other oriental goods, between Europe, Africa and Asia and between Christians and Muslims, through an elaborate network of land and sea routes. Turkic militias disrupted these trades for centuries, thus populations of pre-renaissance Europe and west Asia would grow up knowing nothing about oriental produce. Some of this trade would be resumed later in the city states of Amalfi, Genoa and Pisa on the Italian west coast, while Venice in the east would have a virtual monopoly in the Byzantine Empire.

Jews converted to Christianity or Islam as self-interest and exigencies dictated; the nature of their trades and occupations scattered them over the known world, at times to escape persecution. For example, the Jewish population of Arabia was large, and by long tradition and learning, members occupied important government and civil positions. They had co-existed with Arab "idol-worshippers" for a millennium and other Jewish tribes had joined them fleeing the Roman campaigns that had crushed the Zealots and other rebel Jewish tribes in Judea.

The nations forming Europe—from the Baltic Sea to the Atlantic Ocean, including the east half of Britain—were a multiplicity of warring Germanic tribes, pagan and illiterate, but for the Roman Christian clergy. They regularly raided one another and often clashed in major battles, sometimes exterminating a tribe, and generally living solely for personal or tribal survival. The poor and weak in such circumstances were easy prey to enslavement or recruitment into serfdoms, which became the organised way of lay and religious society.

In pre-history, tribes were ruled by consensus and cooperated to hunt and gather food, living a communal lifestyle. Some among them had the talent to organise and lead and so became first among equals. When the ice-age came to an end, and weapons developed—especially those that could be launched from afar, such as spears, catapults, arrows, and others that were silent, such as poisons—sneak attacks became an easy way of defeating a foe. However, warfare was probably not much used for survival when populations were small and competition for food unusual.

The popularity and successes of ancient warfare initially came from raiding neighbours, killing fighters, enslaving captives as a source of labour, and getting new women, despite the certainty of retaliation. This gave men—they were mostly men, barring a few famous women, like Boadicea in Britain, and legends of other warlike Celts, e.g. Amazons—an incentive to build strong militias and thereby seize and acquire more land, to settle and to extract raw material. They thus gained greater and more secure access to food, shelter and clothing, and in time the freedom to produce surpluses for trade. Often the need was for better quality of land, or a more salubrious climate, or simply to find labour and women and new pastures for stock. Tribes went to great lengths to get these, to the extent of involving all members as permanent militias, to provide a steady means of attack and defence, able to move when their numbers and their resolve gave them a reasonable chance of success.

Mergers often occurred, based on kinship and other bonds, especially intermarriages among leading families, which added strength and increased over decades or centuries. Wars grew from intertribal skirmishing to determined raids, when material or sociopolitical needs were supported by a religious philosophy that promised salvation and panacea even to the meanest, with ideas like faith, repentance, forgiveness and rewards that would involve all. Allegiances between neighbours and beyond tribal confines created larger groups that could quickly become an invading force when some charismatic leader arose, like Mohamed, who promised and delivered more loot than one tribe could obtain alone.

With success, tribal chiefs morphed into large landowners, military and/or religious leaders, heading formidable forces. As time passed, the most successful among these became the kings of territories, some acquired by conquest, creating a hierarchy and succession to maintain sovereignty. It mattered not that greed among heirs frequently led to unplanned changes of leadership; but at least the disposals or murders needed to become leader were family affairs, and only secondarily involved others unlucky enough to be seen as too close to a target.

Thus tribal societies changed with time from cooperatives to monarchies, where rulers commanded the lion's share of communal goods. Those that served them most skillfully and loyally, and safeguarded their person or chattel, became their generals, mandarins and Brahmins. The rest worked for those in power and to care for themselves as best they could; they were free to own and manage land and carry on business or a profession, as long as they paid a percentage to maintain the rulers and the government. It was natural that as kings became further and further removed from the plebs—their ultimate ancestral roots—that they would believe and impose on others the myth that they were specially endowed by "God" to wield authority over, and dispense good fortune to their followers or subjects, and reward them for merit, whether spiritual or lay. The concept of the *Divine Right of Kings* followed naturally and had related at an earlier date to the appointment of Popes.

The plebs in European societies were left to supply the labour, until the industrial revolution of the 18th century provided machines for much manual work, rendering large groups of people worthless. It is providential for many that the expansion of religion and the refinement in writing in Charlemagne's late eighth-century Holy Roman Empire created new skills that slowly allowed Europe to emerge from "the dark ages". Thus they began to follow in the footsteps of the established peoples of the Orient, India and the Middle East, where writing had gone beyond rune stones. Most cultures had developed a uniform alphabet and established a writing style, following the invention of paper in China. In time, paper would replace papyrus in Pharoanic Egypt, and prepared leaves and tree bark in parts of South Asia. Libraries, a feature of these literate societies, existed in most cities of the Middle and Far East, where education was more widespread, though later affected by the destruction of schools at all levels by the armies of Rome, Christianity and Islam, as they rampaged through the Mediterranean, Middle East, North Africa and elsewhere.

Muslims, although contained within Andalusia, were a constant worry to the Papacy and to western European kings in the centuries after Charlemagne's truce with Haroun al Rashid. The hardships faced by pilgrims travelling to Christian sites in the Levant, and the Pope's desire to control the Holy Land, fostered a campaign to agitate for military action. Popes throughout the 11th century promoted this, and convinced a syndicate of established European states to mount the equivalent of the Islamic jihad, the Crusades, to conquer and hold those lands, perhaps under rule of the Byzantine Empire. The first crusade was launched in 1095; five major ones followed, the last in 1272 (the fifth and sixth are not usually numbered. (See map p. 130) They created nearly three centuries of turmoil in the Middle East and major changes in Europe—geopolitical, national, religious, economic and social—and led to new alliances and changes, particularly the expulsion of Muslims from Spain.

A particularly vengeful and gory crusade, called the Albigensian Crusade, led initially by the bloodthirsty Abbott Arnaud Amaury, followed by the hated Baron Simon de Montfort, then his son, among others, occurred between 1208 and 1244, when Pope Innocent III (!) authorised the persecution of the Cathars of Languedoc, in south France. These were a self-sufficient and exemplary group of Christians, with an enlightened approach to life, and highly moral, far closer to Christ than anything then or now in Europe. They criticised the depravity and debauchery of the Roman Catholics and were in turn reviled for vegetarianism, unwillingness to kill animals, belief in reincarnation, and other similar crimes! In 1209, 20,000 Cathars were massacred in the Mediterranean town of Beziers; the remainder was hunted down in neighbouring areas, so that four decades later, very few would be left alive of those who had not accepted Catholicism by force, been killed by the blade, or burned at the stake in Languedoc and Toulouse. The Church never regretted this dastardly act of ethnic cleansing.

Because the majority of principals at the van of crusaders were English, French and other landed aristocracy, kings increased their holdings when they acquired lands of war victims who had no heirs (*doctrine of lapse*) or from special fund-raising. Two to four million died. Survivors returned with new knowledge, from skills learned in war to, more importantly, products met for the first time: spices, sugar, silk, jewels, art etc. They saw applications of science and mathematics, including advances in ship-building and navigation, and prospects for exploration and trade (Marco Polo, John Mandeville and others). The Church and the Papacy gained prestige, power and enormous wealth from donations of money and land, or cheap purchase of individual property to finance the wars. Socially, contact with the more refined people and products of the East improved European manners and behaviour, at least among the upper classes, a benefit that is often overlooked. It is said that even serfs benefitted from the softer manners of their lords. Doubtless the greatest benefit was the enlightenment and stimulus it provided that led to the European Renaissance.

The Albigensian massacre authorised by the Pope Innocent III ; expulsion of citizens of Carcassonne after the town's capture (Wikipedia upload by Dencey)

(L),Pope Innocentius III excommunicating the Albigensians (Wikimedia)
(R):Massacre of the Albigensians by the crusaders 1208-44 (British Library, Royal 16 G VI f. 374v) Albigensian crusade. P.147 Photos.

Inquisition tortures authorised by Pope in 12th century and used for centuries in Europe: a small sample; the first was in Aragon in 1238.

"Contemporary illustration of the auto-da-fé of Valladolid, in which fourteen Protestants were burned at the stake for their faith, on May 21, 1559." Public Domain (Uploaded Wiki, by Archaeogenetics: July 16, 2011) The Spanish Inquisition notably ordered arrest of Protestant Unitarian Michael Servetus, who was later executed.

Saladin and Guy de Lusignan after battle of Hattin in 1187, by Said Tahsine (1904-1985) *Syria; http://www.discover-syria.com/photo/11177*

1694-1774. One of the greatest French writers and philosophers

Francois M. Voltaire

"I am convinced that everything has come down to us from the banks of the Ganga – Astronomy, Astrology, spiritualism, etc. It is very important to note that some 2,500 ago, at the least, Pythagoras went from Samos to the Ganga to learn Geometry… But he would certainly not have undertaken such a strange journey had the reputation of the Brahmins' science not been long established in Europe."

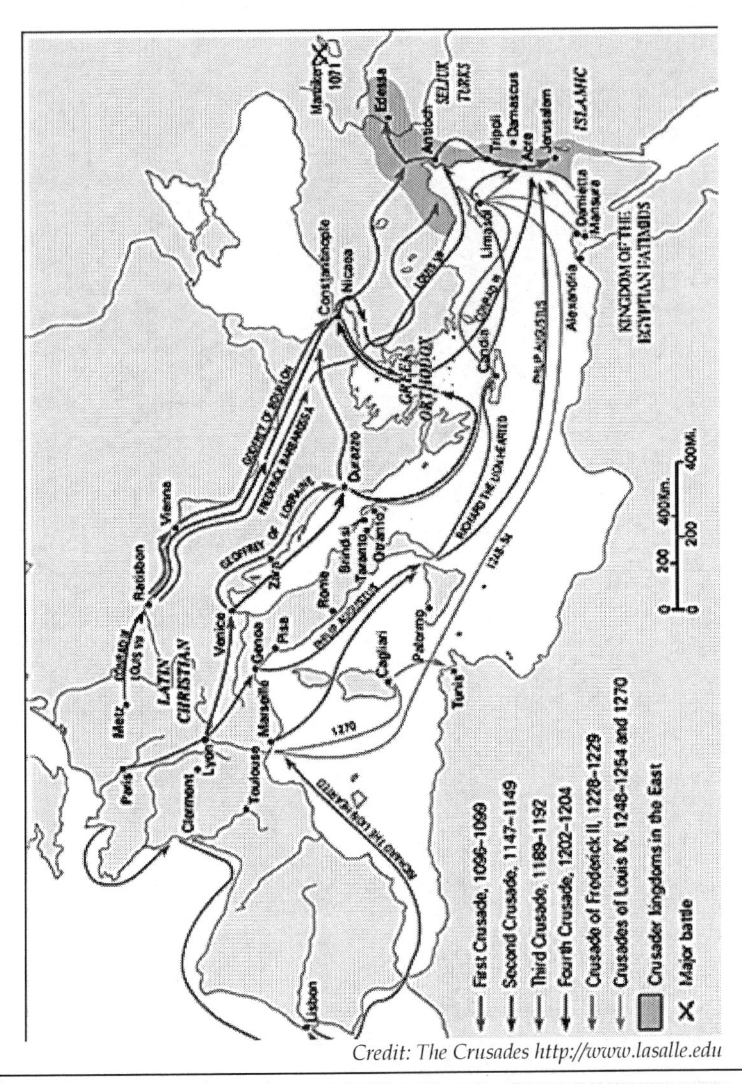

Credit: The Crusades http://www.lasalle.edu

The Crusades confirmed the usurpation of politics by religion, as the two strongest forces went for each other's jugulars, literally. More blood has been and still is spilt through religious hatred and striving for supremacy than wars of conquest. The first crusade left a trail of looting and carnage from Europe to Jerusalem, and saw Fatimid Arabs side with the Christians against Abbasids. Half a century after Saladin's recapture of Jerusalem Hulagu Khan would see the Tigris flowing blood as he destroyed Baghdad and its people. Islamic powers have never ceased fighting, whether among themselves or someone else. The savaging of India by Islam's Caliphs and Christian British followed in the next centuries. Today Islamic forces spread indiscriminate terror and death as they seek a new hegemony.

Chapter 8

"A physician who fails to enter the body of a patient with the lamp of knowledge and understanding can never treat diseases. He should first study all the factors, including environment, which influence a patient's disease, and then prescribe treatment. It is more important to prevent the occurrence of disease than to seek a cure".

Charaka *Samhita*

Advance and Decline: Muslim invasions

By the 10th century, Indian society had advanced considerably, with the north reunited, first under the Gurjara-Pritiharas and then the Pala dynasties, in a volatile peace, and the southern half stable under the several dynasties, including Rashtrakutas (753-982, Karnataka); Cholas (300s-1279, Tamil Nadu); Pandyas (Tamil Nadu, ca. 600 BCE); Cheras (Kerala, 3rd-12th century, CE); Chalukyas (Andhra Pradesh 624-1189); and Hoysalas (Tamil Nadu, ca 1000-1343).

Science and religious insights had addressed community issues and problems of the day in each region of the country. The range was wide, from Kashmiri philosophical treatises on aesthetics—such as Abhinavagupta's nine flavours *(rasa)* of responses to art, music, dance[63] etc.—to such pragmatic economic activities as development of improved textiles e.g. light muslins for clothing; architectural and engineering innovation to counter heat and humidity, manage water in the Rajasthan desert and elsewhere, build reservoirs in Kathiawar, and artificial lakes in central, south and western regions; and expand research in astronomy.

New observatories were built in Ujjain, Mathura, Varanasi, New Delhi, among others—to improve the data base for determining auspicious times for various royal and community functions, and for predicting the weather. Increased agricultural output spurred research in food preservation, with discovery of pickling and other techniques. Progress in medicine and allied sciences, such as pharmacology, extended the seminal work of Sushruta, Charaka and their successors, with new discoveries that placed India at the van of medical sciences. Textbooks on *Ayurvaidic* medicine were well-known locally and abroad and covered studies of the natural history of diseases, their prevention and treatment; the use of autopsy to describe and classify them; anaesthesia to facilitate surgery such as cataractectomy, craniotomy, fracture repairs, caesarean sections, plastic and other procedures; technology to devise suitable tools,

---

[63]Abhinavagupta's nine flavours were: *abhuta* (awe-inspiring), *bibhatasa* (unappealing), *bhayanhaka* (terrifying), *hasya* (comic), *karuna* (compassionate), *raudra* (angry), *shanta* (peaceful), *shringara* (erotic) and *vira* (heroic). To evoke a flavour, a work must stimulate and the viewer sophisticated enough to receive aesthetic stimuli. Thus an experience of art in any form is an interaction between viewer and the art.

medicines, disinfectants, dressings, ointments and cleansing agents; and the promotion of medical education, quality of care and ethics.

Along with scientific advances, came—inevitably and from the earliest days of the civilisation to this day—the "science" swindlers, soothsayers and dream-peddlers, assorted con-artists and others hawking superstitions and myths, which tainted the practice of medicine and the sciences—even as they do today, worldwide, now with enhanced speed, vigour and corporate protection. But these distractions did not prevent advances in science and technology. In every region of the country enterprising scientists were busy. Chemists refined sugar, produced glass, acidic and alkaline substances for commercial and industrial use, extracted oils, compounded spices, cosmetics and beauty aids. Agriculturalists created a huge dairy industry, produced varieties of rice, wheat, other grains, barley, corn, pulses, peas, beans, lentils, a wide variety of vegetables, fruits and roots, spices and the finest dyestuffs, which became major exports. Artists expressed the spirit and reality of progress in paintings using materials that have lasted to this day.[64] Miners found sapphires, rubies, diamonds, silver and gold; silver became the basis of Indian coinage until terminated by the British.[65]

Indian technology took directions from the support provided by the rulers of its kingdoms. Many from the earliest Vaidic times were, as already mentioned, enlightened men who supported the sciences, technology, mathematics, religious studies and learning in general. Several were distinguished scientists, such as King Shuchi of Magadha and 11th century polymath Rāja Bhoja of Dhar-Malwa, who achieved great engineering successes in his reign, including an artificial lake, roads, iron and steel structures, town planning, and mechanical inventions such as chronometers. His *Somarangana Sutradhara* is a textbook of engineering and one of 84 books that he authored covering a wide range of topics on sciences, religion, construction, grammar and philosophy. He was deeply engaged in the research and manufacturing of prestige articles, arms, luxury goods, including jewellery, fine fabrics and furnishings; he built structures and monuments, often of great size and complexity, as were many of the temples, palaces and government buildings.

Rome and Europe were at this time embroiled in religious politics, engaging in the first crusade, which led to refinement of war machines, an activity Europeans would eventually dominate.

---

64 Wall paintings in the Ajanta caves have survived for 1500 years, exterior paints on temples at Ellora have lasted over 1200 years. Indian miniatures have maintained their richness for many centuries. Dyes were exported to the Middle East and Roman Empire.

65 This was probably the most cruel act by British administrators in India. See page 252.

Each region of India could boast of centres of excellence in manufacturing, which made their owners and regional rulers prosper, developing a considerable middle class of artisans, professionals and other specialists, whose skills sustained the success of Indian industries. But this was a two-edged sword, as industry became complacent and overly reliant on skilled labour—because it was plentiful and produced enough for its privileged employers to maintain a healthy profit and lavish lifestyle, with many servants—and did not see the need to spread prosperity to those less privileged, even as they neglect to do today, the few philanthropists notwithstanding. A factor in the complacency of Indian manufacturers was the benign climate, with a long growing season that allowed the populace to obtain food, clothing and shelter fairly cheaply. The peasantry survived stoically at a basic level while the elite lived in luxury, a situation promoted by the "caste" system which became more complex as invaders e.g. Turks and British, added other layers.

In temperate zones the pressure to provide for and cope with seasonal changes was a strong stimulus for innovation and growth, even though Catholicism had convinced a large sector of society—the poor—as did *karma* in India, that their lot should be endured for the greater comforts that awaited them in the "other" world! Islam too offered many post mortem rewards, for acts, including lethal ones, committed for religion.

Indian industry was more developed than most, at this early time, and relied heavily on the skills and knowledge of its workers and managers. It could have taken greater advantage of expanding external (and internal) markets by increasing research, production and reach. This required substantial additional investment in special education to increase the work force, and scientific research and experimentation to develop a wider range of products and more, better and cheaper devices required for mass production. But with the smugness that came from success of their traditional methods, too many Indian business and political leaders seemed to have forgotten that competitiveness required innovation, and that called for diligence, special insights, research and cultivation of new skills, to avoid getting stuck in a rut.

Nor did they know much about northern Europeans and that the novelty, spread and promise of education had created in them a thirst for knowledge and discovery, which, coupled with their ignorance of the world beyond Europe's borders, induced a feeling that they were pioneers in every field and that everyone was at the same primitive stage of development! Besides it suited their aristocracy to promote this belief.

India's large population allowed it to defer any action to broaden its industrial base by mechanisation, or to discover how others solved human problems. It was thus ill-prepared for the contest with the heavy mass production that would transform Europe during the industrial revolution a millennium later, and send Europeans scouring the world for markets for their factory goods. Yet in some fields, notably the textile industry, Indian machinery, although manually operated, (India was well-supplied with technicians and other skilled labour), was among the world's best and was copied by British "inventors".

The spread of Hinduism, Buddhism and Jainism between 1500 BCE and 1000 AD through India, Lanka, Indonesia, Indochina and southern China—with establishment of Indian settlements in several of them—created a demand for Indian products, spurring international trade, again mainly in goods for the wealthier classes. The huge demand for exports stimulated shipping, ship-building and packaging industries and Indian ports were among the world's busiest. By the 18th century the Wadias of Bombay (Mumbai), would become well known for the quality of their ships. Even though one could with hindsight clearly see that India had missed an opportunity for worldwide expansion of its industry, the fact is that its standard of *privileged* living was the envy of the old world, and made it a target for every warlord with a craving for luxury and power.[66]

One of the more stable fragments of the Gupta Empire was the Hindu Shahi kingdom of Gandhāra and Punjab in the northwest, a prosperous and self-sufficient realm that had remained aloof from the trading ventures of Turkic Muslims from cities along the silk route that altogether did not constitute for Shahis a large enough market. Seljuk Turks had by this time integrated with their Persian conquests and had adopted their language. They had eliminated the Hunas, who had been expelled from India, and gained control of most of Central Asia east of Anatolia, and had made inroads into the weakened Byzantine Empire. Traders, including Afghan Ghori slavers, coveted Indian wealth, agricultural plenty and large population—a source of high taxes and slaves—tempting frequent *razzias* into the Shahi kingdom, whence a conqueror could invade, and perhaps subjugate all India by *jihad* (holy war).

Various Islamic rulers had maintained their assaults on the region for centuries, from 636 to 870 CE against Gandhāra, and from 870 to 1030 CE attacking the Punjab. North Indian armies, like their counterparts to the south, had repulsed waves of invaders for centuries. Yet, it is amazing that these gifted fighters had failed to see the great risks they were running by failing to mount, at this stage, a united defence to finally study and destroy the invader. They had missed previous opportunities, the first when Islamists invaded the Rai kingdom in Sindh, and the second when the Chalukyas defeated them at Navasari in 739 CE, and yet again

[66] Harry Vere lst (Senior Officer of the East India Company) described Bengal before Pilashi (Plessey) quite succinctly: "*The farmer was easy, the artisan encouraged, the merchant enriched and the prince satisfied.*"

when Mihir Bhoja (836–885 CE), though aware of the foreign danger, waged war against the Bengali Pālas and the Rashtrakutas instead.

In 1001, Mahmud, son of the expansionist Sabuktigin of Ghazni, a central Afghan state, after 17 failed attacks in 30 years, entered the Shahi kingdom with a strong Turkic force, which overwhelmed Raja Jayapala Shahi's armies at Peshawar and later defeated his son Anandapala. Jayapala Shahi had responded to repeated attacks by Ghazni by attempting to destroy his base, but the Ghaznavids repelled his attack and his subsequent efforts also failed. He committed suicide. Ghazni had followed the route used by Darius in 512 BCE, and later by Greeks under Alexander in 326 BCE. But these two had failed to hold on to their conquests. Ghazni, however, soldiered on. He had weapons, a growing army and a purpose—besides cupidity—that previous invaders had lacked: religious fanaticism. It is uncertain whether the Shahis had sought the help of neighbouring Indian kingdoms, by treaty or urgent request.

With the Shahi conquered, Ghazni waged *jihad* and plundered cities along the northern Indus, including Muslim ones like Multan, thus suggesting that prey and booty were more immediate objectives—although eradicating Ismaili, Sufi and other Shi'a sects might have been a more insistent purpose, a factor that weighs in all Islamic conflicts.

Ghazni created vassal states along the way to be governed by vanquished Hindus, Buddhists or Jains and reduced the population to *dhimmis*—people who could retain their religion, rights and privileges but at a cost of the *jizya* or poll tax, which Muslims did not pay. Thus conversion was coerced especially among the backward classes or the poor, who remained under-privileged, since Islamic Turks and Persians did not observe the principle of equality among Muslims, showed biases against the dark-skinned *(al muhammam)* and a more rigid casteism than existed then among Indians. Princes who converted retained status and privileges; those who did not, were invariably murdered, like apostates. The similarities with European experience in the 7th-11th centuries and the way Romans and Charlemagne spread Christianity are uncannily close. They point to an innate trait of man to impose his will and doctrine when he accepts a belief and finds it a reliable and easily exploited source of power. This the Romans had found in Christianity, as expounded by Paul and the disciples, but assimilated into their practices the Roman way.

From Punjab, Ghazni moved south and east, through Punjab and Rājputāna, and in 1017 sacked Mathura, birthplace of Lord Krishna. He was repulsed by the Chandela king, Vidyadhara, the builder of the magnificently sculpted and erotically decorated temples at Khajuraho, in the decadent fashion of the time. Seven years later, the persistent Ghazni reached Somnāth and destroyed the Shiva temple, after seizing its riches and killing some 50,000 defenders; he built a mosque thereon. This success initiated a series of raids and stimulated other Islamists to seek their fortunes in India. It was the game of *razzia* on a grand scale by zealous raiders now fired by the reality of untold wealth, gripped by a militant religion, with scores to settle, and impelled by "holiness" and promises of pleasurable rewards, if martyred (heaven and 72 virgins). Many of the hated Shi'a had found asylum in India, from as early as the first Caliphate. Hundreds of thousands of civilians and children were impulsively slaughtered, numerous others enslaved, especially artisans and labourers, and sold into Asian markets hungry for skilled workers.

L: Rishabha of Kosala founded Jainism; Khajuraho statue. (photo: ne.Berger@unil.ch)
R: Bāhubali, second son of Ṛishabha, monolith at Shravanabelagola, Karnataka, 978-993 CE
Photo by Ilya Mauter (Creative Commons CC-BY-SA-2.5)

Meanwhile, Raja Bhoja of Dhar-Malwa (1018-60 CE), had allied with Rajendra Chola and Kumara Gangeyadeva of Kalachuri in a campaign to seize Chalukya's Gujarat kingdoms, but unexpectedly strong resistance forced him to return home. It was an ill-advised campaign and only served to highlight the strong residual tribalism of the kingdoms and the divisive forces that fractured attempts by the Gurjar-Pritihara alliance to restore north India to a level of strength and unity approaching the Gupta Empire. They repelled repeated western invaders up to the eleventh century, by which time the realm had, by internal wars, fragmented into small states, each too weak to repel Ghazni and his successors. Islamists slaughtered millions of Indian "infidels." Rāja Bhoja regrouped in Dhār and drove the Ghazni forces from Somnāth back to the Punjab.

In 1031, Sayyid Salar Masud, 16 year old nephew of Mohamed Ghazni, born in Ajmer and already a 6-year war veteran, led a large army to recapture cities his uncle had lost. Realising the Islamic threat and its strength, Rāja Bhoja forged an alliance of Rajput Hindu states, which succeeded in driving Islamic forces as far north as Lahore, after annihilating Salar Masud and his army at Barraich, Uttar Pradesh. Set to take Lahore, the last stand of the fleeing Muslim forces, Raja Bhoja's allies squabbled over division of conquered lands and, reaching no agreement, defected, leaving Rāja Bhoja to carry on alone. He was forced to split his armies to fight erstwhile allies, and moving to defend his capital, was killed by an *Indian* opponent's arrow.

Bhoja was a polymath: poet, engineer, military strategist, philosopher, temple builder, a good ruler and founder of the fair city of Bhopal. His mistake and India's regret was to prosecute a war of expansion—or unification, depending on one's sympathies, perhaps to rekindle the glory and international prestige of the Guptas or Mauryas—when powerful and fanatic marauders were already threatening the northern approaches to the rich cities of the Yamuna-Ganga valleys, close to his. Despite their initial failures, the raiders of these early incursions had confirmed the wealth of the country, fuelling their resolve.

A culture of divisive internecine war had developed since the fall of the Hephthalites (Hunas), as northern Indian kings jostled for power. Thus engaged, they overlooked or underestimated, until too late, the power, fanaticism and unorthodox character of Islamic warriors that propelled them to victories, which would have been near impossible against alert unions like the Mauryas or Guptas. India repelled the invaders for a millennium or more, until disunity and weakness in border kingdoms, following the breakup of Empires, allowed the invaders to triumph in succession: the Kushans, Indo-Greeks, Hephthalites, Islamists, and later the British, who fomented disunity as a conquering strategy.

Bhoja made a strategic error in ignoring the vehemence and organisation of the Turks in Central Asia, and failing to form an alliance to drive Ghaznavids out of India (and Gandhāra), when he had Ghazni on the run from Somnāth. It is arguable whether such an alliance would have had any better outcome than the actual later one against Salar Masud which collapsed on the brink of a final and decisive win, when the endemic rivalry and hunger for possessions rent the alliance and allowed a vicious enemy to escape and regroup for successful re-invasion. It is not difficult to imagine the resulting carnage at Lahore had the tables been turned, with Hindus fleeing Islamists. India would regret the failure and blame the rivals to this day for failure to protect her, as further waves of frenzied Islamists stormed across the Punjab to seize, pillage and murder, to destroy Indian kingdoms and work to end its civilisation.

The brutal treatment of civilians as booty by Islamists shocked Hindus. Many thousands of people from Rajasthan and Sindh fled them and eventually settled in the west, and in Asian and European countries, where they became known as "Roma"; some adopted a nomadic life-style and today remain generally reviled by host nations.

Hindus witnessing the carnage by Islamic forces were shaken, not just by its intensity, but that it was happening at all. The Hindu warrior class (*kshatriyas)* waged war against *soldiers* and *armies,* not civilians, among whom casualties were largely accidental, not the result of vengeful and deliberate killing, as if targets in a blood sport. Muslim writers of the time marvelled at the lack of *"messianic zeal"* among Hindu fighters, and socially at the way the men treated women as partners to be consulted, unlike the savagery shown by Turkic Muslims, who treated women as chattel. Hindus were astounded and repelled by the difference and began to resort to various stratagems to protect their women and children.

Al Biruni had travelled with Ghazni as his chronicler and wrote: *"Mahmud utterly ruined the prosperity of the country and performed those wonderful exploits by which the Hindus became like atoms of dust scattered in all directions...their scattered remains cherish, of course, the most inveterate aversion towards all Muslims. This is the reason too why Hindu sciences have retired far away from parts of the country conquered by us and have fled to places, which our hand cannot yet reach, to Kashmir, Benaras and other places."*

The loss of Northern India would be complete, with Mohamed Ghori's victories, between 1175 and 1206 CE, in Punjab and part of the Ganges Valley. The prolonged period of continuing warfare against over-zealous Muslims seeking plunder and taxes would be but the first phase of the decline of India that would progress inexorably to the present.

The long years of failed invasions attest to the determination of the defenders. But had they possessed the Muslims' fanaticism and philosophy of *jihad,* or shown less of a philosophical difference and more collaboration and nationalism among Buddhists, Jains and Hindus, or prompt incorporation of artillery and gunnery into their defensive strategies, the conquest of India would hardly have occurred. Even though conscious of *ahimsa,* Indians held out for 570 years from the early eighth century, and the Mewaris, Marathas and southern kingdoms would stem the Islamic tide for another four hundred years, until finally quelled by Babur's answer to the might of Indian elephants.

Pre-Muslim India was undoubtedly the most advanced country in technology, agriculture, politics and economics, all coveted by Asian nomads, now driven by Islamic zeal. Their fury would cost India its glamour and wealth, as the contest shifted away from *kshatriyas,* who observed traditions of honour, even when engaging enemy forces that were crude, mercenary and vicious—not the types that fought a *"gentleman's war"* —as al Biruni had noted.

To illustrate further, the 12th century Indian writer Chand Bardai, court poet and companion of the Ajmer King Prithviraj Chauhan, reporting on the defeat and capture of the Turk Mohamed Ghori at the first Battle of Tarain in 1191, wrote: "*Muhammad Ghori was brought in chains to Pithoragarh, Prithviraj's capital and he begged his victor for mercy and release. Prithviraj's ministers advised against pardoning the aggressor. But the chivalrous and valiant Prithviraj thought otherwise and respectfully released the vanquished Ghori.*" A year later the tables were turned at the second Battle of Tarain, and Prithviraj was taken prisoner to Ghori's capital in Afghanistan. "*Ghori ordered him to lower his eyes, whereupon a defiant Prithviraj scornfully told him how he treated Ghori as a prisoner and said that the eyelids of a Rajput's eyes are lowered only in death.*"

Ghori retorted by blinding and torturing Prithviraj, a common practice then. Prithviraj salvaged his honour, according to Chand Bardai, by committing ritual suicide.

The defeat of Prithviraj illustrates the risks of disunity among Indian kings, occasionally trifling, but often deep-seated and related to tribe, *jāt* and other loyalties. It shows the ethics of war cherished by Kshatriyas which forbade injuring non-combatants or wounded soldiers; fighting after sunset (warriors needed rest, like everyone else); or involving women unless they were fighting as soldiers. They abhorred raids and stealthy actions, such as Islamists routinely carried out, and followed strict rules in guerrilla warfare; they treated all opponents alike, even kinsmen who fought for the foe, but executed traitors. They took roles seriously, fought valiantly and expected their enemies to do the same. But they had not reckoned with the fanaticism and unusual ethics of Islam.

Ajmer and neighbour Kanauj were traditional allies and the two strongest Rajput kingdoms of northern India. An enmity had developed between them because 17 years earlier, Prithviraj had eloped with Sanyogita, the daughter of Jaichandra, king of Kanauj, at her *swyamavara* (ceremony to choose a spouse). It is said that the irate king shunned his son-in-law and left him to face the invaders alone. Jaichandra allowed peeve to obstruct national security and is even said to have helped Ghori militarily. He would soon regret this folly and betrayal, when Ghori attacked and conquered Kanauj! This was a replay of the schisms within the Rāja Bhoja alliance where self-interest had led to a ruinous defeat.

It did not help that Indian society was becoming more rigid in use and observances of *varna* and outright segregation of the lower classes while Brahmins terrified Hindus with tales of doom that would follow neglect of the rituals, which they imposed on everyone. These included paying homage to Brahmins, giving them gifts and virtually pampering them and the rulers. Successful businessmen became Brahmin patrons and helped to consolidate this sorry state of Brahmin hegemony. The teaching of Sanskrit was suspended in schools and restricted to the higher castes. (Similarly the Roman Catholic Church would later confine the reading of the Bible to the clergy, and condone various practices: simony, peddling penance and other indulgences, all strongly criticised by Wyclif and Hus in medieval Europe and ridiculed in Chaucer's *Canterbury Tales.)*

The arrogance of Brahmins and their actions helped to alienate the majority, who declined to help the ruling class, when the invading Islamists besieged and treated them with the savagery for which they had become notorious, in their obsession to create an Islamic world. Their approach was opposite to Buddhist, Hindu and Jain tolerance and welcome, which had made Indians react too late. Besides, Indian rulers, with advice from scheming Brahmins, had failed to involve the people in their own governance and defence, contrary to Ashoka's advocacy; thus it was no surprise that they had fallen to Islamic *jihad*. Brahmins would have time to regret their self-interest and shortsightedness.

Mohammed Ghori had crossed the Himalayas and conquered Punjab in 1185 CE. Eight years later Qutb ud-Din Aybak founded the first Sultanate of Delhi, starting the Mameluk dynasty that would rule for ninety-seven years. Muslims advanced across North India and by 1200 CE had gained control over the Gangetic plain, having plundered and destroyed great Hindu and Buddhist institutions of learning and culture.

One of his generals, Ikhtiyar (Bakhtiyar) ud-din Khilji, who led the advances east, destroyed the University at Nālandā, killing thousands of monks, students and civilians, thus eliminating a major human and educational base of Buddhism. This was one of the worst examples of barbarism in human history, above or equal to other atrocities such as the Roman burning of libraries, including the great one at Alexandria, Egypt, a thousand years earlier, which had destroyed most of the recorded knowledge of Mediterranean peoples, pre-Roman Jews and Egyptians. (Later other tyrants—from Roman Catholic authors of the Inquisition to Hitler—would similarly burn books and other stores of knowledge). By this act Ikhtiyar joined the ranks of the most loathsome of men, those who destroyed, not structures, nor life alone, but *knowledge,* the very foundation of civilisation, and the expression and repository of man's loftiest and most illustrious attainments. The loss to Buddhism was irreparable. Islamic forces were unrelenting in their pursuit of worshippers and clergy, and almost destroyed the religion across the north and wherever they went. Survivors fled to all points of the compass, and re-established Buddhism or enlarged its following in Tibet, Burma, Ceylon and China, while some Indian Buddhists seemed to have merged with Hinduism, from shared beliefs and rituals.

Having completed the plunder of North India and established the Sultanate of Delhi as the major force in northern India, Islamists looked south, but they had little success, apart from a group reaching Cape Comorin at the southernmost tip of India, in 1300. The wealthy Vijayanagara Empire of South India, which was established in 1336 by Harihara and Bukka Raya I, united South Indian kingdoms (Chalukyas and Rashtrakutas) against Islam and lasted through many vicissitudes, until it finally fell in 1646 CE. By this time the British had come to trade, making agreements with the Mughals, and would eventually overthrow them, ravage the country in a way that made their predecessors look like amateurs, and retard and debase Indian religion, education, science and technology that the Muslims had already savaged.

Indian trade with the West and East continued despite the changes in governments. The decline of her strength coincided with an explosion in knowledge, which came to Europe's aristocrats with the Renaissance and later Reformation, and their spread by forces that challenged Rome's hegemony. Slowly Indian and Chinese knowledge came to Europe in translations—especially Arabic and Latin—and was taught in Europe's first institutions of higher learning such as the Salerno Medical school, the universities of Cordoba, Bologna, and later Paris and Oxford, all of which thrived on classical Roman, Greek and Arabic learning; these included copies of Indian teachings in the sciences, mathematics and literature, but were not so credited. Indeed, Europeans knew nothing of the universities in India that were established in the millennia *before* Christ.

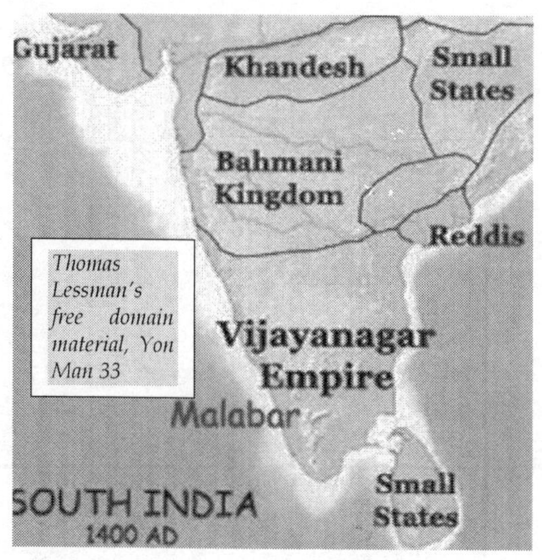

Thomas Lessman's free domain material, You Man 33

Unlike Hindus, who were greatly influenced by the teachings of that unique *Upanishad*, the *Bhagavad Gita*, and Buddhists and Jains by the precepts of *karma* and *ahimsa*, Europeans—from Romans onwards—had no qualms in transforming Christianity into a militant political force and an excuse for world conquest, having grown tolerant of continuous fighting in Europe for millennia. They used the new knowledge that came from Asia, e.g., explosives, to make tools and weapons that facilitated territorial expansion and industrialisation. These enriched the victors and helped them to reverse the negative balance of trade with India and China that had been an initial stimulus to explore so far away from home.

In the mid-11th century the Chinese had invented the compass and moveable type and had refined the use of gunpowder which Indians too had earlier discovered as a mixture of saltpetre, sulphur and charcoal, and used in small arms and artillery. Neither major power exploited these innovations in the way the Europeans did when they came to know of them, following Greek excursions, and later Marco Polo's epic journeys to the East. Note that the Greeks in 678 CE had used the same mixture, to which they had added petroleum, in their successful defence of Constantinople against the Arab Muslims.[67]

A major social and political change took place in Europe beginning with England's Magna Carta in 1215, which, although benefiting aristocrats only, did provide a benchmark for those pursuing the tough, plodding and incomplete process of relief from serfdom, where lower classes could aspire to some freedom and perhaps a rare taste of the foreign luxuries flaunted by their masters, the aristocrats and merchants. To do this, they had to be delivered from the rigid European brand of casteism and gain access to education and rights before the law.

But Magna Carta did nothing for the plebs. Emancipation was a long and fierce struggle of the masses versus the rich that brought out the best and worst in humankind. European aristocracy opposed reforms and notions of fairness, justice and equality for the masses, and what little measure was eventually achieved came only after murderous civil strife and revolutions in Britain, France, Russia and Spain.

Asian dynamics changed radically with the conquest of the Abbasid caliphate in 1258 and the destruction of Baghdad by the Mongol, Hulagu Khan, who exterminated all the inhabitants of the city, except Christians, and razed all buildings except churches. He humiliated the Caliph Mustasim who had earlier ridiculed Hulagu's invitation to surrender on arriving outside the city; he then had him trampled to death by horses.

---

[67]"When I teach about India, I always stress this," Dr Brahmam had poignantly said, "because that was when this country, which was so powerful and almost impregnable, lost focus and allowed her wealth and culture to fall to two warring religions, Islam and Christianity—because of egotism, hatred and disunity; personal wealth and power displaced the Hindu virtues taught by the *Gita* and the great sages. When Ghazni tried to take Punjab, Pālas and Chandellas could easily have repelled any invader with united defence, like Gupta or Ashoka, or Gurjar-Pritihara. Later Kalachuris, Chahamanas, Parmars, and Gahadvalas also failed to unite against Ghazni's successors. Indians were complacent; we didn't modernise our armies and so lost early battles against Mughal cannons. We didn't just lose land; we lost our heritage, our command of science, direction and drive to excel. We became slaves!"

The 1272 CE visits of Marco Polo to the Orient had profound effects, not only on Venice, but on Islam and India, as he described the opulence and culture of the East to his Venetian sponsors. The consequent trade arrangements established Venetian monopoly over the spice and silk trade with Europe which flourished for centuries, while the rest of Europe battled among themselves, pausing briefly from killing one another—like WW1 soldiers in a European field, calling a spontaneous cease-fire at Christmas, 1939—to mourn the death of millions of fellow citizens, among the 75 millions who died in the eastern hemisphere, killed between 1347 and 1351 by the *Black Death*, the plague caused by the bacterium *Pasteurella pestis*.

The actions of the Rashtrakutas recapped the movements of their ancient ancestors who are alleged to have taken their commerce and culture north from Karnataka, four or more millennia earlier, suggesting that the religion of India spread north from the Deccan to the northern plains after the great thaw. This movement also belies VA Smith's two-nation conjecture based on his belief that the Vindhya Range and the great rivers provided a barrier to any mixing of north and south. Instead it favours PK Srinivasa Iyengar's opposite theory of a single shared Hindu culture that flowed in both directions. One must recall that to the British the little Thames was a large river.

Varanasi 1922 (Library of Congress)

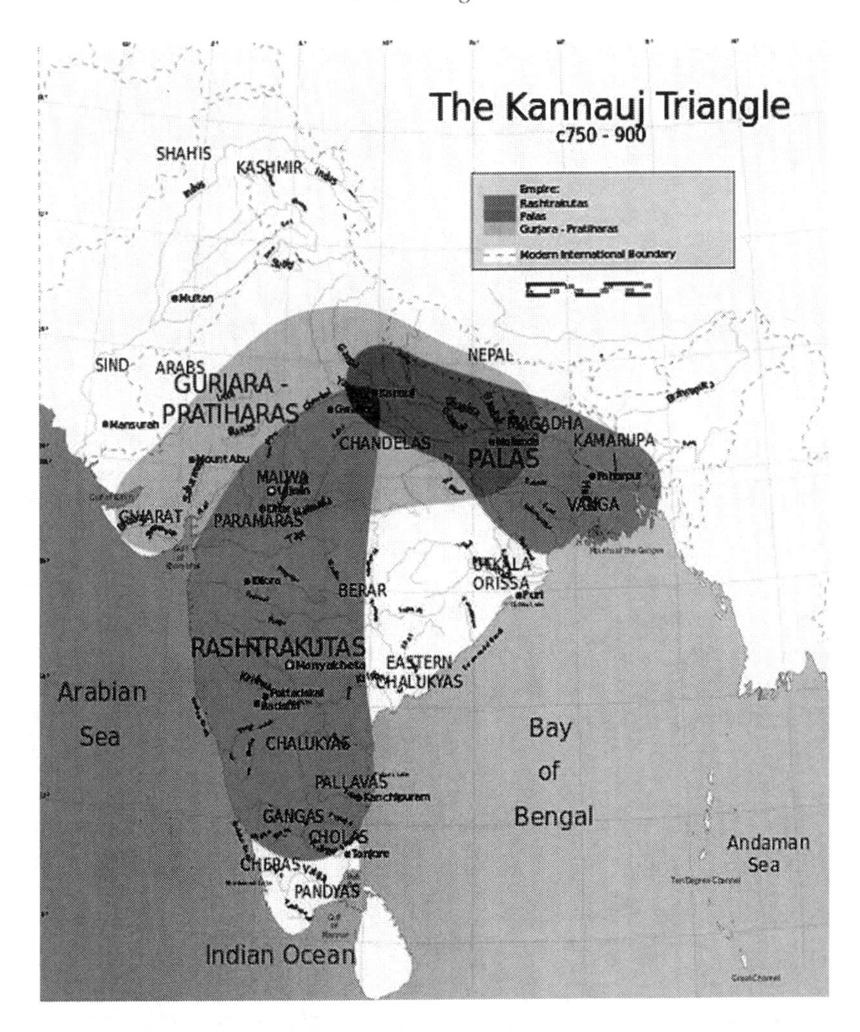
The Kannauj Triangle
c750 - 900
Empire:
Rashtrakutas
Palas
Gurjara - Pratiharas
Modern International Boundary
SHAHIS
KASHMIR
Multan
SIND
ARABS
GURJARA -
PRATIHARAS
NEPAL
MAGADHA
KAMARUPA
CHANDELAS
PALAS
Mount Abu
MALWA
Ujjain
PARAMARAS
VANGA
UTKALA
ORISSA
Puri
Ellora
BERAR
RASHTRAKUTAS
EASTERN
CHALUKYAS
Arabian
Sea
CHALUKYAS
Bay
of
Bengal
PALLAVAS
Kanchipuram
GANGAS
CHOLAS
Tanjore
CHERAS
PANDYAS
Andaman
Sea
Indian Ocean

Chapter 9

Let no consideration of relationship or selfish interest weigh with you. The Satan is at large; it may tempt you. Rise above all temptations and perform your duties in accordance with the injunctions of Islam.
Caliph Umar, 7th Century

"Thou art so busy in winning easy victories over the poor Hindu friars and beggars there. Why dost thou fight so shy to face the Hindpati himself? Thou hast lost fort after fort in the fair field here: that is perhaps why thou art distinguishing thyself by pulling down unoffending convents, churches and chapels there! Art thou not ashamed to call thyself Alamgir, conqueror of the world, wheyself standest vanquished by the Hindu Emperor Shivaji?"
Bhushana

The Mughals

Europeans had traditionally paid for Indian and Chinese goods with gold and silver, which were becoming scarcer and costlier, and the goods more expensive, as Venetians tightened their grip on Oriental trade. The layers of intermediaries ramped up the price of Asian goods, to a point that influential and wealthy European consumers and businessmen felt pinched enough to desire direct trade with the East. They lobbied governments to find an alternative route to India, to avoid the routes controlled by the Venetians and other seafarers, and by those controlling the Silk Road. Up to the sixteenth century, Europeans had neither the scientific knowledge nor indigenous capital to do this, and had to purchase gold from West Africa to pay for oriental goods. Advances in navigation, shipbuilding and exploration led to the discovery of gold and silver in the Americas which paved the way for colonisation of America, decimation of its natives, and seizure of the world's wealth, to enrich Europe.

The Spaniards had led in this massive holocaust and seizure of mines throughout Central and South America. A single mountain at Potosí, in what would become Bolivia, produced enough silver to enrich all Europe. Drake's 1588 defeat of the Spanish Armada off Plymouth unleashed a free-for-all on the Atlantic Ocean, with royal English assent to piracy (Elizabeth I). Atlantic plunder provided capital, first for trade, then for the eventual conquest of India, once England had established naval supremacy over all Europeans, in two centuries of bitter fighting, culminating in the defeat of Napoleon.

The race to find a sea passage to India made names for Portuguese King Henry the Navigator, Vasco da Gama, the German businessman and explorer Martin Behaim, who helped Portuguese explorers of the African coastline. Later, Cristóbal Colón, Ferdinand Magellan, Amerigo Vespucci, Henry Hudson, Francis Drake, Martin Frobisher and others would benefit. While India welcomed the traders from the West, the Ming Chinese reacted differently to commerce with them, by banning travel there in the 1430's, pulling down the first "bamboo curtain".

Yet, a few years earlier, China had celebrated the epic voyages of Admiral Zhang Hê, who died in 1433. Hê had thoroughly explored the Indian, Atlantic and western Pacific Oceans between 1405 and 1433, in what was described as the grandest flotilla ever assembled, the flagship being 499 feet long, enough to house, on deck, Cristóbal Colón's three ships, with room to spare! The book, *The Marvellous Visions of the Star Raft,* records his travels, and "his" remarkable and controversial map predates anything from subsequent Europeans. Its accuracy raised questions on authenticity, especially as the Chinese did not capitalise on the discovery of friendly tribal lands in the new continents, by subverting them to their own use, as Europeans did with America, after Colón's reports, and later in Australia and South Africa. Instead, China became isolationist for 400 years. Whether or not Zhang Hê reached the American coasts is still a matter for debate, as is the map.

A 1763 copy of a 1418 map, said to be Zheng Hê's, exhibited in London in 2006. This is presented to show the changed outlines as explorations expanded geographic knowledge .

Yet Zhang Hê's discoveries might well have underpinned Portuguese exploration, since the maps they followed included data not yet discovered by Europeans, and might also have been the basis for Cristobal Colón's confidence in reaching India by going west into the Atlantic—further than any European was known to have done—as Zhang's map shows. Colón had clearly been carried from the Canary current into the westward flowing North Equatorial Current, thence into the Antilles current, which sweeps by the Bahamas, encountering the Sargasso Sea, with hopes of nearby land. Later, da Gama sailed closer to the coast of Africa and found a way to India, and Magellan rounded South America to enter the Pacific Ocean. da Gama's journey, capped a century of effort by Portuguese seamen to sail the west coast of Africa, and he was able to reach India, after successfully rounding the Cape of Good Hope. Indian traders welcomed discussions and sought agreements, recalling their historic trading association with Radhanite Jews. In 1519, Magellan started his round-the world journey via the South American tip at Tierra del Fuego. Soon after, other explorers from Britain and France found routes to the east coast of North America, the Spanish and Portuguese having seized the Caribbean, Central and South America. The result of these journeys was the usurpation of aboriginal lands throughout the Americas; the destruction of the major Mayan, Aztec, Inca, Hopi and other American cultures, by war and European plagues; and the subjugation of residual populations, as new European countries seized their lands and built colonies. Some colonies united to form the USA, which would become paramount among modern nations.

Twelve years after da Gama's arrival in India, a Portuguese force overwhelmed the surprised people of Goa and seized the area, with much carnage, as a base for trade. Their main interest was pepper, more particularly the peppercorn best known as blackpepper (or whitepepper, when processed after removing the nutrient coat). The Spaniards, French and British started similarly in the Americas.

The Portuguese were, of course, staunch Roman Catholics; their zealous religious proselytising became a model of conquest in the cause of mercantilism and Christianity that Europeans would follow for the next four and a half centuries, equalling the fanaticism of Islamic invaders. But Portuguese success in Goa, in business and proselytising, was not matched by Europeans elsewhere in India. Multinational corporations and their Indian acolytes have expanded it recently, and pursue it a bit more cunningly, but no less brutally.

The Portuguese dominated the 16th century Indian spice trade by sea and would lose eventually to the Dutch and British, but gain a tremendous prize when they found, after a long and bloody search, the source of the coveted cinnamon in Ceylon (Sri Lanka).

The major development that would eventually threaten their desire to control and plunder India was undoubtedly the ambition of English King Henry VIII, whose aspirations for grandeur—it is believed due to the effects of tertiary syphilis, known to induce delusions of grandeur in its victims—spurred him to create the best armed navy of the time which his daughter, Elizabeth, would use to good effect. Henry's engineers built cast iron cannons that were far cheaper than bronze, enabling him to equip his fleet, first the *Mary Rose*, each with more guns than other nations' warships.

Earlier that century, a major change had occurred in Islamic hegemony over India. In 1526, Babur the Mughal (1483-1530) had conquered the sultanate of Delhi—an Islamic centre of intrigue—and initiated the dynasty that ruled for the next two and a half centuries. In 1528, he destroyed the Hindu temple at Ayodhya, the ancient birthplace of the avatar Rāma, and outraged Hindus by erecting thereon a Muslim *masjid*. He built a retreat at the bird sanctuary of Sultanpur, near Delhi.

His grandson, Jalal ud Din Mahammad Akbar (1542-1605), became Emperor at age 13, on the death of his father, Humayun, whose reign had been challenged for 15 years by Sher Shah Suri and Hemu Chandra. In 1556, Hemu Chandra followed a series of victories up the Ganges valley, captured Agra, then defeated the Mughals at Delhi, to become Emperor of India. He had been "supplier of Food items, Cannons and Gun Powder" to Sher Shah Suri, chief Advisor to his son, Islam Shah (1545-1553), Prime Minister-cum-Chief of Army of Adil Shah Suri, and virtual king from 1553-56.

Hemu had planned to expel the Mughals and follow them to Kabul. But sooner than he expected, the Mughals counterattacked; in the defence, which he led from an exposed perch atop his elephant, a chance arrow landed in his eye, felling him, at a time when he is said to have been on the verge of victory. Meanwhile, the youth Akbar and his regent Bairam had stayed safely eight miles to the north, where they received the news. On his fall Hemu's army panicked, lost focus and gave the enemy the chance to win the day. Hemu was captured and taken to Akbar's camp, where the youth wounded him, establishing his claim to be a *ghazi*, slayer of infidels, and Bairam beheaded him, in the customary Islamic way. Such was the brutality of jihad, alive and thriving today.

The young Akbar—assisted and protected by Bairam Khan—became the best known of the Mughal rulers (1556-1605, cf. Elizabeth I, 1558-1603) and a celebrated polymath. He professed a love for jihad and used all means to expand his kingdoms. One unusual device, a peaceful one, was his success in "persuading" Bharmal, the Hindu Rāja of Amber (Jaipur) to allow him to marry his daughter, Rajkumari Hira Kunwari (Harkha Bai), one of many women with whom he had "fallen in love".

The Rajput king became Akbar's army commander; he and his successors fought for the Mughals for 150 years—an unbelievable alliance, considering Muslim cruelty to Hindus and Buddhists, such as the looting and destruction of temples; the practice of beheading Hindus and building victory pillars with heads of the slain; and the imposition of punitive *jizya* tax on non-Muslims, which forced the poor to convert to Islam or be executed for debt.

Samrat Hem Chandra Vikramaditya, Hindu emperor. Here (bazaar art, 1910s) he is reimagined in a courtly Mughal style, and glorified in Hindi, Persian (from the Akbarnamah), and English, as "the last Hindu emperor of Hindustan", his genius certified by the Imperial Gazetteer

Akbar's marriage to Rājkumāri and his close relationship with her father, Rāja Bharmal, exposed him to Hindu beliefs and practices; for a time he was less cruel in treatment of Hindus, abolished *jizya* and engaged Hindus, Sikhs, Jains, Parsis and Jews in philosophical discourses. He started a new religion, *Din-ilahi,* which included the best features of all religions and proclaimed that *"No man is to be interfered with on account of religion, and anyone is to be allowed to go over to a religion that pleases him."*[68] Today, his alleged fairness in dealing with Hindus and his attempts at tolerance and separation of religion from government, is much doubted. Although he did encourage art and literature, the emphasis was on things Persian, not Indian, and he chose to expand Islamic influence, proclaiming himself a *ghazi,* a slayer of infidels.

The raiders of India over several millennia had encountered many leaders, who did not easily capitulate or join them for personal gain, as many Rajput princes easily did, when wooed by Muslims. Bharmal was notorious among them, to an extent that they could be called traitors to India. More memorable leaders were those Kshatriyas, steeped in virtues of nobility, honour and fairness, despite their formidable reputations and record as instruments of war and death, at a time when war involved the likelihood of hand-to-hand combat, mounted or on foot.

Heroes abound in Indian history. Others have shone in the resistance against Islamists, and are remembered for acts of chivalry that lost them advantage, and may even have led to their defeat. One may argue which is the better strategy, to win at any cost, even your good name, or to lose with honour. India's conquerors, it seemed, Muslims and British, often with the help of Indian princes or rulers, had chosen the former. Enough Indian leaders, however, had chosen honour, providing memorable examples: Jayapāla and his son Anandapāla, and Rāja Bhoja against Mohamed Ghazni; Prithviraj Chauhan in battles against Mohamed Ghori and Hemu Chandra against Humayun and Akbar.

Hammir Dev Chauhan was a member of the Sisodia clan and descended from Jain king Prithviraj Chauhan, who had fought and lost to Ghori. He restored rule over Ranthambor from 1282-1301, won major battles against the Sultan of Delhi, Jalal-ud-din-Khilji, and some years later against Ala-ud-din Khilji, who had murdered Jalal and assumed the sultanate. Islamists had destroyed the temple at Somnāth and the Shiva *linga,* whose fractured pieces were recovered after the victory, and distributed to several temples. Hammir was well reputed and praised for these, but a lack of social skills is said to have provoked his step-brother and finance adviser to a thoughtless defection to the invaders. In 1301, facing famine after a long siege by Khilji, two of his generals, Ratipal and Ranamal, accepted Khilji's bribes and deserted. Facing defeat, women committed *jauhar* (ritual suicide when capture was inevitable; see also p. 154-5). The men fought on to the death, to preserve their honour.

---

[68] V.A. Smith: *Akbar, the great Mogul,* Oxford, the Clarendon Press 1917 *(Bibliography)*

As ruler of Mewar, Rana Kumbha (1433-68, *pictured*) fortified the region with a perimeter of thirty forts and made Chittorgarh, his capital, famous in India as a centre of learning and the arts. Besides satisfying his first calling to defend successfully against Muslim invaders, he was known for musicianship and poetry. He had captured Ranthambor fort, famous as the scene of conflicts between Islamic forces and Rajput kings: Prithviraj, Hammir Dev Chauhan and others. It fell finally to Bahadur Shah in 1532, and to Akbar in 1559.

Rana Sanga ruled Mewar from 1509 to 1527; he gained control of Malwa and defeated the sultans of that region, including Ibrahim Lodi; by 1520, he had reached Agra. He was poised to begin the eviction of the Muslims, when he heard that Babur had advanced on Delhi and killed Lodi. He and his allies moved against Babur, lost the initial battle because of treachery and defection to the enemy of his vassal Raja Shiladitya (Silhedi), taking with him his contingent, the largest force in Rana Sanga's army. This was one of the many key occurrences of betrayal in Indian history. The battle was fought at Khanwa near Agra, and saw a major use of cannon and musket in Indian warfare, after the Bahmanis of the Deccan sultanate, initiating a *Gunpowder Empire* in India. Rana Sanga died encamped en route to meet Babur, of an illness thought to be poisoning, perpetrated possibly to prevent another bloody war with the better-armed Mughals. He fought despite loss of his left arm and a crippled leg. His bravery was outstanding and had fired Indians' hope of a Hindu victory.

Krishna Deva Raya (1509-1529 CE) ruled the Vijayanagara Empire at its peak; he was probably the last hero of the realm, earning the title, *Hinduraya Suratrana.* The Vijayanagara Empire of southern India was founded in 1336 by Harihara, after the neighbouring kingdoms had been occupied by the Islamists, Khilji and Tughluk, from the Delhi Sultanate. Harihara and later Bukka I strengthened their defences, and over the next century, most of South India and parts of Lanka and Burma came under Deva Raya (1424-46). Later, he consolidated the Empire, strengthened it and added parts of the Bahamani sultanate to its north. He lived long enough to see the sultanate break up in 1518 into five small entities of Ahmednagar, Berar, Bidar, Bijapur and Golconda.

The death of Krishna Devi Raya in 1529 heralded a period of decline of Vijayanagara, which allowed Akbar, in 1565 CE to besiege the city and destroy it, paving the way for the fall of that empire, 81 years later. Vijayanagara had become known for its patronage of fine arts and literature, which reached new heights in the major languages of the south: Kannada, Telugu, Tamil and Sanskrit, while Carnatic music evolved into its current form. The Empire created an epoch in South Indian history that transcended regionalism by promoting Hinduism as a unifying factor. Its fall told instead of the power of royal ambitions.

Krishna Deva Raya (1509-1529 CE)

Twenty years later another Mewar hero, Pratap Singh, gained fame defending his realm against Akbar—who had christened his sword with the blood of Hemu Chandra, the last Hindu ruler of Delhi—and had wooed and won over most Rajput princes, by bribe or threat. They included Pratap's younger half-brother Jaimal, who, like Prince Kunwar Mansingh, had become one of Akbar's military commanders. Mewar stood virtually alone against the invader despite great odds and limited resources.

Mansingh was given command of the Mughal army charged with subduing Mewar. He clashed with Pratap Singh's much outnumbered force at Haldigathi in Rajasthan. The battle ended in a stalemate. Pratap was wounded, but he escaped with loyal followers and faithful Hindus, who had also refused the bribes of the Mughal ruler. They fled into the rugged heights and ravines of the Arevalli hills, surviving on the fruits of Nature, like Rāma of old. After struggling with many doubts, he resumed his duty—some say after hearing from Prithiraj, a Rajput prince and poet in Akbar's court—and resumed guerrilla warfare against Akbar, recapturing all of Mewar save Chittor, which remained in Mughal hands.

Pratap is revered as a trusted and honourable leader, an exemplary Kshatriya warrior, foremost among Rajput kings and the major upholder of Rajput honour at the time. His guerrilla tactics were analogous to those used a century later by Marātha leaders like Shivaji of Puné and later Malik Amber of Ahmednagar. His was the outstanding success against the invaders, highlighting the weakness of Rajput kings, major and minor, who preferred servitude in luxury under Akbar to the tough discipline and deprivations of resistance to the invader, whom they might well have liquidated, had they chosen to defend in unity.

Maha-Rana Pratap Singh: 1572-97CE

Prithiraj was a Hindu prince of Bikaner and a poet in Akbar's service. Having been shown Pratap's plea to Akbar for relief he wrote, presumably without Akbar's knowledge: "*The hopes of the Hindu rest on the Hindu; yet the Rana forsakes them. But for Pratap, all would be placed on the same level by Akbar; for our chiefs have lost their valour and our females their honour. Akbar is the broker in the market of our race: he has purchased all but the son of Udai (Singh II of Mewar); he is beyond his price. What true Rajput would part with honour for nine days (nauroza); yet how many have bartered it away? Will Chittor come to this market? From such infamy the descendant of Hamir alone has been preserved. The world asks, from where does the concealed aid of Pratap emanate? None but the soul of manliness and his sword. The broker in the market of men (Akbar) will one day be surpassed; he cannot live forever. Then will our race come to Pratap, for the seed of the Rajput to sow in our desolate lands. To him all look for its preservation, that its purity may again become resplendent.*"

Pratap may have suffered from the envy of Rajput princes, as few had the grit to emulate him. He is recalled in poetry and song, and nostalgic legends extol his valour against Akbar's armies, and his dedication to the people. More tales have been spun about him than almost any opponent of the Mughals. After his death in 1597, his son,

Amar Singh, a brave and gifted soldier, withstood Akbar's fury and that of Jahangir, his successor, for eighteen years, until depletion of resources and the plight of his subjects forced an honourable treaty. Amar ruled Mewar until his death in 1620.

The Muslim, Chand Bibi, achieved a similar just reputation for resisting Akbar in Ahmednagar, 1596-99. She was the daughter of Hussain Nizam Shah I and an accomplished warrior; she was finally killed at age 49 by the combined effects of male chauvinism and intrigues among other Mughal leaders, to the extent that false rumour was used to stir her own troops to murder her.

She was a brave woman, in the tradition of Raziyya Sultan, who had become, from 1236 to 1240, the first, and only female Sultan of Delhi in a male-dominated Turkic Mameluk hegemony. Her father, Shams-ud-din Iltutmish, had wished Raziyya to succeed him, but the Council of potentates opposed this, despite her qualifications for the job and the known weakness of her brothers. They insisted on a male successor and installed a son, Rukn Ud Din, who ruled jointly with his mother for six months, until his debauchery drove the powers to arrange their murder.

Raziyya succeeded to the sultanate, and was assisted by her closest ally, Jamal-ud-Din Yaqt, an Abyssinian (Ethiopian) Siddhi slave, said to be her lover. Their relationship and her position were ahead of their time, and stirred rebellion, first from a revolt led by a rival chief, Malik Altunia, a childhood friend. She lost the battle, and Yaqt was killed. She was induced to marry Altunia, but majority support for her brother, Bahram Shah, led to further fighting, and they had to flee. Both died in flight, of uncertain cause, or whether together or separately. Ibn Battuta, in his *Travels,* thought that she was alone and killed for her jewellery. As a ruler, she was a religious liberal, promoted education and saw to it that schools taught a broad curriculum, besides the Quran, including ancient philosophies and Hindu sciences, astronomy and literature.

Chittor was a major Jain centre and has a place of pride in Rajput history, having seen brave acts of *jauhar* and *saka* that used to define a Rajput, not the cowardly and selfish defections to a perverse enemy by so many leaders from the rest of Rājasthān. The fort (Chittorgarh) had been assaulted in 1303 by Ala-ud-din Khilji, who coveted Rana Rattan Singh's wife, Padmini, only to lose her when she led the immolation of wives by fire, while Brahmins chanted Vedic mantras *(jauhar*). The following morning, the men—dressed in their saffron *kesariya,* with tulsi leaves in their mouths and the ashes of the women marking their foreheads—went out to fight the enemy to the death *(saka).* This sequence was repeated in 1535 when the Muslim ruler of Gujarat besieged the city, and in 1568 when Akbar's forces razed it.

There are many instances of this sacrifice – the preference to preserve honour and integrity, rather than serve the enemy. For the women the alternative was sexual surrender, and for the children slavery. Unwanted people and spectators were slaughtered. Akbar's forces, for example, are said to have killed some 40,000 spectators at the 1568 battle at Chittor.

In 1559, the hill fortress of Ranthambor had fallen, the site of a holy Jain *tirtha*, and had flourished under the Jain rulers, starting with Prithviraj Chauhan, and has a legacy of Buddhism and Hinduism. The region, like its neighbours, had seen both southern and eastern influences in social and cultural matters, and by the 16th century, northern India had had considerable interchanges with southern kingdoms. It is possible that memories of the unity and strength existing through the Maurya, Gupta and later dynastic periods – during which the Islamists had toiled unsuccessfully to raid India – moved some kings to recover that strength. Briefly, there was hope that a cooperative outlook might develop and repel the waves of invaders, who had never before penetrated so deeply into Indian territory. Sadly, the conqueror could find any number of disaffected aristocrats willing to take bribes in exchange for positions of power, or a chance to get even, as many Rajputs did. The capture brought Rājputāna to the Mughals and thus control of northern India from Sindh to Bengal.

The excesses of Akbar's successors angered the country, but the loyalty, strength and Islamic fanaticism of the Mughals and their armed forces – many ironically led by Hindu vassals – and with the inherent disunity of Indian leaders, kept the population underfoot. Shah Jahan was a wastrel, who squandered a fortune to bejewel the "peacock throne" and to build the Tāj Mahal, completed in 1647, for his favourite wife, on what was probably a Hindu palace or temple. He then finished the Red Fort in Delhi.

He was succeeded by the zealot, Aurangzeb (1618-1707), the last of the major Emperors, whose cruelty undid the little gains in goodwill Akbar might have won among Hindus. He expanded the Empire by invasions south into the Deccan and east to Assam, where the Ahom army defeated him in 1682. He maintained the *jizya* tax on Hindus, already suffering tremendous hardships. In 1675, he executed Sikh Guru, Tegh Bahadur, and by 1688, had razed all temples in Mathura, said to number 1,000. Muslims destroyed over 60,000 Hindu temples in India, and built mosques on 3,000 of them. They annihilated a vast number of Hindus, including those who refused conversion to Islam. K.S. Lal has noted (*Bibliography*) that the Hindu population *decreased by 80 million* between the invasion by Mohamed Ghazni in 1000 AD, and the battle of Pānipat. Another 20 million Hindus were killed by Mughals in the north

Chittorgarh, showing the tower Vijaya Stambha

and central India and by other Muslim sultans in the south. Koenrad Elst concluded that the slaying of about 100 million Hindus is perhaps the biggest holocaust in world history![70]

Aurangzeb's rebel son had fled to the safety of the Marātha Empire, which Shivaji had founded by retaking Vijapur (see Ch. 11). Aurangzeb invaded the Empire to punish it, beginning a 27 years' war, ending in 1705 with his defeat by Rani Tarabai at Malwa, heralding the end of Mughal power in India that had begun in 1526.

In 1708, a year after the death of Aurangzeb, Govind Singh, the militant tenth and last Sikh guru, was killed, presumably at the command of the new Mughal emperor, Bahadur Shah I (formerly Prince Muazzam, eldest son of Aurangzeb, who had defeated his brother Azam in fighting for the throne). He was a weak ruler and presided over the disintegration of a vast Empire that had expanded beyond the resources and the vision of its rulers. It had become weak, fractured and crippled

---

[70] "Nadir Shah made a mountain of the skulls of the Hindus he killed in Delhi alone. Babur raised towers of Hindu skulls at Khanuaj when he defeated Rana Sanga in 1527 and later he repeated the same horrors after capturing the fort of Chanderi. Akbar ordered a general massacre of 30,000 Rajputs after he captured Chittor in 1568. The Bahamani Sultans, who had revolted against Mohammed bin Tughluk and taken charge of a large area of the Deccan and Central India, "had an annual agenda of killing a minimum of 100,000 Hindus every year. The history of medieval India is full of such instances"(Anon). A similar bloodthirstiness and behaviour, the making of pyramids or columns of skulls of their victims, were key features of Assyrian armies in their campaigns of expansion throughout the Middle East in the 8th to 7th C. BCE.

with intrigue and conflict among its many princes, and the Europeans (see Ch. 10) who bribed them, and survived mainly by Indian disunity.

Central government had become increasingly reliant on regional governors or Nawabs, making it easy prey to the machinations of plotters, especially, at that time, the Arabic Sayyid brothers. They had great influence among Mughals, claiming descent from Mohamed, through Fatimah and Ali. They disparaged non-Arabs and searched for their own types to fill the power vacuum, playing king-makers in a fragmenting Empire; they instigated five changes in 12 years, until their final choice, Roshan Akhtar Mohammed Shah, organised their execution!

Meanwhile Nawabs had begun their own intrigues to secure full control of their domains and, by 1720, Asaf Jah I had declared himself the independent Nizam of Hyderabad in the south. In the East, Alivardi Khan, a deputy governor of Bihar became Nawab of Bihar, Orissa and Bengal after deposing Sarfaraz Khan with the Emperor's approval; soon, he too asserted self-governance. These developments had left the Emperor with Delhi and surroundings only, and at the mercy of his Nawabs. Nadir Shah, a Persian tyrant, had risen to the throne of Iran, after boldly driving Afghan occupiers from Khorasan, the capital, in 1725. He had become regent to a boy king whose convenient death left Nadir at the helm. In 1738, he invaded and captured Ghazni and Kabul, and moved into India where the Afghan ruler Nasir Khan had been on an expedition. Khan was easily defeated and Nadir Shah advanced across north Punjab to capture Delhi in 1739, and seize the treasures of the Peacock throne, including the *Koh-I-Noor* diamond. He returned to Afghanistan with thousands of captive young men and women, leaving a trail of horror and innumerable atrocities against opponents. (For this Hindus might say his first name Nadir was well chosen!)

Sikh defenders trailed the departing armies and were able to attack their rear, re-capture much of the treasure and release large numbers of captives. Mohamed Shah was reduced to a tributary to Nadir Shah. The region remained in a state of anarchy, peppered with skirmishes led by Afghans, Mughals, Sikhs and Marathas.

Following Rani Tarabai's victory, the Maratha Empire had consolidated the gains previously made by Shivaji. By 1760, they had regained all of central India. But there was much internal squabbling among the Maratha chiefs so that when the Afghan, Ahmed Shah Durrani, also called Abdali, perpetrated another of his raids into Punjab, he was able to overcome the forces of the Maratha military Commander-in-Chief, Sadshivrao Bhau, who was sent from Puné to expel him in 1761. Durrani was a Pashtun, who had succeeded Nadir Shah and founded Afghanistan. The Maratha forces fell at Pānipat, mainly from failure of supplies to troops and horses, which were too exhausted from hunger to complete the final decisive battle against the Islamists! In that battle, lasting eight horrifying hours, up to 200,000 Hindus are said to have been killed, warriors and civilians (see p. 182).

Durrani reinstated Alamgir II as Emperor and left Delhi for Afghanistan, two months after, with his loot of 500 elephants, 1500 camels, 50,000 horses and more than 22,000 women and children. This was not his first such trove. Five years earlier, he had invaded India, established his overlordship of the Mughals, sacked Delhi, removed tons of valuables, installed Shah Alam II on the throne as puppet, and on his way back to Kabul had cavalierly raided the Golden Temple at Amritsar and humiliated the Sikhs by filling its sacred pool with the blood of humans and cattle. Sikhs have not forgiven this abomination. The victory heightened Sikh-Muslim tensions, did nothing to improve the chances for restoration of the Mughal Empire, and placed India once more at the mercy of the most resolute among those competing for her hand.

Babri Mosque constructed on a Temple destroyed by Babur's general Mir Baqi

Chapter 10

"I have given my general command to all the kingdoms and ports of my dominions to receive all the merchants of the English nation..." Jahangir to King James, 1615

The European Raiders

The subsequent capture of India had been charted, unintentionally as it were, a century and a half earlier. In 1588, Queen Elizabeth I of England (ruled 1558-1603) realised her father's dream of English naval superiority, when her navy triumphed over the invading Spanish *Armada*. In 1600, she granted a new company of 216 aristocrats and merchants, headed by the Earl of Cumberland, a Royal Charter to trade exclusively in the vast region between the Cape of Good Hope and the Straits of Magellan, under the rubric *Governor and Company of Merchants of London trading with the East Indies* (the East India Company, EICo, British EICo after 1707[71]). This should assure her a steady supply of India's finest opium, not to mention silks, muslin, spices and other luxuries. Thus began a series of events that led to the brutish subjugation of India, and the seizure of Indian wealth. The Company's actions spared few, even the poorest, from the fury of British greed, which lacked none of the brutality of the Mughals' that it would replace; the British simply substituted foreign thieves for local ones! The Queen's Charter was valid for fifteen years, but the Company became so profitable, and so quickly, that James I in 1609 granted the Charter *"in perpetuity"*![72]

Meanwhile several Dutch merchants—amid lingering hostilities between Holland and Portugal/Spain, which had disrupted their supplies of spices from Portugal to Antwerp—had already realised astronomical profits from pilot ventures trading directly with Indonesia, one trip returning in 1599 realising 400% profit! This and other factors led to the formation in 1602 of the United Dutch East India Company *(VOC Vereenidge Oost-Indische Compagnie),* which obtained a monopoly

---

[71] One of the first known joint stock Company was the *Muscovy Trading Company* that grew in Moscow in 1555 from the *Company of Merchant Adventurers to New Lands* formed in 1551 by English adventurers wishing to profit from new land discoveries and a Northeast Sea route to China. It was granted a monopoly of trade between Moscow and England and a whaling monopoly off Spitsbergen by Elizabeth I in 1577; the trade monopoly ended in 1698 (cf. *below*).

[72] This was annulled in 1694 under pressure of merchants wishing to compete with EICo. In 1698 an *English Company Trading to the East Indies* was formed but EICo quickly bought a controlling interest and the two merged in 1708 as the *United Company of Merchants of England...Indies,* after years of squabbling. Contrast this with Maratha disunity in India at that time and the failure of other Indian leaders to expand education, reform caste issues and involve more people in government.

Charter to trade with Asia and behave independently, even to wage war and establish colonies, in the European tradition. Soon they set up quarters in Batavia (Jakarta), finding it more suitable than Bantam, which was further west and had also become home for the EICo. By this time, Java had come under Muslim influence.

As noted above, Europe had changed significantly since the end of the dark ages, and had advanced in education and geographic exploration, spurred by the need for resources, in times of peace, as in war. Henry VIII's divorce from the Roman Catholic Church brought England a new Church, separating the country from continental Europe, which remained steadfast to Rome, until unsettled by the Reformation and the schisms in 15th century Europe. The Vatican had remained troubled by Muslim expansion, which by the 14th century had consumed Turkey and made it the Western hub of Islam, the Ottoman Empire.

Aftermath of the Battle of Nicopol,1396 CE: Turkish killings of Christians in revenge for the massacres of Turks by Vlad Dracula at Rahova and other sites in Wallachia; he had up to 50,000 Turks impaled (credit: Cristian Chirita)

As in previous centuries, Popes nursed the hope of final victory and encouraged assaults on Islamic states, so that, by the 15th century, a number of new crusades had been fought. Perhaps the bloodiest occurred in the Slavic state of Wallachia, which was a vassal to the

Hungarian Empire that had formed from tribal conquests in Eastern Europe and fragments of the Byzantine Empire. Mehmet II had become caliph of the Ottomans, and Vladimir Dracul(a) the head of Wallachia-Bulgaria, when they clashed. Dracula massacred 22,000 Turks by impalement, including members of the revered Turkish janissaries (*yeniceri*). He followed by killing another 20,000 or more, suffering the inevitable retaliation at the battle of Nicopol. His adventures were the last of the "crusades"; soon after, eastern Europe would be rearranged according to dominant tribes.

European companies, vying for monopoly, fought one another frequently in the Indian Ocean, to eliminate rivals, like brigands, just as they were accustomed to do in Europe. Only the scene had changed and the vastness of the prize. The EICo failed against the Dutch in Java but defeated the Portuguese in 1612 in the *Battle of Swally*. After appropriate diplomatic agreements between King James I and the Mughal Court of Nuruddin Salim Jahangir, mediated by Sir James Roe, EICo received a permit to establish an exclusive factory, i.e. place of business, at Surat, Gujarat, where they had ostensibly been visiting since 1608.

Jehangir wrote to King James in 1615: "*... I have given my general command to all the kingdoms and ports of my dominions to receive all the merchants of the English nation as the subjects of my friend; that in what place soever they choose to live, they may have free liberty without any restraint; and at what port soever they shall arrive, that neither Portugal nor any other shall dare to molest their quiet; and in what city soever they shall have residence, I have commanded all my governors and captains to give them freedom answerable to their own desires; to sell, buy,* and to transport into their country at their pleasure. *For confirmation of our love and friendship, I desire your Majesty to command your merchants to bring in their ships all sorts of rarities and rich goods fit for my palace; and that you be pleased to send me your royal letters by every opportunity, that I may rejoice in your health and prosperous affairs; that our friendship may be interchanged and eternal...*"

With such fulsome and unctuous generosity had Jahangir given to Europe's most avaricious nation, the uncontrolled expropriation of Indian wealth, and its transfer to Britain, which started straight away.

In 1611, EICo set up a trading post at Masulipatam at the mouth of the Krishna River on the south Coromandel Coast of the Bay of Bengal, and soon after, was granted the right to trade. At that time, Europeans had scant knowledge of the cultural, educational or religious attainments of eastern nations, and were themselves barely at the threshold of learning or developing a stable or predictable culture. Their growth had been stormy, with deep tribal conflicts and unremitting enmity between major groups, such as the French and English, and internal conflicts as in Germany. Thus they were not mentally or intellectually ready to deal with new societies, customs or religions, except to abide by strict Christian attitudes of rejection. Ironically, at that time, much of European education had derived from Arab renditions of Hindu science, grammar and mathematics. Latin continued as the language of learning and literature, and tribal European languages did not emerge as literature until the 14th century. The wonders of the great Indian, Persian and Indo-Chinese religious centres were totally unknown to them.

Similarly, South and East Asians knew little of European peoples and tended to welcome them as traders, assuming that peoples who had mastered ocean crossings had similarly developed in social, moral and religious ways. Little did they know that Europe's pagan cultures had to adapt to Roman values that were based on a prophet who was familiar to the historians of Hinduism and Buddhism, and whose mausoleum existed on Indian soil, in Srinagar! That gave Europeans credence to the Indians, even though that knowledge was unknown to them, and remains unacknowledged, despite the evidence so carefully preserved to this day by the Ahmadiyyas of Kashmir (Faber-Kaiser).

By 1652, Europe was entering a period of relative tranquillity, following the *Peace of Westphalia* – a series of treaties held at Osnabruck and Munster which ended Europe's 30 Years' war in the Holy Roman Empire (1618-48), and 80 years of war between Spain and Holland (1568-1648), severing the latter from Spain. In India, the EICo had grown to 23 posts (factories). In 1662, King Charles II of England received Bombay as a gift from the Portuguese, on his marriage to Catherine of Braganza.

In exchange for a large sum, he granted the Company wider latitude – beside trade in textiles, dyes, spices, etc., authorising it also *"to make peace or war with any prince or people not being Christian."* Six years later, he leased Bombay to the EICo for £10 per annum. The Company then developed a post at the site of a village on the Hooghly River, after failing to hold on to the port at Hijli, about 80 miles west, which its Capt. Nicholson had captured in 1687, but the Mughals had regained. The village became the city of Calcutta and the Company's headquarters. It grew as two cities: a white Calcutta of fine homes, parks and clean streets – capped with a palatial mansion for the head of the Company – and a brown Calcutta of overcrowding, squalor and deprivation, ruled with a stingy and iron hand, just like the colonies.[73]

[73] Calcutta, now Kolkata, became the capital of the British Raj until 1911. In 1803, Richard Wellesley built the Governor General's palace as Belvedere House was not opulent enough: *"India should be governed from a palace, not from a country house."* From this base he changed the British role in India from that of traders to brash imperialists. The palace became the Governor's mansion when the capital moved in 1912 to New Delhi, designed as the capital with wide tree-lined streets crowned with a vice-regal palace (*Rashtrapati Bhavan*) and supplemented with luxurious summer lodges in Shimla, all paid for by penniless Indians!

Lacking competitive sea power, the Mughals had come under pressure from the Portuguese, and from Shivaji, the first Indian king to build a navy, and had, as a result, granted the British increasing trade and military concessions in exchange for naval protection. Weakened by conflicting ambitions and infighting, the Mughal Empire was unable to police the English traders who, with new charter powers, openly courted Indian princes, while backing each side in the clashes among Mughal heirs vying to succeed Aurangzeb in 1707. In 1708, Mughals killed Govind Singh, the last Sikh Guru, and Raja Jai Singh II began building observatories in Delhi, Ujjain, Varanasi, Jaipur and Mathura.

The British had by this time clearly shown their intent and had begun to behave more like tricksters than traders and had thus achieved far more freedom than in China, where, for example, the trading season was regulated and foreign merchants confined to three cities only; they, were not allowed within city walls and had to leave at the end of each year. In India, however, they had ingratiated themselves with Mughal rulers at all levels and used the resulting influence to assist favourites. They seized on the chaos among Aurangzeb's successors and influenced the succession. By plotting and other devious acts they acquired territory and *diwanis* which allowed retention of tax collected. One major success was the grant in 1717 by the frail and submissive Emperor Farruqsiyar, Aurangzeb's grandson, of tax-free trading rights in Bengal in exchange for a mere ₹3,000 per year. India's population in 1700 was 167 million.

In both major trading areas, Bengal and the Coromandel Coast, the main rival was the French, who had built trading posts and fortifications at Pondicherry (Puducherry today) on the Coromandel Coast and at Chandrānagar in Bengal, while the British were ensconced in Fort George, Madras, Masulipatam and other Coromandel sites, and in Calcutta and Dhaka in Bengal. The prime object of Bengal trade was cotton and the fine cloths made from it and the vibrant colours that flowed from a sophisticated indigo industry in Bihar and Oudh.

The outbreak of wars among Europeans—the Wars of *Jenkins' Ear* and *Austrian Succession* and the *Seven Years War*—occupied nearly all of Europe, from 1739 to 1763, barring a few short breaks. It spread British-French hostilities to three continents: Europe, Asia (India), America, (including Canada and the Caribbean) and wherever they met on the high seas, creating a real world war.

The rivalry between the two nations had existed for a millennium or more—perhaps an inherent hatred derived from the conquest of Saxon tribes in the fifth century CE by the Salian Franks, forcing their flight to the British Isles, a humiliation that Saxons had nursed into a deep hatred for the Franks, and aggravated by later conquests. In India, each plotted against the other, recruiting to its cause local chieftains, whether Hindu rājas or Muslim rulers, by various stratagems – bribery, deceit, treachery, breaches of contract, coercion, and so on. As wars erupted and raged in Europe, each developed a metastasis in India, manifesting there as three *Carnatic Wars* between 1746 and 1763 and the first Mysore war from 1762 to 1764. At the start, France had captured Madras, but released it in 1748 when the *Treaty of Aix-la-Chapelle* ended the *War of Austrian Succession*.

By 1750, the Mughals had lost much of the west and northwest to the Maratha confederacy, the east to Nawab Alivardi and his successor Siraj ud Daulah, and the south to Nizam ul-Mulk (later Hyderabad), to the Raja Wadeyar of Mysore[74] and Haidar Ali, his commander, who later became Nawab of Mysore. The crumbling Mughal Empire thus provided excellent grounds for shysters and opportunists, who materialised like flies from a faecal dump, led by the British and French, the Dutch having been relegated to an outpost at Negapatam and to Ceylon, after ousting the Portuguese, at the request of the Kandyan King Rajasinghe, and confining them to the western coast of India at Goa, Daman and Diu.

The Portuguese – by then known for cruelty to natives wherever they went, like the Spanish and other Europeans – had committed many atrocities in their quest for cinnamon, which they eventually found in Ceylon, after killing many of the inhabitants of that country. They held fast to Indian territories, like limpets, and profited enormously from the spice trade, until finally driven off by the Indian army in 1961, six years after Portugal had massacred 22 unarmed *satyagrahis* in Goa. In the more than four centuries of their settlement, an enterprising breed of Catholic Indians had arisen, who bore Portuguese and apostolic names, bred inwards and held fast to orthodox Catholic teachings. (They continue to confuse unsuspecting diasporal Indians, who have difficulty making a close connection between their names and faces. And even when they did, they could hardly believe that these dark folks could be such staunch Catholics, knowing the historical violence of that denomination.)

Anglo-French wars in India lasted over six decades, each using agreements, intrigue, bribery and other chicanery, to exploit the ambitions of Indian princes and drag them into conflicts, which allowed the European victor to gain Indian territory, and usurp Indian rights. The wars also forestalled Indian alliances to prevent political and territorial expansion by foreigners. By the time the first Carnatic War had started, the Marathas had gained control of the west and north, and Nawabs, the east and south. Here, the Nizam ul Mulk in Hyderabad had begun a series of skirmishes against his southern neighbour Mysore,

---

[74] This was one of several regional kingdoms that had emerged from the collapse of the Vijayanagara Empire occupying the region of ancient Pandya and Chola.

plotting with the British Company, after initial flirtation with the French, who sided with Haider Ali of Mysore and Shinde of Gwalior, a Maratha ally. Anglo-French hostilities became a contest for control of South India, and thus untold wealth, which, to Richard Wellesley (Lord Mornington) in 1800, was ample replacement for the US loss.

In the *first Carnatic war,* the English roughneck, Robert Clive, had emerged as a natural soldier. Seemingly bipolar in personality, he had come to India as a BEICo clerk, was imprisoned by the French in Madras in 1746, and came to the notice of army commander Major Lawrence by escaping to Fort St David. This earned him a commission as ensign which lapsed with the 1748 *Treaty of Aix-la-Chapelle* that ended the *War of Austrian Succession.* France saved some face in regaining Louisburg on Cape Breton Island, Canada, in exchange for Madras (Chennai).

Returning to the Company, Clive took up its cause, in the conflicts among the Islamic rulers of Hyderabad, in which merchants jostled for the huge spoils of war and the revenues from trade monopoly and territorial control. In 1751, Clive, then 26, was made a Captain by Lawrence, and distinguished himself as a military leader, capturing the fort at Arcot that year. He received signal honours in England and went there in 1753, returning two years later as governor of Fort St David.

In Bengal, Siraj ud Daulah had succeeded his grandfather Alivardi Khan as Nawab. He protested British expansion at Fort William and elsewhere and their sheltering of treasury thieves; he resented their tax-free status given by a naive Emperor, heedless of British duplicity and indifference to Indian welfare. (Tax exemption had traditionally applied in pre-conquest India to Brahmins and certain Kshatriyas for teaching or performing public service, or in the case of Kshatriyas, defending the realm. But they had managed to enjoy the exemption even when they were freely participating in businesses, and often quite wealthy.)

The British responded to Siraj's order to stop their illegal property seizures by waving the Emperor's *firman* across his face, affirming its legality in *English* law![75] They ignored him and continued as before. Siraj decided to drive them out of Bengal, captured the fort at Calcutta in 1756, and held some prisoners overnight in a small room, where some were overcome by heat. The incident received exaggerated publicity in Britain with an inflated number of victims, as related by a captive, Holwell, enough to fire the British with revenge. The captives were held in a room said to be 23 x 20 sq.ft or 20 x 20 sq.ft or, as others guessed, 20 x 12 sq.ft. According to Holwell, 146 men were held overnight and only 23 survived. But there were 190 soldiers in the battle, of whom 95 were killed and 95 imprisoned. Yet Holwell blithely inflated the number taken

---

[75] Compare similar tactics of British agents in Africa, against Zulus, and in America.

to 146, knowing that nationalistic sentiments in England would favour his lie and bring him profit[76]. He thus concocted a grim tale of cruelty which he related and gained immediate fame and fortune, when the British East India Co. exploited its propaganda value to gain government support for its land grab in Bengal and on the Coromandel Coast.

So great was the depth of racial and religious bias that Holwell could have claimed the torture of thousands that night, in total disregard of the truth. In like vein, the British would announce in 1792 that French rebels had killed 12,000 in Verdun, when the true number was 1,200. They used this to dissuade ordinary British citizens from thinking of rebellion as an end to their woes, urging them instead to give thanks that they had a stable government and that they were living in England!

Clive was sent to Bengal to oust the Nawab. In 1757, his army and naval forces regained Calcutta and took the French post at nearby Chandrānagar, as an extension of the *Seven Years' War*. From there, he moved to attack the Nawab at his capital Murshidabad. Meanwhile Siraj had led a force out of the city, having arranged with Mir Jafar, his grand-uncle and head of his main army, to flank Clive and attack upon his signal. Siraj met Clive at Pilashi (Plessey), unaware that Jafar had conspired with Clive to betray him, in return for the position of Nawab of Bengal, Bihar and Orissa. On his grand-nephew's signal at a crucial point in the battle, Mir Jafar led the main army *away* from the fray, instead of attacking the vulnerable British force. Siraj lost and was later captured and murdered.

Mir Jafar would earn the opprobrium of history and the label of traitor *(gaddar-e-abrar)*, joining the parade of Indian leaders, like Jaichandra 550 or so years earlier, and many Rajputs, and other traitors since, who had sold their country for brief personal gain. Thus Bengal fell to the Company and gave the British a stronghold and base for the subsequent campaigns to seize India. Clive became Governor of Bengal and Jafar the Nawab. His treachery was bitter-sweet. He had to pay compensation of £3 million sterling to the Company, £1.5 million for military expenses, plus other settlements totalling a further £1 million! In 1760, Jafar was deposed in favour of his son-in-law, Mir Qasim, by Clive's successor, Henry Vansittart. By this time, the Mughals had lost most of central, west and north India and Orissa to the Marathas, but held on to control of Delhi and Oudh, tenuously.

As the *Seven Years War* intensified, the French had planned to invade England, having abandoned a similar plan in 1744 (ironically, from

[76] Germany's Goebbels used propaganda during WWII to misinform for political and military ends, but the British preceded and out-performed him in India, as the use of this, and the Verdun incident, by the BEICo illustrates.

Dunkirk, 200 years before WWII allies landed *at* Dunkirk to liberate France from Germany! France laid siege to Madras late in 1758-9, but retreated on the arrival of a British fleet, giving Britain a victory, one of a string worldwide that included Wolfe's defeat of Champlain in Québec; naval victories near Lagos, Portugal; at Quiberon, Bay of Biscay; and others in Europe and the Caribbean. With so much going their way elated Britons dubbed 1759 *Annus mirabilis,* the Wonderful Year, much to the joy of PM William Pitt, the elder.

Robert Clive and Mir Jafar (gaddar-e-abrar) after the Battle of Plassey, 1757
(National Portrait Gallery)

The defeat of France in Canada and India gained Britain two rich prizes and led to the *Treaty of Paris,* ending France's power overseas. France was allowed to keep its trading base at Chandrānagar and posts on the Coromandel and Malabar coasts, but could not keep an army. Bengal was the richest province of India then, with a large population of some 30 million, who bore the burden of paying the oppressive taxes levied by the Company and Nawab. Its capture and control, free of French interference, laid the foundation on which Company agents: Clive, Hastings, Cornwallis, Wellesley and others, indemnified by the Crown, would begin to subdue the rest of India, by arms, conspiracies and treaties, for the next hundred years, and effect King Charles' arrogant order of 1662: *"to make war"* on any prince who was *"not Christian"*. Clive and Hastings were the early leaders among a host of amoral officers in an immoral Company who lied, cheated and abused trade agreements to seize Indian lands from rightful rulers, replacing trading pacts with outright land theft and military overthrow.

From secure bases, the Company's militia—made up, by a curious irony, largely of Indian *sipahis* (sepoys)—launched excursions under Clive and others to seek greater treasures inland. Thus the Company that had been allowed to trade, stayed to raid deep into Indian territory, aided and abetted by the decadence of Mughal rulers and the creeping collapse of their Empire, which had already ceded certain eastern regions to the Company, and others in the west, south and north to the Maratha Confederacy.

This duplicitous behaviour was already well-known and glorified in British leadership circles, where intrigue and in-fighting among the aristocracy had become an art form, titles a coveted end for the aspiring middle-class, while the tortured poor were left to rot in the slums of London and every major British city, providing a wealth of material for cartoonists, and novelists like Charles Dickens, to exploit. Many Company protagonists would earn titles and extract great wealth from India, through deceit and subterfuge. Surprisingly, few would have to endure the ignominy of having their dirty work dragged into the English limelight, with ten thousand miles of protective buffer, and that only rarely, when honest men sought justice. Hastings, one of the most evil of Englishmen, was impeached for treason, but acquitted, earning British adulation for territorial gain, and the hatred of India's millions.

While Clive schemed with Muslim rulers to dispossess the Emperor in the south, Hastings sought the same in the Ganga and Yamuna valleys and central India. In 1764, he defeated a disjointed alliance of Mughal Emperor Shah Alam II, Mir Qasim of Bengal and the Nawab Jala-ud-din Shoja of Oudh, at Buxar in Bihar, which gave the Company control of the lower Ganga River. Hastings extracted from Shah Alam the *diwani* of Bengal (or right to levy land and business taxes), which allowed the Company to fund military adventures and send remittances home to satisfy the lavish lifestyles of Company aristocrats.

The effect of this fulsome generosity was to impoverish rural India and by extension, cities, by gutting the system of local government that had developed to a high degree over millennia throughout pre-Mughal India (described in *Smritis* and *Mahābhārata*). Each village was governed by an annually elected *pānchāyat* (council of five), which had evolved from individual *sabhās* (assemblies). Pānchāyats were responsible for all village affairs, including land allocation and other executive and judicial functions, including tax collection for the kingdom. Regional and municipal councils (*janapadas* and *nagara sabhas*), with appropriate supervisory and executive functions, intervened between the village and the central government. The Mughals dismantled this structure and created governors or large landlords—possessors with or without ownership—to manage the land and remit to the emperor a portion of its revenues, and usurped the authority of the *pānchāyats*. This system was prone to corruption by officials. Hastings allegedly gained from it.

His successor, Lord Cornwallis, used Pitt's India Act of 1786 to create the system of *"permanent settlements"* which vested lands in *zamindars* (landowning aristocrats), whose tax collectors (*tehsildars*) administered the properties (except police services); they taxed individual holdings *(ryotwari)*, districts *(mahalwari)*, and remitted the appropriate amount to Government. Police, judicial and other services were provided from a central or regional pool, as appropriate.

The British destroyed all local land registries and substituted an official *(patwari)*, who kept records for several villages, and found it easy to falsify these to his advantage, especially when he had, as allies, an equally crooked buyer and magistrate to legitimise land deals. The rigid hierarchy ensured that the villagers kept within their class limits, remained enfeebled, reduced to slavery, with no political representation to address grievances. Thus local rulers stifled complaints from the poor, and even reduced the chances of insurrection.

The system had removed a known area of official corruption among Company officers, but created another far more vicious, and it enabled the Company and its landowners to acquire and use lands to maximise profit, regardless of the people's needs for food. Thus commercial crops supplanted rice and wheat, the major food crops, placing millions at risk in times of famine, people who still had to feed themselves and pay taxes, though deprived of the means to do so! Zamindars became wealthier and with the connivance of officials soon found ways to acquire and commercialise land—a new development for Bengal.

British administrators exploited the fickle and corrupt behaviour of some Indian rulers, and generally reviled all Indians as perfidious, maligning them thus in Britain, where they stood defenceless, to justify enforced changes to Indian society and education e.g. closing village schools. Sir William Jones, encouraged by Warren Hastings, made telling remarks in 1786 re Sanskrit that forced serious attention to India's treasury of learning, science, religion and literature: *"The Sanscrit (sic) language, whatever be its antiquity, is of a wonderful structure; more perfect than the Greek, more copious than the Latin, and more exquisitely refined than either, yet bearing to both of them a stronger affinity, both in the roots of verbs and the forms of grammar, than could possibly have been produced by accident; so strong indeed, that no philologer could examine them all three, without believing them to have sprung from some common source...both the Gothic and the Celtic, though blended with a very different idiom, had the same origin with the Sanscrit; and the old Persian might be added to the same family."*

Charles Watkins' ground-breaking translation of the *Bhagavad Gita* in 1785 astonished European scholars and spread it to America. Its unique philosophy exposed the dishonour and evil of mindless materialism that Europeans practised globally, and incited the British into astonishing levels of rapacity, self-serving and brutality, in the 19th and 20th centuries, in India and the colonies. The *Gita* would later empower Gandhi in his strategy to achieve freedom for India.

The events of the three and a half centuries following the British arrival in India illustrate the evils of human behaviour when one nation or group seeks total dominion over others. The worst emerges when the targets are deemed to be an inferior colour, race or religion. The conduct of the British in India belied the teachings of Christ, whose name gave them purpose and justification, just as Islamists cited Mohamed. A few acts of compassion and petty kindnesses, usually outside of government, were excessively glorified, while the masses suffered.

The hegemony of the BEICo expanded on the basis of conquest, flaunting Parliament often—such was the power and stature of the directors. It savaged the land further, exploited ambitions and caste and fomented wrangling among Indian kings and regions, led by a ruthless succession of imperialists: Wellesley, Curzon, Dalhousie, and others, who systematically proceeded to loot Indian kingdoms and *transfer their wealth to Britain.* Not content, they imposed heavy taxes on Indian production, enterprise and labour, dispossessed millions, impoverished a hundred times that, and began the importation of Britons to do the work of Indians in *India's* civil and military services, at rates of pay far in excess of any in Britain or in India. So blatant were the abuses that Tom Paine was moved to say, in 1792, *"The Government of England is as great as, if not the greatest perfection of fraud and corruption that ever took place since Governments began."* In 1813, the BEICo's own charter noted, *"The Empire ought to be a moral undertaking rather than a wholesale looting by either the EICo or its servants"*.[77] But neither criticism changed the transgressions of the British or the extent of corruption of Indian princes by Company officers. Thus were the generations of British carpetbaggers fattened—as H. Hyndman, a UK parliamentarian called them a century later—and on retirement would sponge on Indian peoples almost in perpetuity.

[77] "Wherever it was possible to put in an Englishman to oust a native an Englishman has been put in, and has been paid from four times to twenty times as much for his services as would have sufficed for the salary of an equally capable Hindoo or Mohammedan official." *(Sen. WJ Bryan, US presidential candidate, 1903)*

The three Carnatic Wars had ended in 1763, with the French restricted to merchandising at Chandränagar (Bengal), Pondicherry, Karaikal, Yanam (Coromandel Coast) and Mahé (Malabar Coast), although they maintained connections with individual rulers, especially Tippu Sultan of Mysore and Raja Shindia of the Maratha Confederacy. The Nizam of Hyderabad was fattened with additional lands taken from the Marathas in the west and Mysore in the south and would remain unshakably loyal to the British until 1947, having been sweetened with the title of *Most Faithful*! [78]

Hastings, Clive, Cornwallis

The naval Canon shot, the hallmark of the 18-19th CE European naval supremacy

[78] The Nizam made TIME cover in 1937 as the World's richest man. In WWI--with millions of his subjects in poverty and lacking even basic education--he had financed an air squadron for the British forces, and later purchased a destroyer, which was turned over, fully equipped, to the Royal *Australian* Navy!

The Chain of Being (Scala naturae)

Image by Didacus Valades in *Retorica Christiana*, 1579. Lines by John Milton:
"The scale of nature set/From centre to circumference,/ whereon/In contemplation of created things By steps we may ascend to God. Paradise Lost 5.509-12)*
This scale of beings was based on the notion that everything was created by God in a strict hierarchy, from God, Higher Angels, Lower Angels, Humans, Birds, Fish, Animals, Plants, Inanimate Objects. This scale was staunchly followed in Elizabethan times and up to today, though much diluted and challenged except by fundamentalists. It was promoted by Plato, Aristotle and others. Thomas Aquinas ranked all things, from God to sand or dirt; Linnaeus put all species and things into three broad classes and Haeckel developed a biological scale from amoeba to man. All women, excepting Elizabeth I, were considered to be inferior to men. Caste is an expression of this scale. A secondary heirarchy existed by religion, race and colour, with ignominy heaped on Jews, heathens and Blacks. The Commoners, not to be outdone, had their own levels, as Tomas Nash in 1593 said, "*The Courtier disdaineth the citizen;/the citizen the countryman;/the shoemaker the cobbler./But unfortunate is the man who does not have anyone he can look down upon!*"It was everyone's duty to accept one's place in this chain, and gain reward from God. Disruption would lead to chaos. It is expressed in several of Shakespeare's plays, e.g., Hamlet, Henry V, Macbeth, King Lear and others. Note fallen angels in right margin and hell at bottom! (image credit to *Lhademmor*)

Shivaji, founder of Maratha Empire

L: Mir Jafar who betrayed Siraj ud Daulah allowing British to gain Bengal, with his eldest son, Mir Miran.
R: Jāt officer in British army, 14th Murrays Lancers, AC Lovett (1862-1919)
Below Left: Madhu Rao Narayan, the Maratha Peshwa with Bitlur and attendants, Puné, 1792 by James Wales
Below Right: Sri Aurobindo, 19th CE

Chapter 11

"As I have often said in public, India is, in fact, now governed by successive relays of English carpet-baggers, who have as little sympathy with the natives as they have any real knowledge of their habits and customs." Henry Hyndman, quoted by WJ Bryan 1898

The Maratha Wars; Holkar

In 1773, following revisions to the Company Charter by the British Government, Hastings was made Governor General of Company territories in India which then comprised Bengal, Bihar, parts of the Carnatic, and lands around Bombay, in addition to tributaries of Oudh and Benares. On acquiring Bengal, the Company raised taxes from 10% to 50% of the value of produce. It also diverted agriculture to commercial crops like cotton, opium poppy and indigo, instead of rice and other grains. Food shortages soon began, aggravated by Hastings' prohibition of the Indian practice of storing a portion of annual harvests (cf. modern Monsanto seed retention embargo!). A famine followed, reaching its peak in 1770, and lasted several years, killing some 10 million people, during which Hastings raised taxes an extra 10%! He did little to help the hungry masses during their suffering and silent calls for aid, their lands seized in lieu of tax, millions dying of starvation.

Needing money to pay for the southern wars, Hastings extorted huge sums from Prince Chait Sing of the prosperous Varanāsi kingdom and from the Begum of Oudh, which had come under Company protection. Varanāsi seemed attractive as a new territorial acquisition, so, using Singh's fear of the army, he coldly and ruthlessly took advantage of the confusion generated by the decline of Mughal power and the breakaway of kingdoms, to seize rich territories and create vassal states or outright possessions. Even before actual conquest, the relationship was corrupt and dictatorial, in which Hastings ordered unjustified levies payable to the Company.[79] By repeated demands of increasing cash sums, he planned to force a Rāja or Nawab to reach a point where the demand would force him to protest; Hastings would deem such protest as criminal non-compliance punishable by territorial seizure! He firmly believed in the primacy and right of force and deception to settle disputes, and on absolute rights to lands won by "conquest", however contrived or fraudulent or evil!

---

[79] *"I resolved to draw from his (Raja Cheyte Sing) guilt (for attempting to break away) the means of relief of the Company's distresses, to make him pay largely for his pardon, or to exact a severe vengeance for past delinquency,"* Hastings said, and took a bribe of £20,000 from Chait Singh but revealed it when it appeared his bosses might find out! So distrustful were they of their rulers that citizens did not readily come to their aid, allowing people like Hastings to get away with coercion, trespass, exploitation and theft.

In Bengal, he was implicated in the death sentencing of one Nanda Kumar, who had accused him of corruption. In Puné, he plotted with Raghunathrao, who craved the Maratha throne, after the murder of his nephew Narayan Rao, the youthful *Péshwé*, in 1773, an act instigated by Anandabai, Raghunath's wife. Raghunath displaced the natural heir, Narayanrao`s infant son, Madhavrao, and ruled for a year until deposed by a council of twelve (*Barbhai mandal*), led by Maratha Finance Minister Nana Phadnavis. Raghunath fled to Bombay and plotted with the BEICo to conclude the deceitful *"Treaty of Surat"*, by which he would regain the Maratha throne as a Company subsidiary, in exchange for Bassein and Salsette, near Bombay. At this time, Phadnavis had allowed the French access to a Maratha port, as was his right. But this the BEICo resented.

Calcutta rejected the *Treaty of Surat;* a new one was signed which Bombay rejected, and sent Coronel Keatinge to seize Puné. A Maratha force under Haripant Phadke stopped him; Hastings seized the opportunity to retaliate. This first *Anglo-Maratha War* ended with a Maratha victory and Bombay had to return all lands previously annexed. In waging war, Hastings was merely continuing the campaign of bullying, intrigue, bribery and theft that had gained the Company Bengal, lands in the south and in the Ganga valley, and aimed to procure and control more Indian lands.

Financial difficulties from plotting, war-mongering, a trade deficit with China, and a lull in the European economy forced Parliament to pass the Tea Act in 1773, which allowed the Company to sell tax-free tea to America without restriction. The taxation provisions led to a revolt among American merchants, the *Boston Tea Party,* and three years later, as taxes were still in place, the American Declaration of Independence. British losses in America pushed expansion in India, facilitated by French distraction by Rousseau's *The Rights of Man,* and the suspension of royal wars, as France's multitudes finally rose in hungry revolt.

By 1758, Mysore had come under Haidar Ali, the hereditary Raja Wadeyar's military commander, and an ally of France. Aided by the Nizam of Hyderabad and the Marathas, BEICo began a series of actions, the four Mysore wars, against him and his son Tippu Sultan. Ali had a cancer and died suddenly in 1783, at the cusp of victory in the second war, which Tippu carried on to win, but at the cost of abandoning a killing and conversion campaign against Hindus on the Malabar Coast. By the treaty of Mangalore in 1784, each side returned captured lands.

The 3rd Mysore War saw action by Lt. Gen Charles Cornwallis, "fresh" from his 1781 surrender to George Washington at Yorktown, Va., which had ended the American War of Independence. He was made Governor General of India in 1786, replacing Hastings. He dismissed the

British commander and forged an alliance with Hyderabad and Bajirao II, the Maratha Péshwé. Together they besieged Tippu Sultan's capital and forced him to sign the *Treaty of Srirangapatnam* which cost him half his kingdom, which the three victors duly shared. This was an incredible event, where two major Indian kingdoms had joined the foreign invader and despot to defeat a third Indian kingdom, also despotic, to advance the invader's agenda of Indian conquest! Indian rulers behaved just like Europeans, whose rulers readily changed loyalty to the stronger king to ensure continuity of power. Religious beliefs often prevented this treachery.

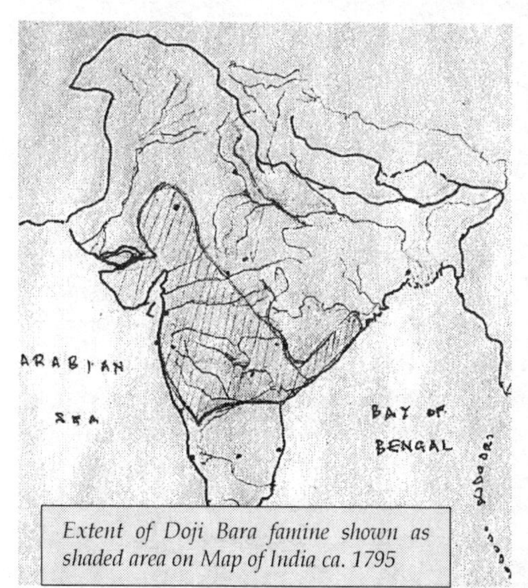

Extent of Doji Bara famine shown as shaded area on Map of India ca. 1795

The great famine of 1791-92 that afflicted Gujarat, Rajasthan, the Marathas, Hyderābad and parts of Karnataka—known as the *Doji Bara* or Skull famine, from the numerous human skulls found unburied at affected sites—was due to severe droughts lasting from 1789 to 1795 CE, caused by failure of monsoons following a major El Niño occurrence. William Roxburgh, a Scottish BEICo surgeon and botanist, was the first British officer to record the climatic details. Droughts due to failure of monsoons had been well known to Indians who had traditionally stored grain for use in such lean years. Hastings had stopped this prudent practice, as well as the customary transfer of grain from unaffected areas to those in need.

At the time of the *doji bara* and other famines, grain was available elsewhere in India but the authorities preferred to continue exports to Britain (see p 310.) Famines had also become more frequent since the British occupation, largely attributable to unwise storage prohibitions and land use practices, dictated by Hastings' seizure of agricultural lands, impoverishment of farmers and switch to commercial non-food farms: cotton, opium, sugarcane, dyes and so on, as already noted.

During his term, which ended in 1793, Cornwallis reformed taxation and administration, eliminating certain corrupt practices of company officials and gave some small aid to the working class, but he was openly racist. Cornwallis wrote of Euro-Indians, "*...on account of their colour and extraction they are considered in this country as inferior to Europeans, I am of opinion that those of them who possess the best abilities could not command that* *authority and respect which is* (sic) *necessary in the due discharge of the duty of an officer"*. Consider this with the concurrent French declaration of equality and the extraordinary careers of two coloured West Indian cavalry generals in the French Army of that time, both with titled fathers. One was the illustrious Count Alex Dumas (Alexandre Antoine Davy de la Pailleterie), Napoleon's contemporary and the father of Alexandre Dumas, the great novelist, who wrote about his father's exploits as France's greatest and most honest general of that time. Racial bigotry replaced *"equality"* when Napoleon became emperor. General Dumas, whom Napoleon envied, was denied the *Legion d'Honneur*, despite his startling successes in Napoleonic campaigns in Italy, Austria and Egypt, some of which Napoleon claimed! Dumas, dispirited and wounded after two years in a Taranto jail, was refused further commissions, and given a small pension. He died at age 40 from cancer (? stomach)"[80] (Weiss).

At that time, the commercial rewards of labour exploitation overrode any notions of morality, and abuse of workers was common and probably the rule in Britain. This saw its worst expression in the excesses of the Slave trade and the horrible treatment meted out to slaves, especially Africans, who were taken in millions to the Americas. All Europeans participated, the Portuguese, French and the British foremost. Employers, and indeed all sectors of British society, accepted slavery and the trade that it sustained on both coasts of Africa, the West being the more heavily publicised and greater in volume, since it supplied the Americas. A small, but increasingly influential group of Britons, including nine Quakers and two Anglicans, campaigned against the trade and the practice. Protests were made, altogether for some two hundred years, but met heavy opposition, before Parliament outlawed the trade in 1807, and the practice in 1834, but it continued covertly.

During its heyday, many prominent politicians, particularly in the trading ports of Liverpool, Bristol, Southampton, London and so on, profited from it. One of the most prominent was the Lord Mayor of London, William Beckford, England's first millionaire, who owned sugar estates in Jamaica. The horrors of the middle passage were dismissed as *"They're only Blacks!"* John Newton, a conservative Christian convert, and later anti-slavery activist, exemplified British businessmen when he said *"(I) never had the least scruple as to its (slave trade) lawfulness.... It is indeed accounted a genteel employment, and is usually very profitable."* Newton in 1747, considered blasphemy his biggest sin, not slavery! (Hochschild). He was not alone in this view.

---

[80] A statue of the tall handsome Gen. Dumas was erected in 1913 in Place Malherbes, Paris, after a fund-raising campaign by Sarah Bernhardt, Anatole France and others. Hitler destroyed it in the hope of cleansing history of "undesirable" races, showing his ignorance of racial mixing in Europe since time began. Hopefully modern France will resurrect him.

Blacks were dehumanised to the point that even otherwise caring individuals discounted them and thought little of treating them worse than work animals. Even the best-selling author, ex-slave and anti-slavery activist Olaudah Equiano, who convincingly displayed all the highest attributes of the civilised, was reviled by opponents of the Anti-Slavery movement. His book, *The Interesting Narrative of the Life of Olaudah Equiano, or Gustavus Vassa the African,* was widely distributed, and had helped him to earn an engagement to coach white reformers!

Eventually, Wilberforce's bill succeeded and Parliament ended the trade. But slavery persisted and sugar was boycotted, prompting importers of Indian sugar to label theirs: *"East India sugar, not made by Slaves"!* How slight the difference between the two would remain hidden as long as British aristocrats and their minions kept control over the news and its dissemination. The importance of this was seen in the campaign, as planters found ship captains to testify about the salubrious, congenial and holiday-like atmosphere on slave ships, which might have delayed or scuttled the bill, were it not for Equiano's powerful retort. Yet it was not easy sailing. The onset of the French revolution, the French abolition of slavery, the revolt in St Domingue (Haiti), British planters' branding anti-slavery action as French—and thus to be shunned—plus Admiral Nelson's support of slavery, caused at least ten years of delay before the trade was ended.

In previous decades in India, Robert Clive had won Bengal, Warren Hastings had consolidated the British presence and Cornwallis had added to British-controlled territory and alliances. In his turn, Richard Wellesley, who succeeded Sir John Shore in 1798 as Governor General, promptly set about to remove all traces of French political influence, subvert the rule of Indian kings, and expand territory, with considerable and decisive help, as noted, from the Indians themselves. Traditional tribal ambitions, inter-regal rivalries, and the valour of the hundreds of thousands of Indian soldiers (*sipahi,* sepoys) sustained his cause.

In 1799, Wellesley started the fourth Mysore War by sending his brother, Arthur Wellesley, later Duke of Wellington, and General Harris to attack Tippu Sultan, who had been negotiating with Napoleon, then in Egypt. Negotiations ended abruptly when Rear Admiral Horatio Nelson defeated the French fleet at the *Battle of the Nile,* which ended the formal French threat to BEICo. Still, Harris and Wellesley invaded Mysore and besieged the capital. Tippu was betrayed in this war by one of his commanders, Mir Sadiq, who, bribed by the British, removed his forces from the defence of the city wall, at the height of the battle, by sending them to collect wages! The lull in the defence allowed the attackers to break the wall and enter the city. Rushing to the scene, Tippu was killed.

His death gave the Company control of South India directly, and indirectly, through forced treaties with weak, confused, divided and greedy local princes. A few exceptions stood out, like the popular and valiant Pazhassi Raja of Kerala. One by one, over the next decades, they fell victims to Wellesley's scheme of "*Subsidiary Alliances*" for conquered states, whereby the native ruler would continue his rule, disband his forces, accept a resident British officer, pay tribute and maintain a Company army! On Tippu's death Mysore became one such, under the older Wadeyar rulers. The death of this genocidal Islamic tyrant was a small exchange for the killing and forced conversion of so many Hindus.

Meanwhile, major changes had taken place in west, central and north India with formation and expansion of the Maratha Empire and its successor Confederacy (1674-1820), which by 1760 had developed the capacity to rid India of all foreigners. It had begun with Shivaji Bhosle's campaigns that established the Maratha Empire. The capital was at Raigad, later moved to Sātārā, restoring Maratha sovereignty over ancestral lands. Shivaji had followed in the footsteps of his father Shahaji Bhosle who had, like Rajput princes, a long and brilliant career as a prince/general in the armed services of Mughals and Nizams of west and south India: Ahmednagar, Vijapur, and Golconda. His abiding ambition was to recapture Maratha lands from the Mughals, restore the Hindu kingdoms of India, curb political meddling by foreign merchants and confine them to trading posts, as China had done. He had passed on this ambition to his sons, Sambhaji, Shivaji and Venkoji, operating from their family base at Puné. From here, Shivaji (1632-1680), brother Sambhaji and their dedicated forces of hardy warriors set out to conquer the sultanate of Vijapur, which had usurped Maratha lands. Sambhaji was killed in the battle of Kanakgiri, in 1654.

Shivaji had seen military action at age ten, when his reign officially began, and after two years of formal training in Bangalore, starting at 12, had returned to Puné. At age 16, he led the first assaults against Vijapur with a series of daring raids, using guerrilla tactics (*ganimi kava),* similar to those used by Pratap Singh a century earlier, to which he added innovations. He captured Fort Torna after a long and arduous campaign, with many ups and downs, including near-death events, and, in battles that have become legendary, he triumphed over the much larger forces of the Sultan Adilshah.

He reorganised the army, developed a navy that challenged the British and Portuguese, established a council of ministers (*ashtrapradhān mandal*) and encouraged public participation in government. He became a popular, virtuous and exemplary ruler, inspiring his people to greatness, with achievements that placed him among the most illustrious of Indian rulers and Maratha's best. Swami Vivekānanda called him "the very incarnation of Lord Shiva." He was crowned king in 1674, with the title of *Chhatrapati* (king of the Kshatriyas). When he died in 1680 from a febrile illness, thought to be Anthrax, control shifted to the *Péshwé* (Prime Minister) in Puné—a position Shivaji's father, Shahaji, had created in 1640, which would become hereditary in 1749.

Soon after Shivaji's death, the Mughal Emperor, Aurangzeb, began a series of frenetic invasions of the Deccan, with the largest army the world had yet seen—500,000 men and some 400,000 animals—to destroy the Marathas and their new king, Sambhaji, Shivaji's son, who had given asylum to Akbar, Aurangzeb's rebel son. Fortunes fluctuated in the many battles that followed; Sambhaji and his talented generals, led by Hambirrao Mohite and Péshwé Moropant Pingle, harassed Mughal forces, waged successful wars against Chikka Devraj, Wadeyar of Mysore, and punished the Portuguese in Goa for assisting the Mughals.

In 1689, on the eve of an offensive against the Mughals in the Deccan Sambhaji was betrayed by a brother-in-law, Ganoji Shirke, captured, tortured for forty days and executed by hanging and quartering. His younger brother, Rajaram, succeeded him, and, with seasoned generals, Santaji Ghorpade and Dhanaji Jadhav, withstood another decade of Mughal assaults. When Rajaram died in 1700, his widow, Rani Tarabai, carried on and defeated Aurangzeb in 1705, expelling the Mughals and heralding their fall in India. Aurangzeb retreated to Delhi, ill and heavily in debt, and died soon after, aged 90.

The decline of the Mughals facilitated new and intense political and military activity, by the Marathas and the British, to gain control of larger territories. For many decades of the 18th century, it had seemed that the Marathas—communities of warriors and cultivators—might succeed in uniting India, especially since the efforts of Péshwé Bajirao I had brought under their control all of the former Empire of Harshavardhan plus the Maratha lands of the western Deccan.

Shivaji and successors—Sambhaji, Rajaram and his wife Rani Tarabai, Shahu (Shambhaji's son), and Rajaram II—and their appointed Péshwés, enlisted *sardars* (generals) and princes from all parts of India. The most dynamic of the Maratha commanders, the most expert after Shivaji and perhaps the first to really believe that the conquest of the Mughals was imminent was Bajirao I, the fourth Péshwé at Puné, appointed in 1719, age only 20, by Chhatrapati Shahuji. He fought the Mughals continuously in 41 battles, winning all, until his sudden death in 1740 of a "fever", cf. Shivaji. Whether this was heat stroke or a virulent infection or poisoning requires details. His death was a great loss to India, and at a critical time, when it was still possible to expel both Mughals and British, militarily. His strategic skills were so impressive that Field Marshal Bernard Montgomery wrote, in *The Concise History of Warfare*, (1972), *"The Palkhed campaign of 1727-8 in which Bajirao I out-generalled Nizam ul Mulk is a masterpiece of strategic mobility."*[82]

By then, his brother Chimaya Appa had evicted the Portuguese from the Arabian coast settlements, except Goa, and he had put the Maratha Empire on a solid footing, well-placed to expel the British, but for one lapse which his premature death left uncorrected. He had appointed local generals as interim rulers of conquered lands but did not establish a controlling and coordinating authority to assist the Péshwé to organise militarily, regulate and administer government, as Ashoka had done, and to prevent bribery, power struggles, subversion, backsliding or treachery, as foreign inducements with quick wealth might accomplish.

Bajirao I

With Bajirao's death, regional governors and urban chieftains were left "on their honour", as it were, free to form alliances to feed desires for personal power, even before they had expelled the foreigners. Some of this conceit flowed from individual military prowess and reflected the same over-confidence that had allowed Islamists to conquer India. Several leaders squabbled within families and among themselves, usually for power, and seemed to have lacked the geo-political insight and vision of a larger India shared by Bajirao I, Shivaji and Shahaji.

Maratha victories had made regional leaders semi-autonomous: the

[82] "Remember that night has nothing to do with sleep. It was created by God to raid territory held by your enemy; the night is your shield, your screen against cannons and swords of vastly superior enemy forces." Bajirao to his brother, Chimaji Appa.

Shindes at Ujjain and Gwalior, Holkars at Indaur, Gaekwads at Baroda, Bhonsles at Nagpur, Dabhade, Bhosale and others, working with the Péshwé, Nanasaheb, at Puné. Allied with other leaders from Rajasthan, Maharashtra and Central India: Pawar (Parmar), a Rajput chieftain, Pandit, Panse, Pantpratinidhi, Patwardhan, Pethe, Phadke, Purandar, Raste, Vinchurkar and many others, they expanded the Empire to its greatest extent, and by 1760 had captured most of the Mughal-ruled territories, amounting to over two million sq.km., and controlled Delhi and the Deccan. They were poised to drive the British from India, from territories they had seized in Bengal and Bihar and from those they occupied in and near Bombay (Mumbai).

This failed, when Maratha Commander Shadshivarao Bhau (p. 158) lost to Ahmad Shah Durrani in 1761 at Pānipat, three years before the Anglo-French war for domination of the Coromandel Coast, the Indian extension of Europe's *Seven Years War*. Péshwé Nanasaheb had sent Maratha forces under Shadshivarao Bhau to repel Ahmad Shah Durrani, returning for another raid through Punjab and the north. Unaccustomed to northern conditions, politics or wars, Shadshivarao chose to confront Durrani without making alliances with local rulers, Hindus and Muslims, and to ensure his supply lines for a long campaign. He may even have upset some Rajput rulers. Burdened with many civilian camp-followers, his supplies ran out, under siege.

Durrani had been invited by the Mughal courtier, Shah Waliullah, to invade India and erase the "industrious and adaptable" Hindus, whom Waliullah openly hated. He was an extremist disciple of Abdul al Wahhab, whom he had met in Arabia on a hajj and study visit in 1726-30. He even claimed Arabic ancestry, so fanatical he had become, in craving an Islamic state. Durrani had allied with Indian sultans Suja ud Doula, Najib ud Doula and Hafiz Rahmat Khan, who had agreed to oppose the Marathas, in Islamic solidarity. After weeks of starvation under siege, the weakened Maratha soldiers and horses engaged the enemy, fought bravely for over eight hours of close combat, and had the upper hand until the death of Vishwarao, the Péshwé's son, created great confusion among Marathas. Trying to rally the men, Shadshivarao Bhau and the cream of Maratha generals were killed, including four of the five sons of Shinde, and up to 200,000 Hindus, including camp-followers and pilgrims. Nanasaheb died soon after, from grief, it is said.

Malhar Rao Holkar and Mahadji Shinde, survived. The Maratha loss on the brink of victory recalls earlier catastrophes of Raja Bhoja, Prithviraj, and others, a recurring theme in Indian history, of alliances failing at the very edge of final triumph. This weakened the Empire, which had stood poised to regain the glory lost to the Mughals which Shivaji and Bajirao I had begun to recoup, and would have succeeded had its leaders been less self-willed; more cooperative; prudent; recall an adage from their own literature, the *Panchatantra*, that cooperation among friends was vital to survival, especially in war. Leaders had allowed differences to cloud their vision of a nation, and stall a true and binding political union. Enough time and events had passed to show that the independence of action in guerrilla warfare had to give way to coordinated military strategies, with disciplined and strong components, modern weapons and a forward plan, to make gains permanent.

Hindus had for decades won key battles, but lacked the unity, discipline, diplomacy and loyalties that the British generals enjoyed, the exploitation of race and caste, and the Company's decision to allow its troops to plunder at will. Indian failures had deepened cynicism among a populace suffering in want amid glaring excesses of the rich; few believed that rulers would work to remove the heavy taxation levied by successive Governments, or the harassment and extortion by officials and police, which kept rulers rich and the plebs in penury and serfdom, relieved temporarily by the efforts of Bajirao I and his son, Balaji Bajirao (Nanasaheb), and, after Pānipat, Mahadji Shinde (1730-92), Tukojirao Holkar (1723-97) and later Yashwantrao Holkar (1776-1811).

Following Pānipat, the foremost Maratha generals—Shinde, Holkar, Gaekwad and Bhonsle (no relation to Shivaji)—lost focus for a while, and allowed disagreements to increase among themselves and with the Péshwé at Puné. The Empire became a loose Confederacy, but rallied, led by the young Péshwé Madhav Rao I, Nanasaheb's son; Malharrao Holkar; Mahadji Shinde; and Nana Phadnavis, to regain, in the next decade, most of the lost ground in the north, and the lands around Bombay, previously annexed by the BEICo. Mahadji had been in service from age 10 and was the last and only one of five sons of sardar Ranoji Shinde to survive Pānipat.

Statue of Ahilyabai Holkar at Datta Temple, Sahastradhara, Uttarkand

In 1766, Malharrao, founder of the Holkars, died and was succeeded by his daughter-in-law Ahilyabai, as astute a leader as any then in India. She was ably supported by her commander and adopted brother, Tukojirao. Warren Hastings had tried to seize control of

Puné and destroy the Maratha Confederacy by concluding the *Treaty of Surat* with Raghunathrao, Nanasaheb's brother, which would make him Péshwé, but subservient to the BEICo in Bombay. This caused the *First Anglo-Maratha War,* in which the combined forces of Mahadji Shinde, Tukojirao Holkar and Mudhoji Bhonsle held the British at bay and forced the *Treaty of Salbai* in 1782, Marathas regaining lands. This inaugurated two decades of peace. Hastings was strongly criticised for his acts, which contributed to his impeachment in 1786, a year after his forced resignation. He was accused of maladministration, injustice, oppression, receipt of bribes, etc. His celebrated trial—in which famous Britishers: Burke, Fox, Sheridan and Macaulay thundered against him—began in 1788, and terminated in 1795 with his acquittal, but cost him his fortune.

The Marathas were once more poised to attain supreme power, but drifted into the same inter-regional squabbling that had led to their defeat by Durrani. Instead of uniting, Shinde and Holkar, two of the four strongest kingdoms of the Confederacy, fought each other, perhaps wishing to dominate a new India, promising their citizens progress and plenty, and enrichment from an expanded tax base. Tukojirao Holkar lost to Mahadji Shinde's troops in 1793, under General Benoît de Boigne, a French mercenary, hired by Shinde to train and lead his army, European style. Although not an officer in the French army, he had proved quite proficient, and was given the title of General.

A year later, Mahadji died, a great blow to India, and was succeeded by 15 year-old Daulatrao Shinde, grandson of Mahadji's brother Tukaram. On Ahilyabai Holkar's demise in 1795, after 30 years of a productive and admired reign, relationships deteriorated further, aggravated by the covert actions of British emissaries who offered sweet deals to each leader, driving deep wedges among them, and reducing them to a number of weak and malleable forces, instead of the powerful army they were as a Union. Early in her reign, 1772, Ahilyabai had warned the Péshwé about the British: *"Other beasts, like tigers, can be killed by might or contrivance, but to kill a bear it is very difficult. It will die only if you kill it straight in the face. Or else, once caught in its powerful hold, the bear will kill its prey by tickling. Such is the way of the English. And in view of this, it is difficult to triumph over them."*

By the end of the century, the British, under Wellesley, flush with the capture of Mysore, and still aiming at the French, or perhaps finding them a convenient excuse for war against Indians, decided to open another chapter of the Napoleonic wars, by moving against Raghoji Shinde, whose French general had defeated the Holkars.

Wellesley exploited the schisms among the Marathas, but was cautioned by the resolute way in which Yashwantrao Holkar had, since his ascent to the throne in 1797, tried to dislodge the British from Delhi, earning the Mughal Emperor's admiration and a hefty title. In 1796, Bajirao II—son of Raghunathrao, whose treachery had caused the first Maratha war—had become Péshwé. He was mean and weak, yet crafty—traits perhaps inherited from wicked and covetous parents and a deprived upbringing. He had the support of the youthful Daulatrao Shinde, but would yield to the prudence of finance Minister Nāna Phadnavis, who unfortunately died in 1800, aged 58, another grave blow.

Yashwantrao Holkar believed that Bajirao II's brother, Amrutrao, would be a better Péshwé. He also resented Shinde who had suddenly attacked him and his brother, Malharrao Holkar II, in 1797, killing the latter. In 1801, Holkar and his brother, Vitthojirao, decided to move against their tormentors, but Vitthoji was taken by the forces of the Péshwé, Bajirao II, and executed. Yashwant then moved against the Péshwé, won many battles and finally defeated him and Shinde at Hadapsar, near Puné. The Péshwé, fearing retribution, declined Holkar's request to return to Puné, and after a delay, during which Holkar announced that he would install Amrutrao as Péshwé, Bajirao II fled to Bassein and agreed with Wellesley, the BEICo Governor General, to cede the Empire to the Company and become a "subsidiary ally"!

The Narmada River from a terrace of Ahilyabai's fort, Maheshwar, Mewar

His defection heralded the *Second Anglo-Maratha War*. He had played directly into the plans of Richard Wellesley, who had prepared for war. His first success was an 1802 treaty with Gaekwad of Baroda, which severed him from the Confederacy. The following year he ordered Lord

Lake, the Commander in Chief from Calcutta, and Arthur Wellesley, his brother in Mysore, to attack the remaining Marathas. They exploited the schism between Shinde and Holkar, intercepted mail and used spies, paid Indian informers and traitors, plots and other forms of "British diplomacy" to secure secrets and advantages that were key to success. In 1803, Lake defeated Daulatrao Shinde and Raghoji II Bhonsle of Berar at Kol (Aligarh) and Delhi, while Arthur Wellesley achieved the same at Assaye and Argaon, Holkar abstaining, until too late.

Throughout 1804, Holkar pleaded with other Maratha leaders to join with him to evict the British; he alone had fought Lake's armies with much success and had defeated several generals that year, including Fawcett and Manson, until, failing to take Delhi, he retreated to friendly Bharatpur, having received news that an Anglo-Indian alliance, including the traitor, Péshwé Bajirao II, had seized some of his territory, and that the British had offered to share his lands among their allies. He and Lake fought to a stalemate at Bharatpur in 1805.

In all these battles, other treachery, besides that of Bajirao II and Gaekwad's premature surrender, was critical to British victory over the Marathas in the second war, whether fighting separately or together. For example, by 1805, Alwar had surprisingly helped the British against Marathas at Aligarh; Deshpande released secrets to Wellesley before Argaon; Cuillier Perron[83] abandoned his strong Shinde army and defected to the enemy, and Holkar was betrayed by his officers, Mohamed Khan and Bhawani Shankar Khatri. Of interest is that Holkar, the most vigorous and nationalistic of the Marathas, the closest in talent and character to Shivaji, Bajirao I, or Mahadji Shinde, played little part in the Shinde wars, having been shown by Wellesley a letter, likely a British forgery, with plans by the other Maratha chiefs and the Péshwé to betray him, after their defeat of the British. The subsequent treaties left all, except Holkar, under British domination.

Back in Britain, the British painted Holkar in very unflattering colours. True to his convictions, he resented the British presence and control and continued his campaign to restore the Confederacy. He pleaded with Indian leaders for new alliances, was promised help from various princes but was rejected by Sikh and Kashmiri kings; others balked, under threats by the British. He wrote defiantly to Wellesley:

---

[83]Perron, Shinde's French commander after Boigne, proved a duplicitous officer who accumulated wealth, which he lodged in British banks, yet preached anti-British rhetoric to his employer and army, and at a critical moment defected to Lord Lake and abandoned his army, bribing river transports to deny them passage across the Yamuna, thus ensuring a Shinde defeat. The British gave him safe passage to France.

"Although unable to oppose your artillery in the field, countries of many hundred miles in extent will be overrun and plundered. British shall not have leisure to breathe for a moment; and calamities will fall on the backs of human beings in continual war by the attacks of my army, which overwhelms like the waves of the sea." For betraying him, Amir Khan Pindari and Bhawani Shankar Khatri received *jaghirs* in Delhi, which are still called *Nemakharam ki haveli* (traitors' quarters)!

Both Wellesleys were recalled from India that year. Richard was replaced by Lord Cornwallis, who ordered an end to the wars, but died suddenly before his order was implemented. Barlow, the new Governor General, promptly concluded a treaty with the capricious Shinde, thus denying Holkar any chance of re-energising the Maratha alliance. Nevertheless, Holkar stood firm, until the British offered an unconditional *Treaty of Peace and Amity* which he signed on Christmas Eve, 1805. One historian noted: *"...As soon as he(Cornwallis) came to India, he wrote to Lord Lake on 19 September, 1805 and stated that all the territory of Yashwantrao Holkar be returned and that he was ready to make peace with Holkar. Maharaja Yashwantrao Holkar refused to sign any treaty with the British. George Barlow was appointed as Governor General, due to the sudden death of Lord Cornwallis. Barlow immediately tried to divide Holkar and Shinde. The British signed a treaty with Daulatrao Shinde through Kamal Nayan Munshi on 23 November, 1805, and in this way, Maharaja Yashwantrao Holkar was left alone to fight with the British."*

Y. Holkar

Six weeks later, Holkar wrote Bhonsle: *"The Maratha state had been grasped by foreigners. To resist their aggression, God knows how during the last two and a half years I sacrificed everything, fighting night and day, without a moment's rest. I paid a visit to Daulatrao Shinde and explained to him how necessary it was for all of us to join in averting foreign domination. But Daulatrao failed me. It was mutual cooperation and goodwill which enabled our ancestors to build up the Maratha states. But now we have all become self-seekers. You wrote to me that you were coming for my support, but you did not make your promise good. If you had advanced into Bengal as was planned, we could have paralysed the British Government. It is no use now talking of past things. When I found myself abandoned on all sides, I accepted the offer which the British agents brought to me and concluded the war."* Even with Shinde's duplicity, Holkar continued in secret to reason with him, convinced that the British were bent on seizing Indian assets at all costs, and would dishonour promises. They came to a confidential agreement on points of defence and attack. Shinde promptly revealed it to his British resident!

In frustration, Holkar decided to fight the British alone. Recognising their superiority in artillery, he proceeded to manufacture his own cannons, at a factory in Bhanpura. He made 200 long and short range guns and assembled an army of 100,000 to attack the British headquarters in Calcutta. Suddenly, in 1811, he died of a "stroke". (Haemorrhage from a ruptured cerebral aneurysm, possibly, or was it something his enemies did?) He had come to the same end as Shivaji and Bajirao I, at a similar stage of resolve. He was just 35! Some accounts assert that he had become insane, but there is no good evidence for this; organic or toxic brain conditions can show confusing signs of "mental illness", but diagnosis required methods not available in the 19th century.

The resulting increased influence and control by the British brought increased suffering to Indians, especially Hindus, but ordinary Muslims, previously lightly taxed by Mughals, now began to appreciate, slowly and belatedly, the misery overtaxed Hindus had endured under the Mughals. Appeals to London generally were slow to arrive and fell on muffled ears, as the rich spoils from India transformed and enhanced the architecture of London and other cities, and dulled the edge of upper crust conscience, which, if any existed, by its close and numbing links with power, would be sure to give a mere token response.

Burke had labelled Hastings a *'captain-general of iniquity'* – among other choice terms – who never dined without *'creating a famine'*! Such were the conceit, immorality and blatant excesses of BEICo executives in India. Subsequent changes occurred that slowly brought increasing oversight by the Government in London, especially after loss of the American colonies, and as controls fell to the Company in each region, by conquest or treaty. London asserted its sovereignty and political authority by various Acts, and had even criticised Bombay's over-reaching in Maratha affairs – a criticism the Company's Bombay directors had ignored. The impeachment of Warren Hastings had failed to awaken the British public to the perfidy of the BEICo and its officers. It didn't help that the practice of repatriating Britons found guilty of wrongdoing in India was stopped, much to Indian regret.

The Indian service attracted the cream of British universities and every military man seeking a fortune. The Company's monopoly yielded such profits that other traders had tried to break it, only to be annihilated by the Company on reaching India. The clergy had kept silent. After all,

Charles II had granted the Company wide latitude, including *"...to make peace or war..."* The continuing conflict had impelled Parliament to seek royal intervention.

In the late 18th century, a new force had entered European politics, the pan-European Rothschild money-lending dynasty, whose acumen and strategies in the financing of both conflicts and industrial development, would soon create new empires and make it the world's most profitable and richest private Corporation. Its reach was global, with Indian, Middle East, African and American footprints, and easily dwarfed its imitators, its wealth equal to or exceeding that of the 14th century kings of Mali.

The French Revolution and the Napoleonic wars that followed deeply affected India, a decade later. The British, like the Rothschilds in Finance, would emerge from this struggle the strongest of the European nations, a far cry from the mean reputation of a millennium earlier, when their ancestors were among the most cantankerous in a collection of squabbling Germanic exiles, trying to find a footing in the British Isles. This they did, partly displacing the natives and Romanised Britons, forming an Anglo-Saxon coalition, until first the Vikings, then the Normans displaced and diluted them. Thereafter, led by single-minded and greedy aristocrats, who fought continuous wars for supremacy among their peers, and for foreign relatives and friends, they developed a hierarchical culture (see p.172), which had become the pattern in all Europe, and which Shakespeare would tellingly illustrate in several plays on Britain, notably *Henry V, King Lear, Macbeth,* and in *Hamlet.*

Europeans benefitted later from the *"age of enlightenment"*, with direction from its many intellectuals and philosophers, as knowledge expanded. In this age, reason and analysis dominated thinking and individualism began to flourish. The romanticists of the next decades would modify it, to be replaced by the "positivism" of the scientist who believed only in what could be seen, studied and measured, only to realise that all was not black and white, that scientific objectivity was affected by degrees of personal biases, and required some consensus or general "agreement" on observations before their acceptance as valid. However, the actions of imperialists did not seem to fit this mould.

Nine hundred years after Angles and Saxons had crudely begun to take over Britain, and to replace the collapsing Roman province, Henry VIII, the dissolute Tudor king, severed connections with another Roman power, the Vatican, which had maintained, since 962 CE, a Holy Roman Empire, an assemblage of German tribes and principalities that had, with Roman support, limped along for centuries, until formally brought to a muted end in 1804. In India, Britain was once more about to take charge of another collapsing Empire, the Mughals

Chapter 12

As early as 1868, age 33, he drafted a memo to himself. He wrote: "...The amassing of wealth is one of the worst species of idolatry. No idol more debasing than the worship of money...the man who dies thus rich dies disgraced." Andrew Carnegie, US steel magnate, philanthropist.

A century of Turmoil and Theft

The dawn of the 19th century had found Europe in its usual state of unremitting tumult. The continent had not seen any peace for more than a millennium. European nations had become known for national and international instability, largely due to the persistence of tribal superstitions and the dominance of oligarchies, despite claims to democracy. They were obsessed with monolithic expansion, pushed by a consuming mercantilism and the imperative for self-promotion, using their adopted religion, Christianity, as a tool, locally and internationally.

For more than a millennium, European aristocrats have disagreed, quarrelled and fought one another, as discussed earlier, each seeking to dominate Europe and eventually the world. The 16th and 17th Century raged with wars of expansion and suppression among British, Bourbons, Habsburgs, Ottomans and Eastern monarchies like Prussia, Poland, Russia and others. The 18th century followed with some forty conflicts and the 19th was no better. Nehru would later call Europe *"a quarrelsome little continent."* This was compounded with the absurd notion that skin tone defined privilege and ability and that the world outside Europe was unschooled and backward, and therefore theirs for the taking. This was supreme arrogance, for which the young, as yet untutored, nations were well known, even as the young and over-confident tend to be, especially when ignorant of any history, including their own. But it was not alone.

South America faced successive revolutions for Independence from Spain, while in Brazil, the Portuguese Emperor, who had ruled from Rio de Janeiro during the Napoleonic Wars, returned to Lisbon, leaving his son, Dom Pedro, as Regent of Brazil. In 1822, Pedro declared Brazil independent of Portugal and after a brief war became Pedro I, head of the Empire of Brazil, a constitutional monarchy. The British wormed their way among the new countries when the *Cisplatino War,* between Brazil and Argentina (1825-8), ended with the creation of Uruguay. The British had gained a foothold in Guiana, and mediated the *Treaty of Montevideo* on August 27, 1828, which formalised Uruguay. Brazil and Argentina gained peace and lost ownership of the Rio de la Plata which was declared "international", allowing the British free access for its mercantilist goals in South America, to complement its gains in India.

Britain was also busy suppressing dissent at home while magnifying Indian "brigandry" by so-called thugs (more often legitimate protesters) numbering 0.04/1000 compared with Britain's 3/1000 criminals, 75 times the frequency! British criminals had been distributed worldwide: Australia, the colonies, USA and Canada. Dissent seethed throughout the 19th and 20th centuries. The Napoleonic Wars lasted from 1792 to 1815. The Poles fought the Russians in 1830-31; the Hungarians rebelled against the Habsburgs in 1848-9; the Danes fought with Schleswig-Holstein, and with Prussians in 1848 and 1864, losing control of the duchies. Between 1848 and 1866, Italians fought the Austrian Empire for unification and independence that brought renown to Italy's Giuseppe Garibaldi. In 1854-6, Russia fought and lost the Crimean War against an alliance of French, Ottomans, British, Germans (Nassau) and Sardinians, ostensibly over control of Palestine's holy places.

The war brought peace to the Ottomans briefly and achieved unforeseen benefits to the care of sick and wounded, prompted by two enterprising British nurses, Florence Nightingale and Mary Seacole[84], the latter a coloured Jamaican volunteer who performed great feats, despite racial prejudice and the animosity of Nurse Nightingale. For the Russians, it spurred the abolition of serfdom, while the British maintained fears of Russian expansion. Soon Russia made treaties with various central Asian states, including Persia.

As a sop to Indians, critical of BEICo's immoral aggression across India, London in 1813 renewed the Company's charter for 20 years only, restricting its monopoly to the tea trade and to trade with China, and requiring separate commercial and territorial accounting. The Act also opened India (and colonies) to missionaries, chiefly the London Missionary and other Christian Societies. This encouraged the *Society for the Propagation of the Gospel* (SPG, UK) to enter the growing business of conversion. They sent missionaries to India in 1820, South Africa in 1821, China in 1863—where the British had established the opium trade—and to Japan and elsewhere, by 1873. They focussed on ministry to poor natives and education of women. From this grew the *Women's Mission Association for the Promotion of Female Education,* recruiting women from the United Kingdom to peddle the gospel. Later, they saw a need for something worthwhile and developed a medical function.

There was another side to the reality that slavery had powerful opponents, besides do-gooders, for purely pecuniary reasons. Slaves cost much less than the wage-earners who worked in the new and expanding factories, albeit at very poor wages, and sometimes were worse off than slaves. Thus factory owners, most with links to the aristocracy, and unable to add slaves to their workforce, argued that slavery was an

[84] She was honoured in the 20th century by the University *of the West Indies,* Mona, Jamaica, which named a student residence after her, and by statuary in Britain.

unfair competition and lobbied successfully to end it. The reformers were allowed to take the credit for the end of slavery in the British Empire; but had less success in the US south, where slave labour *was* the economy! A vicious war would be fought, three decades later, to end it.

Despite abolishment of the *Slave Trade* by Britain in 1807, slavers had continued to trade with the USA. In 1812, Americans had been driven from Canada, relieving British forces and freeing army resources to serve in India. British views of Indians were influenced by Charles Grant, a dissolute man turned religious, who had served as Chairman of the BEICo in 1805, and earlier under Cornwallis, agreeing that Britain had a duty, not just to secure India for merchandising, but to rescue its inhabitants from Hinduism, civilise and convert them, by allowing Christian missions to operate (see Duff below). The Company had long opposed this as a distraction from business! Mill and Macaulay would take these arguments further in the next decades.

Napoleon's fall rewarded Britain with colonies in the Caribbean and Guianas, and accelerated its expansion in India by the hallowed techniques of coercion, bribery and deceit. Holkar's sudden death in 1811, leaving a child as heir, had energised British preparations to tackle the Marathas a third time, coinciding with the publication of James Mill's derisory *History of British India,* which he wrote solely by reviewing Company accounts. He did not allow his total ignorance of India to affect his trashing everything about it: history, literature, culture, religions, social customs and even the climate. Mill's motto seemed to have been: *"What I don't know is not worth knowing!"* And while attacking Indians he ignored the misery and hopelessness of Britain's landless poor—over 80% of its 14 million population—made so, and kept so, by their own aristocracy, with the help of toadies like Mill! His denunciations, despite their unreason and some criticisms of the Company, were a godsend for imperialists. The book was widely circulated, and used to justify abominable British behaviour in later years, including war.

The *Third Maratha War* began with the British-instigated murder of the Holkar regent Tulsibai on 20 December 1817, followed immediately by a huge and rash invasion by Sir Thomas Hislop to start the *Battle of Mahidpur.* This ended with the surprise defeat, in 1818, of the Maratha Confederacy, despite its fractured and weakened state, giving the Company—then headed by Lord Hastings (no relation to Warren)—dominion over most of India, either as direct colonies, or subsidiary alliances. Hislop would have fallen to the Holkar forces led by 11-year-old Malharrao Holkar III, 20-year old Harirao Holkar and their 20-year-old sister, Bhimabai Holkar, had betrayal, so common in Anglo-Indian history, not supervened. This time, it was the critical defection of Nawab

Abdul Gafoor Khan—a commander in the Holkar army appointed by Yaswant in 1808. Like Raja Shiladitya in Mewar, Mir Jafar at Pilashi, Bengal, Mir Qasim in Mysore, among others mentioned elsewhere, he pulled out his forces, already poised to deal a decisive blow to the British army, and scuttled a crucial part of the battle plan of the youthful Holkars. They had trusted their commander of ten years and had no inkling that he had sold out to the British; in retrospect his treachery explained Hislop's reckless attack. The Péshwé, who had belatedly realised past errors, especially his lack of vision and mistaking the heroic nationalism of Yashwantrao Holkar, had fought with Bhonsle alongside Holkar's children, almost as a penance. To start the War, the British forces had moved against the Pindaris, groups of mounted raiders, about 20,000 strong, led by three Pindari chiefs, who regularly attacked and looted British settlements, and, at times, fought alongside the Marathas. They were defeated in the War, having split into three; one leader was killed by a tiger, the rest resettled in Gorakhpur, United Provinces.

The treaty, signed at Mandsaur on January 6, 1818, rewarded Khan's treachery with Jawara, a mere pittance for having dealt India the *coup de grâce*, which ended the Maratha Confederacy and gave India to the British. Bhimabai rejected the treaty, and continued guerrilla attacks against the British. The BEICo came to dominate India except for the Northwest and Nepal, reducing Indian *rajas* to mere "subsidiary allies".

The Holkars lost territory to the Nizam of Hyderabad and other British allies, retaining only the princely state of Indaur, the rest absorbed by the Company's Central India Agency. The Péshwé was banished to Bithoor, and the once proud and expansive Maratha realms reduced to small princely states including Kolhapur and Sātārā. Puné came directly under Bombay. In a form of poetic justice, even those who had sided with the British—Shinde and several Maratha sardars—lost their best lands, much to their surprise and shame, and were allowed to retain restricted holdings as humiliated subsidiary allies—the rewards of betrayal! Yashwantrao Holkar and the others who had pleaded for unity were amply vindicated.

The Maratha victories had shown how relatively easily India could have expelled both Mughals and British by the mid-18th century, had the Confederacy prevailed, Indian Rājas been smarter, had inspired their people with nationalism, self-respect and confidence, and studied developments in Britain. A reversion to pre-Mughal education, spreading it to all classes and to higher levels generally, would have helped, especially if advantage were taken of technological advances in the wider world, peaceful and military, adopting those of strategic or socio-economic value, including Mysorean rocketry, which had been claimed instead by William Congreve, a friend of the Prince of Wales.

Individual empowerment by enfranchisement within the rule of law would have propelled the drive to social equality and justice. An appropriate legal and representative structure was already known. Governments would be structured to follow an agreed constitution with a code of standards, responsibility, accountability and moral conduct. It is doubtful, however, if any more than a handful of Indian rulers had a national outlook, or democratic feeling, having been nurtured to promote and expand clan holdings and interests, which had kept them in conflict with neighbours and in a constant state of disunity, since the fall of the Gupta Empire, through internal strife. This singular inability to escape tribal confines would dog India to this day and keep her at the mercy of sly foreign "diplomats", schooled in the art of deception and "divide and rule" policies. India's combined military strength was enough at all periods in history to prevent inroads by foreign armies, despite the force of *jihad* that fired Islam, and the strengths of the British: the navy, their disciplined forces, mostly Sepoys, bribery, megalomania, artillery, and greed. Shivaji had effectively begun to counter them at sea, as did Bajirao I and Yashwantrao Holkar on land. Sadly for India, these three undefeated champions had each died at the height of his powers, of a similar acute cerebral event, under suspicious circumstances. Those familiar with the morals of *Panchatantra* or the lessons of *Arthashastra* will not fail to see their close parallels with events of Maratha history.

As a piece of poetic justice, however, India, the land, if not the people, exacted a toll; a cholera epidemic starting in Bengal in 1820 soon affected the whole country, killing some 10,000 British troops and numerous unfortunate Indians. It is said that only one in ten employees of the British Company survived their tours of duty. As for the Indian masses, centuries of foreign domination, heavy taxation and dispossession, had impoverished and subjugated them to the point that paid servitude (indenture) seemed like a reward.

Systematic denigration of Hinduism set it against Islam, widening divisions that Akbar had tried to bridge. As facts contradicted James Mill's guesses and denunciations, which are echoed even today by Indian Marxist historians writing about Vaidic India, the British began to dismantle Hindu village life and malign Hindu scriptures to make its vast literature look petty, despite high praise by knowledgeable Company officials, like Sir William Jones, co-founder of the Asiatic Society, and Charles Watkins, translator of the *Bhagavad Gita*. Mill's book, later modified with corrections by Sankritist H.H. Wilson, remained a reference for the British, as its flawed arguments fell in line with British aristocratic thinking and their *"Subdue India"* and *"Forward"* policies. James Mill's condemnation of India, on hearsay, seemed then like an account of the Jews written by Adolph Hitler, or vice versa.

As the British consolidated gains, educated Indians sought accommodation to the new hegemony. One early and determined activist was Ram Mohan Roy (1772-1833), a Bengali scholar and religious iconoclast, founder of *Adi Brahmo Sabha* in Calcutta, with Debendranath Tagore which aimed to incorporate Islamic and Christian ideals, using a common language, noting that the many languages of India hindered easy communication and united action, even though many Indians were polyglot. He then appealed to Lord Amherst to *compel* learning of English as *the* lingua franca! This was an unwise, if not sycophantic idea.

The first girls' schools had been set up a year or so earlier by Baptist and Anglican missionaries, who targeted the lower classes with lessons in basics, plus needlework and the Bible. The schools were small and increased to less than 500 students in 20 years. But the need here was great, as this largely uneducated class had been badly exploited for menial labour, at less than subsistence wages, a practice that would survive colonialism and remain one of India's social scars.

In 1817, Roy, with David Hare and Radhakanta Deb, founded the *Hindu* (later *Presidency) College, Hare School* and *Vaidanta* College in Calcutta. The Muslims had changed Indian education drastically to studies of Arabic, Persian or Sanskrit, and basic arithmetic, quite unlike the extended curriculum they had replaced. Roy wished to change that, re-introducing science, humanities and mathematics, and adding English. After debate, girls were *excluded* from the schools.

Roy had campaigned against *sătí* and saw it banned in 1830. He remained Brahmo Hindu and published extensively. He died in England in 1833 of "meningitis" having travelled there in 1831 as emissary of Akbar II, the Mughal emperor who gave him the title of *Raja.* Akbar II was reduced by then to a mere pawn of the British.

In pushing English, Roy had joined Thomas Carey's Mission and anticipated Macaulay by 20 years. It is likely that Roy was disillusioned by his experiences in Britain, not the least being the revelation that Britain was an aristocratic oligarchy that only mouthed democratic principles on demand. His death prevented any dissemination of this disquieting knowledge, new to Indians, and that the British in India was not a true sample of their people at home. There, the ordinary people faced as great a tyranny as the Indians in India, contrary to his expectations; and having exhausted their islands, the British were plundering the world, not for Christianity, but to gain resources, and enrich and aggrandise the aristocratic and moneyed BEICo shareholders!

At the time, Britain was involved in a debate on human rights that confirmed its domination by a few aristocrats, who dismissed domestic dissidents and the poor, as swiftly and summarily as those in the colonies. For example, authorities in 1819 sent a yeoman cavalry rampaging, with swords drawn to hack their way through a crowd gathered in St Peter's Field, in Manchester, to protest lack of proper representation in Parliament. All Lancashire, including its major cities, had only two representatives, while a few "rotten" boroughs, some with hardly a dozen or so people each, enjoyed one or two. There were over 50 of these in the UK, all controlled by the gentry, and through them, Lords could exert strong influence on the Commons! But the protesters were merely seeking what the British were boasting to the world: representative government, even using the word "democracy" to describe it! The Lancastrians called the episode their *Peterloo!* Swift suppression cooled protests.

Dissent did not stop, however; ultimately, mass action forced reform in 1832, but the Bill had rough passage, virulently opposed by Lords, who nursed fears that the revolutionary fevers of France would consume England and topple their mansions, castles and elegant townhouses, built on the backs, and with the sweat of slaves and minions. This fear continued for a century and guided London's policy overseas. The rich saw their wealth as sacrosanct and should only change by addition or multiplication! They felt that small plots of land, the labouring and domestic jobs and other minuscule concessions were enough to satisfy the plebs. Surely the rabble would not know what to do with the vote, or worse, with education or money! Thus, the Lords, lay and spiritual, twice defeated the Bill despite its large Commons majorities. Aristocratic attitudes had not changed for a millennium.

The Bill was finally passed in a weakened form on the third try, but only after King William IV had privately urged Lords to come down to earth and see reality. The Bill's first passage had defeated Arthur Wellesley's conservative government but briefly restored him when Earl Grey resigned as Prime Minister after the second rejection.

Once in the House, Wellesley made the following pompous and ignorant remarks, (quoted here as it appeared in the formal third person, author's emphasis): "He (PM Wellesley) was fully convinced that the country possessed, at the present moment, a legislature which answered all the *good purposes* of legislation—and this *to a greater degree than any legislature ever had answered, in any country whatever*. He would go further, and say that the legislature and system of representation possessed the full and entire confidence of the country...He would go still further, and say, that if at the present moment he had imposed upon him the duty of forming a legislature for any country—he did not mean to assert that he could form such a legislature as they possessed now, for *the nature of man was incapable of reaching such excellence at once – (he would refuse)*. As long as he held any station in the government of the country, he should always feel it his duty to resist reform measures, *when proposed by others.*"

Two weeks later, he lost a non-confidence motion and was gone!

The Bill's passage had an unfortunate consequence for the proletariat whose members had given their lives in the struggle. Enfranchisement required £10 worth of property which few labourers had; this effectively split the reform movement. (The same problem of expanding the franchise would become an issue later among members of the Indian National Congress).

In practice, the First Reform Bill had failed the majority British poor and given them grounds for continued agitation. Labour unions awoke, and formed alliances, which were promptly deemed illegal, but they joined with the poor and continued to agitate. In 1838, *The Peoples' Charter* was published, initiating the *Chartist* movement, which has continuously exercised social historians and dispassionate academics since. It led to many demonstrations including the huge Kennington rally, one of whose organisers was a black Englishman named William Cuffay, whose father had come from St Kitts to London presumably as a house slave. Like his father, William was a tailor and had previously led a failed protest to improve wages to six shillings a day. Under sedition laws, passed to curb and punish dissent (as in India during the century of opposition), he was falsely convicted of planning armed uprising and sent to Tasmania, where he continued in labour politics until his death in 1870. This illustrates the harshness of government response to dissent.

The behaviour of the British aristocracy was as stingy at home as it was in the Empire. Complaining colonials found to their dismay that the cruelty existing in the colonies were no less brutal in Britain. In a sense, this reflected the fact that the ruling minority classes were from two original German tribes, adulterated in the next centuries by injections of Scandinavians, mainly Norsemen, and French (of Frankish origin). Native Britons remained in relatively low estate, barring natural tendencies of a few to rise socially and politically as they acquired wealth. An alliance soon sprang up between the nouveau industrialist and the aristocracy to their mutual benefit, the one rising socially, the other financially. When the abolitionists raised their case, it clashed to some extent with that of the equally disadvantaged British poor seeking emancipation. But while the abolitionists succeeded in freeing slaves, or so they thought, the aristocracy sought every means to prevent joint action by the poor or unionised. One measure was the *Poor Law Act* which reduced benefits and created "union" workhouses—not trade union—where workers were forced to live, thus separating them from families; another was the imposition of a 4d stamp tax on newspapers which made news too expensive, until some newspapers refused to pay or found ways of diluting the tax, such as reading groups!

These and many other impositions illustrate the extent of oppression of the masses of that time in Britain that spurred the Chartist movement. If the treatment of labourers in the "mother" country was so disgraceful, it was small wonder that colonial work conditions were worse, and workers heavily exploited, reflecting British reverence for established hierarchy, and thereby disdain for the plebs, which writers like Charles Dickens portrayed so vividly! It was unlikely that British lords would treat coloured workers any better than their white serfs! Indian colonial indentures were therefore not specially selected for exploitation, and some actually argued that colonial workers were protected! For example, Lord John Russell, a member of the Whig party, became head of the Colonial Office in September 1839, and believed that while the export of indentured labour to British Guiana had failed initially, sufficiently stringent regulations should protect from slavery Indians going to Mauritius, under a one year contract of indenture. This belief was based on the opinion that *"coolies travelling to Mauritius would receive higher wages and better conditions than what were available in India."*

The Chartists' demand included universal male suffrage at age 21, ballot voting, annual change in parliaments, equal representation and an end to property requirements for members of Parliament. The movement had gained considerable strength among British workers by 1838, the year *The People's Charter* was published. Relations with abolitionists were often confrontational, as Chartists felt that the plight of poor white workers was similar, but overlooked in the campaigns to end the slavery of Blacks. Generally though, the two groups shared philosophy, and membership, including leaders. For instance, Joseph Sturge, one of the founders of the British and Foreign Anti-Slavery Society, was a Chartist.

In May 1842, Parliament summarily rejected a Chartist petition on representation. The Chartist paper, *The Northern Star*, made this comment which would have resonated with Indian and colonial peoples: *"Three and half millions have quietly, orderly, soberly, peaceably but firmly asked of their rulers to do justice; and their rulers have turned a deaf ear to that protest. Three and a half millions of people have asked permission to detail their wrongs, and enforce their claims for RIGHT, and the 'House' has resolved they should not be heard! Three and a half millions of the slave-class have holden out the olive branch of peace to the enfranchised and privileged classes and sought for a firm and compact union, on the principle of EQUALITY BEFORE THE LAW; and the enfranchised and privileged have refused to enter into a treaty! The same class is to be a slave class still. The mark and brand of inferiority is not to be removed. The assumption of inferiority is still to be maintained. The people are not to be free."*

By 1850, the Chartist movement was in decline. Earlier, it had been supported by the popular Richard Cobham, a wealthy capitalist and politician, then campaigning for free trade, under the banner of the *Anti-Corn Law League* to repeal Britain's *Corn Laws.* He was believed when he said that their repeal (1846) would lower food prices. But the ACLL supported Chartism from self-interest only. Cobham's platform was "*We advocate nothing but what is agreeable to the highest behests of Christianity—to buy in the cheapest market, and sell in the dearest!*" (So Cobham had made Christ a trader; but Christ *had* driven the bankers from the Temple!)

After the repeal of the Corn Laws, British manufacturing did see significant productivity rises, while British agriculture ultimately went into decline due to import competition. The *free-traders* had duped the general public as they would continue to do, more viciously, today.

The Second and Third Reform Laws (1867, 1887) gave the franchise to males, and again created a split among the activists, this time between men and women! Some of the Lords' justification for this make distressing reading, but understandable from the viewpoint of an elite group who regarded all below their lofty station as worthless dogsbodies fit only for menial drudgery!

In 1832 the British population was 17 million; the first Act increased total voters from 440,000 to 717,000 males (4.22% of population), with conditions of residence and employment. The subsequent Acts added about one million middle class voters, but still excluded women. That would remain so until 1918—see p. 249.

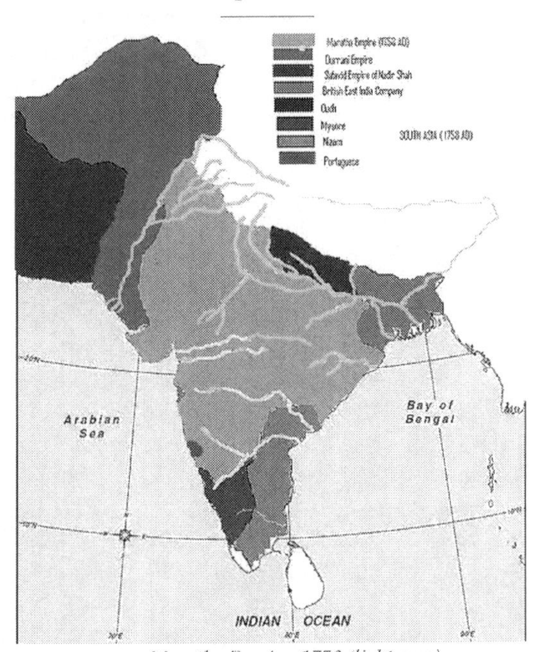

Maratha Empire, 1758 (light grey)

Chapter 13

In order effectually to relieve the suffering of oppressed Hindoos, they humbly conceive a series of enlightened, humane, and comprehensive laws must be substituted for those which exist; and the present system of mis-government be entirely abandoned.

British and Foreign Anti-Slavery Society

Under modern civilisation the spirit of adventure had created a class of men who, when they went among uncivilised people, seemed to lose that humane and benevolent relationship which those at home retained. They had been rightly described as prospectors "who belonged to no country and who owned no moral law."

Wm H. Byles, Lib MP, UK

Struggle for Independence; Macaulay's message

These events and conditions in Britain clearly showed how unrealistic Indians were to expect any goodwill, honest dealing or justice from the British. Those who visited and lived there for a while came to know details, but the first Indians to go to the UK were from the wealthy or ruling classes, few of whom would have spontaneously visited the guts of British city slums or exercised either mind or body for Indian plebs, and would begin to change a little, only when harsh repressions began to affect them.

Contemporaneous with Mohan Roy's lead, other groups became active, especially in Bengal, initiating the *Bengal Renaissance,* which saw a scintillating succession of bright minds who began at last to see beyond their own interests and beyond the *kāla pāni*—dark water, associated with the trip across the Bay of Bengal to the infamous British prisons of the Andaman Islands. Early among these was the *Young Bengal,* an eclectic mix of Hindus, new Christians and atheists, underlining the tolerance of the society at large. It was dominated by the half Portuguese, anti-imperialist and proudly *Indian* youth, Henry Derozio (18 April 1809–26 December 1831), who wrote fairly mature poetry in the romantic style of Lord Byron, and precociously taught English at the *Hindu School.* He influenced many students to examine their beliefs and political attitudes, and to speak for women's rights. His group was styled *Derozians* and adopted the motto *"He who will not reason is a bigot, he who cannot reason is a fool, and he who does not reason is a slave."*

Derozio died prematurely at age 22, but his students became a lively group of movers and shakers in Bengal who influenced the rest of India. They became teachers, writers and businessmen, who called for expanding education and social reform and addressed certain issues such as *săti,* female education, widow remarriage, child marriage, polygamy, the erosion of Indian values by missionary teaching, and the oppressive nature of the government, which was eroding old nurturing values and placing them at permanent risk. These were vigorously debated in papers such as Debendranath Tagore's *Tattwabodhini Patrika* (truth-seeking paper), which discussed science and non-religious topics, and the need for patriotism; its variety attracted a wide audience.

Pyari Charan Sarkar, like Mohan Roy and colleague, Vidyasagar before him, promoted the education of girls, and in 1847 started the first of several schools, including an agricultural and technical school. He wrote textbooks in English for the new schools which made him wealthy, when they were translated into major languages. (It is said that Macmillan & Co. unethically obtained the revisions prepared for the local printer, who had already begun printing, yet Macmillan published the books, after a settlement that was forced on the bilked publisher!)

Leading educators included Ramtanu Lahiri, who saw the opening in 1848 of the private *Krishnanagar College* with Capt. D.L Richardson as head. The writer and businessman, Ramgopal Ghosh, helped in 1849 to establish the *Bethune School* for girls in Calcutta. Indian women would become the world's first female medical doctors; the first was a Bethune graduate trained in Calcutta, the second in Pennsylvania (see p. 246). But there was much anguish before that point was reached and much more after. Journalist Harish Chandra Mukherjee earned the wrath of British plantation owners for championing, in his paper *Hindu Patriot*, the cause of small farmers and workers, who had been forced to plant indigo, for trifling returns, under slavery conditions, cf. Bechu, a Bengali in British Guiana during the late 1890s, who severely criticised a Mr. Bethune, the manager of an estate, Enmore, for criminal abuse of workers (Ragbeer).

In 1831, a group of Bengali zamindars formed the *Landholders Society* acting, no doubt, out of self-interest and only when their interests were threatened. They cared little for the millions of *raiyats* (tenants), toiling for them—a situation similar to British hegemony that inspired the UK Reform movement (see above). Their names, like *Young Bengal* are famous in Indian historiography—Dwarkanath Tagore, Prasanna Kumar Tagore, Radhakanta Deb, Ramkamal Sen, Bhabani Charan Mitra, and others—who described a formal constitutional path to protest and to assert rights; it was overtly upper class, like the *Magna Carta*, but it was hoped that any gains it made might trickle down to the *raiyats*.

The BEICo received a new Charter in 1833 giving it political and governing powers for 20 years. William Bentinck became Governor General, subject to a Board of Control, specially charged with codifying the laws of the land. The Company lost all commercial monopolies, as the industrial revolution created a need for large markets, which subjugated India provided and China promised. Indians were allowed to hold Company positions but in practice few "qualified" (see Bryan, Footnote, p. 170); by the end of the 19th century only one Indian, RC Dutt, had penetrated the invisible ceiling.

Thomas Macaulay, an ardent Christian, with a Presbyterian father and Quaker mother, was a parliamentarian, writer, classicist and literary critic, who served the BEICo in India, from 1834 to 1839, as President of the Supreme Council of India, under Governor General William Bentinck. Macaulay was aware of the prevailing opinion as expressed by previous Company executives—Lord Cornwallis and others—that Indians were *inferior* to Europeans (see p.177-8) and may have been shown Ram Mohan Roy's views of Indian education. He had already noted the obsequiousness of the subjugated Indian maharajahs and could be forgiven his lack of sympathy, since he blamed their plight on failure to teach modern science and technology.

Macaulay had fixed views on governance and did not believe India was ready for any form of democracy, since it lacked essential and stable representative institutions, including a national language, laws, suffrage or unity. He marvelled *that "a handful of adventurers from an island in the Atlantic should have subjugated a vast country divided from the place of their birth by half the globe ... a territory, inhabited by men differing from us in race, colour, language, manners, morals, religion."* This justified his unshakeable belief in British superiority and underpinned his proselytism and other anti-Indian actions. He preferred to ignore the fact that in Britain only 4.2% of the total population could vote—or 8.4% of adults, assuming half are below 21—hardly the stuff of democracy, which he so pompously touted. He admitted, however, to some reassuring quality in the native: *"That the average of intelligence and virtue is very high in this country is matter for honest exultation. But it is no reason for employing average men where you can obtain superior men. Consider too, Sir, how rapidly the public mind in India is advancing, how much attention is already paid by the higher classes of the natives to those intellectual pursuits on the cultivation of which the superiority of the European race to the rest of mankind principally depends."* He then outlines his tactic.

"To the great trading nation, to the great manufacturing nation, no progress which any portion of the human race can make in knowledge, in taste for the conveniences of life, or in the wealth by which those conveniences are produced, can be matter of indifference. It is scarcely possible to calculate the benefits which we might derive from the diffusion of European civilisation among the vast population of the East. It would be, on the most selfish view of the case, far better for us that the people of India were well-governed and independent of us, than ill-governed and subject to us; that they were ruled by their own kings, but wearing our broadcloth, and working with our cutlery, than that they were performing their salaams to English collectors and English magistrates, but were too ignorant to value, or too poor to buy English manufactures. To trade with civilised men is infinitely more profitable than to govern savages. That would, indeed, be a doting wisdom, which, in order that

India might remain a dependency, would make it an (sic) *useless and costly dependency, which would keep a hundred millions of men from being our customers in order that they might continue to be our slaves.*

Are we to keep the people of India ignorant in order that we may keep them submissive? Or do we think that we can give them knowledge without awakening ambition? Or do we mean to awaken ambition and to provide it with no legitimate vent? Who will answer any of these questions in the affirmative? Yet one of them must be answered in the affirmative, by every person who maintains that we ought permanently to exclude the natives from high office. I have no fears. The path of duty is plain before us: and it is also the path of wisdom, of national prosperity, of national honour."

His views were conveyed in a Minute dated Feb 2, 1835 to the Commission. He decided that moneys spent on educating natives in their historical/cultural language reaped no practical or uplifting value, and, concluding that this was either Sanskrit or Arabic, and taught to all scholarship holders, asked rhetorically, *"Why then is it necessary to pay people to learn Sanscrit and Arabic? We have to educate a people who cannot at present be educated by means of their mother-tongue. We must teach them some foreign language."* To justify this conclusion, he invoked the "support" of "orientalists", a term then used for Europeans specialising in "Eastern" studies. *"I have never found one among them who could deny that a single shelf of a good European library was worth the whole native literature of India and Arabia..."*

With this baseless and incredibly pretentious remark, he proposed the elimination of all scholarships and substituting English as the language of instruction, stressing, even more fulsomely and with greater conceit, *"The intrinsic superiority of the Western literature is, indeed, fully admitted...It is, I believe, no exaggeration to say, that all the historical information which has been collected from all the books written in the Sanscrit language is less valuable than what may be found in the most paltry abridgements used at preparatory schools in England. In every branch of physical or moral philosophy the relative position of the two nations is nearly the same. The claims of our own language it is hardly necessary to recapitulate. It stands preeminent even among the languages of the west."* The tenor of this diatribe was no different from that of James Mill, whom Macaulay fulsomely praised as the greatest British historian since Gibbon (*The Rise and Fall of the Roman Empire).*

From this, one would conclude that Macaulay, the classical scholar, had extended his study, as any objective intellectual would have done, to these two languages, if only to recognise them in print or by ear. Macaulay, however, proudly proclaimed, *"I have no knowledge of either Sanscrit or Arabic."* And so he had denied himself knowledge of the great

Shastras of India, with the mathematics and science that had awakened Europe, and other knowledge that is still not fully used.

This and following paragraphs are a fine example of hyperbolic linguistic chauvinism, easy to achieve when extolling his specialty, in contrast to another, of which he knew nothing, and got so carried away as to lose the objectivity he had invoked as a prime virtue. His Minute includes these gems:

"We are not content to leave the natives to the influence of their own hereditary prejudices..."

"It would be manifestly absurd to educate the rising generation with a view to a state of things which we mean to alter before they reach manhood." (See also Al Hajjaj re Khwarazmians, p.118)

"Yet an intelligent English youth, in a much smaller number of years than our unfortunate pupils pass at the Sanscrit College, becomes able to read, to enjoy, and even to imitate not unhappily the compositions of the best Greek authors. Less than half the time which enables an English youth to read Herodotus and Sophocles ought to enable a Hindoo to read Hume and Milton." (Is this not a compliment to Indian students?)

His summary defined the program for the Committee for Public Instruction *"...we ought to employ them* (funds) *in teaching what is best worth knowing, that English is better worth knowing than Sanscrit or Arabic, that the natives are desirous to be taught English, and are not desirous to be taught Sanscrit or Arabic, that neither as the languages of law nor as the languages of religion have the Sanscrit and Arabic any peculiar claim to our encouragement, that it is possible to make natives of this country thoroughly good English scholars, and that to this end our efforts ought to be directed.*

"...We must at present do our best to form a class who may be interpreters between us and the millions whom we govern – a class of persons Indian in blood and colour, but English in tastes, in opinions, in morals and in intellect. To that class we may leave it to refine the vernacular dialects of the country, to enrich those dialects with terms of science borrowed from the Western nomenclature, and to render them by degrees fit vehicles for conveying knowledge to the great mass of the population."

His final dismissal of Indian education was vehement: *"We* (Board of Public Instruction) *are a Board for wasting the public money, for printing books which are of less value than the paper on which they are printed was while it was blank – for giving artificial encouragement to absurd history, absurd metaphysics, absurd physics, absurd theology – for raising up a breed of scholars who find their scholarship an encumbrance and blemish, who live on the public while they are receiving their education, and whose education is so utterly useless to them that, when they have received it, they must either starve or live on the public all the rest of their lives. Entertaining these opinions, I am naturally desirous to decline all share in the responsibility of a body which, unless it alters its whole mode of proceedings, I must consider, not merely as useless, but as positively noxious."*

While Macaulay was busy denigrating Indians, 25-year old Ardésar Cursétjee Wādiā, a Bombay Parsi, built a 60-ton ship in *1833,* called the *Indus,* and later fitted it with a steam engine of his own design. In 1834, he showed the Governor of Bombay, John Fitzgibbon, Earl of Clare, that public lighting could be powered with gas. It seems unlikely that Clare was unaware that by then many cities in England had been using gas-lighting, e.g. London, on Pall Mall, since 1807. At age 29, Wādiā became a member of the Royal Asiatic Society, and in 1841, at age 33, a Fellow of the Royal Society of Great Britain for marine science, one of the youngest and the first Indian to be so honoured.

Macaulay had made serious blunders in allowing his bias and megalomania to blunt common sense and good judgement. Like James Mill, 20 years earlier, whose book was being "modified" by HH Wilson that very year, Macaulay had proudly broadcast his ignorance of India and Indian literature, yet proceeded to treat the country as if it were one nation, failing miserably to realise that a more apt comparison would have been with Europe with its many nations, all *white,* where he wouldn't dare reduce any of their languages to mere dialects, as he had done, so cavalierly, to those of India, stupidly assuming that Arabic and Sanskrit were *the* native languages!

As a classical scholar, he had failed miserably in not rising above crude bias to examine these older languages, and to discover that their role in religion was similar to that of Latin in Christianity, even in his time. So obsessed with narcissism was he, and so cowed was Bentinck with Macaulay's scholarly pretensions that Bentinck allowed him to execute an astonishing and swift rejection of Indian languages, culture and all literature! Endorsement by Bentinck, an ordinarily liberal person, silenced the Committee; all criticism was dismissed, and Macaulay's rash opinion became the basis of British educational policy in India!

At the same time, Macaulay chaired the Commission to establish an India-wide penal code, many of whose clauses he personally drafted and perfected. The model followed two principles: crime suppression with the least agony, and determining truth in the shortest possible time and at the least cost. This Commission's work was applied in all provinces, although Muslim rulers could follow *Sharia* law, as before. Throughout the exercise, he maintained his trenchant and derisive attacks on Hinduism. By these two major thrusts: education and law reform, Macaulay launched the mission to transform India's urban middle class into a group loyal to the British crown, and in every aspect Englishmen, (see above), save for the small detail of the colour of their skin (*coconuts*). This would never become an issue since they would remain in India to propagate their learning and new behaviours, always under the direction of *proper Englishmen* and at arm's length from them. There would be no socialising or intercourse.

Macaulay's plan was diabolically simple: educate the Indians to University level, according to a British curriculum, and make the graduates a dominant social and business elite, but always subservient to a British chief. Educated Indians would thus become the untouchables of the British and would naturally keep their distance from their lesser fellows, family ties notwithstanding.[85] Three flagship universities were built in Calcutta (Kolkata), Madras (Chennai) and Bombay (Mumbai), which soon became the prime ends of Indian educational ambitions. Others followed. Today, 2011, there are 687: 45 central, 322 state, 192 private and 128 with "deemed" university status.

By the 1870's, graduates of the first universities had, like religious converts, become British proselytes and, indeed, began to exceed Macaulay's cherished hopes. Indian aristocrats were isolated from meaningful contact with citizens; their offspring were brain-washed, mainly in British public schools. They became display *coconuts.* One early success was the father of Sri Aurobindo, Dr Krishna Ghose, who was so anglicised that he took excessive care to make sure his children were raised *free* of any Indian influence! Yet two of three became militantly anti-British and served the cause of Independence, Aurobindo becoming quite renowned, and his *ashram* a learning centre in South India.

Features of Jantar mantar, 8th C. Delhi Observatory. These are two of the precision astronomical instruments constructed by Raja Jaisingh and were remarkably accurate.

---

[85] It is said that he had "reported to Parliament" in February 1835 thus: *"I have travelled across the length and breadth of India and I have not seen one person who is a beggar, who is a thief; such wealth I have seen in this country, such high moral values, people of such calibre, that I do not think we would ever conquer this country, unless we break the very backbone of this nation, which is her spiritual and cultural heritage, and therefore I propose that we replace her old and ancient education system, her culture, for if the Indians think that all that is foreign and English is good and greater than their own, they will lose their self-esteem, their native culture and they will become what we want them, a truly dominated nation."* This quote is not in his Minute of Feb 2, 1835, but is consistent with his thinking and may have been a private (off the record) report.

The "Rape" of Indian Industry: the Mellor cotton mill in Marple near Stockport (1802) exemplifies this. It was built in 1790-93 by Samuel Oldknow, England's leading manufacturer of muslin, which used to be made only in Dhaka, East Bengal. The building was six stories high, and the mill was powered by a waterwheel fed from a nearby river, diverted into a series of mill ponds. The cotton-spinning machines requred constant lubrication; the oil used, shale oil, caused a cancer of the scrotum among mule-spinners, first reported in 1887. This was one of the first studied industrial and occupational cancers.

The impeachment of Warren Hastings in Westminster Hall, 1789. Engraver; Pollard, R.; Jan. 3 1789. Downloaded by Fowler& Fowler, Talk, 22:04, 23 March 2008 (UTC) from the British Library Web Site

Chapter 14

"Multiply your ships and send them forth to the East. The nation that draws most materials and provisions from the earth, and fabricates the most, and sells the most of productions and fabrics to foreign nations, must be, and will be, the greatest power on the earth."

William Seward, 1867, U.S. Secretary of State

Constitutional, legitimate, appropriate and pragmatic (CLAP), like the opium trade enforced by the British from India to China, at least from the tyrant's point of view! *Author*

Fall of the Mughals; war of independence

In 1839, with India subdued, the British ironclad *Nemesis* sailed up the Yangtze to "coax" China into accepting the opium trade—*First Opium War, 1839-1842*—and part with Hong Kong. Seven decades earlier, Warren Hastings, on becoming Governor General, had exploited the Company's monopoly on the trade with China—and the opening of Canton (Guangzhou) to foreign trade in 1785—to increase export of opium, whose cultivation he had ordered in Bengal and Bihar. India's Ayurvaidic physicians had for millennia used a weak decoction of opium to treat diarrhoea and impotence. Chinese rulers had rejected the import of opium when Arab traders had brought the Egyptian (Theban) variety to China in 400 AD, and reaffirmed the ban in 1500 AD when the Portuguese had tried to induce the Chinese to *smoke* it.

To maximise revenues, and to avoid shipping risks and clashes with the Chinese, Hastings had decreed that all opium contracts must be auctioned in Calcutta; buyers would pay the taxes and ship the goods to China on Company ships. Soon, the sales enabled the company to pay for Chinese tea, prized in Britain, and very lucrative. The Chinese wished payment in silver, but its rising cost and an official end to Atlantic piracy of Spanish ships forced Britain to find new funding sources.

The opium trade quickly attracted smugglers, including several Americans, some famous, like John Jacob Astor *(American Fur Company, N.Y.)*, and John Cushing *(J. & T. H. Perkins Co,* Boston*)*, creating multi-millionaires and large commercial houses, many extant today. T.H. Perkins was a prominent Boston aristocrat and one of the wealthiest men in America. But the best known opium trader was Dr William Jardine, a founder of *Jardine, Matheson and Co.*, a leading Hong Kong firm today, and one of the world's largest. Dr Jardine was ironically a BEICo ship's doctor charged with preventing and treating illness! Like other officers, he was allowed the space of two tea chests—together 0.4 cubic metre—for personal business cargo, provided it was "local" and did not compete with the Company. In 1802, Jardine quickly discovered that smuggling opium to the Chinese was far more profitable than practising medicine! On one voyage, his ship was captured by Napoleon's Navy and its cargo seized; Jardine lost his chests, but met and soon partnered with a fellow passenger, an Indian named Jamshedji Jeejeebhoy, nicknamed *bottlewalla* (bottle merchant). Jardine campaigned relentlessly against Company monopoly, which ended in 1834. Two years earlier, Jardine and an associate, Matheson, had formed the Company, in which Jeejeebhoy, one of modern India's wealthiest names, had a substantial interest.

Meanwhile, Europe had developed a cult of opium use: chewed, imbibed, inhaled and later injected, popularised by writers like John Keats, Thomas de Quincey, Elizabeth Barrett Browning and André Malraux. BEICo users included Clive, Hastings, the Wellesley brothers and other Indian adventurers. British generals used and fed it to Sepoys. Bonaparte used it in France, as did Rhodes in Africa. Keats' melancholy verses, as he slowly died of tuberculosis, are especially moving, and suggest why the drug was so popular: *"My heart aches, and a drowsy numbness pains/ My sense, as though of hemlock I had drunk,/Or emptied some dull opiate to the drains/One minute past, and Lethe-wards had sunk"* and *"...Fade far away, dissolve and quite forget/What thou among the leaves hast never known/The weariness, the fever and the fret/Here where men sit and hear each other groan."*

British gunships, in two *Opium Wars, 1842 and 1856-60,*"convinced" the Chinese to accept the opium trade. The *Treaty of Nanking,* in 1842, ceded Hong Kong Island to the British. Eventually, over 120 million Chinese would become opium-addicted, eliminating 25% of China's population and ending the Qing dynasty in Nanking. In 1860, a combined British-French invasion of Beijing ended with the looting and destruction of the magnificent Summer Palace and Imperial Gardens (*Yuanmingyuan* or *Gardens of Perfect Brightness),* and transfer of treasures to Britain and France, an act described as barbarity by French writer Victor Hugo. The destruction was ordered by Britain's Lord Elgin, supposedly in retaliation for the capture and torture of an army "peace contingent", which included Indian sepoys. Thus did the Europeans display to the world the cruelty of power and the heartlessness of civilised greed. Coupled with racial superiority hypotheses, then becoming intellectually popular in Britain, Europe and America, they persuaded even ostensibly humane physicians to promote addiction and succumb to immorality and crime. The loot was scattered across Europe.

At this time, Britain moved to secure the India's NW frontier by turning Afghanistan into a buffer zone against Asian invaders. British imperialists had long viewed the imposing Hindu Kush Mountains as a natural protection from northern invaders and had conceived the *"Forward Policy"* to seize all lands between Delhi and the mountains—which included parts of Afghanistan—to gain control, and thus security.

When Napoleon fell, the likeliest threat to Britain became the surging Russian Empire, with whom Britain played the "great game", as British writers dubbed it, to win the Middle East and Central Asia. In the 1790s, Russian Emperor, Paul, had allied with Britain against Napoleon, and in 1801, sent an army of Cossacks on a mission to conquer south central Asia and perhaps India. With Paul's assassination, the mission aborted near the Aral Sea, less than a thousand miles from home; but the fact that the mission had taken place, heightened British paranoia, caused further cooling between Russia and Britain and eventually led to war.

Russia had already penetrated the regions south and east of the Aral Sea and Amu Darya, and had formed an alliance with Persia. In 1838, Lord Auckland, British Governor General, arrogantly issued the *Shimla manifesto (a dawah),* detailing the conditions to be met by Afghanistan, to avoid hostilities. Needing a malleable and greedy strongman as British puppet, he chose Shuja Shah Durrani as the ruler, while the Afghans generally preferred Akbar Khan, son of Emir Dost Mohamed. Auckland sent an army, mostly of Indians, under two William's—Elphinstone and MacNaghten—which had initial successes and later captured the fort at Ghazni, by the tried and true technique of bribery of an enemy officer, euphemistically called "strategic alliance" or, more aptly, "sharing the trough", which remains a most potent and universal tool today!

The corrupt Afghan enabled the invaders to blow up a city gate. However, the battle see-sawed and came to a stalemate. After two years of skirmishing and negotiations, all in bad faith, MacNaghten tried to bribe Akbar Khan into letting the British remain, by offering him the position of Afghanistan's vizier, while spending lavishly on potential traitors to assassinate him! How typical of imperial Britain's double-dealing and immorality! Akbar found out and attended a planned meeting, where the plotter MacNaghten and three officers with him were summarily executed! Poetic justice, you might say.

MacNaghten's body was paraded through Kabul streets, and in the ensuing flight of army and civilians only a few, all captives but two, survived the harsh winter's trek to Jallalabad. The dead included families that had joined the troops in Kabul, in the wake of initial British victories, so confident of conquest had been their commanders. This defeat undermined the fearsome reputation of the Company, and the British lost considerable face. Their failure to take Afghanistan was a sober lesson in resistance hardly heeded by Indians, who seemed to have forgotten how feuding Kalinga and Magadha had agreed to an alliance two millennia earlier, to repel Alexander's Greeks, should they invade.

Anxious to protect western India from the Baluchi allies of the Afghans, the British invaded and conquered Sindh in a bloody campaign in 1843. (*"Peccavi!"*[86] General Charles Napier telegraphed Calcutta, with pride. When Queen Victoria got the news, she is alleged to have said, "Get the poor man a priest!")

In the north Maharajah Ranjit Singh had created a Sikh kingdom composed of Punjab, Multan, Peshawar, Jammu and Kashmir. His death in 1839 left the state at the mercy of factions, and weak or young successors, whom the British attacked and eventually subjugated in two wars, from 1845 to 1849, led by Sirs Hugh Gough and Henry Hardinge, Bengal's Governor General. Sikhs lost Kashmir and other land to the British, who exacted steep tolls. When the Sikhs failed to pay, BEICo sold Kashmir to Jammu's Raja Ghulab Singh for £1 million. The Sikh loss is especially poignant in that the young Rāja Duleepsinghi (1838-93) lost his possessions, including the *Koh-I-Noor*, the famous diamond, and his home. He was parted from his mother, who was exiled to Nepal, while he was forced into exile in Britain, where he spent the rest of his life[87].

Raja Duleepsinghi

Sikhs should have won the first war but were plagued with divisions and incompetence, and the treachery of their commanders Lal Singh and Tegh Singh, who "allowed" the enemy to win key battles! Under the Khalsa, Sikhs had lost the sympathy of their neighbours, barring a brief alliance with Afghans under Dost Mohamed Khan. The Sikh Wars illustrated once again the failure of Indian rulers to recognise the high cost of insularity, disunity, internal squabbles and personal ambition. Nor did they seem to appreciate the stupidity of opportunistic responses

[86] Latin: *"I have sinned"*, a translingual pun!

[87] He converted to Christianity as a ward of the BEICo and was allowed to return to India to bring his mother to England in 1860 and three years later to return her ashes. Both visits were under close guard. He reconverted to Sikhism seven years before his death. He was called the Black Prince of Perthshire and his eight children, by two wives, one Coptic, the other English, called 'dusky tadpoles,' died without heirs, officially ending his line. In the late 1880s he failed to persuade the Czar of Russia to invade India. The Indian Government maintains its claim to the *Koh-i-noor*.

to foreigners who wished to gobble up the country and loot its wealth; nor how eager the BEICo was to sacrifice Indian sepoys to do this!

In the four decades after the last Maratha war the British expanded relentlessly, seizing lands worldwide, by treaties, stratagems, chicanery, deception, criminality and war, plundering countries shamelessly, just as English colonists in New England had done, two centuries earlier, by cheating the Natives of their lands. This behaviour stemmed from the imperial conviction that mercantilism was good for rulers, who could share in the profits, while overlooking the shameful fact that merchants would simply gouge the populace to maximise profits. (Sociologists ponder the magnitude of plebeian poverty and the rising prevalence and concentration of extreme wealth. It's simple, really. The total populace produces wealth, of which 90% is grabbed by the leading 10% to make them rich. A tenth of these acquire enough to become wealthy, and a tenth of them so rich as to gain absolute power and control over nations and the souls of people, hoping to use that wealth to assure survival and ascendancy when empires collapse, as they inevitably must.)

The residue of Mughal rule disintegrated over several decades by intrigue and attrition. Their decline, like the British domination, showed the contrast in the styles of two brutal conquerors: the one erratic and idiosyncratic; the other, their successor, more organised, devious and bullying; both greedy and steeped in religious dogma.

For the Mughals India had become home; they were finally secure and settled luxuriously in a land of plenty with a sophisticated, developed and learned society beyond anything they had known. They relied on Hindus and Buddhists for economic strength, social stability and progress, knowledge and skills, but reserved the higher executive positions for Muslims, thus inducing many Indians, including royalty, to convert to Islam as a sure route to increased wealth and power. Wealth remained in India, enriching the rulers, while the majority was taxed into serfdom. Skilled Hindus kept their jobs and trades, albeit at a down-graded social level. Mughal rulers enjoyed this symbiosis for seven centuries, until chauvinism and religious zeal led them to destroy the very things that had made them so prosperous. Akbar had recognised this when he tried to accommodate Hinduism, by separating government from religion. But his success eventually dissipated in his murderous approach to the peoples of non-Mughal India, mainly in the south, creating another line of division among Indian peoples.

By contrast, the British in a cold and calculated raid over three and a half centuries, raped India and transferred its wealth to Britain, where much of it still lies in the hands of aristocrats and royal families. While the Mughals coveted wealth and invaded India openly to get it, they stayed and recycled their booty, but the British came as "wolves in sheep's clothing" and took the plunder home.

Not to be outdone, Indian merchants seized opportunities for profit-making by serving the invader as diligently as the defender, in the way the patriarch of the Rothschild fortunes had advised his sons, i.e. never to favour one side in granting loans to warring kings and governments! Profit flowed whether the borrower won or lost; the wars profited both Indian moneylenders and the Rothschilds.

British oppression took on a new and crushing face under Governor General Dalhousie (1848-56). The harshness and excesses of British hegemony had increased steadily since the fall of the Maratha Confederacy and Britain was flexing its muscles in Europe, Australia and Africa. India seethed for forty years, before a rebellious spark was lit. In that time, the spread of British imports into India's heartland had ruined its artisans, while heavy taxation was ruining farmers. The dispossessed soon became desperate enough to cross the *kāla pāni* (dark water) to get work. First, it was to Mauritius and Réunion in 1834, then British Guiana in 1838; others followed steadily, establishing the Indian Diaspora.

On Dalhousie's arrival, he proclaimed the autocratic European *Doctrine of Lapse,* whereby entities which had become *Subsidiary Alliances* would fall to the Company if the ruler died without a direct heir, or were deemed incompetent. He promptly began a tyrannical programme of annexation of princely states and subsidiaries, ignoring past agreements and custom. He took Sātārā that year, Jaipur and Sambalpur (1849), Nāgpur and Jhānsi (1854), and Oudh (1856), all for shallow reasons that no court in Britain or Europe would have upheld e.g. *late* payment of tribute! He divested the ruler of Tanjore of his title in 1855, in a breach of agreement, and denied Nana Bithur a pension inherited from his father, according to British rules!

University construction began, in line with the Macaulay plan, and in 1853, a vigorous campaign of railroad building and installation of telegraphy for rapid military deployment, speedy communication and commercial distribution that, with the isolation of *rajas,* put an end to any notion of military revolt. Two hundred miles of railway track were built by 1858, five thousand by 1869, 25,000 miles in 1900 and 35,000 miles 10 years later. The network expanded steadily to reach over 50,000 miles by 1950, to become the world's largest, saddling India with a huge and lasting debt.

The railways reached the smaller villages fairly quickly, destroyed immense acreages of India's forests, devastated the environment and ruined much local industry and agriculture. Even though new kinds of jobs and opportunities were created, they were regrettably at the lowest levels, substituting poorly-paid labour for displaced artisans, small businessmen and aspiring administrators.

The British could have made some amends for the job losses their policies had caused, had they given the displaced any worthwhile positions with the railways. Mass migration to cities and overseas began, chasing crumbs from British factories while Indian rulers remained impotent and compliant. Did any ponder, as Macaulay had criticised, how they had missed chances presented by the industrial revolution to build new tools and industries, and perhaps internal alliances to resist invaders, instead of squandering capital in opulence and squabbling?

Some did pursue new opportunities, especially Parsis of Mumbai, a few brighter members of royal families, and intellectuals. But the spirit of the Mauryans, Guptas, Shivaji, the kings of Vijayanagara, Chalukya, Pandya and Chola, and many other heroes, was stifled in disunity. Instead, princes saved their skins and continued to live well, while village artisans and farmers—more than 80% of the population—suffered, and at times of famine or disease, millions starved to death; a few chose survival in migration, bravely breaking long-standing taboos.

British harassment, bullying and contempt for Indians (see Macaulay in *"The Impeachment of Warren Hastings")* raised increasing alarms among Indians and even stirred critical responses in Britain, mostly from missionaries who came to India to proselytise, concentrating on key figures and the poor. Ram Mohan Roy was an early link. (An associate of missionary Thomas Carey tried to convert Roy to Christianity but instead became a Hindu!)

The Missions established Christian schools in many parts of India. In the period to the war of Independence, various attempts were made to improve the lot of ordinary citizens but the resulting Associations, some with English direction, only belatedly addressed grassroots issues and faltered, until John Drinkwater Bethune, a lawyer and member of the Governor General's Council, proposed a law to bring British subjects under Company jurisdiction.

White objections to this, which they called *Black Acts*, led Indians to greater introspection, especially as the Company Charter was due for Parliamentary review in 1833. The leaders grappled with the complexities and contradictions of the need to place Indians in a civil and just society with guaranteed rights, especially equality of treatment, regardless of wealth, ethnicity, colour, or class biases, British or Indian.

Vaidic scholars knew that there were four interchangeable *varnas* but Brahmins had listed a fifth, the untouchables, people with insanitary jobs, restricted in what they could do or claim in Indian society. This recalls the exclusion of Blacks by Americans, and by the French in Haiti, at the time of their independence, on the grounds of race. The British had reduced all but the indispensable and wealthy to the economic level of "untouchable" leaving only a few cracks to allow squeeze-through passage for the inventive and resolute. Thus Indians had to decide how to reconcile potentially divisive reforms of Hinduism, or piecemeal adoption of western ways, with the need to form a unified force against tyranny. As the 16th century poet, Prithiraj, had noted, *"The hopes of the Hindu rest on the Hindu…"* (p.153).

Indians enlisted British Unitarians who sought similar goals and seemed kindly and understanding. But these posed two hurdles: Christian proselytising (as most were missionaries) and loyalty to the Crown. Neither of these was acceptable to the majority, for the tyrant needed to learn that his time at the helm was limited. The British would depart; the only question was when, and by what means. Sober minds conferred and formed successive associations to bring together the thinkers to fashion a plan that would see transitional devolution of decision-making; redress imbalances e.g. the British were paid 5-10 times what Indians earned in an equivalent position; Indians were denied promotion to the highest ranks, in spite of talent, deprived of education, health care and job opportunities, or relief from taxes. Women's rights and freedoms were curtailed, plebs abused by landlords, employers, the military and police, and suffered a multitude of other social ills.

Ram Mohan Roy had approached reform by joining with Scottish Baptist missionary, William Adam, to form the *Calcutta Unitarian Society.* When this failed, Roy switched to Hinduism and formed the *Brahmo Sabha* as a reform vehicle. In 1839, a delegation of *Landholders* led by Dwarkanath Tagore visited the *British India Society*, an anti-slavery UK group, to study their programme. On return in 1840, with George Thompson, an English abolitionist, in tow, they joined with *Young Bengal* to form the *Bengal British India Society,* led by Thompson, Tarachand Chakraborty, Ramgopal Ghosh, and others, to address issues on a Pan-Indian basis, while remaining loyal to the Government. They publicised in the UK paper, *British Indian Advocate,* Indian conditions needing redress. It is uncertain whether their message went beyond intellectuals.

At that time, the *Committee of the British and Foreign Anti-Slavery Society* had commented: *"In order effectually to relieve the suffering and oppressed Hindoos, they humbly conceive a series of enlightened, humane, and comprehensive laws must be substituted for those which exist; and the present system of mis-government be entirely abandoned. All partial expedients to relieve the misery which so extensively prevails in that vast country, can, in their judgement, only have the effect of retarding the introduction of those searching reforms which the exigencies of the people, and the prosperity and security of the empire so immediately and peremptorily require."* This shows clearly that there was a segment of conscionable British society, perhaps a majority, almost all non-aristocrats, and therefore powerless, which disagreed with the Government's India policy. But that was not enough; India, as US Senator William J. Bryan later remarked, quoting H. Hyndman, was run by British carpetbaggers who did not allow morality or reason to intrude into, or influence their methods.

Meanwhile Rev Alex Duff had started the Scottish Church College (Presbyterian) in Calcutta in 1830, with the aim of inducing high caste Indians to accept Christianity, having persuaded his home Church to fund education, on the theory, later promulgated by Macaulay and Müller, that when Indians were educated in western science, humanities and the Bible they would abandon Hinduism and its "*myths*". By educating the higher "castes" they expected that knowledge would "filter" down to those below!

This of course did not happen, and only exposed the ignorance of an alien and intolerant culture that did not have the collective wit to suspect that an old and accomplished society must have had some mathematical, scientific and socio-economic basis for its governance, development and prosperity, some profound ethical and spiritual philosophy to nurture and satisfy hundreds of millions, for millennia, and must be capable of analysis and reform from within, and not by foreign neophytes.

Duff's constricted and elitist approach to conversion, and his belief that dull Hindus would see the shining Christian light, led them only to snigger. What he had failed to see was that Hinduism was neither rigid nor petulant; it was inclusive, tolerant of diverse religious views and could lay claim to have educated Jesus Christ! This was anathema then, as it still is, in Christian circles. (This is amazing; Christianity stands to lose nothing by this. Indeed, only gains can come from shedding ill-founded biases and moving closer to true ecumenism, if not beliefs based on common core principles that allowed individualised worship.)

The *Brahmo Sabha* had languished on Ram Mohan Roy's death, until Debendranath Tagore, the co-founder's son, a religious man, founded in 1839 the *Tattwabodhini* (Truth-seekers*) Sabha* (TS), attracting the polyglot Akshay Kumar Datta and the polymath Ishwar Chandra Vidyasagar, a professor at Fort William College. They taught and wrote, including textbooks, and promoted female education nationwide; they attracted reformist members of the snobbish Kulin Brahmins of Bengal, dipped into Christianity and Unitarianism, and adopted faith in God and public worship as adjuncts to Hindu standards. This inevitably angered Kulin Brahmins leading to schisms. *Tattwabodhini Sabha* merged with the Brahmo Sabha in the 1860s, to form the *Brahmo Samaj,* and spread the reform throughout India, while each religion could devise its own ways of expression. It maintained its anglophile stance and support for the *Rāja*, a position Akshay Kumar Datta did not share.

The seeds of political rebellion matched the religious in number and had been widely sown, but Indians remained divided by old habits, exploited by an unscrupulous and cunning merchant-conqueror before whom they stood cowed, powerless and subdued. Scattered skirmishes did occur across the land, only to be hastily punished, most often by hanging someone, anyone, more to terrorise than punish; a conviction in each instance seemed so easy to achieve as eye-witnesses cropped up everywhere, even in pitch blackness, desperate for a few rupees!

Indians smarted under the repressions, denial of equal rights and any voice in governance, the favouritism and exclusivity given whites in the Indian Civil Service which would increase relentlessly in the 20th century so that Nehru could remark that the Indian Civil Service was neither Indian, civil nor a service!

Taxation fell harshly on those least able to pay; the imposition of British culture and denigration of Indian religions weighed heavily on Indians. Suddenly a catalyst for rebellion was supplied in 1856, when the Company callously and arrogantly introduced a new Enfield rifled musket whose cartridge casings were greased with animal fat—beef or pork—which the soldier had to bite off to access the powder. Sepoys refused to do this, Hindus rejecting beef and Muslims pork. The army's cold and unsurprising response was that the soldiers could supply the fat, clearly a mean, impractical and cruel suggestion certain to inflame anger and conflict.

The resulting uprising began in Bengal in 1857 and fuelled the wider War of Independence, perhaps prematurely. Certainly there were grounds enough, and forces enough, had Indians decided to unite for once against a foe that had become increasingly punitive, despotic and aggressive. The Sepoy revolt followed the annexation of Oudh, where many had their roots and lands, and feared loss of perquisites and overseas service bonuses, plus having to pay heavier taxes to the colonial rulers. Many had served in the 1856 Anglo-Burmese War.

At that time, the total army under direct Company command was 350,538—including 38,977 military police, probably all Indians. The Bengal Presidency had 159,003 troops—cavalry, infantry and artillery—of which Indian nationals were *137,571* or *86.5%*. Interestingly 14% of British troops were in artillery compared to just over 3% of Indians. Bengal Indians represented 44% of Indians in the Company's total army and almost all joined the revolt. However, the *British Indian Association,* the upper echelons of Bengal, the armies of the Madras and Bombay presidencies, the Nizam's troops, and Punjabis—including Sikhs whom the British had humiliated earlier—stuck with the Company. Of these, the Sikhs, rather than stay clear, fought harder than their fellows to defeat the rebellion, much to the dismay of Indians who had hoped at last for unity against a vicious occupier. Indians behaved true to form, subdued again by treachery and threats. Influential Bengali Associations and reformers forgot BEICo's cruel record and incredibly sided with it.

The revolt involved many brave and talented men and women, old and young. They achieved early success, capturing Kanpur and Delhi, but failed to hold them, largely through disunity and the stranglehold the British had over Indian kingdoms and provinces. Nāna Sahib of Bithur, an adopted son of Bajirao II, Tantia Tope, son of a nobleman in Bajirao's court, and Rani Lakshmi Bai of Jhānsi became the major leaders. They fought valiantly, scored initial victories but were let down by rājas, who had grown soft and lazy under British sinecures and defeated by propaganda and other mind games. Tope was a brilliant guerrilla fighter, but was betrayed by an associate, Raja Man Singh of Narwar, and eventually executed on April 18, 1859 in a brutish act, contrary to accepted legal canons of *"rebellion against an invader"*. Civilian casualties bothered rebels, but hardly fazed the British.[88]

"It is true that Tantia Tope was responsible for waging war against the British government, but, it was no crime to fight against a foreign invader."[89] In *Revolt in Central India*, British writer W. Milayson noted: *"It is doubtful whether the succeeding generations will accept the verdict as correct, the verdict of a British War Tribunal. Tantia...was not bound by the legal dictates of foreign occupiers who had deprived his Peshwa of his estate and ruling power."* Yet the British relied on such dictates and skewed the laws to gain convictions throughout the Empire. Earlier, Lakshmi Bai and her Dalit double Jalkari Bai, had met death, with thousands. Begum Hazrat Mahal of Lucknow had proudly led rebels and when Lucknow fell, spurned British terms of surrender and escaped to Nepal, where she died in 1879. These and others are famous as martyrs, despite British smears and efforts to erase their names from popular memory, and degrade the rebellion to a simple mutiny. Sepoy leaders were hanged and thousands of others were sentenced to *"transportation"* and indenture in British Honduras.

A number of nationals had secretly given time and money to the independence struggle in the action against Delhi, often at great cost.

---

[88] The Rajputs of Jaipur were said to own the world's largest cannons at the time of the 1857 War of Independence. Yet, none was ever used against the British who "succeeded in conquering the sub-continent without ever having to fight the country's best equipped armies, thus demonstrating that technological progress is not an end in itself." It also underlines the divisions and rivalries that have plagued the rulers of India for a millennium, and the successful manipulation and separation of Indian rulers by British businessmen and militia.

[89] T. Foryst, a British chronicler quoted in M S Gill in *Trials That Changed History.*

Many were arrested for acting or speaking suspiciously at the time of Lakshmi Bai's murder and the British recapture of Delhi. This saddened everyone involved, and put whole villages and towns into a state of high alert, especially in view of the tempting rewards offered by the British for information on rebels. The citizenry was terrorised, some arrested, and for decades tension remained high. A number of sympathisers and participants enlisted for indenture overseas to escape the unrelenting searches and arbitrary arrests.

British success was due as much to the ease with which they exploited internecine rivalries as to the quality of their armaments and naval strength. They suborned Rajputs to stay out of the conflict. Decades earlier Haider Ali of Mysore had ruefully noted that it would be difficult to defeat an enemy that had a strong Navy, and had hoped that the rockets he and his son Tippu Sultan were developing could change that. They were too late.[90]. Britain would later achieve the acme of world power with the suppression of the Indian rebellion, and the scientific, industrial and metaphysical changes brought on by the Industrial Revolution that made Britain supreme among European nations.

The search for dissidents and revolutionaries continued, marked by periodic disappearances of young men and women. However admirable the rebels, they—perhaps caught unprepared by the spontaneity of the sepoy uprising—had failed to engage the public at large, whose historical memory may have been far superior to that of their leaders. The populace may well have seen the revolt as merely the efforts of the dispossessed elite to regain their former fiefdoms, with no real concern to improve the lives of the needy masses. A great irony and error was the rebels' hasty choice of 80-year old, politically emasculated *Mughal* "Emperor" Bahadur Shah, as an icon of freedom; he had been confined to the Red Fort for 20 years, and was unlikely to rouse a spontaneous support by Sikhs, a probable explanation for their antagonism.

Having quelled the revolt, the British government replaced the Company and formally swapped Mughal rule for an even more oppressive and extractive administration: the British *Rāja*. It lasted 90 years and made Victoria Empress of India, when Disraeli became Prime Minister in 1874. Britain then claimed Bengal, Bihar, Orissa and Awadh in the east; Punjab, Multan and Sindh in the west; Nagpur in the centre; and south, the Malabar and Coromandel coasts, Carnatic, Sarkars and Ceylon. Rājputāna, Gujarāt, Mysore, Hyderābad, the former Marātha kingdoms of central India, and a number of principalities across the country remained subsidiaries as they had been since the last Marātha

[90] William Congreve, a protégée of the Prince of Wales, seized Mysorean rockets, added some flourishes and his name and got the British Army to use them in the US War of 1812.

war in 1818. Only Kashmir, Nepal, Bhutan and the north-east remained independent. The French and Portuguese kept their trading posts.

With regard to the Sepoys, many have marvelled that so many Indians had been recruited to fight for the British, almost from the first year of the Company's arrival in India, despite meagre incomes and discriminatory selection criteria, favouring the so-called *"martial races"* —kshatriyas, cultivators and certain brahmin groups—who had no qualms fighting fellow Indians. The poor among them were believed to be the bravest and thus good *cannon fodder.* They were held by petty gifts of land or small favours and by pitting them in war against traditional rivals, usually under the influence of opium. Loyalty was also ensured by status, coercion and threats to family, and fomenting divisions. After 1857, sepoys were recruited mainly from among Sikhs, Ghurkhas and other groups, to separate the Army from the general populace.

The sepoys generally gave loyal service, despite harsh treatment by cruel leaders. There is evidence of secret episodic planning for revolt that could not easily mature into concerted action, because of communication barriers, lack of leadership, and animosities, which the British exploited and nurtured to keep the groups apart, and loyal to them by default; for example, the BEICo's Bombay Army of Mahars fought against their fellow Marathas and won a crucial battle in 1818. Rajputs, Bengalis and South Indians did the same in Mughal and British wars and put self-interest before national security or integrity [91].

It is worth repeating that whatever little unity Indians had was based almost wholly on the dharmic religions—Hinduism, Buddhism, Jainism—and that Indians were never ethnically homogeneous any more than Europeans, nor any less quarrelsome! Indeed French, Dutch and even English soldiers had fought for the Mughals, Marathas and Tippu Sultan against the British. It is said that Hitler would have found little difficulty in raising a British division to fight against their fellows in a conquered England, given appropriate incentives.

British India assumed the territories ruled directly by the BEICo and by the *Sanad* deed continued to recognise the rule of princes in Bundelkhand and Bagelkhand over their states, in return for signed bonds of allegiance *(ikrarnama)*. Eleven of the 148 princely states were

---

[91] Many have noted that the Hindu Rajput kings of Jaipur have long been vilified for their staunch allegiance to the Mughal Emperor, a relationship they rarely developed with Hindu sovereigns. Even as late as 1963 Indian leadership still lacked a truly national vision and was quite likely to succumb to foreign blandishments, initially the USSR, later the USA, that threaten the Union. Americans were always waiting in the wings, certain that India will crumble under corrupt leaders, and are busy promoting and exploiting that, using bribery, the CIA, missionaries, corporations, NGOs and other agencies, to grab the pieces as they fall, just as the British had done!

held by treaty: Gwalior, Indaur, Bhopal, Dhār, the two Dewas States, Jaora, Orchha, Datia, Samthar, and Rewa while the remainder answered to a larger state. The British either mediated the terms of association or guaranteed to the states continuation of their rights and privileges existing at the end of the Pindari War (3rd Maratha War).

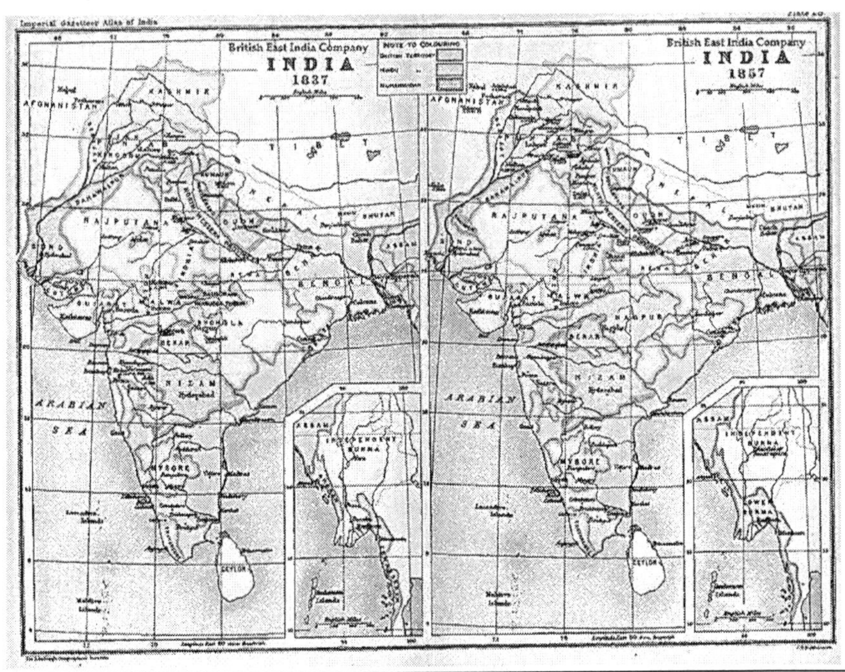

The War of Independence had smouldered for a century since the days of Clive as India teetered between the excesses of the British and the disunity of Indian rulers. Mangal Panday, the young soldier who fired the first shot in outrage against his Sgt. Major and adjutant, finally showed what must be done, but mercifully did not live to see the carnage that reprisals brought. The British press gloated and screamed for blood, praising the brutality of their own and condemning Indians, even the many civilians killed. Britain proceeded to gut India, seize its industries, scuttle its state-of-the-art manufactures and substitute shoddy goods. They destroyed peasant farming, bribed rulers or else "legally" eliminated them, plotted to undermine India's major religions and transferred her wealth to Britain—*the most egregious example of international theft in history, eclipsing the Romans.* The US today, it seems, is aiming to outdo the British in rapacity, raiding the world's nations, using a variety of peaceful instruments, from treaties and free trade agreements to bribery, and when swifter and more convincing, war.

Begum Hazrat Mahal and Tantia Tope

British Reaction to 1857 War of Independence, a sample. You would think India had invaded the UK!

..."... All the city's people found within the walls of the city of Delhi when our troops entered were bayoneted on the spot, and the number was considerable, as you may suppose, when I tell you that in some houses forty and fifty people were hiding. These were not mutineers but residents of the city, who trusted to our well-known mild rule for pardon. I am glad to say they were disappointed." (*Extract from a letter published in the "Bombay Telegraph"; reproduced in the British press, 1857.)*

"It was literally murder... I have seen many bloody and awful sights lately but such a one as I witnessed yesterday I pray I never see again. The women were all spared but their screams on seeing their husbands and sons butchered, were most painful... Heaven knows I feel no pity, but when some old grey bearded man is brought and shot before your very eyes, hard must be that man's heart I think who can look on with indifference..." (Edward Vibart, a 19-year-old officer.")

"All honour to you for catching the king and slaying his sons. I hope you will bag many more!" General Montgomery to Captain Hodgson, on his massacre of Delhiites, 1857.

"With all my love for the army, I must confess, the conduct of professed Christians on this occasion, was one of the most humiliating facts connected with the siege." Capt. Hodgson, British Army in India, 1857.

British soldiers looting Qaisar Bagh, Lucknow, after its recapture. The Times correspondent looks on at the sacking of the Qaisar Bagh, after the capture of Lucknow on March 15, 1858. "Is this string of little white stones (pearls) worth anything, Gentlemen?" asks the looter. Who's the barbarian and who is the thief?

British officers executing captured Indians by blowing them from guns! This had taken on the aura of a sport, as brave as hunting tigers from the safety of an elephant's back

The hangings, a favourite British blood sport, cost less than cannon shots; victims lined up for their turn

"And England, now avenge their wrongs by vengeance deep and dire,/ Cut out their canker with the sword, and burn it out with fire;/ Destroy those traitor regions, hang every pariah hound,/ And hunt them down to death, in all hills and cities 'round."
Martin Tupper, stirring bloodthirsty hate in Britain, *Wrath of the Lion*, NY Times reprint, 1857, emphasising the slaughter of Indians.

JUSTICE.

Women of India (Ch. 26) Rich and Poor:

Below *L: Mastani, wife of Bajirao 1; Right: Rural young woman whose family lands were seized by British and passed to zamindars. Today US corporations do the same, with collusion of Indians.*

"There are some parts of the world that, once visited, get into your heart and won't go. For me, India is such a place. When I first visited, I was stunned by the richness of the land, by its lush beauty and exotic architecture, by its ability to overload the senses with the pure, concentrated intensity of its colors, smells, tastes, and sounds. It was as if all my life I had been seeing the world in black and white and, when brought face-to-face with India, experienced everything re-rendered in brilliant technicolour." - Keith Bellows (Editor-in-chief, National Geographic Society)

R: Lakshmi Bai of Jhansi, heroine of 1857 Indian War of Independence, killed in action

Below: Sipahis (sepoys) in action in Indian War of Indevendence, 1857

1876 Punch cartoon captioned "New crowns for old ones!" PM Disraeli (1804 – 81) making Queen Victoria Empress of India!

Below:
Residence of businessman Sir Jamsetjee Jejeebhoy, 1st Baronet, 1858, a Parsi, notable for his alliance with Dr Jardine in opium trade with China. His palace is lit to welcome the British monarch. As businessmen, Parsis were generally aloof from others and tended to support the Rāja, in the hope of favours returned. They control the film industry, in which they retain their biases, especially colour.

Chapter 15

"All differences in this world are of degree, and not of kind, because oneness is the secret of everything."
Swāmi Vivekānanda

Even a much shorter time ago than that, if you travelled in a railway train with an Indian, or drove in a motor car with an Indian, you were supposed to be lowering the British Raj.
Major Graham Pole, British House of Commons, 1929

Conquest by Hoax: Macaulay and Müller

As efforts to convert Hindus miscarried, the British sought an Englishman, knowledgeable in Sanskrit, who could render the *Vaidas* in such a way that the Indian, newly educated in English, could be led to discard them in favour of the *Bible*. They found none, but in 1847, came upon Frederick Max Müller, ardent young Christian and German nationalist, an unemployed classical linguist and Sanskrit student, who eagerly accepted a grant from the BEICo to translate the *Rg Vaidas,* at £4 per sheet. Müller expected to show, by comparative linguistics, that India's past achievements and advances, the *Vaidas* included, were either the work of foreigners, or a collection of myths. This he dutifully did, despite the ancient structures and contradictions, and received the same favourable reception from an ignorant and biased audience as Mill's book had; the BEICo trumpeted it world-wide.

In 1866 Müller wrote, *"This edition of mine and the translation of the Vaida will hereafter tell, to a great extent...the fate of India, and on the growth of millions... in that country. It is the root of their religion, and to show them what the root is, I feel sure, is the only way of uprooting all that has sprung from it during the last 3,000 years."*

Müller had settled in Oxford as a philologist, not a scientist; his Vaidic work and discussions revealed several errors in translation, and in astronomy and mathematics. Main examples were, as already noted, the capitalising of the Sanskrit adjective *"aryan"*, meaning *"noble"*, giving it a racial meaning absent from the original Sanskrit, and so invented an "aryan race" which he claimed was nomadic, central Asian, invaded India, fought and evicted indigenous people, invented Sanskrit and composed the *Vaidas,* all in an incredibly brief period, all without trace. Knowledge of astronomy and mathematics would have shown this to be highly improbable, according to references in the same *Vaidas.*

As a Christian, Müller believed the Bible literally and thus had to discount Vaidic chronology to create a version of Indian history fitting the Old Testament account of creation which is said to have occurred in 4004 BC. Thus he compressed 10,000 or more years of pre-Christian Indian history, to 2,000 years. He also ignored *Vaidic* references, such as to ocean or sea, neither of which is to be found in central Asia. His error was made at the time of German unification under Bismarck, the rise of nationalism and search for identity, and was used to "prove" their belief that German peoples had descended from this mythical superior race, and migrated west, most likely from *Sogdiana* in Central Asia.

The rebuttal and censure of this British propaganda—presented mainly in Indian languages and papers—hardly made the western press. The propaganda remains manifest and dominant, chiefly among Indian secularists, converts and anglophilic intellectuals, however reputable or respected, who even now repeat and promulgate this flawed hypothesis, despite Müller's retracting his original stance: *"If I say Aryas, I mean neither blood nor bones, nor hair nor skull; I mean simply those who speak an Aryan language…To me, an ethnologist who speaks of Aryan race, Aryan blood, Aryan eyes and hair is as great a sinner as a linguist who speaks of a dolichocephalic dictionary or a brachycephalic grammar."*

But he had retracted too late. The British had publicised it and Germany had developed a keen interest in Sanskrit and "Indology", a bastard hodgepodge of beliefs and approaches reflecting the "scholars", not the subject, starting with the teachings of Frenchman Joseph de Goubineau (1816-1882), who, in *The Inequality of Human Races,* declared the "Aryan race" as superior above all and of aristocratic hierarchy (see p. 172). That boosted German race theories and led, later on, to Adolf Hitler's "Aryan" racism and his misappropriation of a mirror image of the *Vaidic* emblem *Swastika* as his party's symbol. Müller's use of "cephalic" reflects the beliefs of that time re phrenology and Caucasian racial superiority.

As their experiment matured and the products emerged, Macaulay wrote *"Our English schools are flourishing wonderfully….The effect of this education on the Hindoos is prodigious… It is my firm belief, that, if our plans for education are followed up, there will not be a single idolater among the respectable classes in Bengal thirty years hence. And this will be effected without any efforts to proselytise, without the smallest interference with religious liberty, merely by the natural operation of knowledge and reflection. I heartily rejoice in the prospect."*

Macaulay systematically peddled disinformation about Indian culture and denial of Indian heroes, recent and remote, their achievements in science, mathematics, governance, agriculture, the military, literary pursuits, religion, history and civilisation. He debased Hindus and Hinduism, and altogether succeeded in destroying the self-esteem of educated Indians, especially urban, by disdaining their background, and consolidated this by curricular indoctrination of students into British ways, at all levels. His vision of transforming the educated Indian middle class into English toadies became a cruel reality. (Today, some of the chief opponents of *Vaidic* culture or education come from among British-educated Indian pedagogues, journalists, politicians, and secularists, most of whom ironically claim to be Hindu. Meanwhile intellectuals in the West are turning to *Vaidic* and other ancient philosophies in search of answers to the complex social and scientific puzzles that they daily confront. Celestial astronomy increasingly favours *Vaidic* beliefs, from the age and form of the universe to the ancient geography of India. Much of this had been misread, mangled or suppressed, often and increasingly by Indians themselves, especially converts to another religion. Regrettably, North America's basic education has regressed and now consistently produces laggards with sparse knowledge of science or mathematics, many of whom confidently believe that the universe was created in 4004 BC, or that the earth is flat.

The establishment of British schools was accompanied by a vigorous imposition of English as *the* language of India and of the Empire.[92] This segregated and emasculated all but the small, urban anglicised moiety of the huge population—the *WOGs ("Western Oriental Gentlemen")* and *coconuts (brown outside, white inside)* and Bengali *bhadraloks ("gentlefolk")*, rewarding them with small benefits (bribes really) like recognition, promotion and a few empty titles, which anglophiles value to this day.

The spirited activities of Christian missions in the *Rāja* led to many conversions, which enhanced the social status of converts. At the same time the rise of Christian fundamentalism, race superiority theory and social Darwinism, made the British more arrogant, oppressive and dismissive of Indian values—including religion and culture, which their pre-revolutionary predecessors had found as mystifying as they were uplifting—and ultimately treated Indians more cruelly. To consolidate this, the British began to classify society using many attributes that Hindus had not traditionally used e.g. religion. This served to segregate people further and facilitated their subjugation and exploitation.

In like manner, the descendants of the Arabs, Turks and Mughals were in the next century allowed to carve East and West Pakistan out of India and hold on to their Indian converts. Thus did the British, by the fruits of the industrial revolution, subdue and control a population ten times their size. They were however assisted by Indian history.

From earliest times, India had been a complex of tribes, races and cultures united by rule, religion and commerce, but separated by distance, language and customs until brought together by Mauryas, Guptas, Gurjara-Pratiharas, Rashtrakutas, Pālas, Gahadvalas, Marathas

---

92 Modern Indian curricula have remained largely unchanged from those developed by the British Rāja, as noted by Swami B.V. Giri in *Early Indology of India* Part 2, and disavow attempts to reinvigorate Vaidic studies.

and others, but easily reverting to original regional boundaries, even to tribalism, steered by opportunity, temptation, stress or fear of losing territory, due to weak central leadership. (Similar movements flourish today: Scotsmen wishing to secede from the British union, Quebec from Canada, or Ulster wishing to unite with Eire.) But India was unlucky to have two ruthless and greedy invaders in succession, zealously exploiting and fomenting these divisions and fears, to amass profits.

Soon a mercantilist battle—promoted by British free trade advocates like Cobham—intensified among continental Europeans to compete with Britain and share the fruits of the new industries, made possible by advances in science and engineering. The USA, too, had forced its way into trade with Japan and was building at home, with British financial partners, despite political differences, an industrial infrastructure, consisting of railway and telegraph networks, roads, canals and power grids. The US was bent on continental expansion, which John O'Sullivan, a New York journalist, in 1845, had called the USA's *"manifest destiny"*, envisaging American control of all lands to the Pacific and even the entire North America. The earlier *Monroe doctrine* (1823) had given grim notice to all Europeans that the western hemisphere was out of bounds.

Territorially, Britain, by the end of the Napoleonic Wars, had eclipsed other Europeans, establishing numerous colonies, acquiring others, and had begun to surge ahead of rivals, as it reaped economic and social advantages from the industrial revolution, and victory in the Indian War of Independence. In the early 1860s, the USA was pre-occupied with a brutal civil war, and with President Lincoln's murder soon after. France, Britain's traditional rival, and also a major colonial power, see-sawed in the five to seven decades following the Napoleonic wars, between the post-revolution republic, according to Rousseau, and a resurgent Napoleonic monarchy. Napoleon III built the Suez Canal in 1869, much to Britain's dismay, as it seemed to threaten Britain's Middle East and Indian interests; this fear eased, six years later, when the Egyptian ruler, Ismail Pasha, sold his 44% share to London, for a mere £4 million. (The Canal was later deemed neutral territory, by agreement reached in 1888.)

About this time, major and defining conflicts occurred between the Prussians and Austrians in 1866, and France and Prussia, 1870-71, Prussia winning both. From this, a united Germany roared into the limelight, attributable to the machinations of the Prussian triumvirate: Otto von Bismarck, Albrecht von Roon and Helmuth von Moltke, led by Bismarck, Chancellor of Prussia, since 1862.

Meanwhile the Dutch plodded on, profiting from colonies and avoiding wars, save by duress. Even volatile Italy achieved a measure of unity, at the expense of the Austro-Hungarian and Ottoman Empires.

The latter continued its slow decline, despite the *Tanzinat Reforms* (1839-1876) with their sweeping changes, civil and religious, and aims to modernise; however, its new constitution of 1876 lasted two years. Various surrogates—Serbs, Greeks and others—began wars of secession and independence, as the century came to an end. The "young Turks" would attempt to revive "the sick man of Europe", but WWI would reduce the Empire in extent and importance. The rise of Kemal Ataturk would end the Caliphate in 1924 and establish a secular state. Indian Muslims opposed this, with Gandhi 's support (Khilafat movement of 1921). It later became clear that the Caliphate was not envisioned in the Quran and therefore was not a religious institution. Arabs opposed any major "head" of an Islamic state that could not be traced to Mohamed!

By the mid-nineteenth century, Britain was drunk with military and industrial strength and the headiness of colonial conquests. During the Napoleonic wars, it had attacked shipping of even neutral USA, to abduct seamen, and justified those events as acts of war! It was thus easy to understand its dismissive attitude to India. But in the 1840s, it experienced an economic downturn, and Ireland saw its worst potato famine, forcing millions to emigrate to the United States, Canada, Australia and elsewhere, and aid American expansion.

The migration caused by the potato famine is a distinctive irony. Farmers did not readily adopt the plant when it was first introduced into Europe. However it was cheap to grow and by the 17th century had become a staple and literally spurred the population expansion in Europe in the 17th and 18th centuries. Potatoes are a heterogeneous tuber, native to the Andes, in Peru and nearby Bolivia and Chile, where thousands of varieties are known, and several varieties are grown at once. In the 16th century, the Spanish brought a few strains to Europe where the cooler climates of the north suited the plants. Selective cultivation of the limited number of strains reduced the plant's resistance to certain organisms, including the oomycete *Phytophthora infestans,* a fungus-like organism, which caused the "late blight" that destroyed the crop in Ireland, causing many deaths from starvation among poorer people and spurring the great Irish exodus across the Atlantic.

The potato, meanwhile, had been carried worldwide from Europe by sailors and merchants, including the BEICo, and became a familiar food choice for Europeans in India, and later in China, joining native favourites. They have the same susceptibility to blight, while Andean and Mexican potatoes, including wild strains, are naturally resistant. Potatoes thus played a vital role in European expansion.

The subjugation of peoples "not Anglo-Saxon" had brought Africa in British gun-sights, as a partial solution to the land needs of migrants.

South Africa, where the colony of Natal had been started, received only few of these migrants, largely through fear of the Zulus on whose territories they would be squatting, despite inducements to build up the critical mass needed for a viable colony. The Dutch had colonised the Cape, but, in 1806, during the Napoleonic Wars, had yielded control to Britain, which carved Natal from the eastern end of the Dutch colony. Both the Cape and Natal relied heavily on enslavement, but the trade was banned in 1807, restricting supply and farmers' profits! The British had responded by driving the Xhosa people from their homes west of Zululand, and in so doing, ,had also inflamed the Boers, who had craved the same lands.

The discovery of gold in 1851, in Victoria and New South Wales, Australia, had attracted over 40,000 Chinese migrants to the goldfields, where they competed directly with the locals. Inevitably, clashes developed, facilitated by the obvious physical differences between the opposing parties. But, if that was not enough, the work ethics of the two groups differed enough to make the Chinese more successful in alluvial mining. Agitation by white miners gave rise to legislation restricting Chinese migration, despite breaching British-Chinese agreements following the Opium Wars, and the need elsewhere in Australia for plantation workers.

"*It is not the bad qualities, but the good qualities of these alien races that make them so dangerous to us.*" Alfred Deakin, a future Australian Prime Minister observed, "*It is their inexhaustible energy, their power of applying themselves to new tasks, their endurance and low standard of living that make them such competitors.*" Edmund Barton, Australia's first Prime Minister, agreeing with the move for racial exclusion, shamelessly declared, "*The doctrine of the equality of man was never intended to apply to the equality of the Englishman and the Chinaman.*"

In 1895, a British Colonial Premiers Conference agreed to ban non-white immigration generally, and two years later the Colonial Secretary, Joseph Chamberlain, conceded in a comment on the "White Australia" legislation of Australian colonies that "*...there should not be an influx of people alien in civilisation, alien in religion, alien in customs, whose influx, moreover, would seriously interfere with the legitimate rights of the existing labouring population.*" And yet, these same people had failed to see themselves as "alien in civilisation, alien in religion, alien in customs" when they imposed themselves on native Americans, Indians, Chinese, Maoris, Australian aborigines and Africans, all with "legitimate rights" of nationality! The supreme hypocrisy of this eluded Chamberlain.

The British benefited from industrial/commercial applications of advances made in Europe, America and elsewhere in science, engineering and technology. They revolutionised printing; the textile industry; transport (railways, iron ships, Suez Canal, underground rail); utilities (electricity); communications (telephone, telegraph, radio); economics; education etc., all of which helped Britain to retain its Empire and expand colonies. Social reform—secret balloting, 1872; free primary schooling, 1891—relieved pressure on Parliament.

Britain became master of the seas with Brunel's launching of the *SS Great Eastern* in 1858, the largest ship built to that time (18,915 tons, 32,000 fully loaded). It came into India's history as the ship that laid the undersea cable between Aden and Bombay in 1869-70 that facilitated control of India, by speeding up British business and Government communiqués; *the telegraph was withheld from Indians generally*.

British commercial profits improved as railways flooded India with cheap British goods, wrecking Indian industries and saddling India, to boot, with a British debt! By the 1870s, Britain had developed the largest unified market, which Benjamin Disraeli, on becoming Prime Minister, wished to enlarge by reviving the defunct *"Forward Policy"* in India to subdue Afghanistan and Burma and win more territory in South Africa. Industrial competition from continental Europe and the USA sought new markets everywhere, while jostling for empire.

At this time, Central Africa was unknown to Europeans and called the Dark Continent. Following his desire to do missionary medicine, but unable to travel to China, Dr David Livingstone, a remarkable man, shifted his interest to Africa, and became the first European to explore Central Africa. He searched for the source of the Nile, in vain, but discovered the Rift Valley, its lakes and peoples and eventually the *Mosi-oa-Tunya* Falls, which he renamed Victoria, on the Zambezi River. He contributed maps and commentaries of his findings, which were widely publicised. His work led to the end of the East African slave trade in 1874, the year he succumbed to chronic malaria. The accounts of Africa attracted Europeans and led to the *Scramble for Africa* a decade later.

In 1878, a notable year of discovery and invention, King Leopold of Belgium *bought* a major share of the huge Congo. The year would see changes in society as radical as the railways (funded by the Rothschilds and other moneylenders), and soon matched by the completion of ironclad ships, the naval screw propeller and the internal combustion engine. North America achieved major breakthroughs, with George Eastman's development of dry photo film; Alexander Bell's telephone; Nicola Tesla's (Westinghouse) transmission of electricity; and Edison's 1877 invention of the gramophone and the electric light bulb, and soon after, the motion picture camera.

In 1879, while famine was killing millions in the Deccan and central India, the British gave grossly inadequate relief, despite the advice of their own medical experts. Robert Temple, the Famine Commissioner, had suffered the Bihar famine six years earlier, and his humane handling of relief had averted many deaths. Yet he was roundly castigated then, so much so, that he responded with stinginess this time, fearing renewed criticism for *generosity*! He not only reduced rations to a fifth but allowed British merchants to export grain freely, just as the British had allowed the export of food from Ireland during the potato famine of the 1840s!

This was the eighth major famine in India since the British occupation in 1769, with total loss of about *43 million* lives! William Digby, a British journalist in India, estimated that this one had killed ten million people. Governor General Robert Bulwer-Lytton, son of the poet, maintained a hard-hearted stance and chose instead to make demands on Afghanistan, which were promptly rejected and the British repulsed. The loss, although not quite as humiliating as Chelmsford's annihilation in Zululand (see below), was an added shame for Britain. Bulwer-Lytton resigned, showing more character than Chelmsford, and Disraeli's government fell. Back in London, Bulwer-Lytton churlishly denounced new PM John Gladstone's somewhat less inhuman approach to India.

Improving economic activity brought some peace to Europe but sadly not shared elsewhere. The British in South Africa clashed repeatedly with the Dutch Boers. Lord Chelmsford, Natal's governor, sharing BEICo's Lord Auckland's arrogant dismissal of natives, decided to rid Zululand of its rightful owners, whose King Shaka had generously donated to the British nearly 3000 sq. miles of land, south of the Tugela River, for a farming colony. Coveting lands north of the river, Chelmsford greeted 1879 by invading the Zulu kingdom, casually remarking—in the prevailing spirit of British immorality that would find a high priest in Cecil Rhodes a few years later—that it was a *"simple campaign of expansion!"*

The Zulu king Cetshwayo, grandson of Shaka, was not amused. Despite his professed admiration for Queen Victoria and the British, and dislike for the Transvaal Boers, he sent an army under his brother Dabulamanzi which annihilated the British assault force at Isandlwana, a remarkable feat considering their primitive weaponry. But what they lacked in armaments they made up in strategy and ferocity. Sadly, the Zulus, and later other native groups would succumb to British armies with their superior training, discipline and above all, guns and artillery.

British greed increased with Chelmsford's destruction of the Zulu capital, Ulundi. Annexing Transvaal, they assumed Boer claims to Zulu borderlands and soon achieved the acme of cupidity in the person of

Cecil Rhodes. It was Rhodes, too, who in 1887 told the House of Assembly in Cape Town that "*the native is to be treated as a child and denied the franchise. We must adopt a system of despotism in our relations with the barbarians of South Africa*". In less oratorical moments, he put it even more bluntly: "*I prefer land to niggers.*" This notion of racial superiority was consistent and a mere repetition of British disdain for Indians and other natives, and would later stimulate apartheid and the awakening of Mohandas Gandhi, who began his resistance in Natal.

Three years earlier, to avert new European wars, this time over ownership of the remaining free world, Portugal had proposed and Germany hosted the Berlin Conference, to discuss Africa, the last "unconquered" continent. The meeting was styled *The Scramble for Africa.* Most of the participants already had some connection with Africa, and at the end of the meeting the flags of major European nations would be planted somewhere on African soil, creating Belgian, British, French, German, Italian, Portuguese and Spanish colonies or spheres of influence, with King Leopold as personal owner of the Congo Free State, leaving only Ethiopia and Liberia truly free.

A photomontage made in Europe in 1889 with the main heads of state in the world.
L to R: Yohannes IV of Ethiopia, Tewfik Pasha of Egypt, Sultan Abdülhamit II of Turkey, Naser al-Din Shah Qajar of Persia, Christian IX of Denmark, Luís I of Portugal, William III of the Netherlands, Pedro II of Brazil, Milan Obrenović IV of Serbia, Leopold II of Belgium, Alexander III of Russia, Wilhelm I, German Emperor, Franz Joseph I of Austria, Victoria of Britain, Jules Grévy of France, Pope Leo XIII, Emperor Meiji of Japan, Guangxu, Emperor of China, Umberto I of Italy, Alfonso XII of Spain, Oscar II of Sweden and Chester A. Arthur of the United States.

The British, French and Portuguese, as expected, had tried to hog all lands for resources and markets. Bismarck was not really fond of colonies but some German mercantilists were, and had sent explorer Carl Peters to represent them. But Bismarck had already traded a prime interest in East Africa for the tiny but strategic North Sea island of Heligoland. This gave to the British territorial continuity from Uganda to the Indian Ocean at Tanganyika, German East Africa, today's Tanzania. The Germans retained Southwest Africa. In 1901, Friedrich Ratzel had begun to advocate German settlement in SW Africa as one option to meet their need for farmland. This was the heyday of white supremacy beliefs and to prove these, the opportunity was taken to experiment on the skulls of the indigenous Herero and Nama people to prove their ethnic inferiority. These were supervised by the notorious anthropologist Dr Eugen Fischer, later to become a Nazi. It didn't take much to conclude that the indigenous Herero and Nama peoples must be annihilated, so the Germans carried out a brutal genocide, led by General Lothar von Trotha, who admitted, *"I destroy the African tribes with streams of blood... Only following this cleansing can something new emerge, which will remain."*

Surviving Herero people after escaping Germans through the desert of Omaheke in German South-West Africa, modern day Namibia

Others involved in the African scandal were Commander Franz Ritter von Epp, and a Dr Bofinger, who treated Vitamin C deficient Blacks with arsenic, opium and other substances, then did autopsies to note the effects! What they did was undoubtedly murder, an extreme example of racism (*social Darwinism*), and most likely set the stage for Nazi experiments in WWII. (One of Fischer's future students was another Nazi supremacist, Josef Mengele, who later experimented on Jewish children at Auschwitz. He escaped Nuremberg to Brazil where he lived under aliases, until his death in 1979.) German overlordship and troop tactics were identical to those of the colonial British, including the use of native recruits to guard the few prisoners they actually took. The British studied the German massacres and published the results as a *"Blue Book"* in 1918, but for unknown reasons destroyed it, in 1926. (Descendants of von Trotha have recently apologised to Namibia publicly for his actions; see *http://www.spiegel.de/)*

The British were clearly in the van of mercantilists raiding the world's wealth, outdoing the Muslims for tenacity, efficiency and zeal. To Indians, their major victims, the failure of the 1857 War had brought severe repercussions and reprisal. The British dealt harshly with dissent; their spies were everywhere, terrorising people with capricious and false accusations, arrests, coerced witnesses, kangaroo courts and hangings, to the point that injustice and fear ruled. Divisions and suspicions were amplified among the people, even within families. It was not unusual for an Indian to be hanged for a peccadillo while an Englishman would be freed for witnessed murder. So tight were controls over movements of people and of goods, and so pervasive the use by the British of bribery and paid informers that few dared to meet to discuss renewing the rebellion, or to correct the tactical errors of 1857. But whatever the British did, they failed to stop the often tragic calls for freedom.

Indians recalled this as a period of great privation in all the villages of India, aggravated by the demands of *zamindars, tehsildars, naibs* and village watchers (landlords, collectors, deputies and assistants). Drought, unemployment and food shortages had reduced families to penury. A drop in value of silver, the monetary standard, had reduced the savings of most Indians.

The prosperity of some villages, based on mixed grain and cattle farming, had shielded them somewhat from the decline throughout the region, and some said all across the north and east. Artisans everywhere were unable to compete with cheap manufactured goods from Britain, made cheaper by the removal of preferential customs duties which, coupled with new taxes on local industry, had made local produce *expensive*, as they did in all the colonies.

Indian merchants seized the chance to make handsome profits by selling British imports, from tools to food and medicine, caring little that the process was ruining millions of their countrymen, creating wholesale suffering and lasting social divisions, while food imports began to cater to a "western cuisine" to accompany Anglicisation. Craftsmen, artisans, tradesmen, farmers—the economic backbone of many villages—grew poor and joined the rapidly rising flood of unemployed who at times of famine grew desperate enough to seek work far from their homes, many moving to the cities while others moved overseas, most on indenture contracts. The continuation of this external traffic would become a troubling issue, by the time the Indian National Congress was formed in 1885. The trafficking in labour continued until 1917.

Conscious of British use of spies, even within families, activists warily pondered solutions to the growing social and economic problems and pressed for the formation of a national self-rule organisation.

The view from the Diaspora is worth noting. The repressions, dispossession and hunger following the 1857 War and subsequent famines had led to the growth of a Diaspora that by 1961 numbered over ten million people, mainly in Mauritius, the East and West Indies, Malaysia, Africa, South East Asia, Hong Kong, South Pacific, a sprinkling in the UK and USA, and an enclave of Sikhs in Canada. Indians had become a majority in British Guiana (now Guyana), Mauritius and Fiji, and a third of the Trinidad population. By 1900, many had achieved enviable success in agriculture and business in the new lands, and had begun to educate their children in professions such as medicine, engineering, accounting, law, education, agriculture and politics. Others had returned home on completion of contracts, disillusioned with the British failure to abide by the terms of those contracts, and instead, had treated them as captive slaves. Unable to find land, or other than menial work back home, some had returned, having reluctantly accepted new contracts, with no guarantees of change.

A famine in the 1870s, in eastern India, had killed millions and one was raging at the time, driving many to take the dreaded ocean voyage. Many recalled the period vividly as the time when they were forced, even shanghaied into British service overseas. Most did not understand the political or economic issues then, but in indenture had developed a grasp of the problems from experiencing British coercion and cheating. New recruits told depressing news of India's continuing humiliation, abetted by princes, professionals, soldiers, police and office workers, trained by the British, and subdued by their guile, or bribed with small privileges. The tyranny was forcing many Indians who had lost their lands to accept the hated indentures, some for the second time, in order to provide for families. To many, the prevailing desperation and lack of opportunity in the villages and towns made struggling in colonial swamps and forests preferable, despite the abundance of natural hazards and, most cruelly, pushy and thieving white men! This appraisal of India was something of a shock, as migrants expected conditions to have improved with the diminishing threat of armed rebellion and the formation of the Indian National Congress.

Migrants were eager for continuing news of India particularly the state of the economy and their prospects should they choose to return as most wished to do. Despite abysmal conditions and discrimination on grounds of colour, language and religion in diasporal lands, many ambitious Indians decided to remain on completing contracts, reasoning, *"Here I can have as much land as I can manage if I work hard and save; there I have to fit in; that would be okay but for the oppressive demands of the British fearing a new rebellion, so they're suspicious of anyone who look half competent or prosperous; the war in 1857 really shook them. Now they see everyone as a revolutionary and they'll hang you for stealing bread!"*

They thus became established in the villages and towns, many coming to own prosperous farms, shops and big houses, fine clothes, their own implements, domestic animals, vehicles including the new motor-cars. By the time of the Great War, some were in commanding positions in commerce, agriculture and the professions and were competing for political and government positions. (Ruhoman, Ragbeer)

Few in the early years thought of any career in public life, even at the lowest level, due to requirement of Christianity and fluency in English, neither of which was enough to compensate for loss of religion or culture. Most maintained their religion and found a way around the biases to teach their children enough Hindi and Sanskrit to understand casual conversation and participate in religious practices. Even those with limited vocabulary learned popular songs from Indian movies, and the classical *bhajans* (hymns) and recitations from the holy books. Thus despite legal, educational and social pressures to adopt English and Christianity, less than 10% of migrant Hindus or Muslims converted to Christianity, except where the total population of Indians was small, as in the Caribbean Antilles.

The huge urban population in India suffered intense pressures for jobs and social success, and wilted under an anglocentric education and constant denigration of their culture. The diasporal Indian, spared competition from that class of British shopkeeper that occupied the shopping streets of British towns and villages, found ways to surmount the barriers and avoid the atrophy of religion that led to Marxist conversions in India; or to atheism and secularism, which hobble India to this day. Besides, in colonial communities, deviation from caste and other repressive practices became a necessity for survival and progress.

In India, dissent grew also among the middle classes, especially the educated and wealthy, as they began to face the barriers and repressions already familiar to the working class. If they had thought the Mughals barbaric and cruel, there was no condemnation strong enough for British rulers, who added race and skin colour to the list of biases, not that Indians under Islam were spared any of these social prejudices. Towards the end of the nineteenth century, the British would develop outlandish theories in support, including the offensive concept of *social Darwinism.*

The feelings in time intensified as intellectuals from Calcutta, Bombay, Varanāsi and elsewhere joined in the demand for economic fairness, justice and an increased say in central and regional government. Many in the Diaspora who had fought the British continued to show scorn for them, describing them as "pushy unprincipled thieves". Even the military, although disciplined, was as ruthless as the Mughals, and dealt harshly with civilians; they had no qualms about brutalising or killing Indian men and corrupting women. Even before the 1857 war, skirmishes had erupted in places, spurred by British breaches of agreements, atrocities against civilians and sepoys, and excesses, especially the desecration of symbols and monuments of non-Christian religions, including holding dance parties at the Tāj Mahal. One Governor looted marble from the Agra fort and is believed to have considered demolishing the Tāj monument to sell its marble to British scrap-dealers, but ceased as the first auctions did not make a profit!

The atmosphere darkened for Indians, and the regular economy worsened. The deadly famine that raged in the 1870s had killed millions and helped activists by attracting attention to the brutality and disinterest of the Rāja. Indians continued to be maligned and savaged in courts for trivial offences, and were often framed for crimes while the real British offenders went scot-free.

The *British Indian Association* was established on the 31st of October, 1851, as a union of the *Landholders' Society* and the *Bengal British India Society*. The first committee consisted of prominent Bengalis—Macaulay's "respectable classes," and *bhadralok*—all as distant as the British from the poor. Raja Radhakanta Deb was President; Raja Kalikrishna Deb, Vice-President; Debendranath Tagore, secretary; and Digambar Mitra, Assistant Secretary. Members included Raja Satya Saran Ghosal; Harakumar; Prasanna Coomar; Ramanath Tagore; Ramgopal Ghosh; Jay Krishna Mukherjee; Asutosh Deb; Harimohan Sen; Umesh Chandra Dutt (Rambagan); Krishna Kishore Ghosh; Peary Chand Mitra; Jagadananda Mukhopadhyay and Sambhunath Pandit.

It was a welcome step with potential to address the major issues openly, but from the start, it was hobbled by its name and elitism. Its founders were well-known Bengali conservatives, except for the more progressive Ramgopal Ghosh and Pyari Chand Mitra, but even they supported the pro-British political agenda. The Association set up branches countrywide to develop a national stance on petitioning Government, but each retained the right to approach its regional authority independently. The potential for divisions on issues, for self-seeking and other abuses, was thus clear, and quintessentially Indian!

They rejected independence and, like most princes, showed strong support for the British in the War of Independence, beguiled by their stipends and by anglocentric versions of history. They seemed ignorant of their own, and of the real European one of discord, selfish ambition, autocracy and militarism. The main interest of the BIA was Brahmo activities, until 1870, when a motion from the *Adi Dharma* faction was carried to address Government on issues of discrimination; employment in the Indian Civil Service; political representation and empowerment. Their opponents formed the *Indian Reform Association* (IRA) in October 1870, led by Keshab Chandra Sen (1838-1884), who was basically pro-British. None of this addressed the plight of India's majority, especially small farmers and the poor; but the hope was that discussions in Committee would have to include those major issues as soon as the more selfish ones of upper- and middle-class privileges were out of the way.

Bengalis and the *Brahmo Samaj* thought that Christianity could contribute to reform and condemned the corrupting of Hinduism by some Brahmins. The continuing disputation did the latter no credit, painting them as obsolete, misguided, arrogant and overly dependent on rituals, rather than principles expressed in scriptures, and setting bad examples re women's rights and child marriages.

Swami Dayānanda Saraswati (1823-83), a Gujarati by birth, emerged from his long training in 1875 and founded the *Arya Samaj* in Bombay, to engage in social service, pursue the education of women and their release from the Muslim veil and other non-Hindu restraints, asserting that this hobbling of women had led to India's downfall! He showed that Hinduism had been degraded by many accretions and practices, some ascribed to Brahminism, and deviating from the *Vaidas*. Reform was therefore necessary, which Buddha had enunciated. Like Buddha, Dayānanda advocated an end to idolatry, child marriage, mandatory dowry and to caste, so that talent may determine vocation. He placed a minimum age for marriage at 16 for females and 25 for males. He toured India, urging princes to support reform and reinstate and expand the *gurukul* system that had served India well, before the Mughals and British depreciated it. The subsequent growth of *Arya Samaj* and gurukuls in the north was heartening. Dayānanda was at the height of his influence, when, on rebuking the Rāja of Jaipur for his dissolute ways, a concubine, Nanhi Jan, poisoned him at a Diwali festival.

His illustrious disciple, Swāmi Shraddhānanda (1857-1926), established the famous gurukul at Kangdi which produced many Indian nationalists, including Lala Lajpat Rai and Ram Prasad Bismil, both of whom were staunch Samajists. He was aware of various Associations that had been formed including the latest *Indian Association* and felt that Lord Ripon, Viceroy at the time, might be too well-meaning towards Indians for his own good, in view of the disparaging attitude of the local Anglo-Indians and British to his rule. With the British so recalcitrant and oppressive, the Swami supported those who thought of renewing armed struggle, among them his disciple Shyamji Krishna Verma (see below).

Dayānanda's ministry overlapped that of other giants of his time, including two Bengalis, the mystic Ramakrishna Parahamsa 1836-86) and his disciple Swami Vivekānanda (1863–1902). They propounded the scientific basis of Hinduism, its logic, spirituality and accommodation of secular views and its lack of bias based on *varna*, race or gender. Thus Hinduism welcomed all ideas. Vivekānanda said, *"All differences in this world are of degree, and not of kind, because one-ness is the secret of everything."* He became famous for his rousing speech in Chicago in 1893 extolling Vaidanta, stressing that all people were born equal, without caste. He taught the true basis of Hinduism, not the local British version in vogue then, and attracted world praise and a vigorous following.

In 1870, Lord Mayo (1869-72) sought, by resolution, to devolve certain funded responsibilities to local government, such as elementary education, medical care and public works, to be financed by local taxes. But the plan languished as villages had long lost their political base, the *panchayats;* moreover, the British administration was unable to supply a reliable and honest mechanism to establish one. They had never paid any attention to the Indian system of local government, perhaps because one did not exist in Britain, which was still a feudal state, until retrospectively claimed otherwise, relatively recently! In any case, the idea of local rule ran counter to British purposes in India: extractive trade and profit, not good government!

Indian leaders were no real help, as they all hailed from the upper and least humanitarian classes, just like the British. Many were also experiencing doubts and changes, and had little contact with the plebs, were mistrusted and had generally become demanding and dissolute. Over the last hundred years, the rājas had become British sycophants, and Brahminism had weakened the leadership of Hindu society. Parsis, Jews and Christians were mostly in commerce, aloof and supported the British, as did many Hindu and Jain businessmen, Sikhs and Muslims.

KC Sen was a religious worker, associated with Unitarians, and had been a member of Tagore's *Brahmo Samaj*, until 1866, when Tagore objected to his see-sawing on, and eventual espousal of Christianity; Tagore renamed the original group *Adi (First) Brahmo Samaj,* when Sen formed a group also called *Brahmo Samaj!* Meeting Queen Victoria earlier in 1870, Sen had affirmed his secularism and loyalty. He was enthusiastic about the Unitarian gospel, and seemed convinced that British "Reform" could be duplicated in India. The Association would therefore advocate "the social and moral reformation of the natives of India", and promote change through "cheap literature, female improvement, education, temperance, and charity." His weekly paper, *Sulava Samachar* (Cheap News), cost one paisa only and brought news to the street. It was a welcome innovation at that time when the underprivileged had little or no access to news and the gulf between the Kulin Brahmins and the plebs was deep and wide.

The changes following the War of Independence had created a morass of controversy and disquiet at all levels of society, especially as more educated youth were emerging from the schools, seeking jobs with higher expectations, and gravitating to one or other religious or political group. (Their numbers are large and details of their identities, roles and intricacies are beyond the scope of this book. See relevant titles in *Bibliography*). It is sufficient to note that Sen was controversial and at times contradictory, perhaps understandable in someone with deep religious roots, struggling to reconcile different doctrines, especially the very dogmatic Christians and Islamists in India, the equally dogmatic Kulin Brahmins in his area, and the mix of objectives in Brahmoism which he was trying to meld together into one rational statement or universal religion. In this he was not unlike his contemporary Lalon Shah, the Bengali poet, who was then probing Hindu, Jain, Buddhist and Islamic traditions to find a coherent thread to tie his art together.

Sen came closer to his aim after encounters with Ramakrishna, whose rough mien had repelled him at first. But Ramakrishna's message was simple: "*Worship God as Mother*" and "*All religions are true*". Sen later lost not only face but his organisation when he went against Brahmo principles and gave his 9-year old daughter in marriage, by family tradition. After this he was left to his personal projects and writing. He died in 1884, a year before the various self-rule movements came together as the *Indian National Congress*.

In 1876, Surendranath Banerjee, producer of *The Bengalee,* and Ānanda Mohan Bose formed the nation-wide *Indian National Association (INA)* – incorporating the *Brahmo Sabha,* and other groups mentioned above – to promote "by every legitimate means the political, intellectual and material advancement of the people". This was easy to say, but tough to envisage, considering the long-standing divisions among Indians – a trait that seemed unusually deeply ingrained and easily exploited by any power determined to subdue the country, as the British and Mughals had done.

Earlier, the first products of higher education for women had emerged, when Chandramukhi Basu, a Christian convert from Dehra Doon, UP (now capital of Uttaranchal), and Kadambini Ganguly, a Bengalee Hindu, obtained BA degrees from University of Calcutta in

1882. Basu earned an MA in 1884 and later became Principal of Bethune College, the first female head of a College in South Asia. Ganguly, as noted earlier, had become the first Indian female graduate in allopathic Medicine in 1886[94]. Anandi Gopal Joshi studied western Medicine in Pennsylvania, graduating in 1886, age 21, the first female Indian with a US degree. (Dr Ganguly's father was Braja Kishore Basu, Brahmo activist and advocate for women's rights. She was one of the six female delegates to the 1889 session of the INC, and also organised the *Women's Conference* in Calcutta in 1906 in the aftermath of the partition of Bengal. In 1908, she had also organised and presided over a Calcutta meeting to express agreement with *Satyagraha*.)

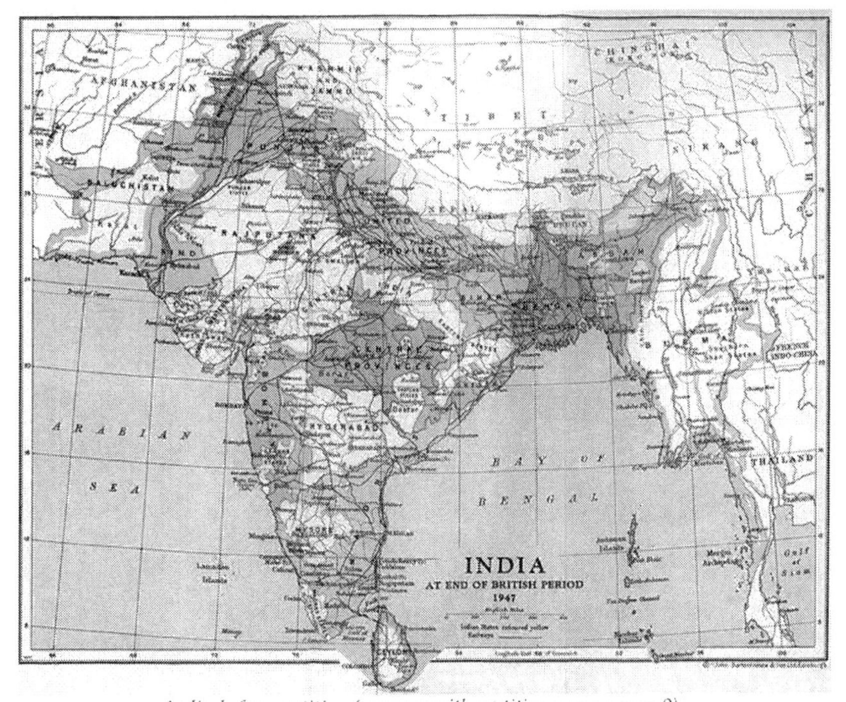

India, before partition (compare with partition map on page 9).

[94] Oxford did not confer any degree on women until 1920, although women were allowed to take examinations since the early 1880s.

Chapter 16

"Swaraj (Self-Rule) is my birth right and I shall have it!" BG Tilak

"A significant fact which stands out is that those parts of India which have been longest under British rule are the poorest today. Indeed some kind of chart might be drawn up to indicate the close connection between length of British rule and progressive growth of poverty." J. Nehru

The Indian National Congress – the uncertain rebels

Lord Ripon (1827-1909) served as Viceroy from 1880 to 1884, succeeding Lord Lytton, who had organised the Delhi durbar in 1877 to install Queen Victoria as Empress of India. Lytton was generally reviled for approving the *Vernacular Press Act in* 1878, which muzzled criticism of Government. Ripon repealed this Act two years after taking office, thus restoring Indian freedom of the press. He also resumed the issue of decentralisation of power by changing the Local Boards from large nominated bodies to smaller elected units; but Anglo-Indians and British citizens – who benefitted most from Board appointments – opposed this on the grounds that natives were not yet ready for an electoral system! *How ironic that the British first destroyed the Indian electoral system, then less than a century later, had the gall to suggest that the ones deprived had no prior knowledge of what they had been deprived!*

That shows how little they knew about knowledge-sharing among Indians, or their own history. Their objection forced Ripon to accept partially elected Boards. He addressed serious abuses of farmers and introduced the Tenancy Acts, which surprisingly returned to *raiyats,* land they had lost under Cornwallis's *Permanent Settlement* legislation.

Lord Ripon, 1880-84

Ripon supported education at all levels (*Education Commission* of 1882), and earlier had passed the Factory Act, to prohibit child labour. His attempt to reform the judicial process, the *Ilbert Bill,*[95] was opposed in Parliament. It sought to ensure equality of

[95]C.P. Ilbert wrote a paper, *Government of India,* in which he said that the post-1857 period of Crown governance, *was followed by "an era of peace in which India awakens to new life and progress."* This MUST have been said tongue-in-cheek!

treatment of all accused, thus removing the preferential treatment accorded whites, and rendering them liable to appear before Indian judges throughout British India, as they already did in the three Presidential capitals: Calcutta, Bombay and Delhi. The House debate on the issue saw some egregious behaviour by so-called civilised British and their Indian hirelings, who turned a small reform into a major issue. They painted bizarre pictures of Indians, with stereotypes derived from false reports of Indians raping English women during the rebellion of 1857. British women claimed that Indians were unfit to be judges as they were loose and fickle, because their women were ignorant and allowed such behaviour! Bengali women replied by ridiculing them as hypocrites who knew that their British husbands kept Indian concubines. Moreover, there was no College graduate among British women in India, while the university of Calcutta had graduated two Indian females in 1882, years before UK universities! This was the fractious and low level of argument, but misrepresentation and recrimination were standard fare.

A probe into India's past would show that women had an exalted role in Vaidic society, which revered *Viraj*, the Female Creative force, derived from *Purusha*, an incarnation of the Supreme, as noted earlier, and the recognition and reverence of deified females. Vaidic women studied scriptures and performed religious rites, just like men. However studies of women's deprived status in Europe, or in modern Islamic communities—whether Arabia, Middle East, Bangladesh, Pakistan, India, Indonesia or elsewhere—revealed their sorry state, except for Muslim or Christian women born into luxury and aristocracy, and recent improvement in women's rights in emancipating western societies. Old religious practices remain, however, and explain the dismissive attitude of Muslims and older Europeans to women in general, which conquerors carried over to female Hindus (see later).

Muslim writers at the time of Islamic invasions marvelled at the partnership between Hindu men and women, unlike the savagery displayed by Islamists, who treated women as chattel. Hindus in turn were astounded and repelled by the barbarism and began to resort to various stratagems to protect their women and children. One of Swami Dayānanda's aims was the re-education of women to their Vaidic status and their release from Islam's veil and other non-Hindu restraints, including, no doubt, British hegemony, asserting that this hobbling of women had led to India's downfall!

Today's secularists would be well-advised to consult some of the earliest writing on Hinduism, and be less hasty in dismissing Hindu literature as mythical, a wild presumption at the very least. On women, for example, Manusmriti *Lib* 3, *Shloka 3* et seq. notes: *"Women should be nurtured with every tenderness and attention by their fathers, their brothers, their husbands and their brothers-in-law, if they desire great prosperity...when women are honoured the divinities are content; but when we honour them not, all acts of piety are sterile."*

After decades of agitation for civil rights, Britain legalised Trade Unions in 1871, but women had to wait until 1918 to be recognised and to vote! In her response to British campaigns for *Women's Rights,* Queen Victoria is alleged to have said, *"The Queen is most anxious to enlist everyone who can speak or write or join in checking this mad, wicked folly of 'Woman's Rights' with all its attendant horrors on which her poor feeble sex is bent, forgetting every sense of womanly feeling and propriety."*

The main opponents of the *Ilbert Bill* were British plantation owners, who feared that Indian judges, strict and morally conservative, might not overlook their many wrongdoings! They ignored the strength and extent of support for the bill, and its intent to extend to all of British India, rights that already applied to 70% of the populace! In London, a resolution in favour was supported by a several speakers, including the very articulate Indian, Lalmohan Ghose. The Bill was watered down but allowed trial by Indian judges in district courts, where Whites were allowed a jury of equal numbers of Whites and Indians.

Ripon gained the respect and admiration of Indians, more than other Viceroys or Governors. Most others were insensitive and dismissive; unfortunately, his successors reversed most, if not all, of the goodwill he had earned. The controversies and recriminations surrounding the overdue reforms he had tackled reaffirmed the raping of India, shamed some British civil servants and inspired the formation of the *Indian National Congress* (INC भारतीय राष्ट्रीय, *Bhāratīya Rāstrīya*) in 1885.

The INC was a natural though weak development of a national voice uniting the regional forces that had by then become active in all regions of India. It was a union of upper class Hindus, Muslims and a few Europeans to promote self-government.[96] At its founding it merged with the INA. The leaders were Allan Octavian Hume, Womesh Chandra Banerjee, Surendranath Banerjee, Manmohan Ghose, William Wedderburn, Dadabhai Naoroji[97], Dinshaw Edulji Wacha and many others. Their first meeting, held in Bombay in 1885, was organised, ironically by Hume, a Scottish ex-BEICo official with a conscience and a passion for birds.[98] The founders were intellectuals, businessmen or bureaucrats who were actuated when their heads began to butt against the white ceiling restricting their social and political development, in

[96] Its first meeting was held on Dec 28-31, 1885, chaired by W C Banerjee.
[97] Later became the first Indian member of the British House of Commons.
[98] Hume was known at Sultanpur near Delhi, my *nana's* (grandfather's) village and home of a bird sanctuary, which Hume often visited.

their own country! Ramesh Chandra Dutt of Bengal was the first to achieve Executive status in 1882, when Ripon was Viceroy (some said as Queen Victoria's token Indian, to keep her 1858 promise of "equality"). The 1886 meeting launched regional committees and debated WC Banerjee's statement on limiting the Council to politics, not social issues.

As to strategy, some proposed armed struggle but Justice Mahadev Govind Ranade (1842-1901), an eminent scholar, like many of his colleagues, had earlier argued for moderation and a measured progress to self-rule; he wished to preserve the tenets of Hinduism with dignity while promoting reforms, especially the elimination of "caste" and certain social prohibitions e.g. widow remarriage. As a respected member of the Bombay legislative council and a judge of the Bombay High Court, Ranade's prestige lent weight to his optimistic view that political progress was inevitable, without force, but Indians needed to modernise and could do so by education without losing their traditional values. He joined the Bombay-based *Prarthana Sabha* (prayer group) that had been formed in 1849, following Brahmo principles. In 1870, he and others started the *Puné Sārvajanik Sabha* (Public Society) to represent the people's interest to the Government. But they had failed so far to build the cohesive nationalist movement required to oust the British.

The reform crusade gained strength as voices coalesced across language barriers, ironically aided by the enforced spread of English as the *lingua franca*, and abetted by the pens of S. Banerjee in Calcutta and Gopal Krishna Gokhale (1866-1915), Lala L. Rai, Bāl Gangādhar Tilak and Bipin Chandra Pal from other cities (*Lal-Bal-Pal* trio). They led the militant and more insistent group, which unequivocally condemned the British for their ignorance about, and denigration of Hindu culture, and their rulers for brutality. At the same time the group recognised and commended those more humanitarian British who sought to "improve" Indian education by incorporating "appropriate" western methods. Invariably, these were private citizens, their programs running counter to that of British business and the agendas of successive Viceroys, starting from Channing.

Tilak and Gokhale shared heritage and education (both were mathematics professors), and helped Ranade to found the *Deccan Education Society* in 1884, in line with commentaries on India's education which the Marquess of Ripon explored during his term as Viceroy. They established a Western-style school in Puné in 1880 (later called *Ferguson College)*.

Like Ranade, Gokhale was a moderate and emphasised social reform to uplift ordinary citizens, while Tilak was militant and insisted on expelling the British, by force, if necessary. He also reminded leaders that the *Bhagavad Gita* had described the conditions under which righteous men were *obligated* to fight an oppressor. The British had amply qualified for that designation. Between 1891 and 1897, the rifts between the two factions grew, particularly in the *Sārvajanik Sabha.*

Lal-Bal-Pal trio (see text)

Inevitably, British excesses in all spheres of life—political, physical, financial, moral—and the increasing penury of the Indian masses, led to insistent calls for autonomy. These were met with needlessly violent reprisals, in brutal displays of authority and arrogance, as if the conqueror had a monopoly on rights. Decisions were made by the administration that seemed to have bypassed the brain entirely! This happened a great deal in India. Ripon tried to change that and to achieve fairness, noting the attempts made twenty five years earlier by the first Viceroy, Earl Canning, a plodder, who had inherited the Independence War, and won it by the time-honoured tactics of bribery and dividing the natives. His successes were negated ever since by his successors.

When a famine and plague ravaged Maharashtra in 1896, Tilak, then a member of the Bombay Legislative Assembly, chastised the Government of Lord Elgin for mismanagement. Protests and reprisals occurred in many ways. In one confrontation with citizens, an Army officer and head of the plague relief committee were killed. Tilak was arrested for inciting murder and jailed for 18 months in 1897 (he served 11 months), and again several times after. His slogan, after serving his first jail term, *"Swaraj (Self-Rule) is my birthright and I shall have it!"* made him a hero, but the British labelled him the "Father of Indian unrest".

In 1893, the British perpetrated one of the most savage and destructive acts against the Indian populace. By a single deft stroke of the pen, the British Governor-General and Council impoverished the majority, without firing a single shot, when they closed the Indian mints to the free coinage of silver—a single obscenely brief moment in history that ruined hundreds of millions of India's peoples. This was the year of economic "panic" that slowed the US economy and allowed passage of regressive laws in various states, especially in the cotton and tobacco belt; it also saw reversal of civil rights claims by Blacks and minorities, and slowed migration of Europe's poor, who had been welcomed in the past two decades to provide cheap labour in the US.

Curzon

WJ Bryan, the American senator and later candidate for the Presidency of the United States, told his colleagues, in an address to Congress in 1897, that *"Mr Leech, former director of the US mint, in an article in the Forum, declared that the closing of the mints in India on that occasion was the most momentous event in the monetary history of the present century. In that speech Mr Wolcott also asserted that the closing of the India mints reduced by five hundred millions of dollars[99], the value of the silver accumulated in the hands of the people."* Bryan cited this casual use of foreign power, of government from afar, to argue against American flirtation with colonising the Philippines. It was just one example of the irresponsibility of foreign administrators, with no local ties or local interest, working only for the enrichment of the home power. He accused the British of particular callousness, which he could see the Americans easily repeating in the Philippines.

The INC had achieved little in 20 years, considering its huge and expectant support base. Some said it was too passive, too upper-crust and cared little for rural or poorer folk, and too steeped in "caste". The frustrations invigorated militant individuals and groups who resented the new Viceroy Curzon who, hardly arriving in Calcutta in 1899, moved to achieve "English" dominance in the *Calcutta City Corporation,*

[99] The economic power of this amount in 2010 was $471,000,000,000!

by cutting 50% of the number of elected Indians and curbing the autonomy of Indian Universities. Ripon's rule was torn apart!

The British hegemony and the atrocities it engendered were aided by stiff laws introduced after the 1857 war, aimed to curtail gun ownership, license owners, limit personal freedoms and facilitate searches. Genuine protest was ignored. Organised militancy began to appear near the turn of the century among Bengali Hindus. They were wary, always mindful of the ubiquitous spies and the violence of British retribution; as one wag said, "Even the *bhagi* must be carefully searched before eating!"

Although many incidents occurred in the last decades of the 19th century, the first organised movement advocating revolution to achieve independence was *Anushilan Samiti* (Self-Culture Association), founded by Satish Chandra Basu and Bengali barrister Prama Nath Mitra, with other men of intellect, who had despaired of any reforms, noting the INC's pro-government stance and its failure to press for the masses, despite Surendranath Banerjee's efforts and his work as an elected member in the Calcutta City Corporation. He had founded the INA and had vigorously opposed Curzon's arbitrary cuts in the elected membership of the City Corporation, playing Muslims against Hindus, calling the latter a Brahmin clique remote from *real* Hindus, an insightful, if unwelcome assessment!

Curzon was immediately disliked; his stifff bearing made him look arrogant and even more unlikeable than he was among political Indians. Even some Englishmen cared little for him, and he had arrived with a negative image earned from his days at Oxford. There was even a derogatory rhyme that people chanted: *"My name is George Nathaniel Curzon, I am a most superior person. My cheeks are pink, my hair is sleek, I dine at Blenheim twice a week."*

He was, however, fluent and convincing in presenting positions; this, no doubt, plus family connections had secured for him important political appointments, including that of Viceroy of India. It was perhaps naive to expect that he would maintain the spirit of liberalism that Ripon had brought to the position, and given such hope to Indians; instead, they quickly learned that his views on colonialism had not changed since the tyrannical comments he had made about the Irish, and that rejection of home rule would apply even more to India. An example illlustrates his mentality: he invaded defenceless Tibet in 1893, to secure British hegemony over the region, convinced that the Russians were threatening from the North; (he ignored the Chinese). When he reached Lhasa, he found *no* Russians there or anywhere near to Tibet!

The *Anushilan Samiti* operated as fitness clubs, to escape British detection. Its *leaders* included vice-presidents Aurobindo Ghosh and Chittaranjan Dās (*CR, Deshbandhu),* treasurer Suren Tagore, famed activists Jatindra Nāth Mukherjee *(Bagha Jatin),* Bhupendra Nāth Datta (Swami Vivekānanda's brother), Barindra Ghosh (Aurobindo's younger brother), Jatindra Nāth Banerjee (later Nirālamba Swāmi), Bipin Chandra Pāl and many others, who formed units in almost every province. Aurobindo established contact with B G Tilak and Sister Nivedita (Margaret Elizabeth Noble), a disciple of the late Swami Vivekānanda, all strong advocates for independence.

By 1901, the British had transferred over £1,000,000,000 ($30B today) of Indian wealth to the UK, including the *Koh-I-Noor,* stolen in 1850 from Duleepsinghi, the Maharaj of Kashmir (p. 212) along with numerous gems and precious objects culled from palaces and temples. Enriched with the addition of the giant *Star of Africa,* they decorate the necks and appendages of British monarchs and their royal crown, sceptre and orb! The rape would continue to the last days, when even the tiny gem inlays on Tāj Mahal tiles would be looted.

Curzon and wife

The British Rāja, at that time, consisted of eight provinces: Assam, Bengal, Bombay, Burma, Central Provinces, Madras, Punjab and United Provinces, each headed by a lieutenant governor or commissioner. They ruled 60% of the subcontinent's population of 350 million directly. The rest, 562 princely states of all designations, were subsidiary alliances, each of which was coerced to provide and maintain a part of the British Army, reaching a total which far exceeded the number needed for the defence of India. They were used mainly as cannon fodder for Britain to crush local dissent and to fight invasive foreign wars, which Britain waged, at India's expense.

The spirit of local revolt was assisted, ironically, by the new universities in India, plus access to the best British schools—Oxford, Cambridge, LSE, London, Inns of Court etc.,—where students absorbed liberal political views on morality, ethics, equality and ideas, methods and other virtues from Locke, Johnson, Ruskin, Spencer, Bentham, JS

Mill, Blake, Marx, Hyndman, the Fabians, and a host of others, literary and philosophical, including continentals from the later 18th century onwards, like Rousseau, Kant, Kierkegaard, Nietzsche, Descartes and others. Those who lived in France heard about Voltaire's views on India.

On graduation, Indians discovered the colour bar to employment and promotion in the *Indian* Civil Service, for which they had prepared so assiduously, and even when employed, were denied the huge salaries paid to British recruits. They faced other forms of bias, as virulent as casteism at its worst. They would discover the truth of the dictum they had heard but rejected as not applying to them that the Indian would *never* earn the same as their British counterpart in the *Indian* Civil Service! And as Jawaharlal Nehru remarked later, *"the Indian Civil Service was neither Indian nor civil nor a service!"*

In 1905, Curzon made a whimsical decision that would affect India's future in a way no one at the time suspected: he divided Bengal into Islamic and Hindu sections, thinking it would make governance simpler, clipping off pieces to Assam and the Central Provinces. This satisfied Islamists, who wished to establish a separate religious state and entrench Sharia law. The Aga Khan, their leader, was delighted with the prospect of an enhanced share of India, in exchange for fealty to the British. The act was condemned by all Indians, and even the English administrator of Assam, Henry Cotton, opposed it. *Anushilan* members severely criticised the act, but Curzon stood by his dismissive view of Hindus.

Anushilan Samiti spread quickly through Bengal and India, especially after the Bengal partition; a branch had been established in Dhākā under Pulin Behari Das. The Samiti was energised by Aurobindo's writings, one of which summarised the frustrations with the INC: "*... that its aims are mistaken, that the spirit in which it proceeds towards their accomplishment is not a spirit of sincerity and whole-heartedness, and that the methods it has chosen are not the right methods, and the leaders in whom it trusts, not the right sort of men to be leaders; in brief, that we are at present led, if not by the blind, at any rate by the one-eyed.*"

In Bengal, the *Anushilan* spawned the *Yugantar* (New Age) paper and party in 1906-7, led by young men, chief among them Bagha Jatin—an expert in martial arts and briefly a civil servant—and the two Ghosh brothers. Disappointed in the direction taken by the INC, and the high-handedness of the Viceroy, *Anushilan* adopted a policy of harassing British interests and personnel, whom they considered turncoats and tyrants. Barin Ghosh went to Paris to learn how to make bombs, while in Calcutta and Dhaka, various people were targeted, some assassinated, others missing. One of those targeted was Judge Kingsford, a Calcutta magistrate despised for unduly harsh punishment of young activists. His movements were studied, but the bomb hurled in his carriage by 18-year old Khudiram Bose and Prafulla Chāki, killed two women instead. Kingsford was, unaccountably, not in the carriage at the time.

Khudiram was a strong believer in justice and had been impressed with the lessons of the *Bhagavad Gita;* he saw the British as more villainous than the Kauravas, and himself as a warrior in Arjuna's army. Prafulla committed suicide, and Bose was tried and hanged. The martyrdom attracted many admirers and new recruits to the movement, which maintained guerrilla actions against the British and Governor General Curzon's policies. Many activists were arbitrarily imprisoned in Port Blair, Andaman Islands.

The partition of Bengal was perhaps the most perfidious and ill-conceived of all autocratic acts in India then, as it promoted a Hindu-Islam division, which the Aga Khan had long been fomenting. The 1909 Morley-Minto "reforms" would cement this division and throttle the quest for unity among Indians of all religions. Viceroy Minto, an anti-Hindu demagogue, allowed Indians a few positions in central and provincial governments, favouring Muslims, upper class or rich Hindus, granting Muslims a separate electorate and twice the number of seats given Hindus in government bodies.

These acts were promoted as an advance on the *Indian Councils Act* of 1892, which had given Indians a few elected seats on District Boards and Municipal Corporations, adding to the advisory roles already played by privileged Indians. Thus, in 1909, Britain was far from the devolution of powers to Indians that it had argued was a *right* to *white* South Africans! The saving grace was that the Act did allow devolution of a few powers to provinces and increased the number of elected members in governing councils. But it left government firmly in the control of the Viceroy and his executive.

In response to Curzon's policies, the INC changed its goal to self-rule. Tilak and his followers began the *Swadeshi* (self-sufficiency) movement to boycott British goods and restore traditional Indian products. Articles in Tilak's paper, *Kesari,* promoted these activities, but lack of political progress and disagreements in the INC on method, led Tilak and his militant followers in 1907 to split the INC into two camps, dubbed the *Garam Dal* ("hot faction"), led by Tilak, and *Naram Dal* ("soft faction") or moderates, led by G. K. Gokhale.

In his paper, *Kesari,* Tilak promoted the philosophy of *Swaraj,* and was soon imprisoned for his support of revolutionary activities. Banerjee in *The Bengalee* had for years exposed the inequities and prejudices of the British, and criticised Curzon's high-handedness and flawed reasoning, so much so, that friends and readers feared that the writers and editors would be arrested in reprisal on some fabricated charge, or perhaps through some sudden or capricious law that criminalised their actions; indeed, to this end, subtle changes to sedition laws had already been made near 1900. As a result, Tilak was jailed for 6 years for sedition, for defending Khudiram Bose's actions, in articles in *Kesari*. On conviction he told the jury: *"... I maintain that I am innocent. There are higher powers that rule the destiny of men and nations and it may be the will of providence that the cause which I represent may prosper more by my suffering than by my remaining free"*[100].

The religious fracture of Indian peoples by the Bengal split, and the award of enhanced privileges to Muslims under the "Reforms," would haunt India from then on and bring lasting discord among Bengalis and Indians generally, even though the Bengal split was reversed in 1911, the year the new capital was built in New Delhi.

Gokhale, meanwhile, had founded the *Servants of India* in 1905, based in Nagpur. Its English paper, *The Hitavada,* started in 1911. On release from prison, Tilak became less militant and supported Gokhale's advocacy of constitutional approaches to self-rule. With Mohamed Jinnah, G.S. Khaparde and Annie Besant, Tilak formed the *India Home Rule League,* backing a federal system with equal states, and Hindi written in Devanagari script as the common language.

At the end of the 19th century, several wealthy Indians in London: Shyamji Krishnavarma, Bhikāji Cāma, S.R. Rāna, Vināyak Sāvarkar, and others, had formed the *India Home Rule Society (IHRS)* and published, with British sympathisers, a paper, *The Indian Sociologist.* Earlier, Shyamji had founded India House as a student residence. When the British threatened arrests, they moved to Paris, forming, in 1905, the *Paris Indian Society,* a branch of the IHRS, under the patronage of Bhikaji Cāma, Sardar Singh Rāna, B.H. Godrej, and included, at various times, Virendranath Chattopadhyaya, Lal Lajpat Rai, M.P.T. Acharya (founder of the Indian Communist Party), Har Dayal, Savarkar, G.S. Khaparde, Rambhuj Dutt and Bipin C. Pal.

In 1907, Bhikāji, along with other IHRS associates, attended the Socialist Congress of the *Second Internationa*l in Stuttgart. There, supported by Henry Hyndman, she demanded recognition of self-rule for India, and in a famous gesture unfurled one of the first Flags of India, made up of parallel bars of green for Islam, orange for Hinduism and red for Buddhism, with a sun and crescent at the bottom signifying Hinduism and Islam, and eight *kamalgattas* (lotuses) at the top, one for each province of the British Rāja. Her reputation soared; enraged British rulers put a price on her head.

---

[100]This is carved on a wall in the Bombay High Court. At Tilak's death, Gandhi called him the *"Maker of India"*.

The Swadeshi movement and Tilak's *Kesari* had ignited feelings of outrage among youth who were beginning to despair for their future in a British-oppressed society, where each day came with the erosion of some Indian value and the substitution of local ways and tampering with religious systems that had long sustained India. The lectures of Sri Aurobindo and Sister Nivedita on nationalism inspired many youths across the country, including the Calcutta martyrs, Khudiram Bose and Prafulla Chāti.

In frustration and a spirit of revolt, Savarkar and other students in London had formed the *Free India* Society and a London unit of the Young India *(Abhinav Bharat)* Society in 1904, who swore: *"In the name of God, In the name of Bharat Mata, In the name of all the Martyrs that have shed their blood for Bharat Mata, By the Love, innate in all men and women, that I bear to the land of my birth, wherein the sacred ashes of my forefathers, and which is the cradle of my children, By the tears of Hindi Mothers for their children whom the Foreigner has enslaved, imprisoned, tortured, and killed, I, ... convinced that without Absolute Political Independence or Swarajya my country can never rise to the exalted position among the nations of the earth which is Her due, And Convinced also that Swarajya can never be attained except by the waging of a bloody and relentless war against the Foreigner, Solemnly and sincerely Swear that I shall from this moment do everything in my power to fight for Independence and place the Lotus Crown of Swaraj on the head of my Mother; And with this object, I join the Abhinav Bharat, the revolutionary Society of all Hindustan, and swear that I shall ever be true and faithful to this my solemn Oath, and that I shall obey the orders of this body; If I betray the whole or any part of this solemn Oath, or if I betray this body or any other body working with a similar object, May I be doomed to the fate of a perjurer!"*

Although the fate of the would-be betrayer was undoubtedly an anticlimax, the zeal was unmistakeable. The Society expanded by 1906 and paralleled Tilak's activities. Savarkar wrote revolutionary tracts, and a book titled *History of the Indian War of Independence*. The British promptly banned it, making it more desirable when it was published in Europe, through Bhikaji Cāma's intervention.

Among the many militant young men swept up by the Swadeshi movement was the articulate Madan Lal Dhingra (1883–1909), who had made news by getting expelled from College in Amritsar for protesting the use of English cloth for his College blazer! His brother, a physician, later sent him to University College, London, England, to study mechanical engineering. He soon learnt of India House, went there and met Savarkar and others. This would give him the opportunity to affirm his views and his national commitment.

The tricolour is, from top: green, orange (with Bande Mataram) and red

Imbued with the spirit of revolt and Swadeshi from his study of British tyranny, he became justifiably angry at the execution, in 1908, of young nationalists like Khudiram Bose, Prafulla Chāti, Kanhai Lal Dutt, Satinder Pal and Pandit Kanshi Ram in India. He seized the opportunity of meeting English officials in London at the July 1, 1909 annual meeting of the *Indian National Association,* to shoot and kill British official Sir William Hutt Curzon Wyllie, and Parsee physician Cowasji Lalkaka, who had intervened in trying to save Wyllie and stop Dhingra.

In court, Dhingra made a statement of purpose that told of the great frustrations of aspiring Indians and the obstacles due to colonialism; they would have endorsed every word he said, but few had the courage or confidence to say them or to support him openly at that time. Mahatma Gandhi condemned the violence, but his statement was unduly harsh and might well have encouraged British administrators and delayed Indian independence. From hindsight, it would have served India better had he kept still on the issue, or confine his remarks merely to a regret that young men were finding it necessary to express themselves with such violence!

Dhingra was exceptionally blunt and prescient in his court remarks: *"I do not want to say anything in defence of myself, but simply to prove the justice of my deed. As for myself, no English law court has got any authority to arrest and detain me in prison, or pass sentence of death on me. That is the reason I did not have any counsel to defend me."*

Earlier in Court addressing the judge, he had said, *"And I maintain that if it is patriotic in an Englishman to fight against the Germans if they were to occupy this country, it is much more justifiable and patriotic in my case to fight against the English. I hold the English people responsible for the murder of*

80 millions of Indian people in the last fifty years, and they are also responsible for taking away £100,000,000 every year from India to this country.

I also hold them responsible for the hanging and deportation of my patriotic countrymen, who did just the same as the English people here are advising their countrymen to do. And the Englishman who goes out to India and gets, say, £100 a month, that simply means that he passes a sentence of death on a thousand of my poor countrymen, because these thousand people could easily live on this £100, which the Englishman spends mostly on his frivolities and pleasures. Just as the Germans have no right to occupy this country, so the English people have no right to occupy India, and it is perfectly justifiable on our part to kill the Englishman who is polluting our sacred land. I am surprised at the terrible hypocrisy, the farce, and the mockery of the English people. They pose as the champions of oppressed humanity – the peoples of the Congo and the people of Russia – when there is terrible oppression and horrible atrocities committed in India; for example, the killing of two millions of people every year and the outraging of our women. In case this country is occupied by Germans, and the Englishman, not bearing to see the Germans walking with the insolence of conquerors in the streets of London, goes and kills one or two Germans, and that Englishman is held as a patriot by the people of this country, then certainly I am prepared to work for the emancipation of my Motherland. Whatever else I have to say is in the paper before the Court. I make this statement, not because I wish to plead for mercy or anything of that kind. I wish that English people should sentence me to death, for in that case the vengeance of my countrymen will be all the more keen. I put forward this statement to show the justice of my cause to the outside world, and especially to our sympathisers in America and Germany."

Madan Lal Dhingra

"I have told you over and over again that I do not acknowledge the authority of the Court. You can do whatever you like. I do not mind at all. You can pass sentence of death on me. I do not care. You white people are all-powerful now, but, remember, it shall have our turn in the time to come, when we can do what we like."

His last words recreated the impression of poignant defiance and daring, *"I believe that a nation held down by foreign bayonets is in a perpetual state of war. Since open battle is rendered impossible to a disarmed race, I attacked by surprise. Since guns were denied to me, I drew forth my pistol and fired. Poor in wealth and intellect, a son like myself has nothing else to offer to the mother but his own blood. And so I have sacrificed the same on her altar. The only lesson required in India at present is to learn how to die, and the only way to teach it is by dying ourselves. My only prayer to God is that I may be re-born of the same mother and I may re-die in the same sacred cause till the cause is successful. Vande Mataram!"*

Dhingra's martyrdom evoked the respect of members of the British Cabinet, and certain aristocrats, including the young Winston Churchill, Under-secretary of State for the Colonies, as reported by diarist William Blunt: in his entry for October 3, 1909: "*Again we sat up late. Among the many memorable things Churchill said was this. Talking of Dhingra, he said that there has been much discussion in the Cabinet about him. Lloyd George had expressed to him his highest admiration of Dhingra's attitude as a patriot, in which he shared...He will be remembered two thousand years hence, as we remember Regulus and Caractacus and Plutarch's heroes, and Churchill quoted with admiration Dhingra's last words, as the finest, ever made in the name of patriotism...*"

Dhingra acquitted himself with poise and dignity, unlike his family members, who, with fashionable Indian *muddle*-class toadyism, declared, through an attorney, that *"they view this crime with the greatest abhorrence, and they wish to repudiate in the most emphatic way the slightest sympathy with the views or motives which have led up to the crime. Further, I am instructed to say, on behalf of the father of this man and the rest of his family, that there are no more loyal subjects of the Empire than they are."*[101]

This statement remains as shameful an act of betrayal and brown-nosing as any in the sorry history of Indians, and stands condemned by the high-minded, esteemed and celebrated patriotism of Madan Lal. It would have been wiser to have remained silent.

The *Indian Councils Act*, Morley-Minto Reforms, was passed in 1909. A year earlier, Tilak was shipped to a Burma jail for activism. Savarkar allied with the *Garam Dal* faction of the INC and joined in armed demonstrations against the Act, for which he was imprisoned in 1910. In jail, Savarkar and Tilak came to experience the punishing life of India's distressed *crores* (1 crore=ten millions) of internees, in conditions described by many as worse than hell, but ignored by their "betters", especially Brahmins. Prisoners, like indentured workers, awoke at 5 am, toiled all day at heavy manual labour, under duress and in silence, even at mealtimes, and were abused and tortured for minor breaches.

Prison gave political and other detainees ample time for reflection, and to Savarkar, ideas to reform Hinduism, which he presented as

[101]There is among them one named Sonam Dhingra who parades her superficiality on the appropriately-named medium, *Twitter*—she may be only nominally connected to the quintessential patriot Madan Lal.

Hindutva. The All India Hindu Congress (*Akhil Bhārata Hindū Mahāsabhā)* adopted it, along with Savarkar's rejection of the *Naram Dal* stance in the INC. He proposed a union of all Hindus—using the term to include Buddhists, Jains and Sikhs—as inheritors of India, there to establish *Akhand Bhārata* (United India) as a *Hindu Rashtra* (Hindu Nation).

The Salt March, Gandhi in centre

J. Nehru and M. Gandhi

Chapter 17

"Unhappily there had never been in the whole history of mankind an instance of a civilised race taking anything like a scientific, much less a humane, method of treating the native question, which seemed always to be settled by the passion, pride, and prejudice of race…"

J M Robertson, House of Commons, 1906

"The visions of men are widened by travel and contacts with citizens of a free country and will infuse a spirit of independence and foster yearnings for freedom in the minds of the emasculated subjects of alien rule." Gurdit Singh, Komagata Maru

Race, Religion and Might; the *Chain of Being* at work

While leaders argued, the disenfranchised, dispossessed and poor masses had become inured to oppression, even by their own people. Hindus and Muslims sought solace in religious activities, in temples and mosques, where spiritual leaders were often their only advocates. Ramesh Dutt, a founder of the INC, came to recognise the centuries-old problem of injustice and crimes against rural Indians, who bore the brunt of British atrocities, often with the help of upper crust and urban Indians, and the lingering vices of the caste system. This the British enhanced, emphasised and advocated, to their advantage, and to degrade Indians and Indian society to a more rigid hierarchical state than even the most opportunistic Brahminist had imagined.

Village administrative *panchayats* had secured the land, and its productivity, through millennia of dynasties and empires. Now, tenants had no assured rights of any kind and paid exorbitant taxes. Since people had no political representation, bureaucrats had no way of assessing their concerns. That applied equally to British or Indian officers, but while the one could be excused by his position as ignorant conqueror, Indian leaders and officers must be blamed for being more aloof, vain, unhelpful and dismissive, and for facilitating the continued subjugation of their peoples, whose ancient rights to address their problems locally had been imprudently and brutally taken away. Indian "leaders" over the centuries had profited from this and had become the go-between for the conqueror, first Mughals, then the British. They also maintained strict class and tribe practices that could only improve if the British had decreed a change in behaviour. That was unlikely to happen, as the prevailing system provided pliable local middlemen and lackeys to collect taxes and do other "dirty work."

It didn't help the self-rule movement that India harboured, among its most privileged citizens, groups of anti-Hindu minorities, especially in the large commercial cities. They readily acted as a fifth column for the conqueror, getting concessions and making huge profits for cooperation and duplicitous inside activities, which undermined efforts to expose and expel the foreigner.

Yashwantrao Holkar of Indaur, Tippu Sultan of Mysore and Pazhassi Raja of Kottayam (Kerala) were among the last Indian princes to resist the British. The former finally agreed to a treaty after a poignant complaint to Daulatrao Shinde whose help he had sought in vain to drive the British out. Tippu, a most obnoxious and cruel prince, but virulently anti-British, anti-Hindu and anti-Pazhassi, was killed in battle, after bribery and betrayal. Pazhassi fought the British, including Wellesley, for two decades, about the same time as Holkar, and was finally ambushed in 1805, betrayed by a former security employee. For the British, Indian princes had become a crapshoot, using fable, bribery, land promises and religion to divide them, then reneging on promises once they had been hooked

It would be invidious to suggest that the Catholic Christians of Goa, Daman, Diu and elsewhere, or the Jews—typified by the Bombay Sassoons or Cochin spice traders—or the non-Indian Islamists, had retarded independence by decades, any more than did Indian princes, Islamists, Parsees, merchants and "Liberals". But Indian Catholics behaved more like Portuguese than Indians, despite their inferior ranking by Portuguese imperialists. They—and the others preferred by the British—did have much to lose, and by the time of self-rule worked to secure important parcels of the country, for example, the ports, or gain irreversible control of the nation's transportation, communications and administration. The Muslims of India will never be "first class" to the Saudis, being non-Arabs and mostly dark-skinned. Parsees and Sikhs were courted by the British, who promoted differences from Islam and Hinduism, to keep them apart. It is small wonder that the tightly related Parsees control business in Mumbai, own the city and manipulate Indian affairs. They maintain their ties and loyalty to India, though, in much the same way as Jewish interests dominate Europe and America today.

Back in Britain, the aristocracy that ruled India and the Empire behaved similarly, with scant care or respect for their own British masses. It was thus unlikely that they would pay attention to the reviled and "lowly" Indian. Even the middle class in Britain had little or no say in the affairs of the nation. Thus, it was no surprise that progress was snail-paced, despite agreement, in Ripon's time, of the need to restore India's *panchayati rāja,* to protect communities and allow them to participate in rural affairs. Moreover, few in the INC, or other political groups, had any real contact with the rural majority. It was as if these learned men had not read their own classics dealing with village organisation and government, or, if they had, had totally disbelieved or forgotten those accounts. It took a British MP, George Campbell to observe, *"in no country in the world are local self-governing institutions more ancient and nowhere were they more effective than when we arrived in India! The country has been truly described as a congeries of little republics..."*

In the two decades to the end of WWI, in which the problem languished, reviews identified the same problems, the same abuses, the same miscreants and the same remedies. These included the 1907 *Royal Commission on Decentralisation,* chaired by C.E.H. Hobhouse, Undersecretary of State for India, affirming the need to reconstitute *panchayats;* the *Government of India Resolution* of 1918, said the same, urging strengthening of local government. The 1919 *Montagu-Chelmsford (M-C) report* passed the issue to provincial ministers, but failed to empower *panchayats.* Indian labour made up 70% of the population and was vital to the nation's economy, but remained too poor to constitute a market. (In South Africa, later, the same situation re Blacks made Botha's regime believe that an *antidote* was needed to prevent them from flocking to Communism!)

The 1919 *Government of India Act* implementing the M-C Reforms endorsed expanded provincial councils, and transferred them to the ministries of education, health and agriculture. Centrally, it created a bicameral legislature with a lower house of 144 seats, 104 elected, and an upper Council of States with 60 members, 36 elected. Nothing was done to restore village-based self-government, as it was not in the interests of British business, and a trivial or even vexed one for the Government. Curzon for one had had no patience for local government, and had seen his role simply to promote *"the interests of government and the English (sic) in Calcutta"*, and to *"cut the Babu down to size"*, both of which he would approach, by shrinking legislatures, not by creating more layers. And so the issue had languished, until Gandhi began his campaign.

The formation of the Congress had an impact beyond Indian politics. It was warily welcomed by many Indian émigrés, whose families had suffered losses due to British policies. In the continuing protests for self-government, many were arrested and imprisoned, without trial, or simply disappeared. Concern was world-wide.

Disunity and the absence of true nationalism continued to dog India, and hobbled progress, its security and integrity, and obstructed resolute action for self-rule. Self-interest, not unity of purpose, or principle, or strategy, governed majority actions, despite hostile and racial responses from Government. The divisions were overt and pervasive, the voices strident on every side, but concerned mainly with maintaining wealth and privilege, with scant thought for the increasingly side-lined masses.

Schisms worsened as more Indians became anglicised, repudiated the past, and the privileged cut ancient ties, adopted British attitudes, values and behaviour, to preserve businesses or rank, or to prevent a shift of power from the upper to lower classes. Anglophilia had benefits.

As the self-rule movement grew and called for better representation of the people, it demanded, *inter alia,* an end to emigration and indenture, largely due to Gandhi's experience at Champaran *(see below)*. Change, however, was not likely to happen until the British monopoly—then crippling India's industry and continuing to extort and export its wealth to Britain—was brought to an end. Measures were needed to deal with the burning issues that impoverished the rural majority, as noted above, especially the authoritarian conversion of individual and family food farms to commercial plantation crops like cotton, opium, sugarcane and tobacco. (This practice continues freely today, with equally crooked Americans and Indians following in the corrupt British mould). The issue of contract migration was controversial and, as noted, opposed by the INC. The British *Rāja* "studied" it and decided to allow it to continue, as long as contracts were legally done and their terms observed to the letter. Among diasporal Indians, as contracts ended, recruits could claim repatriation, but employers reneged and readily found ways to deny it.

With the formation of the INC, the *Rāja* tightened surveillance of dissident activities. By Queen Victoria's death, the British Empire had reached its zenith. The larger white colonies had already achieved a measure of self-government: colonies in Canada and Australia had federated—1867 and 1901 respectively—and South Africa was next. The USA had advanced steadily by aggressive mercantilism, conquering all of America to the Pacific Ocean, between Canada and Mexico, defeating the latter, liberating the Philippines and the Spanish Caribbean from Spain, holding Cuba and Santo Domingo in fief, and Puerto Rico as a colony. Earlier, in 1854, Admiral Perry's warships had convinced the Japanese to forego *sakoku* (isolation) and accept US trade. By this time, the British had already smothered the out-gunned Chinese with opium.

The policy of the INC before the end of the century was class-based, aimed to achieve equality of opportunity in Government services, desegregation of public facilities—including vehicles such as railway carriages—and elimination of the many barriers to promotion of Indians. What was particularly galling to Indians was that they had to tutor new recruits from Britain, employed on hugely inflated salaries, paid for by Indian labour and taxes. Employers banked business profits in Britain that should have been shared with the local employees, who had made their businesses profitable, or else invested in India. By 1883, this was even less likely to happen as white people, academics even, became increasingly influenced by Francis Galton's ideas on *eugenics*, which impressed hierarchical and racially-bigoted Europeans and Americans, especially politicians, giving them a feeling of superiority, and excuses for the boorish behaviour they flaunted in India, the Far East, Africa America, Australia, Canada and the Caribbean.

The later 19th century had seen the spread of eugenics and ideas of a super race. Europeans saw themselves as the acme of perfection, of breeding, appearance and intelligence, forgetting their fairly recent rise from the dark ages, compared with the older and more mature and tolerant non-Islamic civilisations of the East, the Mediterranean and Northern Africa. Soon, with military conquests, the aura of superiority became so consuming that whites began to believe that non-white peoples were inferior, could do with less, and that exploiting or robbing them—by slavery, indenture or captivity, as in colonies—was acceptable and indeed desirable! If an inferior race died out through enslavement, so much the better. Countries like the USA, Sweden, and Germany actively promoted negative eugenics, i.e. preventing conception among "inferior" peoples, or, God forbid, racial mixing.

In 1907, Indiana enacted the first compulsory sterilisation laws, having previously labelled masturbation—then called *onanism*—as a cause of "early disease, disability or death", a syndrome identified as "degeneracy" in the 17th century. Galton however favoured a positive approach, to encourage desirable races and those of *"high genetic worth"*—following his classification of British society—to out-procreate all others, and prevent a *"reversion towards mediocrity!"*

By then, too, proselytism, which had for long played an important role in national identities, became more aggressively promoted, as both major branches of Christianity began the extensive missionary work of conversion—which British protestants had not pursued seriously until the nineteenth century. Quoting the Biblical condemnation of the degenerate Amalekites, they targeted Hindus in India and the Diaspora. To aid conversion, Christianity was made the official colonial religion, a necessity for jobs in the public services, and for legalising marriages.

Regrettably, conversion was not easy and did not bestow the promised equality, less so with the rising importance of race superiority, based on ideas of phrenology, craniometry and similar quack hypotheses in human biology. It was in this race superiority climate that British missionaries worked and must be pardoned for feeling so rewarded for rescuing and bringing luckless non-whites into the fold of Christianity!

The Indian National Congress announced its plan for self-government *within* the Empire, even as India's sister states in that

Empire were planning to pass discriminatory legislation denying Indians equality and the right of free movement within the Empire. This principle had allowed the British to move freely across the world, and was an implied, if not stated, guarantee in treaties signed, as Indian rulers ceded territory or swore allegiance to Britain.

The British had come to India with a firm purpose to trade and make profits; they cared little about Indian people or their customs, beyond what either could contribute to fatten the British purse. They thus dismissed Indians, without consideration, superimposed their own beliefs and practices, for ease of control, and spared no effort to find new ways to exploit conditions: domicile, religion, occupation, caste, social status, dress etc. to divide people into malleable units.

Hindus and Muslims had accommodated to one another over a period of several centuries, and the majority lived in integrated or contiguous communities, rural and urban. Muslims had accepted the anthem *Bande mataram,* knowing its Bengali origin, and that most Bengali Muslims shared heritage and language with Hindus and Buddhists. Hindus regarded the Muslim man-in-the-street as a fellow victim and ally, but generally judged Islamic military men and administrators—who were mostly of non-Indian origin: Afghan, Arab, Mughal, Persian and Turk—as self-seeking, ambitious, unreliable, devious and insecure, who suddenly decried the anthem as too "Hindu".

Reaction to the British *Rāja's* narrow-mindedness, arrogance and the dismissal of the INC, perhaps because of the latter's internal disagreements, led to activities which resulted in the arrest of Lala Lajpat Rai and Sardar Ajit Singh in 1907, and their deportation to Burma. Convinced of British invincibility, Lord Montagu in 1908 fulsomely proclaimed, *"The British Raj will not disappear in India so long as the British race remains."* (Note that the British are far from being a single "race" and he was not the first or last of that nation to show this ignorance.)

The *Morley-Minto Act* promoted the spread of religious divisions down to the lower classes and to rural populations previously living in harmony. The formation of the *Muslim League* in 1906 made Muslims believe themselves entitled to more of India than their importance or numbers might justify. The British might have regretted this outcome but Islamic leaders, who feared loss of power in a unified India, grabbed it and promoted it vigorously, until partition occurred, although the idea of separate states did not gel until just before WWII, having earlier been a tacit wish of non-Indian Muslims only.

On February 10, 1906, Britain launched the *HMS Dreadnought,* the most advanced battleship of its time, just months after the keel was laid, and completed it on October 3, a year and a day after starting. This impressive record tells of Britain's industrial strength at that time. The act spawned other dreadnoughts in major economies—even Brazil and Argentina—and a naval arms race that kept British and European shipyards very busy. This activity and its implications contributed to the tensions that morphed into WWI, where a regional dispute between Austria and Serbia soon provided the excuse for a major war. This was hailed by salivating European bankers, who would earn huge profits from a war, as Austria and Serbia embroiled their allies and treaty partners in Europe, the *Triple Entente* and *Triple Alliance*, respectively.

Although the dreadnoughts had caused such a stir, they did not last much beyond the Great War and were superseded, their heyday ending with the 1922 Washington Treaty that briefly ended the naval arms race. But, for the British and India, the *HMS Dreadnought's* guns, armaments, range and speed were a cause of fear throughout the Empire. The publicity warned subjects of the carnage and destruction that the ship could do to major cities like Bombay, Madras and Calcutta *(Mumbai, Chennai and Kolkata)*, and the myriad smaller coastal towns that could be annihilated with a barrage or two from the formidable 12" guns. Yet there is little evidence that this affected revolutionary activity inside India or in the many cells outside.

HMS Dreadnought, British Battleship, launched 1906

In 1902, Britain had concluded three years of bitter warring against the Boers of South Africa, ostensibly to secure aboriginal rights, though the arguments in parliament hung on securing property and wealth, mainly gold and diamonds, for the British. Gold had transformed the Boer territory of the Transvaal into the richest region in South Africa and a magnet for investors, among whom British corporate miners, headed by Cecil Rhodes, stood out, resisted by Paul Kruger, the Boer leader.

During that war, the British had used the unethical practice of imprisoning civilians, women and children, in dirty concentration camps, given half-rations and their farms burnt. Not that the Boers were any paragons of virtue; they were Dutchmen, who had come to southern Africa as members of the parent VOC, and established a camp at the Cape to supply their trading ships sailing to and from Indonesia and India. Failing to coerce the native Koisans to work for a pittance, they invaded their lands, and, with superior weaponry, captured and enslaved men, women and children.

Dutch trade with the East prospered enough to allow a thriving settlement to develop, the Cape Colony. The Napoleonic wars gave Britain, which had already encroached on Natal, the excuse to seize Dutch colonies. The Boers responded with the Great Trek north across the Vaal River, and there established the Republic of Transvaal, by expelling native tribes. They lived as thrifty and militant farmers, until gold was found in the arc of rocky land known as the Witwatersrand, and made them as acquisitive as, and perhaps even more racially corrupt and xenophobic, than the British.

Questions of self-rule emerged in London, and parliamentarians seemed to have no qualms about granting it to white people, while just as easily denying it to coloured races. Among the latter, the Indians and Chinese of South Africa were an anomaly, and not as easily dismissed as the "uncivilised" Black tribes. Unfortunately for the latter, the king of Swaziland had squandered his gift of self-rule, at a time of strong antipathy for Blacks, explaining British denials for new freedoms! White politicians focussed on preserving, for whites only, all ventures that were profitable or influential, denied Indians the full franchise, business licences and other concessions, thus highlighting the colour and racial prejudices that governed British decision-making.

Gandhi had been in the thick of these activities, from 1894 until his return to India in 1914, where he received the title of Mahatma, to recognise his fearless and principled battles in Transvaal and Natal. In 1909, the four South African colonies had come together as the Union of South Africa, preserving white interests, but distinctly threatening the rights of non-white inhabitants: the majority Blacks (Zulu, Khoisan, Sotho, Ndebele, Bechuan, Xhosa, Venda and others) and the minority Indians, Chinese and mixed races. Africans had settled in certain regions of India, taken there as slaves by Islamic merchants, and by the 19th century, their free descendants were fully a part of the Indian scene.

In debating colonial self-rule in South Africa, William Byles, MP for Salford N. aptly and sympathetically summarised the situation: *"Under modern civilisation the spirit of adventure had created a class of men who, when they went among uncivilised people, seemed to lose that humane and benevolent relationship which those at home retained. They had been rightly described as prospectors, who belonged to no country and who owned no moral law…The Boer record with regard to their treatment of the natives was not a good one; the British record had been no better. Both contained many stories of harshness, cruelty, and encroachments on the rights of natives and of slaughter. Both Boer and Briton believed in the doctrine of freedom, but it was the freedom of the white man to 'wallop his own nigger.'"* (HC Debate., Hansard 28 February 1906 vol. 152)

After remarking on the inequalities and changes made in the Transvaal, and making a case for protection of natives, he had argued, *"Why should a white Government destroy the system of communal land owning, which in many ways was a far better system than the system of the private ownership of land that we had in this country? Why should the happy tribal life of natives be broken up, and why should the native races be forced to labour in the bowels of the earth to dig gold which enriched only a mere handful of speculators?*

In response, Winston Churchill, then 32, Liberal Undersecretary of State for the Colonies, affirmed, *"In fact, the native supports the whole economic fabric on his despised and dusky back. It is he that has built our railways; without him the working of our mines would be impossible… The responsible government of a Colony is a great gift: it is, I think, the greatest and best gift that we can bestow"* (on South Africa).

In 1899, during the second Boer War, Churchill had served in the South African Light Horse and had thus learned of the issues. He stressed the adverse reaction of natives witnessing a lethal conflict between two white races which had the effect of lessening their regard for Whites. That was compounded, he said, by the work of *"coloured missionaries belonging to the African Methodist Episcopalian Church, a branch of the Methodist Episcopalian Church in the United States, one of the oldest, certainly the most powerful and the most remarkable organisation to which Negroid civilisation has yet given rise. Missionaries of this Church wander to and fro among the native tribes and villages of South Africa. They repeat the story of Esau and Jacob, of Esau the stronger and the elder who was robbed of his birthright by the craft and fortune of a favoured younger brother. They represent the white men as intruders and robbers who have deprived the native of his inheritance, and they say 'Africa for the Africans' and other disconcerting propositions of that character…In the presence of such an issue all the harsh discordances which divide the European population in South Africa vanish.*

Farmer and capitalist, Randlord and miner, and Boer, Briton, and Africander (sic) forget their bitter feuds and are all united...There were 630,000 whites in 1891 to 3,000,000 natives; in fourteen years' time in 1904, 1,135,000 whites, to 5,200,000 natives. In the United States the proportion of white men to natives is eight to one, and even there I believe there is sometimes something approaching to racial difficulties, but in South Africa the proportion is one white man to five natives. I ask the House to remember the gulf which separates the African Negro from the immemorial civilisations of India and China. The House must remember these things in order to appreciate how the colonists feel towards that ever-swelling sea of dark humanity upon which they with all they hate and all they love float somewhat uneasily. In this land of bewildering paradox good produces evil and evil produces good. The gold mines, so long needed to repair the annual deficits, have proved to be the greatest of curses, overwhelming the land from end to end with blood and fire, leaving an evil legacy of debt and animosity behind...We will encourage as far as may be in our power a careful, patient discrimination between different classes of coloured men..."

Despite the overt racism and patronising tones, or perhaps because of them, restrictions against coloured peoples became law in most of the British Empire, Europe and the United States, based on ancient hierarchies, still prevalent, and bolstered by the new hypothesis of white racial superiority. The white colonies of South Africa were granted self-rule, well ahead of the brown and black or yellow, regardless of mental and historical maturity and precedence. Perhaps whites feared that coloured peoples might not harbour the same emotions, loyalties and affiliations, hence propagandists needed more decades to brainwash them to think like whites, already imbued with the doctrine of favouring your own group (*apana jaat* in Hindi); this was a soothing panacea, to be conveniently invoked in every inter-racial transaction. Despite their racial bias, British Parliamentarians, in debating the Afrikaaner-British conflict, perhaps missed the depth of feeling of the former for Africa, which they had embraced totally, having severed ties with Holland. This is the same with North Americans, who had secured their pilfered nests by killing off the cream of the native populations of America.

The ruling dynasties and classes of India had been, by 1917, methodically browbeaten by the succession of acts effected during the past century. Unwilling to protest to regain ancestral rights, they remained humbled as the *Rāja* paraded, in its support—as if it needed any—the *Council of Princes,* made docile and dissolute by privileges. Their subjects had no independent voice. It devolved on people like those mentioned above, to assume a voice for all, and give substance to protest and rebellion, and claims for freedom.

The princes had been uniformly humbled, perhaps deservingly, in view of their supercilious attitude to their subjects, from whom they had grown more distant, as the British wooed them with gifts, bribes and compliments. This had started in the earliest days of trading, and grew as the traders learnt to differentiate among the religions, then existing quite amicably in the land, and how that knowledge could be used to divide the population by caste and religion, assisted, as appropriate, by bribes, threats and treaties, to gain primacy in key territories, Bengal in the east and Bombay (Mumbai) in the west. Then, by a combination of *doctrine of lapse*—highhanded by any view—and *subsidiary alliances* (i.e., *'I order you to ally with me on my terms'!*), enforced by arms and an official Resident, backed by artillery and a network of spies, Britain came to control the half of India that they had not conquered, and thus extended their field of theft to the entire country. They brainwashed millions of ambitious Indians, trained by Macaulay's anti-Hindu curriculum of deception and misinformation, to believe that Britain was a superior country, flooded with milk and honey; the British a superior race; Christianity the acme of religions; and Hinduism mere myth. They bought the assertion that English was the world's foremost language, that in Britain everyone was prosperous and educated, and that the coloured races were degenerate in proportion to their lack of whiteness. By serving loyally, in the British way, they would gain rewards, material and social, become eligible to join the world's best and most talented nation, and on death, qualify for a place in heaven!

A surprisingly large number of Indians bought this drivel, but just as many—the millions dispossessed—seethed with disbelief and discontent. When circumstances suddenly provoked it, a haphazard and poorly-supported war for independence occurred. It was predictably unsuccessful as most princes remained loyal to the *Rāja*. In the cleansing that followed, the British found that the majority of Hindus had spurned their arguments and that most converts were among poor urban dwellers, who naively believed the British propaganda, hoping to improve their status and escape neglect. Undoubtedly a few did; those who managed to sustain school attendance, pass British examinations and get jobs, did indeed feel elevated above their fellows.

However, despite loyalty and hard work through many decades, few advanced beyond the middle grades, while whites came in, learned from them and got promoted in a steady stream to the highest positions. And even the few Indians who reached near the top found that their British equivalents were paid up to five times more for the same job (Bryan). Then came the *coup de grâce:*, the teaching and worldwide spread of Müller's doctrine that Indians had acquired their learning and culture, their language and religion, from an ancient foreign invader, the mythical "Aryans" of central Asia. Some of them had migrated west, to Europe, some east to Persia and India. The British presence was thus a simple reunion of ancient tribal brothers, and their take-over the natural and desirable act of enrichment of the lesser by the stronger and more advanced family! His "proof" was a mistranslation of *Vaidic* words and passages, whose correction at the time, by Indians, was ignored. It was an error of great convenience and timing for the British *Rāja,* which exploited it thoroughly to indoctrinate the uninformed.

The falsification has been examined earlier, but it is worth recalling that it was a time of grave ignorance and venality in the world; poor communications; limited ability to verify information; divisions and restricted freedoms in society—educational, economic, political, societal; limited travel; widespread distrust; spying and exploitation of the poor and weak, in fact, much like today! British dogma flourished, especially among those with a weak religious upbringing or a shaky belief system.

Indian princes could have made a difference, but they were hogtied by treaties, most of which were only legal under the invader's laws. No prince arose to expose or challenge the British lies. Almost to a man they remained loyal to the British in 1857, and some were thereby rewarded with additional property and rank.

The "aryan" fable was taught in India from the mid-19th century; eager students swallowed their lessons to pass examinations and spread them to their children, so that in a few generations these fables became the "truth", sanctified by the "pukka English", and the basis for upward mobility or recognition in British India, especially for Christian converts.

It is easy to understand why Hindus believed the British fables, once education was in English and excluded any study of Sanskrit texts. The appraisals of Indian history were the work of 19th century BEICo officers, especially William Jones, H. H. Wilson, T. Macaulay, F. M. Müller, and F.E. Pargiter, the last three being among the most virulent opponents of Indian writings and religions, some descriptions amounting to abuse and hate. Immersed in British dogmatic teaching for over a century, Indians can be forgiven for rejecting things contradictory to their schooling, especially those that had been trashed as myth or falsehood. That they passed on their view of things to later generations is natural and also forgivable, but a dismissal of modern contradictory evidence is not.

Indian workers in colonies kept to their religions, perhaps because they were few, weak and unimportant, and removed from India's masses. Colonial authorities hoped to restrain any curiosity by banning all non-Christian and non-English religious publications. Yet Hinduism offered a far more engaging set of values for community living, in town or country, and thrived in the Diaspora, despite vigorous efforts by evangelists to spread Christianity, except among those aspiring to a British life style, or government positions, or occupations denied to Hindus or Muslims, as an incentive to conversion. .

Chapter 18

We will encourage as far as may be in our power a careful, patient discrimination between different classes of coloured men..."
W Churchill

Divided India; "a despotism controlled from home"

By 1920, few of the 562 princely states had any say in the running of the Rāja. The largest four or five were solidly pro-British. The richest ruler was the Muslim Nizam of Hyderabad, whose excesses were legendary. Few princes were well-regarded by the time of Independence, most being seen as well-paid lackeys of the British. They retained nominal authority over their subjects; some were treated with dignity and concern, but British Residents held the real power.

Elephant Carriage of the Maharaja of Rewa at Delhi Durbar of 1903

Most princes avoided criticising the Rāja, and preferred diversions such as sports, whisky, cars, or games, especially polo, cricket or hunting, all sorts. The Nizam bagged over 200 "wives" and allegedly became a father every four months. A few, however, like Jai Singh of Alwar, deigned to criticise the *Rāja* in the first three decades of the 20th century. Lord Reading (Viceroy 1921-6) referred to Jai Singh's "eccentricities and defects of character" as "thoroughly worthwhile", and Montagu had earlier praised his "knowledge and reasoning power".

In general, Princes maintained—and in some cases increased—their customary pomp. Many rulers descended into profligacy and waste that would have shamed their ancestors who had fought the invaders. The Holkars of the last century are examples, Tukhoji Holkar having to abdicate in 1926 in favour of his equally spendthrift son, Yaswant, whose ancestral namesake had almost single-handedly held off the British in the early 19th century, a feat his descendants might find unbelievable.

Princes (a demotion from Rājas or Kings) spent little time and money to educate and elevate their subjects, preferring personal adornment, families, courting British overlords by gifts and entertainment, so that many became the butt of jokes, circulated across the Empire. Visiting dignitaries to India might "grace" a palace and confer an award, or perhaps host a visit from a princely ally, at the palace of the British

Resident. The debasement of Indians followed logically, especially in America; intellectuals felt alienated, except for those parlaying their talents to gain favours from the *Rāja* or from princes.

During the Great War (WWI), the Viceroy created a *Council of Princes* as a reward for their commitment and support for the *Rāja* locally and internationally, especially for the War, to rubberstamp British use of Indian troops and money in that pointless European moneylenders' war. What justification was there for Indians to kill Germans or Italians? Perhaps if Indians knew any real history, of India or Europe, they might accept the chance to avenge past assaults by the Turks, but thanks to Macaulay and the succession of Indian secular historians, little factual timelines remained or were allowed to be taught in Indian schools.

Photograph (1894) of the 19-year old Shahaji II Bhonsle, Maharajah of Kolhapur, visiting the British resident and his staff at the Residency

As further reward to princes for their support in WWI and WWII, some were accorded military ranks based on their level of support, their own martial skills and gun-salute status, which had to do with historical agreements, lineage, heritage etc. Thus the Maharaja of Bikaner and Nizam of Hyderabad were made Honorary Generals of the British Army in WWII, a rare award. The princes of Gwalior, Kolhapur, Patiala, Jaipur, Jodhpur, Jammu and Kashmir contributed heavily to WWII; they were made Lieutenant Generals. Princes entitled to salutes of 15-guns or more were dubbed Major-General/Air Vice-Marshal e.g. Baroda, Bhopal, Mysore and Travancore. Some lesser princes were given ranks from Lieutenant to Brigadier, or equivalents, according to status. Some gave active and loyal service to the Crown, in India and in the UK; others served on commissions in colonies, or in junior diplomatic posts.

By 1920, after two or more generations as subsidiary allies, the Princes of India, whatever their personal obloquy, were softened and conditioned progressively by a British "public" school (upper crust) education, anglocentric immersion and Indian cultural denigration; they accepted the changes, complete with brainwashing, and displayed them with great aplomb—enhanced with turbans, elegant robes and fabulous jewellery—at international gatherings. They became a confirmed and smug bunch of impotent figureheads and showpieces, circus clowns, Macaulay's *coconuts*, who uncritically endorsed the decisions of the *Rāja,* giving them local credibility and binding their subjects to their service.

Most princes had lost lands, prestige and power. Only 120 out of 562 headed *"salute"* states, i.e. meriting a gun salute between 9 and 21, and commanded little more than local allegiances. As noted earlier, few had shown either interest or vision to throw off the yoke. By 1900, they had become mere lackeys of British largesse, barring none. Prior to WWII, Yashwantrao Holkar II, the descendant of the great Maratha fighter, had abused his wealth to acquire palaces in the USA, France and India, and a glitzy collection of custom-made sports cars, in which he sped through his principality, after ordering the police to clear the route! His ancestor would surely weep. Yet his profligacy is no worse than the excesses of India's modern industrial rich, who slavishly copy Western "celebrities" or merely mimic the princes of the British *Rāja.*

Those who prospered became progressively more anglophile and "liberal" in their politics, so that a wealthy class of officers, businessmen and administrators in both the *Rāja* and the princely states could be relied on to support the governments, while the mass of Indians, held in check by lack of schooling, remained oblivious that the wealthy and influential few had become spokesmen for all. The *Rāja* would quote the princes without qualms whenever it needed to publish an "Indian" opinion, emphasising the millions that that opinion represented.

Little would the world know or care that those millions, however impressive the numbers, excluded the large mass of impoverished, unheard and unseen megamillions, who laboured to eke out a sparse and tenuous living behind the princely pomp so glamourised in romance novelettes of the time. They would remain poor and underserved. Some lost kith and kin *(jāt)*, who had "debased" themselves by accepting overseas contracts, where many had outperformed their peers from other races, and emerged free and cleansed of the impediment of caste. They prospered by talent and enterprise, whenever they got a chance to use them. Some reunited with kin in India; more than half did not.

In reality, wealthy Indian princes had been paraded so often as a British success that any well-dressed Indian in certain places in the West was assumed to be an aristocrat. Sirpaul Jagan of British Guiana was treated in the 1950s as an aristocrat by a New York hotel, paying homage to the "Sir" in his name, which was simply *Shri*, mis-spelled.

Group portrait Chamber of Princes- meeting of 1941, albumen print, stamped A.R. Datt, Delhi. Image about 575 x 320mm. Date 17th March 1941 Author A. R. Datt

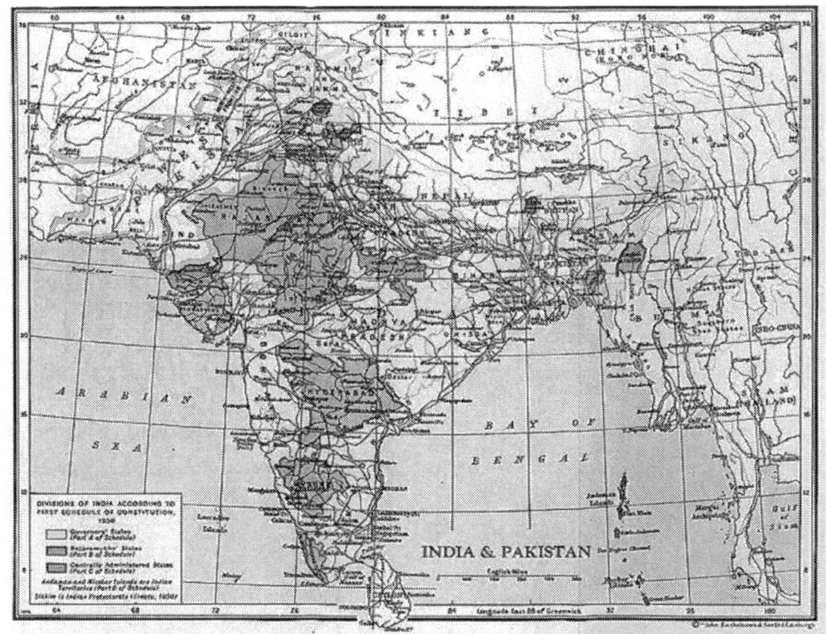

*The princely states shown situation post-1947 independence, scanned from *Majumdar, R. C. et al, Advanced History of India. (Bibliography), and photoshopped by MaGioZal from the original copy in Wikipedia uploaded by Fowler & Fowler «Talk» 17:37, 18 September 2007 (UTC).*

It was not surprising therefore that while a clamour was taking place for independence a group of Anglophile Indians would form the *National Liberation Federation*, however short-lived, sycophantic and non-viable, and left their members floundering.

Dayānanda's critique of the Maharaja of Jaipur could have applied to any prince at that time! The Nizam of Hyderabad—dubbed *"The Faithful"* by Victoria, and rewarded with a plaque—basked in the positive publicity he received from the British on whom he lavished gifts, in peace and war, including aeroplanes and a warship, spending millions that should have been spent on infrastructure, health and education for the teeming millions under his rule.

At this time, the Viceroy, supported by Parliament through the Secretary of State for India, responded to Indian protests by jailing anyone for adverse criticism, however slight! The *Prevention of Seditious Meetings Act, No. 10 of 22nd March, 1911, India*, was one such act. Aimed to curb protests, it awarded six months in jail, plus or minus a fine, for trivial breaches and effectively shut down meetings. It remained in force until 1927, but has lived on, to this day, as a model of similar capricious old British laws in the Empire and Commonwealth. Before its end, it had enabled many arbitrary incarcerations; more tellingly, it had exposed the total subjugation and spinelessness of princes, and the frailty and ambivalence of the INC, provoking another split. No wonder people like Montagu and Churchill were convinced that the Indians could never succeed in overturning British rule, a point that was noted by Earl Winterton, the Assistant Secretary of State for India, during the 1927 debates on the India Bill, (see Hansard), and retold to diasporal Indians seeking colonial independence after WWII. The phenomenon of British convicts completing reform in Australia and gaining independence, was cited in favour of whites, and as a change that could not happen to Indians of similar class, due to defects of race, religion and ethnicity!

In the optimistic belief that all British citizens had an equal freedom of movement, groups of agricultural Sikhs and Hindus had ventured into America and Canada, attracted by the wide plains and valleys, since losses due to substitution of food crops, famine, adverse weather, wars and politics had changed their livelihood at home. Diasporal white politicians were not all racists, but those who favoured racial segregation won key elections—defeating forces of morality and fairness in Australia, South Africa and Canada—that led to the "Whites only" immigration policies, adopted by these countries.

British Columbia and Canada's abominable treatment of a shipload of Indians—340 Sikhs, 24 Muslims, and 12 Hindus—who had arrived in Vancouver on May, 23, 1914, on the Japanese ship *Komagata Maru,* has become a symbol of the most objectionable elements of racial bigotry and breach of trust, as expressed by Canadians and British during and after the event, clearly showing that racial animosities and ingratitude had existed for a very long time. Their two months of imprisonment on board ship at Burrard Inlet and denial of food and water, followed by forced deportation—the first act of the Royal Canadian Navy's lone warship, *HMCS Rainbow*—reflected the callous lack of even elementary civility by the highest levels of the *Christian* governments of British Columbia and of Canada. They would repeat this to Jews in 1938.

Canadian antagonism to brown folk had developed before that. By 1900, there were merely 2,000 Indians living in Canada, mostly Punjabis, proud of their British citizenship and more loyal to Britain than to India. As numbers rose and began to include more Hindus—Canadians called all Indians Hindus, with generous injections of the epithet "savage"—H.H. Stevens, on becoming head of the *Asiatic Exclusion League* in 1907, explained that the League's mission was to keep Canada white. He pontificated that *"the destiny of Canada is best left in the hands of the Anglo-Saxon race,"* demonstrating straightway his ignorance of the origins, meaning and history of "Anglo-Saxons" and of Canadian settlers, and of the proper use of "race". Exclusionary legislation followed as did sanctions against domiciled Indians, including Canadians by birth. (They would have to wait nearly fifty years for any semblance of fairness, but equality would continue to elude them to this day.)

The *Komagata Maru* and its passengers were forced out of Burrard inlet on July 23, 1914, except for 24 passengers who were allowed to stay in Canada, because they were returning residents. As the vessel entered Indian waters heading for Calcutta, the British seized it and off-loaded the passengers at *Baj Baj,* an island outside Calcutta. They refused to obey orders to board a train for the Punjab and headed for Calcutta instead. This prompted a barrage of gunfire from a contingent of British riflemen, summarily murdering twenty people and wounding nine others. The survivors were jailed, the leader Gurdit Singh for five years.

The *Komagata Maru* massacre was publicised and condemned in British India. Yet, despite the horror and injustice of these actions, the INC at the outbreak of WWI that same year, agreed to support wartime austerities and the recruitment of Indians for the war in exchange for *British guarantees* of constitutional reform, a decision based on an oxymoron (italicised) and widely denounced. Tilak too had "forgiven" the British, and had written King George V approving India's support!

The massacre at Baj Baj, 1914

The decision to endorse the use of Indian soldiers in the War was not generally agreed. As it happened, over a million Indians fought bravely in many major campaigns in Africa, the Middle East, Italy and France, in which 36,000 were killed, and a hundred thousand others injured. They distinguished themselves at Ypres, in Flanders, and in Mesopotamia where Townshend imprudently led 12,000 to their deaths against the seasoned Turks. India contributed, in cash or kind, some £400,000,000 to Britain for WWI, yet merited barely a footnote in British accounts of that war. Punjabis, who comprised about half of the British Indian Armed forces, were disillusioned and hurt to find on demobilisation that they had reverted to their "native" status and were denied the honours paid to their white counterparts. Savvy Indians would smile at their naiveté.

At the start of the Great War, there were many nests of Indian anti-British revolutionaries world-wide. The best known groups were the militant *Ghadar Party*, formed in California and British Columbia; *the Hindu-German Conspiracy* in WWI; the *Indian Home Rule Society* (IHRS) in Britain; and Japanese and other groups, all favouring Independence. The Germans were willing to commit arms in WWI, when Indian activists seemed willing to grasp any helpful military hand, Germany's foremost. But this had petered out.

The actions supplemented civil disruption on Indian soil and attacks on the British, with loss of life on both sides. British vigilance and Indian divisiveness and treachery impeded political progress and led to arrests, imprisonment and execution for sedition, even for non-violent activities, including the execution of the respected 35-year old intellectual leader Bhadra Jatín, in 1915. By 1916, many hundreds had been hanged, and this would continue after the War. The INC then had fully expected that the British would keep the promises made in exchange for endorsing the use of Indian troops in WWI, and would leave India at its end.

The *Ghadar* movement had begun in 1913 among Sikh Punjabi members of the *Hindustani Workers of the Pacific,* led by Har Dayal and Sohan Singh Bhakna, to seek Indian independence, by armed rebellion, if necessary; they urged Indian soldiers (sepoys) to revolt.

The war provided a convenient milieu to canvass support in the USA, India, Germany and elsewhere, through the publication *Hindustan Ghadar,* and by contact with prominent militants such as Rashbihari Bose and Taraknāth Das. Das was a Bengali activist and scholar, with an MA from Berkeley and a PhD in Political Science from the University of Washington. He had been a professor of political science at Columbia University and visiting faculty in several other American universities. He had, earlier, organised Indian migrants on the West Coast in favour of Indian independence and had formed the *Indian Independence League.*

Das had added a strong academic input to the independence struggle and had had discourses with Tolstoy, already well-known for his ideas on non-violent resistance, as he discussed in *The Kingdom of God Is Within You (1894)*, an exposition of Christ's non-violence. Gandhi, too, had read this book in South Africa, and had discussed his ideas and methods at length by mail, before Tolstoy died in 1910. Henry Hyndman, Krishnavarma, Madame Cāma and others endorsed Tolstoy's maxim that *"the sole meaning of life is to serve humanity."*

The *Ghadar Party* viewed the aim of the Congress-led movement for dominion status as modest and the latter's constitutional methods as soft; they ignored Tilak's arguments in favour of the middle ground. *Ghadar* preferred the campaign to entice Indian soldiers to revolt, and to that end, established in November 1913 a press in San Francisco to produce a newspaper and other nationalist literature.

Soon after, the party established contact with prominent radicals in India, including Rashbihari Bose. But the group was infiltrated by British spies, especially one Sikh "activist", and when members tried to carry out projects in the Punjab, the forewarned British were able to neutralise them. At War's end, it split along ideological left/right lines and was inactive by 1919. It was, however, a valid quest for independence which ran parallel with, but often counter to Gandhi's *Non-Cooperation Movement.* It sadly illustrated the difficulty of uniting even intellectual Indians, and, moreover, how easy it was to divide them, even in small diasporal communities.

A few Indians, mostly Sikhs, had settled in western USA and Canada. Many in the USA had intermarried with Americans and Mexicans. Most were academics, agriculturalists or businessmen. A few had become politically active, mainly in Indian affairs, but only much later—after the 1946 *Luce-Cellar Act* made it possible for Indians to obtain citizenship—could they participate in US politics.

At that time, Dalip Singh Saund became active in California politics and was the first Indian US congressman elected by the state. He served from 1957-63. The *Asian Exclusion Act* was in force when Saund came to the USA in 1920 as a graduate student, and California was ahead in race supremacy activities, led by Dr. Paul Popenoe, Charles Goethe, a banker and Paul Gosney, businessman (*See http://historynewsnetwork.org/*). While allowed to remain and work in the country and *pay taxes*, Singh, like other Asians, was labelled inferior, denied the vote, entry into public service and other privileges, due almost entirely to the state's eugenics practices, one of the harshest in the nation, and more rigidly observed than in the British Empire. The condemned *inferior* races or *inferior* "genetic strands" faced compulsory sterilisation, and even euthanasia for certain conditions; some states outlawed mixed marriages.

Eugenics indeed so pre-occupied the white races of Europe and America that they supported it, on the flimsiest of evidence, during that immature state of western scientific development. Anthropometry was probably credited for more mistakes in the USA and Europe than the followers of Plato or the Spartans ever made in the name of producing the fittest race. Racial "purity" was practised well into the 1960's. Ironically, Nazi defenders at the Nuremberg trials invoked American Eugenics laws in defence of German practices in WWII!

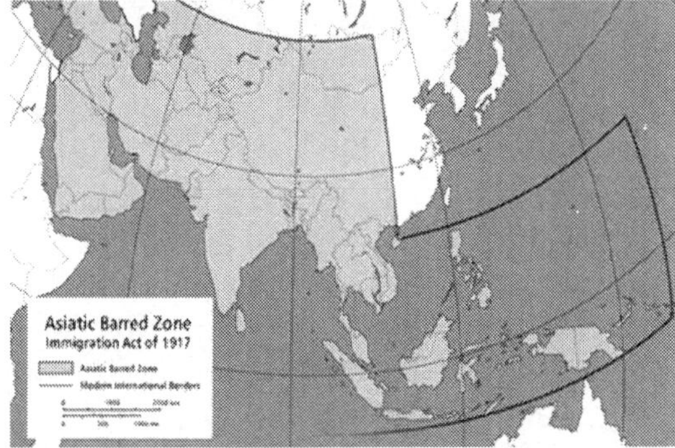

Top: 1946: US President Harry Truman signing Luce-Cellar Act, which allowed an annual migration of 100 each Indians and Philippinos (the Philippines became independent in 1946). The Act allowed resident Indians such as Dalip Saund to qualify for citizenship and thus obtain the vote, buy land and homes, and apply for family unification (US Govt. photo)

Bottom: the Asiatic exclusion zone by US law of 1917 (shaded and outlined area)

Guru Nanak, (1469-1539) founder of Sikhism, with Bhai Bala, Bhai Mardana and other Sikh Gurus (uploaded to Wikipedia by Jujhar.pannu). Sikhism was conceived as a practical monotheistic religion, free of complicated rituals. Nanak said, "*Realization of Truth is higher than all else. Higher still is truthful living.*" The Sikh aims to unite with Akal, the Timeless One; to do this, one would have to vanquish the five "thieves": *ego, anger, greed, attachment and lust.* The genders have equal rights and Sikh women have led prayers from the inception of the religion. Sikhism coincides with the Bhakti movement in North India and the life of Kabir, the great poet. There are over 25 million Sikhs worldwide, 60% in Punjab, and a large Diaspora.

Chapter 19

"To protest against all tyranny is a service to humanity and the duty of civilization."

Taraknath Das

(The Government of India is) *"a despotism controlled from home(UK)"*.

Sir Charles Wood, the second British Secretary of State for India

"(It is time) *to teach the Indians a lesson, to make a wide impression and to strike terror throughout Punjab.*" Punjab Governor O'Dwyer, before Jallianwallah Bagh massacre.

Gandhi; the young martyrs

Gandhi (1869-1948) returned to India on January 9th, 1915, after years of activism and peaceful protests (*hartal*) in South Africa, punctuated by jail terms for civil disobedience, (ironically, he was decorated by the British for humanitarian work during the 1899-1902 Boer War and Zulu Rebellion). He had made gains for workers, which he would repeat in India, where he soon became involved in helping rural workers, peasant farmers and urban labour to organise protests against discrimination.

The problems—low prices for produce, poor wages, violence from enforcers working for British landlords, over-taxation and other impositions—were then particularly burdensome in Champaran, Bihar, and Kheda, Gujarat. Both were afflicted with famine, an inevitable consequence of having all farmland diverted exclusively to the production of the commercial crops: cotton, opium, indigo and tobacco. This pattern of land use was begun by the BEICo, enforced by Warren Hastings and carried on by the Government of India. This profited the *Rāja*, the merchants and landlords but impoverished farmers through high taxes and loss of personal sources of food. Indentured workers barely subsisted on eroded wages; living in filthy huts in unhygienic villages; exposed to casteism; and at high risk for disease and alcoholism. Champaran had seen two uprisings, both ruthlessly quelled. Public outcry had gone unheeded.

Gandhi and co-workers in 1917 waged a campaign *(hartal)* of refusal to pay taxes or submit to legal and other threats. They were harassed, assaulted, jailed and otherwise vilified. But resistance did not waver and in time forced the governments of the affected regions to sign agreements suspending taxation in times of famine, allowing farmers to grow crops of their own choice and get increased pay for crops. Political prisoners were released and regained all seized property and lands. It was the biggest victory against the British imperialists since the American Revolution.

Gandhi was from Gujarāt but had thoughtfully left his Gujarati colleague, Sardar Vallabhbhai Patel, to lead the Kheda reaction. Patel proved an excellent choice and later became Gandhi's closest associate. The Champaran and Kheda actions were the first major break in the post-Tilak period and propelled Gandhi to the forefront of the INC. Grateful farmers dubbed him *Bapu* and *Mahatma.*

Gandhi was influenced by Jain and Hindu principles, and by the ideas of famous foreign advocates of non-violence, from antiquity to more recent exponents, including H D Thoreau and P B Shelley, whom he often quoted. On learning of the massacre in St Peter's Field, Manchester, in 1819 (p.197), Shelley promptly wrote a condemnation in his poem, *The Masque of Anarchy,* on "Passive Resistance", ending segments emotively with, *"Ye are many, they are few."* One stanza succinctly reflected the doctrine of peaceful defiance, which must have been in Gandhi's mind as he rallied his forces: *"Stand ye calm and resolute/Like a forest close and mute,/With folded arms and looks which are/Weapons of unvanquished war."*[102] Since then many in Asia, Europe, America and Africa have followed Gandhi, but little has changed in human interaction, as tyranny gets worse, at times more subtle, as corporatism takes over.

By this time, the Indian National Congress had existed for over 30 years and remained little more than a body that the British could keep an eye on and placate from time to time with a little sop, while selecting one or more from among them for special favours, either reward or punishment! The INC had lost focus and its main achievement had been the reunion of moderate and militant factions. It continued to behave as a reclusive upper-class body, remote from the vast population of Indians, predominantly Hindus, whose voice in decision-making became less and less forceful, as special interest groups and Islamic agendas gained ascendancy.

The INC naïvely believed that the British would keep their promise of constitutional reform, in exchange for supporting the use of Indian troops in WWI. It maintained its vision of Dominion status within the British Empire, a limited relationship, little different from the subsidiary one so roundly criticised as of "lower social status by those with fewer

[102] This account re the Gandhi era is drawn partly from experiences of Indian physicians at the Georgetown Hospital, who hailed from all major regions of India and had anecdotal or direct experiences of the events.

axes to grind," that is, the large mass of urban and rural underprivileged, who were daily exploited by both British and Indians. Only Gandhi seemed to understand and relate to this majority and only the INC seemed surprised that the British promptly forgot their promises of reform hardly had the War ended!

Gandhi joined the INC and persuaded it to adopt non-violence and non-cooperation as its major tools in breaking the British yoke. "The government we dream of," he said, "I describe as *Rāmarājya* (Rāma's kingdom); Swaraj alone can be such Rāmarājya."

Rather than keep its war-time promise to the Indian people, the British *Rāja* added salt to Indian wounds with the passing the *Rowlatt Act* in 1919, over strong opposition. This extended the 1915 war emergency measures—a shameful and treacherous imposition that broke earlier agreements and set aside discussion of plans for Indian self-rule—and suppressed protest, by jailing leaders and "wrong-doers"!

In one incident in Amritsar on April 10, 1919, two Punjabi leaders, Drs Saifuddin Kichloo and Satyapal, were seized and deported by a deputy district commissioner, Miles Irving. Gandhi had travelled to Amritsar to join the protest, but was arrested at the provincial border and ordered back to Bombay, by the lieutenant governor of Punjab, the hated despot Michael O'Dwyer. The followers of the arrested men marched to Irving's camp to demand their release, but met fire from British troops; several were killed. This provoked a response in which a few Britishers died, two women were attacked and banks burned.

At this time, the city of Amritsar was busy preparing for the annual *Vaishaki*[103] and Sikh *Kalsa*[104] celebrations, and thousands had come to the city to participate. On April 13th, nearly 10,000 people had assembled in Jallianwallah Bagh, an enclosed square, and co-incidentally became part of a peaceful protest against British action against the Indian leaders.

Gen. R. Dyer arrived from Jullundur with a brigade to assist O'Dwyer, and without warning or reason penned the essentially peaceful crowd in the Bagh and ordered his men to open fire "to preclude the spread of mutiny," having decided to shoot even before he had reached the Bagh! Dyer admitted to this in hearings of the Hunter Committee of enquiry, and Churchill confirmed it in a speech to Parliament in July, 1920. The number killed varies from a minimum of near 400 to thousands—the British physician on the spot claiming the number to be 1,800—including women and children, and over 1,200 wounded. This act was condemned worldwide, but hardly fazed the

---

[103] This is an ancient festival marking the first day of the month *Vaisakh*, in the *Nanakshahi* solar calendar, (April 14th).

[104] This means "Servants of God", founded by Sikh Guru Gobind Singh in 1699.

British *Rāja.* It left indelible marks, however, on the tender minds of several youths who had joined the *Non-Cooperation Movement.* Many would be moved to retaliate with violence, including Bhagat Singh and colleagues (p.297), and Udham Singh.[105] It is clear that O'Dwyer was fully aware of Dyer's plan to shoot without provocation, having said earlier that it was time *"to teach the Indians a lesson, to make a wide impression and to strike terror throughout Punjab."*

The Hunter Committee in 1920 censured Dyer for a "mistaken concept of duty". Parliament fired Dyer but a London paper, the *Morning Post,* declared him "the saviour of India" and raised £26,000 for him, a third coming from within India!

In 1920, Chakravarti Vijayaraghavachariar (1852-1944)—Tamil politician, friend of Allan Octavian Hume and a founding member of the Indian National Congress—became INC President. He helped draft its constitution, and felt that the Congress should be political, with economic and general social aims, while others opted short-sightedly for politics only. He helped frame the *Swaraj Constitution.*

In 1921, Gandhi became head of the INC, with the goal of *Swaraj* (self-rule), choosing the process of civil disobedience, or *Satyagraha* (soul force), which he had used in South Africa, and Egyptians had copied against the British in 1919, to force independence, obtained in 1922.

In August 1921, Mappila Muslims in Kerala began a bloody revolt against their landlords and the British, but focussed their venom against Hindus, and in a short time, before the army could reach them,, killed 100,000 Hindus, converted many, seized property, raped women and burnt houses and temples. As President of the INC, Gandhi, instead of a swift reprimand to Muslims for the slaughter, urged Hindus to forgive, perhaps out of his passion for Hindu-Muslim solidarity in the quest for independence, and his support for the Khilafat movement. The details, as recorded in *Young India,* showed his blunted judgement and may well have emboldened Muslims to increase their anti-Hindu violence.

Among many nationwide rallies, the one at *Chauri Chaura* I Feb., 1922 ended badly, when Police assaulted and shot stragglers dispersing from it. Seeing the carnage, the crowd ahead turned on the Police who retreated to their station *(chowki);* this was set on fire and 23 men died, either from burns or from attacks while trying to escape. Gandhi concluded that the deaths would weaken the basis of his protest—*truth and non-violence*—and cancelled the *Non-Cooperation Movement (NCM).*

This was a controversial, if not unpopular decision. The NCM had started two years earlier, had a wide following, including overseas

[105] Udham achieved martyrdom for killing O'Dwyer on March 13, 1940 in London having stalked him for two decades.

Indians, had raised Gandhi's profile and had put great pressures on the government to the extent that many saw imminent victory. Moreover, it had taught discipline, solidarity and sacrifice as tools of resistance, and showed that the masses had high motivation, stamina and courage. NCM had taken politics from upper crust city parlours into rural huts and villages. Many believed the accusation that the *Chauri Chaura* affair had been engineered by British Police to frame Indians and provide the excuse for reprisals against leaders, and a justification to Parliament for further oppressive legislation. British tacticians were often accused of using this reprehensible type of scheming, throughout the Empire, to frame individuals and embarrass or quell opposition.

Militants thus blamed the British, pointing to other brutal actions: the suppression of Ghadars and Sikhs; wholesale detentions and unknown losses of lives in jails and secret places by firing squads; the rape of the Indian economy to help finance WWI; and the post-war Jallianwallah Bagh massacre of innocents. Infuriated leaders organised many protests, including a "*hartal*" on April 6, when Indians stopped all business and fasted in protest (*Rowlatt Satyagraha*). Protests increased, resulting in several incidents of fighting, breaching the principle of *ahimsa*. The British responded with habitual ferocity, killing many, jailing more, including Gandhi.

An incident at Viakom, Travancore, in 1924, helped Gandhi and the cause of the INC. Temple authorities and the Diwan, also head of the temple, had prohibited Dalits from entering the temple or using neighbouring roads. This provoked a strong protest by temple Hindus and Dalits, led by T.K. Madhavan which he called the *Viakom Satyagraha*, the first to gain national attention and approval. The Diwan callously decided to set police against the protesters. All India was outraged; support came from far and wide, including the Diaspora. Gandhi felt that it was a Hindu issue, which Hindus should resolve sensibly. But the Diwan was inflexible and prevailed, as the matter seethed. When a petition, brought before the local government on referral by the Rani of Travancore, tied at 21 each, the Diwan forced the brother of a highly-respected physician to cast his vote against it; so intense was the reaction against the voter that he is said to have ended his days in disgrace. It took a year to obtain a more acceptable, though incomplete solution.

The *Viakom Satyagraha* had brought Gandhi to Kerala in 1924, and had the positive effect of showing the concord among Hindus, Sikhs, Christians and Muslims, and the interest of overseas Indians in human rights protests, illustrating the basic tolerance of India's peoples, and the chauvinism of those with extreme views, which prevail only by the power they hold and exercise. It also increased the popularity of the INC, hitherto remote from the lower classes, and from the Diaspora, and gave hope that the taint of caste might finally begin to fade. Six years later the *Satyagraha* at Guruvayoor, Travancore, occurred and resulted later in mandatory temple access for all Hindu castes in the region.

Gandhi's action attracted members from the ordinary citizenry, thus changing the INC from an elitist to a more inclusive movement. He spread the resistance country-wide. His aims were comprehensive: national unity and solidarity; religious tolerance; reduction of poverty; restoration of Indian village life; expansion of women's rights and an end to untouchability, to bring dignity and rights to those affected. He called them *harijans* (God's children). Dr B.R. Ambhedkar, a Dalit member of INC, and a highly respected lawyer and economist, disliked the term, pointing out that Dalits were, like others, intrinsic to Indian society. (The term is now being used abusively by militant Indian Christians to falsely accuse Gandhi of naming *harijans* the children of *devadasis,* or temple servants, with no known fathers. Ambhedkar remained with Gandhi and became Nehru's first Law Minister, only to see a Congress Government delay, then virtually kill his Hindu Code Bill. He resigned and became a Buddhist just before his death.)

Motilal Nehru criticised the suspension of NCM, as it relieved the British, and many agreed. Members demanded a change in policy. With Gandhi imprisoned, a split developed between those who wished to continue passive resistance—"no-changers": R Prasad, V. Patel and Gandhi—and the more militant members who wished change—"pro-changers": M. Nehru and C.R. Das. The latter started the *Swarajya Party* to contest elections, in accordance with the 1919 Government of India Act. *"The truth is we cannot get anything from England except by proving our strength,"* Motilal Nehru opined, suggesting that the duplicitous and untrustworthy British would yield only to military action.

Disagreeing with the idea, and not wanting to appear to be cooperating with the oppressor, Gandhi resigned to allow room for free debate among the wide-ranging political and economic camps, from conservatives of all kinds, and bureaucrats, to socialists, labour unions, student radicals and communists.

By this time, the Bolsheviks had gained control of Russia, and socialism was spreading across Europe. Menshevism succumbed and Stalin wormed his way to the leadership. The success of Marxism, and later Marxism-Leninism, over the previous two decades, had impressed many seeking independence from European imperialism and inspired the more militant and younger Indian *'revolutionaries,'* including members of Bengal's *Anushilan Samiti.* They contacted Marxists, studied their philosophy and methods, and keenly promoted the armed overthrow of the *Rāja*. Their enthusiasm led them to a series of actions complementing those already taken by the *Anushilan Samiti* and Punjab's *Ghadar Party*. The *Swarajya Party* contested elections in 1923 and became the opposition, facing a majority of British appointees and bureaucrats. They managed to delay finance and a few activities.

In 1922, Gandhi suffered an attack of appendicitis and was released from prison. He remained irrevocably on the side of *ahimsa* (non-violence), just as Motilal Nehru and CR Das were diametrically opposed. Responding to criticism and pressure, the Viceroy's *Repressive Laws Committee* in March, 1922, repealed the Rowlatt Act, press censorship and over twenty other pieces of legislation, perhaps goaded by the *Chauri Chaura* incident of the previous month, the festering discontent everywhere, and periodic outbursts of frustration or rage.

Regrouping quickly, and deploying British or Indian forces controlled by the *Rāja*, Police began reprisals against Indian leaders, whose retaliatory militancy was not surprising and might have been what the British wanted; but Gandhi remained firm and rejected it.

In Bengal, the *Hindustan Republican Association* (HRA) was formed as an offshoot of *Anushilan Samiti*. Among the leaders were Pratul Ganguly (later a member of the Bengal Legislature), Narendra Mohan Sen, and Sachindra Nath Sānyāl, who famously argued with Gandhi, opposing his gradualist approach to independence. HRA's manifesto noted *"...Official terrorism is surely to be met by counter terrorism. A spirit of utter helplessness pervades every stratum of our society and terrorism is an effective means of restoring the proper spirits in the society..."*

HRA promised to refrain from terrorism, for terrorism's sake, and to use it only *"...when expediency will demand it..."* The aims of the Association included universal suffrage and religious freedom. Its orientation was socialist, with inspiration coming from Bolshevism, which had finally taken root in Russia and its former empire.

KB Hedgewar

About this time, KB Hedgewar, a congress activist and medical student, who had spent a year in jail for anti-British activism, formed the *Rashtriya Swayamsevak Sangh* (RSS) in 1925 as a community based organisation to educate people and to campaign for rights. The focus was non-political, primarily Hindu rebirth, and to stimulate a love of, and loyalty to India, to achieve social reforms and improve the economy of Indians. It had no formal membership, and in promoting Hinduism, included in the term all Indian religions, "tribals and untouchables", as in the Indian constitution today. There was no caste structure in any of the groups, a surprise to visitors, including B K Ambhedkar. RSS quickly attracted many young people but avoided formal membership; it encouraged support for Gandhi's *Salt Satyagraha* and *Purna Swaraj*. But it was quickly branded as an extremist group by Islamists, socialists and secularists, and the Rāja, a charge that still stands. The leadership chose to ignore the accusations.

Hedgewar was jailed for his part in the Salt March. The RSS stopped short of supporting INC cooperation with Islam and rejected division of India. In 1934, the INC responded by banning support for RSS, and forbade its members from joining it, the All India Muslim League or the Hindu Mahāsabhā. Hedgewar regretted this but maintained focus. In 1940, he was succeeded by MS Golwarkar who advanced the idea of a Hindu state: "*The non-Hindu people of Hindustan must either adopt Hindu culture and language, must learn and respect and hold in reverence the Hindu religion, must entertain no idea but of those of glorification of the Hindu race and culture ... In a word they must cease to be foreigners, or may stay in the country, wholly subordinated to the Hindu nation, claiming nothing, deserving no privileges, far less any preferential treatment – not even citizens' rights.*" (This is similar to the US pre WWII, or the Saudis re pre-eminence of Islam in Arabia, and the apical position of Arabs in Islamic hierarchy.)

Golwarkar avoided confrontation with the INC or AIML on the issue. At partition, RSS in Delhi is said to have prevented the Muslim overthrow of Nehru's government, according to noted theosophist, Bhagwan Das. Implicated in the Gandhi assassination in 1948, as Nathuram Godse was a supporter, Golwarkar, and other leaders of the RSS, were arrested and the group banned. Despite lack of evidence, it took T.R.V. Shastri, former Advocate General of Madras, to intervene directly with Sardar Patel to get the ban lifted, seventeen months later. The RSS grew to over 40,000 branches, and remains a strong advocate for Hinduism. It has been implicated in defensive and retaliatory anti-Islamic events; but instances of crimes against Christianity charged to RSS are said to have been committed by Christians associated with *World Vision*, the NGO. *(See http://bharatabharati.wordpress.com/2010/02/02)*

Frustrated with the lack of progress and needing money to purchase arms, several HRA members organized a train robbery at the town of Kākori in 1925. The incident is notorious for the publicity and excessive severity of the sentences. There were five executions: Swaran Singh, uncle of Bhagat Singh; Ram Prasad Bismil; Ashfaqullah Khan; Rajendra Lahiri and Roshan Singh; and several life sentences. Their defence involved most of the leadership of the INC, headed by Govind Ballabh Pant, later Chief Minister of the United Provinces. Lord Irwin, the

Viceroy, denied many appeals for clemency. Jogesh Chandra Chatterjee, a member of *Anushilan Samiti,* received a "short" sentence of ten years. On release he became an INC member, left to form his own Party, then rejoined and became a member of the Rajya Sabha, serving until his death in 1969. Several others had similar experiences.

Chandrasekhar Tiwari (Azad, 1906-1931), close associate of the militant Bhagat Singh (1907-31), Yogendra Shukla and others, changed the HRA into the *Hindustan Socialist Republican Association* (HSRA), to reflect the socialism, which they felt was sweeping the colonial world, as Russia advanced and became a more convincing model of revolt.

Students of LL Rai's school; Bhagat Singh is fourth from right, standing

Bhagat Singh's father was a Sikh and also an Arya Samajist, active in the *Ghadar Party,* along with two brothers. Bhagat was educated in a Vaidic school, as his father—some say grandfather—like so many other Indians, had rejected the pro-British education of the Sikh school, in response to Gandhi's call. He later attended a high school founded by Lala Lajpat Rai. Rai was a widely respected leader of the Freedom Movement and was among the leaders of a peaceful demonstration in 1928, in Lahore, supporting the All-India boycott of the *Simon Commission,* which had been appointed in 1927 to study Constitutional reform for India, without an Indian member!

This had provoked a brisk debate in the British House of Commons and exposed the extremely partisan approach to Indian affairs, as if what mattered most was the welfare of UK aristocrats and of the Conservative Party, and that little or no account would be taken of the lives and hopes of 300 million Indians who would be affected, some irreversibly, by Government policy. Ellen Wilkinson,[106] Labour MP for Middlesbrough East, criticised the Government for its alleged role in facilitating the

[106]Future Minister of Education in Clement Attlee's government 1945-7)

writing and circulation to the opposition of a scatological account of life in India. The book, *Mother India,* by an American, Katherine Mayo, painted a malicious portrait of Indians, skewing social and labour practices of certain sects to taint the entire nation. Opposition parliamentarians condemned the book in London, and quoted the writer's profile as a notorious racist and colour-prejudiced WASP (White Anglo-Saxon Protestant), supported by fundamentalist conservatives and the central intelligence arm of the British *Rāja;* she named one member, a J H Adams. Gandhi said of it, *"If Miss Mayo had confessed that she had come to India merely to open out and examine the drains of India, there would perhaps be little to complain about her compilation. There is a general feeling that the book was not written without Government connivance."*

In fairness to her critics, Mayo could have tried to remove the "motes in her own eyes" before tackling India's, making her motives self-seeking and more like a hateful smear campaign, "commissioned" by the British Government, and not a spontaneous piece of investigative reporting. For that, or even for smears, she could have looked at her own country's sordid side, the myriad crimes of prohibition, the "rackets" culture, occult slavery, ghettoes, homelessness, corrupt politicians and thieving bankers who would soon precipitate a prolonged depression: her own country was replete with black marks. Not so long ago, white slave owners proudly tagged American Negro slave girls for use as "bed-warmers", selecting them from among new virgins as soon as they had reached age 11, and tagging them with red scarfs for easy identification.

Perhaps to further improve perspective and fairness, Mayo could have mentioned the advances and sterling achievements by Indian women, including enfranchisement and political office. For example, Dr Muthulakshmi Reddy had become the first woman legislator in 1926-7 in Madras (Chennai). She could also have noted that the University of Calcutta (Kolkata) had granted degrees to women 38 years *before* Britain's Oxford University; two Indian women had graduated as physicians in the mid-1880s (pp. 245-6). The first British woman physician, Elizabeth Blackwell, had completed her basic studies in the USA in 1849, and not in Britain, but was allowed post-graduate time at St Bart's Hospital, London. India had universities 3000 years ago, and the country had thrived until looted by Mayo's ancestors for more than two centuries. And it was Mayo's people too who had withdrawn the franchise from women in Dutch colonies, acquired by the British at the end of the Napoleonic wars. In identifying all that was wrong in India, she was really condemning the British aristocrats who ruled India for allowing the practices and lack of amenities that she found so damnable!

When the Commission on India was proposed in 1927, Earl Winterton harshly and stubbornly rejected consulting the Indian assembly, as proposed by Mr Saklatvala, a Parsi Marxist and the sole Indian in the House of Commons, which had led to some acrimony. The following excerpts from the record convey the flavour of the remarks made in the House of Commons (HC, 22-11-27 vol. 210):

Saklatvala: *"...many unjustifiable and untruthful assertions have been made by the Noble Lord, the Under-Secretary of State for India..."* and *"I want to remind the Noble Lord that he has been guilty of deceiving the British people and the whole world by placing unrepresentative Indian Princes on the League of Nations to speak in the name of India. Some of those Princes are corrupt men who are afraid to go back to India... I cannot see why the Noble Lord should not incorporate my Amendment in the permanent Act in order to secure that the Indian Legislature will be consulted in the future...the Noble Earl, when he made the sweeping assertion that it is merely shifting the date, that there is no opposition in this country or in India, misinformed himself as well as the House, and that there is bitter opposition in responsible Indian circles capable of expressing themselves against this Bill... which looks so innocent and harmless, which, even in the characteristic Parliamentary hypocritical manner, looks so generous and charitable, is merely a trap for the people of India".*

Wheatley: *"...our treatment of India up to now has not been a great success. It may be that we have made money there; it may be that we have added to the numbers and the prestige, in one sense, of the British Empire, but there are many improvements possible in the condition of the Indian people that have not taken place under British rule in India... it is of the utmost importance that we should have the goodwill of the Indian people in the steps we are now taking, and that we should take every step to assure ourselves that what we are doing has their heartiest support. It would be most unfortunate if we were to embark on a course that led to friction, when we are attempting to produce harmony. I think the Bill in its present form is more likely to do harm than good, and for that reason I am opposing the Third Reading.*

Beckett: *"What we object to is the utter flouting of all conscious Indian opinion, a deliberate declaration that 'We are the all-high, endowed, aristocratic Englishmen, who can tell the Indians and the Chinese and the British workers and everybody else what they are to do, and they are to be very grateful to us.' That is not the way to move the world now. Right hon. and hon. Members opposite may have been able to do that 30 or 40 years ago, when no one else knew much about gunpowder except themselves. This Government is exactly like the Bourbons; it learns nothing and forgets nothing. It conducts itself as if it has still only to rattle the sabre and everyone else will shake. That is not the case. India cannot be held for ever by these brusque methods of conducting negotiations...Everyone who listened to the Debates then visualised a consultation with the Indian Legislative Assembly and a careful combing of all the facts by the Government. I and all those with whom I have discussed the Bill were under the impression that the Statutory Commission referred to in the Act would be an inclusive and expert Commission. No Government has ever dreamt of calling a Parliamentary Committee an expert Commission. No Government, if it really wanted to find out facts or get a thorough investigation, has appointed a Committee of Members of Parliament... The Act of 1919 met with the approval of considerable numbers and influential sections of the Indian community. The Bill of 1927 meets with the approval of no representatives.*

Buchanan: "*... I would ask the Noble Lord, therefore, in the interests of courtesy to give the Committee a short explanation of this Clause.*

Wheatley: "*I hope I shall not say anything that will restore in the House the unfortunate atmosphere created by the Noble Lord who is in charge of the Bill. I think it was most regrettable that he should have introduced the Measure to the House in the superior tone which he felt it his duty to adopt; not that I think anything which he said would leave any deep impression on any Member of this House. I regret it from the effect it may have in India, and among people who do not understand the Noble Lord as well as do the Members he was addressing this afternoon.*"

Wilkinson: *Why are we having a persistent refusal on the part of the Noble Lord to bring forward these Resolutions? Surely it is not correct for the Noble Lord, with all the resources of the British Government at his disposal, with the permanent officials sitting below the Gangway and messengers crowding the House, to say that it is not possible to get these Resolutions from the India Office... If they are not in the India Office, why did the Noble Lord quote them in support of this Measure?*

Shaw: *I have said that I know of no responsible body of Indian opinion which is against the move being made. I hold in my hand a telegram from the Indian referred to by the right hon. Gentleman for Shettleston (Mr Wheatley), which seems to indicate that it is not the move which is opposed, but the constitution of the Commission.*

Maxton: "*I know that a great deal has been made in various speeches of the claim that there is no such thing as responsible Indian opinion that can be consulted. I am quite sure that that is not true. I am prepared to believe that you cannot get one man who can speak for the whole of India. I am quite satisfied that you cannot get one man who can speak for the whole of Great Britain. I question whether you can get one man who can speak in a really responsible way for the whole of the Conservative party...*"

Beckett: "*...but the Noble Lord was preposterously amazing a little while ago when he got up with an air of outraged majesty and dignity and said, "Why, you are doubting my word!" I do not think there have been many cases in Parliamentary history when an Under-Secretary of State has been given so trustfully and completely by the Leaders of the Opposition a blank cheque for him to fill in.*"

Winterton had entered a long tirade against Saklatvala, assailing the liberty he had taken to comment and damning his bonafides. Winterton was appropriately chastised for improper conduct, and although several speakers objected to his lack of decorum and the disparaging remarks about Saklatvala, he was unrelenting.

Lala Lajpat Rai was assaulted by Police in Lahore on Oct 30, 1928, as he led a protest march against the Simon Commission; he died of his injuries eighteen days later. Bhagat Singh is said to have witnessed Police Supt. James Scott brutally beating Rai with a lathi. Singh was incensed by this wanton assault and swore vengeance, which he and colleagues, Shivarām Rājguru, Jai Gopāl and Sukhdev Thapar plotted. Thāpar mistakenly killed Assistant Superintendent Saunders instead of the target Scott. They escaped, and later, Bhagat Singh and an accomplice, Batukeshwar Dătt, threw radical leaflets and two bombs in the Legislative assembly, which caused no injury. Jailed for the offence, Bhagat promptly started a prolonged fast demanding to be treated as a political prisoner. While in jail his role in the Saunders killing was revealed, and a trial led to a death sentence. An appeal to the Privy Council in 1931 failed.

Lala Lajpat Rai

On March 26, 1931, Gandhi said, "*Bhagat Singh and his two associates have been hanged. The Congress made many attempts to save their lives and the Government entertained many hopes of it, but all has been in vain. Bhagat Singh did not wish to live. He refused to apologise, or even file an appeal. Bhagat Singh was not a devotee of non-violence, but he did not subscribe to the religion of violence. He took to violence due to helplessness and to defend his homeland. In his last letter, Bhagat Singh wrote, 'I have been arrested while waging a war. For me there can be no gallows. Put me into the mouth of a cannon and blow me off.' These heroes had conquered the fear of death. Let us bow to them a thousand times for their heroism. But we should not imitate their act. In our land of millions of destitute and crippled people, if we take to the practice of seeking justice through murder, there will be a terrifying situation. Our poor people will become victims of our atrocities. By making a dharma of violence, we shall be reaping the fruit of our own actions. Hence, though we praise the courage of these brave men, we should never countenance their activities. Our dharma is to swallow our anger, abide by the discipline of non-violence and carry out our duty.*"

Memorial to Bhagat Singh, Rājguru and Sukhdev Thapar

Bhagat Singh

Jatin Das, Singh's associate

Chapter 20

"It is easy to kill individuals but you cannot kill ideas. Great empires crumbled but the ideas survived. Bourbons and czars fell while the revolution marched ahead triumphantly".

Shaheed Bhagat Singh

"It takes a loud voice to make the deaf hear" — Edouard-Marie Vaillant, French Rebel

"*Samrajyavad murdabad*" (death to imperialism), — Indian Bolshevik Slogan, 1917

Repression and Oppression

A year after the L. L. Rai incident, Rufus Isaacs, Marques of Reading, Assistant Secretary of State for India and previous Viceroy, *(Hansard 1929 HL Deb 05 November 1929 vol. 75 cc 372-426),* explained that an Indian was not needed on the Simon Commission, as the team's purpose was only to gather information for Parliament, prior to any constitutional discussions or decisions, at which time involvement of all parties would be appropriate. He quoted from the terms of reference: *"The Commission shall report as to whether and to what extent it is desirable to establish the principle of responsible government, or to extend, modify, or restrict the degree of responsible government then existing therein."*

The Simon Commission boycott, which Mohamed Jinnah had supported, had already spread throughout the country. Motilal Nehru, then President of the INC, had prepared a draft constitution demanding Dominion status, like Canada's, to be achieved within one year. A year earlier, Jawaharlal Nehru had moved a motion demanding *"complete national independence."* Gandhi had opposed this because at that time he did not "require" full independence. The Muslim League and the pro-British Liberal Party of India rejected the 1929 reports of both Motilal Nehru and Mohamed Jinnah.

Recapping the events, which the Asst. Secretary of State had found so troubling, and calling Motilal Nehru's request for Dominion Status premature, Under-Secretary Isaacs had declared: *"The very mention of the term 'Dominion status' conjures up at once a position, to some extent at least, in advance of what might be ascribed to responsible government. It means in any event arriving at the full status of Dominions such as Canada, Australia, New Zealand – the ideal, the ultimate goal we seek to reach in due course."*

In a long and rambling speech Isaacs suggested that India was not ready, that the previous plan of a graded increase in responsibility should not change then, and in any case, no change should be made before the report of the Simon Commission. He continued, referring to the Congress statement of aim: *"It is a statement issued by the conference of political leaders and signed by a number of very prominent politicians, beginning with Mr Gandhi and including Pandit Motilal Nehru, Pandit Malaviya, Pandit Jawaharlal Nehru, President of the Congress which is to meet in December, and Sir Tej Bahadur Sapru. The importance of it may not be quite so apparent to some of your Lordships as it is to me. These are politicians of various shades of opinion – if it is right to include Mr Gandhi in the term 'politicians'. I am not quite sure that it is; but at least he has taken part in this matter and has signed this statement. Sir Tej Bahadur Sapru is a distinguished member of the Bar in India. He was Law Member, which is analogous to the position of Attorney General in this country, in the Viceroy's Executive Council during my period in India. He was a leader of the Moderates or Liberals, but I find him in conjunction with those who are certainly not either Liberals or Moderates. Pandit Motilal Nehru is the leader of the Swarajists and his son, Pandit Jawaharlal Nehru, is to be President – either he or Mr Gandhi – of the National Congress which is to meet in December.*

"Perhaps your Lordships may remember why they are meeting and the resolution they proposed last year at the Congress. That resolution last year at first stated that, if Dominion status was not granted at the end of the year, there would be civil disobedience throughout the country – a very, very grave threat. If I remember aright, it was Mr Gandhi who then appeared on the scene and moderated the severity of this resolution by postponing it for one year and it is that resolution which is about to be considered in December of this year at Lahore. The object of the resolution is to determine that, unless Dominion status is given by the end of that year, civil disobedience with all its consequences will ensue."

And then he said what must have made every one of the hundreds of thousands of political prisoners in British imperial jails laugh in derision at his arrogance, self-deception and lack of insight: *"I do believe that our rule in India, marvellous as it has been throughout the whole period and especially, may I say, in more modern times, depends far more upon the fairness and the justice with which we administer in India, the purity and integrity of our purpose, the responsible sense that we have of the burden imposed upon us and, above all, the scrupulous fidelity with which we insist upon maintaining promises and pledges given to India. India has learned that she can rely upon us. Far more, therefore, does our government of India rest upon these qualities than upon the armed forces which of course, in any civilised country, must exist in case of need."*[107]

However, Indians had not expected this obscenely flattering and narcissistic effusion, and had hoped for better, maintaining the demand for at least Dominion status at the end of the year, failing which the

---

[107] (*HC Deb 18 December 1929 vol. 233 cc1501-60)* Isaacs would rise to an Earldom becoming the highest ranking Jew in the House of Lords. He was implicated in a scandal related to conflict of interest and insider trading of stocks in the new Marconi Company which his brother headed; he was alleged to have helped his brother obtain contracts from the British Government.

country would begin civil action. Opposition Parliamentarians agreed with that possibility, feeling that the central government in 1919 had made too stingy an offer to Indians re self-rule, while advocating white majority legislatures in Africa, as Lord Delamere had done in 1927 for Kenya, when the white population there was only 12,500, Africans 2,500,000 and Indians 26,500! The chauvinism of some debaters in the House of Lords reached the nadir of human morality.

In a House of Commons debate a few weeks later Labour MP James Horrabin, dealing with discontent in India, cited the lack of a free press, and quoted a court trial of a newspaper editor: "*...the magistrate informed counsel that if the present Prime Minister had used or written those words in India be would have been liable to prosecution for sedition...(This) is helping in no small measure to exacerbate that distrust which is making so difficult a real full-hearted co-operation at the present time... a list of books has been published in this country as having been banned by the police in one district in India, including poetic works of ...an eminently respectable Poet Laureate, Robert Southey. I have not seen any explanation as to what particular part of Southey's works came under the police ban, but I am sure the ghost of the Poet Laureate must be anxiously awaiting some explanation. I take up one page ... of an Indian newspaper published in English:* 'A religious preacher sentenced to one year's rigorous imprisonment.' *Two columns afterwards:* 'A professor sentenced to one year's rigorous imprisonment.' *In the next column*: 'What is sedition? Editor sentenced to one year's rigorous imprisonment'. *I do not want to touch on the details of those cases, but I wish to urge that almost all of them...are definitely cases in which the question of the legitimate expression of political opinion arises, and in regard to which the question of incitement to violence or murder produced long legal arguments during trial. We ask that in cases of that sort the benefit of the doubt should be given to the prisoner, rather than against him.*

We urge that at all costs there should be avoided the sort of deadlock which comes about by one side regarding as necessarily innocent every person charged and the other side regarding as necessarily guilty every person charged.

Col Charles Howard, Conservative member for Chelmsford, preferred self-praise, and echoed Isaacs "marvellous rule" speech and in part the Earl of Birkenhead's "pathetic contentment" of India's vast majority: "*Whether one goes to the aborigines with their bows and arrows, or to the cultivators in the United Provinces, one never hears a word of politics spoken. They are a happy and contented people. Why bring discontent all of a sudden to them by introducing politics? The Maharajah of Benares said the other day: The ever-indulgent British Government, eager to reward India for its war service, made a fateful announcement in 1917, anticipating the actual state of things by at least half a century, and trying to build a twentieth century constitution with materials of the Middle Ages.*"

Both the Viceroy and Parliament had uncritically concluded that Indians were not ready for self-rule, some actually believing that it would be a long time before Indians could qualify for Dominion status, a vague specific at the best of times, and clearly no more than a general framework, which must be adjusted to each situation. Some parliamentarians went so far as to impugn the integrity and knowledge, if not wisdom of Indian politicians, and scoffed at their propensity to exploit "caste", as if the British were free from that particular sin! (see *"Chain of Being", p 172.*)

The British however were the first to admit India's strengths and achievements. Sir Charles Eliot,[108] British diplomat and colonial administrator, wrote in his book, *Hinduism and Buddhism*: "*In Eastern Asia the influence of India has been notable in extent, strength, and duration…Scant justice is done to India's position in the world by those European histories which recount the exploits of her invaders and leave the impression that her own people were a feeble dreamy folk, surrendered from the rest of mankind by their seas and mountain frontiers. Such a picture takes no account of the intellectual conquests of the Hindus.*"

Readings from Hansard about this time reveal the distressing lack of insight, at key times of decision-making in Britain, when the views of some of Britain's most thoughtful, wise and fair were overlooked or frankly rejected or scorned. The remarks of James Maxton (MP, Glasgow Bridgeton), have been quoted on p. 296. Other revealing remarks made in Parliament include:

"Unhappily there had never been in the whole history of mankind an instance of a civilised race taking anything like a scientific, much less a humane, method of treating the native question, which seemed always to be settled by the passion, pride, and prejudice of race…" J. M. Robertson, *Commons, 28 February 1906, vol. 152 cc 1212-47* (see "eugenics", above).

"Everywhere subject peoples have a new sense of national existence. Everywhere they are seeking education. Everywhere they are seeking political and economic liberty. There is no force on earth that can prevent that movement of liberty from ultimately reaching its achievement." Fenner Brockway, *Commons, 18 December 1929 vol. 233 cc 1501-60.*

"Even a much shorter time ago than that, if you travelled in a railway train with an Indian, or drove in a motor car with an Indian, you were supposed to be lowering the British Raj." Major Graham Pole, *Commons, 18 December 1929 vol. 233 cc 1501-60.*

At the same time Indian thinkers were saying the following:
Sri Aurobindo: "*The most vital issue of the age is whether the future progress of humanity is to be governed by the modern economic and materialistic mind of*

[108] Charles Norton Edgcumbe Eliot (1862-1931), *Hinduism and Buddhism, vol. I*, p.12

the West or by a nobler pragmatism guided, uplifted and enlightened by spiritual culture and knowledge...."

Rabindranath Tagore: *"The significance, which is in unity, is an eternal wonder. The tendency in modern civilisation is to make the world uniform...Let the mind be universal. The individual should not be sacrificed. Men are cruel, but Man is kind. Facts are many, but the truth is one."*

The *Rāja* justified most of its decisions, claiming wide support from "responsible" Indians. These, however, were largely self-interest groups, fostered by the British and benefitting from British largesse or goodwill, such as the *Council of Princes*, businessmen, industrialists, zamindars, Christian converts, Islamists (AIML), Anglo-Indians, a few intellectuals, British residents, officials and others with scores to settle, exploiting the British propensity and willingness to reward traitors and sycophants. Most of this group, except for the AIML, had organised in 1910 as the pro-British *Liberal Party,* although some of its members favoured independence within the Empire and rejected partitioning.

Some had broken away from the INC when Tilak and colleagues had begun to talk in radical and militant terms. Zamindars and city employers, fattening off the labours of low-paid, half-starved workers, felt certain that empowering rural folk was a mistake, as the masses were generally ignorant—meaning unschooled, not stupid; true, but that was quickly changeable—and might expect more from a vote than just the emotional agreement to choose someone they liked, without knowing whether he could deliver anything of benefit. For this reason, they said, olden democracies had enfranchised only those with something to lose: property owners, the educated and the aristocracy.

These men feared that rural folk taught to protest effectively in the promotion of *Swaraj,* and restoration of the *pānchāyat rāja* (village governing councils), might believe that success would permanently free them from taxation, while others believed that it was essential for persons to own property, in order to safeguard the condition of the masses. By this view, every farmer, however small his holding, should regain the vote, which ancient Indians had, at their village councils. However, under the Muslims and British, the majority had lost their plots to the new landlords, moneylenders and other middlemen, local and foreign, and farmed only as tenants in fee.[109] Obviously an education programme could supply the knowledge base to the exploited, change

[109] In *Rerum Novarum* (1891), *paragraph 16* Leo XIII said, "*The main tenet of socialism, that is community of goods, is directly contrary to the natural rights of mankind...The first and most fundamental principle, therefore, if one would undertake to alleviate the condition of the masses, must be the inviolability of private property.*" It is ironic and sad that the Papacy did not apply this principle to native rights to their ancestral lands.

perceptions, broaden horizons and inculcate in learners, as in others, *critical thinking* on political issues, without which the franchise was a waste, despite wealth or status.

Jawaharlal Nehru, through charisma and socialist beliefs, had become fully established in the van of the left wing of the Congress Party. He had risen, under the mentorship of Mahatma Gandhi, to the position of Congress President in 1929-30, and had opposed his father's proposal of dominion status and willingness to seek office in the Central Legislature, advocating instead complete independence from British Imperialism. His main rival as successor to Gandhi was Vallabhai Patel, the ailing but, to many, the superior candidate.

On Dec 23rd, 1929, six weeks after the quoted debate in the House of Lords, Viceroy Irwin met with Gandhi, Nehru, Patel, Jinnah and Sapru to develop a plan for Dominion status, which, at this time, many in Parliament had labelled as premature, as, in their opinion, Indians were too backward and had not reached the development level of the established dominions!

How ironic all this was, that the English, who had known civilisation and prosperity for just a few rapacious centuries, should conclude thus about a nation that had been among the first to develop stable political, economic and educational systems, and become rich, until looted by Muslims, and by the British they had trusted. Like so many before him, the Marquess of Reading knew little history, as he concluded in disdainful ignorance that India was innately unable to govern itself!

The Government ignored the INC position, buoyed by the support of their toadies, the *Council of Princes*, the minority *Liberals* and the *AIML,* and lulled by the dispassion of the masses and Gandhi's hesitation at J. Nehru's proposal for total independence. However, Indian self-rule was inevitable, regardless of what strategies were used to procure it, or how many or who favoured the British. Only the path to sovereignty remained undecided. Eight days later, at midnight on December 31, 1929, the Congress, led by Gandhi and Jawaharlal Nehru, raised a national tricolour flag in Lahore and published the *Declaration of Independence (Purna Swaraj* or complete self-rule) on January 26, 1930. The declaration included, inter alia, the readiness to withhold taxes, defy forest laws and stop doing business with the British.

The declaration contained this statement: *"We believe that it is the inalienable right of the Indian people, as of any other people, to have freedom and to enjoy the fruits of their toil and have the necessities of life, so that they may have full opportunities for growth. We believe also that if any government deprives a people of these rights and oppresses them the people have a further right to alter it or abolish it. The British government in India has not only deprived the Indian people of their freedom but has based itself on the exploitation of the masses, and has ruined India economically, politically, culturally and spiritually. We believe therefore, that India must sever the British connection and attain Purna Swaraj or complete independence."*

Jawaharlal Nehru had become INC President in 1929. The Working Committee of the INC assigned Gandhi the decision to choose a protest action. He decided to galvanise and unite the independence movement on the basis of *Satyagraha* (civil disobedience). He chose to begin his attack on British hegemony by marching 241 miles from his Sabarmati ashram in Ahmedabad, to Dandi beach salt deposits on the Gulf of Cambay, Gujarat, beginning on March 12, 1930. This action would emphasise the gravity of the *Purna Swaraj* declaration. Gandhi's choice of *salt* as the subject of the action mystified his colleagues, even his closest comrades, Patel and Nehru, who were perhaps too polite or shocked to question his sanity, as many did. Viceroy Irwin scoffed, declaring that he would lose no sleep over it and the pro-British press and Liberals openly chuckled. Patel had favoured boycotting land revenue instead.

But Gandhi had chosen well. Prior to the British taxation act, Indians had been free to harvest salt, and this was often the sole means of livelihood of a large number of coastal people. Gujaratis regarded it as a "gift from God". Everyone used it, every day, from the lowliest to the mightiest, among all people and among all religions. As Gandhi said, "Next to air and water, salt is perhaps the greatest necessity of life in a climate that sweats!"

The 1882 Salt Act sullied Lord Ripon's period as Viceroy and was his most unfavourable intervention, and echoed the BEICo's earlier tax. The Act made it suddenly illegal and criminal for anyone, other than the British Government, to harvest and sell salt. It was taxed and brought in 8.2% of the British Rāja's total tax revenue, a huge amount "stolen" from the poorest Indians. The Act was seen as denial of a common birthright, and turned a natural resource and a free general necessity into a trading commodity, whereas before, only the labour to harvest it commanded a price. Salt manufacture, as a cottage industry, abruptly died, and workers became employees of the state, under conditions of near slavery. As a result, they earned much less than they had done as independents. Many defied the ban, were arrested, fined and/or imprisoned; some were even killed. (Compare US biopiracy and patenting practices today).

This shameful extortion of a poor man's staple had lasted nearly forty years and ruined many on the Gujarat coast. It was almost forgotten among the numerous arbitrary seizures of Indian sources of living. Salt manufacture was not a middle class, urban, Brahmin or princely occupation; most of the activity occurred in the background! Gandhi's perspective on people and his place among them allowed a superior grasp of issues. He was one of them, not above them, a position that seemed to have obscured the vision of Motilal, with all his heart, Tagore with his knowledge, or Jawaharlal with his confidence. None of the proffered alternatives had the same high impact. To their credit, the Working Committee of the INC allowed the march, despite doubts. But soon enough, they were singing an opposite tune. Gandhi's entourage swelled with each mile. The march (photo) lasted from 12 March to 6 April 1930, by which time thousands had joined him. "It seemed as though a spring had been suddenly released," J. Nehru remarked.

C. Rajagopalachari understood Gandhi's viewpoint. Publicly he commented, *"Suppose a people rise in revolt. They cannot attack the abstract constitution or lead an army against proclamations and statutes...Civil disobedience has to be directed against the salt tax, or the land tax or some other particular point – not that that is our final end, but for the time being it is our aim, and we must shoot straight."*

The British were dumb-founded. Lord Irwin not only lost sleep over it, but lost his perch the following year! As a follow-up to Dandi, Gandhi wrote Irwin that he proposed to march to the Dharasana Salt Works on May 6th; but he and key colleagues, including Jawaharlal Nehru and Sardar Vallabhbhai Patel, were jailed before the set day!

The INC Committee had already arranged Gandhi's standby, as his Dandi action was, under current laws, punishable by custody. In those tumultuous years, it seemed that the British would hastily pass knee-jerk laws banning every criticism – by word or deed – or right of Indian citizens, blissfully abandoning the principles of fairness and justice in society, freedom of speech and association, which Englishmen were wont to tout as the inventions that had made them a "superior" nation.

But in India, as in Africa, such rights were applicable only to whites!

The march occurred as planned, led by a retired judge, Abbas Tyabji, and Kasturbai Gandhi. On the way, they were arrested, quickly tried and jailed for three months. Sarojini Naidu and Abdul Kalam Azad took over and admonished the marchers to observe *ahimsa,* even in the face of extreme provocation. As expected, Police stopped them and ordered them back, but they parked on the wayside, and when, on May 21, 1930, they tried to remove the wire fence at the Works, Police assaulted them with steel-tipped lathis, killed two and injured 320, some near death.

Lord Irwin flippantly reported to King George: "Your Majesty can hardly fail to have read *with amusement* the accounts of the severe battles for the Salt Depot in Dharasana. The police for a long time tried to refrain from action. After a time this became impossible, and they had to resort to *sterner* methods. A good many people suffered *"minor injuries"* in consequence."(Emphasis added).

However, an American journalist, Webb Miller, told the real story: *"Not one of the marchers even raised an arm to fend off the blows. They went down like ten-pins. From where I stood I heard the sickening whacks of the clubs on unprotected skulls. The waiting crowd of watchers groaned and sucked in their breaths in sympathetic pain at every blow…I felt an indefinable sense of helpless rage and loathing, almost as much against the men who were submitting unresistingly to being beaten as against the police wielding the clubs...Bodies toppled over in threes and fours, bleeding from great gashes on their scalps. Group after group walked forward, sat down, and submitted to being beaten into insensibility without raising an arm to fend off the blows. Finally the police became enraged by the non-resistance....They commenced savagely kicking the seated men in the abdomen and testicles. The injured men writhed and squealed in agony, which seemed to inflame the fury of the police...The police then began dragging the sitting men by the arms or feet, sometimes for a hundred yards, and throwing them into ditches…"* Such were Irwin's "sterner methods" and "minor injuries"!

Former Speaker of the Assembly, Vithalbhai Jhaverbhai—eldest of four political Patels, of whom Sardar Vallabhai was the youngest and best known—watched the massacre and remarked, *"All hope of reconciling India with the British Empire is lost forever. I can understand any government's taking people into custody and punishing them for breaches of the law, but I cannot understand how any government that calls itself civilised could deal as savagely and brutally with non-violent, unresisting men as the British have this morning."* (Compare the *Peterloo* incident, p 197). Irwin responded by imprisoning over 60,000 people!

The following extract from *Hansard,* July 1930 is instructive: *"The chief event of the week has been the declaration of the All-India Congress Working Committee as unlawful association under the Criminal Law Amendment Act. The Committee consists, at full strength, of about 15 persons.*

For a considerable period they have been playing a prominent part in organising and directing the civil disobedience movement. Not only have they passed a number of resolutions urging the public to defy the law and to refuse payment of taxes, but they have circulated widely an incitement to the troops and the police to fail in their duty in dealing with the Civil Disobedience Movement. Simultaneously with the notification of the Committee, the President, Pandit Moti Lal Nehru, and the secretary, were arrested, and were subsequently sentenced to six months' simple imprisonment each. Following on this action there were hartals in various towns, but many of them were incomplete and there have been no clashes between the authorities and the public. Popular demonstrations have been most marked in Bombay City, where conditions continue to be unsatisfactory, and the mill-hands suspended work for two days. The day before the Committee was notified, a meeting was held, the results of which have now been reported in the Press. A number of resolutions were passed, the general sense of which was to urge the continuance of the Civil Disobedience Movement with increasing vigour. The Committee confirmed the resolution inciting the troops and police to fail in their duty, reference to which has been made above, and they urged all Congress organisations to give the widest publicity to it, in spite of the fact that the resolution had been proscribed under the Criminal Law.

§ "During the week the Governor-General promulgated an ordinance for the purpose of controlling effectively the seditious bulletins and news sheets which, since the issue of the Press Ordinance, have been published in many places in deliberate defiance of the law. These bulletins consist largely of falsehoods and misrepresentations, and their object is to stir up racial and anti-Government feelings. In spite of the vigorous activities of the Congress, the situation shows distinct signs of improvement in several directions, as already noted. The position on the frontier is rapidly returning to normal. In parts of Gujarat there are indications that the movement is losing some of its vigour, and most of the Provinces report a slackening of effort. The conviction that the Civil Disobedience Movement cannot succeed is growing and commercial and industrial circles are showing increasing concern regarding the dangerous consequences of its continuance. There is an increase in constructive effort towards a constitutional solution of political problems, and Muhammadans (sic), in particular, are devoting much thought and attention to the presentation of their case at the London Conference. While the situation, therefore, has still many unstable elements, these are not so numerous or so pronounced as a few weeks ago."

Motilal Nehru died on February 6, 1931, gratified that Jawaharlal and Gandhi had come to see him in his last days. A month later, Viceroy Irwin met with Gandhi and agreed to free political prisoners, once civil disobedience was halted. He allowed Gandhi to attend the *Round Table*

Conference on India in London, but this did little for constitutional advancement and failed to address major issues.

Irwin gave way to Lord Willingdon who, when Governor of Bombay Presidency, had met Gandhi in 1915 and had called him a *Bolshevik*. He promptly re-arrested Gandhi, turned the clock back, but failed to deter him or the inexorable *Swaraj* campaign. Three attempts were made on Gandhi's life, of uncertain instigation. When the Government of India Act, 1935, granted Indians limited self-rule, the INC—which had adopted a socialist stance—won a majority of seats and formed governments in six provinces, initiating *Congress Rāja*. Bengal was the only province with a Muslim government, secured as an alliance with pro-British groups.

Gandhi returned to active politics in 1936, with Nehru as president and head of the parliamentary majority. The intractability of the Islamist position led Congress—itself prone to factionalism and still mainly middle and upper class—to decline coalition with the All India Muslim League (AIML) in several provinces. In 1937, Congress dominated provincial elections, while the AIML failed to form a government in any of the Indian provinces.

Subhas Chandra Bose became INC President in 1938 and clashed with Gandhi over policy regarding the path to independence, Gandhi insisting on non-violence, while Bose had more faith in armed alliances, then being pursued with Japan and Germany, a move Nehru did not support. In 1939, Viceroy Linlithgow committed India to WWII, without consulting Indian ministers. Those from the INC resigned in protest, but Jinnah opportunistically pledged Muslim support. As war began, Bose and the Congress government resigned *en masse* over Britain's endorsement of the Viceroy's unilateral decision to drag India into the war. They accused the British of hypocrisy in declaring Nazis *tyrants*, when they were just as tyrannical, or worse, in India, where they had already supervised the killing of scores of millions of Indians. It was disingenuous and disgraceful, not just paradoxical, to refuse India its independence, while "fighting for democracy" in Europe. Gandhi had earlier given Britain qualified "non-violent" support, but sided with Nehru and the INC and withdrew it. The AIML remained solidly on Britain's side, expecting further political preferences at war's end.

Stafford Cripps' had been sent to India to negotiate with Indian leaders and secure Hindu and Muslim support for the war, the reward being Dominion status when the war ended. Churchill and Linlithgow rejected Cripps' proposal. Gandhi distrusted the delegation and called Cripps' offer of Dominion Status a *"post-dated cheque drawn on a crashing bank"*. The INC declined and announced instead the *Quit India* movement in 1942, and was disappointed that Jinnah balked. Cripps was said to have spent more energy at meetings grandstanding, instead of diplomatic negotiation, and of following the time-honoured British policy of '*divide and rule*' at a time when unity was sought.[111] His actions, the Viceroy's conceit and British lack of a strong policy on India allowed divisions to deepen between Hindus and Muslims, despite Gandhi's agreeing to guarantee Muslims an excess of seats in the Indian Parliament. The Muslim League had demanded a third of the total seats for 10% of the population! Savarkar had insisted on one man, one vote.

Gandhi intensified the call for independence and pushed the *Quit India* resolution, to which the Government responded, with Churchill's approval, by arresting half of India, killing thousands and imprisoning *hundreds of thousands*, including all Congress leaders, until 1944. The government even refused to allow relief to reach famine-starved millions in eastern India. Pockets of opposition, particularly among young Indians, were ruthlessly crushed; most escaped to reorganise in ineffectual groups in or near Nepal. This is a particularly shameful example of imperial tyranny and social bias at their worst, with a devastating effect on India.

The 1943 Bengal famine, like many other famines in India, was multifactorial, the prime element being the marginalisation of small farmers through an erosion of their position by a millennium of Muslim and British exploitation, more so by the latter, who had, as already noted, seized farmland and commercialised agriculture, exporting most of the grain produced. The acreage under cotton doubled between 1875 and 1900, bankrupting millions of small farmers, as a result of land seizures, which reduced them to bare subsistence, with no reserves or surplus for emergencies, or to accommodate growing families.

So, when adverse climatic conditions, such as an El Niño Southern Oscillation (ENSO), caused a prolonged drought and crop failure, as in Bihar and Bengal in 1942-3—or previously there and elsewhere; see pp. 175-6, 229 etc.—millions starved even though there was enough grain in India to aid the needy poor. Millions were allowed to die, in the presence of hoarding by businesses; price gouging; inflation; continuing export of grain to Britain; failure of the British *Rāja* to use promptly the internal transport systems to take relief to the affected regions; "unavailability" of vessels to bring in grain from Burma due to the war; and finally, Churchill's refusal to take advantage of Australia's offer of grain, bare-facedly asserting that shortages and high prices were simply market forces at work! The millions who died of starvation in 1943 must be

---

[111] Gandhi, addressing a youngish British delegate, marvelled sarcastically that such an untried mind could deign to carry out policies that demeaned, exploited and sacrificed people, "not in any subtle way, you understand, but overtly"!

regarded as one of the largest exterminations of the 20th century. It joined with the many previous famines that killed millions, especially under British control or rule, as Nehru observed.

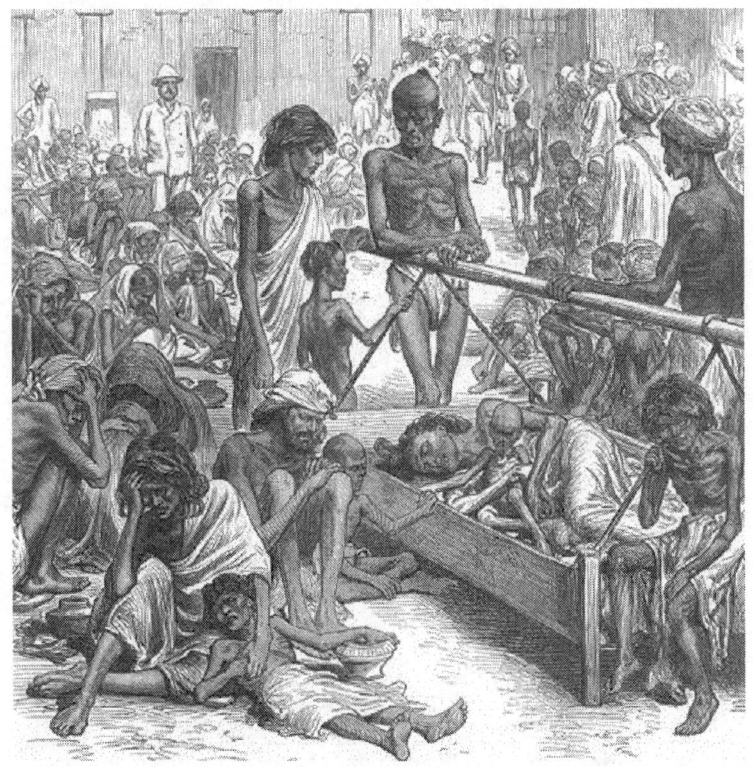

Famine: Waiting for Relief at Bangalore, 1877 (Illustrated London News, scan by Adam63).

American writer Michael Davis wrote, *"Between 1875 and 1900 – a period that included the worst famines in Indian history – annual grain exports increased from 3 to 10 million tons" (enough to feed 25 million people for a year!) "Indeed, by the turn of the century, India was supplying nearly a fifth of Britain's wheat consumption at the cost of its own food security."* Compare Irish exports of food to Britain in the 1840s while locals starved from failure of the potato crops.

Davis further noted: *"Already saddled with a huge public debt that included reimbursing the stockholders of the East India Company and paying the costs of the 1857 revolt, India also had to finance British military supremacy in Asia. In addition to incessant proxy warfare with Russia on the Afghan frontier, the subcontinent's masses also subsidised such far-flung adventures of the Indian Army as the occupation of Egypt, the invasion of Ethiopia, and the conquest of the Sudan. As a result, military expenditures never comprised less than 25 percent (34 percent including police) of India's annual budget..."* The burden of this fell on the backs of the poor; it was thus small wonder that they succumbed in droves.

Mr Frederick Pethick-Lawrence, the MP for Edinburgh East, opening a House of Commons debate on Nov 4, 1943, poignantly set the scene and said, *"I would remind Hon. Members that this House is ultimately responsible. If this terrible death-rate had occurred in any one part of the British Isles, the Member who sat for that locality would have been vociferous in demanding that something should be done. He would not have allowed any member of the Government to rest while such terrible things were happening, and this House, every day and all day, would have been continually confronted with the need for drastic remedies. In this House there are no actual Members for that immense part of the British Empire – the Sub-Continent of India – and that fact must not be allowed for one moment to let this House, responsible as it is for India, forget its grave responsibility."*

The political situation did not help, not with INC leaders under detention, rendering provincial governments ineffectual. Speaking for the Government. Flight-Lt. Raikes, endorsed by John Armstrong, Chancellor of the Exchequer, admitted, *"It is no good saying that we must release the Congress leaders. That would only bring nearer the spectre of civil war."* Instead, they blamed the Bengal provincial government for the failure of famine relief! (Hansard HC 4/Dec/1943).

Gandhi had replied to the Viceroy's actions with a "do or die" declaration to gain freedom. He and his Working Committee were imprisoned from 1942 to 1944, along with his wife, Kasturbai, and his secretary, Mahadev Desai—curiously, at the Aga Khan's Palace in Puné. Desai died from a heart attack, six days later; and Kasturbai died in prison, after being there for 18 months. Gandhi developed a fever soon after, probably Malaria, and was released to undergo surgery that year.

The resignation of INC legislators across India allowed the AIML to flourish; Jinnah increasingly advocated partition and was able to win general support, a remarkable *volte-face,* but explicable with all INC politicians in jail, including Muslim leaders opposed to partition. But Jinnah's success was not a blessing; his militancy frightened many. His popularity waned, and by 1945, more moderate voices had risen, and might have changed the outcome for India, but for one of Gandhi's worst mistakes. On release from jail, he decided to negotiate with Jinnah, some say, against evidence and advice, and thus restored Jinnah's credibility and his stance. Jinnah in turn smartly seized the occasion, betrayed Gandhi, and championed his absolute demand for an Islamic Pakistan.

WWII ended with a Labour Government in power, thus assuring India imminent independence. Britain was broke and had mortgaged India and every corner of the Empire. The allies had won the war, but the real winners were the moneylenders who had financed the war, chief among them the Rothschilds and their ilk. Gandhi ceased *Quit India* actions; INC leaders and over 100,000 political prisoners were released. Churchill lost, after all, to the "naked fakir" and did preside over the Empire's trip to the brink, leaving Attlee the final pleasure of pushing it over. The fall fractured India in three and shattered the Empire into little pieces, some no bigger than thumbnails, several falling hopelessly to tyrants. Churchill however did have a revenge of sorts, in supporting the toxic creation of Pakistan by combining India's Islamic majority regions. This division destroyed all chances of a united secular India where all religions could exist in peace, under the same set of laws.

The writing for a divided India[112] had been on the wall for a long time. After years of membership in, and support of the INC for independence, a few powerful Muslim leaders had broken ranks and in 1906 had formed the All India Muslim League (AIML) in Dhaka, with Sir Sultan Mohammed Shah, Aga Khan III, as President. They declared the League a political party, seeking exclusive Islamic interests, to counter the united pan-religious stance of the Indian Congress, of which many were still members. The ambivalence had seethed and taken various turns through the next two decades, and Jinnah had, like the *Jamaat e Ulama Hind,* supported the one-India policy. His divergence from Gandhi coincided with a growing interest in poet-philosopher Iqbal's 1930 motion for a self-governing Islamic state (*see footnote112, this page*).

It is possible that for Islamist politicians the future of the sub-continent had already been decided, when Curzon divided Bengal, and reinforced in 1909 by the Morley-Minto "Reforms". Minto was an anti-Hindu demagogue who favoured princes and rich Hindus when it suited, and granted Muslims a separate electorate and other favours, including twice the number of elected seats in later governments.

Jinnah's antagonism to Hindus had increased through the 1920s, and had infected even ordinary Muslims, who had a generation or so earlier been non-Muslims, animal-lovers and even vegetarian. Jinnah's feelings

---

[112] On a visit to India and Bangladesh in 1974, as a Commonwealth Fellow, I met many officials and ex-officials, one a retired Muslim physician in Dhaka who had been in the All India Muslim League and had treated victims of riots and the war; he gave me this quotation from *Speeches and Statements of Iqbal,* A.R. Tariq ed. Lahore, 1973: *"I would like to see Punjab, North-West Frontier Province, Sindh and Baluchistan amalgamated into a single state. Self-government within the British Empire or without the British Empire, the formation of a consolidated North-West Indian Muslim state appears to me to be the final destiny of the Muslims, at least of North-West India."* Iqbal, whom he knew well, really "wished a Muslim state in the northwest as a self-governing *part of a strong federated India,* perhaps a buffer against new invaders, not a separate nation." Thus, united India would be safe and strong. Tara Chand's *History of Freedom Movement in India* Vol. III, 253, New Delhi, 1972, supports this.

were difficult to understand, despite signs of back-sliding over the years on several issues previously agreed with his INC colleagues. He was a *secular* Muslim, spoke only English, loved whisky, cigars, Saville Row suits, and was an early member of the INC. In 1913, he and GK Gokhale had journeyed to Britain and founded the *London Indian Association.* He did not join the AIML until 1915, and almost immediately moved to establish a joint committee of Congress and the League to bring about Hindu-Islamic unity. The result was the *Lucknow Pact,* pushed by Jinnah and Tilak, which brought the two organisations together to pressure the British. The Pact healed many breaches between Hindus and Muslims until the twenties when various forces worked to weaken and destroy it.

Jinnah resigned from the Congress in 1920, allegedly pressured by Islamists, who stood to gain from further favours through the *Montagu-Chelmsford Act* of 1919. Jinnah had long resented Gandhi's Indian-ness, his simple clothing, lifestyle and food, contrasted to his ultra-anglophilic and foppish ways, shared with many AIML officials. In 1929, at their Delhi meeting, the AIML adopted Jinnah's views and rejected Motilal Nehru's judgment of the Simon Commission. Relations between Jinnah and the Nehrus soured further when the INC rejected Jinnah's *Fourteen Points,* despite agreement on the boycott. The religious groups were now targeting each other, encouraged by Arabic imams and, some say, fostered covertly and facilitated by British commercial interests, using the financial and civic resources of the *Rāja.*[113] Jinnah's subsequent 1934 election as Permanent President of AIML cemented his withdrawal from the INC and established the League's campaign against an intact India.

Jinnah's speech, at the League session at Lahore in 1940, argued for separation, based on the "irreconcilability" of the two religions, an argument he had not made before and now found expedient. In 1943, he presided over AIML's Karachi session and fired up the crowd, saying: *"We have got millions behind us; we have got our flag and our platform; and what is more we have now the definite goal of Pakistan."* His tour of India raised a storm, a proper *jihad,* with advocacy of a two-nation decision.

Jinnah and AIML may well have been puppets, manipulated by an entrenched Arab-Islamic aristocracy and British business. Division can be traced in the writings and career of Saeed Ameer Ali, a jurist, who had founded the *Central National Mohamedan Association* in Calcutta in 1877, urging Muslims to take advantage of English education, then becoming available, as Hindu leaders established schools (*see above*). Like the Aga Khan (Sultan Mohamed Shah), Ali was loyal to the British,

[113] This is akin to the revolving door practice existing in the USA between federal departments and US corporations, notably FDA and Monsanto, weapons manufacturers and the Armed Forces, DOT and vehicle makers etc.

perhaps recognising in them the covetous qualities of his ancestors, who had come to India to plunder, by *dawah* and *jihad*, get rich and spread Islam among the Hindus. His influence secured separate electorates for Muslims and he was active in the AIML until his death in 1928. Before Ameer Ali, Sayyid (Syed) Ahmed Khan had also urged Muslims to secure a British education and had founded a college in Allahabad, which would become the Muslim Aligarh University. He vigorously promoted the cause of an Islamic state, supported the Muslim League, but hypocritically suggested that the Indian National Congress—a nonreligious body led by tolerant Hindus—was not to be trusted!

Islamic politics had already come under divisive influences, with the formation in 1928 of the radical *Muslim Brotherhood* by Hassan al Banna in Egypt, seeking Islamic states governed by *Sharia* law, welcoming "death for Allah" by jihad. It had no direct say in Indian affairs but indirectly influenced radical Islamists, such as imam Abu Ala Maudoodi founder of the *Jamaat e Islami*, which agitated for a unitary India as an Islamic state, to be attained by gradual takeover of political leadership and changing society top-down, an idea alive today. Partition scuttled this plan; Maudoodi moved to Pakistan, to promote an Islamic state.

Sayyid Khan was perhaps the earliest influential voice for separation of Muslims from Hindus. Mushtaq Hussain (1841-1917), Nawab Waqar-ul-Mulk Kamboh (Kamboja), was a founder of the AIML and credited with inducing Jinnah to join. Khwaja Salimullah Bahadur, fellow founder and contemporary, supported the partition of Bengal. These were a small though powerful sample of the many rich and well-placed Islamic relics of the Mughal past who led the move to fracture India. They were landowners, lawyers, bureaucrats, businessmen and military officers of the AIML, nurtured by the *Rāja* and paraded conveniently at *durbars* as representatives of *Indians*. While the majority of Muslims were Hindu converts, these men were largely of Mughal, Arab, Persian, Turkic and other non-Indian descent, with privileges under the Mughals and British, strictly hierarchical in outlook, and anxious to maintain or gain high office after independence. The Aga Khan had already enjoyed the title of Prince since 1844. Arab Islamists generally put down non-Arab Muslims.

Fearing dilution of their powers in a free India, they had begun a campaign of intrigue and civil destabilisation, currying favour with successive Viceroys of India, gaining preferment, in the early 20th century, from the more anti-Hindu ones e.g. Curzon and Minto. The schism they promoted was a disappointing development for the beleaguered forces of Indian unity, and a sad prelude to the intrigues that had led to Mohamed Iqbal's 1930 proposal for a Muslim state in the Northwest, but within India, which Jinnah had enlarged in 1939 to mean "partition". This he promoted with vigour and achieved with threats and a bloody *Direct Action* program. When asked to explain, Jinnah retorted peevishly: "*Go to the Congress and ask them their plans. When they take you into their confidence I will take you into mine. Why do you expect me alone to sit with folded hands? I also am going to make trouble.*"

Earlier, he had begun to argue that India was not *a nation*, thus the idea of invoking a nationalist feeling was misplaced. India had become two distinct cultures, socially and by religion. But India, as Hindustan, had sheltered many religious groups, including Shi'a fleeing the early caliphs" (632-661), and had seen later Islamic dictators become rich and powerful. Now their descendants wanted huge territories, and sought unique social and political solutions *(sharia)*, which could happen peacefully only in separate states. Buddhists, Jains, Christians and others were irrelevant. The pros and cons are buried in time.

In 1946, PM Attlee sent a Cabinet Mission to India to discuss the Wavell plan for self-rule. Lord Wavell, who had replaced Linlithgow as Viceroy in October 1943, had convened a meeting, in Simla, in 1945, but discussions stalled on the question of Muslim representation, Jinnah claiming sole right of such representation and rejecting nominees from the INC. The 1946 group was headed by Lord Pethick-Lawrence (quoted above, p.311)—who had become Labour's Secretary of State for India and Burma—and consisted of Sir Stafford Cripps, President of the Board of Trade, who had headed the 1942 mission to India for the same constitutional reason, and A. V. Alexander, First Lord of the Admiralty. Wavell did not participate.

Between late 1945 and early 1946, the British court-martialled three members of the armed forces—Colonels G.S. Dhillon and Prem Sahgal, and Major General S.N. Khan. They had joined the Indian National Army and fought with Japanese forces. National protests then had united Hindus and Muslims, giving some hope of political accord. Although convicted, they saw their sentences commuted, as the British feared an Army-wide revolt, especially when the Royal Indian Navy mutinied in Bombay (Mumbai) and Karachi, against poor conditions and the racism of white officers. But the unity quickly dissipated, in the terrors of *Direct Action Day*, August 16, 1946.

Inflammatory press reports stoked violence. The Muslim President of Bengal declared the *Direct Action Day* a holiday in Calcutta which Muslims observed, but Hindus did not, thus laying their businesses wide open to the goons, men with grudges, religious fanatics, and assorted riff-raff wielding *lathis* and other weapons, fired up by the urgings of Jinnah and other partisan demagogues. They terrorised urban and rural areas, with violence ranging from personal attacks to looting, arson, riot and murders. Islamic agitators were told that Police would look sideways! In 72 hours, 4,000 were dead, mostly Hindus, and over 100,000 homeless. The press noted the thousands of Hindus killed, but the Muslim press denied any fatalities!

Britain's conservative government had ardently wished to hang on to India, despite the twin realities of British impotence after WWII and the resolve of Indians, however disunited, to get rid of them: either they left on friendly terms or waited to be driven out, ignominiously. In 1946, their Commander-in-Chief in India, General Claude Auchinleck, advised of this. Ironically, were Britain to battle India then, it would have had to rely on the same sepoys and other native troops that had fought for the Allies in WWII. But for them to fight against fellow Indians in a civil war was problematical. Some Sikhs, Muslims and Ghurkhas might have done so, for pecuniary or religious reasons, but even they would have had to overcome the appeals of their fellow Indians and later live with them.

Calcutta: Vultures feast on victims of religious riot in India, Direct Action Day, 1946 (Photo by Margaret Bourke-White) http://life.time.com/history/-

In early 1947, Lord Mountbatten, with Attlee's approval, had supervised the calamitous turn of events and ignored the entreaties of strong delegations opposed to partition. Attlee, as Prime Minister, had shown little interest in India beyond its socialist leaders and affiliations. When unrest among militants was growing in Indian cities, he had chosen to withdraw troops from the country, leaving a mere skeleton to deal with the disasters that followed. (At about the same time, he withdrew troops from Palestine, leading directly to the success of Zionist terrorism under the Irgun, Stern Gang and other groups, and could be blamed for the bitter feuds between Palestinians and Jews that shame humanity to this day). Attlee had claimed that the cost of maintaining troops in these areas was too high, blithely overlooking the fact that India had contributed more than enough in the past and to the Allies in WWII, and did not merit desertion at a time of crisis. Mountbatten's excuse was a desire to avoid involvement in a civil war! This, from a tribe of aristocratic hypocrites that had fomented and profited from civil strife among native peoples the world over, for more than four centuries!

In WWII, Indian troops had fought in the Middle East, Italy, North and East Africa, in Hong Kong, and Malaysia. Overall 36,000 had died, 64,000 wounded, and over 60,000 had been taken prisoner by the Japanese in Singapore. But in 1946-7, with all the unrest in the land, discontent and looming strike in the Royal Indian Navy, and Britain's debt, the prospect of Britain surviving a war with a determined India, with an army of nearly 2.5 million, was highly unlikely. Another truth was that India and its riches had filled the pockets of British aristocrats, and what little had trickled to the British poor were just that, trickles, whose source few ordinary Britishers recognised and thus would hardly have sacrificed their lives to fight a war with India that benefitted only the upper classes. But this excludes the power of patriotism and Britain's well-oiled anti-India propaganda machine.

It is said that partition suited British policy as it created two entities which could, for trade and aid, be played one against the other in the upcoming jockeying for bilateral preferences and hegemony, in a region familiar to the British, and in which they had controlled or owned the major financial stakes (and in cases still did). It was unlikely that either would break away from the Commonwealth of Nations, even if it served only as a modest protection from the pending clashes of major powers.

In the upcoming fight for sway in the subcontinent, Pakistan was expected to prevail over India, as it was more driven by passion of a militant form of Islam that aimed for supremacy and did not recognise any other. Saudi Arabia, its source and direction, tolerated no other religion on its soil. India, however, despite its larger population, was weakened by competing multiples of races, religions and a tenacious caste system that made it a rather discohesive mosaic. Knowing this, the British—by see-sawing support in India between secularism and Islam—could keep India and Pakistan on leashes. Stafford Cripps (parodied then as *Stifford Craps*) may not have been that crass after all. Later, partition added meaning to the dictum: *India is a geographical term. It is no more a united nation than the Equator.*

A major question was the constitutional designation of India as a secular state, when indeed Indians—the Hindu majority, that is—were highly spiritual, tolerant and accommodating, and preferred to see India set on a moral course that protected and supported all religions, rather than merely shrugging them off, as secularism seemed destined to do, if

Islamists would allow. Some saw it as a dissolute ideology or crutch for leftist fanatics and doctrinaire atheists. Nehru favoured it. Independent India was launched, therefore, on a misconception, by denying its Vaidic foundation and heritage, and its role in founding major philosophies. Instead it adopted secularism, a euphemism, at best, for atheism or communism, and erred when it failed to devise a common civil code.

The INC thus surrendered India to known and inflexible enemies that had ruled it for centuries, reviled its major cultures and religions, and had in the process allowed minorities to spurn and constitutionally devalue the 85% Hindu majority and claim the country. These promptly and systematically set about to assail Hinduism, self-aggrandise and seize the land. Better to have chosen outright Communism, like the Chinese, to enforce equality and unity, as the folks in Kerala wanted, and have an early showdown with political Islam, to forge a *modus vivendi* that would establish mutual respect between the new nations, restrict the activities of destabilising forces and ensure peace and harmony. But that was clearly unthinkable by the secular leaders of that time, and, if considered, as Patel must have done, dismissed as wishful thinking.

The British, with customary cunning, had supported secularism, branding Hindus as terrorists, belittling their religion as idolatrous, cheap, foolish and full of demeaning practices, despite its moral and spiritual strengths. In the Diaspora, this denigration only served to strengthen the will of Hindus, especially those who had stuck to the land and continued traditional activities, and in some places added new and diversified agricultural pursuits, responding to their community's needs, as when *gwalvansh Ahirs* found it necessary to add grain, fruit and root crops to their traditional immersion in the dairy industry.

http://www.hindu.com "Subhas Chandra Bose "*(1897-1945); Hindu patriot and nationalist, President of INC 1938-9, sought Axis help to expel the British from India but failed as his Japanese ally lost the Pacific and Indian wars. Bose died in 1945, the British claiming fatal burns from an airline accident in Formosa (Taiwan), but his body was not there. Others believe he was murdered, like the later Shastri, Bhabha, Sarabhai and others at key stages of Indian resistance or breakthrough. The Indian government is still to release classified documents; the investigation is still open.*

Vallabhai Patel, MK Gandhi, Mrs VL Pandit at Ānanda Bhavan, Prayāg, 1940 . http://proudindian123.tripod.com/great/photos.html)

Damodar Savarkar, RabindranathTagore

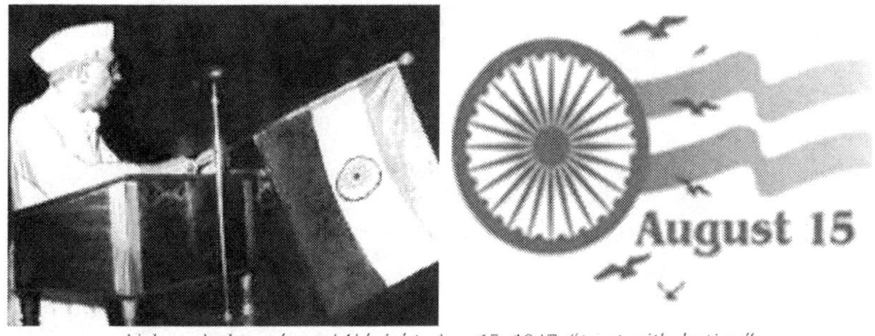

Nehru: Independence Midnight, Aug 15, 1947, "tryst with destiny"

Chapter 21

The significance which is in unity is an eternal wonder.
The tendency in modern civilization is to make the world uniform... Let the mind be universal. The individual should not be sacrificed.
Men are cruel, but Man is kind.
Facts are many, but the truth is one. R. Tagore

"Long years ago, we made a tryst with destiny and now the time comes when we shall redeem our pledge... At the stroke of the midnight hour, when the world sleeps, India will awake to life and freedom." Jawaharlal Nehru

A Bloody Independence

Bloody conquests by nations on the rampage have punctuated history and, if anything, have gotten more vicious, even if more subtle; they are notorious for the carnage created and the millions of innocent victims killed. India has suffered this type of slaughter on many occasions, but rarely in such numbers, so quickly, at the hands of its own people. The Mahābhārata War was the best example of a massive purge, but it was fought by armies for right and justice, the classic "good" versus "evil", not for conquest or loot.

Jawaharlal Nehru being sworn in as Prime Minister August 14-15, 1947

It is said that wars of independence tend to be prolonged, with rebels ranged against the conqueror, and much spillage of blood. In recent times, many entities were born bathed in blood. The American War of independence, the French Revolution, Simon Bolivar's campaigns in Latin America, the Bolshevik seizure of Russia, the Chinese war against Japan, the Cuban revolt, Vietnam and others in SE Asia, were all aimed at the overthrow of an oppressive force that resisted the call for reform. Rarely have rebels won by non-violent means, as India did, and yet soon sank into blood-letting, as if the change could only happen on blood-soaked soil, as Islamists split the land into two religious and three geographic entities. Both sides watched people turn on one another to slaughter and uproot, as if they wished to release pent-up hurts and mark in blood the victory they had won. But the blood spilled was that of their friends and fellow victims, not of conquerors and oppressors!

Trains laden with refugees escaping Pakistan

Partition was not easy for India, because its peoples—Hindus, Jains, Buddhists, Sikhs and most Muslims—shared original Hindu roots, or as strangers, were welcomed long ago by Hindu, Buddhist or Jain rulers. While those who historically had resisted conversion to Islam might have resented their fellows who did, relationships had survived, by virtue of traditional occupations and practices. Yet, partition acted as a catalyst in the holocaust of murder and pillage and was almost entirely avoidable, had the political forces been more sagacious, or patient, and the leaders set aside current resentments in favour of lessening the fears of the diverse groups making up Indian society. There was hardly an issue that could not be settled by intelligent action, granting, however, Islam's rigidity and refusal to establish a truly secular state, one with a common civil code. In this matter the surprising pro-partition lead taken by Jinnah in the late stages of the *Rāja*, seemed guided by self-interest and emotion rather than the good sense he had shown up to his abrupt change. The partition decision cost more than a million lives in senseless massacres mainly in the two Pakistans, where an eerie madness plunged people into a frenzy of religious chauvinism, as leaders, uncertain of their positions, fumbled and failed to stem the fury they had unleashed.

There were many stories in the press and on air about the terrors in mixed communities, especially in cities, where fortunes were made and lost, from insurance scams to property deals, those fleeing a place losing the most. The hurt was greatest along the new India-Pakistan borders, east and west, especially the latter. Escapees told a variety of tales; the story of a businessman who had fled into the Diaspora illustrates the tragedy of partition.

A Sindhi Hindu, who described himself as of Ahir-Arora lineage, managed a furniture store belonging to a Sindhi international chain; he had fled Karachi, Pakistan, to escape murdering squads of Muslim muhajirs. His forbears had preserved Hinduism in the face of increasing Islamisation of Sindh, which had reduced Hindus from 100% of the population in 700 CE to 25% in 1947. Yet they had hoped that the good relations that had existed between the two religions in the preceding 200 years and the apparent softening of Islam, as they worked together over the centuries, would promote co-existence and preserve the prosperity that urban Hindus had maintained in Sindh, from commerce. But at partition, which few Sindhis wanted, hate-mongers sent hordes of *jihadis* prowling streets, ripping apart whole communities, looting businesses, raping and murdering hundreds of thousands of Hindus in Karachi and other cities, while Muslim Police stood by and watched or joined in, as Hindus fled abandoning all possessions. His family was among them.

"We hoped that Pakistan Government would stop killings and help us return to our people and businesses. After all, we give the most to economy of region and nation too; but they curse us, call us Jews of India and give away our property to looters. But we are resourceful people and will make good wherever we go. See how well we do here. But we will always mourn those we lost, family and friends; we had community that language, customs and heritage had made one. Now all gone! Invaders took all. Sindhis who became Muslim, now get more rich; some we know stole our business; others took what little we had when they chased us away. Not one rupee they gave us!"

He paused, choking on his words, recalling the losses, the bloodshed and wasted lives. *"It's our bad karma. It was same long ago when first Muslims came among Sindhi Jāts; they were like us, merchants and traders; most of us were Hindu, some Buddhist, few Jain, all living in peace. Then other Muslims came, many Sunnis, with horses and camels, weapons and swords. They say 'pay taxes and become Muslim, or we kill you and take your women.' Our people split; some become Muslim, others, especially Buddhists, accept terms; they are allowed to live and work; only few resist in our small town and all are killed, their bodies defiled, their heads piled in a mound, their leaders on pikes and paraded. Many thousands were killed in Multan, and they destroyed many stupas and temples. Our people are very unhappy. But Sindhiyat stayed strong in our blood, to this day. It is our culture, our bond with dharti māta, mother earth. We had learned to live well together. Now mujahedeen destroy all that. Over three quarter million of our people fled to India.*

"Same thing will happen to Hindus in other colonies, in Africa and Caribbean, only this time Police who will watch us burn and bleed will be African, not Pakistani. Many people now agree with Subhas Chandra Bose that pacifism, Gandhi style, allowed Islam to destroy India in the same way that Sindhi merchants and pacifist Buddhists allowed Islam to settle, back in 712."

India in 1947 consisted of British provinces, union territories and princely states. Vallabhai Patel, with help of Maulana Azad, persuaded most princes to join the Indian federation although some Muslim-ruled areas wanted linkage with Pakistan, even when separated from Pakistan by substantial territory or having a minority of Muslims. One in Gujarāt, though small, had to be forcibly taken over, and Hindu majority Hyderābad in South India—larger than many countries, including its erstwhile patron, Great Britain—was invaded, as later was Goa and other Portuguese colonies, some of whose inhabitants persisted in calling themselves Portuguese. By 1956, the last obstacles to a republic, the covenanting states, were joined with others, ending *rajpramukhs* (governorships by previous princes).

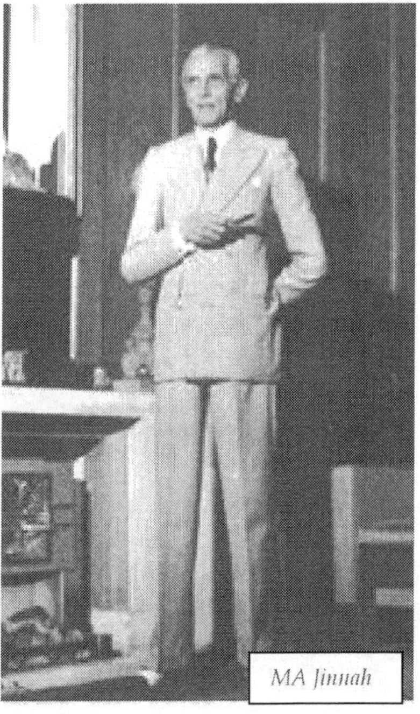

MA Jinnah

One of the most disputed regions was the heavily-populated Punjab, a diverse and rich agricultural region of the five tributaries of the Indus: Jhelum, Chenab, Ravi, Beas, and Sutlej. It consists of five interfluvial doabs (land between two confluent rivers). These are the Sind-Sāgar (Indus/Jhelum); Jech (Jhelum/Chenab); Rechna (Ravi/Chenab); Bari (Beas/Ravi); and Bist (Beas/Sutlej). The Punjab Boundary Commission's conclusion was a compromise among competing claims of Sikhs, Muslims and the INC. (See map next page).

With the shifts in population, Delhi—a relatively small city of less than a million people—doubled its population by 1950. Some 14 million people were displaced, about equal numbers of Hindus and Sikhs moving out of Pakistan, and Muslims out of India. Estimates of those killed range from half to one million. Many blamed the British, targeting Mountbatten, but the error was made before that, when Britain failed to grant self-rule by the mid-thirties, and created an atmosphere where Islamic separatists were allowed to flourish and further divide the two religions, mostly for pecuniary reasons.

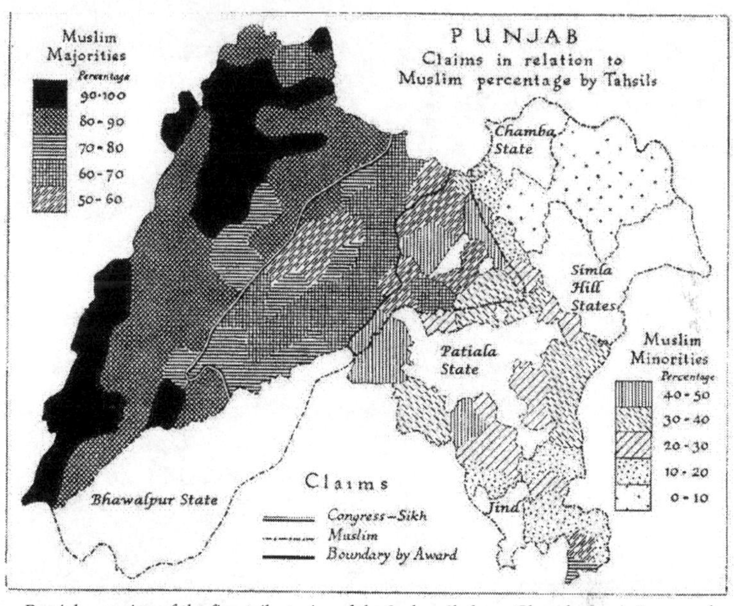

Punjab – region of the five tributaries of the Indus: Jhelum, Chenab, Ravi, Beas, and Sutlej, with a population of various religious groups, and boundary awards.

Mountbatten was handed cards with no trumps, as Attlee had no resources or will left to defuse the schism that had reached the streets, where the ordinary man simply acted on instinct, not by reason. Britain should have left India, latest after WWI, as a planned and peaceful withdrawal. But Curzon's dictum: "*the loss of India would mean that Britain drops straight away to a third rate power*", kept it going and the spoils were irresistible goads to continue, many British lords justifying this by insisting that the Indian was incapable of ruling responsibly!

Gandhi's error in preferring Jinnah to Azad as the Muslim patriarch, restored Jinnah's primacy among Muslim leaders, as already noted. Unapologetic about his role in the partition murders, Jinnah strutted through his first year as Governor General and revealed his latent dictatorship when he usurped the role of Prime Minister Liaquat Ali Khan, and made himself head of an Islamic state, adopting appropriate dress and cap! He even made speeches in Urdu and showed others how to flout a constitution. He died on September 11, 1948.

Meanwhile, Nehru had become the inaugural Prime Minister of independent India. In 1948, with rumours of an affair with Edwina Mountbatten behind him, Nehru faced a nation with a 23% male literacy rate, lower for females; few and poor facilities for primary education; socialists and communists everywhere, with unproven loyalties to India; and a privileged upper class that fully intended to keep its privileges and foreign leanings. The nation was divided, with millions of potential spies and other traitors, enemies east and west, and a governing elite steeped in British ways, even Hindus, and not ready, or in some cases, not willing to come from under that awful but familiar shadow. Indeed, many seized the opportunity to flee India! Loyalty was shaky, but that was probably because the secular—as distinct from multi-religious or multicultural—policy of the INC had unfortunately, or perhaps deliberately, down-graded the cause of Hindus, who formed over 80% of the population.

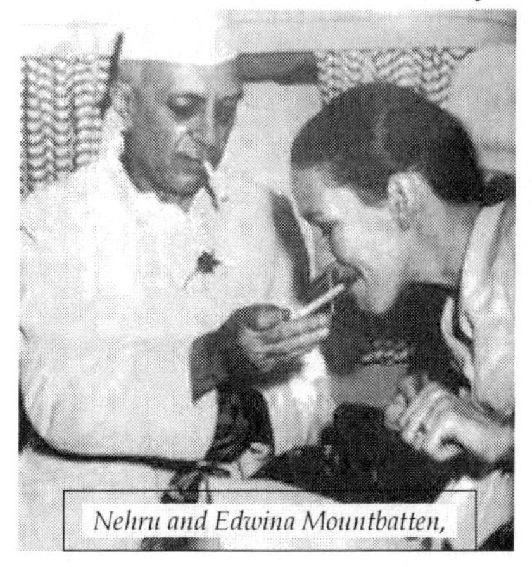

Nehru and Edwina Mountbatten,

Over the years, the INC has taken few steps, if any, to correct the historical falsehoods circulated by the British, and which they maintained in school curricula. The INC was even accused of being anti-Hindu as, like the atheists, they vilified "Hindutva" (literally "the way of the Hindus", a *cri du coeur,* really), claiming that India had traditionally followed many religions, not just Hinduism, ignoring the numbers. This claim, of course, depends on how far back one probed. Nevertheless, it misrepresented the position of Hindutva, as Savarkar had conceived it, emphasising culture and claiming inclusion of Buddhists, Jains, Sikhs, atheists and all *indigenous* Indians, including those who followed Mohammed, Christ, Ahura Mazda or other religious figures.

Nehru visited the USA in October 1949 and was cordially, if coolly received. India had criticised the USA's arming of Pakistan, and their pact, with deployment of the newly-formed CIA, fresh from its funding triumph in manipulating Italian elections and thwarting communists there. The CIA "persuaded" a trusted member of Nehru's Cabinet to spy for them; he served for decades and fed Cabinet decisions to the CIA, including Shastri's and Indira Gandhi's plans re Pakistan, until discovered in the seventies; he has been protected from publicity since.

The Communist bloc concluded the Warsaw Pact in 1955, a political and military alliance of Communist governments. The Cold War combatants were thus confirmed. Nehru's grasp of parliamentary practice, coupled with his concerns for the indigent, enabled him to pursue a moderate socialist agenda and one of "positive neutrality", as the Cold War raged

Among his close friends and supporters for the two previous decades was VK Krishna Menon, a Communist sympathiser from Kerala, who, in the 1930s, had settled in London, England, where he became a left-wing journalist, Labour Party politician and lawyer. Soon after, he became a founding editor of *Pelican Books*, the non-fiction branch of Allen Lane's *Penguin Books*. He was a prominent activist in the India League, which regularly and effectively lobbied the British Government on the independence issue. He had friendly relations with high profile Labourites including Fenner Brockway, Bertrand Russell, James Horrabin, Ellen Wilkinson, Michael Foot, JBS Haldane and Harold Laski. He had studied under Laski at the London School of Economics, earning Laski's praise as his best student ever.

Menon became Indian ambassador to Britain in 1947 and served to 1952. He puzzled many with his friendships and meetings with senior politicians on both sides of the Cold War e.g. Russia's Molotov and Stalin, so that the British Secret Service opened a file on him. He was quick-witted, fearless and forceful, and wrote and spoke eloquently. Once, during WWII, on criticising UK actions, he was asked for his preference for a ruler, UK or Hitler; his reply came in a flash: *"(you) might as well ask a fish if it prefers to be fried in butter or margarine!"* Similarly, when he commented that the USA had aided Pakistan in attacking India by selling them weapons, John Foster Dulles protested, emphasising that those weapons were meant to defend against a possible Russian attack. Menon retorted, *"The world has yet to see an American gun that can only shoot in one direction!"*

Menon was sharp, acerbic even, and smart. Serving as India's ambassador to the UN (1952-62), he coined the word "non-alignment" when he was sure that neither the USA (NATO) nor the USSR (Warsaw Pact) had it right, and that neither deserved unequivocal support. Nehru accepted the idea and it spread to over half the world, as he became a key spokesman for the non-aligned countries of Africa and Asia, many of these were former British colonies that wanted to avoid dependence on either of these major power blocks, which had coalesced from the fall-out of WWII, now aligned as *Cold War* combatants.

Gandhi's insistence on placating Muslims e.g. Mappila, 1924; his "resurrection" of Jinnah after WWII; and failure to recognise Pakistan's territorial ambitions, or to strongly condemn the Muslim invasion of Kashmir in 1947, were seen as a grave oversight and weakness. He was assassinated on January 30, 1948 by a disgruntled journalist, Nathuram Godse—allegedly to advance the militant views of Savarkar, who earlier had openly advocated armed rebellion against the British, and had paradoxically supported British enlistment of Indians for WWII, because it would give them training in the use of modern arms, up to then denied them in India. Indians, he argued, had become too soft. (Gandhi was the first of three heads of state murdered over the next forty years, the other two being Indira Gandhi, 1984, and son Rajiv, 1991.) In 1953, a patrolman removed a bomb from the path of Nehru's express train, seconds before it arrived at the site (*Daily Collegian, 53,136,5/5/53).* Other likely murders were LB Shastri, Homi Bhabha and V.Sarabai.

Photo of men accused of Gandhi's murder. ***Standing:*** *Shankar Kistaiya, Gopal Godse, Madanlal Pahwa, Digambar Badge (Approver).* ***Seated:*** *Narayan Apte, Vinayak D. Savarkar, Nathuram Godse, Vishnu Karkare (courtesy PD-INDIA). N. Godse and N. Apte were convicted and hanged. Savarkar and others were freed*

Hindus generally had become aggrieved at having, in practice, fewer constitutional rights than minorities in their own country, and had suffered terribly in the partition murders. Pakistan's new *Inter-Services Intelligence* (ISI, a ward of the CIA) and the CPI (Communist Party of India) were sponsoring terror attacks in India. Some 6,000 communists were jailed in 1948-9. A rumour had spread that Hindu volunteers from the RSS had hurried to defend sites of intrusion, and that another group had intercepted an Islamic gang sent to kill Nehru and seize Delhi! This is unverified but believed by many. Vallabhai Patel, Gandhi's compatriot and a strong voice for pragmatism, fell ill and died in Dec., 1950, aged 75, a great loss for India, as it left Nehru unopposed as head of government.

Within two months of independence, more serious and lasting problems developed in Jammu and Kashmir (J&K), the princely state which had hoped to remain independent. On October 22, 1947, Pakistan invaded Kashmir, using Pashtu militias *(lashkars)*. Kashmir appealed to India, but Indian military response was delayed until Maharaja Bahadur Singh had signed the article of accession to India, allowing India to legally defend it. A prompt military response could have limited the incursion; Gandhi's Muslim policy was wrongly blamed for the delay.

After a year of fighting, Pakistan was driven north, holding on to about two-fifths of Kashmir. Indian forces were poised to drive the Pakistanis back to their border, but Nehru incredibly stopped the advance, and asked the United Nations to intervene! A line of control was agreed, to India's disadvantage and continuing regret. Nehru, the secularist, was criticised for being soft on Islam, or pressured by the USA and UK. But perhaps his own ambivalence to J&K as part of India must have influenced his decision to cease fire. In earlier statements, he had inferred that a J&K plebiscite would choose Pakistan, so why push for a different solution? Maybe Jammu was enough for him.[114] Islamic terror has persisted, driving over 400,000 Hindu Kashmiris (*pandits*) from their homes, killing thousands, while media and the INC ignored the crimes.

Sometime after independence, it transpired that the British Minister in charge of Indo-Pakistan affairs in 1947-8, Philip J. Noel Baker, had taken an anti-Indian stance in the United Nations, contrary to instructions from Attlee's Government. US Secretary of State, George Marshall, was more pro-Indian, and the USA had accepted Kashmir as legally part of India. Noel-Baker, however, falsified American and Indian positions to his Government, while persuading the US to float a UN draft resolution allowing Pakistan to send troops into Kashmir, if India agreed. He was reprimanded by Prime Minister Clement Attlee in a *"Top Secret and Personal"* telegram: *"I find it very hard to reconcile the view*

---

[114] The assaults on Kashmir have continued from Pakistan-based terrorists, notably the *Lashkar-e-Taiba* and *Jaish-e-Mohamed*. The former was founded in 1990 by Hafez Saeed, Abdullah Azzam and Zafar Iqbal, the latter by Masood Azhar, immediately on his release to Pakistan in exchange for passengers of a hijacked *Indian Airlines* airplane. They have carried out murderous raids in India, including the Delhi Parliament building, and in Mumbai. They are among 35 banned terror groups in India, including a women's group, *the Dukhtaran-e-Millat*. Add to the list many others named by the UN Security Council. All aim at a separate Kashmir ruled by Sharia Law, or a separate Muslim nation in India. Most terrorist groups, whether based in Pakistan, Afghanistan or Bangladesh, espouse Wahhabi extremism and recent members are largely graduates of Wahhabi schools. They reject secularism, democracy and nationalism, yet maintain a strong Islamic presence in India.

which you express as to the attitude of the Indian delegation with the representations I have received through the High Commissioner from India here. It appears to me that all the concessions are being asked from India while Pakistan concedes little or nothing...The attitude still seems to be that it is India which is at fault whereas the complaint was rightly lodged against Pakistan."

Zafarullah Khan, Pakistan's legate, had argued that Pakistani raiders in Kashmir were not "raiders" but "seekers of justice, peace, and the people's will", which, he was reminded, had already been expressed by Kashmir's choosing to join India!

Krishna Menon, India's ambassador to the UN (1952-62), argued India's position in a marathon 8-hour speech at the UN, countering Pakistan's insistence on a plebiscite, even though it had not fulfilled the conditions. He was particularly critical of their overlooking their aggression and illegal occupation, coupled with denial of rights to their own people. One telling passage illustrates his passion: *"Why is it that we have never heard voices in connection with the freedom of people under the suppression and tyranny of Pakistani authorities on the other side of the cease-fire line? Why is it that we have not heard here that in ten years these people have not seen a ballot paper? With what voice can either the Security Council or anyone coming before it demand a plebiscite for a people on our side who exercise franchise, who have freedom of speech, who function under a hundred local bodies?"*

In November 1948, J.F. Dulles was acting leader of the US delegation in the Security Council; he complained to the State Department that the *"present UK approach (to the) Kashmir problem appears extremely pro-GOP (Govt. of Pakistan) as against (the) middle ground we have sought to follow."* (Das Gupta). A stale-mate resulted, and tensions have remained high along the line of control. Pakistani intrusions have continued, punctuated in the last decades by attacks by Islamic terrorists, *Lashkar-e-taiba, Jaish e Mohamed,* and many others, which have involved threats, raids on transport and buildings, city bombings, ambush and murder, forcing the majority of Kashmiri *pandits* into refugee camps.

While India, under Jawaharlal Nehru, moved to create a stable and less vulnerable democracy with a socialist, non-aligned agenda, Pakistan became a military dictatorship in 1958, under General M. Ayub Khan, after a chaotic decade. The Muslim League, which had promoted partition and fomented bloodshed, disintegrated in 1953. Jinnah would mercifully not live to see how quickly and brutally his notion of an Islamic state would destabilise and radicalise the new country. Pakistanis generally remained oblivious of the real forces at work. India's shakiness was underlined by Pakistan's alliances with the USA, which had entered the Cold War with bases at every strategic point around the USSR, some as close as Turkey.

A major naval base was established in Karachi to patrol the Indian Ocean and incidentally destabilise India's independence, through the many quislings among Indians, anxious to maintain and expand the sources of wealth that the British had allowed them and which a socialist regime seemed likely to threaten. Movements of Indians – brown people generally – had been severely restricted for many decades, and only slightly improved by India's sacrifices for the Allies in WWII. Efforts were made to secure a higher quota of visas to the USA, barring students, as many middle class Indians in the UK were willing and eager to forego fish and chips for a hamburger or hotdog. (The British had long ago, it seems, inserted into Hindu scriptures a line or two claiming that ancient Hindus ate beef and other flesh! See Prakashānanda)

The partition of India was fairly sudden for most Indians, and the preparations for take-over by India and Pakistan inadequate. Moreover, post-WWII events had stirred animosities between Hindus and Muslims. Incidents of violence and disruption occurred in religious ghettos, but the transition was relatively peaceful in places remote from the borders. The civil and armed services were maintained almost intact, just as the British had left them, with its systems, language, methods and laws, some lingering obscurely, some actively and usefully, from the days of the BEICo and the British Rāja; others remained, as unjust as when created. From that perspective one could not tell that the British had left.

Many continued to migrate to the UK, to avoid being trapped in India or Pakistan. But, British tolerance slowly ebbed, and attitudes changed from curiosity to avoidance and rejection, once brown newcomers became permanent settlers, and the smells of Indian curries spread beyond British University perimeters. In India, British policy had created divisions more menacing than the tribal enclaves of primitive peoples; it prevented social integration, deemed essential to unite the nation and accommodate its many ethnic and linguistic groups, and to secure its well-being. The same effect was seen in every country of the Empire with a multiracial or multi-religious population. Even if wiser and more efficient management had prevented internecine strife – which many feared that partition had entrenched – India would need much thoughtful and painstaking work to purge its social and educational systems of two centuries of intensive distortion that had corrupted Indian history, by turning ancient facts, religious beliefs and practices – which could sustain inter-regional relationships – into disruptive and absurd 19th century British "myths and falsehoods."

India has been criticised for its slow adoption of western industrial innovations. This is only partially true, and belies Indian successes before the conquests, and many since, despite British suppression. Hindu choices gave way to those of Islam and the British for the many centuries of their rule. The latter had expropriated Indian rocketry and textile manufacturing, transferring technology to the UK (picture p.208), and had denied Indians the chance to participate in the railway and other heavy industry. India was not unique, nor as negative as Pope Gregory XVI, who, in 1836, had banned railways from the Papal States, bluntly calling them "*ways of the devil.*"

But in its favour, Indian technology was quite advanced during the extinct Saraswati/Indus civilisation; it had built sophisticated sanitation systems 4-6 millennia ago, while it was not until 1855 CE that the city of Chicago developed the first sewage system in the USA. India accounted for nearly 25% of world GDP prior to British rule, but less than 5% at independence. This tells the compelling story of the wholesale theft of a nation's industry and production, of extortion and degradation unparalleled in human history. The European rape of America's raw materials and decimation of its peoples rank high in the annals of invasive pillage, but that was done by several countries and involved extraction of raw materials and produce mainly, not the uprooting and theft of centuries of industrial growth and accumulated wealth, and the debasement of a sophisticated culture, religion and literature.

The scrapping of Indian industry and control of all formal learning prevented the transmission of skills, knowledge and techniques that would naturally have flowed and evolved from one Indian generation to the next, so who is to say what industrial goods could have resulted in India, what technological innovations, considering the mathematical, scientific, medical and other skills already possessed, and advances made in agriculture, astronomy, metallurgy, textiles, medicine, rocketry, flying, etc., all usurped by the British? Indeed, Mysorean rockets were claimed as an invention by William Congreve, a protégée of George IV.

It is instructive to note that since independence India has not shown the degree of emancipation one expected—perhaps credit to the efficacy of British brainwashing—except for achievements in computer software and rocketry for US corporations or agencies, like Microsoft, Sun, NASA and others. In the past, Indian scholars had discovered principles and developed a broad range of innovations in mathematics—beginning with computational systems we use today—medicine, such as cataract and stone extraction, mental illness therapy and practice of preventive and holistic medicine (*Ayurveda,* and *Unani,* an Arab system practised by Muslims), *Siddha* and other sciences, religion and governance. Six generations of British hegemony had dulled freedom and self-confidence and Indians are yet to discard the yoke of colonial dominance, subservience and methodology. They have come to accept things British as a standard, from industrial techniques to processed foods and table manners. Many of India's early projects were thus slavish copies of western themes, like the Ambassador car, and still include those that "failed" in the west, e.g. malls and suburbia. The copycat mentality permeates all aspects of life, and it seemed aimed to duplicate the worst elements of US and western profligacy, waste and ecological damage: in housing, business, food, transportation and so on, instead of indigenous solutions.

Another frequent criticism is India's indifference to child labour, a clear result of poverty, and lack of education and opportunity, not culture, as in Britain itself, and most of the world. In 1838, mining accidents in Britain caused 122 deaths in children under 18, of whom 58 were under 13. The hours of work were long, unregulated and exhausting. It was not until 1847 that the UK Parliament passed a bill limiting the work week of women and children to *63* hours!

Yet this did not stop exploitation, no more than did Britain's compulsory colonial education bill of 1876 stop coercive child labour on colonial plantations, or enforce schooling laws. Even the threat of Marxism—beginning with Karl Marx and Friedrich Engels' 1848 *Communist Manifesto* – failed to influence employers. In the turmoil of the next 140 years, Marx's fears of corporations and labour have been realised. Marx's opening salvo: *"The history of all hitherto existing society is the history of class struggles"* remains a fair and fairly obvious comment. In 1839, British conservatives defeated a reform bill with violent protests in Wales, Birmingham, Glasgow and Newcastle.

As noted earlier, Arab Bedouins and Mughals were acquisitive and enticed by the luxury of India, and adopted it as their home; they spent most of their amassed wealth in India, whether lavishly or sparingly, but they pushed conversion to Islam, by threat or taxes. Previous invaders or migrants who settled in India had largely integrated with the Indian population, e.g. the Iranians, Kushans, Greeks, and adopted an Indian religion. This is plain for all to see. The British, by contrast, spent their Indian loot on monuments and palaces in Great Britain, and stingily has still not acknowledged the debt (nor spoils from other lands stored in mansions and museums). The major industrial project of the British Rāja was the railway network, built chiefly to serve commercial and military purposes, and its running excluded from Indians until WWII. The telegraph was similarly kept from Indians, and was a prime factor in enforcing British control. But, ironically, today's Indians might be having a curious "revenge" by buying up the most expensive of prime real estate in London's Mayfair and Kensington!

Rashtrapati Bhavan, New Delhi

R. M. Lohia

Feroze Gandhi
(WP: NFCC#3 Uploaded by Rayabhari)

J. P. Narayanan

Raj Narain

Chapter 22

In the long run, it would be in the interest of all to forget that there is anything like a majority or a minority in this country, and that in India there is only one community-Indians.

Sardar Vallabhbhai Patel, August 1947

Non-alignment, 5-year plans and leaky borders

The INC had since the thirties grown more bourgeois, as evidenced by the choice of candidates for elections: fewer farmers, and increasing numbers of people who could pay their way and likely raise funds for the party. Thus rural members (*kisān*) were disappointed to see business as usual, with the same old hierarchies in place and the same vested interests. A few changes did happen such as the success of cooperatives.

A meeting of the Kisan Sabha

The Bihari *Kisān Sabhā* (Peasants or Farmers Party) was formed in 1929, under Swami Sahajanand Saraswati, to advocate for peasants against predatory landowners (*zamindars*). It attracted leaders of other provincial peasant groups, including southern communists, E.M.S. Namboodiripad, later Chief Minister of Kerala, and N.G. Ranga.

Soon, a national body was formed, the *Akhil Bhāratīya Kisān Sabhā* (ABKS, All-India Farmers Party). Other leaders were Ram Manohar Lohia; Jayaprakash Narayanan; Acharya Narendra Dev; Bankim Mukerji; Pandits Karyanand Sharma, Yamuna Karjee, Yadunandan Sharma; Rahul Sankrityayan and P. Sundarayya. Other major activists included Raj Narain—a descendant of Chait Singh, whom Hastings had defrauded. Narain was a student leader in Varanāsi, frequently jailed by the *Rāja* for his pro-independence activism. He was the first to oppose J. Nehru, and later clashed with Indira Gandhi over election misdeeds (p. 360). Lohia, JP Narayanan, and many others, were well-known, pre- and post- independence. Lohia consistently advocated for the poor (the OBCs and Dalits), for women's rights and equality, and for Hindi, not English, as the national language, while acknowledging the other major tongues. He was as controversial as he was original, and his ideas guaranteed regular clashes, if not attempts at put-downs from INC supporters. The ABKS had allied with the INC, until its leaders found that the INC was using, not helping them. They clashed on policy and practices of the Communist Party of India (CPI) when the *Rāja* legalised it, hoping to gain communist, thus anti-Hindu support (Rasul, M).

By 1950, the scars of partition still raw, it was obvious that the only way for Indians to advance together was to regain self-esteem and pride, by reclaiming culture and heritage, and eradicating the ills that retarded society, especially poverty, lack of education, social segregation and stagnation. India's challenge was to bring her peoples out of the morass of mutual suspicion, antagonism and rejection, in which generations had been trapped, and replace them with trust and cohesion.

With independence, India was promised quick changes. But change for the sake of change was not a worthy objective, unless it restored and spread to all the traditions of spirituality, learning, industry and discovery, as promoted by the *dharmic* Hindus, Buddhists and Jains, and by others, but sadly sapped by wars, conquest and alien vilification.

Buddhism had declined through centuries of Islamic suppression, and its symbols were destroyed, most recently in Afghanistan. Christianity and Maoism were favourably received by the secularists. But those whose education had significant *Vaidic, Agamic* and other native inputs, confessed to a deep cynicism that India's leaders could guide and protect the country to regain the wisdom, wealth and respect that had made her the hub, if not the cradle of world civilisation, the originator of higher learning, of contemplation and expertise in grass-roots democracy (*panchayat rāja*)[116].

These virtues had crystallised in the Mauryan and Gupta periods and remained solid enough to survive the vicissitudes of dynastic change, until dissolved by intrigues, rivalries and conquest, first by the Mughals, some Brahmins, ambitious and divisive regional kings and

---

[116] With regards to rural reform, the Constitution (Article 40) required States to organise *Panchayats* but it was not until 1992 that the government acted *"to enshrine in the Constitution certain basic and essential features of Panchayati Institutions to impart certainty, continuity and strength to them"* (the 73rd Amendment).

then by Britain. In 190 years since Plessey, the British had impoverished India and decimated its population through a series of holocausts (famines and killings) on a far greater scale than the little one which the Jews have made into a major profitable industry and a flail for Germans.

British greed and profiteering had extorted excessive taxes from the dispossessed poor, and corrupted officials, while draining India's wealth to enrich British aristocrats. They had forced subjugated princes (subsidiary allies) into further taxation to support large armies for British needs (Egypt, Sudan, WWI, etc.), gutted its coinage and destroyed individual savings. Infrastructure—roads, electricity, communications etc. that benefit the majority—was neglected and there was minimal investment in India of the fruits of Indian labour. Village education was maliciously destroyed, and much talent used to distort, debase and deny Indian history and religion, its astronomical, scientific, mathematical, linguistic and other achievements that had existed to a high degree for more than a millennium before civilisation had even touched Europe.

The British exacerbated social classes and exploited them to create greater divisions, perverting society at large by favouring and empowering a subservient fraction of Indian converts, anglophiles, to their cause, who then facilitated the suppression of the majority. In this way, they maintained a brutal *Rāja* that is the shame of history. Their depredations have not ceased, only changed in expression and direction, now inescapably under control of the USA and an elite Euro-centric Indian upper class.

In the course of three centuries, many British Indophiles, or at least people of conscience, did emerge. Some are named above. Most resided in the UK, but a few showed their mettle in India. One of these—and poles apart from the Lords, whose relationship with India and Indians was similar to that of Hitler and his Nazis with Europe and the Jews—was Charles Bradlaugh, a railway contractor and parliamentarian, whose support for the Freedom movement and Indian self-government earned him a cancellation of contracts and expulsion from India! Annie Besant, Madame Blavatsky, Sister Nivedita, Bertrand Russell, Octavian Hume, Charles Wedderburn and thousands more—teachers, writers, administrators, clergymen, physicians, and the vast unnamed and unsung—contributed just as much as the headlined names. Without them, and the Vaishyas and Sudras of society, the more pretentious British mandarins and arrogant local Brahmins did not amount to much.

India was massively supported by the weak and lame and poor, who, together, gave lives and property, in greater proportion than all the wealth of the mighty, who have now inherited the nation, and continue to fatten themselves at the expense of the downtrodden. Who among India's growing wealthy will lift a finger to help their fellow citizens retain what little they might have squeezed from a greedy, ungrateful and stingy ruling class? The INC drifted back to its elite roots and forgot the power and inclusivity of the mass argument that Gandhi had so ably and eloquently made and shown that it would free India.

To say that Independence arrived with bloodshed is to accuse not Gandhi, nor the ideas of *Satyagraha* or *Purna Swaraj* or *Quit India*, but the ambitious around him, even though he had failed his policy when he revived the waning Jinnah in the mid-forties, and when he impulsively cancelled the *Non-Cooperation Movement* at the height of its success after WWI (p.289). Instead, he should have exploited the *Chauri Chaura* violence for what it was: the result of tyranny, just as Dhingra's act had been, and explored the notion that the British had deliberately provoked the incident to justify their harsh delays and brutal police reactions. It, no doubt, postponed independence, and allowed Britain to loot India for decades more and force its involvement in another costly war in Europe. Those passing years aged and took away some of India's brightest talents: Patel, Gandhi, etc.—whose leadership was sorely missed.

It is amazing that British Governors-General and administrators, for whom Macaulay had claimed such stature, sagacity and honour, could each ignore the simple connections between their oppression and the reactions they encountered: hatred, protest and revolt. And so profound were their blunders that even when the moderate Lord Ripon tried to achieve one just reform, and correct a great inequality, he would be practically pilloried by fellow British and promptly recalled! So blatant was their hatred that not a single British Indian attended his Bombay send-off, held by the people of that Presidency. At least he was spared the ignominy shown to those of his countrymen who dared to deal with India sympathetically and humanely.

And as for Clive, Hastings, the Wellesleys (Richard and Arthur), Dalhousie, Curzon, Minto, Irwin, Linlithgow, Wavell and the rest in India, and Chelmsford, Rhodes, Kitchener and others in Africa, the honours they gained were truly "rooted in dishonour", as Tennyson, one of their ilk, whose pen was his sword, had said, "*And faith unfaithful, kept him (them) falsely true* "(to *the throne*)! The lords were however true to form, continuing to debase all classes below them yet demanding their service, loyalty and allegiance to the model of royalty and kleptocracy—as preserved from the Dark Ages—that had brought England to a place among the world's foremost nations.

Meanwhile Western and some Indian "scholars" have paid scarce attention to recent discoveries that definitively repudiate British 19th century distortions of Indian history. India has discovered lost knowledge and expertise to the extent of independently venturing into extra-terrestrial exploration, which many had long anticipated, from tales in the epics and from recent work of scientists, from Homi Bhābhā to Abdul Kalam and his forerunners in astrophysics.

The ringing phrases of the *Ramāyana* and *Mahābhārata* dealing with ancient travel and warfare echo in the mind, with new impact, and invoke an ancestral race, with knowledge and skills beyond our grasp, and doubted today. In ignorance and an almost despotic narrowing of the boundaries of time, space and civilisation by three bellicose Middle East religions, people had meekly accepted the discounting of their past, while *Vaidic* scholars have tirelessly and stoically shown the validity of *Vaidic* lore, repudiating the inventive history of Abraham's children!

To recap, recent findings confirm that the course of the Saraswati River was remarkably close to that described in the *Rg Vaida,* with its many towns and settlements. Each discovery brings the age of the current Indian "civilisation" nearer to 12,000 years. Much of this old history antedates handwriting, but experience with the oral tradition—where each child practises, virtually from birth, memorising long passages from epics and holy books—gives credence to the accuracy of orally-transmitted knowledge. The same is true of Chinese and most other ancient history. It is remarkable that the *Vaidic* (Hindu) tradition has alone survived, albeit with some add-ons, through the last twelve millennia, while others have expired or been destroyed or supplanted by newer doctrines.

Historians have written extensively about the last six decades of Indian history. Analyses vary, but the main events are established and provide amply for current affairs discourses and the perennial dance of nations, which twist and turn, plot and posture to gain ascendancy, like competitors on a stage. The account that follows is abbreviated and the reader is urged to explore, for detail, some of the titles in the Bibliography, noting that the worldwide web is bountiful, but unedited, and a treacherous source for information on India. The history of India is presented, mainly with the British dates, but annotated; that of Pakistan varies, as some of its protagonists revise its history, making the British fictions pale in contrast. It seems as if Pakistan's revisionists have simply substituted *1947 BCE* for 1947 CE as Pakistan's birth, and conflated all of Hindu past history into a fiction called "ancient Pakistan". This ignores the fact that "*Pakistan*" was first used in 1933 by Choudhry Rahmat Ali, a Muslim lawyer, in proposing a carving up of India into a jigsaw puzzle, with Islamic islands in Hindu seas. Jinnah and Nehru rejected the idea, and at independence Pakistan's PM Liaquat Ali Khan expelled Rahmat Ali from Pakistan. Some revisionist historians avoid reference to Hinduism or *Vaidas* and pretend the religion did not exist west of the Indus. *(See* Wynbrandt; *http://en.wikipedia.org/History of Pakistan; http://www.brecorder.*

http://ancientpakistan.info/). The reference to "ancient Pakistan" as a geographic entity before 1947 is dissembling and disingenuous.

The Cold War erupted hardly had WWII ended, but even before that, Churchill had proposed an assault on Russia, carrying the war into Eastern Europe and Moscow, to end communism. His military men fittingly dubbed the idea, *Operation Unthinkable (*Reynolds*),* and rejected it, but considered instead what they would do if Russia were to advance on England! Churchill was reliant on American strength and hoped that Pres. Truman might have agreed with him. But calmer heads prevailed, and the USA shifted to the Pacific war. In the aftermath, it found itself in a face-off with Russia on ideological grounds. In short order, half the world rallied to one or other side in this conflict and the Cold War began, as noted. Churchill had his *Operation Unthinkable,* after all. Eventually, he would discover that Europe was already in shambles.

The North Atlantic Treaty Organisation (NATO) was formed on April 4, 1949, as a military alliance following the inauguration a year earlier of the Organisation for European Economic Co-operation (OEEC), which operated the Marshall Plan for European renewal, in which Moscow declined to participate. It had formed the Communist International to unite workers and to eliminate bourgeois elements. Its major organ was the magazine, *Communist International*. For various reasons—some say pressure from Roosevelt and Churchill—Stalin dissolved it in 1943, but transferred his international interests to a department of the Russian Communist Party. With WWII over, the activities were subsumed by the new bureau founded in 1947, called the *Communist Information Bureau* (Cominform). Rejection of the Marshal Plan at the 1947 Paris Conference led to formation of *the Council for Economic Assistance* (*Comecon*), in 1949, to offer members an alternative to western inducements and to maintain solidarity through mutual assistance.

Nehru became India's Prime Minister in 1948 at the head of a socialist government, which followed the Soviet economic model based on five-year plans. Stalinism was the dominant socialist doctrine, though rife with slaughter or massive imprisonment of opponents. The Maoist version of Marxism had that year triumphed in China; Chiang Kai Chek and his nationalists retreated to Formosa and fortified it.

Strapped for cash, Mao united half a billion people, with arms and the slogan, *"to each according to his needs, from each according to his ability to pay"*. The problem was, then as now, who decided on ability to pay and what levels were set. Invariably, even the most leftward felt the limit was set too low, so low in fact that even landless peasants might have had to contribute by way of tax! The British *Rāja*, and following its example, the princes, had already reduced India's poor to desperation with hardly any benefit to flow from Independence. To them the transition was from white to brown exploiters, and for the millions of Dalits and untouchables – a distinction that did not appear in the Diaspora, allowing them to proceed on merit mainly – the yoke of caste was not removed in practice, but conflated with a bastardised version of *varna* that replaced heredity for ability as a criterion of *varna*.

Thus, in the India ruled by Indians, the poor and the neglected hardly had any hope for betterment in the near term, despite the hope and ringing nationalism in the Constitution, and the extravagant claims of the Communists. Yet the latter, which came to power early in Kerala, outperformed the others in education and training for several decades; but it neglected to find work for graduates, thus exporting its talent, to enrich the West and continue the plunder of India, now also by Indians! The ranks of Hindu-bashers swelled wherever they went.

With its diplomatic relationships, its non-aligned status, its parliamentary democracy and basic governmental structure – figure next page – and US-like federation, one expected that India would outperform China economically. But that did not consider India's burden of the *Rāja's* cumbersome and pretentious bureaucracy, its entire Civil Service – a baggage Mao had cut loose – with its myriad privileges carried over from the *Rāja*, like everything else British, including expensive pensions for the departing officials, and compensation to the BEICo! For what, one may ask? Surely it should have been the other way around, and India should demand the return of stolen treasures.

The cupidity of Indian inheritors in every way matched or outdid the British they had succeeded. Some of them took their nationalism and independence literally and seriously, and tended to be even harsher in their dealings with the public than they had been under the *Rāja*, just to show how serious and loyal they had remained! More common was the favouritism shown to wealth, caste and *jāt* by the inheritors of India. It was said that twenty million or so, the secularists, with their rejection of all religions, were the main beneficiaries. The language and many laws designed for a Christian government remained despite their obvious irrelevance to secularism and a majority Hindu population, and their shameless verbal touting of socialist values, which, ironically, the wealthy have learned to manipulate and turn India into one of the most corrupt countries globally. Incredibly, traditional Indian beliefs and their following remain subservient to British-style mores.

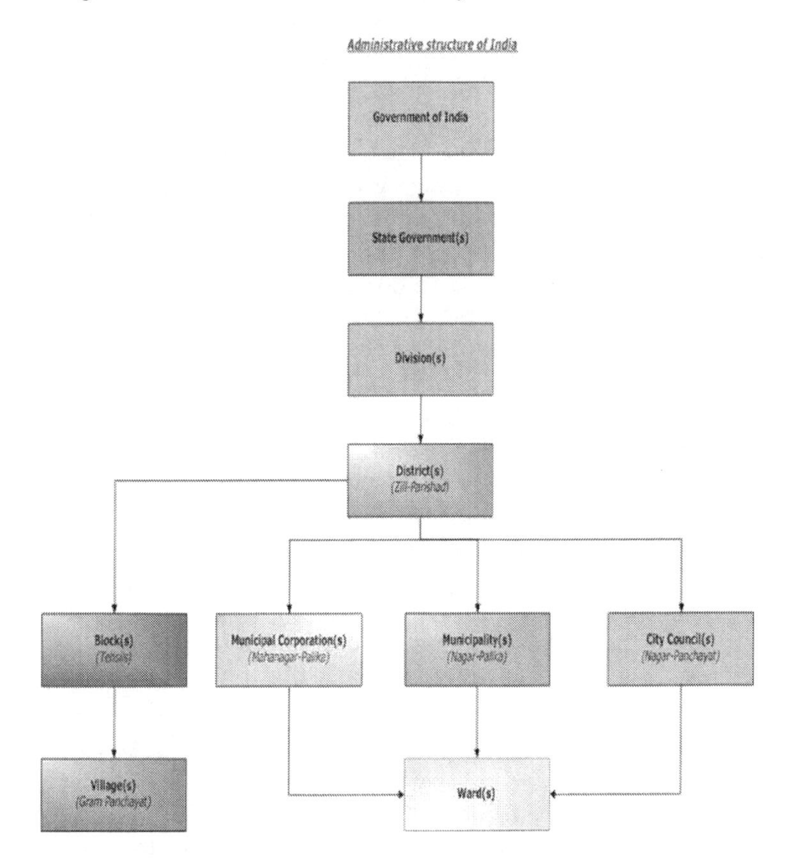

The nation began as a socialist state, kept a friendly distance from the USA, which had "adopted" Pakistan, supplied it with arms, ostensibly to contain the USSR's southern reach and counter the rising powers of Mao's China and non-British Asia. Hardly had the weapons arrived, than the Pakistan Army invaded Kashmir, aiming at conquest of North India, as their forbears had done centuries earlier. Pakistan abruptly, and China later, has each clipped a piece off India's northern boundary, just like thieving money-changers of old who would clip off narrow strips from the margins of smooth-edged gold and silver coins, until milling and wordage made the act not just detestable, but detectable! Nehru witnessed both, and at the time missed the import of these acts. The West continued to pressure India indiscriminately, a liberty they might not have taken so easily with Menon or Shastri.

Menon had a noteworthy career in the UN, followed by many years in politics in India, including five years as Minister of Defence (1957-62), which he resigned following China's seizure of Aksai Chin. He accepted responsibility for defeat, even though the seizure might have been historically justified, or merely a result of Nehru's poor grasp of border issues and smug belief in China's friendship *("Indee Chinee bhai bhai": Indians and Chinese are brothers)!* In fact, China was "allowed" to complete their road from Tibet to Sinkiang through Aksai Chin, during the late fifties. Nehru had failed to recognise that Mao Zedong's fortunes had changed by 1959, and that he needed to impress Beijing once again. Nehru had poor data on China, just as he was cavalier about Pakistan's motives in the northwest and their undermining of Jammu & Kashmir.

Some had considered Menon as Nehru's ablest Minister and many regretted his resignation—Muslims didn't—arguing that India could not have stopped China then, and that India has not had a better Defence chief. This opinion overlooks Menon's pro-communist views and the possibility that he too was overly tolerant (or ignorant) of China's aggressive intentions re sections of India's borders, and that historically Tibet was not part of China. In either case, Nehru's lackadaisical approach to India's borders with China, explains much of the problems today with China's adamant claim on Arunachal Pradesh and ostensible willingness to trade Aksai Chin for it.

Nehru has been criticised for believing too much in his own doctrines and spending too much time on his role as "non-aligned" head, when Pakistan, aided by the USA, and China were pushing at his borders in several sensitive places. Thus he missed the cues to China's intentions on the frontier, when it overran Tibet and seized it. Today Arunachal Pradesh remains under threat. It is possible that a stronger frontier policy in the fifties, when China was relatively weak, could have avoided or mitigated these incursions.

The Cold War split the world's powers into two combative and ideologically opposed groups. Outside of Europe and the USA, a substantial number of sober minds saw the Cold War for what it was: a symptom of the addiction for war games that afflicted Europeans and had defined their history for nearly two millennia; and when not fighting one another, they carried their aggression to other continents, seized lands and condemned defenders for being fierce and aggressive! The manoeuvres of the main Western powers, led by the USA, UK, France and West Germany, and the counter-manoeuvres by the USSR, dissuaded outsiders from trusting either side. The group led by Nehru:

Soekarno of Indonesia, Abdel Nasser of Egypt, Josip Tito of Yugoslavia and Kwame Nkrumah of Ghana, met in Belgrade in 1961 and formally founded the Movement, which, as noted, India's Foreign Minister, Menon, had dubbed the *Non-Aligned Movement (NAM)*, when describing the concept at the UN in 1953. The Movement adopted the principles that Nehru had earlier set out for relations between India and China:

Mutual respect for territorial integrity and sovereignty;
Mutual non-aggression;
Mutual non-interference in domestic affairs;
Equality and mutual benefit;
Peaceful co-existence.

The NAM grew to 120 nations. And even though today the Cold War has "ended," nations remain polarised, splintered on several fronts, some internalised. Most are beholden to the lone superpower, the USA, while conscious of others, especially China, now rich and flexing sizeable muscles, and Russia under Vladimir Putin. The Cold War has given way ideologically to an undeclared but quite obvious struggle between Christianity and Islam, both imperialist, and intent on crushing the other religions, by hook or crook, notably the next most populous, Hinduism.

Islam got its big boost with the discovery of huge quantities of oil in Arabia and the Middle East, starting in the early 20th century, and projected to last at least until 2030, at current rates of extraction. The crucial moment was the action by the Organisation of Petroleum Exporting Countries (OPEC), in 1973-4, spearheaded by Saudi Arabia's King Faisal ibn Saud. The cartel increased oil price from about US $2.75/barrel to $12.00/barrel, sending Americans wild; it almost closed the nation down. People in heavily-taxed countries adjusted, as did those living a more realistic, less materialistic and dream-besotted existence, as they did whenever oil corporations capriciously increased prices or reduced supply, having become inured to the demands of GATT in favour of the USA. They were affected but didn't panic. The USA panicked, fuelled by rumour and Orson Wellesian incidents, such as the "joke" on NBCTV's *The Tonight Show,* of a looming shortage of toilet paper! A similar rumour in Japan also caused a run on toilet paper!

The steady rise in prices in the next decades made oil exploration or production profitable from more costly fields, such as Canada's tar sands, however environmentally destructive, and off-shore sites in various seas; it spurred the search for oil in new locations. The major beneficiaries were Russia, north-western Europe, Mexico, US Gulf states, Alaska and Canada. By 1980, Russia became the world's largest producer. The economies of nations like India and China and most non-oil-producing third world countries were badly affected. Some explored alternative sources of energy, besides nuclear power. Soon solar power supplied most of Israel's heating needs. Although its war with Egypt and Syria had contributed to the Arab embargo on exports to the USA, parts of Europe and Japan, Israel suffered relatively little from OPEC action.

Nehru in USA, 11 Oct.1949, (U.S. National Archives and Records Administration)

The effects continue its ripple today as prices increased steadily and the industry invested heavily in Canada's tar sands, Gulf of Mexico, the North Sea, Nigeria and elsewhere. Less directly-poisonous sources of energy, such as wind and sun, are being developed, but slowly, offset by increased use of coal and consequent air pollution. India is a major user of coal and imports most of its oil. The USA is also a heavy user of coal, contributing massively to air, land and water pollution, and to global warming, and lags behind countries like Germany in promoting non-fossil sources of fuel. It has taken to fracking for natural gas and oil, a polluting activity that has become widespread, but boosted US domestic supply and lowered its reliance on Islamic sources. Of note, Germany's major wind generation is based on Heligoland, the little island in the North Sea which was obtained in exchange for German East Africa (see p. 237), during the *"Scramble for Africa"*, a decision for which Bismarck was chastised by German businessmen.

With Nehru leading, the INC government developed the economy on the framework of five-year plans prepared by the Planning Commission, an agency of government that consisted of economists, chaired by the Prime Minister India had inherited a plethora of ills from the British, and Nehru had made many promises, in the emotion of the independence moment..[117]

The first 5-year plan concentrated on commerce, not social amelioration, and stifled free enterprise among the general population. Nehru appeared merely to continue the practices of the British, who did not educate the masses, nor facilitate industrial research and development in the 19th and 20th centuries. For example, in the early 20th century, Jamshedji Tata could not get start-up loans from British banks for a steel mill.[118] Many less persistent or affluent Indians with ideas moved overseas, and did well in the Diaspora, especially in the USA, in academia (teaching or seeking higher degrees), business, industry or personal enterprises. America denied food aid to India in 1949 and rigidly screened migrants, but that did not stop Indian migration. The success of Indian migrants is now legendary, and they have risen in corporations, academia and government, in Canada, UK and USA.

After the first five years of slow growth, Nehru had placated the nation, (even as his daughter later would do with her slogan *"garibi hataao"* [banish poverty]), when he said, *"I shall not rest content unless every man, woman and child in the country has a fair deal and has a minimum standard of living…Five or six years is too short a time for judging a nation. Wait for another ten years and you will see that plans will change the entire picture of the country so completely that the world will be amazed."*

The world was indeed amazed, but not as Nehru wished. Dr D Gadjil, of Nagpur University, commenting on Nehru's rule, and the shift of the INC from the socialist focus of 1938 and restatement of 1947, over to the right, wrote, *"A group of leading capitalists have virtually taken over the economy, politics and society. The ugly businessman is the major character in the Indian scene, making large profits, promoting corruption, securing the support of officials and manipulating the administrative machinery*[119]*…At the same time the share of foreign companies in gross private sector profits had gone up to 33%. Foreign capital transactions had increased from 2,176 million rupees to 6,185 million in 1964. To make the matter worse, rural folk had seen a 400% increase in taxes, while facing a drop in prices for their produce."*

"I come from a class of bourgeoisie," Nehru said in admitting the miscarriage. Part of this was presumed due to the continued subsidies to princes and the failure of land reform to achieve its worthy goals. And even when farmers increased production, they found that central planners had not secured the internal market, presumably still flooded

---

[117] See Bibliography: *UPSC Guide* http://www.upscguide.com/Accessed 17/3/2013 and http://en.wikipedia.org/wiki/Five-Year plans of India. These are highlights.

[118] See M. Ragbeer, *The Indelible Red Stain* for similar hurdles in other colonies.

[119]See also Herdeck, Margaret L and Parimal, Gita, *India's Industrialists, Bk 1,* Lynn Reinner Publications, Colorado, USA, 1985

with British imports and governed by British tastes instilled over twenty decades.[120] Indian industrialists like Tata, Birla, Wādiā and Dalmia had openly endorsed the socialist agenda, knowing fully that their objectives will not be impeded in any way, so weak were socialist efforts to "control" big business. By 1947, the Congress party already had a majority of middle class and business members.

Nehru had fallen short in most aims, except the aggrandisement of the rich and powerful, as Lohia and others had pointed out. Yet in 1960, Nehru had derided the *Swatantra Party*—a coalition of parties formed to oppose the INC—as confined to "*the middle ages of lords, castles and zamindars,*" referring to the high percentage of the princely, rich and upper crust, most of whom had defected from the INC, just as the farmers union had done. Acharya Kripalani's successor, Rajendra Prasad, supported Nehru, but in 1950 Puroshottam Das Tandon became INC President, despite Nehru's lobbying against him. Kripalani and Tandon had advocated a strong stance against Pakistan's anti-Hindu aggression, which was producing numerous non-Muslim refugees in West Bengal. Further action by Nehru against these two rivals eliminated their "threat" but did not curtail their services to India, and did little about the border breaches or land reform.

Lohia, as noted above, was an intelligent but exacting person; usually leftist and sometimes volatile; but he criticised communism and capitalism equally, suggesting that these were European tools to enslave Asia and Africa! He was scathing in his criticism of caste and the lifestyle of high officials. As early as 1951, he had observed that thriving Indians were nearly all well-off Anglophones of high caste, whose forebears the British had conquered with guns and enslaved with English, and ensuring their position by Lord Risley's caste distinctions.

To begin emancipation of Indians, Lohia had advocated the creation of municipal schools to replace private schools so as to ensure attendance by all students of all classes, arguing correctly that segregation would only perpetuate caste and force people into narrower and narrower circles, whereas learning together would eventually break barriers, widen circles and promote unity. He thus considered his loss of the anti-English language campaign a betrayal of the independence movement. In 1963, he moved a no-confidence motion against Nehru, remarking, no doubt sarcastically, that after sixteen years of governing, Nehru's major domestic success was his command of ₹25,000 a day when the poor man's wage was ₹0.2/day, giving Nehru a multiple of 125,000! JP Narayanan upbraided Nehru, *"You want to go towards socialism, but you want the capitalists to help you in that!"*

---

[120] http://planningcommission.nic.in/reports/articles/venka/index.php?repts=mland

Much has been written about Nehru but few have condemned his egotism and scheming when good talent had appeared ready to do what was needed. The last thing that the 80% of India's struggling uneducated poor needed was an apologist, and zamindar at heart, to speak for them. He might have been okay for the twenties or thirties but post-war resurgent India needed someone with more empathy and insight, and better organisational, managerial and operational skills. Nehru was first a Fabian socialist, fiscally conservative, keen on industrialisation as a concept, including heavy industries, largely under central control and owned by the public, though not excluding his favoured private entrepreneurs. Nehru could handle non-alignment, but the reins of government should have gone to someone else.

Modern commentators criticised India's slow adoption of western industrial technology and often blamed Mahatma Gandhi's advocacy of a return to cottage industries, which he saw as gainfully occupying the unemployed or those displaced by textile and other mills. Heavy industry, and even some light industry, required much capital and a steady market. Tata was successful in operating a textile mill with American equipment and Egyptian long staple cotton that produced a better product than Britain's, so he was as good a prospect for bank support as India possessed. Yet British banks had denied him that, to avoid competition with British mills.

When the railroads were expanding and needed supplies, rails and continuous maintenance, the facilities, personnel and technology were restricted to British hands. Although local shops could have fabricated parts, every piece, large or small, *had* to come from Britain! In any case tenders for contracts had to be made in London, thus eliminating Indian bidders. Menial and non-technical jobs were the only ones given to Indians, regardless of qualification. The same applied to all colonial jobs before WWII. Finally Tata founded his steel mill, TISCO, before WWI, on subscriptions from thousands of small investors in India. But not until WWII did he get an order for rails from the British *Rāja* or a State Railway. India was then well supplied with skills, but underfunded.

There have been twelve five-year plans from 1951 to the present, with a few intercalary years in the late 1970s and early 1990s.[121] Many in-depth analyses of these have been compiled and are included in the bibliography, and several are available on-line. The account below shows highlights, which depend on the listed sources and a personal review of the plans. The first one was launched in 1951 and stressed agricultural development, with a budget of ₹2,069 crore: 27.2% allotted

[121]www.planningcommission.nic.inw/plans/planrel/fiveyr/welcome.html

to irrigation and energy; 24% to communications and transport; 17.4% to agriculture and community development; 16.64% to social services; 8.4% to industry; 4.1% to land rehabilitation, and the remainder to other sectors and services. The state dominated each of these; it was felt that India's economic weakness demanded careful management to improve capital and foster savings.

Bhakra and Hirakud Dams and other irrigation projects were begun, to retain water from monsoons, regulate supply and provide for hydropower. The population grew, largely due to reduction in infant mortality, good rainfall, peace and increased productivity. Net domestic product increased by 3.6%, lower than expected and derogatively described as the Indian rate of growth, contrasting it with the more aggressive rates of many post-war economies and new states, especially in Asian neighbours.

Indira Gandhi and Jacquie Kennedy, 1962

Statistics Professor Prasanta Chandra Mahalanobis was recruited to the Commission in 1953 and oversaw the Second Plan (1956-1961), with a budget of Rs. 48 billion, to be spent on foreign trade, five new steel plants (at Bhilai, Durgapur, and Rourkela), hydroelectricity, five Institutes of Technology (IITs), increases to Universities, plus scholarships in nuclear physics. This was regrettably not matched by a similar emphasis on the more urgent need for primary education, curricular reform and prompt correction of Indian history. The result is today's education deficits at one end and, at the other, an enormous and continuing brain drain to the West. The *Tata Institute of Fundamental Research* was established. More coal was produced and railway lines added in the north east.

Mahalanobis put much effort into operations research, hoping to discover the best investments for maximum growth in a closed economy focused on capital imports. A growth rate of 4.27% was achieved falling just short of the projected 4.5%. A notable loss was the sudden death of Parsi legislator, Feroze Gandhy (name changed to Gandhi after marriage), husband of Indira Gandhi, on Sept 8, 1960, age 47, ostensibly from cardiac arrest. Gandhi was the first anti-corruption crusader and had earlier led a charge of financial wrongdoing against industrialist Ramakrishna Dalmia, a long-time INC member, and Nehru's friend.

Gandhi had fallen out with his father-in-law and was seen as a threat to the smooth functioning of the party; it is uncertain whether Indira shared his concerns.[122] His death remains suspicious.

The Third Plan (1961–1966) focussed on agriculture and wheat production in Punjab, new cement and fertilizer plants and rural elementary schools. Elections at the *panchayat* level were held for the first time, and states given more responsibility for education, energy, road building and transportation. Dhaman and Diu and Pondicherry were incorporated, and the eastern state of Nagaland created.

The Kennedys visited India March 1962, where Jacquie revisited her dislike for Indira Gandhi, but discovered a fascination for saris and assembled quite a collection. The Kennedys were lavishly treated, quite in contrast to the cool reception they had given the Nehrus in the USA.

The 1962 war with China in Kashmir revealed Nehru's lax China policy, leaks to CIA, and India's lackadaisical defence policies, belatedly forcing measures to improve the army. It was felt that a border war with a potential ally was unnecessary, but fear of Maoism was great in India then, especially after the easy seizure of Tibet. Nevertheless, his loss was inevitable, sending poorly prepared and equipped troops against a seasoned Chinese army. Nehru was criticised for laxity, and Defence Minister Menon, as noted, resigned. Even the separatist DMK supported India, backed by founder C.N. Annadurai, who had become a member of the Rajya Sabha, and, in 1963, dropped the call for *Dravidasthan*.

Nehru's health declined and he died in 1964.

In spite of shortcomings, Nehru's projects enabled India to fuel agricultural expansion and the needs of industry for energy and transportation. During the first five year plan, he had started infra-structural projects for water control and hydroelectric energy, with a generous rise in spending from 1% GDP in 1951, to 5% in 1963, finishing construction of several impressive dams across the country.[123] He did start to repair the physical damage done by partition, though Hindus may not have agreed with his spending on Muslim mosques while withholding funds from Hindu temples and Sikh gurdwaras.

---

[122] Feroze would be busy today investigating his late wife and son Rajiv and his wife Antonia (Sonia), for the many allegations of graft amounting to billions of dollars, and other illegal acts, and also son Rahul: See http://www.ekakizunj.com/Sonia_Gandhi

[123] See *The Political Economy of Infrastructure Development* Rajiv Lall & Anupam Rastogi, 2007; www.idfc.com/pdf/white_papers/idfc_peidpII_report.pdf. Seeing Bhakra, Nehru enthused, *"Bhakra-Nangal project is something tremendous, something stupendous, something which shakes you up when you see it. Bhakra, the new temple of resurgent India, is the symbol of India's progress."*

The Hirakud dam on the Mahanadi River, Orissa (Odisha) is one of world's longest at 25.8 km., while the Bhakra dam on the Sutlej River in Himachal Pradesh, completed in 1963, is India's largest to date. Others were built on the Chambal tributary of the Yamuna, between Indaur and Kota in Madhya Pradesh. The Nagarjuna Sagar on the Krishna River in Andhra Pradesh was completed in late 1960s and is known for being the world's tallest masonry dam, and for the matchless persistence of its major advocate Muktyala Rāja, who, almost single-handedly, persuaded Nehru to approve the site.

The Tungabhadra dam in South India and the Damodar Valley Corporation in West Bengal were welcomed; the latter addressed an old problem of flooding in Bengal in the valley of the Hooghly and its tributaries. These and other projects consumed up to 23% of the first plan and were the first of many as energy needs mounted. Four hundred and ninety-nine (499) dams were built in 1961-70, and 1,296 in the next decade. Today, there are 4,847 completed large dams and 348 under construction across the country; most are in Maharashtra, Madhya Pradesh, Gujarat and Andhra Pradesh.

The Rourkela Steel Mill, Odisha, (initially *Hindustan Steel*), took three years longer than planned at twice the cost. The same applied to dams[124] and fertiliser plants, the delays necessitating importation of fertilisers and food grains. Taxation measures included wealth tax, gift tax and expenditure tax, but an efficient collection system was not established. Tax avoidance was thus quite high; even ministers, like Jagjivan Ram, did not file income tax returns for years. Nehru had promised to hang black marketers and anti-socials, but that did not happen. Had he done so, he might have sacrificed most of his friends and colleagues! He complained about ministers and officials who lived in big houses, while he, a self-styled socialist, lived in a mere mansion!

Nehru achieved little for early education, but promoted tertiary education that fed Indians to the West. The first Indian Institute of Technology (IIT) was founded in 1950 at Kharagpur, 75 miles from Calcutta. At the convocation in 1956 Nehru promised to recapture the past glory of Indian mathematics and technology, and said, *"Here in the place of that Hijli Detention Camp stands the fine monument of India (IIT) today, representing India's urges, India's future in the making."*[125]

---

[124] National (Indian) Register of Large Dams; included are all dams over 10 metres high; see http://www.cwc.nic.in/main/downloads/New%20NRLD.pdf

[125] The British had built the Hijli Detention Camp in 1930 to hold freedom fighters; it became the seat of a University just as the WWII Gibraltar Detention Camp in Jamaica had become the site of the University of the West Indies. Being Europeans, the detainees in Jamaica were treated rather more gently than the Indians in Indian camps! Kharagpur has the world's longest railway station (1km), no doubt to accommodate the thousands of

By 1961, the fourth IIT was opened in New Delhi, followed by others, restoring India's dominance in Mathematics and Engineering. Many of their graduates left for the West, though, especially for the USA, after US immigration, social and citizenship laws relaxed in 1965. (The traffic had increased from the mid-1940s when the quota of Indian migrants from all sources—India and the Diaspora—was raised to 7,000 annually in recognition of India's role in WWII). The exodus was predictable, and in line with the persisting pro-western anglophile curricula of Indian schools at all levels, instilling pro-British loyalties and serving western, not Indian interests. It remains embarrassing to note how poorly educated in Indian history its secular and non-Hindu professionals and businessmen are.

Under Nehru, the rich got richer and the poor poorer, with more people below the poverty line (BPL), and getting worse. PM Manmohan Singh's response recently was to lower the poverty line to incomes below a minuscule ₹816/1000 month (rural/urban), thus instantly decreasing the numbers of the needy! The suggestion (Rangarajan) for 2011-12 is ₹972/1407 giving a total of BPL population as 270 million!

The right shift in the INC had occurred early, when socialists like Narendra Dev and other legislators resigned from the party and lost their seats on re-election, from lack of financial support. In this way, Indira Gandhi, having ended princely subsidies in the 70s, would later purge INC of dissidents and gradually change the party to one that represented vested interests and cronyism, not the masses, which it would still return to and woo quite successfully at election time.

Women's procession in Bombay during the "Quit India" movement, 1942

---

detainees sent regularly to Hijli. These included Mahatma Gandhi and the youth Bhagirath. It was here that the British murdered two unarmed detainees Santosh Kumar Mitra and Tarakeshwar Sengupta in 1931, one of the numerous blood stains that the British left all over India.

Chapter 23

Greed, lust and other evil tendencies should be discarded so that our inner self may become illumined. Bhajan, translated by Pandit Sitaram, Toronto

There are about 7 billion people in the world, half of whom are poor and marginalized and half are prosperous; if the boundaries between the nations are removed and one person helps another, the entire world will be prosperous and all will lead joyous lives. *B. Pathak, SISSO*

Border wars; PMs and scientists

In the six and a half decades since Independence, India has been ruled by the INC, except for a break under the Janata Party (JP), 1977-9, and another under the Bharatiya Janata Party (BJP), 1999-2004. As of May 16, 2014 the BJP/NDA faces the failures of the INC and its culture of disappointment. Much was expected of Nehru, but, on his own from 1948, his policies fell short, both in foreign relations and at home, though he avoided an overt treasure hunt by the victors. In the federal structure, shown on p 342, the INC controlled each level of Government and had a blueprint which Nehru had laid out in his *"Tryst with Destiny"*.

Secular intellectuals and atheists, e.g. Amartya Sen, spend much ink and noise on criticising Hindus, while overlooking the invasive behaviour of Islamic Wahhabists and Christian proselytisers today, and pretending that the huge loss of Hindu life and property—under successive Islamic and British rulers in the last millennium—did not occur. Of Islamic behaviour, the American Will Durant has written: "*the Islamic conquest of India is probably the bloodiest story in history. It is a discouraging tale, for its evident moral is that civilisation is a precious good, whose delicate complex order and freedom can at any moment be overthrown by barbarians invading from without and multiplying within.*"

Some critics of Hinduism exaggerate the role of the other religions—even the tiny groups of Parsis, Jews and Baha'i, which together total less than 1% of the population, but carry much economic clout and are apparently quite satisfied, aloof and prospering. They remain free to migrate anywhere, and many do, but a billion Hindus have only India to call their home. Some detractors even fabricate scenarios to assert that Hinduism was a creation of the British, thus revealing their deep ignorance of the complexity and content of the religion, its enormous literature, intellectual stature, its science, arts and crafts, industry, music, cuisine, manufactures, and agriculture that had developed long before the enlightenment in Europe and the birth of Islam in Arabia.

There has never been a period of peace since the repulse of Islamic invaders of Jammu & Kashmir in 1947-8, as the vantage point ceded to them allows Islamic terrorists, encouraged and funded from Pakistan, to systematically launch raids into Jammu and Kashmir's Hindu districts.

In the course of several decades, they have succeeded in ousting nearly half a million Hindus, who still occupy refugee camps in J&K and neighbouring states, as silent, unsung victims of Islamists that Indian and Western media never seem to notice in their tirades against Hindus.

Killing raids are frequent; an especially heinous one occurred in 2002 when *Lashkar-e-taiba* militants, dressed as Indian soldiers killed a busload of tourists, and, a few minutes later, wives and children of the regular soldiers before being themselves killed. This almost started a war with Pakistan. A similar expulsion of Hindus took place from East Pakistan into West Bengal. Pakistan now claims J&K as of "right", because of the Muslim majority. By this logic, Pakistan should claim other states like Afghanistan, Iran, Malaysia, Indonesia, the Middle East, Saudi Arabia, Turkey, North Africa and others!

When Nehru died, the seasoned South Indian INC activist, Kumarasami Kamaraj, declined the succession and promoted instead the appointment of Lal Bahadur Shastri. Less than two years later he intervened again, in the appointment of Indira Gandhi. Kamaraj had become Chief Minister of the state of Madras, now Tamil Nadu, in 1954, and was noted for appointing opponents to his Cabinet! He promoted free primary education and provided students a midday meal and uniforms, to equalise appearances among them.

Shastri, a reserved personality, was chosen to succeed Nehru. His rule was a short 19-months (9 June 1964 -11 Jan 1966), but quite eventful. He was resourceful and decisive; arguably the best PM India has had so far (2012). In September 1965, Pakistan shot down an Indian private airplane, killing two pilots, the Chief Minister of Gujarat, B.R. Mehta, his wife, a journalist and three staff, having previously invaded Kashmir. Shastri reacted quickly, and in 17 days Indian forces had repelled the invaders and had almost reached Lahore, when a UN-Russian-US initiative stopped the war, against Indian army advice. In 1966, peace terms were agreed and signed in Tashkent. A day later, Shastri died suddenly, under troubling circumstances; his wife believed he was poisoned. Despite requests from the family, Delhi has denied information, for example, findings of an autopsy, if one was done, even after appeals under the Freedom of Information Act. The controversy and speculation surrounding his sudden death persist to this day, and the role of the CIA remains to be clarified. Shastri had changed his mind on nuclear power, approved its development and in 1965 had appointed Vikram Sarabhai to head India's Space Research Organisation (ISRO). India's infrastructure and technology needs retarded communications to the villages and among them, and slowed efforts to locate underground resources. It was hoped that ISRO's efforts might bypass laborious and costly ways of achieving these aims and thus advance development.

In 1944, Homi J. Bhābhā, a noted physicist, known as the father of nuclear power in India, was the first to report on nuclear energy to the INC, advocating its development and proposing to use thorium as fuel, which is plentiful in Kerala, (where modern anti-nuclear, pro-US Christian proselytes have bought much of the ore-bearing land).

In his short tenure, Shastri made thoughtful reforms in official procedures, such as using water instead of lathis to control crowds, a small thing seemingly but of considerable impact at the time. He appointed women to railway positions, eliminated the luxury class in trains, thus making more space available to the people; he addressed corruption and set an unmatched example of honesty in public services. Not surprisingly, he died poor. The 5-year growth rate was 2.4%, less than half the projected rate of 5.6%, due largely to the war.

Left: Homi Jehangir Bhābhā (1909-66), nuclear physicist, died in airplane crash widely believed caused by CIA, to derail India's nuclear programme. Compare the sudden highly suspicious death of successor Vickram Sarabhai (right) (1919-71), p.359

Shastri was a life member of *the Servants of the People Society* and served a period as its President. All this was very much in the Gandhian tradition and welcomed by millions. Many still remember his slogan during the Pakistan war: "*Jai Jawan, Jai Kisan*" ("hail the soldier, hail the farmer"), and rue the loss to politics of this prime exemplar of honesty, moral strength and concern for the public. The Hungarian Government paid him the tribute of a stamp in 1976 (p. 354).

After a two week period under Gulzarilal Nanda, pending elections, Indira Gandhi became Prime Minister. The disruption of the plan just ended led to temporising with annual plans for the next three years. Indira Gandhi had filled the role of Chief of Staff to her father from 1947-64, during which she had made contact with the Kennedys, which sadly ended too soon. Still, relations with the US had remained cool, the US distrusting India, because of its ties with the USSR. It is more than likely that the Nehrus learned about the Alianza (*Alliance for Progress)* and its predecessor, the *Economic Charter of the Americas,* which Truman had foisted in 1945 on all Latin America. That had given US Corporations—heavily subsidised, and backed by the military—free access to Latin American resources, in exchange for a market and some limited help with industrial development, provided that it did not compete with US companies. This scuttled Latin American hopes to see benefits of industrialisation go to their citizens to raise living standards, rather than boost US corporate profits. They were promptly disabused of their misunderstanding of US priorities and urged to respect its stature as top dog in the world order. Nehru's subsequent behaviour suggested that he had appreciated the problems of bedding down with a gluttonous and hungry pit bull.

The rupee was devalued by 57.5% in the first year of Indira's rule on 6-6-66 and India concluded a 20-year treaty with the Soviet Union. The fourth 5-year plan began in 1969 and saw momentous changes: major banks were nationalised; agricultural output increased to self-sufficiency (the *green revolution,* which was not without critics because of the heavy use of chemical fertilisers) and another war, in 1971, with Pakistan.

PM Gandhi had complained about Pakistan's massacres in the East, and the sequel of over 10 million refugees crowding West Bengal. In the put-down of the revolt in East Pakistan, West Pakistani troops are said to have killed 3 million easterners and raped 300,000 women. The USA and China had ignored India's pleas for relief, until a full scale war between India and Pakistan began, after Pakistan bombed airfields in India.

India's triumph in East Pakistan prompted Nixon in December 1971 to send the 7th fleet, headed by the *USS Enterprise,* on an intimidatory visit into the Bay of Bengal, all bristling with mighty armaments—the modern equivalent of the British *Dreadnought* of 1906—while the British Navy also steamed into the Arabian Sea, to defend West Pakistan by threating India's west coast. The appearance of the Russian Pacific fleet off India's south coast sent the British retreating to Madagascar and stopped any aggression by the USA. India won the war and could have destroyed the Pakistan army and charged its leaders with ethnic crimes.

However, Mrs Gandhi allowed President Bhutto to get his way at the 1972 Simla conference, and discovered that she had been betrayed to the US by a spy in her cabinet, said to have been a close associate of her father's. He had served as a CIA agent from 1947, as confirmed by the recent release of US documents (*see theconspiracyofsilence.blogspot.ca/ 2009/01/*). Relations with Bangladesh were cordial for several years and during that time Indians were welcome in the country.[126]

Nixon's actions and anti-Indian behaviours continued the period of relatively cool relations between India and the USA. His support for the Pakistan dictator, Yahya Khan, was matched by a pejorative attitude to India's success in maintaining democracy. As PM, Indira Gandhi was often cited for harshness, arrogance and family bias, and called a threat to that democracy, especially when, by constitutional amendment, she ended the Privy Purse that Sardar Patel and VP Menon had negotiated with the princes in exchange for their 48% of India's territory. This had hardly been a major financial cost compared with the dishonour to the country: in 1947, the total pay-out to the 555 princes was ₹6 crores, on a reducing scale that by 1970 had brought it down to ₹4 crores, a cheap price to pay for a nation's integrity. (see AP Datar, *The Hindu*, 24-4-2013.)

In the following years, Indira Gandhi tried to help small farmers by pushing ground water irrigation through the use of pumps. She increased rural electrification and gave free power and fertiliser subsidies to growers and food subsidies to consumers.

Earlier, in 1968-73, a US-USSR détente had developed but did not stop activities between their allies. The Vietnam War had been active since 1956 and had sparked numerous protests in the USA, with defection of young men, mainly to Canada, to avoid the draft. South East Asia was generally pro-US, despite active Communist parties. The US supplied Pakistan with ordnance from its base in Saigon, as the Vietnam War raged and Pakistan remained hostile to India.

The USA had naval treaties with Pakistan, but Indian attacks in Operations *Trident* and *Python* in the 1971 War had quickly crippled the Pakistani Navy in Karachi. The US had thereupon concluded an agreement with Britain to develop a base on Diego Garcia, a tiny island south of the Maldives, and part of the British Indian Ocean Territory (BIOT). To do this, they abruptly and callously expelled the Chagossians, the people of Diego Garcia, to the Seychelles and Mauritius, allowing the USA to construct, without reparations, a naval base and housing for their permanent military personnel in South and South East Asia.

---

[126] As an Indian I was welcomed in Bangladesh in 1974 and travelled fairly freely in the country barring limitations due to infrastructure deficits, and war damage. The heavy bureaucracy was most frustrating however, worse than India's and much slower.

American intrusion, atrocities in Viet Nam and neutral Cambodia, and their overt anti-Buddhist and anti-Hindu attitudes were not likely to win them friends in Asia. The Socialism of the post-WWII "democracies" in East Africa and Indo-China, and the Vietnam War, had begun to strain American patience, at war and at home. The image of the *ugly American* was widely circulated and acknowledged.[127] Protests against anti-socialist US actions were common e.g. following their assault on Cambodia, resulting from a legal seizure by Cambodia of a US container ship, the *Mayaguez,* in 1975. The American Navy and Marines reflexly jumped to the wrong conclusion that the crew had been harmed, when in fact Cambodia had already released them, well *before* the US attacks. Relations with the US soured and Communism gained ground.

When China invaded India in 1962 and took Aksai Chin, an uneasy truce had followed, as China seemed clearly intent on establishing land contact with the Arabian Sea, through Pakistan. Nehru had met with Kennedy in 1962 and hosted his Indian visit later that year. Two years later, China conducted nuclear tests, and helped Pakistan build a deep water harbour on the Arabian Sea near Gwadar, which opened in 2007. The Chinese have planned an overland road/railway from there to Tibet and have built a rail link from Lhasa to Shanghai, opened in 2006.

Mrs Gandhi responded to China's sixth explosion by appointing Raj Ramanna to conduct weapons research. This led to the *Smiling Buddha* test in 1974, India's first nuclear test explosion, almost as a late response to the US 7th fleet in the Bay of Bengal. The test, later called *Pokhran 1,* part of India's energy programme, earned vociferous criticism from the Americans, despite their sitting on a malignant stockpile of nuclear weapons and a huge deployment of troops worldwide. Under NATO and other treaties, they sought fights like prowling vigilantes, and thought little of launching their favoured weapon of trade embargos on defenceless nations. They exerted enormous pressure on India to halt any further development of nuclear capability, or status, and continued to demand, vainly, that India sign the *Nuclear Non-proliferation Treaty.* At US behest, a *Nuclear Suppliers Group* was formed just to monitor and

---

[127]A novel, *The Ugly American,* by Eugene Burdick and William Lederer, published in 1959 portrayed a "good guy," based on the work of a real American in Burma (Myanmar), whose deeds were negated by the arrogance and egomania of his countrymen, pithily summarised in the book by a Burmese journalist, "*...the [American] people I meet in my country are not the same as the ones I knew in the United States. A mysterious change seems to come over Americans when they go to a foreign land. They isolate themselves socially. They live pretentiously. They're loud and ostentatious.*" (cf. British behaviour in the Empire, as described in *The Indelible Red Stain,* Ragbeer, Bibliography, and that of Caucasians today). It is said that John Kennedy modelled USAID on the work of the real hero, and in 1960 gave a copy of *The Ugly American* to each Senator, reminiscent of the British Conservatives' circulating the hostile *Mother India* to Parliamentarians in 1927 to sway their vote against India.

control India's access to nuclear materials. India's insistence on its plan to develop nuclear power for peaceful purposes failed to sway the USA, which responded by CIA assassinations, facilitated by access to Indian Cabinet secrets. On August 1, 2008, India was finally able to obtain certain nuclear materials for peaceful uses. India's industrial development funds were diverted in this period to a defensive war, the fourth against Pakistan, reducing the growth rate to 3.3%, far short of the target of 5.6%, as in 1965-6.

The pace of nuclear research slowed under PM Morarji Desai in 1977, but resumed in 1980, with Ramanna restored, to develop a hydrogen bomb, while Abdul Kalam, a rocket scientist at ISRO, later President of India, took charge of missile research in 1987. This resulted, by 1995, in the Prithvi missiles, whose tests were approved by PM Narasimha Rao, but halted when US president Bill Clinton intervened with India and Pakistan. India obliged. Narasimha Rao had been impressed by Clinton; in any case, India's testing site was out in open desert and easily tracked. But Pakistan, under Benazir Bhutto and the Army Chiefs, continued secretly in the mountains of Baluchistan and exploded *Chagai 1* on May 28, 1998, following India's *Pokhran 2* tests on May 11-13, 1998. May 11th is celebrated in India as *National Technology Day* and May 28th is Pakistan's *Youm-e-Takbir* (great day).

Internationally, both nations were condemned. India's critics included two very hypocritical ones: China and Pakistan, the latter claiming that its test was a response to India's, as if a nuclear weapon could be developed on the spur of the moment. Pakistan further announced that it was determined to match India in every way. Yet it neglected to mention that it had been conducting nuclear tests in the Kirana Range, Punjab, since 1983. PM Vajpayee settled for declaring India a nuclear state.[128] The INC, like the US and UK, was strangely hostile. France and Russia did not comment.

The Indian achievement no doubt surprised the Americans. Shastri had endorsed the nuclear program recommended by Bhābhā, just before Shastri's shady death. A few weeks later, in 1966, Bhābhā was also killed,

---

[128] In India in 1974 as a Commonwealth Fellow, I saw how the nuclear explosions had boosted the morale of people: civil servants, academics, physicians, hotel staff and people in general, regardless of religion or station in life. The taxi driver who took me on tour one day to my nana's village was especially pleased. His extensive contact with Americans at the hotel had led him to conclude that they were patronising and conceited, even the young USAID and Peace Corps workers, and, increasingly, the growing proselytising NGOs. I heard the same criticism in Calcutta, Dhaka, Varanasi, Agra and Bombay, plus comments on their lack of up-to-date knowledge on simple facts about India, their general ignorance of essential differences between Muslims and Hindus, which no amount of tutoring about the clues inherent in names really helped, and how aggravating that was to the already poor relations with Pakistan. See also Fn 129.

when an *Air India* aeroplane exploded over Mont Blanc, Switzerland, believed due to a strike from a CIA-arranged air-to-air missile. His successor, Vikram Sarabhai, also died suddenly in his hotel room after arriving at Kovalam, Thiruvanthapuram, Kerala, in 1971. He had just attended a successful rocket launch, and opened a railway station built to serve the installation. The cause of death was unknown, but his health was excellent and the circumstances were suspicious. Since then others in the nuclear program have met the same fate (see *PMO unconcerned about scientist deaths, Madhav Nalapat, Guardian, New Delhi, 26-10-2013).* Iranian physicists have suffered similarly, believed due to Israel's Mossad; Iran publicised the events while India's INC and media remained relatively silent about Indian killings. President Obama urged Israel recently to *"stop killing Iranian scientists!"* (D Raviv, *www.cbsnews.com/* Mar 1, 2014). Iran actively protects its scientists and recently jailed a US citizen, Amir Hekmati, for spying. Sarabhai was succeeded by Satish Dhawan, who died in 2002, aged 81.

In 1971, Mrs Gandhi was accused of election fraud by defeated opponent Raj Narain (see p 328). A judge, Jagmohanlal Sinha, ruled in 1975 against her, voided her election, ordered a new one in her constituency, and barred her for six years from any future candidacy. She ignored the order and on June 25, 1975, got a weak President Fakhruddin Ali Ahmed to declare a State of Emergency, under which all normal processes of government were suspended, opponents arrested, unions banned, the press muzzled, and a dictatorship ensued which lasted for 21 months.[129]

Her younger son, Sanjay, already tagged as an intemperate bully within the INC, was allowed to impose his will on elected politicians, including Ministers, famously I K Gujral, Minister of Information and Broadcasting, and became *de facto* director of many Government

---

[129]Part of my Fellowship (Fn 128) was spent examining the training of auxiliary health care workers, I was invited to join in the deliberations of India's NIHAE over a two week period as guest of the Government. This allowed me to see the range of problems and gauge the attitudes of people, especially the more "intolerant" Brahmins, who proved more ill-informed than intolerant. I had a chance to debate with a few who had agreed to do so, on what I thought were (and are) millstones on India's neck, and the factors most likely to sabotage its security and its prosperity. These included the prevailing caste practices, even among Muslims; poor basic education; poverty and ritual untouchability—apart from avoiding someone smeared with filth—which forward thinking Brahmins were discarding. Many in the Diaspora, of all varnas, had long ago shed the major trappings of caste. NIHAE agreed on a national promotion of hygiene at all levels, with efforts to end open defaecation. Adherence to sanitary practices and to proper personal and community hygiene was the most constructive step to promote health, prevent disease, increase the well-being of communities, and spare resources, both human and material. Dr Pathak had just announced his timely invention (p. 369 et seq,). Inflation was high then, corruption rampant, and Mrs Gandhi was blamed for all.

programmes. One of these was compulsory sterilisation, launched under Emergency rules, and promoted by the World Bank and IMF, both fearful of India's population growth and thus happy to find two corruptible so-called socialists running the country!

Sanjay was earlier awarded a contract to build the first indigenous Indian car, the *Maruti Udyog*, although there was no bidding and he had neither training nor experience in automotive production. His main advisor was Bansi Lal, Chief Minister of Haryana from 1968–75, (also 1985–87 and 1996–99), who became Defence Minister during the Emergency, and later Minister of Railways and Transport. Lal quit the INC in 1996 and started the *Haryana Vikas Party.* (Sanjay's wife, Menaka, and their son Varun also quit and later joined the BJP.)

Throughout her career, PM Indira Gandhi had given every indication of her strong will and contempt for rivals, but the tactic of declaring an emergency was barefaced and astonishing. The INC lost the elections of 1977 to the Janata Party under Jaiprakash Narayanan (no relation to Raj Narain), and she lost her seat. Earlier when she was found guilty of violating electoral laws by the Allahabad High Court, JP Narayanan called for her to resign, and advocated a program of social transformation which he termed *Sampoorna krānti* (total revolution). Instead, the proclamation of a national Emergency on June 25, 1975, forestalled that, and she asked the military and the police to disregard unconstitutional and "immoral" orders. JP, opposition leaders, and dissenting members of her own party—the "'*young Turks*"—were arrested. The decree of "Emergency" was not justified by any evidence of a *grave emergency* threatening the security of India as mentioned in the promulgation. There was no assessment or report on the files; no report on any "internal disturbance"; no major threat to law and order, or mass violence from any State Government, or Central or State agency.

Prime Minister Indira Gandhi's letter to the President on June 25, 1975, saying that '*there is an imminent danger to the security of India being threatened by internal disturbance*' was all! That assertion abruptly changed a working democracy into a personal autocracy on the basis of a false and hasty declaration by the Prime Minister. The files show signatures of the President and Home Minister but none of the Prime Minister's. Only a typed copy of the original letter sent by her is available. So dispirited and passive had the nation become that the Gandhis were able to impose this on the people, and other acts, such as sterilisation and the bull-dozing of slums in cities. (*See http://www.rediff.com/freedom/30rajan.htm.)*

One of the troubling issues at the time was the way Mrs Gandhi had pushed amendments to the constitution, apart from those required by creation of new states or language recognition or change of status. Any that tended to alter the structure of the constitution was questioned, such as the 21st amendment of Nov 1971, which allowed Parliament to "dilute fundamental rights". Mrs Gandhi's unabashed desire to dictate and assume more and more power as Prime Minister—directly or through Parliament, rather like Jinnah at the birth of Pakistan—was widely known. The protection of the Constitution from a threat to its integrity—and directly to democracy—was the essence of the case brought against the Government in 1973 by Kesavananda Bhārati.

Lawyer N. A. Palkhivala argued for the plaintiff, Bhārati, and a 13-judge panel narrowly ruled 7-6 in his favour. The 39th Amendment sought to overlook malpractice in the election of the President, Vice-President, Speaker and Prime Minister, while the 41st barred anyone from *ever* filing any type of complaint against these officers or the governors. Both were obvious attempts to quash Judge Sinha's 1975 ruling against Mrs Gandhi and were brazenly done. In the ensuing years, the INC has erected many permanent memorials to her memory but, not unsurprisingly, none to those who saved democracy from her anger and tyranny in the turbulent 1970s. The Supreme Court has since struck down the "law" banning senior prosecutions.

The performance of the INC in its first thirty years had displeased many. Internal critics were ignored and many left the INC in disgust. They included famed multilingual Sankritist and Professor Dr Raghuvira (also written Raghu Vira), whose extensive expertise and achievements included study of Buddhism and Hinduism in China, a monumental English-Hindi dictionary, coinage of over 100,000 Sanskrit-based words for Hindi, and a translation of the Indian constitution into Hindi. He was a member of the INC and the Rajya Sabha, had disagreed with Nehru's China policy, and saw his warnings ignored; he was amply justified when China invaded Tibet in 1959 and India in 1962.

He thus left the INC, joined the *Jan Sangh (JS)*, became its President and supported JS's Deendayal Upadhaya's concept of *integral humanism,* announced in 1965—but known in India since 2000 BCE—which urged a middle course between capitalism and communism, and advocated *Swadeshi* (self-sufficiency) and decentralisation. It reflected the essence of Gandhian humanism indicated by Gandhi's *"seven social sins: (1) politics without principles; (2) wealth without work; (3) commerce without morality; (4) knowledge without character; (5) pleasure without conscience; (6) science without morality; and (7) worship without sacrifice."* It was argued that *"the twenty-first (century) should bring a synthesis of science and spirituality, socialism with human rights, social change with non-violence, national sovereignty with world citizenship."*

Upadhaya's *integral humanism* was supported by many intellectuals, including Justice V.M. Tarkunde, a defender of civil rights, and was adopted by the Jan Sangh and later the BJP. Dr Raghu Vira was killed in a car accident on May 14, 1963 at the height of his genius and has proved irreplaceable. Five years later, Upadhaya was persuaded to accept the Presidency of the JS, but was killed shortly after in a train, and his body discarded near the junction at Mughalsarai, UP. Thus, in short order India lost three of its most gifted political intellects, its top nuclear physicist and in 1971, his successor, a man of similar genius, all under suspicious circumstances!

This period of discontent also saw the rise of the Naxalite Communists, started by Kanu Sanyal in 1967 in the West Bengal village of Naxalbari, a largely agricultural district, agitating for rights in Bihar, Odisha, Madhya Pradesh, Maharashtra, Kerala, Andhra Pradesh and wherever land reform was an issue. Also, they wished to curb the hegemony and corruption of land owners, but their message failed on the clash between Maoists and Marxists-Leninists. Indian Maoists were thought likely to resort to violence, if threatened with eviction.

Recently, Maoists have promised peaceful protest with focus on preventing the corporate take-over of tribal lands in states identified as rich in minerals, and wish to protect forest lands as well. Mining would destroy both agriculture and forests and pollute surface and underground water—ending a way of life for many, just to enrich a few—with dire long-term consequences. Some affirm that *swidden* agriculture, which has saved forests and soil for millennia, would be just as rewarding, preferable and of long term benefit, by providing food and shelter to local inhabitants, rather than wealth to multinationals and their Indian partners, and poverty to the poor.

It seems that India is bent on following the development model of the United States, based on individualism, materialism and laissez-faire capitalism through multinational corporations, supported by a modern Christian ethos that allows these things and regards them as "inalienable" rights and values. But this model has failed to safeguard ecosystems or the interests of majorities, and has poisoned the bulk of North America in less than 300 years of existence. Perhaps India should revisit its US deals and promote only those that have preserved pure water and soil. And rein in profligate uses of pure water for toxic industries, like "soft drinks". Coca Cola, for instance, uses 3 litres of water to produce one litre of Coke and has a long history of pesticide-contaminated products (India) and poor human relations (Colombia). Recently, it lost a decision in Varanasi and was ordered to close a plant.

A similar order closed a plant in Kerala 10 years ago and a compensation award for affected users has still to be paid. The losers here are the poor consumers who have swallowed the advertising line and its tainted drink, and bought an American craze, assuming that the product is the same and has some merit. But while Indian Coke had about *36 times the pesticide residues allowed*, US samples had none! What this reveals is that Coca Cola is a callous bully that breaks Indian laws with impunity. The actions against Coca Cola, and, separately, PepsiCo, came from farmers and consumers' complaints, not inspection! One can guess why, in a climate of such pervasive corruption and bribery as India's. *(See www.slideshare.net/madhavtarun38/coke-india-case).*

A major problem, inherited from the British, was the shortfall in food grains in certain states, and the fears of adequately feeding the growing Indian population. In 1961, Minister C. Subramaniam invited American geneticist Norman Borlaug to India to discuss the strain of microbe resistant wheat he had announced in a 1953 paper.[130] In 1965, the Minister headed the development and planting of a high-yield strain of rice, and by 1970, India had expanded production, initiating the *Green Revolution*. The key elements were use of high yield seeds, e.g. K68 wheat developed by Dr MP Singh; and irrigation to promote a double crop in suitable areas, since monsoon-reliance will cover one crop, and chemicals to control weeds and pests, plus tube wells will support the other.

The *Green Revolution* was pushed by the USA's Rockefeller and Ford Foundations globally, and by USAID, other US agencies and Canada's International Development Research Council (IDRC), hoping that its success would weaken Marxist political and economic positions. The International Rice Research Institute (IRRI) was established in the Philippines and was breeding several hybrid seeds to meet specific needs. The Indian Government adopted their IR-8 semi-dwarf variety of rice, which improved yield, but needed costly irrigation and fertilisers.

By hybridising IR-8 with other varieties, Dr Gurdev Singh Khush at IRRI had by 1990 developed numerous variants, including 1R 36, 1R 64 and 1R 72. IR 36 became popular worldwide, matured in 105 days, vs 130 days for IR-8, and a month longer for regular strains. Annual rice output rose from 257 to 626 million tons. New water-resistant strains promised relief for flood-prone areas.

The current involvement of the Gates Foundation in food genetics continues the funding support given by the above-named Foundations to food research through IRRI, International Food Policy Research Institute (IFPRI), Washington, DC, USA, and similar bodies. IFPRI is funded in part by the US government and is said to have a CIA footprint.

By 1974, India became self-sufficient in wheat. This brought prosperity to Sikh farmers who began to relax the constraints of Sikhism in spending their new wealth, favouring western "toys", especially TV's,

---

[130] Borlaug, N.E. *New approach to the breeding of wheat varieties resistant to Puccinia graminis tritici.* Phytopathology, 43:467 1953. Borlaug owns the patent. See also *http://www.indiaonestop.com/Greenrevolution.htm*

stereo systems, appliances and cameras, then trickling in under licences and regulations. Sikhs were rebuked by their clerics for failing to wear the five Ks that identified them: *Kacchera* (piece of undergarment), *Kangha* (small wooden comb), *Kara* (steel or iron bracelet), *Kesh* (uncut long hair) and *Kirpan* (short dagger). In that year, India and Iran settled their differences stemming from the Bangladesh war and signed an oil agreement, whereby Iran supplied some 75% of India's crude oil needs.

In 1975, Sikkim and Arunachal Pradesh became new states. For two decades, the Kashmiri line of control had remained ill-defined at the remote and lofty eastern end. In response to requests from mountaineers, both India and Pakistan had begun to issue permits allowing access to the area. The uncertainty of ownership had existed for over a decade. Increased Pakistani movements in the area of the Siachem glacier prompted India to secure their claim. It launched *Operation Meghdoot* in April 1984, by air and land, secured the passes to the glacier and established India's position days before the Pakistanis reached the area, only to be defeated yet again. The Indian Army secured, and now controls the 70 km. long Siachem glacier and its tributaries, plus the three key western access passes.[131] The glacier remains a point of dispute between the two countries.

About the same time a movement led by Sikh cleric Sant Jarnail Singh Bhindranwale inveighed against the moral breaches among his fellows and firmly promoted the resumption of basic values, taking his message across the Punjab, but generally avoiding politics, particularly the issue of a separate state *(Kalistan)*. He spoke harshly of his critics and when one of them, a newspaper editor, was killed in 1981, Bhindranwale denied involvement, but nevertheless was arrested; he was later cleared of the crime. His militant advocacy continued, and, in 1982, he was allowed to occupy the Akal Takht complex in the Golden Temple, Amritsar; he continued to speak out against various individuals and amassed weapons, causing fears of a Sikh uprising.

In June 1984, Mrs Gandhi responded to this with Army *Operation Blue Star,* to disarm the Temple. Gunfire ensued, with casualties, and the Army invaded the temple. Both sides suffered losses, dead and wounded: 83 killed and 249 injured for the army, and 493 and 86 for Sikhs, including Bhindranwale. In the aftermath, Pakistan was accused of supplying the Sikhs with weapons, which included AK47s.

But a worse fate befell Indira Gandhi, when her Sikh bodyguards killed her four months later, in October 1984. Thousands of Sikhs were assassinated by INC followers to avenge the murder. Her rule had

---

[131] http://www.bharat-rakshak.com/MONITOR/ISSUE6-1/Siachen.html

angered many, but she had managed to forge ahead, in her imperious way, and had achieved some gains. The economy grew by 5.4%; agriculture improved, and the inflation rate was contained. The balance of payments remained a challenge and deteriorated during the seventh 5-year plan, headed by Rajiv Gandhi, who was pulled, by his mother's death, from his Air India job to the Presidency of the INC and the Prime Ministership of India; this began 32 days later.

Like his mother, he was a populist; he focussed on developing communications technology, easing central control and the need for licences and regulations. He supported and participated in the growth of a globalised economy, but was fairly loose with spending and became entangled in several scandals: the Bofors gun funding, Union Carbide poisoning of Bhopal (p. 375-6) and Shah Bano (p. 398), among others. India's withered reputation for official honesty worsened, if such was possible, and regard for the welfare and betterment of the poor fell far short of the plan's promises. The poor continued to get poorer, while a series of scandals consumed the nation, some with foreign involvement. This involvement in corruption led to the INC defeat in 1989, and his failure to fulfil the wishes of the LTTE *(Liberation Tigers of Tamil Elam)* re their struggle for independence in Sri Lanka, led to his killing, in 1991, by Tamils, during his campaign for re-election.

L: Indira Gandhi
R: Rajiv Ganddhi http://www..iloveindia.com/indian heroes/rajivgandhi.htm)l

Chapter 24

"At least two thirds of our miseries spring from human stupidity, human malice, and those great motivators and justifiers of malice and stupidity: idealism, dogmatism and proselytising zeal on behalf of religious or political idols. Aldous Huxley

Globalisation, America, Toilets and Terrorism (GATT)

The decade of the 1990s would show, unfortunately, that the extravagant promises and euphoria of the *"Green Revolution"* would fade and result in hardship and high cost, and even suicides. With use of select varieties and growing aids, as noted,—chemicals, drenching and genetic modification—rice yields in India had increased from 34 million to 74 million tons in 1990 (*source: Directorate of Economics and Statistics*). But the shift to commercial large-scale farming, with export contracts that profited a limited set of businesses, brought hardship and malnutrition to the poor by changing land use from food e.g. pulses, ground nuts and vegetables, to grain and export crops, and favouring inorganic monocultures, with attendant loss of species, as in BEICo days. Those opposed to monocultures argued that traditional ways preserved crop varieties and relied on manure, natural selection and symbiosis for healthy cultivations; they used less water and avoided chemicals whose run-off killed aquatic life—a source of protein—and edible "weeds" (for man and animals) that flourished in rice fields.

Indian governments have been over-eager to dump indigenous methods for highly-touted foreign, especially "scientific" American ones, some poorly tested, but powerfully supported, from the start. The Indian populace was already seduced by US glitz, slick advertising, bribes, obesity, prizes and other inducements, rather than safe, dependable and reliable outcomes. For Rao's government, it didn't help that he had succumbed to the narrow economics of privatisation, globalisation by multinational corporations, and low corporate taxes, which *prima facie* seem the last things that would benefit the bulk of the Indian population.

The middle class, and aspiring generations, were more easily enticed by things American than the poor, who were less exposed to, spared being mesmerized by the flashiness portrayed on TV and movie screens, then spreading across the nation. American corporations established themselves quickly, as soon as the *World Trade Organisation* (WTO) was formed on January 1, 1995, and essentially replaced its creator GATT (the *General Agreement on Trade and Tariffs*). India had joined GATT in 1948, an instrument of American corporatism, which *happened* to benefit mainly capitalists, Indian and other, and under WTO rules, India, like other countries, has grown billionaires, improved GDP, but failed to improve the lot of its 300 million poor, who have instead gotten poorer.

If Indians today recalled the BEICo, the *Rāja*, Naoroji's speeches on the drain of valuables from India to Britain *(Bibliography)* and the size of the US deficit, now 17 trillion and rising, they might think differently, eschew short-term wealth, and concentrate on achieving true independence and prosperity. Those who dismiss the past and urge "let's move on", forget that moving on calls for a clear start, a goal and a firm track on which to move.

India forgets, or so it seems, that it can muster a billion consumers to back a sensible and fair programme. But its loyalties must become, as Y. Holkar had said 200 years ago, "country first". If any Government can build trust in its population—mainly by being fair and considerate—it would have the force and the stamina to resist the inevitable censures and sanctions, which Western hegemonies (currently G7, G8, BIS) are quick to dispense, from self-interest. By improving the purchasing power (PPP) of the average citizen, India can thrive on internal commerce for long enough to convince the world that it could eschew the WTO, IMF and World Bank, all of which are tools of American business, and the US army the means to ensure compliance. The recent formation of the BRICS bank is a welcome development, if the partners can avoid Rothschild, gain autonomy and have the nerve and stamina to sustain and expand it.

Leaders of Brazil, Russia, India, China and South Africa (BRICS) held closed-door talks in Brasilia with counterparts from Argentina, Chile, Colombia, Ecuador, Venezuela and other South and Central American nations. Modi is front, third from left. (www.kaieteurnewsonline.com)

An example of defiance is the advance in nuclear physics that India achieved, when it was forced by American obstacles to find ways of filling its own needs. US embargos lasted nearly 30 years until 2005; in that time, diligence and the need to be self-sufficient in nuclear fuel enabled Homi Bhābhā to develop the thorium-based model for the long term. Scientists also discovered a way to obtain uranium from carbide to feed its atomic reactors for energy. In 1985, Ramanna noted that the Indian nuclear industry was the first to use a plutonium-uranium carbide fuel and did not need enriched uranium, a product not made in

India. By ending the embargo, the US shared in, and benefit from the technology, four decades after the killing of Bhābhā, its creator.

Between May and July, 1999, Pakistan infiltrated Kargil, J&K. India retaliated and drove them out, both sides losing troops *(Time, July 12, 1999).* One month later, a Pakistan Air Force *Atlantique* surveillance aeroplane was brought down inside Indian territory at the Rann of Kacch. 16 Pakistanis died, including five naval officers. A month later, a Pakistani jet fired at an Indian helicopter carrying newsmen near the border. The Kargil action ended with improvement in India-US and India-Israel relations. But it took "cricket diplomacy" – Pakistan's desire to resume international cricket – to improve relations between India and Pakistan. Still, that softening of official relations did not altogether stop acts of *al Qaeda* terrorism; they have continued.

On Sept 11, 2001 the destruction of the World Trade Centre in New York gave US President Bush the excuse to wage war against the Taliban and Osama bin Laden, the Arab credited with the disaster, and last seen in Afghanistan, which Bush duly invaded. It is instructive of US methods that it had armed bin Laden to fight against Russian invaders of Afghanistan in 1989, and thereafter destabilised the entire region. The 10-year duration of the war gave cover to terrorist groups and continued support to Pakistan's dictator, Gen. Musharraf, whose deep animosity towards India kept both sides on high alert, and the MIFC very pleased.

While these events were taking place, a quiet revolution of equal human and environmental significance had begun, complementing the work of Dr Vandana Shiva and others promoting organic farming and exposing the evils of corporate agribusiness (Monsanto Corp. and others in the USA and Europe), which had obtained a heavily tainted foothold in India, against scientific advice. An unusual scientist, Dr Bindeshwar Pathak, a Bihar Brahmin, undertook the daunting task – really a Government responsibility – of emancipating some of the most neglected people in Indian society and enhancing their lives: the *impures* (Chamars and Daushads), and *untouchables* (Doms) – now called Dalits – whose main livelihood was scavenging and other menial tasks, e.g., removal of faeces from homes. At that time, and still in many places today, people defaecated in buckets in their premises, or outdoors on any vacant lot, among which railway property and open spaces were popular.[132] Open defaecation is a common ancient practice; but it remains a health hazard.

[132] The first faecal field I saw was in Dhaka, Bangladesh in 1974, quite close to the medical school, which the Dean said was a sign of the country's social neglect by Pakistan. The WHO's local representative Dr Sam Street, a Jamaican friend for years, and of Indian ancestry, had prepared a comprehensive water control and sanitation plan for the city and

It is and social embarrassment, worsening as populations expand. It must be curbed, if for no other reason than to promote elementary hygiene, improve human dignity and, especially, to reduce the economic burden of diarrhoeal diseases which had been costed at many times the provision of public toilets. Dr Pathak found that few homes had toilets; the well-off had installed septic tanks, and only about 250 cities out of some 5000 had a sewage disposal system. While others had slowly gained ground since 1947, scavengers had remained untouched by reform grants, neglected even by Mother Teresa's billions – most of which have not been seen anywhere, not even in Kolkata, her HQ. Focus on the sanitary issue changed when Dr. Pathak began, 40 years ago, to study Dalits and live and work among them. He came with Master's degrees in Social Sciences and Literature, and two doctorates: Philosophy and Literature, on *"liberation of scavengers"* and environmental sanitation. His studies led to the invention of a simple, clever, hygienic and effective technology to dispose of, sanitise and recycle human excreta. The basic unit consisted of a twin-pit, pour-flush toilet system, an ecologically friendly unit needing only 1.5 litres per flush; he called it the *Sulabh Shauchalaya.* In 1970, he founded the NGO *Sulabh Shauchalaya Sansthan* – today *Sulabh International Social Service Organisation (SISSO)* – to carry out reforms.

Dr B. Pathak

His system converted excreta to manure and captured the released biogas for use as a source of heat. Odours were channelled underground and rarely, if ever, escaped. The design could be scaled to available space, indoors or out, and a commercial model was available for public places; large apartment and office buildings; and meeting places like railway stations, temples, halls or equivalent. Most importantly, it eliminated degrading work, improved sanitation and reduced risks of diarrhoeal diseases. As workers gained relief from the shame of their daily lives, their rehabilitation and social elevation became Dr Pathak's focus. His invention freed females from the risks of toileting in the outdoors, usually at night, for privacy, if they could not afford the bucket service, which had reduced to "untouchables" those providing the service, a status that had imprisoned them for millennia (Pathak).

---

delta which the Government was keen to implement, in stages. Later I saw similar elimination along railway tracks near Delhi and in city slums quite close to first class city hotels. In London, England, I had walked along faecal streets where slop was regularly emptied;,and I had seen human faeces floating in a small stream on the outskirts of Paris.

What Dr Pathak did was extremely brave, self-effacing and far-seeing, and in a sense his innovation was as explosive locally in 1974, as Mrs Gandhi's "emergency" was nationally. He endured the wrath of family and friends which he has poignantly described in his book. In the 40 years since its start, SISSO has installed 1.2 million bucket conversions and 7,500 industrial units for municipalities, hospitals, apartment buildings, schools and temples. The largest of these, an impressive structure at Sai Baba shrine in Shirdi, Maharashtra, serves 30,000 users daily, purifies and recycles waste water for lawn irrigation and produces enough biogas for heating water and lighting. The solid residue is odourless and is used as a fertiliser. The system eliminates the need for bore-hole and pit latrines anywhere.

Girls and women wait for dark to go to the fields, checking that there are no men around. "The lotas are a giveaway," regrets one. But note figures lurking in the shadows.
Source: Express photo by Praveen Khanna)

Over 120,000 scavengers have been emancipated and trained to perform skilled work as artisans, clerks, auxiliaries etc. A key benefit is improved rates of "caste" and religious acceptance, and a change in attitude of Brahmins and others who have seen the transformation and become aware of the high international praise, which Indians value above all. The UN recognised both Dr Pathak and the former scavengers, who toured New York in their emancipated roles. Dr Pathak thus realised one of Mahatma Gandhi's major aims, perhaps the most impressive act towards Gandhi's dream that has occurred in India. The UNDP has recommended SS for use in deprived areas of Latin America, Africa and SE Asia. SISSO has created *Sulabh Sanitation and Social Reform Movement* (SSRM) to educate and inform, helped by thousands of volunteers, including the highest in government, to achieve social change and improve mobility, opportunity and respect for all. In 2010, he took a group of 36 women to the UN, where they displayed their new, enhanced skills in jobs previously closed to them and received an award.

The technology has created over fifty thousand (50,000) jobs and has been made available in Africa, Asia and Latin America, *free of royalties*. A small museum of toilets, at its headquarters in Delhi, summarises Dr Pathak's work as one of the most far-reaching reforms in India. The selfless release of his invention worldwide contrasts starkly with the greed and inhumanity of Westerners who patent first, put profit ahead of human need and dignity, and squeeze all they can, even from the poor. It is a refreshing contrast and highlights the endemic corruption of Indian politicians, businessmen, bureaucrats and police.

Dr Pathak has not found it easy. He complained, "*I have been working for the last 40 years, but not without opposition, criticism, hindrances and barriers, the wrath of some journalists, politicians, bureaucrats and others. Total abolition of scavenging, restoration of human rights and social dignity for the scavengers, total elimination of untouchability from society, promotion of a safe system of human excreta disposal in urban and rural areas as well as ensuring the security and safety of our natural water sources are the basis of our future dream and vision...Keeping in mind that technologies developed by me are free from patent, any organisation or country can adopt the same free of charges without any royalty and could help other countries to achieve the Millennium Development Goals not only on water and sanitation, but also on health, human rights, poverty alleviation etc.*"

One of the targets of the Millennium Development Goals for 2015 is to reduce by 50% the number of people without sustainable access to safe drinking water and sanitation. Noting that rivers and lakes make up only 0.6% of the world's 71% water, he emphasises the urgency of preventing waste and pollution. *Sulabh* can be justly proud. For his seminal work Dr Pathak became the 2009 *Stockholm Water Prize Laureate* at a Royal Award Ceremony and Banquet during World Water Week in Sweden. The citation read, in part, "*...Dr Pathak's endeavours constitute one of the most amazing examples of how one human being can affect the well-being of millions.*" This comes on top of 33 awards received since 1984 from Indian and international groups, including the UN, Vatican, Dubai and Brazil. The UN Environment Programme awarded Dr Pathak the *Global 500 Roll of Honour*, and more recently he gained the UN-Habitat *Global Urban Best Practices Award* and the *Scroll of Honour*.

The 2011 Indian census (see *www.censusindia.gov.in/2011)* showed a total of just over 247 million households; 53% had no latrines (69% rural, 18% urban), compared with 64% in 2001, i.e. an improvement of only 11% overall in ten years, despite having a cheap secure technology that in any other environment would have been adopted wholesale, or else legislated into general use. To that date, the Indian government had installed 54 million toilets, a fraction of the need.

Insanitary practices are more demeaning today, especially when the country can claim many billionaires—in US $ terms—any one of whom can provide 5 million households with a basic Pathak's toilet for half the cost of one lavish wedding in India or Europe. Billionaire steelmaker Lakshmi Mittal—whom Lewis Mumford (*Bibliography*) would call a *"carboniferous capitalist"*—paid an estimated $60 million (₹350 crore) for his daughter's Paris wedding, in 2004, to the banker son of another Indian tycoon. With all the extravagance, the event was beyond lavish, and just another vulgar display of self-indulgence among similarly well-heeled people, aiming to impress or outdo the others, a childish game still played by the world's wealthy or insecure Mittal lives in Britain and is one of many who prefer to pay taxes to India's erstwhile captor and exploiter. *(India Today,* July 5, 2004, *http://www.bigindianwedding.com*)

Mukesh Ambani lives in a 27-storey high-rise overlooking 19 seething millions in Mumbai, half of whom have no place to live, much less with dignity (*http://www.globalcommunities.org/*). How does one create and enjoy a palace of gold next to a filthy ghetto of cardboard and scrap? Similar callous excesses have been shown by other mega-rich Indians. Perhaps the Ambanis and their ilk will see the poor one day and finance a decent shelter for them, with some forward vision to help them help themselves, for their very survival is proof of their resourcefulness. Sai Baba is an example of a spiritual icon with a wide following and wealthy donors; he too could spend much more on the very poor instead of on structures and fetishes.

But rich Indians do donate huge sums *(see http://www.forbes.com)*. In 2012, Azim Premji of *Wipro* donated $1.34 billion (₹8,000 crore; 1cr=10M). Other large donors were HCL's Shiv Nadar $500M, G.M. Rao $124M and N & R Nilekani $89M. Education benefitted most, totalling $2.03B; social development $202M; healthcare $180M; rural development $94M; environment $30M and agriculture $6.7M. Vineet Nayyar, Rohinton Screwvala, Indu Jain, Kallam Reddy, PC Menon, Rakesh Jhunjhunwala and others remain consistent donors. It is hoped that a heavier emphasis on primary education will occur and enable the very young to gain its many benefits. Indian tycoons should consider a permanent mechanism to assist the hundreds of millions who lack education and opportunity. Perhaps a pool could be set up in each region to provide learning centres and nutrition programs. They could be coupled with other initiatives e.g. SISSO, to improve sanitation and curb diarrhoeal diseases in India's 690 districts. Better education is a prime catalyst for community upgrading.

Financial reports show that India has 65 billionaires, the richest Mukesh Ambani, whose charity is kept secret and probably confined to family projects. A contribution from him and many wealthy is likely to be small, and will probably remain so until Indians—most of whom are self-indulgent, new to big money, and have made hefty fortunes only since Rao's changes—can feel confident in government, in NGOs, in public trust, and get taxation support from Government. *Hurun India,* a Chinese publication, has listed 31 Indians who gave over ₹10 crore ($1.6 million) during fiscal 2012 (April 1, 2012 to March 31, 2013). Some potential donors are troubled, and thereby inhibited by the lax running of NGOs, many failing to meet business standards, and waste or misuse funds. Premji and others retain control of their Foundation Boards[134] to monitor and ensure prudent use of their donations. It is hoped that the climate of philanthropy will improve and encourage the rich to really assist the poor. The sheer magnitude of the need will call for something like the Gates-Buffet "pledge" to build, maintain and manage a sizeable fund. A few donors have begun this. But change in social attitudes must also occur, with acceptance on the basis of character and talent, not caste.

Respect for sanitation and cleanliness was one of the oldest expressions of Hindu culture. The Indus/Saraswati civilisation—Harappa and Mohenjodaro, each with about 100,000 people, were the first studied—had complex indoor plumbing, waste disposal systems, communal baths and other sophisticated infrastructure. The technology, like others of that time, was lost in whatever catastrophe ended that civilisation. Today's Indian cities must cope with enormous mounds of garbage, which, despite the revulsion they evoke, continue to be mined by humans for recyclables. Armies of workers, usually the poor and uneducated, mostly female, sort through the messy heaps, for $1 or so per day. This disgrace persists in the shadow of the filthy rich!

When ex-Minister Jairam Ramesh remarked in Oct., 2012 that India had more temples than toilets—an obvious exaggeration, unwisely made and poorly-timed (he could have said mosques or churches)—some Hindus, BJP and the INC, bristled and responded, equally thoughtlessly, that temples were more important than toilets! They had missed the point entirely, prompting Dr Pathak to intervene and restate India's need for secure toilets to improve sanitation and women's rights. Hopefully, Ramesh's critics would look objectively at this national social disgrace and its implications for public health and female safety,[135] and the part his government had played in prolonging it. The high incidence of rape at night—when darkness offers the poor some privacy but also hides the

---

[134]http://www.forbes.com/sites/johnkoppisch/2013/05/29/
http://www.rediff.com/business/slide-show/www.reuters.com/.../us-india-philanthropy
http://www.deccanchronicle.com/content/tags/mukesh-ambani
[135]*http://www.thehindu.com/news/national/sulabh Oct 7, 2012*

work of rapists—should have already prompted authorities to install permanent structures to reduce female risk, and take advantage of SSRM's services to educate and inform, and to overcome ingrained barriers. Ignorance must give way to education, from programs to teach parents at home and children at school. Many charities try, but without serious impact. Perhaps INC President Sonia Gandhi, might consider applying a percentage of her alleged $2B fortune to this cause, the stated aim of the *Rajiv Gandhi Foundation*, and would commit her beyond Bareilly and Amethi. In Oct., 2014, *Swacch Bharat Abhiyan* (Clean India Mission) was launched by new PM Modi to replace the ailing *Total Sanitation Program* (INC, 1999), whose benefits had escaped rural Indians.

Since 1980, India has seen six 5-year plans, each with clearly stated objectives, about which much has been written. "The Sixth Five-Year Plan marked the beginning of economic liberalisation," ending price controls and closing ration shops. "Food prices and the cost of living rose. Nehruvian socialism ended."[136] Family Planning was encouraged or enforced to contain population growth. Birth rate fell naturally in thriving communities, where health care and sanitation had improved; it stayed high among the poor and in Muslim communities. There was no mandatory family size, as decreed in China.

The seventh Five-Year Plan had a shady start. Like the ones before, its aims were laudable, but the immediate events were alarming, to say the least. The Bhopal incident and other political scandals rankled. The economy provided new jobs, at 4% annual increase, to meet an expanding labour force expected to reach 40 million, (more than the entire population of Canada), and aiming for self-reliance by 2000 CE. Some controls were loosened.

On December 3 1984, an industrial tragedy occurred in Bhopal, Madhya Pradesh, at the Union Carbide Chemical plant, maker of *Sevin*, a pesticide. The factory process involved use of the deadly neurotoxin *methyl isocyanate* (MIC), which escaped; its vapours killed between 2-30 thousand people acutely, injured 558,125, many seriously maimed, most chronically disabled to some degree, with prolonged hospitalisation and regular premature deaths. Deemed the world's worst such event, it was attributed to poor maintenance and oversight, and criminal neglect by the owners. Two years earlier, an audit by UCC had shown "*a total of 61 hazards, 30 major, 11 minor in the dangerous phosgene/methyl isocyanate units*".[137] UCC Chairman, Warren Anderson, and ten others were

---

[136] Five year Plans of India *en.wikipedia.org/wiki* and *http://www.upscguide.com* et al.

[137] Total population exposure was estimated as well over 700,000. A Government affidavit in 2006 claimed 558,125 injured. UCC was initially sued for damages of $4.3 billion, which was reduced to $450 million, $200 million paid into PM Gandhi's Disaster Relief Fund.

criminally indicted in 1987, but Anderson had been "helped" out of India two days after visiting Bhopal in 1984, by persons alleged to be the Prime minister Rajiv Gandhi and/or Arjun Singh, Chief Minister of Madhya Pradesh, though the latter, who had hidden for two days in Allahabad at the time, would deny that in his autobiography (*Bibliography*). Singh claimed that Rajiv Gandhi had kept silent on the issue of Anderson's arrest after the event, and Gandhi had later enjoined him to confidentiality and secrecy, a promise Singh never broke. Singh died in 2011. In 2010 eight Indian officials in Bhopal were fined nominal amounts and received token "jail" sentences (Lapierre).

The matter has dragged on to today, and in the 1990s, implicated PM Narasimha Rao. The US Government refused to extradite Anderson, and various US courts have refused to hear a case against UCC (or later Dow Chemicals, which bought UCC in 2001). Mr Anderson, initially well-intentioned, retired and "disappeared". Victims have not been adequately compensated, and many still wait; animosity against the American principals runs high. It is interesting that in the immediate aftermath, UCC (USA) disclaimed any responsibility, attaching that entirely to UC India Ltd! India originally claimed over $4 billion in compensation, but Gandhi settled for $470 million. Consideration of the amount of compensation revealed an interesting valuation of foreigners by Americans. Estimating an American life as worth just under $600,000, an Indian was less than $6000, based on comparisons of the GDP of the two countries at the time. (Later on, in 1991, Larry Summers as chief economist for the World Bank, would justify exporting toxic US trash to poor countries, on the basis of comparative values of US versus third world citizens, in the ratio of 1:11; he had noted how easy it was to buy dumpsites from local officials in many countries, including India!)

The Bhopal tragedy, which is still in dispute, occurred soon after the Government had agreed in 1984 to purchase 410 Bofors field howitzers for $1.3 billion, Sweden's biggest arms deal ever. Rajiv Gandhi allegedly used a Sicilian friend, Ottavio Quadrocchi, as middleman, to handle millions in kickbacks that Bofors had agreed to pay to INC leaders. By the 1970s, graft had increased, like a rolling snowball down a snow-covered hill, so that by the end of the century, India had become one of the most corrupt places on earth, if not *the most*. Chitra Subramaniam was the journalist who exposed the Bofors scam, with data obtained from a Swedish whistle-blower. After years of tracking dishonesty in Indian politicians and officials, she was moved to write *"India is for sale"* (C. Subramaniam). Unfortunately, this accusation can be made of all governments, but some stand out; India's high-level corruption is matched or exceeded only by a few, including the Vatican, as detailed in the *Shroud of Secrecy* (Marinelli) and *God's Banker* (Posner), and had reached high levels in Canada under Brian Mulroney (Cameron).

Rajiv Gandhi had paid four visits in five years to Moscow and renewed ties and agreements with the USSR. Gorbachev had come to India in 1986 and 1988. The relationship remained sound. The negative external trade balance was expected to continue as an economic millstone. However, growth was reported as 6.01% vs the anticipated 5%. In 1988, anti-corruption laws were promoted, and as early as 1969 an ombudsman *(lokpal)* was mooted, to inspire transparency, but failed in Parliament, possibly because politicos were reminded of the dictum: *"there but for the grace of God go I"!*

Rajiv Gandhi gave way to VP Singh, from 1989 to 1990, Chandra Sekhar from 1990 to 1991, and Narasimha Rao for the term 1991-96; they all struggled with the balance of payments deficit; while in Eurasia, the USSR, under Boris Yeltsin, disintegrated, ending the Cold War, and adversely affecting India's $6 billion trade with the Soviets. Soon after, the USA invaded Iraq, to restore Kuwait and secure that source of oil.

The Dec 6, 1992, destruction of the Babri Masjid in Ayodhya, an act of desperation and frustration, led to the killing of over 3,000 people in irate exchanges between Islamists and Hindus. Islamists provoked it by irrationally rejecting Hindu claims of a destroyed temple there, despite the Archaeological Survey of India's evidence of the presence of a temple at the site, as noted in *Vaidic* texts. Interestingly this fact was not in question in those parts of the Diaspora that were spared the British *Rāja's* suppression of India's true history, nor in places where the history of Hinduism was learned at *kathas*, not from English textbooks.[139]

Secularists tend to dismiss everything Hindu as myth— easy to do as so much is written as metaphor or elaborate imagery—and thus disavow almost all of Indian history BCE. The Indian press as usual sympathised with the Islamic view. However, the *New York Times* and *Agence France Presse* headlined on Dec 8, 1992, *"Pakistanis Attack 30 Hindu temples"*. Muslim gangs damaged Air India offices and Hindu businesses in Pakistan and Bangladesh, clashed with Hindus, resulting in 900 dead. In 1993, the Mumbai Muslim mafia, headed by Dawood Ibrahim, Tiger Memon and others, bombed several sites in Mumbai and other cities, killing 350 Hindus in Mumbai and injuring 1200. Taslima Nasrin earned a fatwa for writing about anti-Hindu terror in her native Bangladesh. In a recent book, the secular Pakistani author, Reema Abbassi, said that *"It was a time that erased over 1,000 historic temples from Pakistan's landscape."*

PM Rao regretted the killings and bombings and offered relief. The aftermath would reveal India's need to prepare better and respond

[139] See this author's *The Indelible Red Stain*, Bk1, pp 11,128, 133 etc., Amazon, 2011

quicker to terrorists, who struck again in Mumbai in 2002, 2008 and 2011. Some convictions and one hanging have followed. But Dawood and Tiger Memon remain at large. The instability added to India's economic crisis. Rao removed controls on business, dismantling the "Licence Raj" and restrained labour activists. Did the USSR's *perestroika* have a role in this, one wondered? With Manmohan Singh as Finance Minister, INC did away with the pillars of Nehru's policies—socialism, non-alignment and democracy—not all prudently, and far more abruptly than warranted; thus, he allowed the country to fall to eager money men. "*Desperate maladies call for drastic remedies,*" Rao told the nation, stunned that this smart but "harmless" academic, this compromise candidate—who had become possible only because of Rajiv Gandhi's murder, while campaigning—had come out with fists flying. "*This is the beginning. A further set of far-reaching changes and reforms is on the way ... we believe the nation, as well as the government, must learn to live within its means ... there is much fat in government expenditure. This can, and will, be cut.*"

Instead, he began the Americanisation of India, its capture by the West, replacing *chapatis* with corn flakes and KFC (*Kentucky Fried Chicken)*; water with Coke; caution with credit cards; and modesty in films with female nakedness, swivelling hips, explicit sex and violence. The language acquired absurd usages of US slang. Copying American styles in food and clothing became a pathetic fad among the privileged as a mark of chic, as it had been before for things British. In 1995, India joined the World Trade Organisation. "*I.Me.Mine*" became the national slogan on billboards and it was finally okay for Indians with means to show off, including nude female bodies to Hugh Hefner of *Playboy*, USA, while the majority of their fellows had little, sometimes nothing to eat.

Prior to this, India had had a close economic relationship with the USSR, cemented by periodic exchanges of visits by leaders between 1949 and 1994, excluding visits prior to 1947. Although initial relations with Stalin was justifiably strained—Stalin believing that Nehru was a Commonwealth stooge—they improved with his successors and led to agreements of friendship and cooperation. The first was signed in 1971, to extend for twenty years. Trade was conducted in national currencies, sparing India scarce hard currency. Agreements also covered arms and military matters, including space technology.

When the USSR collapsed, India had to revise its relationships with all the constituent republics, but retained its reliance on Russia for certain technologies, notably in the space and nuclear programs. One special aid was the provision of cryogenic engines for ISRO, but US sanctions against the Russian space agency, *Glavkosmos,* prevented delivery. Nevertheless, ISRO carried on with its researches to develop a *Geosynchronous Satellite Launch Vehicle (GSRV)* and did eventually get some engines from Russia to speed its work. It was its own engine design, however, that helped launch the GSRV in late July 2014, though not without some controversy, two scientists being accused of giving secrets to two females from the Maldives in an alleged sex plot, later disproved. *See http://spaceflightnow.com/gslv/d5/140105launch*

Under Rao's plan, the nation prospered, at least its businessmen, their American partners and the middle class. This came about, as already noted, by *laissez-faire* capitalism that ignored the poor, and long-standing promises to help them. They became poorer still, as if that were possible for the portion of the nation, who had less than nothing. They were uneducated and lived in squalor, which Dr Pathak was valiantly trying to ease, for his part, by improved sanitation. But, following WTO rules, business taxes were eased to an extent that the richest paid little. The West praised Rao, as they swarmed India to cash in. The GNP rose. Money exports zoomed. The rich got richer; the poor remained poor.

Rao improved relations with his neighbours, came to terms with Israel and welcomed PLO leader, Yasser Arafat. Meanwhile, Indians at large groaned under the burdens of supporting the extravagant lifestyles of the very rich. These were few while nearly 500,000,000 (out of a total~850M) struggled to eke out an existence, burdened by high prices for simple basics: rice, clothing, shelter. That his eagerness to conform to globalisation dictates, his policies too hastily executed, his methods undemocratic and dictatorial even, and his legacy a gift to the West, cannot be argued. His policies led to the decline in morals in the film industry, the day he allowed Hollywood laxity and immorality to swamp Mumbai[140]. An increasing number of Indians sought economic opportunities in the expanding Persian Gulf states.

Rao guaranteed the continued malnutrition of hundreds of millions by allowing American processed (fast) foods to entice the gullible middle class with fancy advertising, which drew them to modish joints that peddled Western poison. A modicum of research would have persuaded him, and subsequent governments, to avoid this fare. The naïve mass of this ancient nation was ill-prepared for the invasions, but was dragged

[140] The catalogue of lowered morals is lovingly displayed by India's press and TV. One recent example fulsomely tells of the extent of decadence; others deal with actresses baring their privates! "*After Sherlyn Chopra, Veena Malik and Poonam Pandey, Nikita will pose nude for the 'Playboy' photo shoot,*" gushes a Marathi website. "*Nikita will bare her assets for the Hollywood adult magazine 'Playboy' founded by Hugh Hefner. Nikita hails from Nagpur and has done a number of modelling assignments in the past. She has recently done the photo shoot for the auditions of the Playboy magazine. These photos have been sent to the selectors. If the photos get approved by Hugh, then post Sherlyn, Nikita will be the second Indian model to pose nude for the magazine.*" (Times of India Feb 17, 2014, 12.36 PM IST). Such demeaning pride and fawning to a hack, from a major paper in a country that produced the *Kamasutra, Koka Shastra and Chandella's* temple sculpture, yet whose females were praised for their elegant modesty.

along by the middle class, which slavishly adopted them, more from adulation and vicarious participation in Americana, than taste, value or quality. Local politicians and businessmen grew rich. A visit to Washington in 1994 buoyed Rao's spirits and his resolve. The US take-over was swift. *"We are now the largest bilateral trading partner and investor with India. We're proud of that, and we want that relationship to grow,"* Bill Clinton gushed, on May 19, 1994. *(See http://www.presidency.ucsb.edu/ws/)*

One of those new trading partners, Monsanto, had long coveted India as a market and had brought chemical "wonders," the latest in biotechnology, promising to revolutionise Indian agriculture yet again, and enrich all, even the poorest. This maker of poisons: DDT, PCBs, Agent Orange (2,4D etc.), bovine growth hormone, and Roundup (the herbicide glyphosate), had stumbled upon a gene, abbreviated *Bt*, from the bacterium *Bacillus thuringiensis*, whose product was resistant to glyphosate. Monsanto could thus modify a seed to make the plant Round-up resistant, allowing closer planting and sure yields—music to every farmer's ears. And so they danced to Monsanto's tunes.

Much has been written to justify the global use of such genetically engineered[142] (GE) seeds. The technique is promising and still requires much independent research to establish its safety, especially in the long-term, to farmers and consumers, and more objective data than a poison-maker's dossier of a 13-week study using 20 rats per group (Burns)!

Genetic modification (GM) of plants is not new. Properly and scientifically performed it should achieve improvements; indeed initial trials by biotechnology companies did show this, but before any new technology can be generally applied, it should be widely tested and harmful effects identified (Shiva). Instead, the zeal of profiteering led to premature usage after inadequate study and abuse of a revolving door practice between Monsanto and the regulators—the US Food and Drug Administration (USFDA) and the Department of Agriculture (USDA)—that harked back to Donald Rumsfeld's tenure, from 1977, as CEO of GD Searle, a pharmaceutical company for which Rumsfeld had "arranged", with President Raegan's knowledge, the approval of the toxic sweetener, *Aspartame*, in 1981, over scientific objections. Searle was acquired by Monsanto in 1985, despite the latter's knowing of the tarnished product.

Armed with US approvals, obtained in the 1990s in similar manner, Monsanto "persuaded" most of North America, and other countries, including India, China, parts of Europe, Australia and most of South

---

[142]Oxfam International (2011) *Growing a better future: Food justice in a resource-constrained world* http://www.oxfam.org/en/grow/reports/growing-better-future (accessed 3 June 2011); and http://responsibletechnology.org/docs/gm-crops-do-not-increase-yields.pdf; also see Bibliography: V Shiva; J. Smith; M. Ragbeer etc.

America to adopt its *Bt* gene-modified cotton, corn and soya seeds, touting high yield, disease resistance and low cost. An early user was Gujarat under Modi, now India's PM, who authorised his head of tribal affairs, Anand Mohan Tiwari, to try "high yield" seeds for maize (corn) crops. Government subsidy for the first two years made seeds affordable; crop successes and growth of tribal farming were credited to GM seeds. One Indian writer endorsed GM seeds and advised, "*Since the government has opened up a virgin market for them, private seed companies must cut down the price of seed to tempt the farmers with bigger gains. The maize research institute must also step up production of the seed. Its Gujarat Makkai-6 hybrid is said to be as good if not better than Monsanto's, and takes a shorter time to mature.*" (V. Fernandes).

But the outcomes were troubling, as with previous chemo-agriculture: seed and soil degradation; killing of symbiotic weeds and beneficial soil microbes; loss of diversity; increased use of water and need for costly irrigation, fertilisers, pesticides and herbicides (essential for *Bt* monocultures); loss of common food crops, e.g., vegetables, pulses, and others, due to seed sequestration by company owners; community squabbling over water; bankruptcies; and so on, the very things that had led to Naxalite protests in eastern India.

The cost spiral was merciless. Farmers traditionally used their own seed stocks, practised crop rotation, used few chemicals, farmed within limits of affordability and usually had excess produce. The GM methods, however, required costly annual seed and chemical purchases, and often loans and contracts for irrigation and regular application of chemicals. The costs bankrupted many farmers, and their small holdings were taken over by larger growers. The Indian record has been poor, with countless failures and over 300,000 farmer suicides up to 2012.

Moreover, long-term adverse effects, biological and social, are slowly emerging. Various illnesses, respiratory and digestive, in farmers and consumers, have occurred, but denied by Monsanto, a dubious claim since it has refused to allow independent study of its *Bt* seeds. However, ill effects have surfaced with experience in the field, and now include an insidious chronic kidney failure—newly identified in the last two decades—among those exposed to use of *Bt* seeds. Many now agitate for proper labelling of GM foods and products, to ensure informed choice, and follow-up of those who consume them. Monsanto resists disclosure, and the US Government itself seems bent on throttling consumer protests. Scientists, farmers and consumers would prefer a moratorium on GM foods, pending proper study of the agents in use or imminent, especially as the US administration has acted so faithlessly, the latest being the threat of prosecution of anyone criticising Monsanto, using HR 933, the *Monsanto Protection Act* passed by US Congress in 2013!

The campaign of Indian activist and organic farmer, Vandana Shiva and others, exposed this danger and highlighted the drawbacks of chemo-agriculture which is invariably monoculture, no different from the former imposition of opium and other plantation crops by the imperial British that led, under their rule, to famines, malnutrition and rural poverty, as related earlier. Traditional Indian agriculture, based on natural multiculture, had fed millions before that, with surplus for export or for lean years, and for seed, as replicated in the Diaspora.

While genetically modified grains have initially boosted calorie intake, they lack flavour and are quite sticky, and fail to supply certain trace elements and vitamins needed to avoid specific deficiency diseases. Moreover, they may be linked to cancer—as alleged in Punjab—blood and lung diseases. Agrochemicals cause chemical poisoning of symbiotic plant and animal life, essential to the diets of the poor, as noted above.

GM cotton treated with the *Bt* gene was introduced to India and accepted by the Government, on Monsanto's word and "persuasion," and US government endorsement, despite protests and knowledge that Monsanto's study lasted a mere 13 weeks. Dr Shiva has explained the devastation to be expected from continued use of Bt cotton, in a well-crafted response to a careless article in the *New Yorker* magazine that blatantly flies the Monsanto and GM flags. She has been careful to point out that in the 1990s, under Monsanto's monopoly, cotton seeds in India went from ₹5-10 to ₹3,555.55 per kg, an increase of 71,111%! (see *New Yorker: Seeds of Doubt, Aug 25,2014.)*

Bhopal, the Bofors Gun scandal, Babri Masjid and the Mumbai bombings were headlines still. But Narasimha Rao, after his Washington visit in 1994, was convinced that Bill Clinton had taken to him and therefore he could do no wrong. Monsanto came in under his watch, when Indian scientists in the wake of Bhopal, were querying the benefits of agrochemicals and molecular manipulation (see *Bibliography*). They were doubly suspicious of Monsanto, which rejected independent scientific study of its products, contrary to normal scientific practice, and as required by US Patent law, to provide objective data on long term behaviour and safety.

Monsanto's caginess and bullying have fed the belief that it is hiding data, and prefer to approach R&D via US executive and political pockets, (cf. Rumsfeld and *Aspartame, http://www.rense.com/general33/legal.htm).* Monsanto retains control of the USDA and relevant Government policy; it stands suspected of bribing key politicians and bureaucrats in many countries, including India—a most fertile soil for bribery—to bypass regulations and get its products approved, despite deficient supporting data, claiming process secrecy and patent protection. It has been quick to sue farmers worldwide whose fields became contaminated with *Bt* seeds. Monsanto is uniformly despised and rejected in many countries, a situation that impedes GM research, but could change, if Monsanto becomes more transparent or civilised. Instead, the US administration has, as noted, bowed to Monsanto's aggressive lobbying and moved to protect it, not the public, by legislation! Even the fact of lowering water tables, in areas with GM crops, has not impressed the US government.

Hardly had India tallied the human cost of Bhopal, Monsanto's Indian agents were peddling *Bt* cotton, soya, potato and other seeds on the banks of the holy Narmada River. When India later gave Monsanto initial assent to start planting *Bt brinjal*—despite partial data, directly and through their Indian surrogates, and against the urging of Indian scientists—T.V. Jagadishan, former managing director of Monsanto (India) testified, *"Introducing Bt brinjal in India will be disastrous."*

Resistance to corporate agribusiness has led to organisations, like *Via Campesina.*[144] In 2003, the Indian state of Sikkim was declared an organic zone; agrochemical subsidies were stopped and replaced by composting and vermiculture.[145] Borlaug and Monsanto defend their patented "cash cows", dismissing organic farming and anything Indian as "primitive."

But their "green revolution" has proven to be one of diminishing returns. Today many rice farmers are switching to the *System of Rice Intensification (SRI)* by organic methods developed in Madagascar by Jesuit priest Henri La Laulanié[146] and championed by Cornell University's Norman Uphoff. Encouraging, if not enthusiastic results of an unexpected increase in yields, have been reported in Bihar among small farmers, without chemicals, plus lowered water use and costs, and improvement in income and nutrition. Large operations, it seems, have balked at the increased labour required, but do not appear to have tested whether the benefits of the new plants offset the increased cost of labour, or whether the social benefits of increased employment lessen the fears of possible reduced profit. India, and other countries that adopt the SRI method, may well be reviving the more natural and sustainable way of farming to supply healthy food to consumers, while avoiding the myriad problems due to hasty inorganic and poorly tested GM agriculture.[148]

Agricultural reform has shown recent gains in method and yield, with the adoption of cleaner, more organic farming methods, which, not

---

[144]Borras Jr., Saturnino M. *"La Vía Campesina and its Global Campaign for Agrarian Reform"*, Journal of Agrarian Change 8, no. 2/3, 1 April, 2008: 258-289.

[145] *"Vision for holistic and sustainable organic farming in Sikkim--the Future thrusts."* Government of Sikkim. Retrieved 13, February 2013.

[146] H. De Laulanié, *Intensive Rice Farming in Madagascar,* Tropicultura, 2011, 29, 3, 183-7

[148] Norman Uphoff for SciDevNet October 16, 2013: *New approaches are needed for another Green Revolution.* See also *National Geographic Magazine*, Oct, 2014.

surprisingly, mimicked those of ancient India; yields were good, sturdy varieties restored and naturally resistant strains and symbionts identified. Multiculture is improving but change will have to await the slow return of new resistant organic seeds, and until India can purge itself of the rampant corruption that skews all major transactions, from seeds to guns and submarines, in favour of the bribing partners. India's secular rulers did not display the moral strength to resist inducements, but there is hope that corruption can be reduced to a trickle or stopped, a massive task, to give the honest man a fair chance to show his wares, if the new BJP sticks to its principles. Anna Hazare's campaign against corruption and for an ombudsman *(lokpal)* may assist the process.

Concurrent with such reforms is the recognised need to stem global warming, which has been having a rough ride, as the wealthy who profit from damaging activities, particularly oil-based businesses, have continued to deny the phenomenon, even though the signs are mounting and have stimulated young entrepreneurs to action. A random example is the engineer, Harish Hande, with a PhD in sustainable energy, founder of the *Solar Electric Light Company* (SELCO) in 1995; by 2011 he had supplied energy to 130,000 customers (500,000 people) mainly in underserved areas of Karnataka, Kerala and Gujarat. Hande is harnessing solar energy that could reduce India's already low carbon footprint of 1.6 tonnes CO_2e yearly (cf. USA's 19.6 tonnes!) But its heavy use of coal may increase these emissions, a challenge for India as it seeks to improve power generation for expanding industries.

Rao's policies did not always please the INC, which has tried at times to distance itself from them. But he did what he thought was best, and his beneficiaries are numerous in the INC, in India, USA and Europe. But not India's poor, who are rarely in the gun-sights of the rich, except at times, literally! Why would they think of those whom they displaced with machines and gunfire—just as the British had used in their conquest—denying them food, schooling and sanitation, for which they had waited so long, so hopefully and patiently?

Powerful groups of steel and power companies have gained control of tribal agricultural and coal-rich lands in certain states: Chhattisgarh, Odisha, Jharkhand, Maharashtra, Andhra Pradesh, Madhya Pradesh and West Bengal, and gained land allocations. People were displaced. Water projects like the Hirakud dam have become less efficient, through silting. Maoists and other radical groups protested, but successive governments have made no real changes, and the displaced poor remains so, while miners got rich. The irregularities in the Central Government's allocation process gained it the condemnatory name of *"Coalgate"*. Lawsuits were started to declare the allocations illegal and perhaps gain reparations and expose the corrupt parties.[149] The people have not benefitted. As Rao said after his term ended, *"Trickle-down economics does not work!"*

The 1996 elections told the true story from the Indian standpoint, while news reports whined and pandered to Americans and wealthy Indians. Corruption increased, even implicating Rao. With venality so pervasive, it is not surprising that the vast population—*the scheduled castes and tribes* (SC/ST) and *other backward classes* (OBCs)—such belittling labels—comprising half the population, most lacking proper education—had improved little, a national disgrace, by any measure.

However approximate the frequency distribution is, the numbers in need are large; 30-50% of the population are poor. Their education was recognised as a top priority at independence, but public programs have been few or wanting, with overcrowding and teacher shortages. A Supreme Court decision in 2008 endorsed the Government's plan, including reserved places for Dalits, 27%, at tertiary institutes and in government jobs. But this mark has yet to be achieved, perhaps because of a low supply of qualified students due to the failure to provide a good enough elementary schooling as a basis for higher education.[150]

In 1996, the INC was defeated, but no one party got a clear majority. For the next two years, governance suffered under various coalitions. The feared *Bhāratīya Janata Party* (BJP)—headed by Atul Behari Vajpayee, and feared because it espoused the Hindu cause—failed to get enough supporters in the two weeks given him by the President to form a government. Deve Gowda of the Janata Dal (JD) became PM, and ruled for ten months, 1996-7, heading a *United Front* coalition, which included the INC. But his government was united in name only, consisting of a broad spectrum of often irreconcilable ideologies. Its collapse, when the INC withdrew support, was not surprising. The INC agreed, however, to support a new JD-*United Front* coalition under IP Gujral, a member of the Rajya Sabha. He lasted for 11 months, 1997-8, until the INC again pulled out, since one of the *Front* partners, the *Dravida Munnetra Kazhagam* (DMK), headed by the flamboyant Jayalalithaa Jayaram, ex-actress and corruption suspect, was indirectly linked with the Rajiv Gandhi killing.

With this failure, the Lower House was dissolved and new elections gave the BJP the most seats, 182, but far short of a majority (273). Jayalalithaa demanded too high a price for support of the BJP, which had taken over from Gujral. Rejection of her demands led to new elections in September, Vajpayee continuing as Prime Minister. The Indian troubles might have induced Pakistan to start a new war in May 1999 at the J&K

---

[149]See http://profit.ndtv.com/news/economy/. Hearings have ended; all coal leases between 1993-2010 have been judged illegal; subsequent steps are to be decided soon.

[150]http://en.wikipedia.org/wiki/Other_Backward_Class#Supreme_Court_verdict

line of control near Kargil. Vajpayee reacted promptly and defeated the invader. Fears that Pakistan's PM Nawaz Sharif—with General Musharraf, a loose cannon and Indian-hater, then partly directing field operations—might deploy their new nuclear missile, led US President Bill Clinton to persuade them to desist and accept liability for the war.

In the September elections, the electorate rewarded Vajpayee with a majority for the National Democratic Alliance (NDA); he continued as Prime Minister for the full term to 2004, although with modified policies to accommodate the INC and regional parties.

By this time, the Russian-Afghan war (1979-89) had allowed growth of the *Mujahedeen,* with help and financing from the USA (Reagan), Saudi Arabia (King Fahd) and Pakistan (Zia ul-Haq). When the USSR withdrew, the *Mujahedeen* displaced President Mohamed Najibullah in 1992 and fought with others for control. In 1994, a Pakistani-backed, Wahhabi-trained Taliban group, under Mohamed Umar, replaced them.

APJ Abdul Kalam, President of India, 2002-7, Credit: K. Ramesh Babu, The Hindu

Wahhabism spread across Islamic Asia, with Saudi largesse, providing a steady stream of eager jihadis willing to become martyrs. General Musharraf seized power in Pakistan (1999-2007), further destabilising the region, and increasing the threat to India, which Bush's prior invasion of Afghanistan to "root out terrorism" and hunt for bin Laden, had already increased. After several campaigns against the Taliban, Bush stopped short of capturing bin Laden and switched to an invasion of Iraq, ostensibly to search for Saddam Hussein's *Weapons of Mass Destruction,* which everyone knew did not exist, and finding none, secured Iraqi oil for the USA, which likely was the primary objective! Halliburton, a nearly-bankrupt oil servicing company, of which Vice President Cheney was ex-CEO, received massive contracts from the US Army for projects in Iraq, despite shoddy workmanship. Osama bin Laden continued to help the Taliban, until finally found in Pakistan, in 2011, and allegedly killed by a US SEAL team deployed for this purpose. President Obama asserted that his body was dumped into the Arabian Sea. In that decade, India had suffered from five major earthquakes, including the third deadliest ever, the Sumatran-Andaman quake at M_w 9.1 and resulting tsunami, killing over 283,106 persons.

Chapter 25

"It is in India, the chosen land that Truth is preserved; in the soul of India it sleeps expectant on that soul's awakening, the soul of India leonine, luminous, locked in the closed petals of the ancient lotus of love, strength and wisdom, not in her weak, soiled, transient and miserable externals. India alone can build the future of mankind Sri Aurobindo

"Unless India stands up to the world, no one will respect us. In this world, fear has no place. Only strength respects strength" Abdul Kalam, former President of India

Corruption and Proselytism

The instability of the late 1990s had restricted the administration to annual plans as happened previously. New 5-year schemes were mooted for 1997-2002, 2002-2007, and 2007-2012 in time for elections in 2014. Dr Manmohan Singh had become PM in 2004, with Sonia Gandhi as Chair of the INC. Like Vajpayee, they continued the Rao formula, enriched many to billionaires, including Mrs Sonia Gandhi. As for the poor and uneducated, the language describing the major parties' promises remained as hopeful as one could get, and far more optimistic than a country with India's massive endemic corruption could ever achieve. Much of this theft was borne by the poor and little evidence exists of any real hardship to the rich. Major political and business hopes fell inexorably into the pockets of corrupt politicos. The gulf between the appreciation of, and attention to urban versus rural realities and priorities, had apparently increased, as cities grew and were provided with amenities that eluded the smaller villages and remote districts.

Mayawati, 2013

The rise of advocacy for the poor was welcome, but so far disappointing. Mayawati, as Chief Minister of Uttar Pradesh (UP) until 2012, and head of the *Bahujan Samaj Party (BSP)*, is particularly frustrating. Her rise as a Dalit promised that this neglected group would have a strong voice in the highest places and see some honest and long-awaited advance. She could have been a model of advocacy for tribal groups in other states, e.g. Chhattisgarh, to support them economically, and help in the defence of their lands and lifestyle against the juggernauts of big industry, local and foreign, which had moved in to exploit mineral resources. Instead, they were allowed to destroy tribal farmlands, displace residents and change their way of life, rather than provide education, health, sanitation and social support. Both state and central governments have failed the poor, special action plans notwithstanding, while senior politicians, including Mayawati, build palaces.

Indeed, the plight of the Dalits is more likely to be relieved by efforts such as those of caring Brahmins like Dr Pathak, than by Dalit Mayawati, whose egocentric lifestyle can only be called perversely extravagant. While she flaunts wealth well beyond her income, only 7% of the Scheduled castes, Scheduled tribes and Other Backward Classes have qualified for the 27% of positions reserved for them. A popular cartoon shows two panels, the top a row of INC stalwarts in 1942, proclaiming in unison, "*Swadeshi*" (independents), the bottom one, the same INC group in 2012 declaring "*Videshi*" (aliens), clearly referring to the sell-out to foreigners.

"*Salwa Judum* began in 2005 and ended in 2011". Meaning Peace March or Purification Hunt in the *Godi* dialect, it began as a "spontaneous" display of peoples' anger against Maoist or Naxal strikes against projects in Chhattisgarh. State politicians backed it as a "militia" and perverted its cause. On ordering its closure, the Supreme Court said: "*This necessarily implies a two-fold path: (i) undertaking all those necessary socially, economically and politically remedial policies that lessen social disaffection giving rise to such extremist violence; and (ii) developing a well-trained, and professional law enforcement capacities and forces that function within the limits of constitutional action*."
(See http://news.oneindia.in/feature/2013/salwa-judum).

In the aftermath several personalities were imprisoned for Maoist insurgency and one, Dr Binayak Sen, a paediatrician, was sentenced to life imprisonment for treason, under a 19th century British law that the INC had condemned before independence! Dr Brahmam (Prologue) had complained ruefully, "*Everything British survives in India.*" (see also Seth).

Repeated promises, as in the ninth plan, to bring "*primary education to all children in the country*" have failed and today the education deficit is at a shameful level, over 20%, and has created a huge dependent population that is a drag on the economy, even though little is actually spent on them. And yet the INC and UPA seem proud to ignore their failures and contentedly repeat their promises as if that were enough. (See p. 373 for role of private foundations)

Tackling poverty through employment had been tried under various names since the nineteen sixties, including the invocation of *Corporate Social Responsibility* (CSR), hoping to shame profiteering corporations into sharing a little with the underprivileged. They did little lasting good beyond enriching or empowering the greedy, including the winners of licences in the pre-1991 period. In 2011-12 those below the poverty line—hence uneducated, underfed and jobless—remained at a high national average of 21.92% (1-40% by state), compared with 37.2% (3-57%) in 2004-5, the worst affected areas being central and eastern India, with Bihar and Odisha leading. The percentage of those considered poor was quite different, 55.4% of Indians overall, ranging from 21.5% in Gujarāt and Goa to 81.4% in Bihar.[151] This is explained in part by the definitions of the poverty line, which might have been set too low for survival.

The most recent *Mahatma Gandhi National Rural Employment Guarantee Act (*MGNREGA), 2005—touted at its launching as the "largest and most ambitious social security and public works programme in the world"—is widely discredited and seems to have faltered, from multiple failures: embezzlement; delayed payments and other bureaucratic errors; and benefits failing to reach the target population that had voted for the INC, because of it.

There seems to be no plan, no process that would escape the eagle eyes of the Indian white-collar thief, yet it seems fairly obvious what stages can be corrupted, and to build safeguards there,[152] bearing in mind that every *new* remedy merely brings a further challenge to the genius of the scammer(s). (If one should go by the unsolicited phone calls one gets from people with Indian accents claiming to be banks wishing to service your credit card or bank account, one can be forgiven for believing that India is peopled only by crooks!) In the *Bhagavad Gita*, Discourse 16, 21 says, *"Threefold is the gate of hell, leading man to perdition–lust, wrath and greed; these three, therefore, should be shunned."*

The tenth plan achieved a 7.7% GDP growth versus the projected 8.1%, compared with the previous 5.4%. The eleventh plan came in on the eve of New York City's financial melt-down that bankrupted Lehmann Bros and caused havoc among American and European banks. Indian banks generally escaped major losses. But in 2009, in the midst of growing accusations of corruption in state and central Governments, and in business, and increasing suffering by the poor, India was shaken by the Ramalinga Raju scandal in Andhra Pradesh, the equally egregious *Fodder Scam* in Bihar, and the excesses of Mayawati in the UP.

Raju was CEO of *Satyam Computer Services* in Andhra Pradesh, and had a stake in a score or more companies—mostly spin-offs from his interests or property. *Satyam* had pioneered outsourcing and served

---

[151] See "*Number and Percentage of Population Below Poverty Line,*" Reserve Bank of India. 2012. Retrieved 4 April 2014.

[152]http://hindu.com/thehindu/thscrip/print.pl?file=20100521271010500.htm&date=fl2710/&prd=fline&

many "Fortune 500" companies for over 20 years. He had developed a grandiose lifestyle, but philanthropy through his *Byrraju Foundation* had won him many friends in rural Andhra Pradesh. In a remarkable letter of resignation (*BBC News, 7, January 2009),* he admitted embezzling ₹71.36 billion (ca. US$1.5 billion), including ₹50.40 billion (ca. US$1 billion) of non-existent assets, and shocked even his critics. Eighty associates were convicted of tax evasion; in December 2014, he received a light 6-month jail sentence, but is yet to be sentenced for the accounting fraud.

The Fodder scam involved Laloo Prasad Yadav, CM of Bihar, and 44 others, including a former CM, Jagganath Mishra, convicted of stealing ₹25 billion from the Bihar treasury, claiming to buy fodder and veterinary services for non-existent cattle. Laloo resigned and was sentenced to five years in jail. The scam was uncovered since the 1990s and involved numerous government members of both *Janata Dal* and the INC. Its unravelling and slow transit through the courts illustrate the power wielded by privileged wrong-doers to escape their crimes, and avoid or delay prosecution, for decades, during which further ill-gotten gains could accrue, while essential relief was denied to those most in need. The poverty numbers increased, even as the economy improved, mirroring, as elsewhere in the world, the enrichment of the rich, and destitution of the poor.

Laloo Yadav's dishonesty is now legendary, though not unique. Among his tricks some years ago was to introduce an Osama bin Laden clone to Muslim electors to get their votes. A colleague of his, Shivanand Tiwari, is also thought to have received ₹106,000,000, which he has denied so far, an almost miraculous escape, if true. To this may be added the endemic corruption of most state legislatures. Those others headed by Dalits are a particular let-down, not for any special moral failure, but because one expected them to be more sensitive and responsive to the needs of the poor, rather than pursue personal enrichment to the egregious levels that some have achieved, even if claimed as gifts.

The extent of official complicity can be gauged by the release of Laloo and Mayawati from the charge of *"disproportionate assets,"* that is, the massive excess of personal wealth over legitimate earnings. Mayawati defended her trove as the accrual from the grateful poor, often as garlands of rupee bills! It is disingenuous enough to make this claim, and even more so for the Supreme Court of India to accept it, hopefully not as a final judgement. Yet Mayawati remains popular, and as an ally of the INC, would bargain for the Prime Ministership of India, in any future UPA win. However, reform-minded voters decided otherwise, and she remains a member of the Rajya Sabha. Recently Jayalalithaa of Tamil Nadu has earned a jail sentence for accruing *"disproportionate assets."*

A chronic problem is the illegal use of children—and teenage young women seeking to earn enough for a dowry—as bonded factory labour for periods of three years, during which employers house them as virtual prisoners. Contracts are often ended prematurely, to avoid terminal payments, leaving workers more destitute than before, with far less than the sum they would need for a dowry. Despite the illegality of dowries, the practice is common, often by extortion, is unprosecuted and an unfeeling blot on the nation's conscience.

India's decline into a dystopian state occurred simultaneously with the spread of massive corruption throughout the world, and consumed nations that allowed whatever moral and ethical values they had, to slide into infamy, from the most powerful to the weakest states, from the most advanced to the newest and poorest start-ups. Such declines have achieved depths of chicanery that shame the USA, Canada, the Vatican, China, Japan and most of the Americas, Europe, Africa, the ex-Soviet Union, and almost all Asian states, including the island of Indonesia and the Philippines. In Africa, old and new, Somalia, Sudan, Libya, Chad, Equatorial Guinea, Eritrea and Zimbabwe, among others, lead the continent, with involvement of the highest ranks of politicians and bureaucrats, earning their countries the label of most corrupt in the world. Among individuals, Silvio Berlusconi of Italy, Mobutu Sese Seko of DRC, Robert Mugabe of Zimbabwe, Sani Abacha of Nigeria, Brian Mulroney of Canada, the late Forbes Burnham of Guyana and Ferdinand Marcos of the Philippines, ranked high among numerous national leaders worldwide who became rich from politics. Among business scams, the Wall St implosions of 2007-9 and the deluge of opportunistic millionaires created by the collapse of the USSR, are mind-boggling.

Meanwhile, India has amassed a cluster of wealthy state Chief Ministers, their take rivalling, if not exceeding that in the most corrupt countries. The following, obtained from various sources in India, is a small sample that tells something of the scale of known operations, and hint at what might be behind the scenes, or buried in secret accounts in India and/or overseas.

Madhu Koda, former Chief Minister of Jharkhand, currently in detention, is alleged to have amassed some ₹4,000 crore (₹40 billion) by 2009, with associates, from mining and other schemes. Mayawati, on being nominated to the Rajya Sabha in 2012, reported her wealth as ₹111.26 crore (₹1.1126 billion). Mayawati invokes "caste" whenever it suits her, and not always in the condemnatory way it should be, since it is unconstitutional. Parkash Singh Badal of Punjab was far behind her, reporting ₹8.6 crore; N. Kiran Kumar Reddy of Andhra Pradesh, ₹8.1 crore; BS Yeddyurappa, former CM of Karnataka ₹5.38 crore; Bhupinder Singh Hooda, CM of Haryana, ₹3.74 crore. Suresh Kalmadi, chairman of the organising committee of the infamous 2010 Delhi games, apparently colluded with a host of politicians, corporate capitalists and bureaucrats, to perpetrate a scam worth a staggering ₹70 billion. Today, Kalmadi and most of his associates have been detained. The former CM of Delhi, Sheila Dikshit, was implicated in the scam, and cleared, until a new probe into her alleged involvement was begun. The enquiry continues.

Independent India started early to cultivate cheats and cheating, facilitated by the *"Licence Rāja"* of the first four decades of Indian independence. The earliest frauds were among licensing, imports and other government officials, many as a legacy from the British *Rāja,* until businessmen, Ramakrishna Dalmia and Haridas Mundhra, became involved in separate massive frauds, which Feroze Gandhi, Nehru's son-in-law, exposed in Parliament. Dalmia had diverse commercial and manufacturing interests and was known for philanthropy, but strayed into financial juggling in acquiring the Bennett, Coleman media concern *(Times Group)* and was sent to jail for two years—a mere rap on the wrist.

Mundhra defrauded the Life Insurance Company of India and earned a 22-year jail sentence, leading to the resignation of Finance minister T.T. Krishnamachary. A mushrooming series of scandals followed, involving every manner of business, and government at all levels, from the prime minister to the lowest cop on the beat, or clerk, in banking, finance, manufacturing, investing, mining, real estate etc., as if in a free-for all, increasing each decade, as illustrated earlier.

Stockbroker Harshad Mehta's finance schemes of the 1990s has been used in films, and he is alleged to have paid "donations" to PM Narasimha Rao, in 1995. Recent probes into allegations of bribery in the Navy's 2003 purchase of the *Scorpene* submarine have features of a thriller and involve one of India's largest bribery totals, some ₹500 crore (about $84 million). In the same year, Abdul Karim Telgi and associates, were jailed for 10 years each, for illegally acquiring ₹200 billion ($3.3 billion) in 11 years by selling fake stamp paper!

Journalist Sujeta Dalal has covered the exploits of a more eclectic and swashbuckling scammer, Dinesh Dalmia, who ranges over India, UK, USA, Mauritius and probably elsewhere, accumulating hundreds of millions of dollars from stock fraud in the outsourcing business. These, though well known by the authorities, have been pursued at snail's pace, while Dalmia lives fast in the USA or India, as he chooses. His associate, Ketan Parekh, was convicted in 2008, and barred from trading until 2017.

The *Saradha* Ponzi scheme in West Bengal started in 2006 and unravelled in 2013; the head, Sudipto Sen, and his deputy, Debjani Mukherjee, were arrested. The scam was wide-ranging, involving 200 daughter companies, touting financial products, media, actual or sham manufacturing, real estate, films and a variety of other instruments, including sports. Its collapse cost investors $4-6 billion. Prominent politicians, media and other public figures are entangled in the scheme which is under investigation. Mamata Banerjee's government is shamed by the wide ramifications and likely involvement of party officers, and has put up a $92 million fund to assist low-income victims of the scam.

The above is a tiny sample of the web of corruption that has enmeshed India. and shows why the country's government has earned the rubric, *Mafia Rāja*. Comparisons can be made with Canada under PM Brian Mulroney whose corruption-ridden tenure lasted from 1984 to 1993, coincidental with many of the hottest scams in India.[153]

A less depressing and more hopeful scene is the one painted by Kiran Bedi, a feisty 64-year old social activist, and a retired Head of the Bureau of Police Research and Development of the Indian Police Services (IPS), and a former prison administrator, who became well known for her work on prisoner reform. She was the first female officer in the Police Services and was fearless in upholding the law, including citing Indira Gandhi for a traffic offence! She voluntarily retired from the IPS in December 2007, and founded two NGO's, *Navjyoti* and *India Vision Foundation*, focussing on urban poor, to assist all ages, children and adults, to acquire or improve schooling and vocational skills.

This is quite different from the thousands of active NGOs, mainly foreign Christian groups with massive funding, like *World Vision,* the *World Council of Churches,* the *Lutheran World Federation, Evangelical Lutheran Church in America, Gospel for Asia,* and others. These, and other NGOs, fund foreign and Indian-born "academics" from prestigious American and European universities, to pursue "religious studies" in India for Western consumption by scholars (via papers), and the public (via lectures, seminars and conferences). Most of this output is distorted, breaching norms of scholarly objectivity, and degenerating to diatribe and hate-peddling. They boost pre-formed biases and serve to prime audiences for donations, by broadcasting erroneous stereotypes about India, particularly the mis-treatment of Dalits, implicating Hindus, but omitting their constitutional protection under secular governments.

The prevailing negative portrayal of India, Indian culture, Hinduism and other religions is a mix of intentional distortions, misreading, half-truths, anachronisms and frank lies. In North America, most of it would be hate literature, and in Canada punishable by heavy fines and/or jail, especially if aimed at Jews, however true. The National Council of Churches of India is a willing participant. Audiences are told that the British should not have left India, omitting to mention that it was Britain

---

[153] See *"A State Unimagined in Law: A Wrong Without a Remedy"*. Arun Shourie. 26 May 2008, (see http://arunshourie.wordpress.com) and Cameron, S., Bibliography

that had created rural India's penury, and ignore the plight of UK's poor, up to today. They claim that Hinduism's virtues were all derived from Christianity, referring extensively to the fiction that Jesus's disciple, Thomas, had preached in the 1st century CE in the south of India and Bartholomew in the West; the presence of these men in India in the first century is, like Britain's Hinduism timelines, pure invention (Sharan).

The *Tirupathi Tirumala Declaration (TTD)* emerged in 2006, following a protest by Hindus against continuing militant encroachment by Christian activists and their acolytes on Hindu lands in the vicinity of the *Venkateshwara* shrine at Tirumala, Andhra Pradesh. The Hindu grievances were many; it did not help that recently converted politicians, including the Chief Minister, Y Samuel Rajasekhar Reddy, ignored their complaints, and proposed the site for a tourism complex! This would be akin to Italy's Berlusconi trying to replace the Vatican with a brothel! The resulting storm revealed that over 40 of the complex's employees were Christian, contrary to rulings, and found that they were using temple facilities for their own purposes, including festivals and conversions. *(See http://www.crusadewatch.org/index.php)*

Hindu frustration sparked several resolutions demanding their rights, with Swami Dayānanda summarising, "*We are not going to support any group, any institution, any political force or the media, which practice anything against Hindu Dharma in this country. From our experiences, we have come to a stand that Hindu religious endowments, Hindu institutions should be run by the Hindu bodies. They have nothing to do with the government. The secular governments should completely hand over all the religious endowments, Hindu properties to the Hindu bodies. This is an appeal that I make to all the Hindus who are not present in this conference that they should join this declaration, and the declaration be called the 'Tirupathi Declarations'. I also request all the Hindus all over the country and all over the world to support this declaration.*" Controversy continues to upset relations, Hindus wanting an end to the sabotage of Hindu practices by non-Hindus and converts, who visit the temple and treat it with disrespect.

Aggressive Christian proselytising has occurred all over India with the conversion target of THUMBS: Tribals, Hindus, Unattached (atheists etc.), Muslims, Buddhists, and Sikhs, funded chiefly, but not exclusively, from the USA, UK and Australia. For each group a specific strategy by proselytising mercenaries operates, following designs to attract, persuade, indoctrinate and buy the weak and disadvantaged, such as Dalits; the hungry and illiterate in India; Russian Jews in Israel; new migrants and refugees in North America; and so on. This has support of Western governments, by policy and by cash (Malhotra & Neelakandan).

One terrorist group, the *National Socialist Council of Nagaland*, Izak-Muivah faction (NSCN, I-M) along with rivals, agitates for a separate state of *Nagalim*, along Mao lines but with a Christian ethos. Their funding is from criminal activities, including murder, extortion and drug dealing, with US and Pakistani (ISI) sources for arms. Much of what they do is illegal, and many activists have been found guilty of crimes, while others remain in custody. Their cause is widely promoted and supported by US and European Christians.

The aim of proselytism in India is to convert Dalits, Tamils and the masses of uneducated poor in Tamil Nadu, Kerala, Andhra Pradesh and Karnataka—altogether styled "Dravidians," to divide them from the northern "Aryans", both fabricated concepts, as already discussed. Activists notoriously proselytise in Orissa (Odisha), and east in Assam, Manipur and Mizoram, preaching dissension and hate. It would be fair if people willingly converted, but many groups, local and foreign, seem untouched by fairness, ethics, respect or tolerance, and, surprisingly, are not accountable to their institutions for content errors re Indian history or culture. Corrections are often late and not stressed or publicised as widely as the original error. Native Indian converts are particularly venomous. Invective prevails and publicity attracts ample funding.

Kancha Ilaiah is a Dalit with a political studies "doctorate" and faculty member at Osmania University, Hyderabad. He is anti-Hindu and rants subjectively for English and Christianity. His invectives are irrational and uninhibited, and distort (or suppress) facts. There is no need of this. Anyone is free to analyse a religion and present the result fairly and openly. Instead Ilaiah has chosen to vilify Hinduism. He is one of a long list of similar militants all across India, but most active in the east, south and parts of the centre, organised either as NGOs or in their support. These are heavily backed by US-, UK- or EU-based groups, most registered as not-for-profit or charitable, thus able to attract activist funds, with noble aims of aiding work in health, education and social services. These groups have multiplied in the last two decades, causing anguish among Hindus, bombarded with campaigns of unfair censure and distortions of Hinduism that stir resentments and make an informed debate on issues impossible. In any case, they exploit the peculiar form of secularism in India that allows minority religions to bully a majority.

The scope of militant religious conversion by Islam is also widening, stoking conflicts and fear in populous communities, dividing them and creating needless ghettoes. The Ghodra train arson and murders in 2002, and their violent aftermath, attracted much attention, fomented by established media biases, local and foreign, against Hindus, and generating many lawsuits, some still unresolved. Few reports of the incident stress the relentless campaign by Muslims for an Islamic state, with encroachment into border areas in Assam and West Bengal and virtual merging of those with Bangladesh. Or the fact that Hindus have been forced from Bangladesh and from Muslim-majority areas in India e.g. Kashmir, and killed in clashes, the deaths totalling many *millions*. The fact that Islamists torched a train to fire the Ghodra incident, and Police reports of Islamic violence before and after, has been muted, especially in the West. The scale of the events is almost irrelevant.

How many recall the massacres of Hindus and Buddhists starting with those by the youthful warrior Mohammed Qasim who in the 8th century killed tens of thousands of Hindus and Buddhists in Sindh for refusing to convert, having already slain all able-bodied men and enslaved numerous women and children? That opening salvo paved the way forward with Hindu and Buddhist blood under Islam's rigid rules, The slaughter has continued. Recently, Muslims have displaced Hindus in Assam, West Bengal and Delhi, encouraged by tales of the INC's granting of ration, citizenship and voting cards to Bangladeshi refugees!

Clashes have occurred elsewhere along India's borders with terror assaults on Hindus, helped by Saudi funding for madrassahs; Kashmir has been almost emptied of Hindus. Throughout India, in Muslim-dense areas, young Hindu women have been for many decades tricked into conversion and marriage *(shādi-jihad),* to become captive baby-breeding "factories". This matter has led to legislative action in Madhya Pradesh, Rajasthan, Chhattisgarh, Jharkhand, Gujarat and Orissa against conversion, except to reconvert to Hinduism.

The Muslim population of India is five times higher than it was in 1951 (p.485); Islamic forces backed by Pakistan's ISI and Bangladesh Security proceed with plans to create a *Mughalstan* by seizing a wide swath of northern India to unite east and west, aided by uprisings. Another tactic is to use the population and aggressive electioneering to win constituencies and control state governments in north and central India. By contrast, the Hindu population of Bangladesh had declined from 28% to about 9%, while in Pakistan it moved down from 2% to 1.6%. Muslim increase is assisted by Indian state and federal laws which provide aid to refugees and immigrants, and promoted by the INC.
(See mughalistan.wordpress.com; Mochahari, M., academia.edu/7189552; http://www.oneindia.com/india/bangladeshi; http://gatesofvienna.net/make-way-for-mughalistan http://www.arunachaltimes.in/wordpress/love-jihad-or-romeo-war; etc.)

This situation has a long history, undoubtedly aggravated by British and Nehru's anti-Hinduism, the militancy of AIML leaders, who alarmed Gandhi (see earlier), and the long political courtship by the Nehru dynasty. That allowed Islam to seize territory, from Kashmir east to Arunachal Pradesh, and south to Kanyakumari. In 1948, both Nehru and Gandhi urged Sardar Patel to use Government funds to renovate mosques, but objected to a cabinet decision to rebuild the Hindu Temple at Somnāth, which Islamic forces had damaged. At the time of the attacks on Kashmiri pandits, Nehru's kinfolk, by Islamic terrorists, Nehru and colleagues gave them little support.

The *Daily Pioneer* reported on October 7, 2003 that the state of Karnataka had "received ₹72 crores as revenue from (Hindu) temples", and returned only ₹10 crores for temple maintenance, while granting "₹50 crores for madrasas and ₹10 crores for churches!"

In 1986, Rajiv Gandhi's government passed an unprincipled law overturning a Supreme Court order for a wealthy Muslim man to pay alimony to his ex-wife, Shah Bano. This heavy-handed intercession in the is widely seen as "proof" of the pro-Islam male bias of the INC in general, and the Nehru dynasty in particular. It still rankles that the legislation, although somewhat weakened, still stands. Indians must know that *Sharia* law was grafted on Islam, is not Quranic and Wahhabis failed to get it approved in Ontario, Canada, stalling its world spread.

While India ponders this extremism, it must also deal with terror tactics, from direct violence to hate emails to Hindus in the most lurid language. *Sharia* is clearly incompatible with secularism. Adoption of a uniform civil code should end it. Islamists are a powerful minority, with voices both schooled and strident, offering nothing to Hindus beyond generous abuse, hate and elimination. Their militants have also targeted *mosques* to inflame anti-Hindu reaction, as in the 2006 bombing of a mosque in Malegaon, Maharashtra, killing 37 Muslims, perpetrated by the *Students Islamic Movement of India* (SIMI). Also difficult to accept is the unconstitutional *fatwa* by the *"All India Muslim Personal Board (Jadeed)"* of ₹500,000, issued March 2007, for the beheading of Dr Taslima Nasrin, the Muslim author and critic of Islam (p. 377). The group's president, Tauqir Raza Khan, said the only way the bounty would be lifted was if she *"apologises, burns her books and leaves."* Surely this threat is a criminal offence? India is not (yet) an Islamic state.

The ups and downs of Dr Subramaniam Swamy, mathematician, economist, politician and Hindu advocate, and once head of the *Janata Party* (and, some assert, the Party's only member), now with the BJP, illustrate the multiple facets of Indian politics. Swamy advocates a casteless society, Hindu unity and cooperation among all Indians, regardless of religion. He has travelled widely in India and in the USA, detailing his views. Swamy is undoubtedly bright and crafty, an inveterate critic of corruption, the snail's pace of justice, and the sloth of investigators even when the facts are agreed. He condemned a 2003 Government directive requiring the Central Bureau of Investigation (CBI) to seek Government consent before investigating any senior civil servant—Joint Secretary and above. His chief accusations were against P.

Chidambaran, the Finance Minister, and Sonia Gandhi.[155] He has urged Government to repatriate "black moneys", about ₹70 lakh crores (₹70 x 10^{12} or over $1 trillion) alleged to be hidden in foreign bank accounts, but doubted that the UPA-INC would act, to avoid self-incrimination. In 1971, he argued that India did not need foreign aid and suggested a market-friendly alternative to Five-Year Plans.[156] By now, it should be plain that bribery and corruption, which had won India for the Mughals and British, will soon do the same for the USA, and their acolytes, Indian businessmen and politicians, the same groups that aided the British.

Money exports (and likely, laundering) are often completed through the *havala* method, which is based on trust between transacting brokers representing parties in a deal. One broker receives money here and asks his colleague to pay there, thus transferring sums from one location to another, within or across borders. All transactions are done orally and therefore difficult to prove. (This method has been in use for centuries and was probably used by the Rothschilds in their takeover of world money.) An example of its use is the late 1990s acquittal of four Jain brothers and several senior politicians: L. K. Advani, Balram Jakhar, Madan Lal Khurana, V. C. Shukla, P. Shiv Shankar and Sharad Yadav, accused of illegally moving vast sums of money through *havala* transfers. The absence of written records, other than diary jottings of payments received, led to their acquittal, even though the diary entries seemed enough to convict. Havala is still common among Muslims in Pakistan, Afghanistan, the Middle East, Africa and India, although India banned it fearing that it would aid money-laundering.[157] The Mumbai Muslim mafia, headed by Dawood Ibrahim, is said to control *havala* in India.

The sixties and subsequent decades were notorious for Cold War arms and military equipment deals, though probably matched by today's transactions. The late Prince Bernhard of Holland was the undoubted early front-runner, serving on a few hundred Boards,

---

[155] On May 6th, 2014 The Supreme Court's constitution bench struck down this directive introduced in 2003 in the CBI Act and the CVC Act by which the CBI was required to seek the permission of the Government for even investigating officers of the level of joint secretary and above "*There are a number of cases which are pending investigation. Now the investigation of those cases will be expedited,*" Sinha added .(*ANI News, 17 May 2014 See also Economic Times, India, 7, Jan 2012*, for others)

[156] *Swamy, S* Indian Economic Planning *Vikas, India, 1971*; *Swadeshi Plan*, Google Books. The first act of the 2014 Modi government (BJP-NDA) was to establish a Special Investigative Team (SIT) to probe the extent of "black money" with a view to recovery. *Global Financial Integrity* quotes the total for 2002-11 as $343.9billion, listing India after China, Russia, Mexico & Malaysia, See EJ Fagan, May 29, 2014, http:*//www.gfintegrity.org/indian-prime-minister-narendra-modis…a*ccessed May 30, 2014.

[157]Supreme Court judgement on 2 March 1998 that quashed CBI charges against LK Advani, VC Shukla and Jain brothers. *See wikipedia.org/wiki/Hawala scandal*

including the Bilderberg Group, and an associate of the Rothschilds. He was exposed by the bribe of over $1M million paid to him by Lockheed Corporation. When asked to explain, he said, *"I'm above such things!"*

Among the infamous of these dealers, as disreputable as the late Prince, is the Arab, Adnan Khashoggi, whose recent money deals involved Indian businessmen, Hasan Ali Khan and Kashinath Tapuriah, who were arrested in 2011 under *India's Prevention of Money Laundering Act*. It is likely that not much will come of this, since records may not be convincing, as in the Jain brothers affair. But that does not excuse the magnitude of the crime or make guilt disappear. Ali Khan is said to owe hundreds of millions of rupees in back taxes.

The neglect of healthcare and primary education (p. 401) is a form of corruption; the UPA under PM Manmohansingh and Sonia Gandhi continued to neglect them. A universal health care plan had been mooted in the 1970s. But health care remains largely private and expensive, thus bypasses the poor. It is riddled with rackets. It fails to reach nearly half the people in need, from shortfalls in manpower, facilities and coverage. Too many are too far removed from health centres; the Government has invested too little in health care and at best has a poor grasp of needs or the value and utility of various alternatives. Public health has to deal with ignorant and opinionated leaders, poor hygiene and sanitation, undernutrition, inadequate safe water, and their extensive sequels such as infectious diseases, poverty, early death and combinations thereof.

Some indices have improved: life expectancy was 27 in 1931, 32 in 1951 and 66 in 2001; infant mortality 80 in 1951, 45 in 2010; female literacy, despite poor performance in absolute terms, is >60% vs. 9% in 1951. Education caters mainly to the middle and upper classes, via a plethora of private schools, which seem to tailor their curricula to the prerequisites of Western tertiary education centres, or for a western life style. India thus exports its educated graduates, whose later higher education in the West ignores or trashes Indian, especially Hindu traditions. The desire for western degrees is rooted in Macaulayism and its sequels, and Western models uncritically dominate Indian education.

An outstanding irony is that the three most popular tertiary educational destinations—the USA, UK and Canada—have large Indian faculties, most of whom received a pre-graduate education in India. Experts in University and College education will agree that much of post-graduate education is self-directed and, except for practical experiments and key demonstrations, largely on-line today. The graduate supervisor often gets more from the students than he gives them: theses, publications, institutional recognition, promotion and tenure. India needs to review its management of this valuable resource which it calmly donates to the West, after preparation at India's expense.

Many billions of rupees are lost in this brain drain, that could be better spent on early education. This applies to all third world scholars who are wooed by the west and so become a poor country's gift to the rich. The main lures are money and life style: *"Double the pay in the USA!"* goes the slogan, but no mention of the higher cost of living.

India's ongoing battle with AIDS among the poor shows how callous US and UK pharmaceutical giants are to oppose Indian production of drugs (Cipla, Mumbai) at a $1.00 per day, a fraction of patented ones. India is a major producer of generic drugs. Mumbai's Sun Pharma recently acquired competitor Ranbaxy, becoming the world's fifth largest pharmaceutical company, and making its owner, Dilip Shanghvi, the richest Indian. It has fended off predatory American companies, which, since 1947, have grabbed, patented and sold traditional Indian medicines and non-proprietary substances e.g. the healing plant, neem, and the spice turmeric *(haldi*); these patents have now been revoked, years after costly appeals by India. Undaunted, American corporations continue to mine the world for profitable and patentable elements, which they would claim as their own, as in the turmeric and neem examples, and lately *yoga*, despite protest. Americans strip them of religious and philosophical roots and context, or modify them, in the case of biologicals and *yoga*, and sell the resulting material, by brazenly claiming that they are non-Indian, or lack "written Indian proof," in one of the six languages accepted by the UN and its agencies, including the WHO. Those six do not include an Indian language!
http://www.goodnewsindia.com/Pages/content/traditions/turmeric.html)

L: Narasimha Rao (PM 1991-6)

R: Sonia Gandhi, President, INC

Chapter 26

"India of the Vedas entertained a respect for women amounting to worship, a fact which we seem little to suspect in Europe when we accuse the extreme East of having denied the dignity of woman, and of having only made her an instrument of pleasure and of passive obedience."

Louis Jaccoliot, French diplomat in India

Women in Indian culture

The so-called lower classes are only "low" as long as they are unable to benefit fairly from the resources of their country. Many of today's rich and powerful were once poor and have gravitated to the centres of power because of wealth and training obtained through years of increasing influence within a social order where their place became established and preserved, by imposed boundaries. But the poor strive constantly, often unsuccessfully, for minimum needs: food, clothing and shelter, hindered often by the wealthy of their own class. While genes do play a part in behaviour, the equal provision of the three basic needs, plus education and the acquisition of useful skills, will give the poor a chance to enhance their social standing and achieve a higher standard of living. Sociability, aptitudes and interests, inventiveness and application will determine their value to community and society.

The Dalits of India have emerged, albeit too slowly, in the last century, not for want of effort or will, but for opportunity and tolerance. The rise of Mayawati, covered in the last chapter, will no doubt be replicated as time passes, hopefully without the negative baggage. The incentive and opportunity were established after independence by reserving places for the designated underprivileged classes. While a useful plan, it cannot help without first providing children a sound primary education in a nurturing environment, to enable them to compete. This means nutrition, and the protection from the harm of caste biases, which prevail, though unconstitutional. India has largely failed in this, as has been said *ad nauseam*, here and by many others.

In 2009, India passed the *Right to Free and Compulsory Education Act* (RTE), adding to the existing *Education for All* scheme (*Sarva Shiksha Abhiyan*), resulting in a jump in primary enrollment to 94%. The total school population is 200 million or more; at that time there was a deficit of some 200,000 schools and over a million teachers, as reported by the *National Council for Teacher Education*. Obviously the task is huge, but the solutions are clear. Enhanced investment in schools and teacher training are needed as well as societal reforms to support expanded programs. It is hardly likely that private facilities would cater to the poor, as family income is spent on schooling only after basic needs are met, and if children are not expected to contribute to family income. There is no doubt that empowering Dalits will in a few generations erase the differences between them and their fellows, and eliminate the labels that so easily divide a people, label by label, and subdue them, as the British had shown, and the Americans have now successfully copied.

The reservation system gives Dalits an accessible place in Indian politics and public life. But the preparatory phase has not proceeded as well as hoped, and instead of near 100% access to a full primary education, as many as 50% are yet to participate. The government is naturally blamed and could tap the wealthy for assistance, either by taxes or outright donations. Earlier chapters contain criticisms of lavish spending by the affluent, who appear not to have contributed enough to those who helped them succeed: their own countrymen, by direct labour or by state provision of infrastructure and other needs. Some however, contribute hugely and continuously e.g. the donations of people like Azim Premji, and the pioneering work of Dr Pathak and his SISSO with untouchables, and its steady emancipation of thousands of people, who can now get to that important first rung of the economic ladder.

Indian societies were accused of suppression of women, but many outstanding women had made their mark in Indian history, from the very beginning, contrary to stereotyping. The *Vaidic* God principle is female, with Saraswati, Lakshmi and Durga as key figures. Hindu women dominate Indian family and religious life. Their successors have filled positions with honour in politics, administration, the military, business, education, women's studies, sport and other leadership callings. They have acted alone or in groups, e.g. *Stree Shakti*, a society of females with multiple talents, or Sampat Pal Devi's *Gulabi Gang* (*Pink Saris)*, a community action group for justice to the poor in Uttar Pradesh.

The invasions of India have revealed many brave and talented female warriors, like Abbakka Rani, a Karnataka queen who led her people against Portuguese invaders in the 16th century; Rani Durgavati, who like Chand Bibi of Ahmednagar, fought Akbar's armies rather than surrender; Rana Tarabai of Malwa who defeated Aurangzeb in 1705, to begin, in 1707, the inexorable collapse of the Mughal Empire. Mai Bhagoji led Sikhs against Mughals in 1707, in the service of Guru Gobind Singh, the 10th Sikh guru. Chennamma, queen of Kittur, Karnataka, attacked the British militarily for imposing the *"Doctrine of Lapse"*. Lakshmi Bai of Jhānsi and her Dalit double Rani Jalkari Bai battled the British against great odds, in the 1857 War of Independence. Rani Avantibai of Ramgarh; Ahilyabai and Bhimabai Holkar of Indaur; Begum Hazrat Mahal of Awadh; the Begums of Bhopal and others e.g. Onaki Obavva of Chitragraha fought valiantly to defend their lands against invaders. Add to these the scores of thousands who sacrificed themselves rather than be captured by Islamic invaders.

Women figured prominently in the independence movement both as leaders and as progressive citizens: Aruna Asaf Ali, Annie Besant (first woman president of the INC), Bhikaji Cāma, Durgabai Deshmukh, Kasturbai Gandhi, Rajkumari Amrit Kaur, Sucheta Kripalani, Sarojini Naidu, Kamala Nehru, Vijaya Lakshmi Pandit, Muthulakshmi Reddy, Rukmini Laxmipathi, and Rani Gadinliu, who, at age 1, led opposition to the British in Manipur and Naga territories. Priti Lata Wadeyar, of Chittagong, and several female medical graduates of that time are well known martyrs, among numerous others who served selflessly.

An entire regiment of Subhas Chandra Bose's *Indian National Army*, called the *Rani of Jhansi Regiment*, was made up of women led by Captain Lakshmi Sahgal. More recently Indira Gandhi became the first female PM of India, and Mayawati of UP has become the first Dalit woman to head a state as well as serve in the Rajya Sabha, despite allegations of corruption.[158] Other Chief Ministers have been Vasundhare Raje Sindhye of Rajasthan who served from 2003 to 2008; Jayalalithaa Jayaram, of Tamil Nadu, now in her fourth term (recently ended by a jail sentence for having *"disproportionate assets")*; and Mamata Banerjee, CM of West Bengal. Pratibha Patil was the first female President of India (2007-12); previously she was the Deputy Chair of the Rajya Sabha, and Governor of Rajasthan. Meira Kumar was the first female Speaker of the Lok Sabha (2009-2014), a position currently held by another woman, Sumitra Mahajan of Indaur.

Late in the 19th century, Indian women became allopathic physicians and educators; Savitribai Phule was the first professional woman teacher in India. Women played an important part in India's independence struggle. In the fifty years since 1917, Vijaya Lakshmi Pandit became the first woman (and only Indian) president of the United Nations General Assembly. On 23 May, 1984, Bachendri Pal became the first Indian woman to climb Mount Everest, and has had a stellar mountaineering record since, achieving other firsts for women's groups, including transit of the entire Ganges by raft—with 18 women—and a record trans-Himalaya trek—with 8 women—in 1997.

Many women reformers, such as Pandita Ramabai, also helped the cause of female upliftment. Kalpana Chawla (1962-2003), the first Indian woman astronaut, sadly died in a US space shuttle crash on February 1, 2003. Women have excelled in sports including at the Olympics and in the Indian craze, cricket, where Mithali Raj (born 1982), is Captain of India's Women Team (2014) and has had a fine batting career so far, along with others of her team. Mithali became the first woman to score a

[158] *http://www.bjp.org/en/media-resources/press-releases/"vision"document,BJP,* released by Nitin Gadkari, 2012 UP election

double century in an inning (200 or more runs) in Test cricket (vs New Zealand, 2004). Indian women won several gold medals at the 2010 Commonwealth Games and in the South Asian Games, where India led the medal trove. An Indian woman, Arati Saha, swam the English Channel in 1959 and Bula Chowdhary was the first female to swim the "seven seas", completing the task in 2004 by swimming the Palk Strait between India and Sri Lanka.

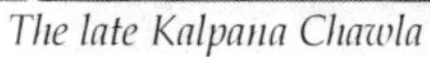

The late Kalpana Chawla

Mithali Raj, star batsman

Today numerous women hold commanding positions in businesses, governance, the professions and politics. Savitri Jindal remains a steel billionaire in a fluctuating industry. Indians are among the most vocal atheists and communists, and include writers and film-makers. Minakshi Ammal pioneered South Indian cookbooks. Indu Jain, the head of media giant, Bennett, Coleman & Co. Ltd, publishers of *Times of India* and other papers, is one of many businesswomen who continue to excel in a world dominated by males, and is one of India's most successful CEOs.

The role of women in Indian society has degraded in the last millennium. The *Manusmriti* (Laws of Manu), (ca. 7,000 BCE), *shloka* 55, had advised that *"Women should be nurtured with every tenderness and attention..."*(see p. 248). Swami Dayananda also warned against the abuse of women.

Hindu treatment of women generally tended to follow *jāti* habits. Louis Jaccoliot—the celebrated French author of *The Bible in India: Hindu Origin of Hebrew and Christian Revelation,* quoted in the epigraph – said of Indian women: *"Here is a civilization, which you cannot deny to be older than your own, which places the woman on a level with the man and gives her an equal place in the family and in society."* This ancient fact alone would astound Europeans and non-Hindus.

Child marriages have been a particularly abusive development, but then one has to recall that European, pre-Colombian American, African and Asian aristocracy had established child betrothals, and even marriage, for political reasons, for over a millennium. Most tribal societies had used puberty as a sign of vulnerability, and found it safer to get a person partnered at that time. Clearly the nature of the society would dictate action, and events that presaged dangers would prompt defensive action. Conquest by Islam endangered Hindus and forced them to protect their female children; early betrothal was one tactic. Europeans generally misinterpreted the inherent place of women in Indian society, since they treated theirs like slaves. The Portuguese and the British were, like Islamists, dismissive or predatory to all but the wealthy or aristocratic, and then, only to advance their interests.

One of the most criticised aspects of Hindu society was the practice of *sătī* (or *suttee*) where a *Brahmin* widow shared her deceased husband's funeral pyre as a religious burden, which European newcomers wrongly imputed to *all* Indian widows, and thus an index of Hindu disregard for women and the "sinfulness" of all Indians, even though Europens at that time (19th century) treated women quite poorly. The Indian practice may have arisen to avoid a fate worse than death: the degradation of a high-caste widow in the hostile society that India had become after the fall of the Guptas (Lata Mani). From the time BEICo gained control of Bengal and success at Buxar, *sati* had become a recurring issue that got buried in the turmoil of the 1780s and later Napoleonic wars, attention returning to it only on their conclusion. Evangelism was by then permitted and preachers seized on it to proselytise and to denounce all Hindus, knowing that corrections of prevarications were not likely to reach or influence the British public, even if they did recall the error.

The arguments of Ram Mohan Roy persuaded the BEICo to declare *sati* illegal in Bengal (British-India) in 1829. The decision was supported by many Indians but the practice lingered on. This was no doubt partly due to the wide publicity of any incident by Christians, as if it captured all that was wrong with Hinduism, and its condemnation all that was right with Christianity, forgetting the old Christian practice—Catholic and Protestant—of burning their critics at the stake!

Despite being unconstitutional, caste and other ritual practices still flourish openly in India, perhaps because the INC has failed in six decades to educate and upgrade the Dalits, and chose instead to blame Hindu practices for their inferior status, an economic one which can be found in the richest countries. This blame perpetuates the division among peoples and improves the chances of the INC's continuing to hold power, the same tactic used by the British to "divide and rule". This lingering drag on society could only begin to be severed by ensuring a solid primary education to improve the chances of Dalits' filling higher education places reserved for them. Those who learn together in a nurturing atmosphere usually live well together, especially when class frictions are curtailed. Germany as a new nation in 1900 was over 90% literate, a major factor in its growth and unification, with the rest of Western Europe trailing.

Perhaps India is seeing the results of millennia of closer breeding within tribes than advised even in the older *Manusmriti.* Unless caste biases are ended and literacy improved, Hinduism will continue to lose adherents; women and poor Indians will remain easy prey to the cheap temptations of Christian proselytes who aggressively bank land, "plant" churches, and buy the conversion of the poor and weak, following the immoral practices of the "Joshua Project", with its massive dossier on people targeted for Christian conversion worldwide, supported by powerful businesses seeking India's huge market (*http://joshuaproject.net/ http://www.huffingtonpost.com/suhag-a-shukla)*

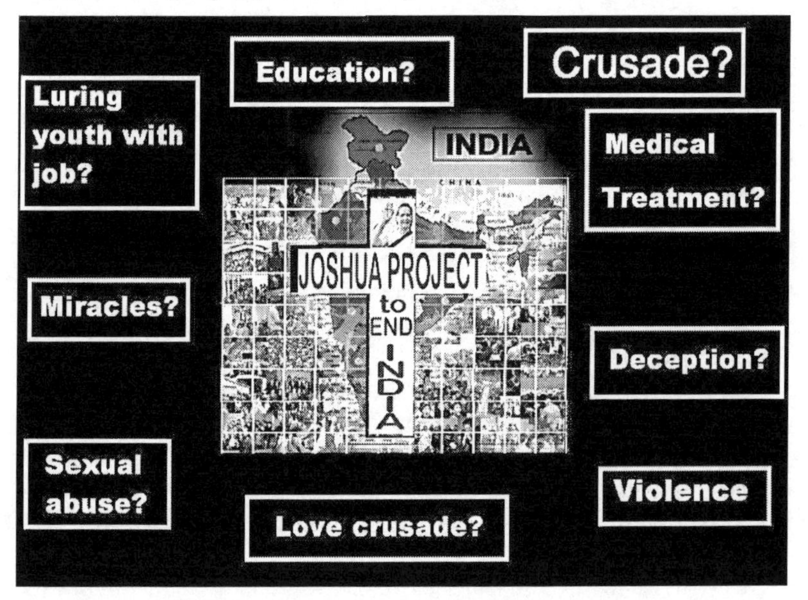

The Christian Church, with about 2% population in India, has exploited its minority position, and gradually acquired state lands to become one of India's largest landholders, and the most influential in Kerala, Tamil Nadu, Andhra Pradesh and Manipur.
(*http://satyameva-jayate.org/2011/03/12).*

Jomo Kenyatta, former Prime minister of Kenya had pithily said, *"When the missionaries came to Africa, they had the Bible and we had the land. They taught us to pray with our eyes closed. When we opened them, we had the Bible in our hand, and they had the land."*

It is well-known that from the late 1980s India has grown at a better than average pace to a GDP some 17 times that of 1951. The growth has slowed in the past few years, ascribed in part to PM Manmohansingh's weaknesses in handling industrial power and tolerating graft among his colleagues. But, as pointed out above, this wealth has not been shared equitably with workers; for example, their wages have not improved, and the increased revenue in good years has not been spent on clean water or sanitation, health, education, power or transportation or similar service to the needy. The country is about 96% electrified, with the northeast still to be completed; half the population lacks sanitation, a grave need, as stressed, that is being slowly addressed.

India has retrogressed in social services and now ranks near last among South Asian countries, even though its GDP tops them all. One of the social and family reforms that would strengthen Indian society is the elimination of so-called "honour killings", which threaten certain categories of women, usually the young. This practice has no place in Hinduism and has all but disappeared in the older Diaspora. In India, incidents tend to occur in conservative upper class families of Rajasthan, Punjab, Haryana, UP and Bihar, among Jāts, Sikhs and Muslims. It is rare or unknown in West Bengal and South India. The defenders claim that the act "purges" religious society of teenagers who have become "too western" or practice sex out of wedlock, reject an arranged marriage, dress provocatively, or commit adultery or homosexuality. *(See http://www.meforum.org/2646/worldwide-trends-in-honor-killings).*

A few instances have occurred in Canada in the past decade among Sikhs and Muslims; one involved a wealthy Afghani who killed three teenage daughters and his infertile first wife, assisted by his son! Canadians reacted with horror; yet seem generally unfazed by the incidence of 42 femicides per year, a high rate!

The 2007 murder of Manoj Banwala, 23, and his new wife Babli, 19, in Haryana, India, created a precedent when, for the first time, perpetrators of an honour killing were handed heavy sentences for the crime. Farouk Omar Idris summarised it thus: *"This was a landmark judgment, in March 2010; Karnal district court ordered the execution of five perpetrators of an honour killing in Kaithal, and imprisoning for life the khap (local caste-based council chief), Ganga Raj, who had ordered the killings of Manoj Banwala and Babli, having judged them to be the same Jaat and ignoring correction. Despite having been given police protection on court orders, they were kidnapped; their mutilated bodies were found a week later in an irrigation canal" (See http://www.slideshare.net/fiu025/honor-killing-32343550).*

On appeal the State High Court commuted the death sentences to life in prison and acquitted Ganga Raj. This is under appeal to the Supreme Court. A weakness in India is that people like Ganga Raj can flout the law and avoid punishment. They should understand instead that the antediluvian views they espouse and expound, with no regard for rights or genetics, are not part of Hinduism, but it gets blamed. It is time to enact fair laws, educate and remind politicians that their prime duty is to defend the weak and poor, not to empty the pockets of the rich. *(See http://newsclick.in/india/dashing-hopes–The High Court verdict).*

In every state old British laws survive that were designed to control and punish people by criminalising petty anti-social acts, not to help or rehabilitate. Often these acts were (and still are) necessities or traditions such as street performing, begging, homelessness, by people who are jobless, poor, uneducated, chronically ill, addicted or abandoned. Jail is not their salvation. Yet middle class India finds no time to improve their lot. The description of the *British Anti-Slavery* society still applies (p 216).

But the rich can commit wanton misdeeds and feel protected. The model Jessica Lal was killed in 1999 by Manu Sharma, son of INC Minister V. Sharma, for failure to serve him a drink, after hours, at an illegal party where she had served as a bartender. With him was Vikas Yādav, the son of D.P. Yādav, a politician and criminal, with a Police Class B rating (not expected to reform). Manu was sentenced to life imprisonment. Vikas and cousin Vishal were later accused of the 2002 killing of Nitish Katara, who had a romantic association in college with Bhati Yādav, Vikas's sister. This was a different kind of murder, an "honour killing", which some Islamic countries mitigate, but not India.

The slow legal progress of this and the Sharma case illustrates the hurdles of law enforcement where politicians and defendants of means and power bribe or threaten, and often harm investigators and case workers. Initially Bhati seemed overcome, assisted police but soon "vanished" to London, England, and hid for years, incommunicado. She finally returned to India, where, in new reports, she denied any romance with Nitish. Her brothers were convicted in 2008 and given life sentences, but they seemed to have spent more time out than in, Vikas being paroled 66 times in 3 years!

These cases illustrate the uneven hand of justice in India, where political influence often trumps sentences for crimes, but a beggar can be jailed for years. Corruption of Police and local Council was invoked in these and other cases of crimes against women. Examples abound and vilify the country, locally and internationally, erode its reputation and threaten its integrity. *(http://en.wikipedia.org/wiki/Nitish_Katara).* Police venality in UP led Sampat Pal Devi in 2006 to form the defensive women's advocacy group, the *Gulabi (pink) Gang*, now over 400,000 strong, mostly poorer women seeking fair treatment and justice; they have become a source of community news, views and strength that Modi cannot ignore.

Thus six decades after Nehru's vain boast, India limps onward, caught, it seems, in the clutches of a different agenda from the one projected in 1947. The successful launch of the Mars probe, concluded at one-tenth the cost of the NASA probe, has boosted the morale of Indians and opens wider this branch of science. Yet it distracts from social imbalances and continues to draw hypocritical comments from US citizens and India-bashers. It is reminiscent of the 1959 success of the Canadian AVRO Arrow (CF 105) supersonic twin-engine jet interceptor, which had out-performed American rivals, yet Prime Minister Diefenbaker allowed US President Eisenhower and Secretary of State John Foster Dulles—acting in the interests of American military contractors, and to advance the USA's aim to have a military base in every country—to "persuade" him to scuttle the aircraft and destroy all blueprints and finished products. This incredible decision cost Canada its aerospace industry, and made it dependent ever since on American manufacturers, selling an inferior product. Redundant scientists and engineers found ready employment at NASA! *(http://www.avroarrow.org/)*

India's experience with its ISRO programme repeats some of the main features of the Canadian AVRO Arrow incident, and the recurring tactic of US manufacturers' use of government pressures to eliminate competition and cover their losses by subsidies, until a monopoly or near monopoly is achieved. The US Military Industrial and Financial Complex (MIFC) remains a powerful monopoly that others emulate, e.g. Monsanto. ISRO will face competitive and other hassles from the US as it seeks to market its space services. India must withstand these.

Comparing India's economic performance with its neighbours, shows that Communist China, starting also in 1948, under Mao Zedong, has eclipsed India in every socio-economic sector. The obvious differences are Chinese language retention; its intense planning; ruthless governance and commercial practices; technological methods, including "ways" of acquiring western ones; and quick despatch of revealed corruption. Not that this has ended corruption. But, were they in China, several prominent Indian politicians and bureaucrats might have been headless today. Even Bangladesh, which in 1974 was miserably poor, has performed better than India in some social indices; Nepal, a Hindu state, exceeds it in several. China is single-minded and high-handed in finding and dominating sources of raw material, outdoing Indians, even in former British colonies. They have assumed control of several, in Africa, Asia and South America, by aggressive means, or by supporting puppets, American style, and corrupting others.

Today we have different Indias: a prominent one where 20% of people flourish, mainly professionals and businessmen, and the rest, the real Bhārat, almost invisible, at least by the rich and the media, of ill-educated poor, in farms and cities, homeless, or poorly housed, who remain exploited and deprived, hounded by police and politician, most below the Tendulkar poverty line. The INC dealt with the poor by shifting food rations and dropping the poverty level, in other words, by a ploy: changing the threshold values to make the INC look good.

This quote from *The Hindu,* Aug 6, 2013, ascribed to Mihir Shah, pithily captures the Indian scene: "*...the 12th Plan clearly acknowledges that even if the figure of people below the consumption poverty line were to fall to zero, removing poverty in India will remain a challenge till every Indian has access to safe drinking water, sanitation, housing, nutrition, health and education. That is the challenge we need to focus on, rather than splitting hairs over the singular estimation of poverty*".

India's Geosynchronous Satellite Launch Vehicle that put a 2.1-ton communications satellite in orbit in January 2014

Chapter 27

"And yet your people(in a British colony) have a much better understanding of Indian history and heritage than most people in India! Especially our secularists and middle class!" Dr Brahmam, 1960

The Indian Diaspora (Table 1)

Recent migrants from India to any country (non-resident Indians or NRIs) have invariably found it difficult to find common ground with previously-settled people of Indian origin (PIOs), especially those from former European colonies (the Diaspora). They were, as it seemed, on different wavelengths, except when sharing language. One constant and impressive feature was that most diasporal Indians—also called Desi, a contraction, now an omnibus term for any South Asian—had escaped Macaulay's direct brainwashing, and the scorn of Indian intellectual atheists and socialists, who had blossomed in the early 20th century, even in the Diaspora, and hungrily imbibed Marxism. The majority, though, had preserved Hinduism and Islam; a few, mainly urban, had converted to Christianity, and most had been forced to adopt English, or other ruling European language, by the third generation.

More impressively, most Hindus had maintained their forms of worship, conducted in Sanskrit and Hindi, and Muslims theirs in Arabic and Urdu, which many could read, however attenuated or dated their vocabulary. Indian cuisine, dress, art, music, dance, games, hobbies were intact, and even farming methods—food crops, fruit trees, vegetables, medicinal plants and other favoured environmental features—had been transported with them and nurtured. Most Indian migrants had come to British colonies on indentures, forced by extreme want due to the seizure of farmlands, trades and businesses in India, by British imperialists.

Indians were subjected to enormous direct and indirect pressure to give up their traditions and convert to Christianity, especially if they wished to advance socially, in cities, or seek a Public Service or similar career e.g. teaching in government or Christian schools. Some did convert, but the majority resisted and maintained their cultural practices, sometimes under protest or threat. Thus, they continued religious sacraments and in many places conducted secret language classes, which were generally ridiculed and often prosecuted by the ruling elements (Mangru; Ragbeer). The coming together of people from different places, *varnas*, religiosity and languages (dialects) gave them the opportunity to modify behaviours, in the interests of conviviality, or even survival. But even so, basic principles hardly changed and were found to correspond across regions, forming a bond that transcended the boundaries of religion, *gotra* and *jāt*. In general, Muslims and Hindus lived well together, as friends, neighbours and even relatives.

Table 1: Population of Indians in the Diaspora, 2011, (figures in brackets from the Ministry of Overseas Indian Affairs (http://moia.gov.in/services), and various countries' census data. The grand total may be an underestimate.

Country	Total	% Population or revised Total
Australia	448,430	
Bahrain	350,000	
Bhutan	33,010	
Canada	1,165,145	3.5 (1,200,000)
China(incl. Taiwan)	54,275	
Fiji	313,798	40.0*
France (Caribbean, Cayenne, Reunion)	145,000	
Germany + Other Europe	913,575	
Guyana	320,300	42.7*
Indonesia	36,050	
Jamaica	53,500	
Other WI &Central America	30,000	0
Malaysia	2,050,000	(2,450,000)
Mauritius	882,220	68
Myanmar	356,560	(2,900,000)
Nepal	600,000	15 (4 Million)
Netherlands + Antilles	219,500	
New Zealand	110 583	2.6
Nigeria	30,000	
Oman	718,562	
Philippines	50,000	
Qatar	500,000	
Saudi Arabia	1,789,000	
Singapore	670,100	9.2
South Africa	1,218,000	2.7 (1,286,930)
Sri Lanka	1,601,600	
Suriname	140,300	33
Tanzania+ Kenya	192,889	
Trinidad & Tobago	551,500	35.4*
UAE	1,750,000	30.0
UK	1,500,000	2.5
USA	2,245,239	3,183,063 Rev.
Yemen	111,000	
Others ME, Asia, Africa etc.	??	
TOTAL	21, 909, 875 +	25 million (Est.)

*Reduced from 51% in 1970 due to migration. See Ragbeer, *The Indelible Red Stain*

The initial scarcity of women in the colonies led to relaxation of caste restrictions in choice of partner, with the result that people from various backgrounds and regions were able to mix and freshen the gene pool; at times Hindus married Muslims, some sanctioned by families, persuaded by the examples of Akbar and other Mughals, and by necessity.

The number of "untouchables", or *avarna,* was small, since recruiters had selected mainly skilled people from villages and cities; what few there were, had converted to Christianity, or, with time, merged with the majority in their communities, or married into other racial groups. Many former "low caste" persons had risen to high positions in the wider society. The main cause of untouchability, the handling of human excreta, had been eliminated in the Diaspora, since most homes had sanitary facilities: pit latrines, septic tanks or flush toilets. Open defaecation was rare except as a rural "emergency." Enamel pots served generally for night use or during illness, for those without indoor toilets.

The first mass migration from India were farm workers who went to Mauritius in 1834, British Guiana (now Guyana) in 1838, Trinidad in 1845, followed by a steady stream, by both push and pull, until 1917, to nineteen European colonies, totalling over 2 million persons. Many died in transit, on cramped, dirty ships, especially on the long journeys (20 weeks) to the Caribbean. Sikhs migrated to North America's west coast, both Canada and the USA, and had a troubled reception as their move coincided with the rise and spread of white supremacy theories (Ch. 18).

In time, PIOs established social, cultural or religious groupings in their new locales, with their unique symbols: Hindus building temples, Sikhs gurdwaras, Muslims mosques, or lay associations for social events and to celebrate special and holy days. Some were non-selective and welcomed members from all religions and regions, while others focussed on a particular group e.g. Bengali, Goan, Punjabi, Tamil etc.

Indian customs have been faithfully preserved in former European colonies, some to an extent almost unknown to modern middle class Indians in India. In 1965 India's President S. Radhakrishnan expressed to a visiting Guyanese hospital executive his pleased surprise at the extent of preservation of "real" Hindu values in Guyana and Trinidad, wishing that India would copy that. The visitor was pleasantly surprised at this reception, having been cautioned that Radhakrishnan was suspected of being more than a bit anti-Hindu.

More recently, the Indian Consul General to Toronto repeated this wish on witnessing a performance by Indo-Guyanese *Tān* singers in Hamilton, Ontario, a city of 500,000 with 18,000 PIOs, home of Mahatma Gandhi Peace Studies, and of a volunteer Networking Council which had sponsored the performance and whose aim was to unite PIOs. *Tān* singing and *Nagāra* drumming are rural activities among Hindus, forgotten in cities. Such events show the differences between the older Diaspora and recent migrants, the former outgoing, welcoming, familiar with Hindu and western practices, the latter reserved and uncertain of both religion and society. The two groups have been slow to integrate, but activists from the Caribbean and the Americas have cooperated to get May accepted as a month for celebrating Indian heritage and to show the culture through its various transitions *(South Asian Heritage Month).*

By the end of the 19th century, Indians had begun to qualify for positions in colonial governments, but those in the USA were not eligible for citizenship, or a Government post, until the *Luce-Cellar Act* of 1946 admitted 100 Indian migrants *yearly,* and permitted those already resident in the USA, some for over 50 years, to apply for citizenship or seek Government jobs or political positions.

Indians had come to North America and Bermuda in the 17th century as employees of the East India Company, the first probably as seamen in the 1790s. Later on, various xenophobic measures: denials of freedom, citizenship, property ownership, voting rights, starting a business etc., were used to discourage Indian migrants. They were mainly Sikhs then, who had loyally served the British and felt special, thus excluded from the prevailing racial biases. US immigration laws, however, permitted entry of Caucasians only, but at least one Sikh argued that he was a Caucasian, which probably helped to keep them coming to the Pacific coast of the USA and Canada, until 1946. In 1917, the *Asiatic Barred Zone Act* banned Indians and other Asians from entering the USA; the *Rāja* terminated British indentures that same year.

It was difficult for Indian contract workers. Once in a new colony, their ignorance of the language and the strangeness of habits—clothing, social norms and cuisine—forced them into the protective preservation of familiar ways, especially when the alternatives were unacceptable to the Hindu e.g. eating beef, or pork (Hindus and Muslims) or cohabiting out of wedlock! Diasporal Indians therefore kept to ethnic clusters, clung to religious strengths, modified with time, and developed a circle of friends among shipmates (*jahajis*), work crews and *jātis* that expanded to become a family, as marriages occurred among their offspring, or among widows and widowers, and a chain of loyalty and trust grew on matters of law, money, social and political relations, land, community and so on.

As time passed and contracts gave way to free choices or were renewed; a proportion chose to stay in their adopted lands, especially as British India was getting less attractive than the colonies, under the same power. The colonies offered more choices, lower population density and hardly attracted European competitors, especially in rural occupations. India was first choice for ambitious Britons choosing a foreign post. *The Indelible Red Stain* (Ragbeer) gives an example of a British major disappointed with his transfer to a top-secret and strategic mission in South America early in WWII, having tasted India and wanting more!

Despite facing harsh conditions, Indian migrants adapted to their new environment, sometimes radically different from the old, e.g. marsh versus mountainside, and in most cases turned it to suit their natures and practices. They accepted the social expressions of other cultures, where harmless, for example, forms of casual dress and observance of feast days, while spreading some of their own virtues, especially cuisine, agricultural and medical systems, and philosophy of accommodation, peace and universality. Of these, cuisine was established early, and Indian entrepreneurs opened fine dining places in most major western capitals beginning in the UK, then elsewhere, as opportunity allowed, lastly in North America and Australia. It wasn't until 1970 that Washington DC acquired two good Indian restaurants. The Clintons were early fans of Indian cuisine, and later Bill Clinton became the first President to dine in an Indian restaurant during his term.

As the Diaspora adapted, it shed the vilifying aspects of caste and ideas of untouchability. For instance, most diasporal Hindus were critical of the widely-publicised prohibition, in 1924, of non-caste persons and "untouchables," the Dalits, from use of temples, or even the roads leading to them, at Vaikom and Guruvayoor in Travancore, South India, a ban that quite likely occurred elsewhere as well.

Traditionally, unions of different castes and tribes were few in India, perhaps because each tribe was so large and thus self-sufficient; but it happened of necessity in the older Diaspora, where cooperation was essential for formal political trust and concord, and to overcome isolationism, language, cultural and other barriers which had, in India, stymied past efforts to unite against the British, e.g. with the Marathas, the rebels of 1857, Aurobindo and *Anushilan Samiti,* and others. Social integration and a real union for Indians were unlikely to occur without the enlightenment that came from progressive education and positive examples, including India's past history.(See p. 452.)

Education is usually enlightening, but can be subverted to impart erroneous views and solidify caste biases, as we have seen among certain Indian nationals, including professionals, in North America, many of whom continue to use caste surnames. This is an orthodox teaching, not a religious concept. It is thus hoped that the *Hindu American Foundation (HAF)* and similar bodies would address the caste issue and champion the extension of Hinduism to all who wish it, and promote needed reforms, although Dalits or "untouchables" are unknown in the West.

Persistence of caste practices would retard attempts to promote the interests and the moral, constitutional and spiritual development of *all* Indians. Many Hindus of the older Diaspora ceased using caste surnames, even when required by colonial authorities. Such attempts were praised as a model of equality that upheld rights and rewarded ability regardless of one's birth, as is inherent in the concept of *varna*, thus sparing the Ambhedkars and Jagans in Indian societies the humiliation that could have soured lesser talents[159].

PIOs, despite their status in the colonies as underdogs and separation from the motherland—or perhaps because of it—have done well economically, wherever they settled after completing indentures. They rose by diligence and honest endeavour to the highest positions in their new homelands, even in segregated societies like South Africa, the USA before Civil Rights legislation, and their more recent destinations in New Zealand and Australia, as primary and secondary migrants.

Alas, those who had been educated only in British schools and for colonial service had learned a false and pejorative version of Indians and their history (Mill, Macaulay, Müller, Pargiter etc.) and, like converts, have tended to dismiss those who were taught the dharmic versions. The dearth of University-educated teachers and professionals in the early 20th century Diaspora lessened after WWII, as colonies acquired universities and colleges. But these tended to reinforce Anglophilia and harden divisions, and did not replace or displace the local self-taught Sankritists, whose years of evening classes had taught Vaidic accounts of Indian history and religion, and traced their progress to modern times.

From the 1950s, many Indian professionals began to fill vacancies in British colonies created by WWII; as a group they were mostly leftists, atheists or both, with scant knowledge of Indian religions, by rejection or neglect. Their pedigree immediately gave them a favoured status among diasporal PIOs eager to connect with kin, but it was soon discovered that surprisingly few were convivial, or familiar with religious lore.

There were exceptions—professionals and businessmen—whose extracurricular schooling had taught them the flaws of the prevailing British version of Indian history (see Prologue). These in turn were astonished to meet diasporal dwellers who had avoided the same propaganda, thanks to their informal evening schools. Even today standard Indian curricula maintain the distortions, which had travelled to America and become entrenched in US education: the invasion theory, caste, the fabricated "arya-dravida" divide, the negation of the epics,

159 BK Ambhedkar, (1891-1956) Maratha lawyer, one of the framers of the Indian constitution, was born into a *mahar* family, considered of low caste; he was a gifted student, but faced harsh biases and endured terrible hardships to achieve an education. Pleased with the INC acceptance of the rights of the lowest castes, he vigorously devoted his energies to constitutional advancement. He became so disillusioned with the INC's failure to promote equality that he and his followers converted to Buddhism. He died of complications of Diabetes. The late Dr Jagan, a Chamar, was the third President of Guyana.

religious chauvinism, the flawed Müller-Pargiter timelines, and the ignoring of newer archaeological evidence, among others.

This parallels the state of equally-misinformed western societies, which still believe in late 19th century race theories and biases. They refuse to accept that a non-white people could have achieved the many inventions in thought, matter and discourse; religion and philosophy; mathematics and sciences; flight; the character of the universe (age, make-up and origin); or gained material insight into matters like water control and agriculture; economics of business and trade etc.—long before white barbarian tribes, seafaring fishermen and raiders of Europe had emerged from the Dark Ages and begun to discover the world.

These were topics covered in "Hindi schools", along with useful general knowledge such as this example of Europe's negative economic impact on India: in 1750 India produced 24.5% of the world's manufactured goods, next to China's 32.8% while Britain supplied 1.9%, most produced manually. By 1830, China's output had dropped to 29.8% and India's to 17.6%. The U.S. share was 2.4% while Britain's had risen to 4.3%, mostly from the industrial revolution and military coercion by the BEICo and its Indian cronies, who profited from switching British for Indian goods, and when they could, by denying others the means to compete with the British (see H. Samuel, *Hansard, HC, 17, July 1929).*

It is surprising that despite their wide publicity, recent discoveries about ancient India are not "welcomed" by secular Indian and Western academics, even some who have risen to high positions in governments, universities and colleges. They continue to believe and teach history as they had learned it, and deny the corrections of the last fifty years. Some North American teachers—mostly ex-Hindu atheists—even question the value of reviewing or revising the British teachings of Indian history. At the best of times few are insightful, courageous or open-minded enough to question what they were taught, much less change them.

Perhaps they need to be reminded how backward, selfish and cruel Europe was just a few centuries ago, perpetrating more heinous crimes than most other peoples of that time. Among these was Church persecution of atheists, while India remained tolerant. For example, Lucilio Vanini, an Italian scholar and priest was burned at the stake in Toulouse in 1619 on *suspicion* of atheism. He was incidentally a racial bigot but that did not seem to have influenced his punishment.

The famous plague and London fire of 1666 were blamed on atheism, prompting philosopher Thomas Hobbes, a respected Englishman, to destroy some of his work lest it be used against him. Today's strident atheist and anti-Hindu could be more objective, and less condemnatory. That excludes campaigning against persisting corruption and favouritism, which too many Indians in India display, and which might explain the deficits in primary education in many states, these past decades, by diversion of education funds to personal use by officials. The Diaspora has suffered from meagre education facilities, but much less so than in Indian communities, where over 200 million stand in need.

In the UK, the education of Scottish and English children began in the 17th century. After some 400 years, it has failed to serve the general population effectively, being largely private, until lately. Disturbing statistics are published in the West to highlight the anti-social effects of poor education[160] and the role of nutrition. Good nutrition underpins education schemes and depends on the ability of parents to feed their children adequately. Indian land laws discriminate against small farmers and their ability to produce food. Mega-farms may be good for short-term profit by corporate farmers, but they displace people whose small plots feed continents. Nor do they substitute for the self-sufficiency and control over their livelihood that enable farmers to earn a decent living and so provide their children a minimum primary education. School attendance laws alone do not place children in classrooms. Diasporal children, unlike Indians, have rarely missed schooling solely from nutritional need.

In the century after colonial settlement, demand rose for post-primary education and for changing or enforcing existing laws. For instance, three Caribbean commissions reported on colonial education in the 1920s: *the Mayhew-Marriot Commission*, the *Pillai-Tiwari-Keatinge Deputation* and the *Wood (Lord Halifax) Report*. All found that instruction was generally poor, and worse in estate schools, with no improvement in 50 years. Private denominational schools (Anglican, Roman Catholic, Wesleyan, Presbyterian, Baptist and Moravian) were run by ministers, not teachers, and vied for students; teachers were expected to proselytise and their promotions were tied to success in that activity. There was a general agitation—joined by teachers—urging governments to take over all schools. This unsatisfactory state continued until after WWII. (See *tera-3.ul.cs.cmu.edu/NASD/...5792.../00000177.htm*.)

The prevailing and uncritical acceptance of British teachings at all levels of Indian society is as astonishing today as it was when Sanskrit scholar, Pandit Dowlat Ram Chaubé—who had gone to Demerara in the nineteen twenties, at the same time as the Pillai team—discovered the phenomenon among educated Indians there, just as he had seen it in India. By that time, Harappa and Mohenjodaro had been found, confirming Vaidic descriptions he had read and tried to pass on. His skeletal grasp of English slowed his efforts, which, however, were

[160]http://www.begintoread.com/research/literacystatistics.html;
http://www.theguardian.com/education/2007/jul/10/schools.primaryeducation

welcomed by the many who could converse with him in an Indian language, Hindi or Urdu, and who, he noted, lived as neighbours.

He felt that it would help Indians to review the achievements of PIOs who were forced to emigrate in the 19th century, and learn what principles and what adaptations had been useful in shielding them from the harsh judgements and intense anti-Hindu or anti-Islamic propaganda of 110 years of exile from pre-independence India. Those could serve as a guide to Indians emerging from British authority in India, especially urban dwellers or loyal servants of the *Rāja.* Many of these had difficulty managing the change, fearing the prospect of serving a Hindu majority, which might be unsympathetic and relationships strained. To avoid the risk, however rare, many fled to the UK or to British colonies.

India's attainment of independence boosted the morale of Indians throughout the Diaspora, despite the negative publicity given to the terrorism and killings on both sides. Crowds were just as fervent as in India or Pakistan and Nehru's midnight message just as moving. In mixed communities, response was subdued, since most colonial Hindus and Muslims shared geographic origins and customs, lived well together and even intermarried. Both groups were horrified by the partition killings and consoled each other, hoping that the two countries find a social remedy. But PIOs did not appreciate the full force of the politics of partition. British censorship of news from India was tight, especially during WWII. In the 1950s, Pakistan opted for an Islamic dictatorship while India fell under Nehru and the INC as a virtual one-party government, until his death. The INC continued for another fifty years, barring short breaks, or with coalitions. It kept out of wars, except to defend against Pakistan. Diasporal friendships between Hindus and Muslims weathered these, until Wahhabism began to intrude, divide and radicalise Muslims, and reject Hinduism and other religions. Pakistan is politically an Islamic state, despite a moderate majority.

The Diaspora had paid close attention to India's agonising journey to independence, praised and criticised the main characters, as occasion demanded and offered ideas. They had lauded the constitutional requirements putting an end to caste and other pejorative practices, and hoped to see real steps to relieve women and the poor, who had suffered the most under foreign yoke, the tyranny of hedonist princes and *zamindars,* dishonest *patwaris* and others who had impoverished them. Comparisons concluded that Indians could benefit from emulating older diasporal PIOs to regain their self-esteem, individuality and culture and stop copying the British, whose life-style and customs were so different. The transition was not expected to be easy or swift for the brain-washed middle class or atheist, or freely accepted by the fully anglicised.

The major question was the constitutional designation of India as a secular state, when indeed most Indians—the Hindu majority, that is—were highly spiritual, tolerant and accommodating, and preferred to see India set on a moral course that protected and supported all religions, rather than merely shrugging them off, as secularism seemed to do. Indeed some saw it as a dissolute ideology or crutch for leftist fanatics and doctrinaire atheists. Muslim clerics followed *Sharia law,* which often seemed arbitrary and inconsistent with the Quran.

By the time India became independent, diasporal PIOs, of both genders, were literate, unlike native Indians, whose general literacy rate was a mere 23%. PIOs were over 90% literate and many had advanced to the highest ranks among professionals, merchants, farmers, politicians etc., in their societies, second to none in India, more broad-minded and worldly-wise, and proud of upholding traditional religious tenets. They lacked the smug superiority shown by Indians of wealth or "high" social class, the type who became the new Indian elite, envoys and migrants to the West, and could afford to travel and misrepresent their homeland!

PIOs saw Nehru's heavily bureaucratised central planning, Soviet-style, as retrograde and ill-advised, as it seemed merely to replace private corporate power blocks with inefficient and equally corrupt state monopolies. Worse, it created a privileged urban minority, while the majority rural Hindus and Muslims remained deprived, isolated and powerless, with inadequate food, education, land or health care—their principal needs; sixty years later, these needs remain unmet. This was surely not what Nehru meant by *"a tryst with destiny."* His welcome by Russia and their agreement on treaties and technical help, while leaving non-alignment intact, led diasporal leftists to follow a similar path.

The slow pace of education, and the heavy hand of centralism, controls, licences and permits in order to do business and remain non-aligned—in what came to be known as *Licence Rāja*—deterred diasporal entrepreneurs, many of whom wanted to re-establish contact with their families in India, and to investigate land claims, bequests and opportunities. Most were Hindus, a few Christians and Muslims. But Indian bureaucrats and politicians seemed to hold these PIOs as inferior people, to be shunned, or treated with condescension, perhaps because most were rural, identifiable by a religion (*Bhāratīyas*), unlike India's educated, who were mostly urban, only nominally religious, and had become "secular", though few could say what that entailed.

Expecting to return to India to replace the departing British, and share their unique perspective and expertise, PIOs were deterred also by the discouraging exodus of Indians headed for the UK and colonies, not realising then that these were Macaulay's despised brown Englishmen. Until the mid-1960s, the USA and Canada restricted Indian migration and Australia maintained a "whites only" policy. Otherwise, many more Indians would have migrated. Thus India was thought to have erred in not encouraging repatriation and entrepreneurship, even if restricted.

Some colonial PIOs did claim Indian citizenship after 1947, but most were deterred by Nehru's left-wing government, even though some of its best-known members were almost communist and entrepreneurial enough to be described paradoxically as leftist capitalists. Avoiding Communism was helpful, since it would undoubtedly forestall factional or ideological violence and avoid overt destabilisation by the CIA, the newly-established US spy agency, which had become active in all British colonies and ex-colonies.

In 1948, India established consulates in colonial capitals; Nehru had advised PIOs to "integrate" with the general population in their places of birth, but there were places, e.g. East Africa, especially Kenya, where Indians were a minority, and felt threatened by a resolute British effort to divide Africans from Indians, as they had done in the Caribbean. Indian activists like Manilal Desai helped form the *Kikuyu Central Association* to coordinate with the East African INC. Soon, journalists Pranlal Sheth, Chanan Singh, Iitzval de Souza and Pio Gama Pinto were alerting readers to the British ploy to grant independence to Kenyan whites, as they had done in South Africa.

Mau Mau uprisings after WWII coincided with the arrival of Apa Pant, the first Indian high commissioner in Nairobi, who, with Pinto, was able to keep Indians from being targeted. Despite Nehru's advice, most of Kenya's 200,000 Indians opted for British citizenship, on independence in 1963. A 1969 decision lost them Kenyan jobs, and they were given three months to leave. The British denied them entry on the grounds of race or colour, accepting only 1500 families annually. Those who could not leave were left to the mercies of charity and advocacy. The plight of Kenyans was soon matched by Ugandans, when Idi Amin, in late 1972, expelled all Indians from Uganda, seizing property and annulling citizenships. British and other Commonwealth governments accepted the refugees. Special deals between the Aga Khan and the Canadian government, enabled all Ismailis to leave for Canada, assured of jobs provided by the Khan's businesses, chiefly in Western provinces.

The treatment of British Indians in other places was generally better, except for South Africa, and Namibia, then under South African administration, under the restrictions of Apartheid. As countries became independent, Indians could opt for local citizenship or retain a European one. As noted, the latter was unreliable and the former dependent on the philosophy of the head of government, as many ex-colonies came under dictators, whose decisions, like Amin's, were often whimsical. Families thus chose to migrate to more hospitable countries, even though the process was disruptive, and most recipient nations were white and possibly racially biased; some communities were openly hostile. Many Indians would wish to re-settle in India, should policies allow.

In 1948, India began to offer scholarships to colonials, regardless of race or religion, to several of India's universities and technical colleges. But anti-India bias had been so effectively disseminated in the Empire and Commonwealth that colonial residents found it hard to believe that one could get a first class education in India.[161] And when they saw the kind of greedy professionals the country was then exporting, it was difficult to change minds. Mrs Dixit, and others from the Georgetown consulate, were too anglicised and rigid in their methods, and ambivalent re diasporal Indians. Anglo-Indian newspapers had seeped into pre-war colonial societies and a few did resume post-war, but generally the INC and Indian press failed to recognise overseas Indians.

Recently, the Ministry of Overseas Indian Affairs separated the descendants of 19th and 20th century Indians—most of whom had been forced into British overseas colonial service—from the group of recent migrants, restricting or denying them any rights in India, even though they may have family ties there and claims to property. (See *moia.gov.in/)*.

There was concern that diasporal Muslims would not show the same loyalty to India as Hindus, despite the very obvious preferences given them in India by the INC, almost as a bribe to secure their votes. These have increased. Most Muslim PIOs originated in UP, Bihar and Bengal, with rare or no Arabs or Persians. Their loyalty has been as expected, and not just a pleasant surprise, both in India and the Diaspora, although it suffers setbacks each time a Pakistani ISI-backed terrorist group, whether home-grown or international—latterly al Qaeda—destroys something in India or assassinates people.

With Pakistan's founding, some colonial Muslims have not only claimed Pakistani origins but given Pakistan an "ancient" history, ignoring its creation in 1947, while Muslims were transported to the colonies a century *before* that. Besides, few colonial Muslims originated in the provinces comprising Pakistan; but the religious rigidity and fear promoted by Wahhabism are paramount and trump geography.

Nehru remained non-aligned and slowly worked to build some capacity within the structure of Government. India needed to regain its technological and scientific excellence, a task Nehru placed in the hands of the new institutes of technology. But India remained ominously at risk to US corporatism and consumerism. It has adopted, rather too

---

[161] This opinion was not shared by the several African Blacks who benefited from the scheme; one of them was a Barbadian who studied Medicine, spoke fluent Hindi and became his country's Minister of Health in 1971.

hurriedly, the worst of western habits and attitudes and seems willing to discard or apologise for the features which are most admirable and distinctive in its traditions. A female Indian in a sari is an elegant and admired sight, but in western casual attire is just another brown woman.

Many university graduates whom India had hoped to retain to rebuild her education, health care, industries and defence continue to surface in the West. Unsurprisingly, they chose migration, whenever possible, mainly to the USA (the US rejects lower classes), and rarely contradict US or UK views openly. They are likely to be pro-West in any stand-off between India and the USA or UK.

It should not have surprised anyone, but it did surprise Indian migrants in 20th century USA that they were still characterised by the standards set by late 19th century eugenicists and racialists. Galton and Broca were among those who believed in social Darwinism and had managed to convince lawmakers in several US states of the validity and significance of phrenology, enough to authorise castration of those deemed unfit mentally or physically to produce the best children, and in some states to prohibit mixed marriages. Early PIOs in the US West found mates in Mexican families, and some adopted Spanish names.

In India, dark-skinned people are believed inferior to those with light skin; this bias was in place in 1947, aided by the discredited British hypothesis of an "aryan conquest" of India. This perverse attitude was recently exposed as alive and well in India, following the selection of a dark Indo-American as Miss USA (pp. 440-2). America did not moderate nor change attitudes to coloured peoples until the mid-1960s, and did accept the dark "queen". Even so, colour prejudices persist, not the least in academia. The mulatto president might well be an experiment and the last one for some time, though some coloured politicians, including at least two Indians, nurture presidential ambitions.

Indian cultural themes, literature, movies, dances, songs, creative arts of various kinds have always been welcomed, and the taste for art forms finely honed, from the earliest émigrés to the present. Tutors arose for every type of activity, group or individual, who have spread awareness and appreciation of various art forms—literature, music, dance, theatre—many with remarkable showmanship and creativity, and many westerners have pursued learning in them, including tutelage by masters in India, often with great success. Many excellent writers have emerged over the last century, and one, Vidia Naipaul of Trinidad, was awarded the Nobel Prize for literature in 2004, while Kenya's MG Vassanji and India's Rohinton Mistry (both now Canadian), have, among others, written prize-winning novels. Numerous others have excelled in business and professional fields—medicine, education, engineering, computing, journalism etc.—and sports, especially cricket, with names like Rohan Kanhai, Basil Butcher, Joe Solomon, Sonny Ramadhin, Alvin Kallicharan, Shivnarine Chanderpaul and others, known worldwide since the 1950s, when they began competing with Indian players.

Most diasporal cities have a number of art schools where children learn basic, traditional and adaptive skills in music, dance and voice; creativity is promoted, and performing encouraged. Indian movies have retained their popularity as have *"filmi"* songs, which have made singers like Lata Mangeshkar global legends. She has, among her triumphs, the most distinguished sound track of Indian films, perhaps all films, *Mughal-e-Azam,* released in 1960, and re-released in a coloured version a few years ago. *Barsaat* was released at the time of independence and was one of the first films that attracted non-Indian audiences in the Diaspora.

JFK, Mrs. and Mr D.S. Saund

The first Indo-American member of the US Congress was Sikh democrat Dalip Singh Saund who served in the House of Representatives from 1957-62. He had been resident in the USA for 26 years before the *Luce-Celler* Act. He became a citizen in 1949 and forthwith entered politics. When he won the election in 1957, he became the first Indian, the first Sikh and the first Asian to become a member of Congress. In 1928, he wrote *My Mother India*, a rebuttal of *Mother India,* a scatological invective against Hindus (p. 294) by Katherine Mayo, the justly-maligned American WASP writer, whose book remains a source of "facts" on Asian and Oriental studies, in some US Universities.

In previous chapters (*Introduction, 15, 17*) comments are made about the migration efforts of Sikhs to North America and their rejection by Canada. But they persisted and became a permanent feature of British Columbia and several western American States. The original Sikh settlers and their descendants prospered but newer migrants tended to arrive with chips on their shoulders and militancy against Hindus, particularly after PM Indira Gandhi's operation *Blue Star* in 1984 (p.365), and out of habit and completeness. Canada has sheltered Sikhs, who demand from India a separate state, *Kalistan*, and began a campaign to promote it internationally, with Sikhs in the USA, UK and Europe.

Separatist militancy, under the rubric *Babbar Khalsa*, alerted security agencies. The Royal Canadian Mounted Police (RCMP) and the Canadian Security Intelligence Service (CSIS), received numerous notices of Sikh intent to target Air India flights, and amassed taped records of conversations among suspected *Babbar Khalsa* terrorists. Yet they failed to prevent attacks. On June 23, 1985, *Babbar Khalsa* bombed Air India's Montreal-New Delhi Flight 182, killing all aboard (268 Canadian citizens, 27 Britons, and 24 Indians). Another bomb had been placed aboard a flight from Vancouver to Tokyo's Narita Airport, where it exploded during transfer of baggage to its target, an Air India flight to Bangkok, killing two handlers and injuring others.

The main suspects were known or presumed members of *Babbar Khalsa*, but their trial was thwarted by CSIS's destruction of wire-tap records, which would have incriminated those arrested. Eventually, Inderjit Singh Reyat, a PIO electrician from Coventry, England, and at the time resident of Vancouver, Canada, was convicted of making the bombs, manslaughter, and of perjury, which had led to the acquittal of prime suspects, Ripudaman Singh Malik and Ajaib Singh Bagri. *(See www.publicsafety.gc.ca/cnt/ntnl-scrt/cntr-trrrsm/r-nd-flight-182/)*

The largest and oldest Sikh community in the West is probably in British Columbia, where they have prospered in Agriculture, Forestry and Lumber, in "small" business and have made solid contributions to politics. Ujjal Dosanjh served as Premier of British Columbia, Canada, in 2000, eighty six years after the same province had expelled Sikh migrants! Later, he served as a liberal minister in the federal government succeeding his colleague Herb Dhaliwal, also British Columbian, and a moderate Sikh. Like most Indians, Sikhs have retained their culture, centred in *gurdwaras* (temples), but have also kept some contentious aspects of family life, such as female foeticide and honour killings, the latter usually a sequel to a female member's breach of strict rules re relationships with males.

Increasingly, Indians are migrating to the West and today number over 4 million in the USA and Canada (see Table p. 412), occupying middle and upper class positions in the major cities, while a militant Christian minority trains in various places for proselytising offensives against Hindus in India. Groups of leftist, secular or communist academics hold positions in US colleges, usually in History, Asian studies, Social studies or Religion, which provide a platform from which they too fulminate against Hinduism, in what has deteriorated into a barefaced hate campaign, packed with half-truths, distortions, inventions and plain lies. Ironically, the harshest critics include Indians who have benefitted from the "reservation" program, have US postgraduate degrees and did not return to India. On campus they are prime targets for Church recruiters.

Indian migrants are not always safe in their new communities, especially as they tend to cluster in settling, work hard to improve their neighbourhood and thus attract attention—welcome and unwelcome—a fact that must be remembered by foreign journalists in India who complain about the less than perfect society that India is.

In 1987, the US was shocked by a spate of murders and serious attacks on Indians in New Jersey that had followed abuse, baiting, vandalism and threats to them by *"dot-busters"* ("dots" referring to *bindis,* the red or orange spots on married women's foreheads). In an academic paper, E. Gutierrez recorded the murders, writing, *"Navroze Mody, Bhered Patel, Jakariya Kirit, Malkiat Singh, and the numerous other Asian Indians who were attacked during the late 1980s were all victims of hate crime."* She cited the prevailing ethnic hatred in US communities, so glaring that the persons responsible in NJ had publicised their intention to rid New Jersey of Indians, in a letter to the *Jersey Journal* signed *"Jersey City Dot Busters"*, as follows:

"I'm writing about your article during July about the abuse of Indian People. Well I'm here to state the other side. I hate them, if you had to live near them you would also. We are an organization called dot busters. We have been around for 2 years. We will go to any extreme to get Indians to move out of Jersey City. If I'm walking down the street and I see a Hindu and the setting is right, I will hit him or her. We plan some of our most extreme attacks such as breaking windows, breaking car windows, and crashing family parties. We use the phone books and look up the name Patel. Have you seen how many of them there are? Do you even live in Jersey City? Do you walk down Central avenue and experience what it's like to be near them: we have and we just don't want it anymore. You said that they will have to start protecting themselves because the police cannot always be there. They will never do anything. They are a week (sic) race. Physically and mentally. We are going to continue our way. We will never be stopped." In India, this would be classed as terrorism, but in the USA, the rewards of ingratiation forced victims to adjust. Some women stopped wearing saris and bindis out of fear. Random attacks continue.

After the 9/11 demolition of the World Trade Centre in New York, ascribed to Arabs, there were many reports of non-Arab South Asians being assaulted by angry racists. Frank Roque in Los Angeles shot and killed Balbir Singh Sodhi, a gas station attendant. Roque boasted afterwards at a bar, *"They're investigating the murder of a turban-head down the street!"* In 2002, Saurabh Bhalerao, a Hindu delivering pizza in Massachusetts, was mugged and beaten for "being Muslim." His attackers told him to go back to Iraq, then bundled him into a car trunk.

Bhalerao escaped and retaliated with a hammer on one of his attackers and was stabbed as he tried to flee.

Indophobia isn't limited to sociopathic racist thugs and wayward teenagers, however. In 2006, Virginia Senator George Allen, with a B.A. and law degrees, wantonly attacked an Indo-American staff worker named Sidarth, and was filmed calling him a *"macaca,"* meaning macaque, the monkey species. Similar terror was sown elsewhere, notably the murder of Sikh worshippers in a gurdwara in Wisconsin.

Racist graffiti on Mayoral Candidate poster, Edison NJ, USA'

New Jersey remains hate prone, but South Asians carry on in the aftermath of the "Dotbusters" and live their lives as any would, trusting in law and order, standing by their high regard for "Amriki" and the promised good sense of most of its citizens, and grappling with continuing chauvinism, as exemplified by the smeared electioneering poster above, America's apparent symbol of welcome to diversity, and an eye-opener for Indians.

http://blog.nj.com/njv_guest_blog/2012/09/ wisconsin_sikh_ temple_shooting.html New Jersey's Dotbusters | NJ.com). (https://www.indiacurrents.com/articles/2010/07/01/

Unsavoury aspects of the Diaspora flourish. Under the British Rāja, aristocrats profiteered in India and exported the proceeds home to enhance their personal holdings, creating a poor model for self-indulgent Indians, especially princes and the avaricious mimics who adopt British mannerisms and speech. The *Rāja* regularly paraded examples to boost its image in the Diaspora and in Europe. Wealthy Indians sequestered monies in foreign havens, rather than invest in productive enterprises in India. They built personal palaces at home and overseas, with exhibitionist zeal, displayed mainly in Europe, especially London—where their numbers and prime real estate holdings have increased steadily—and in the USA, especially in California. Indians have continued to migrate to Britain, are attracted to British real estate and give generously to western institutions.

Today Lakshmi Mittal maintains three or four of the most expensive properties in the exclusive Kensington district of London. His company, *ArcelorMittal,* is the world's largest steel maker, a global conglomerate, with Indian roots, and branches in North America, Trinidad, Europe, Asia and Japan. Other Indians continue to invest lavishly in choice London properties and a few have "attained" peerage positions; currently 23 are serving in the House of Lords, in three political parties.

Three others recently died. While India's public medical institutions starve for cash for basic needs, Mittal's son and daughter-in-law, both London residents, with fortunes derived in India, gave £15 million in 2008 to London's Great Ormond Street Hospital. Perhaps the Mittal family and others of wealth had not heard that it was the British who had drained India of its riches, stolen its jewels, changed social customs, enslaved its people, imposed their language and an anti-India curriculum in schools, and brainwashed the educated into loyal *"coconuts",* claiming thus to have civilised India! (cf. usage of WOG, *"western oriental gentleman,"* which the British used for rich Egyptians).

The Mittal Foundation has contributed to three tertiary education centres in India and to others in North America, but so far no public records show that they have given to primary education or sanitation, the areas of greatest need in India, with potential to emancipate some 300,000,000 neglected people oppressed by desperate poverty.

Ratan Tata (*Tata Foundation*) gives to Indian charities, but gave to Harvard University $50 million fairly recently. However internationally impressive or personally satisfying the program that huge gift will support, it's merely taking a few lumps of coal to Newcastle, or, like the gift of California's toilet businessman, Crane, who, after WWI, gave boxes of Californian dates to Ibn Saud, King of Saudi Arabia, when dates were that country's only export! (Lacey). The *Harvard Alumni Association* gave a Harvard Medal for donations to the university to Ānanda G Mahindra, Chairman of *Mahindra and Mahindra*, an Indian industrial group, the first Indian to be so honoured: another case of Indians buying foreign favours, awards or titles. Like the Ratan Tata gift, Mahindra's could end up funding one of Harvard's anti-Hindu activists! Does India not steadily give the rich US enough in manpower? Should that money not have gone to an Indian University, to make a real impact?

The number of Indians in the Diaspora has grown over the last fifty years, naturally and from migration from India; regional shifts have occurred from one country to another (*secondary migration*), spurred by the 1965 changes to North American immigration laws, and the expansion in the USA of professional and business positions in health care, education, industry and computing. Indians are high average earners among US residents. Political hostility stirred a massive exodus from Guyana and East Africa, Guyana losing nearly half of its 51% Indian population, many professionals, one of whom recently cured a child of AIDS. Idi Amin's repression in Uganda, in the early 1970s, emptied the country of skilled and wealthy Indians and influenced the migration of East African Indians, Muslims getting help from the Aga Khan. Many Indians have also left Trinidad, Fiji and Suriname, exposing them to Western chauvinism and the stereotypes left over from the era of race superiority, which lingers on, particularly in North America, which lacks a knowledge of things Indian: history, geography and culture.

As allies of Pakistan, a conservative Islamic state dictatorship, the USA, in its ignorance, ungenerously viewed Nehruvian socialism as evidence of a backward people, unfit to govern themselves. In 1947, many Americans felt that India would in time disintegrate into chaos, and threaten world stability and peace. The negative prognosis was repeated, even among educated Indians India's non-aligned status was viewed with much suspicion. The posturing of Communist parties in India may have influenced the post-1965 migration to the USA of conservative, individualistic and ambitious Indians. Many, from recent and older generations, have advanced in political parties in the US, UK, Canada, and elsewhere, as noted

The last two hundred years have seen increasing attempts to convert Hindus to Christianity, following the enforced conversions of millions to Islam by the Mughals. In the last five decades, this activity has surged with venom throughout India and the Diaspora, driven by external funding, and the actions of the INC, secularists, communists and other native anti-Hindus: V. Mangalwadi, K. Ilaiah, Meera Nanda, Yoginder Sikand, and others in India, and their foreign counterparts, like Ravi Zacharias, who thunder against Hindus. Older PIOs remain surprised at the anti-Hindu hostility of so many South Asian Christians, having come to attach such witless fanaticism to born-again Caucasian Christian demagogues, whom they had met in the former colonies. Hinduism has withstood much and welcomes informed critiques, not distortions; it was, with its variants, among the earliest belief systems, apart from spotty atheism, and was nurtured with thought and extraordinary insights, until India's prosperity attracted predators, with their religions.

Deepak Chopra, Vijay Prashad, Romila Thapar, Dinesh D'Souza, Angana Chatterji, Biju Mathew, Vinay Lal, Deepak Sarma, and others in the USA, are frequent and harsh Hindu critics. Balmurli Natarajan venerates white missionary professors, and, like the others, is quite likely to condemn Hindu groups like *Sangh Parivar* and demand that they stop using concept words like *Hindutva,* yet would not ask Islamists to abandon *Sharia*, or Christianity the *Ascension*, a display of hypocrisy, petulance, unfairness, arrogance and intolerance. Any show or public defence of Hinduism is deemed *Communalism*, while the same for Islam or Christianity is not. Surely the religions can co-exist, with tolerance and in peace, as they do in many places, and did in India, before the bombardment of Hindus by Islamic and Christian proselytes.

Communalism has a derogatory meaning in India, signifying blind partisanship and religious bigotry, a historically inaccurate portrayal of

Hinduism, which welcomed and accepted other religions in India, along with their institutions, whether church, mosque, synagogue or Parsi fire temple. Saudi Arabia tolerates no other religion on its soil, a fact hardly mentioned by enemies of Hinduism, least of all the USA, which ignores the paradox. Proselytising Hindus, if such existed, would not be allowed on the Seven Hills of Rome, or the Vatican, but Christians had defiantly invaded the Seven Hills of *Sri Venkateshwara Swamy Vāri Temple* in Tirupathi, Andhra Pradesh, one of the most sacred places in Hinduism.

Anti-Hindu forces seemed to have gained increasing strength and wealth since Roman Catholic Bishop Caldwell first entered the lists in 1856 with his divisive and erroneous Dravidian "dark race" hypothesis. It mattered little in the 19th century what falsehoods were concocted as long as they sounded true and aided the British cause. Lies from white clergy carried more weight than the truth from brown or non-clergy opponents. (It could be called the *Caldwell-Muller Axiom*. Bishop Caldwell and Max Müller are equally wrong in blatantly promoting a mere conjecture as truth. But Müller, knowing the flawed conclusions, did issue a late retraction).

Their fantasy has resisted correction and has, instead, become incorporated in the rantings of modern proselytes, active in India and the Diaspora, such as the Billy Graham zealot, Ravi Zacharias, who injects his diatribes with things imagined, while blissfully ignoring or disdaining the real *facts.* Archbishop Ussher's calculation that the world was created in 4004 BCE—the "*Ussher numeral* "seems an apt name—is part of this cluster of "facts", widely quoted to condemn the Hindu idea that the universe is trillions of years older, a hypothesis more in keeping with modern astronomic discoveries, even though Black Hole theorists say, with uncertainty, just over a billion; physicist Stephen Hawking now disagrees with the "event horizon" concept and calls for a grey hole!

The demolition of NYC's Twin Towers (World Trade Centre) on Sept 11, 2001 gave PIOs a dose of reality, more than any previous event had done. Suddenly, brown people were labelled Islamic jihadists and terrorists, and Hindus, generally a passive group, smarted under these labels. They were screened and questioned at airports and profiled by police and security. Their homes were threatened, their children assaulted and their temples desecrated or destroyed. One flagrant example of the last occurred in Hamilton, Ontario, where a Hindu temple was destroyed by arson; city reporters kept referring to it as a mosque, despite corrections delivered to their editor at a public forum convened by the city to provide information. It did not help that the pro-US speaker was unable to separate the religions. The incident exposed anti-India animosities in North America and the ignorance of things Indian, masked by cordiality to INC governments. US impatience with

India is fairly obvious, and stems, it seems, from intolerance to any act of independent thinking on political issues, or reference to Hinduism.

The publicity of happenings in India is usually negative. The 2004 tsunami in the Bay of Bengal surprised regional Indian governments by the speed of the wave: three hours or less from its Sumatran origin to India and Thailand. Casualties were high, though mitigated by flight to high ground. Yet India was criticised for not acting early enough. A tsunami warning system for the Indian Ocean, as there is for the Pacific, would have helped. Not much was discussed about this in Western media, despite the number of countries at risk from a future event. The threat remains, since there is no good way of telling whether the 2004 subduction had released all the stored energy in the colliding plates.

Rich nations have not offered help, though they too are at some risk, e.g., the US base at Diego Garcia. But the Bush Government showed little interest in environmental matters then, and his staff was singularly lethargic in the *days* it took hurricane *Katrina* to reach New Orleans, in August 2005. Had this sloth been India's, the western media would have hammered it. Similarly, the western response to the *Ebola* outbreak in West Africa is so skimpily supported, and mainly by adventure-seeking North Americans, barring personnel from *Médecins Sans Frontières* (MSF). Greater support is needed for local African crews: supplies, medicines, food, etc., not just sanctimonious comments re "poor Africa", a geographic blank to most Americans, who act as if Africa is one country, and expect that the Ebola virus will avoid the white and wealthy. The role of Canadians, Chinese and others in invading forest habitats in pursuit of precious minerals, plants and oil seems contributory.

Some PIOs seeking high office in the USA have switched from Hinduism—e.g. US-born Bobby Jindal, of Punjabi Hindu heritage, now Republican Governor of Louisiana, has converted to Roman Catholicism. He supports a creationist timetable, which his government allows in school curricula, a surprising position for one with a major in biology. He aspires to the Republican nomination for the Presidency in the near future, and has already begun to pander to "big oil" by blatantly dropping scores of lawsuits against British Petroleum and others, re the Deepwater Horizon oil spill in the Gulf of Mexico in 2010. It is hard to ignore the cosiness. But maybe the reprieve is more for Dick Cheney's Halliburton, whose error apparently caused the spill, than for BP.

Nikki Randhawa Haley, another Punjabi and an extreme rightist, is governor of South Carolina and is angling for the Tea Party nomination for the next Presidency. As a Democratic nominee, Bikram Mohanty lost the 2014 race for the 8th District State Senate seat in Georgia.

PIOs, born in the west, speak with the accent of their birthplace, which relieves them of the "Paki" slur common two to three decades ago, and allows new horizons to expand traditional occupational succession in families, often radically. Stand-up comedy, especially "live" is one of the more daunting pursuits, at which several have become expert in North America, UK and Australia, including Russell Peters and Shaun Majumdar of Canada, Aasif Mandvi, Kalpen Modi, Mindy Paling, and others in the USA, Danny Bhoy (Chaudhry) of Scotland and Australia, Papa CJ and others in Britain. PIOs also do well in print and visual media, as reporters, editors and columnists. Analyst Fareed Zacharia has held senior positions in *Time* and *Newsweek* magazines, and regularly appears on US TV and radio stations. The late Freddie Mercury (Farouk Bulsara) was a Parsi rock star from Tanzania. Ben Kingsley (Krishna Banji) is noted for excellent cinema portrayals of Mahatma Gandhi in *Gandhi* and Itzhak Stern in *Schindler's List.*

Infosys is a known success in India, and its founders have all become wealthy. The retiring CEO, Shruti Shibulal, has invested heavily in real estate in India and the Diaspora, owning 700 apartments in the US Northwest, mainly in Seattle, and smaller holdings in Europe. He has been donating to education in India for the last 15 years (2014).

In colonial times, many princes exhibited themselves and their excesses on roads, in halls of entertainment and luxury, and in fashion centres of the world, while continuing to milk their subjects and fellows in India. Among the more flamboyant in India and well-known in Los Angeles, before WWII, were Yashwant Holkar II and his father Tukhoji III. Both squandered Indaur's wealth on capricious and extravagant toys, of which the son's custom car collection, from the world's costliest stables, cannot be admired, even in retrospect, when millions around them starved. Tata and others' gifts to Harvard University and that of the Nizam of Hyderabad's 1940 gift of a warship to Australia and 15 Spitfires to the UK, while his people remained poor and uneducated, and few citizens could get an Australian visa, are equally egregious.

October, 2014 marked the 200th anniversary of the sudden death of Yashwant Holkar I while spending a fortune to build cannons to expel the British! He would probably be ashamed of his self-indulgent descendants and marvel that the pressures against the well-meaning in the land have not eased. Today' excesses are as much magnified and exemplified by Dinesh Dalmia in the USA, and the Mittals and others in Britain and India.

State Department's Richard Rahul Verma, UK-born Surgeon General Vivek Murthy, NYC prosecutor Preet Bharara, Rajiv Shah, Sanjay Gupta and Amrit Singh are among many government officials. Verma, a first generation Indo-American lawyer, son of a University professor, became

US ambassador to India in Dec 2014, having served with Obama since 2008 and in the State department since. Murthy is an internist from Boston and founder of *Doctors for America.* Bharara is noted for his contentious prosecution of Devyani Khobragade, India's former deputy consul general in New York, for violating labour laws—a criminal charge—for which she was expelled from the USA. The matter was clumsily handled by US authorities and created discord with India, prompting the INC to expel a US diplomat and revoke certain US embassy privileges in New Delhi. The USA retaliated by cancelling the planned visit to India of Assistant Secretary of State for Asia, Nisha Desai Biswal, a PIO. Bharara is also involved in actions against mega-banks, so far only two, one French, one Swiss; many hope that he and the US Attorney General will soon probe US banks, which no doubt are greater contributors to the 2008 Wall Street debacle than foreigners. They include *"Sharia banks"*, the latest tool of Arab money. Gifts to US politicians may have shielded them so far.

Rajiv Shah is a medical doctor and health analyst who headed USAID for the last five years; he was among the nation's most honoured under 40s when he guided US efforts after the Haiti earthquake, in 2010. He has changed the way USAID uses its $20B budget to achieve targets, using an evidence-based approach. His work is praised by both political parties. Dr Gupta is a neurosurgeon at Emory University and peripatetic TV and print media personality and author. Amrit Singh is a civil rights lawyer and senior adviser for National Security known for her report *"Globalising Torture"*, the CIA's *"secret detention and extraordinary rendition"* activities. These are just a few examples of those who have advanced in US politics, government and the major professions.

PIOs have generally succeeded wherever they settled. Elsewhere, Navin Ramgoolam has become Prime Minister of Mauritius where Indians have been head of government since the 1960s. In Trinidad, Kamla Persad-Bissessar has been Prime Minister since 2010, while Basdeo Panday served from 1995 to 2001. Guyana's President 2011-5 is Donald Ramotar, succeeding Bharrat Jagdeo (1999-2011) and veteran Cheddi Jagan (1992-1997). Jagan, a communist, had been a colonial Premier (1957-64), but gave way to another communist, Forbes Burnham, with MI5 and CIA assistance! (Ragbeer). The 2014 Vice-President of Suriname is Robert Ameerali, a PIO, and other Indians have been Presidents and Vice-Presidents before him. PIOs have filled major bureaucratic, professional and technical positions, in civil society, government and academia in all the ex-colonies; they did this, while maintaining their culture, and tend to dominate in agricultural pursuits.

PIOs hold or have held leadership positions in the UK, Canada, Australia, Malaya, New Zealand, Singapore, Myanmar and Sri Lanka.

Indians began indenture in Natal, South Africa, in 1860 and now make up 2.5% of the South African population. They played a strong role in the resistance to *apartheid* in South Africa, starting, over a hundred years ago, with Mahatma Gandhi's *Natal Indian Congress*. They identified with the *African National Congress* from the beginning, speaking and acting against racial segregation policies. They prospered economically, and many talented members have spread worldwide. Indians have remained with the ANC and comprise about 10% of the membership of the National Assembly.

PIOs make up slightly less than half of the Fijian population; one of them, Mahendra Chaudhry, was a Prime Minister until removed, through agitation by native Fijians which forced many Indians to migrate to Australia, Canada and the USA. Chaudhary remained and now leads the opposition. Champion golfer Vijay Singh is one of the best-known Fijians. Anand Satyanand, former Governor General of New Zealand (2006-11), and born there, is of Fijian parentage.

The USA attracts many rich and scholarly Indians, especially in computer-associated pursuits, business or academic. In business, venture capitalists Vinod Khoshla of Los Angeles and Gururaj Deshpande of Boston, both billionaires, are well-known as founders, respectively, of *Sun Microsystems* and *Sycamore Corporation,* which they left to become venture capitalists. Silicon Valley, like similar locations elsewhere, is home to many pioneering Indian computer scientists, including inventors of flash drives, microchips, Hotmail and other software. Others have excelled in North America, UK, and in Europe (now European Union, EU), for half a century. They are well represented among executives in Information Technology, Industry, Engineering, Banks and other financial institutions. They occupy all levels in Colleges, Universities and Hospitals, NASA, Communications and other Corporations. Satya Nadella, the recently promoted CEO of Microsoft, was born in Hyderābad, and is a long-term employee. Indra Nooyi, CEO of PepsiCo, is also South Indian. From Madhya Pradesh comes Vodafone's Arun Sarin (not to be confused with the chemical neurotoxin *Sarin,* which was used by Saddam Hussein in Halabja, Iraq, in 1988 and by anarchists in Tokyo's subway system in 1994 and 1995).

In its December 2009 issue, Forbes Magazine writer Megha Bahree listed prominent western PIOs in medicine, finance and in academia. In an article on May 14, 2014, titled *Indian Americans: The New Model Minority*, the Magazine writes this about Indians: "*...although constituting only one percent of the U.S. population, they amount to three percent of the U.S.'s engineers, seven percent of its IT professionals, and eight percent of its physicians (and surgeons). When admitted for surgery myself some years ago in Cambridge, England, I was surprised to be introduced to two Indian surgeons.*

(By the way, the surgery was successful and I was able to walk and run again). ...Whether a result of self-selection in immigration patterns or other factors, the reality is that the Indian talent has been demonstrated in highly competitive environments, and one is left to wonder what would be the limits of India's economic potential if such talent were to be fully unleashed at home." (http://www.india-briefing.com/news/).

An index, despite flaws, of whether a group has "arrived" in US "society" is the choice of one of their members to speak at a College or University "commencement" gathering (the graduation ceremony). Several American PIOs featured in the 2014 list of speakers.

There are numerous societies and associations of Indians in the Diaspora, where, as in India, disunity is a characteristic, and PIO groups could be as far apart as Cold War combatants, waiting for a Gorbachev! However, some have come together with timely formation of the *National Federation of Indian-American Associations* (NFIA), whose aim is unity. The major outcome of its inaugural convention, in August 1989 in New York, was the formation of the *General Organisation of People of Indian Origin* (GOPIO), to increase dialogue among Indians from India and with those from the Diaspora, and review diasporal contributions to the motherland. The BJP government, under PM Vajpayee, responded by holding a conference on June 9, 2003, under the rubric *Pravasi Bhāratīya Divas* (Non-resident Indian Day), choosing to meet on January 9th, the anniversary of Gandhi's return to India from South Africa a century ago.

The Ministry of Overseas Indian Affairs (MOIA) was created in September 2004, under Minister Agnihotri, who, noting the sameness of issues among American groups, suggested the obvious: that a unifying or coordinating body would facilitate discourse, as it was not possible for him to meet with each group or person (p. 5). MOIA has since held an annual convention, in a major Indian city, co-sponsored by the Ministry of Youth and Sports and GOPIO, at which Diasporal groups can network with Indians, discuss issues, seek ways to reduce disunity and cliquism that exist, along the lines of colour, caste and religion that the British had enhanced and exploited, which remain almost intact among Indians.

South Asian Heritage Month (SAHM) was a PIO initiative starting in in Trinidad, then Ontario and Canada; it is also recognised in the USA for honouring Asians and Pacific Islanders. GOPIO now marks SAHM and chooses that time to recognise deserving PIOs.

Hindus continue to be plagued by divisions and enmities, fostered by groups of Indian academics, and their American allies or leaders hostile to Hindus. These include the *Association for India's Development* (AID), formed in 1991 by Balaji Sampath, Ravi Kuchimanchi, and other leftists. It is allied with the *Tamil Nadu Science Forum* (TNSF); Sandeep Pandey of *Asha for Education*, a CPI (Marxist) group, ironically linked with the Taliban; the *Forum of Inqualabi (Revolutionary) Leftists* (FOIL); *Friends of South Asia* (FOSA); and *Act Now for Harmony and Democracy* (ANHAD). ANHAD is headed by Shabnam Hashmi, and funded by US Christian evangelists, despite its pro-Muslim stance, communist/atheist ideology; leftist historian, KN Pannikar, is a trustee. FOIL is satirised as *The Forum of Intentional Liars* in a website by Abhimanyu Arjun (See *http://thetruthaboutliars.wordpress.com/-*). In June 2013, FOIL's Raja Swami registered an anti-Hindu website in Texas, USA, supported by ANHAD.

It is instructive that the US would fund Indian Communists in the USA who regularly trash America and its policies, as a survey of their websites will show. Enemies will lie on the same bed, if the passion is shared, the cause worthy or rewards great! Other activists supported include aggressive evangelical demagogues like Ravi Zacharias, a Billy Graham acolyte.

Anti-India PIOs operating in the USA are particularly voluble, abrasive and spiteful, like the Hinduphobic Dinesh D'Souza, who opposes *affirmative action* in the USA, *employment equity* in Canada, *positive action* in the UK, and the *reservation* program in India. Touting morality, he was found guilty of immoral behaviour—an extramarital tryst in a NY hotel, which led him to resign his position at King's College, a tiny Christian rightist school in Manhattan. His anti-Hindu rants are published in various western media, which lack an equal platform for rebuttal. In January, 2014, he was indicted on charges of using straw donors to make illegal political contributions, during the 2012 US elections. His prosecution was led by fellow PIO, NY's prosecutor, Preet Bharrara. On May 20, 2014, he pleaded guilty in the U.S. District Court for the Southern District of New York and may likely treat readers to an insider's rant on life in a US jail.

An intensive battle to rectify false anglocentric versions of Indian history was waged in the California Board of Education (CBE) in 2005-9, where a case was made by Hindu groups for correcting errors re chronology, religious beliefs, interpretations, terminology, social divisions and practices in Hinduism, all very reasonable, and in any other religion fairly non-controversial, which the CBE accepted.

But a protest was mounted by *non-Indian* and Indian *anti-Hindu* "heavy-weights" in the US, mainly *Christian*, vested-interest "scholars" linked with heavily-funded proselyte groups in India. They vigorously opposed most changes, arguing that they were not shared "generally", meaning, by Christians! Hindu groups relied on their religious expertise, while their opponents were atheists, Communists, Christians and Muslims, none free of internal conflict, Christianity foremost. Islam is deeply divided, with an on-going war between the major Sunni and

Shi'a groups, while Sufis and Ahmadiyyas have been driven out of Pakistan into a Canadian and Indian exile[162]. Hinduism is spared such bellicose fanaticism, belying the ravings of K. Ilaiah, e.g. "*...for Hindu dharma, resolving of a conflict is only by killing. There is no other discourse. Debate is not there. You have to kill the enemy.*" (Ilaiah, *Why I am not a Hindu*, quoted in Bhailal Patel: *https://www.facebook.com/worldwithoutborders2013/posts/*).

What Hindus wanted for US grade schools was a statement of core principles, and an account of traditional variants. But the protest seemed focussed by one person's bias, a Dr Michael Witzel, an opinionated German at Harvard, who had assembled a côterie of associates, all hostile non-Hindus, to oppose a *Hindu* presentation on Hinduism! This reaction was akin to opposing the Pope and the Curia for presenting the *Roman Catholic* version of Christianity! Despite the bigotry, Witzel's views prevailed at the CBE over those of India-born Dr Bajpai, emeritus professor of Hinduism at the University of California. The submissions by other religions to CBE were not challenged Unable to appeal, the

---

[162] The spread of Wahhabism has transformed North America and Europe into passionate and militant Muslim camps espousing Saudi Arabian fundamentalism, which I had experienced firsthand, in Jeddah and Riyadh, in the 1980s; by all accounts they are much worse now, since the Saudis began to fund large organisations, like the *Muslim Students Association (MSA), the Islamic Society of North America (ISNA), the Council on American-Islamic Relations (CAIR),* and others; they have gained the ears of North American leaders, who generally are quite ignorant of Islam (Fatah). As I noted elsewhere, they often confuse Islam with Indian religions and are now wont to consider all brown men as Muslim, and, since the 9/11 incident, as terrorists. In the spirit of reconciliation, George Bush was photographed with fundamentalist imams in Texas, and holding hands with King Abdullah. Other American leaders and Canadian politicians have given extended attention to Wahhabi mullahs and their mosques. In the late 1990s, two short essays in a local Newsletter (multicultural) on the changing trends in female cover-ups – *hijab, niqab, khimar, burkha or chador* – stimulated by the invasion of Wahhabism, drew harsh criticism from Muslim members, who had been known for secularism and ecumenism, an attitude that had begun to change in the Greater Toronto Area, as the Wahhabi doctrines spread. A talk given some years earlier, warning of this and of the hard line from Riyadh re Sharia had been well received. One Muslim graduate student complained of the inappropriate use of the term "rightly-guided" for the first Medina caliphs, noting their bad example of fomenting murder and strife, failure to establish a sound government structure and succession for Islamic states, and the bloodthirstiness of caliphs, including the " rightly-guided"! In the debates in Ontario re introduction of Sharia, championed by the imams of Canada, it became obvious that Canadian politicians knew little of Islam, nothing of Sharia law nor of the environment in which Mohamed formulated his missives, and that *Sharia was not among them*. Indeed, several key tenets of Sharia Law conflict with the Quran, for example, beheading, or any punishment for apostasy, or stoning of adulterers. The Caliph was the promoter, often capriciously. To this day most Muslims continue to follow trends preached by clerics in mosques, and many cannot justify their regurgitations by quoting directly from the Quran. Moderate Muslims suffer as a result. Ontario rejected Sharia Law and though the issue seethes, it is not likely to be approved in this country. Canadians are generally poorly informed on Islam, and generally err in its favour. The viciousness of ISIS and al Qaeda has opened eyes to the capture of that religion by extremists.

Hindus initiated a lawsuit that ended in a way that left them stunned. Christian errors on Hinduism would prevail in California, despite testimony exposing Witzel's apparent conflicts of interest in the affair.

The matter is a vexed one, as many of the objectors, who joined with Witzel, are not only anti-Hindus, but allied to wealthy Christian proselytising projects in India, which unsettle Hindu communities and foment class divisions, at a time when reform of their religion is badly needed to unite *all* who practise it. This, of course, is a difficult goal and needs a sage, kindly and sensitive hand, not ill-informed antagonism and intrusions by Christians, whose own schisms are self-incriminating and anti-Christ. Besides, proselytes who study Hinduism seem to do so with the sole object of finding negative and dated ideas in its scripture, so as to trash it, a fairly simple task. Witzel seems merely to repeat Max Müller's recanted invasion view, still widely publicised by the British and Americans, and never reversed as it supports their purpose. Shri Aurobindo called it at the time *"a conjecture based on conjectures"!* Correcting Indian history requires knowledge and perseverance.

Belgian scholar Koenraad Elst is a staunch advocate for the truth; his internet essays on Hinduism and allied subjects are well worth reading and expose the hypocrisy in the actions of academics at prestigious institutions, West and East, who maliciously use their academic network to muster opposition to Hinduism, and spread condemnations.

The stakes in this matter are high. Conversion in India is a billion dollar industry, enriching thousands of Westerners and Indians. Some Indian enforcers are trained to act as Hindu extremists, inciting conflict with Christians in the name of Hindutva, so that a complaint can be made under minority rights laws! NGO and NGO missions solicit donations widely in Western media, using emotional visuals of starving children, Indian and African, implying that gifts go only to the welfare of the sufferers portrayed. Indian Christians with US accents are often used in heart-rending campaigns that get prime publicity and a positive donor response from largely ignorant audiences who believe that Indians are "heathens" and "barbarians", who must be saved!

Yet the reality is different. In Indian communities targetted for conversion, Christian activists behave in a provocative manner that would not be tolerated elsewhere; they belittle native beliefs, bait the poor and exploit hunger and other wants to obtain a conversion. They push American values in the same uninhibited and bullying way that Islamists and British used centuries ago to browbeat and convert Hindus. The large pool of people below India's designated poverty line ensures a constant audience for zealous missionaries with their petty enticements. The Diaspora viewed with concern the Pope's declaration of 2000 as "the year of conversion" and was amazed that he received so little criticism in the West, or in India, where he was a guest at the time. The current Pope has confirmed that "evangelism" is the main purpose of the Roman Catholic Church. *World Vision*, anti-Hindu zealots like Vijay Prashad and Black Americans of the *Joshua Project* have recently backed VT Rajshekar's Afro-centric and anti-semitic beliefs to advance the postulate of a shared African-Dalit ancestry for "*dravidians*", based on a hypothetical joint origin in the primeval continent, Lemuria. His anti-Hindu rhetoric paints all Hindus as Brahminist and anti-Dalit, and adds a militancy that reminds one of an invasion.

In the 1780s, William Jones agonised to make Vaidic chronology congruent with Mosaic history and to connect Sanskrit with European tongues: the concept of an Indo-European family of languages. The tug-o-war with Indian culture and values was engaged and became fiercer as the British *Rāja* was established; English became the language of education and gained paramountcy. Modern proselytes have gone further to invent a new chronology of Hinduism to make it mesh with Christianity, and some even postulate that Hinduism was derived from Christianity! This is just one of many lures, fabrications and devices used to secure new converts; most are bought anyway with food, water and access to their schools, which try to consolidate the conversion.

Mother Teresa (Agnes Gonxha Bojaxhiu of Skopje, Macedonia), the tainted saint, Nobel Peace Prize 1979, was the Vatican flag-bearer for conversion for decades. Her campaigns for funds made Calcutta (Kolkata) synonymous in the West with poverty, misery and illness. For its relief, she collected billions of dollars, cowed Presidents and Kings, and acquiesced only to the Pope. Her "relief works" in Calcutta were widely publicised in the Western press and lavishly praised. She was known to bully India's prime ministers but was cordial with Indira Gandhi. When she died in 1997, aged 87, India famously gave her a state funeral. Yet Teresa was more a myth than a fact. Her existence and the "company" she formed, the *Missionaries of Charity*, were remote from the citizens, especially those in need and it is reliably reported that the sisters/nuns, mostly South Indian, insisted on speaking English, had neither hospital nor ambulances, nor in fact a school for 5000 children. Where are the billions of dollars she collected? No accounting of this has been done. Indeed it seems that private missions do not account publicly in India, and reject enquiries, even though they could be a conduit for illegal money or terrorism. This may be a major reason for NGOs to include preaching in their work, and other ecclesiastical activities, so as to avoid an audit.[164]

---

[164]The literature on conversion and Mother Teresa is extensive and an internet search is worthwhile under any subject. A few are given, randomly. This matter is explored in India

The American Civil Rights Movement was a critical point in the US search for justice and culminated in various measures, under President Lynden Johnson, to legally emancipate the black and coloured peoples of America which Abraham Lincoln had started a hundred and fifty years ago. Although Indians were excluded from segregation practices, they had no right to vote or become US citizens until the *Luce-Cellar Act* of 1946. Rejection of dark coloured peoples had characterised 19th century American and European society; some progress has been made but deep pockets of rejection persist. India and PIOs cannot complain if they become victims, as they too show preferences for light-skinned people.

Nina Davuluri, a PIO, became Miss New York in 2013 and was crowned *Miss America 2014*. A certain racial type, to whom white is beautiful, reacted negatively to her dark colour. Stephen J. Gould in *The Mismeasure of Man* describes race theories and the fraudulent pseudoscience that they spawned. The greatest period of deception, barring none, was the last two centuries of concentrated fabrication and outright lying, perpetrated by the British and their acolytes to justify colonialism, slavery, and a classification of humans in the infamous eugenics series—from white through mongol and other coloured races to black. This deception has thrived since 1800, countered by history and science, including the genetic origin of white races *(?albinos)*. Ironically, Ms Davuluri's win raised the same ogres of racial bias that Rev. M. L. King denounced so eloquently in 1963 in his *"I have a dream"* speech.

Ms Davuluri is not the first Indian diasporal "queen." US comments re her award have been supportive. Her dance routine in the contest was a fusion of western with classical *Bharatanatyam*, Ms Davuluri's routine was directed by noted choreographer Nakul Dev Mahajan, who operates an Indian dance studio in Artesia, California; he notably was invited by Michelle Obama to conduct a Dance Clinic in the White House in November 2013. Fusion is a rising trend as musicians of East and West discover one another, and experiment with the different styles, rhythms and instruments. Indian music was introduced to the US by the eminent sitarist Ravi Shankar and his partner, tabla player Ali Akbar Khan. Ms Davuluri's win is an indictment of those Indians who judge beauty by lightness of skin, an absurd obsession, degradingly similar to the eugenics and phrenology horrors of a century ago, that Mark Twain satirises so well in *The Adventures of Huckleberry Finn,* where swindlers sell poor white folk superiority after a phrenology test!

---

and the Diaspora in print, on film, and websites by a variety of talents and fidelities, by Indians who teach English, by schools and by Christian proselytes. See http://www.thesundayindian.com/en/story/explosive-confessions-of-an-ex nun/14/36133/. Also www.facebook.com/ChristianAggression etc. For Mother Teresa, see Chatterjee or Hitchens or Wuellenweber, *Bibliography*.

The reaction to Ms Davuluri's brave win highlighted the tolerance of most Americans and the hypocrisy of Indians (See "*Pigment of our imagination*", Editorial, *The Hindu,* September 19, 2013: *"Why Nina Davuluri's win is more important than you think it is"* by Veena Tripathi, *India Tribune,* Chicago, Oct 13, 2013, and many entries under Nina Davuluri on the internet. It is sad to note that this attractive girl would *not* have won an Indian beauty contest, especially noting that an Indian girl of Sonia Maino's social and educational status would hardly have become wife to Rajiv Gandhi. Arabs regard Blacks as inferior. Even dummies in Indian clothing stores are almost all white or pink. Mumbai and the film and clothing industries should display all racial types, like Hollywood, and not march backwards, pushing Indian morality deeper into Western sleaze. It may simply be that Indians are waiting for a Westerner to light their way forward and provide them with something to copy, as they've done for nearly 200 years, craving white acceptance: *"crave for foreign"* as Vidia Naipaul phrased it in *An Area of Darkness.*

Chemical skin lighteners are popular in India and may lighten the skin a shade, as might treatment with herbs, such as turmeric paste, but none alters the genes which determine skin colour. Perhaps Nina Davuluri's tours as Miss America might have shamed Indians into looking more closely at the millions of beautiful darker people that it routinely dismisses, and remind them that a chemically lightened skin indicates vanity, not beauty. It is getting worse, not better, since there is much profit to be made by druggists who have made skin "lighteners" so popular that even men fall for "male" treatments, which are proudly endorsed by male actors, a testimony to human gullibility, prejudice and conceit, fattening the bank balances of drug makers. This recalls the period in US history when Blacks went to ridiculous extremes to straighten their hair with everything from chemical pomades to heat.

Indians have always enjoyed all styles of music and dance, as Mahajan shows. More experimental "fusion" is occurring, spread by the current generation, and with this happening, westerners, including PIOs, are increasingly studying and performing the various genres. Resident and visiting classicists from India regularly perform with popular artistes a wide range of opuses, including their original works, sponsored by local societies, organisations and temples. Thus the Diaspora is well served musically, and the events attract all Indians, regardless of religion. In the last two decades, however, many diasporal Muslims have begun to avoid these concerts, which they used to support and enjoy, or to play musical instruments, openly rejecting common ones like the piano, violin, sitar and tabla. In a certain medical conference in Saudi Arabia some years ago, the only instrumental performance by the Saudis was an orchestra consisting of one instrument, the *daff,* a dull monotone drum thumped by a score of men for an hour playing "different" tunes, all of which sounded the same! When a physician from Arkansas thought it polite to clap, he was quickly squelched by a Saudi colleague. Even the Muslimfest of Toronto, started in 2004 by Chicago's Sound Vision, a Saudi-backed company, and others, denied a place for female singers! The Emirates thrive on 80% Indian and Pakistani Muslim slaves, but, like the rest of rich Islam, they do not apologise for this bondage of the *mawali* (non-Arab Muslims) or the *muhammam* (blacks). It is a tradition.

PIOs have advanced other disciplines in the West that are benefitting Indians and society generally. One is the identification of a major heart and arterial problem afflicting Indians, with genetic and dietary links to lipid (fat) metabolism. Plaques of fat and fibre form in and narrow the small arteries that nourish organs, with lethal risk when those to the heart (coronaries) or brain (cerebrals) are affected. The major event is a "heart attack", so common in Indians that it is referred to as the *"East Indian heart disease"* and linked with effects ranging from no symptoms, distressing chronic debilitation to sudden death. It was first noted in Trinidad in 1959, then in 1963 by a PIO pathologist in Guyana (Ragbeer), and later in the UK and India. It is now vigorously studied in many UK and North American Universities, notably McMaster, Hamilton, Canada, by other PIOs and associates. The disease did afflict the well-off in India and those who lived beyond age 50, but the burden of illness nationally was dwarfed by the great infections, so apparently attracted little academic attention, until the diasporal reports became known.

Dr Ānanda Mohan Chakrabarty, a Calcutta microbiologist, is famed for launching the biotechnology industry, while working for General Electric Co in New York, USA. The development has created over 7.5 million jobs in the USA. He succeeded in 1980 in patenting his gene-modified strain of bacterium, *Pseudomonas putida* that could metabolise components of an oil spill. Initial patent application was denied on the basis that life forms were not patentable. But both the United States *Court of Customs and Patent Appeals* and the US *Supreme Court* allowed the patent, the former ruling, *"the fact that micro-organisms are alive is without legal significance for purposes of patent law"*, the latter, *"A live, human-made micro-organism is patentable subject matter under [Title 35 U.S.C.] 101.*

US Patent #4,259,444 was the world's first patent on a living organism. Professor Chakrabarty is now busy with his two companies, *CDG Therapeutics* (Delaware), based on his work at the University of Illinois (Chicago) on cancer, and *Amrita Therapeutics Ltd.*, Ahmedabad, Gujarat, to "develop therapies, vaccines and diagnostics." His patent success has unfortunately unleashed an army of US and European biopirates who have been avidly combing the third world for unique molecules, from human to plant and microbes, ironically from India, that can be made marketable by GM technology. With Gujarat support, Amrita has succeeded in bringing US-style patent law to India, claiming that it would aid research. Now that Modi is Prime Minister, *Amrita* may feel empowered, but hopefully Modi would put the interests of Indians before those of this company, clearly brandishing its all-American (CEO) credentials and glib publicity. Its biotechnology methods will hopefully be transparent. *(See http://www.monitor.net/monitor/9610a/genepiracy.html.)*

Anti-Hindu feeling thrives in the Diaspora. The *Hindu American Foundation* (HAF) actively responds to critics, many seemingly agents of American anti-Hindu groups, composed of US and Indian citizens, emboldened by the Pope's declaration of Year 2000 as *Year of Conversion*. They are fuelled by American and Indian "academics" like Donegal, Witzel, Nanda, A. Sen, R. Guha, and a plethora of others who have made a career of promoting Hinduphobia. Deepak Chopra suavely distorts aspects of *Ayurveda* to suit his line on *Transcendental Meditation (TM)*, the Vaidic relaxation technique that Maharishi Mahesh Yogi introduced and taught worldwide, beginning with a world tour in 1958. By the time he retired in 2008, aged 90, a month before he died, the Maharishi had reached millions, and his name and TM had achieved household usage by people ranging from Indian politicians and academics to western musicians like the Beatles. *Time* magazine placed him on their October 1975 cover, about the time he taught about *"yogic flying"*. He introduced the *Science of Creative Intelligence* based on *Vedanta*.

Chopra is one of many people in academia and the arts who had learned TM and built a business based on Yoga, severed from Hinduism. He has crossed swords with the HAF's Aseem Shukla over his glib and ambivalent anti-Hinduism and HAF's reminder of the Vaidic (*Sanatan Dharma*) origin of yoga (Hinduism in modern parlance). Meera Nanda is another anti-Hindu claiming that Yoga, a key concept in Hindu medicine, is non-Hindu; it's like denying the role of Christ's crucifixion in Christianity! Nanda wields a wild hatchet in dismissing HAF's claim as ludicrous, when the same epithet could aptly describe her position and arguments. Chopra tries to obfuscate his biases by avoiding use of the word "Hinduism", although his bona fides are clearly Hindu or dharmic. Their essays come close to hate. Obviously they are avoiding the inferior image of Hinduism among richly-endowed evangelists. http://www.faithstreet.com/onfaith/2010/04/30

The Ramakrishna and Chinmaya Missions, the Hindu American Foundation (HAF) and the recent *Hindu American Seva Communities* (HASC, an Obama initiative), support the various forms of Hinduism and dharmic religions. Ramakrishna Mission emphasises *Karma Yoga*, one of three yogic principles that describe a path to spiritual progress. Chinmaya stresses *Advaita Vedanta* of Adi Shankaracharya. Both have centres worldwide and have released a number of English translations of Hindu scriptures and epics; many of these have now been circulated or been made available for consulting via the worldwide web.

Anju Bhargava is head of HASC, a service organisation formed as a response to a remark by President Obama that seemed to accept Hindus finally into the American fold, almost seven decades since the Luce-Cellar Act: "*... our patchwork heritage is a strength, not a weakness. We are a nation of Christians and Muslims, Jews and Hindus, and non-believers.*" In 2009, Obama formed an *Advisory Council on Faith Based and Neighbourhood Partnerships* which made "recommendations on key development issues of national importance." HASC *"brought an awareness of the needs of the Hindu American community and identified infrastructure capacity gaps in providing (members) a sustained service. Currently, HASC is working to develop ways to serve and bridge the gaps. It is also partnering with Let's Move initiative." Let's Move* is championed by Michelle Obama.

Ms Bhargava was the Hindu representative on Obama's Committee. She went into the task to deal with a Panzer division, when she did not even know how to use her pistol effectively! Hindus were diverted to local service *(seva),* leaving Judaeo-Christian activists to lead the Committee. Obama clearly ignored his promises to minorities not to repeat George Bush's lack of even-handedness. In 2011, he added several Christian and Judaic members to the Committee, but no Hindu, Muslim, Buddhist or Jain. The website, accessed recently, shows that membership includes a Chinese Buddhist, but still no other Dharmic or Muslim member, not even Ms Bhargava! So much for that Council, whose purpose now seems a clear religious route for the US government to take towards its Asian agenda, by funding Christian proselytism.

Indians whose names suggest a Hindu ancestry have proven particularly good at anti-Hinduism, both in India and abroad, and provide the foreigner with that aura of authenticity that takes the *Hindu American Foundation* hours to rebut and correct. Meanwhile, Hinduism is attacked, and western publishers are glad to publish such critique, just as they are reluctant to publish a rebuttal. It is difficult not to feel that many of India's erudite still wear the mantle of humility in the presence of whites, amplified by an education in the Anglocentric dogmatism of the last 150 years, which India's private schools continue to follow.

Indians in India and the Diaspora need to know more of their history to improve self-confidence and resist the urge to mimic an alien culture and take pride instead in their own. Indians reared in th West can get confused by the prevailing distortions and the curricular errors taught by ill-informed Wesrerners. Most anti-Hindu propagandists are socialists, secularists, atheists etc., opinionated and articulate, steeped in their own myths, and tend not to look into the distant past or believe what it tells them, if different from their beliefs. One cannot stop history and start at any arbitrary point, as if prior events did not exist, or, existing, did not matter. This is the weakness of belief systems that pretend to have a finite start, e.g. Judaism, Islam, Christianity, Sikhism, Marxism, Fascism and so on, and a prescribed end. Hinduism is, on the other hand, with all its faults, open-ended, timeless almost. It is hoped that India would adopt some of the reforms that the older Diaspora had found useful, enhancing interaction and strengthening basic beliefs and practices. You cannot roll on half a wheel!

In the UK, as elsewhere, propaganda in the centuries of European wars was aimed to strengthen citizen loyalty to the Crown, and one ploy was the belittling of foreigners. British citizens were thus told that beyond Dover the continents were hostile, backward, with poor living conditions, unpleasant and depressing people and horrible wildlife. Walter Raleigh's initial description of South American natives as *"men whose heads do grow beneath their shoulders"* is especially egregious. African commentators talked of men with tails! These images discouraged travel to many places outside of Britain, and illustrate an excess of *inhabitiveness,* in the language and era of phrenology. The messages extolled the triumphs and wealth of Britain, thanks to the wisdom of their lords. Citizens believed this diatribe which pervaded Britain until well after WWII, when the recovery allowed an expansion of travel and migration, changing perceptions somewhat, and exposing the sordid side of imperial life to any who wished to see it.

The educational deficiencies in America and other parts of the West today—in history, geography and languages—allow errors by Indian writers on India, tend to consolidate the bigotry re foreign realities and hide the role of western exploiters—governments and corporations—in the mounting poverty of many tropical and sub-tropical countries. Thus, the stereotyping of Indians, according to old British ways, continues today, except that Americans have now become principal perpetrators.

Diasporal explorations of culture, origins and subversion of Indian languages require much mental and tricky vocal training. Thus, PIOs who speak English well, do so at some sacrifice to their parent language, but do quite well with religious Sanskrit and Hindi songs, lyrics and recitations from the classics, which they had learnt from childhood. Recent migrants and students from India are often astonished at the flawless rendering of Sanskrit *bhajans* (hymns) and Hindi or Urdu *ghazals* (songs) by PIO artistes who do not ordinarily speak these languages.

Older PIOs have revived their search for roots in India and many have regained contact with ancestral villages, facilitated by easier travel, the worldwide web and organisations like the Ministry of Overseas Indian Affairs, willing to help with searches. Many travel agencies, in the Diaspora and in India, promote group tours of Hindu holy places. Some North American PIOs have gained entry to Indian universities, and have appreciated the experience, though medical graduates must seek further qualification to become licensed in the USA or Canada. Professional migrants also suffer long delays in getting a license, and often have to accept lesser jobs e.g. clerks, taxi-driving, shop-keeping, work in restaurants etc. Thus, Americans have tended to link Indians with 7-11 and other 'fast-food' stores, motels and gas stations, and prior to 9-11, to call all brown people Hindus, a label that included Muslims and Sikhs!

Indians have held an unjustifiably romantic view of the USA. The fascination even survived the denigration of Indians a century ago, and in the decades thereafter, as already noted, in the USA and Canada, and despite harassment. They have yet to understand that they are tolerated today because they are good business. Thousands of Indians completing post-graduate education in North America have remained hooked by its freedoms and "easy" living, *("more pay in the USA")*, the unfettered materialism, the relaxed attitudes to custom and tradition, and the uninhibited mingling of classes and genders in daily life, despite their own caste biases. This perhaps reflected the fact that the majority of Indians in the US are middle or upper class economically, quite self-indulgent and opinionated. The earliest Indian businesses, too, were somewhat exclusive, dealing mainly with high-end products: jewellery, gold, fine cloth and clothing, Kashmir wool, carpets, art, cultural and religious artefacts.

The current generation of PIOs is changing; many are involved in social and cultural activities, often cutting across racial and religious lines. Mixed marriages occur and are more accepted today than a few decades ago, although some groups, notably Sikhs and Islamists, remain opposed to breaches of tradition and will even commit the crime of "honour killing" to prevent them. Such incidents are given wide publicity in North America, and treated with horror, as its basis denies a valued personal freedom, and is culturally repugnant. The same denunciation applies to Indian women who practice foetal gender selection—now that several medical facilities in the USA, as in India, offer ultra-sound diagnosis, and abortion of female foetuses.

Hindu religious and social groups have been a real support in the Diaspora against forced conversion and bigotry. Several hundred such groups exist in North America and dozens in smaller countries. The experience of HASC suggests an urgent need to amalgamate most of these for effective US lobbying, even though current advocacy has increased tolerance and goodwill. But bigotry is alive in the USA, which trumpets its "democracy" and equality, yet provides the most egregious examples of intolerance, class and religious prejudice, especially anti-Hinduism, and lethal personal violence against Indians and Blacks. The feelings recall the intense proselytism of newly-independent India by rich US "charities", with large-scale "buying" of converts. The British had recognised Marxist parties, and Nehru neglected Hindu rights and stood by, while Americans and their rival Marxist ideologues confused and converted poor Hindus. Today, American angst re job losses should be directed at US corporations, instead of attacking Indians, who are unfairly blamed for the outsourcing practices of corporate America.

According to the 2010 US census, Indians are one of the fastest growing ethnic groups in that country. Indian-Americans include some 35,000 physicians, while recent immigrants have founded more engineering and technology companies between 1995 and 2005 than immigrants from UK, China, Taiwan and Japan combined, according to a joint Duke university-U C Berkeley study. Pew research data indicate that the median household income of Indian Americans is $88,000 as compared to $66,000 for other Asians and $49,800 for the total US population. The percentage of Indians with higher education is also higher than other Asian ethnic groups.

In the USA today, Hindu groups are becoming more active in defending their integrity and securing their community presence. They face a formidable task of countering, much less overcoming the insistent behaviour of Christian proselytes and Islamic antagonists in their midst, especially in student dormitories on college and university campuses. These have long been hotbeds of religious sanctimony, and push to "join" and "become part of a Christian community" by groups like the *Intervarsity Christian Fellowship (IVCF)*, or the *Muslim Students Association* (MSA), which exist on every campus. They are well-funded; IVCF can sick converted Christian cats – instructed on how to entrap prey – among the freshmen pigeons, busily trying to adjust and conform, and not to make waves. Meanwhile, Wahhabi *jihadists* teach them about the Islamic state and the joys of fighting for a return of the "rightly-guided" caliphs.

This campus activity is matched by other pressures on Hindus by Islam, Christianity and other anti-Hindu forces that abound in India and the Diaspora. The intensity is a marvel when one recalls that there is no *intellectual* argument that could dislodge Hinduism from its primacy as a scientific and spiritual force that has tolerated all religions and beliefs, but wishes to be spared forced conversion, and perhaps emulate the Swiss city of Berne by building multi-religious houses of worship.

The Middle East is torn apart. Wahhabism's harshest expression has gelled in land seizures and killings in Iraq and Syria by ISIS, the al Qaeda group, which seeks to re-create a fanatical Islamic caliphate and spread it worldwide, following Ala Maudoodi (*Jamaat e Islam,* Pakistan), Syed Qutb and Hassan al Banna (*Muslim Brotherhood,* Egypt). They have grown and spread in the west, recruiting young Muslims to the cause of violent jihad, exploiting their naiveté and frustrations, whether British, Canadian or American, their prime soil. *Jamaat* had started in India in 1941; it opposed partition, aiming to Islamise all India. Its leaders are in charge in Pakistan and Bangladesh, and continue to harass India from these bases. In the West, meanwhile, Indians, assumed to be Muslims, especially if young and bearded, are insulted and assaulted, just like the "old days" when every brown skin was a "Paki". NRIs in the US tolerate the abuse; older diasporal PIOs tend to retaliate. The young join ISIS. The challenge for Islam is to find, and for India to nurture a peaceful *modus vivendi* for all religions and races, and tolerance for all social classes.

Nearly two decades ago, American historian, Gore Vidal, remarked, *"From a barbaric Bronze Age text known as the Old Testament, three antihuman religions have evolved--Judaism, Christianity, Islam. These are sky-god religions. They are, literally, patriarchal--God is the omnipotent father--hence the loathing of women for 2,000 years. The sky-god is a jealous god, of course. Those who would reject him must be converted or killed for their own good...When the white race broke out of Europe 500 years ago,... inspired by a raging sky-god, the whites were able to pretend that their conquests were in order to bring the One God to everyone, particularly those with older and subtler religions... Many of the Christian evangelists feel it necessary to convert everyone on earth to their primitive religion, they have been prevented- so far- but they have forced most tyrannically and wickedly - their superstitions and gumph upon others. So it is upon account that I now favour an all-out war on the monotheists."*

Manmohan Singh and President Obama, White House, Nov. 24, 2009.

Chapter 28

Despite ...overwhelming evidence of the existence of a unitary civilization, the divisive and unfounded themes of domination, suppression, and segregation continue to be presented as the theme songs of Indian history. Muslims... then appear as simply one more group in the long list of immigrants. The fact that the previous settlers (Kushans etc.) thoroughly immersed themselves in the Hindu tradition and in no way disturbed the tenor of the land becomes a mere technical point, often overlooked at that.

Menakshi Jain, 1998

Transition

The 2014 victory of the BJP/NDA is an outcome of the complacency, if not anti-Hindu hostility of the secular Indian middle class, to whom media, hence news and views, are slanted, though a few keen probes do penetrate this shield. It is noteworthy that only *Chanukya* among pollsters correctly predicted the outcome of the elections. The results have astonished many, particularly the INC's leaders, and Western anti-Hindu press like the *Economist* and *New York Times*. They smugly dismissed the BJP and its leaders, and misjudged and maligned Narendra Modi. Shortly after Modi's campaigning speech in Amethi, Priyanka Gandhi, who had already left for New Delhi, said, "*Inhone Amethi ki dharti pe mere shaheed pitaa ka apmaan kiya hai. Amethi ki janta is harkat ko kabhi maaf nahi karegi. Inki neech rajniti ka jawaab mere booth ke karyakartaa denge. Amethi ke ek ek booth se jawaab aayega.*" ("The BJP has shown disrespect to my martyred father on his home ground, Amethi. The people of Amethi will never forgive this insult. My workers will respond to their low-level of politics. The answer will be there for all to see from every single booth in Amethi.") On Sunday, while campaigning at a rally in Jagdishpur, Rahul Gandhi promised to "*convert Amethi into England*!" Such is the reverence accorded the English image.

PM Modi (standing, front row extreme left) poses with his 45-member Council of Ministers. (Express Photo by Neeraj Priyadarshi, original in colour, June 9, 2014)

The silliness and pro-British servility and obsession of the remark were lost on him. On Monday 19th May, the streets of Amethi were nearly "saffronised." More objective and less strident reports followed of the significance of the Modi victory in terms of bolstering the confidence of Hindus. They had been made to feel inferior and apologetic by local and foreign press, which insisted that Hinduism was unstable and inherently bad for India, as any internet search of just those two papers will confirm. They are foremost among Western anti-Hindu publications and must the treated as biased and hostile. Perhaps someone might tell them of Hinduism's long record of tolerance, unsurpassed by others.

In his post-election address, President Pranab Mukherjee said the government is committed to improve the quality of life in villages and end the rural:urban divide—a monumental task, but an urgent and crucial one for the salvation and integrity of India.

President Mukherjee

Over 200 years ago, in attempting to muster Maratha kings to help him rid India of the invading British, Yashwantrao Holkar wrote, *"First Country, then Religion. We will have to rise above caste, religion, and our states in the interest of our country. You too must wage a war against the British, like me."* But the appeal lost, as related in previous chapters.
(See *also http://en.wikipedia.org/wiki/yashwantrao holkar)*

The priorities have not changed, but have become more urgent. India must put country first, religion next and "rise above caste", finally enforcing this aspect of the constitution, which sixty years of INC rule has failed to implement. The INC had chosen "secularism" as its ruling philosophy, while the population was 80% Hindu, 12% Islam (and rising by a high birth rate), and the remainder Buddhists, Sikhs, Jains, Christians, Parsis, atheists, Jews and other minorities. Secularism was in line with Nehru's socialism—an acceptable adaptation of leftist philosophy, without adopting Communism. But it failed to deliver what it promised: a separation of "church" and state and a neutral, symmetric treatment of all religions, to ensure freedom and fairness. Instead it has become a sop for Islamic and other minorities, who form a solid vote bank for the INC, along with the majority poor Hindus, who remained loyal to the Mahatma/Nehru partnership, and by reminders of the favourable handling of incidents like the Travancore temple access, in support of their rights. The preferred treatment of Muslims, with

Maulana Azad as a senior minister, kept Muslims in India, where they were spared Arab arrogance and assured of more rights and freedoms than in either East or West Pakistan. Indeed, it was believed that Nehru had promoted Maulana Azad in the INC and made him Minister of Education to prove INC's secularism, while Azad's prime aim was to gain India for Allah! Azad, a so-called 'liberal' and 'secular' Muslim, put his religious interests ahead of others, and was known to have opposed *Vande Mātaram* on the grounds that it was "anti-Islamic"! In his book "*India Wins Freedom*", Azad admitted that he had opposed partition, because the creation of a separate Islamic state would divide the Muslim population and hinder *the Islamisation of India*. Yet Nehru called him a great "*nationalist*" leader.

Another Islamic flouting of the secular principle was the denial of scriptural readings from non-Islamic holy books at the funerals of Zakir Hussain, Azad and Fakhruddin Ali Ahmad, unlike the multi-religious readings at the funerals of these Hindus: Mahatma Gandhi, Jawaharlal Nehru, Rajendra Prasad and Indira Gandhi.

The constitution gave individuals the right to "propagate" their religion, i.e. to establish missions, thus allowing Islamists and Christians to proselytise, since Hindus, Buddhists, Jains, Sikhs and Parsis did not. Hindus believe that this religious asymmetry should stop, some going so far as to say that all efforts should be made to retrieve every Hindu lost to coercive proselytism—such as Mother Teresa's in her lifetime—and reverse Pope Benedict's impolite and insulting proclamation, aimed at Hindus, when he visited India in 2000 and declared it "the year of conversion." The Joshua project details the Christian intent (Shukla). The Vatican, WCC and other proselytisers know the pitfalls, but they have the money to press on. (See *(http://religionhumanrights.com/Research)*.

Hindus recognise the need for reform, and have done this quite capably down the ages, as seen in the work of major reformers like Buddha, Mahavir, Nanak, Dayānand Saraswati, Vivekānanda, Mahesh Yogi, inter alia, who introduced new ideas and forms of expression.

The concept of *Varna* was a helpful classification of labour that merged with the notions of wealth and pedigree in nearly every society. Hindus regarded people as free to change from one *varna* to another as occupation dictated, and untouchability and what was called "caste" reflected occupations, not birth. Roman Catholics and early Protestants did not educate lower classes, and the former actually decreed that only clergy could read the holy books. Prior to Charlemagne's reign in Europe, anyone who could read was assumed to be a priest. Hindu Brahmins did the same and probably would have changed that, had Hindus not been subdued by the British, who exploited caste practices, and entrenched and enlarged them, when Lord Risley made it a classification requirement in the 1901 census. The method was then applied throughout the Empire, and the results used to "divide and rule", by favouring the few upper class to ensure enslaving the majority.

Hindu ideas on untouchability may have had a similar origin as the practice among some Native Americans of shunning strangers, associating them with disease and death, a major threat from Europeans which the natives realised too late, and which decimated tribes from Alaska to Tierra del Fuego.[166] It is no different in principle from hand hygiene in hospitals and clinics. However, enough is known today for Hindus to stop the practice of untouchability, and require Government to improve education, health care, land reform and nutrition among *avarnas* (non-status folk) and work with Hindu leaders to accept and include them. The examples of Vidyasagar, an exemplary Brahmin who, over 150 years ago, dined with untouchables and admitted lower class students to Sanskrit College, and of Dr B. Pathak, the pro-Dalit sanitation reformer for the past 40 years, among others, are worth emulating.

This kind of action is well within the meaning and practice of secularism, and could soften some of its excessive and intolerant anti-Hindu statements. Secular intellectuals and atheists usually aim their polemics against Hindus, and tend to dismiss as Hindutva any reference to a need to learn the *Vaidas,* other Hindu religious treatises and epics, as a judge recently advocated, earning the wrath of another judge.

The rejection of ancient Indian history and culture stems directly from Macaulay's formula for controlling India which, as already noted, involved educating Indians to be English in all attributes, but separable by skin colour! This intolerant and harsh treatment of Hindus by secularists contrasts with their gentler treatment of Christians and Muslims and their literature, which they never, or hardly ever criticise, despite many errors, and tend to ignore the invasive spread of Islamic Wahhabism. Tangible signs of official and academic fairness would soften opposition and improve relationships.

However passionate may be the case for secularism, much of its arguments draw lamely on weak US experience and fears of Hindu dominance, forgetting that original Indian kingdoms were united by Hinduism, and that Jews, Parsis, Muslims, Sikhs, Christians, atheists and others had lived in peace and prosperity, under Hindu and Buddhist rulers, before the Islamic conquests, and that the spread of Hinduism and Buddhism throughout China and SE Asia had united east Asia, as Professor Raghuvira had shown decades ago. It should be recalled that a Hindu is free to choose his form of worship or not, yet remain true to his roots (*see www.swargvibha.in/aalekh/all_aalekh/Dr.%20Raghuvira.htm).*

---

[166] But see Pathak, Bibliography

Religious difficulties attended Muslim and British occupation, partly from conversions. The regional wars among Hindu kingdoms in the pre-Muslim era remain a criticism, but most flowed from intrigue and geopolitical differences, not religion, which instead tended to unify, although the narrow and selfish interests of some Brahmins created schisms, even among rulers, and made them vulnerable to invaders.

Secularism is viewed today with frustration, as a failure, parodied as "*sickularism*", and it does not help that its rather emotional defenders are largely INC stalwarts, atheists and leftists, who give critics ugly names and blame all opposition on "Hindutva". This criticism almost maliciously ignores the tenets of Hindutva, as proposed by Savarkar and others. India comprises, after all, a Hindu majority, warts and all, who have no other home, as their critics often have, commuting easily among western institutions, supported by western funds and absorbed in western values that sometimes include a Nehruvian disdain for Hindu social and religious habits and economic behaviour. Indians in North America include some of the harshest critics of India anywhere, as if by doing so, they were currying favour with white ruling authorities.

Savarkar, the initiator of Hindutva, included all Indian religions but regarded Islam and Christianity as different since they focussed on Mecca and Jerusalem, with heroes outside of India. Critics of Hindutva rightly regard this view as dated, since one has to deal with the reality of the "nation" today. In reaching for an accommodation among all sectors of society, it would be helpful if secularists become a bit introspective and consider, not their narrow and somewhat arrogant Hinduphobia, but the views of the less well-endowed or favoured, and remember that Savarkar was one of a long list of Hindus – he called himself an atheist – who had advocated abolition of caste and untouchability, long before secularists jumped on that bandwagon. Many Indians habitually practice caste as foisted on them, often by authorities, like Lord Risley's 1901 census edict, but they would hail Dr Pathak as a hero. Though professing different religions today, South Asians share a dharmic pre-Christian ancestry, and were largely free of religious violence.

It also appears as if India's intellectuals, especially those with one foot on American or British soil, are consciously continuing the British, now American, "*divide and rule*" policy, as already noted! So far in its aim to destroy Hindus by assaults from many angles, in which coercion to convert looms large, there is a denial of a millennium of Islamic and British atrocities against Hindus, and the painful memories of tragedies and loss of many lives and property. India clearly suffered a prolonged mega-holocaust that was accompanied by looting and destruction of numerous temples and other holy places, and other repositories of wealth, so extensive that Hitler's brief efforts seem like a Sunday picnic.

Akbar is nearly always praised for his failed attempt to infuse Hindu principles into Islam, which the later poet Kabir did accomplish. Akbar's temporary reprieve to Hindus did not balance his destruction of Hindu life and property. There is little reflection by secularists on pre-conquest Hindu and Buddhist champions, barring grudging praise for the Mauryas, Guptas, and spiritual sages, perhaps because there were no Muslims or Christians then! Did Babri temple exist? It is axiomatic that the INC would always pander to the Islamist, Christian, Parsi—and Dalits, whom they seem to have suddenly discovered, Ambhedkar notwithstanding, for their votes—and continue to avoid an empathic connection with Hindus, except their privileged members. Small wonder that political unity gets more elusive.

It is a revealing testimony to the British legacy to read accounts in favoured western works that perpetrate the cover-up, for 200 years, from James Mill, through Macaulay, Müller, Mayo, Thapar, to present academics like Sen, Guha and others of India, and Donegal in the US. Criticisms of Anna Hazari, the modern social activist who campaigns against corruption, fall in with the anti-Hinduism argument.

Similarly there is little secular censure or media outcry at the forced conversion of simple folk whose poverty or illiteracy or low social class makes them helpless. Certainly, all efforts to elevate them are overdue, perhaps none more so than education and nutrition. But to exploit their weaknesses and exact their conversion or vote in exchange for food and/or education seems a social crime. Saudi Arabia does not permit Christian proselytising, or even the mere show of another religion on its soil. Nor does the Vatican welcome non-Catholic evangelism.

At the trial of the men accused of killing Christian proselyte Graham Staines, an Australian, and his two pre-teen sons in 1999, in the Odisha village of Manoharpur for "forced conversions," the judgement read in part, "*Our concept of secularism is that the State will have no religion. The State shall treat all religions and religious groups equally and with equal respect without in any manner interfering with their individual right of religion, faith and worship.*"

While condemning religious conversions, even when voluntary, the Court commented that former President of India, K.R. Narayanan, had pointed out that "*Indian unity was based on a tradition of tolerance, which is at once a pragmatic concept for living together and a philosophical concept of finding truth and goodness in every religion. We also ...hope that Mahatma Gandhi's vision of religion playing a positive role in bringing India's numerous religions and communities into an integrated prosperous nation be realised by way of equal respect for all religions. It is undisputed that there is no justification for interfering in someone's belief by way of 'use of force', provocation, conversion, incitement or upon a flawed premise that one religion is better than the other."*[167]

Six decades have passed since independence, mostly under INC rule, yet the nation continues to allow over a hundred million Hindus to be plagued daily by aggressive "Christians" pressing conversion, in exchange for a meal or schoolbook. Surely INC governments could have provided that, to protect India's children, if not religions, from shame and exploitation by wealthy foreigners abusing India's minority laws?

While Hindus remain tolerant of all religions, Christians and Islamists seem intent on capturing and monopolising India, never mind the prospect of a face-off between the two. It is troubling and stressful to the uneducated, poor and hungry, when they have to cope with complex issues of religious conversion, the strange ideas, unfamiliar language, people and practices that threaten their way of life, all in exchange for a morsel and shelter. In the Staines investigation, reports contained the following: *"The trouble starts when a handful of converts defy age-old traditions and customs."* and *"38 Adivasis complained to the police that they were duped into converting on the false promises of jobs"*. Hinduism has the means and the motive to end or at least mitigate their need; it falls to Modi to address it finally. *(See http://ibsresources.org/articles/staines.shtml)*

The Christian situation is troubling in view of the unconstitutional link between US foreign policy and proselytism, through such wealthy corporations as *World Vision, Campus Crusade, Youth with a Mission, Samaritan's Purse, USAID* and others (Malhotra), including a recently formed Fellowship of South Asian Christians (FSAC), which aims to convert diasporal PIOs wherever they may be (see *www.IndoLink.com*). Increasingly, Indian courts have been dealing with charges of forced conversion among Dalits, a disturbing moral and ethical issue, increasing daily and by now catalogued in detail. These expose the wealth, and the wide and intricate network of proselytising agencies, their outrageous claims and threats, including serious injuries or death to Hindu activists by Christian converts. They also show the volumes of detailed data, circulated daily, about target populations e.g. by the Joshua project, headquartered in Colorado, and the Pope's "*Conversion 2000*".

The transgressions of these proselytes, their flouting of the law and of Hindu rights while clamouring for their own, are helped enormously by the fact that most of them are white, exploiting the Indian weakness for light skin. A brown or native Mother Teresa would have failed. That partly explains the uphill battle of people like Vandana Shiva to "save" Indian agriculture from the ruin that Monsanto has "sown" so widely.

---

[167]http://judis.nic.in/supremecourt/imgs1.aspx?filename=37394. Rabindra Kumar. Pal @ Dara Singh vs. Republic of India, 21 January, 2011; retrieved 15April, 2011

Shiva has to battle not only Indian greed and corruption, but their new ally, Americanism, and its halo of whiteness and wealth.

In 1992-3, Narasimha Rao pleased Indian businessmen with his headlong shift to an open economy. Greater freedom and fewer regulations facilitated US investments in, and control of, Indian businesses, and exporting of profits. But he had neglected to begin by eradicating the heavy burden of corruption, inherited from the British *Rāja* and princely states. This had increased in independent India, and by the 1990s, had infected all levels of government, and become epidemic in society. Rao's reforms had resulted, quite early, in the very problems that Nehru and others had faced with the British, and hoped to avoid.

The United States became an entity because the units (states) shared origins and values, in a vast land. Even if a classified society did exist, it was informal, unlike Britain, and the chance of achieving high rank was easier than anywhere else on the globe. Furthermore, the nation shared religion and language, which even entered its coinage: *"In God we Trust"*. The slogan sustained the US through two world wars until it became the world's most powerful nation, indulging a loose and hedonistic living that it had developed in tandem with Christian fundamentalism, and lately Judaism; it no longer needed trust in God!

The rise of Jewish financial power, through the 19th century to today's supremacy, was powered by the German Rothschilds, lifting with it the mass of European Zionists in the first half of the twentieth century, with paradoxical "help" from Adolf Hitler. Ultimately, it gained them the land of Palestine and created of it an America in the Middle East, fortifying US authority there, and providing a nuclear-armed base to hold Asia in thrall. Meanwhile, the Rothschilds have taken control of the world's central banks performing a function that each nation can easily do, and save enough to finance their national health and education programs, by saving the interest they now pay into central banks!

Iran is one of the few nations without a Rothschild bank; is this why it is Israel's target? Recent campaigns have secured Iraq and Islamic North Africa for the USA, while technological and political realities have kept Pakistan a virtual subject. The US is gradually conquering India, by Christian proselytism, bribery and by stoking armed revolt in southern and northeastern border states, via US missions, or via Pakistan's ISI. They also make enough Indian business associates so rich as to be above country and honour, and at one with similar Americans. By their colour, though, most will be excluded from the innermost seats of power, except as rich but unwelcome tokens, such as Queen Victoria had created. When Dadabhai Naoroji made his first attempt for a seat in the UK House of Commons in 1886, Lord Salisbury snidely welcomed his campaign thus, *"Colonel Duncan was opposed by a black man; and however great the progress of mankind has been, and however far we have advanced in overcoming prejudices, I doubt if we have yet to go to that point of view where a British constituency would elect a black man?"*[168] What a gem! Or consider Major Graham Pole's revealing comment in the House of Commons, in 1929, *"Even a much shorter time ago than that, if you travelled in a railway train with an Indian, or drove in a motor car with an Indian, you were supposed to be lowering the British Raj."* (*Hansard*, HC, 1929).

As long ago as the mid-19th century, the US had bullied Japan into a trade deal. India is buckling under the same relentless corporate invasion from the US, aided by greedy fifth columnists from within who do not understand the dangers of playing with this fire, that the heat of US craving is all-consuming, just like the greed of the British aristocrats who had looted and impoverished India for nearly three centuries. But the US is now invading Indian *culture*, which the British had largely left alone. Indeed, the British had adopted many Indian fashions, food and materials, and incorporated Hindi and Sanskrit words in their language.

Indian restaurants are everywhere in Britain, and British university staff and students thrive on their fare. The US, however, wants to change and own Indian tastes and choices, regardless of local traditions or religions, and be free to sell its products, doctrines, etc., under international agreements that it had concocted in the first place. India is part of the American squeeze of Asia aimed eventually at containment, if not control of Russia and China, having secured south central Asia, except Iran, and, in the east, Japan, the Philippines and South Korea.

For a while, it looked as if India had learned from history and might fend off the USA, but Indian business leaders have failed the country yet again, and are playing loyal US surrogates, while continuing to fool themselves that they can gain world power, equal with the West, by aping them in every way. Instead, they sink deeper into the US net, maintained by spying, threats, deception, a permissive life style and compelling advertising of Americana that entices the gullible, and captures the young and shallow; ultimately military and monetary might will triumph, just as the film industry has done.

Much as India's caste-riddled and divided middle class might admire themselves, their guile is like an immature child's before a seasoned manipulator dangling twin lollipops! Indians have become adept at petty thievery and civil corruption and have lost knowledge and respect for their own mores. They have become attached to things that the British aristocracy had foisted on them (as well as on ordinary British citizens, the long-standing and loyal victims of aristocracy). They have yet to learn how to defend against the American juggernaut and

---

[168] Antoinette Burton, Essay, 2000 *Society for Comparative Study of Society and History*, p.633

the financial leeches it feeds through advertising and international banking.

From the very beginning the problem was defined in India's adoption of a western-dominated form of government and constitution, because it suited the bureaucratic elite that the British had trained, who would maintain the administration during the power transition. Not much appeared to have been done to create a strong *moral* basis for government, particularly a common civil code to administer all religions and groups fairly and equally, as indicated in a multicultural society under a secular government. Honesty, trust, reliability and consistency did not displace favouritism, casteism, bribery, power plays and other corruption rampant in administrations and businesses, correctable, however slowly, by example, laws, good governance, education, reward systems, and elimination of prejudicial, repressive and outmoded social practices. Instead, India fell to graft, opportunism and bullying.

The indulgent lifestyles of Indian princes had left them soft and the payola they received enough to keep them loyally hooked, rarely to achieve true learning or enlightenment, the pre-requisites for unity. Many neglected their subjects as they pursued a sybaritic life style. The rich, if anything, barring a few far-seeing thinkers, regretted the departure of the British. Independence, to aristocrats nurtured by the British *Rāja*, was a foolish idea, as they felt that India could only be kept united and compliant by foreigners with strong arms and expensive enticements; India was too malleable, too clannish, with too many loyalties and tribal taboos to unite with an agreed set of respectable values, except under a really superior or even dictatorial force, like China's. They forgot the dictum that most advances in a nation come from the studious and ambitious middle class, not from its aristocracy.

But India's middle class today have been so subjugated and shorn of the strongest values of its original religions and heritage that they accept American crassness rather than strive to restore or enhance the virtues that had made India unique, rich and attractive, and to protect and preserve those elements at all social and economic levels. Indeed modern Indians watch idly, while swarms of Americans, many toting Bibles in one hand and Bribes in the other, impose their values, while others loot what they can, animate or inanimate, turning pilfered things Indian into popular American goods, through predatory patenting, that tyrannical instrument of American greed. Witness the illegal patenting of toys, neem, turmeric, and others, or the theft of marketable sections of Yoga by zealots with financial clout, who care little for preserving meaning, context or associations, or who misconstrue the ascetic's renunciation—a concept unknown to materialists—as servility or lack of ambition.

The West is founded on materialism and anything spiritual is just that: ephemeral, distracting, of little value, unless it can be commoditised and profitably sold! In this vein, India is seen as a huge market ripe for all the gadgets and innovations that enrich western manufacturers and beguile people, and thus would need the most spirited defence to keep the foreign elements under control. It may come to a showdown such as the US has had before, as Britain's ally, with China over opium, and with Japan, Korea and the Philippines over trade. When Mark Twain's fictional 19th century *Connecticut Yankee* gained authority over King Arthur's 6th century kingdom, the first thing he wished he could introduce was patenting! (Twain). Compare *Amrita,* p. 443.

Indians are too disparate and too consumed by social hierarchies to come together readily on common ground. The census of 1901 by the British Rāja entrenched caste, *jāt* and *gotra* practices throughout the Empire, eroding Vaidic *varna,* which was versatile and flexible, with interchangeable classes reflecting education, aptitude and choice, not heredity. The USA's attraction was equality, the notion that any man could feel free to develop and use his talents gainfully and honestly, and keep the proceeds. Not that it ever achieved it, but it did come close. It used to be that a grave digger could hob-nob with the best, or command an audience with the President. In India, that was sometimes possible, before the British made it unthinkable during the British *Rāja.* Indian historiography is full of instances where access of the meanest to the highest, the monarch, was not barred; a republican system called *Gana-Sangha* (equal assembly), or *Gana-Rajya* (equal government), did thrive in ancient Vaishali and Videha *(vide ante).*

The more sinister and imminently destructive threat is by Islam, from within and across India's borders, and from anti-Hindu media, which cannot see or think beyond PM Modi's *chai* history, honourable though it is, or the Godhra incident, as if either could define character or ability, once and for all. Thus PM Modi has found India, at the edge, about to fall, pressed by enemies and witless locals. Can he save her?

India's collapse this time could be swift and final, balkanised to become a jigsaw puzzle, such as AIML zealot Rahmat Ali had proposed in 1933, each piece under a chieftain, like post-Gupta India, its trusting peoples divided and betrayed. It will once again become subservient, either to Islam or, this time, to America, to fill its need for cannon-fodder—as the British had classed *sipahis,* and the US its Hispanics and Blacks—in the inevitable clash with China and Russia, as the world engages in a two- power "Warm War": the West versus the Rest!

It is not too late for India to avoid the fall. Stepping back, though, will be tough for it stands on a narrow ledge and would require more grit, less pro-US and pro-Islam sycophancy, sharper oversight of local,

US and other foreign operations in India and border countries, including identifying spies, who have always been plentiful in Indian society. Flagrant proselytising must be stopped, amending the constitution, as needed. Government organisation must improve, with enhanced ruling skills and transparency, and determination to eradicate corruption and resist the world's bribes. It should institute controls on its free-wheeling pro-west, anti-religious materialists, in fact do some of what China had done for three decades, and modify policies so as to halt the cheap sale of India to the USA. The refusal of the USA to assist India's nuclear program, even as it sought Indian business, is evidence enough of its paramount self-interest, and a warning that it will not hesitate to trample on India once again, at the least hint of any non-compliance or threat.

Undoubtedly, India has the expertise to develop in an ecological, sustainable way, gradually spreading good to all its citizens, not explosively, as mimics of the American way would selfishly want, and sell out to the West to get it, as already seen. But to use its human wealth to set achievable goals to enhance the quality of life for *all* its people and learn from the *Vaidas* the true principles of *'live and let live'*, and from the old Diaspora how to cast off the shackles of caste and ignorance, to bring out the best in all, to find the hidden Ambhedkars and non-corrupt versions of the Mayawatis of India, and not merely to export its best, or, in Naipaul's words, *"crave for foreign"*. If Indians desire a US or other western lifestyle, let them go there for it. But they should refrain from pushing Americanism to their fellows, through advertising, media biases, religious pressures and false British versions of Indian history, still common on US campuses, even in courses taught by Indians. World media have gelled into a dozen news factories, pushing US cant, not truth. Hence India cannot rely on getting fair publicity in the USA.

The streets in the USA are not paved with gold, not even metaphorically. In fact they're pathways of danger for coloured peoples, Recent videographed police killings of Blacks in US cities, including an older Indian visiting family in the south), and the cited New Jersey incidents illustrate this (pp. 426-7). Indians should find comfort and confidence, from knowing their heritage, values and virtues, and work to preserve and promote them, without fear.

The US Government has ignored or even endorsed the aggression and immorality of US multinationals overseas, as they continue to hog resources, deny global warming and the US's huge industrial carbon footprint. Global warming, like released radioactivity, is a public concern and a threat to all life forms; it should therefore be the first priority of governments, especially those who threaten the most. Climate change discussions began in "earnest" in 1991 and continue today with hardly any advance beyond small-scale CO_2 swapping by polluters for tropical forests. In fact, the discussions have been so much hot air! Greater reliance should be placed on renewable sources of energy such as the sun and wind, rather than dirty sources, like Canada's tar sands, and 'fracking' in the USA. In Mumbai, armies of the working poor comb through dumps sorting items for "re-use and recycle"; they also find far too many items made of harmful non-degradable materials.

Government leaders generally, and some specifically, like current PM Harper of Canada (2014), mesmerised with the earnings side of dirty fuel, are prone to misinform people about the severity of environmental damage. Similarly, they overlook the rising cost of food, as corporate agribusiness grabs control of its production. Home gardens, even urban, conserve energy while a strict regulation of chemical agriculture and banning poorly-tested GM foods and crops can save water and money, avoid GM-related diseases, and prevent bankruptcy and suicides by farmers, as in India. GM crops have been blamed for rat tumours (Séralini) and an insidious chronic human kidney failure (Jayasumana).

To conserve fuel in WWII, private pleasure driving was curtailed in many places, and mass transit improved. Surveys today confirm American distaste for this *(www.nationalgeographic.com/greendex)* and other ways of conserving, e.g. water, now at lowering levels in the USA, and in every major country. Many are too set in their ways to change; habits die hard; the time to start teaching conservation is in childhood.

The cited National Geographic survey showed that one US child in its lifetime will have as much negative impact on the environment as 13 Brazilian children! Yet the response is an enigmatic shrug, and pity for the Brazilians! Little thought is given that affluent societies, and individuals, are among the most wasteful and greedy, and create the most harmful impact on the environment. These tend to be less than 30% of most populations in western nations. The US's 4.5% of world population consumed 40% of world production and produced 5.8 billion tonnes of CO_2 in 2013 or 18.35 per head (compare India 2.16). Yet, even in the USA, large numbers of people are barely able to make ends meet, are poorly educated, live in insanitary environments and dilapidated housing, while US Governments ignore their cause, and boast of wealth.

Climate change has steadily increased over the last fifty years, and threatens to be as momentous as the previous global natural disasters like glaciation, meteor landings and pandemics, or man-made events such as wars of conquest, slavery, imperialism and racial intolerance. Perhaps *Ebola* might be the great equaliser as it joins with any or all of the others to begin the final menace, as past plagues had introduced.

The workings of US National Security (NS) are usually kept from the fickle public, so is known only to the Edward Snowdens of this world and to government heads. NS is their salvation, and protection from the public, which may turn on them if it realises that NS is invasive, perpetrated by a corporate-run government, for profit. Under it, the "asset forfeiture" law, part of the "war on drugs", is used by state and local police to extort money and personal details from drivers stopped for simple traffic violations. Police target Blacks, Hispanics and visible minorities, force a search and any money found is retained. Victims may be forced to wait a year or more for a court to order return of seized money. *"Under the Obama administration, police have made more than 22,000 such seizures worth about $1 billion..."* The Washington Post reported, after a study. Complaints have not stopped arbitrary or capricious use of this power. *(See http://www.washingtonpost.com/sf/investigative/2014/09/06).*

From its inception, American nuclear programming included the idea of a nuclear winter, which Americans feel they could survive in suitably provisioned underground bunkers, or by escaping into massive orbiting spaceships, carrying select thousands, and able to grow food—a theme one sees in science fiction, but possible, as ancient Vaidic tales suggest. If we are near there—who knows what experiments American secrecy and security have conducted—some may well escape the final disaster, but will the world be habitable again, when they have to return? One guess is that they will have far less chance of survival than the most primitive tribe of the most remote and protected tropical jungle.

As the vistas of the defunct Saraswati-Indus civilisation continues to expand with each discovery, the tales in the *Ramāyana* and *Mahābhārata* sharpen in focus and suggest that India had seen an advanced society, using novel forms of energy to achieve air and space travel, and nuclear arms. This civilisation could have had a nuclear ending, although the more plausible suspects, in terms of today's knowledge, remain earthquakes, tsunamis, drought or other natural disasters.

But the finding of sunken structures in the Arabian Sea, glazed earth and brick on land resembling those of Hiroshima or Nagasaki, bodies grouped as if facing disaster, and the formation of large deserts in the area suggest a nuclear calamity. A likely scenario is described by science fiction writer, Walter Miller, in his book, *A Canticle for Leibowitz.* He tells of a degraded society, much like Earth today, where a few survive the final nuclear confrontation, and relearn basic existence. In the course of a millennium or more, they discover much of their previous knowledge, thinking it is all new, and that the primitive state of their origins precluded any prior advances in science and technology. They become rich by selling their inventions and by promoting consumerism. A few centuries later, torn apart by egocentricity, anger and hate; they reach for the nuclear switch, and another cycle of man's trial on Earth begins!

Successive US presidencies have failed to restrain industry from poisoning the planet, or to reduce foreign wars and promote peace. The US *Military, Industrial and Financial Complex* (MIFC), which profits from war, is solidly in charge. Its global activities are more troubling than the family skirmishes between Russians and Ukrainians. A promise by Bush Snr. to Gorbachev to leave East Germany out of NATO, in exchange for unification of Germany, was promptly broken and the breach endorsed by Clinton. Gorbachev's wrath was countered with the boorish remark that their's was just a gentleman's agreement! Obviously there were no gentlemen left in the US administration! Recent records show that the Government has not changed the way huge contracts are awarded to contractors e.g. Kellogg, Brown and Root, Halliburton etc., a lesson the world, especially exposed India, must learn, if only to reject US methods.

Can any today be trusted, even the US President? The recent destruction of the Malaysian Airlines Flight MH17 over the Ukraine was promptly portrayed by US/NATO interests as an attack by Russia. The Russians, equally promptly, publicised an opposite accusation of the US/Ukraine alliance, with far better evidence than the USA (CIA) had presented. The hot words from the US cooled, and the vision of WWIII receded; but uncertainty remains, following the use by US Secretary of State, John Kerry, of a fabricated photo to accuse Syria's Assad of using chemical weapons against rebels. Fake material has long been a CIA weapon, and no doubt used by other states, but over the past 50 years the USA seems to have made increasing use of it. Remember George Bush's accusing Sadam Husain of hiding weapons of mass destruction?

India must beware of this two-faced beast that will just as snappily feast on its own members to satiate the corporations that profit, each bite it takes, no matter how safe some PIOs may feel, as they get cosy with US leaders. The colour of their skin, and, for this generation, their accent, will always expose them, unless they transform themselves with one of India's skin lightening creams, or copy the late American performer, Michael Jackson's whitening process!

US coolness to India increased when India declined to support sanctions against Russia and Sri Lanka. Both had looked like bullying, the former under cover of NATO. The US is active on Russia's doorstep. What would the US do, if Russia tried to revive its base in Cuba? The US base at Guantanamo Bay, Cuba, served as an interrogation centre where post 9/11 detainees were said to have been routinely tortured by the CIA, without any useful outcome. President Bush denied the accusation but is alleged to have approved the acts, including "waterboarding", a technique of torturing the victim by repeated near-drowning.

The US should pay heed to its many fair thinkers and activists and do what is right, from foreign (military) policy to food. This is a sore point, as US Corporations are wont to ignore or undermine other nations' laws and customs, in the name of profit. There is no diplomacy. It is plainly immoral for a strong country to use force or bribery to empower its own companies to seize the assets, whether productions or food, from a weaker or poorer one, or to endanger it. That's despotism. A nation's food is its own concern, its unique choice and property, and should be held sacrosanct, unless an emergency dictates otherwise.

India must support and improve Hinduism, for its over one billion followers (2001), for whom India is their only home, and must secure the interests of *all* citizens, especially the poor and weak.. Hinduism is an ancient and pragmatic way of life and has the rare virtue of tolerance for other philosophies, and respect for doubt and debate. It does not seek world conquest, unlike Christianity or Wahhabist Islam. It encourages self-realisation, material and spiritual. It has suffered centuries of oppression, strayed from its heritage and hardened with resistance, instead of thriving with introspection and discourse. Modi has inherited the religion in its degraded state, since Hindu issues were ridiculed and neglected for over 50 years, and the BJP attacked when it tried to rectify conditions, twelve years ago. The anti-Hinduism of "intellectuals" does not help; it postpones reform that is sorely needed to improve the lot of the most needy. Modi's followers expect quick changes, but one would prefer a cautious and thoughtful approach, making changes that remain tolerant and fair, respect others, and avoid reprisals for past wrongs.

In his book *Indian Philosophy* Vol. I, pp. 22-23, the late Dr. Sarvapelli Radhakrishnan, former President of India, and a critical scholar of Hinduism in his time, wrote, "*The Hindu religion is a reflection of the composite character of the Hindus, who are not one people but many. Unlike other countries, India can claim that philosophy in ancient India was not an auxiliary to any other science or art, but always held a prominent position of independence...In all the fleeting centuries of history, in all the vicissitudes through which India has passed, a certain marked identity is visible. It has held fast to certain psychological traits which constitute its special heritage, and they will be the characteristic marks of the Indian people so long as they are privileged to have a separate existence*".

In a major case the Supreme Court of India examined the nature of Hinduism *(http://legalservices.co.in/blogs/entry/Case-laws-defining-Hindutva-and-Hinduism)* and recorded this opinion, cited here at some length from Dr Radhakrishnan. The Court noted: *"When we think of the Hindu religion, we find it difficult, if not impossible, to define Hindu religion or even adequately describe it. Unlike other religions in the world, the Hindu religion does not claim any one prophet; it does not worship any one God; it does not subscribe to any one dogma; it does not believe in any one philosophic concept; it does not follow any one set of religious rites or performances; in fact, it does not appear to satisfy the narrow traditional features of any religion or creed. It may broadly be described as a way of life and nothing more...Though philosophic concepts and principles evolved by different Hindu thinkers and philosophers varied in many ways and even appeared to conflict with each other in some particulars, they all had reverence for the past and accepted the Vaidas as the sole foundation of Hindu philosophy. Naturally enough, it was realised by Hindu religion from the very beginning of its career that truth was many-sided and different views contained different aspects of truth which no one could fully express...The development of the Hindu religion has always been inspired by an endless quest for truth based on the consciousness that truth has many facets: Truth is one but wise men describe it differently. The Indian mind has consistently through the ages been exercised over the problem of the nature of godhead, the problem that faces the spirit at the end of life, and the interrelation between the individual and the universal soul. 'If we can abstract from the variety of opinion'*, says Dr. Radhakrishnan, *'and observe the general spirit of Indian thought, we shall find that it has a disposition to interpret life and nature in the way of monistic idealism, though this tendency is so plastic, living and manifold that it takes many forms and expresses itself in even mutually hostile teachings '*

"The development of Hindu religion and philosophy shows that from time to time saints and religious reformers attempted to remove from the Hindu thought and practices elements of corruption and superstition and that led to the formation of different sects. Buddha started Buddhism; Mahavir founded Jainism; Basava became the founder of Lingayat religion, Dnyaneshwar and Tukaram initiated the Vārakari cult; Guru Nanak inspired Sikhism; Dayānanda founded Arya Samaj, and Chaitanya began Bhakti cult; and as a result of the teachings of Ramakrishna and Vivekananda, Hindu religion flowered into its most attractive, progressive and dynamic form. If we study the teachings of these saints and religious reformers, we would notice an amount of divergence in their respective views; but underneath that divergence, there is a kind of subtle indescribable unity which keeps them within the sweep of the broad and progressive Hindu religion...

"The Constitution-makers were fully conscious of this broad and comprehensive character of Hindu religion: and so, in guaranteeing the fundamental right to freedom of religion, explanation II to Art. 25 has made it clear that in sub-clause (b) of clause (2), the reference to Hindus shall be construed as including a reference to persons professing the Sikh, Jain or Buddhist religion, and the reference to Hindu religious institutions shall be construed accordingly."

It is clear that the way forward for India must include the reform of education so that all children pursue a common syllabus in a caste-free setting, accommodating all religions, so that the poor can take advantage of legal reservations to aid their progress. Governments must eliminate corrupt pathways, so that services can reach those in need; and above all, establish *a common civil code* so that all citizens are treated equally, share values, observe the same laws and remain free to practise or change their religion, and be safe from threats or pressure from greedy proselytes.

The zamindari system was abolished early, but India needs further land reform to assist the rural poor and ensure that city tycoons do not trample on their rights e.g., in seeking mineral rights. Integrity and lack of favouritism in government services, especially Police, are sorely needed, no less than in business and in the professions, where even physicians trade organs obtained from the poor and redirect casualties to private clinics, among other disgraceful crimes. The current status is perhaps the deepest rut from which India must extricate herself.

The role and activities of foreign governments and corporations in the affairs of others are fruitful grounds for corruption and need close scrutiny. The example of American Free Trade Unions (*North American FTA, Central American FTA* and the looming *FTAA—Free Trade Area of the Americas*—should be warning enough to India, against the destructive effects of WTO policies and "global" sorties on small farmers, weakening this backbone of reliable world food production. Sadly, this field is violated today and increasingly appropriated by global agrichemical giants, which seize farmlands, force small farmers out of business and promise plenty, but deliver little, aiming only to satisfy shareholders.

According to Global Exchange, an international Human Rights organisation: *"'Free trade' agreements to date have been little more than code words for US business expansion across the globe. In theory, these agreements assume a level playing field between partners. However the United States has yet to follow the rules. Just recently, the US Congress approved a $70 billion agricultural subsidy for the next 10 years. This largely benefits corporate agribusiness while undermining small farmers both in the US and across the globe. One of the most glaring attacks on food security and agribiodiversity has been US corn exports to Mexico under NAFTA…"*
(See *http://www.globalexchange.org/resources/ftaa/biotech).*

India is following the path of the USA whose policies foster growth of corporations, by buyout of small businesses or crushing them by crooked competition. Some in the US, like Monsanto, gain control of a government function, via a revolving door arrangement, and thus direct policy. Traditional practices are threatened by unproven or unhealthy American ways that have already spread too far. Americans entered India by force (WTO), bribery and other corrupt practices, caring little for the values lost, especially in food production and cuisine.

A report entitled *"Food Security, Farming, and the WTO and CAFTA"* on this issue, as it affects North America, contains the following: *"Since NAFTA was implemented, 38,000 small farms have been lost in the United*

States, and 11 percent of Canadian farms have gone bankrupt. A mere 2 percent of farms in the United States control 50 percent of American agricultural sales. Over 73 percent of the nation's farms share less than 7 percent of the market value of agricultural products, while 7.2 percent of farms receive 72 percent of the market value of products sold. Eighty-two percent of U.S. corn exports are controlled by three agribusiness firms- Cargill, Archer Daniels Midland (ADM), and Zen Noh. While family farmer incomes have plummeted during the first 7 years of NAFTA, ADM's profits went from $110 million to $301 million, while ConAgra's grew from $143 million to $413 million."

Dealing with the effects on farmers in Mexico, the report states, *"Under NAFTA and the WTO, over one and a half million Mexican farmers have lost their sources of income, forcing them to abandon their farms. This has created a massive farmers' migration to big cities and other countries in search of jobs. In 2002, an average of 600 Mexicans was forced off their land each day. Annually now 500,000 Mexicans per year attempt to cross the U.S.-Mexico border to find a way to feed their families. In the past five years, 1600 Mexican migrants have died while trying to cross the U.S.-Mexico border searching for jobs. Under CAFTA, Central American corn, rice, beans, and sorghum farmers, as well as poultry, pig, cow, and dairy producers all stand to be driven off their land by cheap imports. In Guatemala alone, experts predict that CAFTA will result in the loss of 45,000 to 120,000 agricultural jobs."*
(See http://www.globalexchange.org/resources/wto/agriculture)

India is already familiar with this scenario, in agriculture and mining, e.g., POSCO, the Korean mining company in Odisha and Karnataka. It must do its utmost to end the sickening greed that propels Corporations, local and foreign, to commit such extensive human tragedy. The US government invariably backs its corporations and increasingly uses advanced technology to invade others—from persons to countries—destroy movable or immovable property and launch lethal attacks with bombs, bullets and drones. Others will follow suit.

India should disengage from ill-considered ventures and sweet deals with the West and remember that its current state of relative backwardness has been the result of a thousand years of misplaced trust in foreigners, who came with no moral purpose, but the dishonourable intent to raid, supplant, harm and steal. That has not changed. *India must never forget that when the British came, India commanded nearly 25% of global GNP, and barely 5% when they left* (p. 332).

India's food and agriculture policy is already at the mercy of several dozen FTAs, which the INC government and city-centred or closeted economists have allowed, while regarding tariffs, and other income safeguards for farmers and their cultivars of food and commercial crops, as obstacles to business profits, rarely as benefits for farmers or society.

The most troubling aspect of NAFTA is its Chapter 11, which allows corporations to sue a foreign government for "lost profits", should it limit or ban a corporation's products, however toxic, or its methods, however untried, or uncertain or antisocial! Settlement is judged in "secret" by an *Investor State Dispute Resolution Tribunal* of three excessively-paid adjudicators with open-ended and slow timetables! They have so far been chosen by the industry, the company and from an independent group. The weighting favours companies. An oil company, *Lone Pine Resources,* is suing the Quebec, Canada, government for its environmental and public safety laws banning fracking below the St Lawrence River bed, claiming $250 million (Feb. 2015).

The US drug giant, *Eli, Lilly,* has sued Canada, based on a surely immoral argument that its drug should be approved because the Company has tested it, even though Canada requires more testing to show efficacy. *(http://www.cbc.ca/Sept 13, 2013).* Suits like these have little chance of success before the regular Courts; thus suitors choose the ISDRT route because it's easier, favours companies, is secret, and can be dragged on, if necessary, forcing defendants to incur costs, or settle, which they often do, as it is cheaper. Many of these cases globally have been brought by mining, oil and gas firms against poor nations acting to save their environments. Corporations can thus throttle Governments.

NAFTA records, available to October 2010, show that there have been 66 cases, 28 against Canada, and 19 each against Mexico and the USA. Invariably corporate challenges were against environmental protection, food and drug safety, control of natural resources and real estate development. Interestingly, none of the cases against the US won, while 5 did against Mexico and 2 against Canada, with nearly half not yet adjudicated. Many of the judgments (awards) are questionable, and up to that date Canada had been fined $157 million and Mexico $187M, when the latter was penalised for passing legislation against harmful high-fructose corn syrup (HFCS) made by the three giants of US corn: Cargill, ADM and Corn Products International. What made this a most egregious result was that Mexico was facing huge hurdles selling its cheaper sugar in the USA. It is amazing that three people can thus repudiate the policies of a government, however well-meaning. For details, s*ee http://www.globalexchange.org/corporateHRviolators.*

The push for globalisation in 1988 was a natural American follow-up to the success of GATT in enabling its Corporations to use their financial muscle to seize the world's assets, without restraint, or concern for local rights, culture or welfare, simply by bribing a few influential people! NAFTA empowered the ultra-rich who profited from the fall of the USSR, and from Clinton's "lame-duck" US deregulations, consolidated by George Bush. Obama made no real move to stop the nasty game.

Globalisation allowed Western multinationals to find the cheapest producer with the least oversight, e.g., Bangladeshi textiles, to start a slavery regime, heedless of regulation or taxation, displacing local and family businesses. Western industry has moved *en masse* to third world countries, where rich owners pay marginal wages by strategic bribing and child labour, and so fatten their take, while Western media and corporate public relations turn a blind eye to the labour abuses.

Local entrepreneurs are only too glad to climb on the troika that jingles lowering of taxes, privatisation and deregulation of corporations, along with reduced public spending. The promise of a trickle-down to the poor never happens, as India's reformist PM, N. Rao, glumly conceded when facing increasing farm poverty in the late 1990s, as millionaires morphed into billionaires. India is facing the same problem as it did with the British *Rāja*, except that trade pacts are doing what the railways, telegraph, navy, subsidiary alliances and taxes then did.

With the world collapsing around it, North America leading, ISIS threatening the Middle East, Wahhabism destabilising it, India has a chance to delink from the manipulative American wagon in most aspects of social and economic action, and heed its best scientists who have been fighting valiantly, even as foreign giants seized lives and livelihood in every state. India has the talents to be self-sufficient, to reject the WTO, to avoid agreements like NAFTA and CAFTA, or bilateral trade agreements (BITs) that have impoverished many while fattening a few. The egregious 2012 award to Occidental Oil against Ecuador is quite a disheartening warning. (*See http://www.citizen.org/documents/oxy-v-ecuador-memo.pdf*). If any trickling has occurred it has been a trickle-up; truly, the rich cup "runneth over". (See also *http://www.citizen.org/RDC-vs-Guatemala)*

To cap it all, the extraordinary rise of multinationals in the USA and the immense power of their CEOs, through clubs, formal and informal, will end what little democracy and decency there is left, the US having capitulated, with Canada and the EU tagging alongside, leashed, like dogs, to the WTO, FTAs and the *Bank for International Settlements*. Can India hope to survive and offer even a rusty rupee to its poorest citizen, when all must conform to this pitiless despotism?

Yet democracy, though tainted by preferment, corruption and dynastic ambitions, remains a plus for India. Indian democracy is not the same as American "democracy", itself a fantasy, which the US tends to promote as a model globally and to woo "sister democracies." India has a democratic structure and constitution, but is still heavily colonised, having allowed multinational corporations to rise in the past twenty years to positions of so much power that they intimidate even big governments, especially by trade agreements, which have so far done nothing for the nations' masses, except steal from them, and remain immoral tools of Corporate greed, abetted by Government lackeys.

India now must revise its values and its aims, and under Modi build new and different links with the USA and others, to prevent steam-rolling US corporations from ravishing country and people, down to the last retail store, and to restrain aggressive Christian proselytes and Islamic jihadists, posing as Hindus and doing wrong, from desecration to physical injury so that Hindus get blamed. In the 1960s, Indira Gandhi had bravely and sensibly rejected President Johnson's pressure to license US corporations in exchange for grain purchases and a share in Norman Borlaug's chemical agriculture. He denied food aid to India. India survived and was spared three generations of chemical poisoning.

Sharon Beder, an Australian Social Sciences professor at the University of Wollongong, in her book "How Corporations Drive the Global Agenda, wrote, *"The undemocratic nature of decision making in the World Trade Organisation (WTO) negotiations has ensured that the trade rules agreed to are skewed in favour of the more affluent nations that are pushing for free trade. Business coalitions have presented a united front through the networking efforts of several key, well-placed people. Transnational corporations such as Pfizer and IBM have been able to utilise the trade negotiations to push for better protection of intellectual property such as patents because of the power that the US and the EU are able to exercise in these negotiations."* and *"The enlistment of regulators, bureaucrats and politicians in the corporate cause has been a key achievement of those lobbying for various agreements within the WTO. This is made easier by the phenomenon of the revolving door."*

The British have left, but the looting continues; today it is done by Indians and their *havala* partners. Havala is the likeliest method of transferring Wahhabi funds between extremist Islamic groups.

Shiva Temple, Varanasi

Ex PM AB Vajpayee

Epilogue

"But we are convinced that if we are to play a meaningful role nationally, and in the community of nations, we must be second to none in the application of advanced technologies to the real problems of man and society."
Vickram Sarabhai

"Make In India"
Narendra Modi

The rise of the BJP under Modi places India's future in the hands of reformist Hindus who hopefully will be allowed to chart a fruitful course for *all* sectors of the population, without surrendering the country once again to foreign predators, this time the USA, and where the word Hinduism can be used without apology. The people wish for change where merit determines a person's place in society. Each individual should be able to develop his/her potential and not submit to restrictive birth lines, to the ridiculous extent it is used in some states, even to justify murder (see p.407-8). Hinduism is fairly resilient, but saddled and weighed down by rigid and outmoded caste practices, especially in rural areas, that, if not checked, can result in its destruction. The poor and weak, heavily exploited for a millennium, and still neglected, deserve justice and better opportunities.

Indians must be able to look at themselves with pride, and enjoy a fair share of the country's worth, of life and livelihood, according to their ability and willingness to strive for them. A just society should give the poor the same start as anyone else, if not a bigger boost, to prepare them for a productive role in society. Poverty and repression limit one's initial options but do not define final potential in anyone. But chronic hunger, from birth through childhood, will have a lasting effect on academic achievement, as shown among the malnourished in several studies in India, Mexico and Central America, East and South Africa, Philippines, Jamaica, Barbados and elsewhere, as any internet or journal search will verify. To counter remarks on the torpid poor, note that India's "backward" Hindu castes (a*divasis)* are rarely credited for the twenty or so rebellions they waged against British oppression, unaided.

One large group of the scheduled castes, followers of the *Sarna* religion *("sacred grove,"* a variant of Hinduism), have become so disillusioned with the ruling classes that they seek recognition as a separate religion. Their rally in Ranchi, capital of Jharkhand, in February 2014, continued the protest they had made in June 2013 against Roman Catholics for erecting a statue of the Virgin Mary, showing her dressed in a sari, and carrying the infant Jesus in a sling, similar to that used by tribal women. The brazen and offensive imposition of a Catholic icon on a Hindu motif and their failure to remove it have incensed the *Sarna;* their protest continued. Their resolve recalls a dictum byAbdul Kalam, former President of India: *"Unless India stands up to the world, no one will respect us. In this world, fear has no place. Only strength respects strength."*

BJP leader Narendra Modi and his mother, 90-year-old Hirabenat in Gandhinagar, May 16, 2014. (Credit: Foreign Photo Service/Zuma Press)

Narendra Modi, centre, surrounded by supporters at the BJP's Gujarat headquarters in Gandhinagar, the state capital, 16 May 2014 (Credit, Zuma Press)

Modi's 2014 victory was not what the US wanted. Under the Obama administration, the US has become increasingly cool towards India. Earlier, in 2005, Bush had declared that the US would deny Modi a visa, having black-balled him following the Ghodra train incident. Obama's visit to India in 2010 was welcomed by the INC; he talked of a *"defining partnership of the 21st century"*, which must refer to the USA's continuing pillage of Indian scientists and thinkers. His grandiose phrases dissipated when India did not slavishly follow the USA's selfish and hostile actions against Russia, Iran and Sri Lanka, while aiding aggression against the former two. The "partnership" ended soon after in a separation, if not a divorce. The US remains basically anti-Hindu.

Indian journalists and economists tend to kow-tow to the power and wealth of the US and over-value the word of their politicians and scholars. Obama's remarks were pure rhetoric. After his election in 2008, he had contacted global heads of state, including Pakistan, but not India, and so halted a decade-old reconciliation, started by Clinton and Bush, following Nixon and Reagan's trashing of the country. In his efforts to stabilise Afghanistan after the Taliban takeover, he ignored India's close and ancient relationship with that country, and that Afghanistan was part of greater India in Ashoka's time, over two millennia before the birth of the USA, when the Western hemisphere was unknown to Europeans, pristine, and protected by its aboriginal peoples.

Christian proselytes, intent on continued falsification of Indian history, to malign Hindus and aid conversion, have now substituted "migration" for "invasion" as the method of "aryan" implantation in India, now that the British-propagated story of "invasion" has been finally discredited. This crude but elaborate hoax was foisted on innocent Indian children through school syllabi, and disseminated for over two centuries, and has proved tough to dispel. Converts are led to believe that a good life would be theirs, once they accept the new religion and discard the old "myths," even if that meant denying family and the solid heritage of Hindu philosophy.

Proselytisers today feverishly attempt to explain "everything" within Christian timelines, gloating about their fifteen centuries of Church tradition, exposing a profound ignorance of world history, forgetting the crimes committed by that Church to attain today's position of dominance (see Bartolomé de las Casas, *Destruction of the Indies*, and Ch. 4-6), and not really caring about the lives and life styles of their own members, who asked uncomfortable questions. How could unlettered 4th century pagans, even urbane Romans, have any basis to debate a new religion, knowing nothing of it or of eastern philosophies, and with the verdict of autocratic rulers already written in stone?

Puzzles remain; for example, the age of the cosmos, and of Hindu scriptures, still "mythical" to the West, whose own also abound in myth. The epic *Ramāyana* refers to construction of Rama's bridge from India to Lanka; underwater stone slabs (p. 36) at the site conform to the location of the bridge and the level of the Bay following the great flood. It is portrayed as an age of air and space travel, levitation and anti-gravity power, Hanuman covering thousands of miles from South to North India and back in hours by air (Prakash). The scriptures talk of avatars mirroring evolutionary biology (see p. 20, footnote 5), thus going back a million years, yet describing explosives and weapons rather like those of today, including nuclear ones. Its perspective is thus infinite. The *Mahābharata* tells of the use of Mercury as a source of ions for spacecraft engines. Was it just their imagination or our primitiveness?

The story of *Lemuria* is probably as old as the *Ramāyana*. The land is said to have submerged about the same time, but the flooding could have been conflated with similar events at other times, indeed up to a million years earlier, if the dating of the building slabs is correct: age 1.25 million years. This corresponds to the *Rāmāyana* events, which occurred in the *Tretha Yuga* of the *Vaidic* calendar, roughly 1.25 million years ago. This finding, though tenuous, illustrates the wonder and cosmic extent of Hinduism and its temporal relationship with the universe and human evolution, a major intellectual attempt to place man in a universal context. This dating corresponds roughly to the postulated timeline of *Homo erectus (ergaster). See http://humanorigins.si.edu/evidence.*

"Hinduism" began when the universe began, as explained by the Vaidic division of time, postulated as 155 trillion years ago (p.39). Its lore is partly in scriptural texts, history, astronomy and geophysics. Its concept of the universe is more in keeping with modern astronomy than that given in the Abrahamic religions, whose timelines might be appropriate simply to their tribal and regional geopolitical correlates.

The common ancestor is Abraham, a caravan leader, said to be from Ur, Chaldea, Mesopotamia (southern Iraq today), who knew little of the races and cultures beyond his immediate sphere. These included the Hittites, Kassites, Aramaeans, Canaanites, Egyptians, Mittani, Hurrians, Moabites, Elamites and other regional tribes of the Middle East, Asia Minor and Egypt. Their timeline is but a moment of cosmic time, starting in 4004 BCE, the "Ussher numeral". The Abrahamic religions claim that "God" was unique to them, jealous and demanding, who gave them power over all humanity—which must mean "*their* humanity" only, as they knew little of land or peoples beyond the lofty mountains to the north and far east. This divine mandate was a smart and convenient device that any demagogue could claim, to justify expansion and foreign land seizures, in the name of an omnipotent God. The Church and Islam continue this mission; their forbears, the Jews, have already gained control of Palestine, North America and Europe. (p. 448, Gore Vidal).

Jews, Muslims and Europeans, coming later to India, many centuries apart, were amazed to find the *Vaidas* and other very old Indian scriptures, ante-dating theirs. The British, accepting the Bible literally, and with little or no knowledge of world cultures, found it intellectually and politically difficult to understand or adapt to the Indian works. Nor could they ignore them. So they found devious ways of squeezing Indian history into Biblical timelines, creating an imaginary chronology which their conquest of India and acquisition of an empire allowed them to preach unopposed. Thus Rāma's journey to Lanka is treated as a myth since the events it describes cannot be fitted into the Bible's time frame. Geographic features such as the Saraswati River, then obscured, like the events of Vaidic civilisation, such as the *Mahābhārata* war, which are all recorded in detail, were similarly dismissed as wondrous apologues.

Schisms are common in religions, as different mentalities, experiences and temporal factors inspire differences of interpretations of the same material, aggravated by translational difficulties. But the Abrahamic ones have produced an unusual frequency of schisms, which have become a source of wealth and power to persons and nations. Each variant develops a following which rejects the others and provokes wars of conquest and dominion. These wars have benefitted tyrants in other ways, by stimulating discovery and invention of increasingly powerful tools for waging war, destroying things, facilitating terror and exercising power. Their use and refinement, and the spin-offs have added economic strength to many nations, to the eventual elaboration of a hierarchy of warlike humans, a few with power and knowledge subjugating the rest and imposing social and political allegiances (see *p.172, Chain of Being*). Thus, when the British met the Hindu *varna* system they promptly degraded and merged it in line with the *Chain of Being*. This inspired avarice, commercialism, consumerism and personal aggrandisement to consume Europe and the USA, which have brought the world to its current state of bias, inequality, hysteria and strife.

China maintained its "freedom" from European imperialists, mainly thanks to its languages. The British gained India by substituting language and culture and by vitiating history and religions. Conquered Indians were rewarded for following the British, and thus lost language, literature, culture and country. They became subservient *coconuts,* and sometimes misfits, in their own country. Independence was a middle class brainwave, a reaction brought on by British tyranny, property theft and personal abuses, and rejection of the INC's meek request for self-rule: *dominion status* within the Empire under his imperial Majesty, King George V. Not until WWII had crippled Britain, would it give up India, to the lingering despair of millions of anglophiles, suddenly rootless!

The usurpation of nations has never stopped and has passed on to the USA, whose Asian agenda plays through its NGOs, USAID and the CIA and recalls much of imperial Britain's. The USA, with only 4.5% of the world's population, will continue to consume a hefty share of the world's resources, currently 30%, generating 50% of global solid waste. One American consumes as much as 35 Indians and 53 Chinese, though the latter's usage is increasing. India ranks first, China second, and the US last of 17 largest economies surveyed re *"sustainable behaviour"*. The US is least likely to feel guilty about it (*www.scientificamerican.com, Energy & Sustainability*). Consumption equates with happiness in the US, and as income improves the rising happiness of American citizens will continue to degrade the environment, at great cost! Rajendra Pachauri, Chair (*2002-15*) of the *Intergovernmental Panel on Climate Change (IPCC*, co-winner, with Al Gore, of the 2007 Nobel Peace Prize) warns that India's growing population cannot afford increased consumption levels. *"We can't support lifestyles even remotely like those in Europe and North America,"* he says. *"We need policy initiatives to assure this doesn't happen. But the movement has to take place in both hemispheres. Awareness has to be raised in both the East and the West to deglamourise unsurvivable consumerism."*

American war mentality—matched by others just as militant, especially radical Islamists, Israelis and Christians—is bringing us much closer to the edge of doom. This must have happened several times in mankind's long history on earth, if Vaidic timelines hold, the current civilisation being just another iteration that took a wrong turn and must run to the end, like a herd of stampeding American bisons, immolating themselves over a cliff. It is likely that unless an avatar intercedes, the stampede could gain irreversible momentum in a few generations.

America's claim to foment democracy, good relations and security is empty camouflage. Lies, theft, tyranny and enslavement will continue to dominate society as Corporations get larger. It must bring a constant rush of "feel good" impulses, or mental orgasms, as each million accrues in their name; otherwise why would they continue the exploitation, cheating and other evils to compile such hoards and drive the poor into deeper hopelessness? Democracy is an ideal. America was never one. Similarly there are 57 or so nations in the Organisation of the Islamic Conference (OIC). None is a democracy. Pakistan, Iran, Saudi Arabia are prototypical Islamic states.

Modi should, like Nehru, avoid too close a relationship with the USA, whose trashing of Latin America (Chile, Bolivia, Central America) and loss of Cuba justified his distance. The later breach of Reagan's promises to Gorbachev, the build-up of NATO on Russia's borders and US bases in the Indian Ocean and western Pacific are loud and clear warnings of ignoble intent, of putting US and its corporate interests above honour and respect for others' rights. The pro-West world is easily duped by reference to a Russian ogre, which allows the US to push any scheme, even the most egregious, if it is presented as anti-Russian. US corporatism cannot dominate or take risks without this armed symbiosis. Its plebs remain unschooled, smug and too gullible to think this through.

Now, more and more these interests are guarded by revolving doors through which Corporations join the US executive and write laws friendly to their core businesses. Similarly, Britain had risen to great power when its mercantile aristocracy ruled and exploited its citizenry and that of the Empire, without inhibitions, and attained rapid industrial growth in a large captive market. Adam Smith had said "*To found a great empire for the sole purpose of raising up a people of customers may at first sight appear a project fit only for a nation of shopkeepers. It is, however, a project altogether unfit for a nation of shopkeepers; but extremely fit for a nation whose government is influenced by shopkeepers.*" The USA followed Britain's example, although it has outsourced its manufacturing to become today a nation of industrial assemblers.

India must reassess its place in the western market; it has the people capacity to do so. It must protect its dharmic religions and autonomy, to avoid absorption by Christianity or Islam. Hopefully, Modi is not afflicted with the blind Anglomania of Nehru, who conducted his entire ministry, befuddled by his pro-British focus, and desire to ensure his daughter's succession when he quit. The result was the neglect of borders and of Hindus, the decades of terror in Jammu & Kashmir and the forgotten 400,000 Hindu refugees from J&K, driven out by Muslims while Nehru and his successors courted the Muslim vote. Nehru's weakness started India on a sorry downward path that led to the astonishing selection of Sonia Gandhi as President of the INC.

President Obama was given the Nobel Peace Prize prematurely, mainly out of gratitude for bringing fresh air into a world grown stale and toxic by the Cheney/Bush/Bilderberg doctrine and its unyielding will to seize the world. Yet, in so doing it allowed Wahhabism, its nemesis, to grow, the two becoming the modern Scylla and Charybdis through which Modi must navigate, like Homer's "mythical" Ulysses. Sadly Obama has disappointed and done an about-face, aiding, unwittingly or not, the Cheney/Bush/Bilderberg agenda to own the world by seizing financial controls through trade agreements, agencies like the *Bank for International Settlements,* and by war. Is this perhaps why he did not impeach the former President and Vice-President, whose crimes cried out for prosecution *prima facie?* Obama, however, may not escape his critics as easily. Modi must cope with all this or lose India.

Indians crave an honest and efficient public service, to deliver education and health, protect food sources and human rights, foster growth and strive to improve living standards. Of Indian households, 25-33% have no electricity. The same, or a higher percentage lacks health care, which, like education, is class-based, and therefore inequitable.

Both are heavily privatised and riddled with corruption. The sanitation problem and lack of toilet facilities remain complex, as merely providing toilets to the poor does not suddenly resolve issues of custom and belief about sanitation that have existed for centuries, while government education programmes lag, and grants-in-aid struggle through the existing labyrinth of corruption to reach qualified recipients. Hopefully, in time, this too will fade, and be replaced with integrity, if education to achieve it proceeds in earnest.

By comparison, in the last two decades, Bangladesh has done well in many indices, aided by microfinance and education from the *Bangladesh Rural Advance Committee (BRAC),* started by Fazle Hasan Abed, now the world's largest and most successful NGO, with a global reach—branches in many developing countries—and its own University[169]. There is a trend to greater involvement of women in the economy, education of girls, fewer children per family, and increase in age at marriage.

The increase in corporate earnings in India feeds GDP and the rich, but must be balanced with fairness through joint action and reform that would channel some gains to reach and boost the ordinary citizen.

In the 19th century, when Christianity needed an intellectual champion, and the British an excuse to own India, they ascribed Indian achievements to ancient Greece, which had just emerged from Turkish domination, to be "discovered" and enthusiastically adopted, if not worshipped by English Romantic writers. Britain took great pains to mythologise the *Vaidas, Sutras* and *Agamas* and decry the work of those, especially the French, their arch-rival, who generally tended to translate Sanskrit texts more faithfully than the British had done (see *Bibliography*).

The BEICo's Sir William Jones had praised Sanskrit and Charles Watkins had translated the *Bhagavad Gita*. The British had also learned from Greek and Indian scholars the real source of *their* Renaissance knowledge in sciences, computation, astronomy and philosophy. Yet they took great steps to suppress and distort this knowledge to belittle Indians, glorify whites (Greeks), in line with eugenics and racial supremacy theories that had become popular by the late 19th century, and to make the conquest of India defensible, if not desirable.

It is worth repeating that today's archaeological and other evidence supports the historical accuracy of *Vaidic* passages and other ancient texts. When this evidence became public decades ago, one expected that Müller's "aryan" hypothesis—the aristocratic British fable devised to impress ethnocentric and gullible 19th century Europe and the world—would have been discarded at last, and the propaganda that the *Vaidas*

[169]Also endorsed by Amartya Sen, economist, Nobel laureate, atheist and inveterate anti-Hindu; but some have questioned the value attached to microfinance per se.

and Sanskrit epics were engaging fables, Indians a Central Asian race, and Indian culture their inspired invention, finally ended. This hoax was perpetrated at a time of poor and slow communication, and by a race that calls itself *English* that arose as an alliance of Danes (Angles) and low Germans (Saxons and Jutes), that grafted itself on native Britons, Romanised or not, and later Scots, Picts and Celts, then became vassals of the Vikings (Norwegians) and Normans (French)—see Chapter 5. So the reality of successive invaders as the source of British civilisation had made it natural for them to accept a similar multinational alien genesis of the advanced, complex and accomplished culture they had stumbled upon in faraway India. The perfidy of the British—*perfidious Albion*[171]—is thereby amply illustrated.

In a spark of honesty, Müller had recanted (p. 230), but few in Britain acknowledged it, since to do so would have been to reject the idea firmly implanted and cultured among Jews and Christians that the world was just over 6000 years old, and that would cost them the status of "chosen super race", the foundation of the powerful and wealthy conspiracy of Synagogue, Church and State that effectively controls the world today.

Other uncorrected issues, promises unfulfilled, continue to fester: untouchability; Islamic terrorism and expansion by coercion; the systematic marginalisation of unschooled hundreds of millions and their feelings of frustration and hopelessness; the persistence of anti-social practices, including aggressive proselytism and the abuse of women and children; and sedition and other harsh laws left over from the *Rāja*. The ridiculously low poverty line obstructs education; as does the failure to extract a fair tax from the very wealthy, who demur, perhaps from knowledge of the theft that goes on by officials, whom they had corrupted in the first place, and whose greed they still find useful!

India is plagued by foreign predators on many sides. Americans and their local hirelings comb the Indian landscape for patentable, thus profitable material and monopoly, just as they have scraped sea floors free of commercial aquatic life. Thus, to protect its heritage from thieves, India must meticulously register or patent all assets, native food sources, art, medicinal plant, animals and other natural life, minerals and other objects; this is a nation's basic right; India has too much to lose.

Internal anarchists—the deadly trinity of Wahhabis, Communists and anti-Hindus—pose a huge problem. Territorially and nationally the greatest threat is the first. Pakistan and Bangladesh have been appeased

---

[171]From *The Indelible Red Stain, Bk 2, 288:* 'Augustin, Marquis of Ximenez seems to have been the first to use the phrase in writing in 1793,..French theologian Jacques-Bénigne Bossuet used the phrase *"perfidious England"* a century earlier; the idea of British perfidy has an older history among Europeans. See Schmidt, H.D. '*The Idea and Slogan of "Perfidious Albion"*', Journal of the History of Ideas, Vol. 14, No. 4 (Oct., 1953), pp. 604–616."

by the INC to secure votes, despite increasing terror. Backed by Arabian oil wealth, mullahs indoctrinate youth into militant Wahhabism, to terrorise Hindus, and make border areas almost uninhabitable. The fall of Iran to the Ayatollahs, started by the USA in 1953, when they deposed Mossadegh, and their continued meddling since, has fuelled the threats.

The major groups are well-known: *Lashkar-e-Taiba, Indian Mujahideen, Jaish-e-Mohammed, Harkat-ul-Mujahideen* and the *Students Islamic Movement of India (SIMI)*. SIMI is banned yet active and operates mainly through fifth columnists in many states. Jammu & Kashmir, and the states bordering Bangladesh, are subjected to daily border breaches, and in the latter, massive population ("refugee") shifts.

Sporadic Islamic forays into major cities like Delhi, Hyderabad, Jaipur, among others, aim to destabilise states, enlarge cells and expand fifth column operations. With the unending turmoil in Afghanistan, Iraq and Syria, al Qaeda has spread; with ISIS *(Islamic State of Iraq and Syria)*, it plans to carry out disruptive internal acts, to coincide with border attacks. They aim to Islamise northern India and create a massive new *Caliphate of Mughalstan*, incorporating Pakistan, northern India (Ganges valley), Bangladesh and the eastern Indian states, touting a corrupt model, the "rightly guided" caliphs (632-661CE). China will probably allow this to happen, despite suppressing its native Islamic groups, e.g., the Uighurs. No doubt China reasons that it could quickly reverse any Islamic gains not in its interests. The moves by Islam are expansionist, and have no basis in irredentism. If anything, Hindus can claim the latter as their reason for any expulsion of Islamic extremists.

Land conquests, unlike entitlements, are reversible. Bangladesh has nibbled away at eastern provinces, and now Islam inhabits most of Bodoland in Assam, a relic of British occupiers and tea planters, who populated the area with indentured Bengalis. When the INC took over, it ignored the rights of native *adivasis* and allowed Bengali Muslims fleeing Pakistani atrocities to occupy Indian territory, and it gained their votes. Muslim refugees, however, repaid the favour by agitation, gained more concessions from a pressured and timorous INC. Later, the West Bengal government gave infiltrators the status of refugees, followed by ration, citizenship and voting cards! Yet, the current Chief Minister, Mamata Banerjee, lambasts the BJP for backing curbs on Bangladeshi infiltrators.

The assaults on India recall the pre-WWII ambitions of Adolph Hitler to take over the Czech Sudetenland, with its 23% population of German origin, recent and remote. By 1938, a volunteer force, the *Sudeten German Free Corps (SGFC)* had begun to destabilise the Sudetenland in a program developed by Konrad Henlein, the leader of the SGFC, and endorsed by Hitler and his War Minister, Field Marshal Keitel. This gave the SGFC a plan to harass the Czechs along the borders to the north and west, in the year before the invasion. A study of their details reveals an astonishing similarity with the campaign of Islamic terrorism in India, and the effective cultivation of fifth columns of India's citizens. The concept of Mughalstan is similar to the Nazi one of *Lebensraum,* the pursuit of additional territory for an expanding German population. The plan had been mooted under Kaiser Wilhelm II at the time of WWI, following an idea elaborated two decades earlier by Friedrich Ratzel and an even earlier plan to settle Germans in Africa (see p.237). It is interesting that Hitler adopted the Ratzel plan, and wanted Polish, Ukrainian, Baltic and European Russian territories, but, unlike Macaulay and the British, he balked at teaching Poles the conqueror's language for fear of affecting the *"dignity and nobility"* of Germany, since the Poles were incapable of expressing their ideas in German (*Mein Kampf*)!

Meanwhile, Indian Marxists and secularists, inadvertently or by plan, join with richly-endowed Christian fundamentalists to subvert Hindus and Hinduism. They get support from political forces at federal and state levels, and especially from the poor, and in south and east India. The southern anarchy may be quite separate from the Islamic one, and coincidental, but whatever the reality, the perception of collusion exists; for non-Muslims, this tactic is perilous, as their inputs would mean little to Islamists, once the latter's objective has been achieved.

The destabilisation creates steady and dangerous work for Indian security forces in many states, threatens government workers and civilians and is often difficult to anticipate, since the perpetrators, as trained fifth columnists, are local, usually Muslim, Communists, atheists or Hindus lured by bribes, threats or grudges. With Islam expanding through high birth rates and *shādi-jihad* (Muslims pretending to be Hindus to marry Hindu girls for conversion and procreation, a tactic supported by Islamic religious policies worldwide), India is again threatened from within, the aggressors this time being the two dominant world religions, not just commerce, although commercial objectives play a powerful hand. Already, a Christian majority obtains in Mizoram, largely by purchase of Hindus with proselyte dollars. Islam owns half of Assam, much by squatting. US corporations own the Indian upper class, especially youth, with food, entertainment, laxity, language and dress.

Can Modi lead a resistance to these changes and save his people? Will he be allowed to, if he started? Someone must assume leadership to save India and the planet. So few qualify! It won't be the West; they're too immersed in profitable dirt. It could be mass movements, but again, who will lead? A mass movement will be up against the most powerful corporations in the world: the US MIFC, arms linked with Big Oil, Banks, Agribusiness and Miners, all armed to the teeth, and exceedingly rich.

Yet, ordinary folk in Odisha have stopped a bauxite mining project, and, like others in several states, demand restriction, oversight and equity. Locally, Modi must confront the spectre of caste, which the INC has avoided for its entire reign, and which the middle class, including BJP members, still observe. He must begin to address this vexed issue.

The world is weighed down by economism, a foil to democracy; it has triumphed over politics and other aspects of social life, degraded by money and the monetising of all life issues, including what used to be sacrosanct: family, love, justice, peace and happiness. India has increased earnings from Western business outsourcing, in services, and some manufacturing and testing. This will end, as outsourcers find cheaper or more secure ways of "doing business." Indians are inventive enough to develop competitive products of all types to supply its rising needs.

Despite Government support by various means and programs, the young are still heading for the West, armed with discredited anglophilic versions of Indian history, which, sadly, they still spread. India must act to encourage the inventive to stay and build at home, first by ensuring that what they learn of Indian history is not what the British or their proselytes teach. Modi's slogan of *"Make in India"* is encouraging, but how cosy with the USA will its pursuit make him? Therein lies danger.

The world has become increasingly unstable. Moderate followers of Jewry, Christ and Mohamed, despite their numerical preponderance in the world, have little say in what is done in the name of their beliefs, just as the decent British masses had little influence on imperial leaders. Nearly a billion poor in India, Africa, the Americas and Asia, suffer neglect, alienation and want. For the majority of the world's ordinary folk, primary personal and family demands consume time and energies each day, while their leaders assemble arms and play the great game of monopoly for world resources, entrenching a culture of competition, confrontation and violence that shames this civilisation.

Money makes this possible. There is nothing or no one that it cannot corrupt or buy, they say; and nowhere that business will not explore for profit. Planting churches and reaping souls now degrade the Abrahamic religions; the atmosphere is contentious. It is time to explore what the dharmic religions can offer to calm or counter this destructive trend. This closing remark, from Sri Aurobindo, is as apt today as it was when he said it: "*The most vital issue of the age is whether the future progress of humanity is to be governed by the modern economic and materialistic mind of the West or by a nobler pragmatism, guided, uplifted and enlightened by spiritual culture and knowledge....*"

END

Appendix 1: Literacy Rate (Pre 1951=British Rāja)

Year	Total (%)	Male (%)	Female (%)	50-yr Increase%
1901	5.35	9.83	0.60	
1911	5.92	10.56	1.05	
1921	7.16	12.21	1.81	
1931	9.50	15.59	2.93	
1941	16.10	24.90	7.30	
1951	16.67	24.95	9.45	11.32
1961	24.02	34.44	12.95	
1971	29.45	39.45	18.69	
1981	36.23	46.89	24.82	
1991	42.84	52.74	32.17	
2001	64.83	75.26	53.67	48.16
2011	74.04	82.14	65.46	

Appendix 2: Percentages of World Population by Region and Year

Year	Total (Millions)	China	India	Other Asia	Europe	Africa	Other
BCE 400	100	27	24	21	18	7	3
200	150	28	21	23	18	7	3
0	170	30	21	18	18	10	3
CE 200	190	32	22	15	19	9	3
400	190	27	25	17	17	10	4
600	200	23	26	24	13	10	4
1000	265	23	30	17	14	12	4
1300	360	23	25	15	22	11	4
1400	350	21	28	18	17	12	4
1500	425	23	25	18	19	11	4
1600	545	28	25	17	18	10	2
1700	610	25	27	16	20	10	2
1750	720	30	24	15	19	9	3
1800	900	35	21	13	20	8	3
1850	1275	35	19	12	22	7	5
1900	1625	28	18	14	24	7	9
*1950	2500	21	18	19	21	8	13
1975	3900	18	20	21	16	10	15
1999 2012	6000 7000	21	21	18	13	13	14

Ref: *Updated from Colin McEvedy and Richard Jones, Atlas of World Population History, Penguin, 1978)* * post-partition India

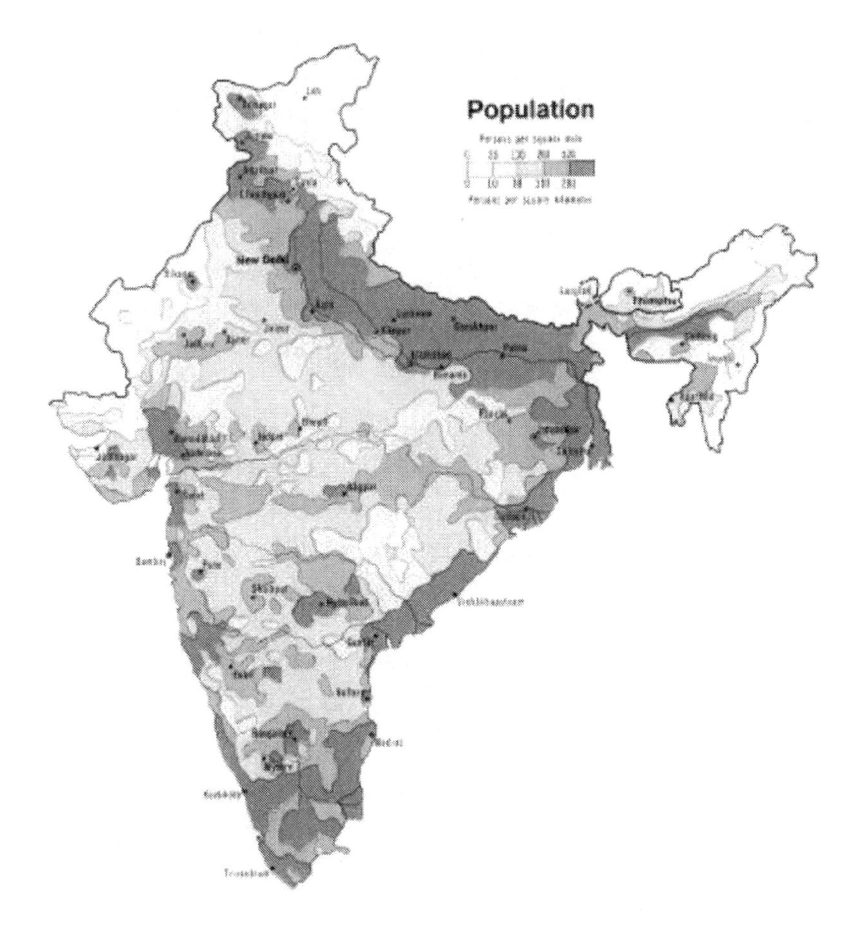

Pre-Partition Population: 340,796,000;
Pre-Partition Area 1,635,337 sq.m.
Area after partition 1,269,338 sq,m (3,283,590 sq,km.), a 28.8% loss
Current Population (2011): 1,210,726,932; urban 32%; 361,088,000 in 1951
Hindus, 2011: 78.35% or 947,866,000 (84.1% in 1951 or 303,675,000; growth rate 14.5% 2001-2011) ;
Muslims, 2011: 14.2% or 180, 000,000; (1951, 9.8% or 35,856,047; growth rate 24% 2001-2011);
Christians, Sikhs, about 2% each; Buddhists 0.4%; others, including atheists: 3.0%, little changed over 10 years. The Parsi and Jewish percentages have fallen.

Bibliography

Abbasi, Reema *Historic Temples in Pakistan: A Call to Conscience,* Delhi, Niyogi Books, 2014

Abdul Kalam, APJ *Ignited Minds: Unleashing the Power Within India,* Penguin Global 2003,

Ahmed, Faruque *Bengal Politics in Britain, USA,* LULU Publishers, 2010

al Beruni, *Indica, quoted by Sachau E. C., translator, Alberuni's India.* New Delhi: Low Price Publications, 1993

Ambhedkar, BR *Essential Writings ed. V. Rodriques,* New Delhi, Oxford Univ. Press., 2004

Arya, Ravi Prakash *Vedic Calendar, 2014 edition, Indian Foundation for Vedic Science, (IFVS),* Rohtak Haryana, India, 2014

Ibid, *India: The Civiliser of the World,* Rohtak, Haryana, India, IFVS, 2005

Aryābhata, *Aryābhatiya, (Astronomy and Maths)* Nālanda University ca.499CE

Aurobindo, Sri *Vande Mataram; The Mother; The Foundations of Indian Culture; The Secret of the Vedas. Mother India and Her destiny; The Hour of God; The Supramental Manifestation, Is India Civilised,* Puducherry, Sri Aurobindo Ashram Press; *India's rebirth,* Paris. Institut de Recherches Evolutives, various dates

Bacon, Francis *Novum Organum Scientarum,(1620)* EC.B1328.620ib, accessed Houghton Library, Harvard University

Bala, Saroj and Mishra, Kulbhushan *"Historicity of Vedic and Ramāyan Eras: Scientific Evidences from the Depth of the Oceans to the Heights of the Skies,"* I-SERVE, 2012

Banu, Zenab *Politics of Communalism,* Bombay, Popular Prakashan, 1989.

Bardai, Chand, Prithviraj Raso, in Satish Chandra, *Medieval India: From Sultanat to the Mughals (1206-1526),* Har-Anand Publications, 2006

Bartolomé de las Casas, *A Short Account of the Destruction of the Indies,* trans from Spanish, Penguin, 1999

Basham AL *The Wonder that was India,* (1954) New Delhi, Rupa & Co, 1981

Bede, The venerable, *Ecclesiastical History of the English People* (1969). Eds. B. Colgrave, and RAB Mynors, Oxford, 1969

Beder, Sharon *How Corporations Drive the Global Agenda* EARTHSCAN, London, UK, 2006

Bhagavad-Gita: with an introductory essay, Sanskrit text, English translation and notes, 1948

Bhardwaj, KK *Combating Communalism in India*: Mittal Publications, 1993

Bhartiya, BL and Arya, RP *Rishi Dayananda,* Rohtak, India IFVS, 2006

Bhattacharji, Arun *Greater India,* New Delhi, Munshiram Manoharlal Publ. Pvt. Ltd., 1981

Bhattacharya, HS *Reals in the Jaina metaphysics.* Bombay, Seth Santi Das Khetsy Charitable Trust, 1966.

Bhushan, Shashi *Feroze Gandhi, Political Biography,* Ann Arbor, .Michigan 1977

Blavatsky HP *The Secret Doctrine,* New York, Theosophical Society, 1888

Bryan, WJ *British Rule in India* New York Journal, Jan. 22, 1899

Buchanan, Iain *The Armies Of God: A Study In Militant Christianity,* Citizens International, 2010

Burns, John M. *3-Week Dietary Subchronic Comparison Study with MON 863 Corn in Rats,* St Louis, MO, Monsanto Corp., 2002

Caesar, Julius *De Bello Gallico* English version, London, Gulliver, Osprey,

Caird John, *Religions of India: Vedic Period–Brahmanism,* Blackwood 1882, digitised by Google Books

Caldwell, Erskine *Tobacco Road,* Pan Books, London 1958

Caldwell, R Bishop *A Political and General History of the District of Tinnevely,* Madras, India, BEICo, 1881

Cambridge History of Early Inner Asia: *http://www.scribd.com/doc/34133754/31/*

Carriere, JC *The Mahabharata, trans P. Brook,* Harper & Row, 1987

Chanukya, *Arthashastra,* ?Pataliputra, Mauryan Empire, India, 3rd Century, BCE

Charaka, *Charaksamhita* Textbook of Ayurvaidic Medicine, 1st century CE

Chatterjee, Aroup *Mother Teresa The Final Verdict,* UK, Meteor Books, 2004

Chengappa, Raj *Weapons of peace: the secret story of India's quest to be a nuclear power.* New Delhi, India: Harper Collins Publishers, 2000.
Chung Tan and Thakur Ravni Eds. *Across the Himalayan gap, An Indian Quest for Understanding China*; Delhi, Indira Gandhi National Centre for the Arts,1998
Chugg, AM *The Lost Tomb of Alexander the Great*, London Periplus, 2004/5
CIA's Eye on South Asia: See Dhar, below
Creasy, ES *The Fifteen Decisive Battles of the World*, Dover Publ. (unabridged ed.), 2008.
Dales, George F *The Mythical Massacre at Mohenjo-Daro.* (also cited Kenoyer, Jonathan. (July 2003) *Uncovering the keys to lost Indus cities.* Scientific American. pg. 67)
Danielou, Alain *Histoire de l'Inde*, Paris, Editions Fayard, Paris, 1971
Das Gupta, C, *War and Diplomacy in Kashmir 1947-48,* Sage Publications, 2002
Della Valle, Pietro *Travels in India,1623-24,2 vols.*, New Delhi, Asian Educ. Services, 1991
Dhammapada, Oxford University Press, *1950*
Dhar, Anuj *CIA's Eye on South Asia,* New Delhi, Manas Publications, 2008
Dickens, C, *A Christmas Carol,* London, Chapman and Hall, 1843, Elegant Ebooks
Druon, Maurice *The Accursed Kings, translated from the French,* London, Hart-Davis, 1959
Duby, Georges *The Age of the Cathedrals,* Chicago, *transl. Fr.* Levieux and Thompson, 1981
Dutt, RC *India in the Victorian Age* London, Kegan Paul, 1904
Ibid, T*he Mahabharata and The Ramayana,* English translation, in verse, condensed, Temple Classics, London , JM Dent & Co., 1899 and 1900, respectively.
Dwivedi, Sharada *The Maharaja and the Princely States of India,* New Delhi, Roli Books Pvt Ltd, 1999,
Eggeling, J. *Sacred Books of the East, XII*, Oxford, 1882 (incl. *Shatpatha Brāhmana*)
Einhard, *Life of Charlemagne*, translated by Samuel Epes Turner, New York: Harper & Brothers, 1880; Paperback Edition, 1960
Eisenman, R. *The Dead Sea Scrolls and the first Christians*, New Jersey, USA, Castle, 2004
Eliade, M. *Essential Sacred Writings from Around the World*, San Francisco, Harper , 1977
Elst, Koenrad *Negationism in India*, New Delhi. Voice of India, 1992
Ibid, *Indigenous Indians*, New Delhi, Voice of India, 1993
Faber-Kaiser, Andreas *Jesus vivio y murio en Kachemira*, Mexico City, Ediciones Roca, 1976
Fanon, Frantz *The Wretched of the Earth, translated from French*, McGibbon and Kee, 1965
Fatah, Tarek *Chasing a Mirage*, Toronto, Wiley, 2008
Ferdowsi, Abolqasem *Shahnameh,* trans. Dick Davis Penguin Classics, New York, 2007
Fernandes Vivian, *Modi: Leadership, Governance and Performance,* Orient Publishing, 2014
Feuerstein, Georg, Kak, Subhash & Frawley David: *In Search of the Cradle of Civilization,* Wheaton, Illinois: Quest Books, 1995, 341 pages
Five year Plans of India en.wikipedia.org/wiki
Fox, Robin Lane *Pagans and Christians,* London, Viking Press, 1986
Frawley, David *The Myth of the Aryan Invasion of India*, New Delhi, Voice of India, 1995
Gandhi, MK *Autobiography,* London, Penguin Books, 1982
Ganguli BN and Naoroji Dadabhai *The Drain Theory* The Journal of Asian Studies: 26.4 (August 1967) 728-*729*, February 23, 2013.
Ganguli KM *The Mahabharata of Krishna-Dwaipayana Vyasa*, in English, Calcutta, published by Pratap Chandra Ray, 1883-1896, *www.sacred-texts.com/hin/m02/index.htm*
Gautier, F *A Western Journalist on India: The Ferengi's Columns*, New Delhi, Har-Anand Publications, 2001
Gibbon, Edward *The History of the Decline and Fall of the Roman Empire*, ed. David Womersley, London: Allen Lane, 1994
Gidwani, Bhagwan S *Return of the Aryans*, Gurgaon, Penguin-India, 1994
Goel, SR, Shourie, A, Narain, H, Dubashi and Swarup, *R: Hindu Temples – What Happened to Them, Vol. 1,* New Delhi, Voice of India, 1998
Gourdon, Carpentier de *Vindicating Traditional Historiography: Ramayana accurate portrayal of ancient India, 10 September, 2012*

Government of India Five year Plans, Planning Commission.nic.in. Retrieved GOI website, Jan 2012

Grab, Walter, *The French Revolution, An illustrated history*, Bracken Books, 1989

Grumeza, Ion *The Roots of Balkanization: Eastern Europe C.E. 500-150.* Univ. Press of America, 2010

Guha, Ramachandra *India After Gandhi: The History of the World's Largest Democracy,* PanMacmillan, 2008

Ibid, Ed. *Makers of Modern India,* Harvard University Press, 2011

Gutierrez Elizabeth *The dotbuster-attacks: hate crime against Asian Indians in Jersey City,* New Jersey Middle States Geographer, 1996, 30-38

Haeckel, Ernst *The History of Creation, Volume 1,* 3rd edition, translated by E. Ray Lankester, London, Kegan Paul, Trench & Co., 1883

Hamilton, Sue *Indian Philosophy: A Very Short Introduction*, Oxford University Press, 2001

Hansard, British Parliament *HC&HL, various dates 1803-1947,* http//Hansard.millbank systems.com HC Deb., 22 November 1927, vol. 210, cc1633-51 1633; ...Lords, 1946 *The government of India Act, 1919; The Simon Commission, 1927, 1929*

Havers, G *The travels of Pietro della Valle in India, from the old English translation of 1664,* Ed. E. Gray, Printed for the Hakluyt Society in London, 1892; Library of Congress G161.H2 no. 84-85

Headrick, DR *The tentacles of progress: technology transfer in the age of imperialism, 1850–1940,* Oxford University Press, 1988

Heehs P *The Lives of Sri Aurobindo: A Biography*, New York, Columbia Univ. Press, 2008

Herdeck, Margaret L and Parimal, Gita, India's *Industrialists, Bk 1,* Colorado, USA, Lynne Reinner Publications, 1985

Hitchens, Christopher *The Missionary Position,* UK, Verso, 1995

Hitler, Adolf *Mein Kampf,* London, Houghton Mifflin, 1971

Hochschild, Adam *Bury the Chains, The British Struggle to Abolish Slavery,* London, Macmillan, 2005 ISBN 978-0330485814

Hughes, David Bruce (Gaurahari Dāsānudās Bābājī), *Śrī Vedānta-sūtra,* Adhyāya 1, NY, Google Books, 2012

Hymns of the Rigveda, trans by RT Griffith, New Delhi, Munshi Manoharlal Pvt Ltd, 1987

India's Rebirth, Institut de Recherches Evolutives, Paris. Distributed in India by Mira Aditi Centre, 62 Sriranga 1st Cross, 4th Stage Kuvempunagar, Mysore 570023

Iyengar, PT Srinivas *Advanced History of India.* 1890, London, Forgotten Books, 2012

Jacolliot, L. *Le Bible dans l'Inde, Paris, 1876,* quoted in Arya RP, *Civiliser...*(qv)

Jayasumana C, Gunatilake S & Senanayake P *re toxicity of Gm crops,* Int. J. Environ. Res. Public Health 2014, 11(2), 2125-2147; (see also Séralini, G.-E, below)

Jha, Ganganatha, *Nyaya- Sutras of Gautama (4 vols.),* Motilal Banarsidass, 1999 reprint, ISBN 978-81-208-1264-2.

Jordens, JTF., *Swāmi Shraddhānanda, his life and causes,* Delhi, Oxford Univ. Press, 1981.

Josephus, Flavius *The Wars of the Jews*, translated by Wm Whiston, Gutenberg Org., File 2850, 2009 (www.gutenberg.org/files/2850/2850-h/2850-h.htm)

Joshi, Lal Mani *Brahmanism, Buddhism, and Hinduism: An Essay on their Origins and Interactions,* Department of Religious Studies, Punjabi University, Patiala, India; Buddhist Publication Society, Kandy, Sri Lanka; The Wheel Publication No. 150/151, 1970

Kak, Subhash *The Speed of Light and Purānic Cosmology* arXiv:physics/9804020 v3 15 Jan 2001

Kalam, APJ Abdul & Rajan YS, *2020, Vision for the New Millennium*, New Delhi, Penguin, 1998

Kalam, APJ Abdul & Pillai AS *Envisioning an Empowered Nation*, New Delhi, Tata-McGraw Hill, 2004

Kamath, Suryanath U. *A concise history of Karnataka.* Bangalore: Jupiter books, 1980. LCCN 8095179. OCLC 7796041.

Kàzí, Ismail *The Chach-nama.* English translation *by* Mirza Kalichbeg Fredunbeg. Delhi Reprint, 1979

Keay, John *India: A History*, Grove/Atlantic, 2001, ISBN 0-8021-3797-0

Keegan, John *A history of Warfare*, London, Hutchinson, 1995

Kenoyer, Jonathan Mark *Ancient Cities of the Indus Valley*, Oxford, 1998

Kimura, Rei *Alberto Fujimori of Peru: the President who Dared to Dream*, Eyelevel Books, 1998

King, Jonathan *'The biotechnology revolution: self-replicating factories and the ownership of life forms'*, in J. Davis, T. Hirschl and M. Stack, eds., *Cutting Edge: technology...* London, Verso Press, 1997.

Kirk, Jason *India and the World Bank: The Politics of Aid and Influence*. Anthem South Asian Studies, London and New York, Anthem Press, 2011

Klostermeier, Klaus *A short Introduction to Hinduism*, London, One World Publ., 1998.

Kokkoka, *Koka Shastra*, 12th Century CE, trans.by Alex Comfort, London, Tandem, 1964

Kolarov, Bojil, *India in Danger: The Offensive of Islam,* Voice of Dharma, Internet Ed.

Kosambi, DD, *An Introduction to the Study of Indian History,* Mumbai, India, Popular Prakashan, 1956

Ibid, *The Culture and Civilisation of Ancient India in Historical Outline,* London, Routledge & Kegan Paul, 1965 *(This and preceding may reflect unacceptable colonial biases)*

Krishnan, Yuvraj *The doctrine of Karma: its origin and development in Brāhmaṇical, Buddhist, and Jaina traditions.* Delhi: Motilal Banarsidass Publishers, 1997

Kulkarni, S.D. *Shri Bhagavan Vaidavyasa Itihasa Samshodhana Mandira*, Bombay, (now Mumbai), India, 1994. Ref p 3

Krishna-Dwaipana (Vyasa) *Mahabharata.* Original in Sanskrit, transl. by Protāp Chandra Roy, Bhārata Press, Calcutta 18881978)

Lacey, Robert *The Kingdom, Arabia and the House of Saud*, NY, Penguin Reprint, 2010 (original 1982)

Lad, Vasant D. *Textbook of Ayurveda, Vol. I: Fundamental Principles* 2001

Vol. II*: A Complete Guide to Clinical Assessment,* The Ayurvedic Press.2007

Lal, KS *Growth of Muslim population in Medieval India*, Delhi Research Publications in Social Sciences), 1973

Lapierre D. & Moro D., *Bhopal, 5 minutes past Midnight*, New York, Warner, 2002

Lévi, Sylvain *Les études orientales*, Paris, Hachette, Annales du musée Guimet, numéro 36, 1911, ANU DS1.P32.t36

Londhe, Sushama, *A Tribute to Hinduism*, New Delhi, Pragun Publications, 2008

Lovejoy, AO *The Great Chain of Being,* Harvard University Press, USA, 1936

Luther, Martin, *On the Jews and Their Lies,* trans. MH. Bertram, in *Luther's Works,* Philadelphia: Fortress Press, 1971).

Macaulay, T. *Minute 2, February 1835, Bureau of Education. Selections from Educational Records, Part I (1781-1839),* edited by H. Sharp; Delhi, National Archives of India, 1920 Reprint, 1965, 107-117.

Mahabharata (see KM Ganguli)

Maharishi Bharadwaja, *Vymaanika-Shaastra* trans. by GR Joyser, Mysore, India, Coronation Press, 1973

Mahmud, Sayed Jafar *Pillars of Modern India, 1757-1947,* New Delhi, SB Nangia, Ashish Publishing House, 1994

Majumdar, RC *History of Ancient Bengal,* Calcutta, Publ. G. Bharadwaj, 1971

Ibid, Raychaudari H C and Datta K. *Advanced history of India,* London, Macmillan 1978

Malhotra R & Neelakandan, A, *Breaking India*, New Delhi, Manipal Press, 2011

Mangalwadi, V. *Five Ways to Salvation in Contemporary Guruism,* Themelios 2,(3),72, 1977

Mani, Lata, *Contentious Traditions: The Debate on Sati in Colonial India* Univ. of California Press, 1998

Mangru B. *Benevolent Neutrality, labour migration to British Guiana,* London, Hansib, 1987

Marinelli, Luigi, *The Shroud of Secrecy*, The Millenari, English Translation, Key Porter Books, 2000

Matilal, BK *Epistemology, Logic, and Grammar in Indian Philosophical Analysis,* Oxford University Press, 2005, ISBN 0-19-566658-5
Matlock, Gene D, *When India Ruled the World,* Journey to Baboquivari, iUniverse, 2002
Matlock, Gene D, *Yishvara*, Amazon, Kindle Edition, 2000
Mayo, Katharine, *Mother India*, Ann Arbor, University of Michigan Press, 1927
McEvedy, C & Jones, R, Atlas of World Population History, London, Penguin, 1978
Mehta Gita S, *The Integral Humanism of Mahatma Maharishi Dayānand, www.bu.edu/wcp/Papers/Reli/ReliMeht.htm* and *www.swargvibha.in/aalekh/all*
Menon, VKK *Condition of India: Being the Report of the Delegation Sent to India by the India League in 1932* London: Essential News, 1933
Meyer, Karl & Brysac, SB, *Kingmakers: the invention of the modern Middle East*, New York, Norton, 2008
Michel Francisque, *La Chanson de Roland, le roman de Roncevaux*, Paris 1869, Amazon, 1998
Miller Jr, Walter, *A Canticle for Leibowitz, in 3 volumes*; USA, Lippincott, 1960
Miller, Webb, *Found No Peace,* New York, Simon and Schuster, 1936
Ministry of Rural Development, India, 2012
Misra, VS *Ancient Indian Dynasties,* Mumbai: Bhāratīya Vidya Bhavan, 2007
Mistry, Rohinton, *Such a long Journey,* Toronto, McClelland and Stewart, 1991
Mittal, DK *Coal Industry*, Anmol Publications Private Limited, 1994, ISBN 81-7041-863-1
Mittal, JP *History of Ancient India: From 7300 BC to 4250 BC, new version,* Atlantic Publishers and Distributors, 2006
Mody, Rekha *A Quest for Roots* (Shree Shakti), 2nd ed., Gurgaon, Haryana, Shubhi Publ., 2009
Mohanty, JN *Classical Indian Philosophy,* Lanham, Maryland Rowman & Littlefield, 2000
Morgan KW Ed. *The religion of the Hindus*, Delhi, Motilal Banarsidass, 1953
Muir, J *Original Sanskrit Texts, Part 1,* Delhi, Oriental Publishers, 1972.
Muller, FM *Rg-Ved Samhita together with the commentary of Sayana,* Oxford University Press, 1890
Müller, Georgina *The Life and Letters of Right Honourable Friedrich Max Müller. Vol 1.* London: Longman, 1902
Mumford, Lewis, *Technics and Civilisation,* New York, Harcourt, Brace & Company, 1934
Naipaul, VS India: *A Wounded Civilisation*, London, Andre Deutsch, 1979
Ibid, *An Area of Darkness*, Middlesex, Penguin Books, 1982
Naithani, Sadhana *In Quest of Indian Folktales,* Pt. Ram Gharib Chaube and William Crooke, USA, Indiana Univ. Press, 2006
Nanda, Meera *The God Market: How Globalization is Making India More Hindu*, India, Random House, 2009
Naoroji, Dadabhai *Poverty and Unbritish rule in India, (1901);* Commonwealth Publishers, Gov. of India, 1988
Narang, Ish *The Science of Agnihotra*, RI Enterprises, New Delhi, 2009
Oman, Charles, *The Dark Ages 476–918 (AD), Period I of Periods of European History*,1893; 5th edition 1905
O'Neill WL *A Democracy at War*, USA, Harvard Univ. Press, Paperback Edition, 1995
Painter, NI *The History of White People,* New York, USA W. W. Norton & Company, 2010
Pal, Bachendri *Everest - My Journey to the Top*, Delhi, National Book Trust, 1988
Pandit Sitaram, *Sangeet Mala, Bhajan #117,* Toronto, ON, Canada, 2012
Pānini, *The Ashtadhyayi of Panini* translated by Srisa Chandra Bose, Benares, published by Sindhu Charan Bose at the Panini Office, 1897, (accessed at Library, University of Toronto, Canada)
Pānchatantra, by Arthur Ryder, Chicago, Ill. University of Chicago Press, 1925. Also by Pandit Vishnu Sharma, *Pānchatantra,* translator: G.L. Chandiramani, New Delhi, Rupa & Co, 1991

Pande, GC *Śramaṇa Tradition: Its History and Contribution to Indian Culture",* Ahmedabad, L.D. Institute of Indology, 1978
Pargiter FE, quoted By Prakashānanda Saraswati, q.v.
Parameswaran N., *Early Tamils of Lanka-Ilankai* Kuala Lumpur, Parameswaran, 2000
Pathak, Bindeshwar, *Road to Freedom*, New Delhi, Vedic Books, 2000
Ibid, *Sulabh Sanitation and Social Reform Movement*, International NGO Journal Vol. 6(1), 14-29, 2011; www.academicjournals.*org*/ ISSN 1993–8225 2010
Pellow, DN *Resisting Global Toxics: Transnational Movements for Environmental Justice* MIT Press ,2007, the Younger, *Epistulae;* www.earlychristianwritings.com/110.96-97
Posner, GL, *God's Bankers: A history of money and Power in the Vatican*, New York, Simon & Schuster, 2015
Prakash, Satish, *The Raamcharitmaanas, What It can teach us,* Arya Spiritual Centre Inc. New York, USA, 1994
Prasad, Leela, Ed. *Live like the Banyan Tree*, The Historical Society of Pennsylvania, 1999
Prakashānanda, see Saraswati, P
Premchand, Munshi (see Srivastava, DR)
Priddy, Robert, *Source of the Dream,* Weiser, 1997 http://www.saibaba-x.org.uk/13/Sai.html
Pococke, Edward *India in Greece, Truth in Mythology,* London, Richard Griffin &Co. 1864; Library of Congress DF220 .P94 1852
Radhakrishnan, S. *Indian Philosophy Vols. 1 & 2, UK,* Oxford University Press, 1923
Ibid, *A Source Book in Indian Philosophy*, Princeton Univ. Press, 1957
Ibid, *British Policy in India, 1858-1905*, Cambridge: University Press, 1965
Ragbeer, Mohan, *The Indelible Red Stain, Books 1 and 2;* Charleston, SC, USA, Amazon, CreateSpace Inc., 2011.
Ibid, *Opeds: Articles on India*, Toronto, IC World, 2004-2015
Rajaram, Navaratna: *The Politics of History: Aryan Invasion Theory and the Subversion of Scholarship*. New Delhi: Voice of India, 1995
Ibid *Looking beyond the Indus Script: Story of Vedic Harappans* – http://bharatabharati.wordpress.com/2012/
Rajaram, N & Frawley, David, *Vaidic Aryans and the Origins of Civilisation*, New Delhi, Voice of India, 1997
Rajshekar, VT, *Dalit: The Black Untouchables of India*: Atlanta, Clarity Press, 1987
Ramayana, Translation by RTH Griffith, 5 Vols., London 1870-5. See also RC Dutt
Ramusack, BN *The Indian princes and their states.* Cambridge University Press. ISBN 978-0-521-26727-4
Rashid ad-Din. in *Encyclopædia Britannica*. 2007.
Raychaudhuri, HC *Political History of Ancient India*, University of Calcutta, 1972.
Reiss, Tom *The Black Count*, Crown Publishers, USA, 2012
Reynolds, David *From World War to Cold War: Churchill, Roosevelt, and the International History of the 1940s*. Oxford: Oxford University Press, 2006
Riddick, John F. *The History of British India: A Chronology,* California, USA, Greenwood Publishing Group, 2006
Robb, Peter Ed. *The Concept of Race in South Asia*, Oxford University Press, 1997, ISBN 0195642686
Ruhoman, Peter *A Centenary History of the East Indians in British Guiana, 1838-1938,* Georgetown, The Daily Chronicle, 1946
Saraswati, Dayānanda *Satyārth Prakash,(Light of Truth)* English Translation by Charanjiv Bharadwaja, New Delhi, India, published by Sarvadeshik Arya Pratinidhi Sabha, 1975
Saraswati, Swami Prakashanada, *The True History and the Religion of India,* Delhi, Motilal Banarsidass, 1999-2002
Sarkar, Jadunath, *Shivaji and his times*, London, Longmans, Green &Co, 1920
Sastri, Nilakanta K.A. *A History of South India, from prehistoric times to the fall of Vijayanagara*, Oxford University Press New Delhi, 1955

Satprem. *Life without death;* and *The Mother's Agenda, 13 volumes.* by Mira Aditi Centre, 62 Sriranga, 1st Cross, 4th Stage Kuvempunagar, Mysore 570023

Saund, Dalip Singh *My Mother India* USA, Pacific Coast Khalsa Diwan society, Inc.,1930

Savarkar VS, *Essentials of Hindutva,* Ratnagiri, 1923; later edition titled *Hindutva: who is a Hindu?* 1928, republished by Swatantrayaveer Savarkar Rashtriya Smarak, 1999

Schmidt, HD *The Idea and Slogan of "Perfidious Albion.* Journal of the History of Ideas, Vol. 14, No. 4 (Oct.,1953), pp. 604-616.

Seidenberg, A. *"The Origin of Mathematics",* 1978, Archive for History of Exact Sciences, Volume 18, Issue 4, 1978

Séralini G.-E. et al. *Long term toxicity of a Roundup herbicide and a Roundup-tolerant genetically modified maize,* Food Chem. Toxicol. (Elsevier) 50, 4221–4231 (2012).

Ibid., *Republished study, as above:* Environmental Sciences Europe 2014, 26:14

Seth, Vikram *A Suitable Boy,* Toronto, Little, Brown and Co., 1993

Sethna, KD *The Problem of Aryan Origins from an Indian Point of View,* New Delhi, Aditya Prakashan, 1992

Sharan, Ishwar *The Myth of Saint Thomas and the Mylapore Shiva Temple,* Voice of India, Third Edition, 2010

Sharma, S et al. *The Indian origin of paternal haplogroup R1a1*substantiates the autochthonous origin of Brahmins and the caste system,* Journal of Human Genetics (2009) **54,** 47–55; doi:10.1038/jhg.2008.2; published online 9 January 2009

Shashikumar, VK *World Vision: Christian NGO engaged in culture murder not social service* – http://bharatabharati.wordpress.com/2010/02/02/

Shea, Mark, Five Myths about Seven Books, http://catholiceducation.org/articles/apologetics/ap0120.html

Shetty BV *World as Seen under the Lens of a Scientist,* USA, ex libris, 2009

Shields, Susan *Mother Teresa's House of Illusions* Free Inquiry magazine,18:1, 1997-8

Shiva, Vandana *Biopiracy the plunder of nature and knowledge,* Boston, South End Press, 1997. See also other books by Vandana Shiva on *worldwide web.*

Shourie, A *Harvesting Our Souls: Missionaries, their Design, their Claims* New Delhi, Rupa & Co, 2001

Shukla, Suhag *The Question of Evangelism in India,* Hindu American Foundation, posted 02/05/11 http://www.huffingtonpost.com/suhag-a-shukla-esq/harvesting-souls

Shukla, KS and Sarma, K.V., *Aryābhatiya of Aryābhata,* Indian National Science Academy, New Delhi, 1976.

Singh, Arjun & Chopra, Ashok *A Grain Of Sand In The Hourglass of Time: An Autobiography,* Hay House, 2012

Singh, Khushwant, *A History of the Sikhs, Volume II: 1839–2004,* New Delhi, Oxford University Press, 2004

Sinha, Nandalal, Mahamahopadhyaya Satisa Chandra Vidyabhusana, *The Nyāyá Sutras of Gotama, The sacred books of the Hindus,* Motilal Banarsidass, 1990 reprint, ISBN 978-81-208-0748-8;MR Manoharlal, 2003, ISBN 978-81-215-1096-7.

SISSO, *Views of the press, Part IV, Multiple Articles.* 111 pages, New Delhi, 2011

Smith, Adam *The Wealth of Nations,* Glasgow, 1976

Smith, Jeffrey M. *Seeds of Deception,* 2003 and *Genetic Roulette USA,* Yes books, 2007

Smith, WD *The Ideological Origins of Nazi Imperialism,* Oxford University Press, 1986.

Sorabjee, S and Dattar, A. *Nani Palkhivala: Courtroom Genius,* India, LexisNexis Butterworth's Wadhwa, 2012 ISBN818038752

Srivastava; DR *(M. Premchand) Soz-e-Watan (Nation's Lament),* Varanasi, Zamana, 1907

Srivastava, Sarvesh *History of Ganit (Mathematics)* in *Facets of India: Ancient and Modern,* http://www.geocities.ws/dipalsarvesh/mathematics.html, accessed March 21, 2010

Subramaniam, Chitra, *Bofors: The story behind the news,* Viking 1993, ISBN-10: 0670845256

Ibid, *India is for Sale,* South Asia Books (May 1997) ISBN-10: 8174761616

Suetonius, *Lives of the Twelve Caesars* ca. 122 AD; translated by A Thomsen and T. Forester London, George Bell 1890

Sungenis, Robert, *Galileo Was Wrong* USA, Bellarmine Theological Forum, 2006

Svetavatara Upanishad *On Shaivism*, (cf Bhāgavad Gita, substituting Siva for Krishna)

Swami Bharti Krishnateerthaji Maharaj (1884-1960 AD) *Vaidic Ganit*, New Delhi, Motilal Banarsidass, 1965

Swami Dayānand Saraswati *Introduction to Vedas* translated by Shri Ghasiram, Delhi, Sarvdeshik Arya Pratinidhi Sabha, 1984

Swami, Subramaniam *Hindutva and National renaissance* Har-Anand Publications Pvt Ltd, 2010, ISBN 8124115273,

Swarup, Rama *Understanding Islam through Hadis*, Smithtown, New York Exposition Press, 1982

Tacitus, *Annals* ca 115-116 CE

Tagore, Sourindo Mohun *The Ten Principal Avatars of the Hindus: A Short History of Each Incarnation and Directions for the Representations of the Murtis as Tableaux Vivants*, Calcutta, 1880

Talageri S *The Rig-Veda, a historical Analysis*; Aditya Prakashan, 2000

Ibid, *The Aryan Invasion Theory, a reappraisal* (debunked) Aditya Prakashan, 1993

Taylor, AJP *The Origins of the Second World War*, London: Hamish Hamilton, 1976

Thapar, R, *Ancient India, Medieval India*, New Delhi, NCERT Textbooks, 1968

The Oxford Dictionary of Quotations, Oxford University Press, 1979.

The politics of History, Publisher: Lustre, The Hindustan Times, Nov. 28 1993.

Tilak, BG *Kesari, multiple editions*, published between 1881 and 1910

Tulsidās, *Śrīrāmacaritamānasa*, Gita Press, 2004

Twain, Mark *A Connecticut Yankee in King Arthur's Court & The Prince and the Pauper, Companion Volume*, NY, Castle Books, 2001

Ibid, *Following the Equator*, Easyread edition, Createspace Independent Pub, 2008

Underhill, *Frequency distribution of R1a1a genes*, adapted from Underhill et al, http://commons.wikimedia.org/wiki/File:R1a1a_distribution.png#file

Upanishads, *The Principal*...958 pages, HarperCollins Publishers Ltd., 1953

Valmiki, *Ramayana, audio version*, http://www.valmikiramayan.net/

Vatsyāyana, *Kama Sutra*, trans. R. Burton and FF Arbuthnot, London, Panther Books,1963

Vidal, Gore *Monotheism and its Discontents*, Harvard, USA, Lowell Lecture, 1996

Voltaire, *The Complete Romances (English version)* New York, Walter J. Black, 1927

Wade, Nicholas *Before the Dawn, Recovering the Lost History of our ancestors*, New York, Penguin, 2007

Wetterhahn, Ralph *The Last Battle: The Mayaguez Incident And The End Of The Viet Nam War*, USA, (Penguin) Plume Publishers, 2002

Wilford, Lt. Col. Francis *Ancient Book of the Hindus, Asiatic Researchers Vol. III*, 1792, quoted by Matlock, Gene D (q.v.)

Williams, Stephen *Diocletian and the Roman Recovery*, London, Routledge, 1997

Wilson, J *The Domination of Strangers: Modern Governance in Eastern India, 1780-1835* Basingstoke, Palgrave Macmillan, 2008

Woodroffe, John *Is India Civilized? Essays on Indian Culture*, Varanasi, Indica Books, 2010

Wynbrandt, James *A Brief History of Pakistan*, New York, Checkmark Books, 2008

Yaska, cited in Lakshman Sarup: *The Nighantu and Nirukta*, Delhi, Motilal Banarsidass, 1998

Yoga-Sûtra of Patanjali, A New translation and Commentary, Rochester, VT, USA, Inner Traditions International, 1989

Index

Made in the USA
Charleston, SC
17 August 2015